BIBLICAL LITERACY

BY RABBI JOSEPH TELUSHKIN

Nonfiction

The Nine Questions People Ask About Judaism
(with Dennis Prager)
Why the Jews? The Reason for Antisemitism (with Dennis Prager)
Jewish Literacy: The Most Important Things to Know About the
Jewish Religion, Its People, and Its History
Jewish Humor: What the Best Jewish Jokes Say About the Jews
Jewish Wisdom: Ethical, Spiritual, and Historical Lessons from the
Great Works and Thinkers
Words That Hurt, Words That Heal: How to Choose Words
Wisely and Well

Fiction

The Unorthodox Murder of Rabbi Wahl
The Final Analysis of Dr. Stark
An Eye for an Eye

BIBLICAL LITERACY

*The Most Important People, Events,
and Ideas of the Hebrew Bible*

Rabbi Joseph Telushkin

William Morrow and Company, Inc.   *New York*

Library of Congress Cataloging-in-Publication Data

Telushkin, Joseph, 1948–
    Biblical literacy : the most important people, events, and ideas
of the Hebrew Bible / Rabbi Joseph Telushkin
        p. cm.
    Includes index.
    ISBN 0-688-14297-4
    1. Bible. O.T.—Introductions. 2. Jewish law. I. Title.
BS1140.2.T45   1997
221.6'1—dc21   97-6645
                                                            CIP

Printed in the United States of America

First Edition

11   13   15   17   19   20   18   16   14   12

BOOK DESIGN BY SUSAN HOOD

To the next generation of our family

OUR CHILDREN
Rebecca, Naomi, Shira, and Benjamin

OUR NEPHEWS AND NIECES
Meir, Nisan, and Sharona
Saul and Sophie
Lena
Sosha, Max, and Zev
Brian, Russell, Scott, and Tracy Rose

May the study of Torah continue through
them and their descendants.

ACKNOWLEDGMENTS

I have been studying the Bible since I was seven. Two particularly influential teachers in shaping my understanding of this holy text were my grandfather Rabbi Nissen Telushkin, of blessed memory, author of *Ha-Torah ve-ha-Olam* (*The Torah and the World*), a three-volume study of the Torah, and my father, Shlomo Telushkin, of blessed memory. I also want to acknowledge the influence of my beloved uncle, Dr. Manoah Bialik, of blessed memory, an extraordinary teacher of Bible and Talmud, and an extraordinary mensch.

I owe much to the Yeshiva of Flatbush in Brooklyn, which I attended from kindergarten through high school, especially my ability to study the Bible and other Jewish texts in the original. Among the outstanding teachers with whom I studied are Rabbi David Eliach, the school's longtime, and recently retired, principal. Rabbi Eliach has a masterful ability to illuminate with fresh insights a biblical text that I, and others, might have read a dozen times, and to do so with a clear notion of its ethical import. Rabbi Amnon Haramati has an encyclopedic knowledge of the Bible and an ability to infuse his students with a sense of its significance. He tried to ensure that we learned many of its most beautiful chapters and verses by heart in the original Hebrew. Today, more than thirty years later, I wish I had been more diligent in carrying out his assignments.

For more than thirty years, my friend Dennis Prager, my classmate at the Flatbush Yeshiva's Joel Braverman High School, and I have spent countless hours discussing biblical texts and how they speak to us today. His insights have greatly helped shape my understanding of the Bible.

Several friends and colleagues generously read and critiqued this book while in manuscript and made suggestions that influenced my writing. I am happy to have this opportunity to publicly acknowledge their help while assuming sole responsibility for any errors or misinterpretations in this work.

Dr. Jeremiah Unterman, the newly appointed director of the Toronto Board of Jewish Education, and the holder of a doctorate in Bible Studies, gave this work a careful reading, and provided a detailed critique. Along with pointing out a number of errors I had made, he deepened my appreciation of verses to which I had devoted insufficient attention. I am grateful for the gift of his time and knowledge.

Dr. Stephen Marmer, professor of psychiatry at UCLA Medical School, read the manuscript carefully and enriched my efforts through his psychological insights and substantial body of Jewish knowledge.

Daniel Taub, a highly knowledgeable student of the Bible, helped improve my style, while offering alternative explanations of some episodes. Rabbi Leonid Feldman also shared with me some very insightful explanations of biblical passages.

Dr. Michael Berger of Emory University, a rabbi and academic with a vast knowledge of the Bible and Talmud, delved into every page of this lengthy manuscript, and thus saved me from errors and misinterpretations. It would be difficult to overstate my appreciation for his work.

This is the fifth book that David Szonyi has helped edit for me, and, as always, he has immensely improved its clarity and readability, while offering insights garnered from his own ongoing study of the Torah. My appreciation for David grows from book to book.

My beloved wife, Dvorah, who currently is engaged in her own systematic study of the Torah, made many valuable suggestions which I have incorporated into the manuscript.

I also wish to acknowledge Dr. Jacob Milgrom's impact on my understanding of the Bible. I consider him the greatest Bible scholar of our age. His impeccable scholarship is accompanied by an extraordinary ability to extract the text's ethical and spiritual meaning. Dr. Uriel Simon, professor of Bible at Israel's Bar Ilan University, and one of the world's greatest experts on Jewish Bible commentators, also has repeatedly deepened my understanding of the Hebrew Scriptures. My understanding of the Bible has also been deeply impacted by the insightful and compelling writings of two of the great Bible scholars and teachers of our century, Dr. Nahum Sarna and Professor Nehama Leibowitz.

My gratitude goes as well to the members of my congregation, the Synagogue of the Performing Arts in Los Angeles, who have heard much of this book's material during five years of sermons. I also am proud to acknowledge my ongoing involvement as an Associate of CLAL, the National Jewish Center for Learning and Leadership. For over two decades, CLAL has played a significant role in educating much of American Jewry's lay leadership in the Bible and in Jewish values. The work of Rabbi Irving (Yitz) Greenberg and of his newly appointed successor, Rabbi Irwin Kula, of Dr. David Elcott and the other extraordinary faculty and staff of CLAL, has made a deep and growing impact on the quality of American Jewish life.

I would like to express a deep sense of gratitude to my two editors at William Morrow, Ann Bramson and Gail Kinn, for their faith in this project. Gail's editing of the manuscript was superb. In several key instances, her suggestions improved the work immensely. As always, Sonia Greenbaum, my scrupulous copy editor, improved the book stylistically, while catching numerous small errors and inconsistencies.

I feel a great deal of pleasure and gratitude in thanking Richard Pine. All writers should be blessed with such an agent, a man whose editorial insights are matched only by his negotiating abilities and loyal friendship. I also very much appreciate the help of Arthur Pine, his father and partner, and of Lori Andiman and Sarah Piel, their two associates.

I am also happy to have this opportunity to thank Maury Coggan, of blessed memory, an unending source of kindness and inspiration, and a man who brought joy into my life and to the lives of all who knew him; to Peter Rodriguez, who inspires me and so many others daily with his friendship and with the reminder that "everything's going to be all right"; and to Jonathan Greenwald, a beloved friend of my family and myself. Jonathan, a paramedic and a teacher of paramedics, has saved many lives, including mine. May God bless him in his holy work. It is to seventeen other very special people in my life that I have dedicated *Biblical Literacy*.

CONTENTS

Introduction   xxi

PART ONE: PEOPLE AND EVENTS   1

The Torah

I. GENESIS
1. In the Beginning   5
2. Adam, Eve, and the Garden of Eden; The Tree of   7
   Knowledge of Good and Evil
3. Cain and Abel; "Am I My Brother's Keeper?"   11
4. Noah's Ark   14
5. Ham's Sin and the Evil Caused by Drunkenness   17
6. The Tower of Babel   18
7. The Patriarchs and Matriarchs   20
8. God Chooses Abraham   22
9. When Abraham Lies to Save His Life   24
10. The Covenant Between God and Abraham   28
11. Ishmael, Abraham's Firstborn   29
12. Abraham Argues with God   32
13. The Sinful Cities of Sodom and Gomorrah   34
14. The *Akedah*: The Near Sacrifice of Isaac   37
15. The Cave of the Matriarchs and Patriarchs   42
16. Isaac: The Man to Whom Things Happen   43
17. Jacob and Esau; Jacob Deceives His Father   46
18. The Bible's First Dream: Jacob's Vision of a Ladder   55
19. Jacob, Rachel, and Leah: The Unhappy Triangle   57

20. Jacob Becomes Israel   60
21. The Rape of Dinah   64
22. The Young Joseph: Beloved Son, Hated Brother   67
23. Tamar (and Judah): The Woman Who Disguised   70
    Herself as a Prostitute
24. Joseph and Mrs. Potiphar   74
25. The Dreamer Becomes the Interpreter of Other   78
    Men's Dreams
26. Joseph Tests His Brothers   82
27. The Twelve Tribes   88

II. EXODUS

28. Pharaoh: History's First Antisemite   91
29. The Two Midwives and the World's First Recorded   92
    Act of Civil Disobedience
30. Moses: The Birth of the Bible's Greatest Hero   95
31. A Portrait of the Hero as a Young Man   96
32. Moses: The Reluctant Leader; The Burning Bush;   100
    "I Shall Be What I Shall Be"
33. "Let My People Go!"   104
34. The Ten Plagues; The Tenth Plague: The Killing of   106
    the Firstborn
35. The Exodus; The Splitting of the "Red [Reed] Sea"   108
36. Moses' and Miriam's Songs at the Sea   110
37. Manna: God's Heavenly Food   111
38. Amalek: Israel's Eternal Enemy   113
39. Jethro: A Most Helpful Father-in-law   115
40. The Covenant at Mount Sinai and the Giving of   116
    the Ten Commandments
41. The Building of the Tabernacle   118
42. *Urim* and *Tummim*   119
43. The Golden Calf; "Whoever Is for God,   121
    Follow Me!"

III. LEVITICUS

44. Priests and Levites   125
45. Nadav and Avihu's Sin and Punishment   127

IV. NUMBERS

46. Miriam and Aaron Sin Against Moses   129
47. The Twelve Spies and the Generation of "Grasshoppers"; 131
    A Land Flowing with Milk and Honey

48. Korah's Revolt Against Moses 134
49. Moses Strikes the Rock and Is Punished by God 137
50. Balaam's Talking Donkey; "How Goodly Are Your 139
    Tents, O Jacob, Your Dwellings, O Israel"
51. Pinchas's Zealousness 142
52. Zelophehad's Daughters: When Do Women Inherit? 143
53. Joshua Is Chosen to Succeed Moses 145
54. Occupying Canaan and Dispossessing 146
    the Canaanites

V. DEUTERONOMY

55. Moses' Final Speeches 149
56. The Death of Moses; "And No One Knows His 152
    Burial Place"

The Early Prophets

VI. JOSHUA

57. Joshua Sends Spies to Jericho; Rahab: 157
    The Righteous Prostitute
58. "And the Walls Came Tumbling Down": Joshua and 159
    the Battle of Jericho
59. Achan's Theft 160
60. The Gibeonite Surrender; The Sun Stands Still 162
61. Joshua and the Conquest of Canaan 164

VII. JUDGES

62. Deborah: Judge, Leader, and Prophet 167
63. Gideon: The Man Who Would Not Be King 170
64. Jotham: Author of the Bible's First Parable 174
65. Jephtah's Murderous Sacrifice 176
66. Samson and Delilah 178
67. "Each Man Did What Was Right in His Eyes": 184
    When Anarchy Prevailed in Israel

VIII. I AND II SAMUEL

68. Hannah: The Woman Who Knew How to Pray 189
69. The Fall of the House of Eli 192
70. Samuel: The Last of the Judges 194
71. "We Must Have a King over Us That We May Be 196
    Like All Other Nations"

72. King Saul: Tragic Hero or Fool?   197
73. David and Goliath   201
74. Saul's Longest Battle: His Maniacal War Against   204
    David
75. David and Jonathan: The Biblical Model of   209
    Friendship
76. Michal: The Woman Who Loved Too Much   212
77. Abigail: How David Meets His Wisest Wife   215
78. Saul Consults a Medium: The Necromancer of Endor   217
79. The Death of Saul: Is Suicide Ever Justified?   219
80. David Rules over Judah, Then All of Israel   220
81. Jerusalem Becomes Israel's Capital   222
82. David, Bathsheba, and Uriah: The Tragic Triangle   224
83. Nathan Confronts David: "That Man Is You"   228
84. One Rape, Two Rebellions: The Unhappy Relationship   232
    Between David and His Sons; Amnon and Tamar;
    David and Absalom; The Revolt of Adonijah
85. Sheva's Revolt Against David   240
86. Joab: David's Ruthless General   242

IX. I AND II KINGS

87. Solomon Becomes King   245
88. The Wisdom of Solomon   246
89. The "Unwisdom" of Solomon   248
90. The Building of the Temple (Beit ha-Mikdash) by King   249
    Solomon
91. The Two Jewish States: The Secession of the Northern   252
    Kingdom
92. Elijah's War Against Idolatry: The Killing of the Priests   254
    of Baal
93. King Ahab and Navot's Vineyard; "Have You Murdered   258
    and Also Inherited?"
94. Elijah Ascends to Heaven in a Chariot of Fire   261
95. Elisha Cures Syrian General Na'aman, a Non-Israelite   262
96. Jehu: From Righteous Assassin to Mass Killer   264
97. How the Ten Lost Tribes Become Lost: The End of the   266
    Kingdom of Israel (722 B.C.E.)
98. King Hezekiah's Illness   268
99. King Manasseh of Judah: An Evil Man   270

100. Josiah of Judah: The Reformer King   271
101. Nebuchadnezzar and the Babylonian Siege of Jerusalem;   275
     The Temple Is Destroyed
102. The Babylonian Exile (587 B.C.E.)   277
103. Gedaliah: The Last Jewish Governor of Judah   278

The Later Prophets

X. ISAIAH

104. Isaiah: A Profile; "The Wolf Shall Dwell with the   283
     Lamb"
105. "Nation Shall Not Lift Up Sword Against Nation":   285
     Isaiah's Dream of World Peace
106. "A Light unto the Nations"   287
107. On "Virgin Births" and "The Suffering Servant of God":   288
     The Different Ways in Which Jews and
     Fundamentalist Christians Read Isaiah
108. Does the Book of Isaiah Contain the Words of More   289
     Than One Prophet?

XI. JEREMIAH

109. The Loneliest Man of Faith   293
110. Was Jeremiah a Traitor?   296
111. Prophet of Hope and an Early Zionist   299
112. Ethics as God's Central Demand   301

XII. EZEKIEL

113. The Valley of the Dry Bones   303

XIII. THE TWELVE MINOR PROPHETS

114. Why "Minor" Does Not Mean "Insignificant"   305
115. Hosea: The Prophet Betrayed by His Wife   310
116. Amos: "Let Justice Well Up Like Water"   312
117. Amos: "You Alone Have I Singled Out of All the   319
     Families of the Earth"; Amos and the Meaning of
     Jewish Chosenness
118. Jonah and the Whale   321
119. Micah: The Three Things God Requires of People   325

The Writings

XIV. PSALMS

    120. An Introduction   331
    121. Psalm 1: "Happy Is the Man Who Has Not Followed   332
           the Advice of the Wicked"
    122. Psalm 15: "Lord, Who May Sojourn in Your Tent, Who   334
           May Dwell on Your Holy Mountain?"
    123. Psalm 23: "The Lord Is My Shepherd"   337
    124. Psalm 44: "Why Do You Hide Your Face, Ignoring Our   338
           Affliction and Distress?"
    125. Psalm 137: "If I Forget You, O Jerusalem, Let My Right   340
           Hand Wither"

XV. PROVERBS

    126. "A Woman of Valor Who Shall Find?"   343

XVI. JOB

    127. When God Gives Power to Satan: The Unhappy Test   347
           of Job
    128. "With Friends Like This"—The Friends of Job   350
    129. "Out of the Whirlwind": God Answers Job   352

XVII. THE FIVE SCROLLS

    130. The Three Peculiar Heroines of the Five Scrolls: Esther,   355
           Ruth, and the Shepherdess
    131. Song of Songs: The Bible's Love Poem   357
    132. Ruth, Naomi, and Boaz: The Bible's Happiest Triangle;   358
           "Your People Shall Be My People, Your God Shall
           Be My God"
    133. Lamentations: A Lament over Jerusalem's Destruction   362
    134. Ecclesiastes: "Vanity of Vanities, All Is Vanity"; "A Time   365
           for War and a Time for Peace"
    135. Vashti: An Early Feminist   367
    136. Haman, the Antisemite   369
    137. Esther: The Beauty Queen Who Saves the Jewish People   374
    138. Mordechai: The Model of a Diaspora Jewish Leader   376

XVIII. DANIEL

    139. Shadrach, Meshach, and Abednego Are Thrown into   379
           Nebuchadnezzar's Furnace

140. Daniel Reads the Handwriting on the Wall   381
141. Daniel in the Lions' Den   382

XIX. EZRA AND NEHEMIAH

142. Cyrus the Great, King of Persia   385
143. Ezra and the Jewish Restoration to the Land of Israel   386
144. Ezra's War on Intermarriage   388
145. Nehemiah and the Jewish Restoration to Israel   390

XX. I AND II CHRONICLES: The Bible's Final Books   393

PART TWO: LAWS AND IDEAS   397

XXI. GENESIS

146. What Does It Mean That Human Beings Were Created   399
     "in God's Image"?
147. "Be Fruitful and Multiply"   400
148. Human Nature: "The Tendency of Man's Heart Is   401
     Towards Evil from His Youth"
149. The Noahide Laws   403
150. "Whoever Sheds the Blood of Man"; On Murderers and 405
     the Death Sentence
151. Circumcision   408
152. Multiple Wives: The Conflicting Views of Biblical Law   410
     and Biblical Narrative

XXII. EXODUS

153. Fear of God   415
154. God Hardens Pharaoh's Heart: Does the Bible Believe 417
     in Free Will?
155. The Ten Commandments: An Introduction   418
156. The First Commandment: Monotheism   421
157. The Second Commandment: Against Idolatry   424
158. The Third Commandment: "You Shall Not Carry the   426
     Name of the Lord Your God in Vain"
159. The Fourth Commandment: "Remember the Sabbath   427
     Day to Make It Holy"
160. The Fifth Commandment: "Honor Your Father and   430
     Your Mother"

161. The Sixth Commandment: "You Shall Not Murder"   433
162. The Seventh Commandment: "You Shall Not Commit   434
      Adultery"
163. The Eighth Commandment: "You Shall Not Steal"   435
164. The Ninth Commandment: "You Shall Not Bear False   436
      Witness Against Your Neighbor"
165. The Tenth Commandment: "You Shall Not Covet"   438
166. Slavery in the Bible   439
167. A Husband's Obligations to His Wife   442
168. The Bible on Kidnapping   443
169. "An Eye for an Eye": Vengeance or Justice?   444
170. Penalties for Stealing   447
171. "You Shall Not Ill-treat Any Widow or Orphan"   448

XXIII. LEVITICUS

172. Sacrifices   451
173. The Dietary Laws   453
174. Sexual Offenses in the Bible   454
175. "You Shall Be Holy"   456
176. To Pay the Wages of a Laborer Promptly   458
177. "You Shall Not Curse the Deaf or Place a   459
      Stumbling Block Before the Blind"
178. "Do Not Go About as a Talebearer Among Your   460
      People"
179. "Do Not Stand By While Your Neighbor's Blood Is   461
      Shed"
180. "Do Not Hate Your Brother in Your Heart"   462
181. "Reprove Your Kinsman and Incur No Guilt Because of 463
      Him"
182. "Do Not Take Revenge or Bear a Grudge"   464
183. "Love Your Neighbor as Yourself, I Am God"   465
184. "You Shall Love [the Stranger] as Yourself"   467
185. Sanctifying, and Not Desecrating, God's Name   468
186. Holy Days   470
187. Jubilee and Sabbatical Years   471
188. Charity   473

XXIV. NUMBERS

189. *Sotah:* The Ordeal of a Suspected Adulteress   475
190. The Nazirite   476
191. The Priestly Benediction   478

192. *Tzitzit*—The Law of Fringes 479
193. The Red Heifer 481
194. Fulfilling a Vow 483
195. Cities of Refuge 484

XXV. DEUTERONOMY

196. *Sh'ma Yisra'el:* The Jewish Credo; The Commandment to 487
   Love God; The Commandment to Teach Torah
   to One's Children; *Tefillin; Mezuzah*
197. To Neither Add nor Detract from the Torah's Laws 490
198. "Justice, Justice, You Shall Pursue" 492
199. The Biblical View of Kingship 493
200. *"Ba'al Tashchit":* The Biblical Law That Forbids 495
   Gratuitous Destruction
201. Firstborn Sons: The Conflict Between Biblical Law and 497
   Biblical Narrative
202. Biblical Laws Concerning the Humane Treatment of 499
   Animals
203. On Building a Safe Roof 501
204. *Shatnez* 502
205. Problematic Laws: Regarding Bastards and Rape 503
206. The Prohibition of Charging Interest 506
207. Divorce 508
208. To Walk in God's Ways 509

PART THREE: THE 613 LAWS OF THE TORAH 511
   IN ORDER OF APPEARANCE

Appendices
   I. The Books of the Hebrew Bible in Order 595
      of Appearance
   II: Dates of Major Biblical Events and Characters 597

Bibliography 601

Index 607

INTRODUCTION

The Hebrew Bible (also referred to as the Old Testament) is the most influential series of books in human history. Along with the Ten Commandments, the Bible's most famous document, no piece of legislation ever enacted has influenced human behavior as much as the biblical injunction to "Love your neighbor as yourself" (Leviticus 19:18). No political tract has motivated human beings in so many diverse societies to fight for political freedom as the Exodus story of God's liberation of the Israelite slaves from their Egyptian masters. The law of "Love your neighbor as yourself" established the imperative of treating people with justice and compassion, and introduced the Golden Rule to the world; the Exodus narrative made clear that, despite the inequities of this world, God intends that, ultimately, people be free.

The stories of the Bible are among the most timeless and moving narratives ever written about the human condition and about man's relationship to God. These stories have long shaped Jewish, Christian, and to a lesser degree, Muslim notions of morality, and continue to stir the conscience and imagination of believers and skeptics alike. There is a universality in biblical tales, for example:

- The murder of Abel at his brother Cain's hand is a profound tragedy of sibling jealousy and family love gone awry (see entry 3).
- Abraham's challenge to God, to save the lives of the evil people of Sodom, is a fierce drama of man in confrontation with God that establishes that human beings have a right to contend

even with the Almighty when they fear He is acting unjustly (see entry 12).

• Jacob's deception of his blind father, Isaac, raises the timeless question: When do the ends justify the means? (see entry 17).

As these examples make evident, the stories, laws, and ideas of the Hebrew Bible have influenced the very thought patterns that govern most of our lives.

Many of us, however, don't know what the Hebrew Bible is. Perhaps it's best to start with the basics. The Hebrew Bible is made up of three categories of writings, the Torah, the Prophets (*Nevi'im*), and the Writings (*Ketuvim*).*

The Torah, the Bible's first five books, is regarded as Judaism's central document. Genesis, the Torah's first book, begins with the story of the creation of the world and of Adam and Eve, the first human beings, who are created in God's image. Unlike much of the rest of the Torah, which contains hundreds of laws, Genesis and the first half of Exodus, the Torah's next book, convey their teachings almost solely through narratives. Here one finds the tale of Noah and the Flood, and the stories of Abraham and Sarah, Judaism's founding Patriarch and Matriarch, and their progeny.

Exodus, the second book, is set in the period after Abraham and Sarah's descendants, known as Hebrews or Israelites, have migrated to Egypt. There, the Egyptians enslave and oppress them, until God commands Moses to lead the people to freedom. But first God inflicts ten plagues on Egypt in punishment for their mistreatment of the Israelites. Afterward, the Israelites flee the country, led by Moses, who takes them into the desert, where he begins to reveal God's will to them. Soon, the people arrive at Mount Sinai. There, Moses encounters God, who inscribes the Ten Commandments, which Moses then brings down to the Israelites.

The Torah's three and a half remaining books, the second half of Exodus, Leviticus, Numbers, and Deuteronomy, intersperse narra-

---

*Observant Jews use the term Hebrew Bible; the term Old Testament is Christian in origin. In Hebrew, the Bible is known as *TaNaKh* (rhymes with Bach), an acronym from Torah, *Nevi'im*, and *Ketuvim*. Christians also regard the Hebrew Bible as a sacred text, second in sanctity only to the New Testament, which tells the story of Jesus and Paul, and the early years of Christianity.

tives about the forty-year Israelite sojourn in the desert with more than six hundred *mitzvot,* the commandments that became the backbone of all Jewish law.

According to Jewish tradition, the Torah is the oldest piece of Jewish literature, and was revealed to Moses by God in the period around 1230 B.C.E., shortly after the exodus from Egypt.*

The second category of biblical works is the Prophets (*Nevi'im*), twenty-one books that trace Jewish history and the history of monotheism from the time of Moses' death and the Israelites' entrance into Canaan, around 1200 B.C.E., to the period after the Babylonians destroyed the First Temple and the ensuing exile of Jews from Jerusalem to Babylon (587 B.C.E.). In English, the primary meaning of *prophet* is one who predicts the future; however, the corresponding Hebrew word, *navi,* means "spokesman for God."

Sometimes referred to as the "Early Prophets," the early books of the prophets (Joshua, Judges, I and II Samuel, I and II Kings) are written in the form of a story; they remain among the most dramatic and vivid histories produced by any civilization. Here one finds the story of Joshua, the military leader and prophet who succeeded Moses and led the Israelites in battle in Canaan. After Joshua's death, a series of judges, most of them military figures, followed, some of whom, such as Deborah and Samuel, stood in the religious tradition of Moses, while others, most notably Jephtah and Samson, seemed

---

*In Hebrew, each book of the Torah is named after its first or second word, while the English names summarize the contents of the book. Thus, the first book of the Torah is called Genesis in English, because its opening chapter tells the story of the creation of the world. In this one instance, the Hebrew name is very similar, since the Torah's opening word, *Brei'sheet,* means "In the beginning." In Hebrew, the second book is called *Sh'mot,* or "Names," because its opening verse reads *"Ay-leh shemot b'nai yisrael—And these are the names of the children of Israel."* In English, the book is called Exodus, because it tells the story of the liberation of the Jewish slaves from Egypt. Leviticus is called *Va-Yikra* in Hebrew; it delineates many of the laws concerning animal sacrifices and other Temple rituals, which were supervised by the Israelite tribe of Levites. The fourth book, Numbers, *Ba-Midbar* in Hebrew, is named for the census of Israelites that is carried out early in the book. The Torah's final book is Deuteronomy, *Devarim* in Hebrew. Virtually the entire book consists of Moses' farewell address to the Israelites as they prepare to cross over to the Promised Land. He knows that he will not be permitted to enter it, but before he dies, he imparts his last thoughts to the nation he has founded.

barely cognizant of the ethical revolution that monotheism had wrought.

The transformative figure within the Early Prophets is David, the warrior king and poet (circa 1000 B.C.E.). David consolidated Israel's rule over the land that became known as Israel, captured Jerusalem, and established it as Israel's permanent capital. Although later dissension sundered David's empire into two separate Israelite kingdoms (Judah in the south and Israel in the north), Jewish tradition—and Christian as well—has long believed that the Messiah will descend from David.

The later prophetic books, which are mainly written in poetic form, are what we usually think of when we refer to the prophetic books of the Bible. The most famous, Isaiah, Jeremiah, Amos, and Hosea, consist primarily of condemnations of Israelite betrayals of monotheism's ideals, and appeals for ethical behavior. In these books, written over several centuries beginning in the eighth century B.C.E., one finds repeated ruminations about evil, suffering, and sin.

The final books of the Hebrew Bible, known as the Writings (*Ketuvim*), have little in common. Some are historical; for example, the books of Ezra and Nehemiah tell the story of the Jews' return to Israel following the sixth century B.C.E. Babylonian exile, while I and II Chronicles provide an overview of biblical history. The Writings also contain the Book of Psalms, one hundred and fifty poems, some of overwhelming beauty, about man's relationship to God. Job, meanwhile, grapples with the most fundamental challenge to religion: Why does a God Who is good allow so much evil in the world? The Writings also contain the Five Scrolls, which include one of the best-known biblical books aside from the Torah—Esther, which tells the story of the joyful holiday of Purim.

In *Biblical Literacy*, I have attempted to retell the Bible's tales in a way that will not only acquaint the reader with each event's most important details, but will also convey the Bible's insights about living: how to raise children, honor parents, serve God, resist evil leaders, be a friend, fight against injustice, and love another person.

The Bible is more subtle than many of us assume; knowing its contents well can empower us when dealing with important life issues. For example, those unfamiliar with the Hebrew Bible may mistakenly conclude that "true religiosity" demands that we uncomplainingly accept "God's will" whenever we are confronted with pain and tragedy. However, if we turn to the discussion of Job (see entries 127–129), and then to the chapters and verses cited from that book, we learn that there is nothing inconsistent between both believing *in* God, and arguing *with* Him. We also learn that while Job is the most famous biblical protagonist to contend with God, such argumentation has a long history, going back to Abraham, whom Jews and Christians regard as the first Jew. When Abraham fears that God is acting capriciously, he challenges the Lord with the daring, rhetorical question: "Shall not the Judge of all the earth deal justly? (Genesis 18:25).

Biblical guidelines have much to offer aside from theology. Readers considering what traits to look for in a partner would do well to consult Genesis 24, which tells the story of Eliezer, Abraham's servant, who, when instructed to find a suitable wife for the Patriarch's son, Isaac, is given only one condition: that the bride come from the land of Abraham's birth. But Eliezer soon develops a longer list of important virtues, among them hospitality, an ability to anticipate others' needs, kindness to animals, and vigor (see entry 16).

The Bible has had a wide-ranging impact on our lives. Several key biblical ideas—the monotheistic belief that the world was created by a single God and hence is subject to a universal morality, that people should dedicate themselves to making one day a week holy, and that the Jews have been chosen by God to spread His message to the world—have transformed how humans have lived and how they have understood their lives' meaning.

Thus, although monotheism is sometimes described as if its *major* contribution came down to numbers, to influence people to believe in one God instead of multiple deities, its major conceptual revolution had more to do with morality. Unlike the amoral, materially demanding pagan gods worshiped by ancient Israel's neighbors, the central demand Israel's God made of His people was ethical behavior, exemplified by such admonitions as "Justice, justice you shall pursue" (Deuteronomy 16:20), as well as commandments obligating people to care for the poor, the widow, the orphan, and the stranger (see Laws 63–67). This biblical conception of God lay behind John Adams's assertion, "The Hebrews have done more to civilize men than any other nation. . . . The doctrine of a supreme intelligent . . . sovereign of the universe . . . I believe to be the great essential principle of all morality, and consequently of all civilization."

Even Jewish chosenness, seemingly the most "parochial" of the ideas enumerated above, has powerfully affected non-Jews. Thus, Christianity argued that chosenness had passed from the Jews (Old Israel) to Christianity (New Israel), while Islam contended that Muhammad and his followers had become God's new messengers.

Language is another sphere of biblical influence. The Bible's language leaves its imprint even on those who have never read it or who regard it as untrue. Thus, the notion that human beings are responsible for one another is underscored by Cain's question to God, "Am I my brother's keeper?" (Genesis 4:9; see entry 3). From the Bible, we have learned to resist the seductions of money, to not "worship[ing] the Golden Calf" (Exodus 32:4; see entry 43), to acknowledge that "man does not live by bread alone" (Deuteronomy 8:3), and to realize that "you can't take it with you" (Ecclesiastes 5:14). We speak of the foolish and the wicked who are unable to recognize the consequences of their actions as not seeing "the writing on the wall" (Daniel 5:25; see entry 140). The notion that punishment should be proportionate to the provocation is expressed in the biblical law of "an eye for an eye" (Exodus 21:24; see entry 169). And many people are surprised to learn that it is the pessimistic Ecclesiastes, not a Greek or Latin philosopher, who first taught, "There is nothing new under the sun" (Ecclesiastes 1:9; see entry 134).

Along with shaping how we speak and think, the Hebrew Bible has also provided many of us with our names. Consider this brief list: Adam, Abraham, Isaac, Jacob, Reuben, Joseph, Benjamin, Moses, Aaron, Joshua, Samuel, Saul, David, Jonathan, Solomon, Jeremy (from Jeremiah), Joel, Jonah, and Daniel for boys, and Eve, Sarah, Rebecca, Rachel, Leah, Miriam, Deborah, Hannah, Esther, and Ruth for girls.

Thus, biblical ideas fill our lives with meaning, its laws influence how we behave toward one another, its stories help us define the kind of lives we should lead, its metaphors help shape the way we think and speak, and its characters inspire the names we give our children. That a series of books written some 2,400 to 3,200 years ago has had this enduring impact seems as miraculous as any of the wonders described in the Bible.

And yet . . . important as the Bible is, its influence for many people today is at best secondhand, mediated through the sermons and explanations of rabbis, ministers, and priests. A 1994 survey of twelve hundred Americans aged fifteen to thirty-five found that a majority could name no more than two of the Ten Commandments.

Even those more knowledgeable about the Bible are subject to information that is vague and imprecise. Thus, one often hears people cite the Sixth Commandment as "You shall not kill," although no such law exists. Like English, Hebrew has separate words for "kill" and "murder"; in Hebrew, the Sixth Commandment reads *Lo Tirtzach*, "You shall not murder." Indeed, to any reader familiar with the rest

of the Torah, only this reading makes sense. For had the Bible legislated, "You shall not kill," how could one explain those verses mandating capital punishment for premeditated murderers (see entry
150) and supporting the right to kill in self-defense? (see, for example, Exodus 22:1–2).*

Biblical Literacy's first part covers biblical events and personalities.
Starting with Genesis and proceeding straight through the Bible's
thirty-nine books to Second Chronicles (Christian scriptures contain
the same books in a different order), it explores the major episodes
and personalities in order of appearance. Jewish readers who wish
to review the narrative content of the weekly Torah reading (the
Torah is read through in its entirety each year during the Saturday
morning service) can easily find the events described. Nonreligious
readers will discover that reading this section straight through provides them with a comprehensive overview of the Hebrew Bible.

As opposed to an encyclopedia, here events and characters appear
sequentially, not alphabetically. To acquaint oneself with David's
life, a person consulting an encyclopedia would have to turn to entries on the warrior poet and king, as well as on the most significant
figures in his life: Goliath, Saul, Jonathan, Bathsheba, Nathan, and
Absalom. Here, one can read about these people and their involvements with David (see entries 73—84) in the way they appear in
the two Books of Samuel.

Regarding the Bible's later books, particularly the literary prophets
and some of the Writings, *Biblical Literacy* cannot adequately cover
each book's powerful poetic images. In these entries, I have tried to
convey what is distinctive about the messages imparted in each book.
To borrow an image from Dr. Jeremiah Unterman, a biblical scholar
and friend, my tour through those works is somewhat like a wine-
tasting expedition, in which one samples many different fine vin-
tages.

Part II focuses on the Torah's most important laws and ideas.
Here, for example, the reader encounters a discussion of circumcision, the Torah's oldest ritual; what the Bible means in referring to

---

*The misconception about the Sixth Commandment's meaning apparently
occurred because most Christian Bible translators translated the Ten Commandments so as to make them consistent with Jesus' teachings. Thus, since
the Gospels cite Jesus as opposing *all* violence, even in self-defense (see,
for example, Matthew 5:39), the Sixth Commandment is rendered as if it
shared this viewpoint. Now that more Christian Bible scholars are fully
conversant with Hebrew, this mistranslation occurs less frequently.

human beings as created "in God's image"; why the Bible commands that people "fear" God, and not just love Him; the biblical view of capital punishment for premeditated murderers; the commandment to love the stranger; and the meaning and significance of each of the Ten Commandments.

Part III was written in response to a question frequently posed at lectures and by readers of my earlier book, *Jewish Literacy*: "What exactly are the 613 laws of the Torah?" Here, I have set down a brief description of each law, and the Torah verse on which it is based. Few people are aware that over three hundred of these laws deal with sacrifices, and purity and impurity, and are no longer practiced.

The appendices contain a listing of the Bible's thirty-nine books in order of appearance, and a listing of the approximate dates of the most important biblical protagonists and events.

One of my major goals in writing this book is to send readers back to the Bible to encounter for themselves its powerful stories of family, of human relationships to God and to other people, and of power and how it should be used. Only through such personal reading and study will the Bible, the most influential book of the past three millennia, remain the most influential book of the next three thousand years.

Two technical notes: In citations from biblical verses, I have italicized certain words (although no such emphasis occurs in the biblical text itself) to underscore a point being made in the entry.

Second, when "Rabbi" is capitalized, this refers to a rabbi or rabbis of the talmudic era.

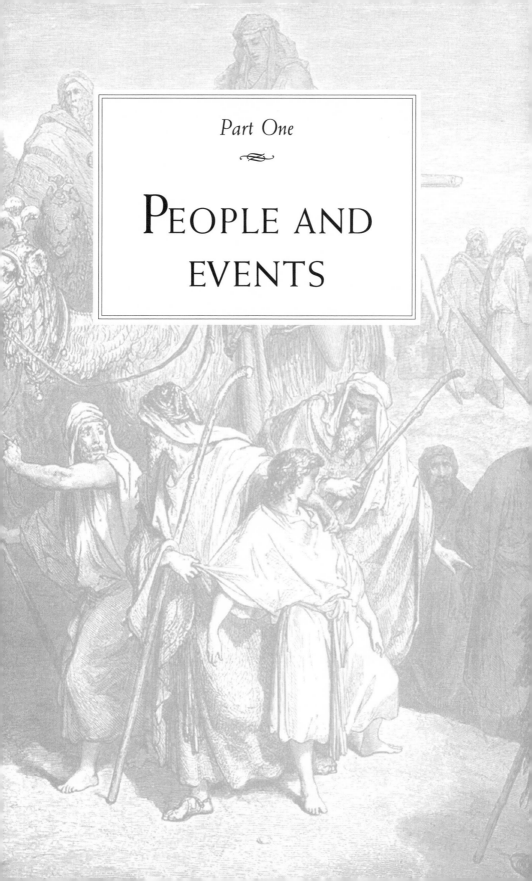

Part One

PEOPLE AND
EVENTS

THE TORAH

GENESIS

EXODUS

LEVITICUS

NUMBERS

DEUTERONOMY

I. GENESIS

1. In the Beginning

GENESIS, CHAPTER 1

"In the beginning, God created the heavens and the earth" (1:1). The first and most important fact established in the Bible's opening chapter, indeed in its opening sentence, is that God, and God alone, created the world. This assertion represents a complete break with the prevailing view at the time, that nature itself is divine. Ancient man worshiped nature; the sun was its most common manifestation. Interestingly, the Hebrew word for sun, *shemesh*, from the root meaning "servant,"* leaves no doubt about the divine order of the universe: that which other people worship as God (i.e., the Babylonian sun god was called Shamash), the language of the Bible makes clear, is but God's servant.

Underscoring God's supreme and supernatural capabilities, the Bible declares that God can create through words alone: "God said, 'Let there be light' and there was light" (1:3).

The order of creation in Genesis 1 is:

Day 1: light
Day 2: the sky
Day 3: the earth, oceans, and vegetation
Day 4: the sun, moon, and stars
Day 5: fish, insects, and birds
Day 6: the animal kingdom and human beings

---

*In Hebrew, *shamash* is the title of the person who assists in the synagogue, while the *shamash* candle on the Hannuka menorah serves to light the other candles.

Despite arguments advanced by biblical fundamentalists, Genesis 1 need not be understood as meaning that God created the world in six twenty-four-hour days. Indeed, given that there were no sun and moon prior to the fourth day, it is meaningless to speak in terms of standardized, modern time units. Many religious scholars understand each of the six "days" as representing eons.

Humans are the only beings described as being created "in the image of God" (see entry 146) and thus apparently represent the apogee of creation.

Many Bible readers have long puzzled over differences in a second version of the creation story presented in Genesis, chapter 2. While 1:27 suggests that man and woman were created simultaneously— "in the image of God He created him; male and female He created them"—2:7–8 speaks of God fashioning Adam alone, from the earth.* Eventually, God concludes, "It is not good for man to be alone" (2:18).† He puts Adam into a deep sleep, withdraws one of his ribs, and from it fashions Eve, the first woman (2:21–23).

Is such an explanation of woman's creation demeaning to women? On the one hand, the claim that man was created first, and woman formed out of a part of him, might suggest the male's inherent superiority. On the other hand, the fact that every new creature depicted in the divine creation is more highly developed than the one that preceded it might indicate that woman, who is last to be created, represents the apex of creation.

In any event, the account in chapter 1, which states that both sexes are created in God's image, clearly suggests that they are equal in God's eyes.

God's initial intention seems to be to create a herbivorous world, and so He directs human beings to restrict their diet to vegetables and fruits (1:29), while also confining the animal kingdom to the consumption of green plants (1:30). Later, after the Flood, God permits humans to eat meat (Genesis 9:3–4).

By the end of the sixth day, God has finished His work, and so on the seventh day, He ceases to create, thereby establishing, as early

---

*There are other differences as well: Genesis 2:7 records that God created man first, and then animals (2:19), the reverse of what is described in Genesis 1:20–28.
†John Milton (seventeenth century) observed in his *Tetrachordon*, "Loneliness was the first thing which God's eye named not good."

as the Bible's second chapter, the tradition of the Sabbath: "And God blessed the seventh day and declared it holy, because on it God ceased from all the work of creation that He had done" (2:3). Much later, the Fourth Commandment ordained that Israel "remember the Sabbath day to make it holy," as a reminder of the very first seventh day, during which the Lord refrained from creating (Exodus 20:8–11).

The biblical view of creation is optimistic. Genesis's opening chapter repeatedly describes the Lord as pleased with what He has brought into being: "God saw that the light was good" (1:4); "The earth brought forth vegetation . . . and God saw that this was good" (1:12); "And God saw all that He had made, and found it very good" (1:31; see also 1:10, 18, and 21, where God pronounces similar judgment on His other creations).

Yet good as it was, creation was still unfinished. The Rabbis of the Talmud deduced from God's ceasing to create that it is humankind's mission to serve as God's partner in finishing His creation and perfecting the world.

2. Adam, Eve, and the Garden of Eden

GENESIS 2:7–3:24

The Tree of Knowledge of Good and Evil

GENESIS 2:15–17; CHAPTER 3

Adam and Eve, the Bible's first man and woman, are the prototype for all people. The Hebrew for "human being" is *ben adam*, a child of Adam.

The couple begin their lives in a paradise, which the Bible calls the Garden of Eden. There, God provides for all their needs, in return for which He imposes several commandments: They are to be fruitful and multiply (see entry 147), fill the earth and master it (1:28), restrict their diet to fruit and vegetables (1:29), and refrain from eating from the "tree of the knowledge of good and evil."* God gives this commandment to Adam before He creates Eve, and offers no rationale for it. Adam simply is warned that "as soon as you eat [of the tree of knowledge], you shall die" (2:17).

Immediately after imposing this prohibition, God creates Eve from one of Adam's ribs. Absent any recorded communication between God and Eve, we must assume that she learns of the prohibition concerning the tree of knowledge from Adam.

Enter the serpent, who we are told is "the shrewdest of all the wild beasts that the Lord had made" (3:1). He speaks human language (the Bible's only other talking animal is Balaam's donkey; see entry 50), and challenges Eve: "Did God really say, 'You shall not eat of any tree of the garden?'" (3:1).

The serpent, in his shrewdness, challenges Eve, who unlike Adam has not heard the prohibition directly from God. Thus, she is more open to disbelieving that God had ever promulgated such a decree.

Eve's response to the serpent's question indicates that Adam may have treated Eve as a simpleton, for she now attributes to God words that He never uttered, but which Adam seems to have told her He had: "It is only about the fruit of the tree in the middle of the garden that God said: 'You shall not eat of it *or touch it*, lest you die.'" Fearing that Eve might be tempted to eat the forbidden fruit, Adam apparently told her that God prohibited them from even touching the tree.

The Midrash, which consists of rabbinic commentaries on the Bible, suggests that the cunning serpent utilized Adam's additional, and erroneous, instruction to convince Eve that her husband had lied to her; he pushed Eve against the tree, waited till she realized that she had remained unharmed, then told her, "You are not going to die [if you eat of the tree's fruit]."

The serpent tells Eve that God wishes to deter her and Adam from eating of the tree because He doesn't want them to be Godlike: "God knows that as soon as you eat of it, your eyes will be opened and you will be like divine beings who know good and evil" (3:5).

It remains a mystery why such knowledge would upset God: Indeed, traditional Jewish theology teaches that the meaning of the creation of people in God's image is precisely that they resemble Him in being able to distinguish good from evil.

*There is no reason to assume that it was an apple tree, although that is how it invariably is depicted in Western art.

In any case, Eve is seduced both by a serpent who urges her to eat of the tree's fruit and by the tree's delightful appearance. She eats of the tree's fruit, then gives a fruit to Adam, who eats it as well.

Now, for the first time, Adam and Eve become conscious of their nakedness,* and cover themselves with loincloths. Soon after, the couple, sensing God's presence in the Garden, hide. God calls out to them, "*Ayecha*—Where are you?"

Obviously, the all-knowing God does not ask this because He can't find them; rather, God wishes to encourage Adam and Eve to acknowledge their sin. But they don't. Instead, Adam responds by explaining that he was hiding because he feared to confront God while naked. The Lord asks him, "Who told you that you were naked? Did you eat of the tree from which I had forbidden you to eat?" (3:11).

We now encounter an age-old problem: the inability of most people to acknowledge their guilt forthrightly but, instead, to "scapegoat" someone or something else. Adam blames Eve, and, by implication, God, for his sin: "The woman *You* put at my side, she gave me of the tree and I ate." In turn, Eve blames the serpent: "The serpent duped me, and I ate."

God now decrees punishment for both the serpent and the two humans:

The serpent will lose his ability to walk; instead, he will crawl on the earth and eat dirt, and live in a state of constant enmity with human beings, who will strike at his head. Strangely, nothing is said about his losing the ability to converse with human beings (perhaps because this was a one-time occurrence, as in the case of Balaam's donkey, see entry 50).

Eve receives two punishments: Childbirth will be painful for her, and her husband will rule over her. Although this is often cited as a biblical mandate for men dominating their wives, the Bible *never says or implies* that this punishment is intended to apply to Eve's descendants. Why should it? Eve alone sinned. All that the text declares is that *her* husband will rule over her, presumably as punishment for her having led him to sin.

---

*This seems to suggest that the word "knowledge" in the tree's name refers, among other things, to sexual knowledge; in biblical Hebrew, "to know" often means "to have sexual relations with." Further, it is sexual knowledge that enables human beings to become Godlike in at least one way, the ability to create life.

Adam is punished by having to labor hard for his food: "By the sweat of your brow shall you eat bread until you return to the ground . . . for dust you are, and to dust you shall return" (3:19).

The final punishment decreed for Adam and Eve is expulsion from the Garden of Eden. No longer will they be surrounded by fruit-bearing trees; from now on they will have to labor for their food.

Reflections: Is the expulsion of Adam and Eve from paradise an unmitigated curse? Not according to the most ingenious interpretation of why Eve sinned, which I heard from the late Jewish educator Shlomo Bardin (founder of the Brandeis-Bardin Institute in Southern California). He explained Eve's behavior through this parable:

"Imagine that a young woman marries a young man whose father is president of a large company. After the marriage, the father makes the son a vice president and gives him a large salary, but because he has no work experience, the father gives him no responsibilities. Every week, the young man draws a large check, but he has nothing to do. His wife soon realizes that she is not married to a man but to a boy, and that as long as her husband stays in his father's firm, he will always be a boy. So she forces him to quit his job, give up his security, go to another city, and start out on his own. That is the reason Eve ate from the tree."

God's words apparently did not mean that Adam would die immediately (see 2:17), but that on the day he ate from the tree he would become mortal and so subject to eventual death. Despite God's warning that on the day Adam ate from the tree, he would die, Adam lives nine hundred years; his and Eve's descendants eventually populate the entire world.

Note: Adam, Eve, and the doctrine of Original Sin: In Christian theology, eating the forbidden fruit constitutes the Original Sin which taints all future human beings with a primal transgression. Such sinfulness can supposedly be overcome through baptism and acceptance of the divinity of Jesus Christ who died to atone for humankind's sins, of which the eating from the tree was the first.

Significant as this episode is in Christian teachings, it does not, as Jewish theologian Louis Jacobs argues, "occupy an important place in [conventional] Jewish theology" (*The Jewish Religion: A Companion,* page 14). The prevailing attitude among Jewish scholars is that people sin *as* Adam and Eve sinned, not *because* they sinned.

However, Jacobs does note that among students of the mystical *kabbalah,* a doctrine similar to Original Sin did evolve that argued that because all human souls were contained as sparks in Adam's soul, all of humankind was contaminated by Adam's sin. However, this kabbalistic doctrine about the significance of Adam's sin remained a peripheral teaching in Jewish life. Furthermore, "even in those [kabbalistic] versions of Judaism in which the idea of Original Sin is accepted, it differs from Christian dogma in that God alone, not a savior like Jesus, helps man to overcome his sinful nature" (page 370).

3. Cain and Abel

GENESIS, CHAPTER 4

"Am I My Brother's Keeper?"

4:9

Although people often think of the world as becoming ever more violent, according to the Bible the violence in men's natures has existed since the beginning. Nothing conveys this somber fact more dramatically than the murder committed by Cain, the first child born to Adam and Eve, of his brother Abel.

Cain's life starts with high hopes: His mother chooses a name for him that means "I have gained a male child with the help of the Lord." A short time later, Abel is born, although we are not told the reason for his name.

When the two brothers grow up, Cain becomes a farmer, Abel a shepherd. One day they each bring a gift to God; Cain brings fruit from the land he has tended, while Abel brings "the choicest of the firstling of his flock." The Bible's choice of language implies that Abel has worked at bringing God something more precious than the gift of his brother.

God responds favorably to Abel's gift, but ignores Cain's. The Lord sees that Cain is upset and immediately challenges him: "Why are you distressed and why is your face fallen?" Cognizant of Cain's anger and cruel impulses, God warns him, "But if you do not do right, sin couches at the door. Its urge is toward you, yet you can be its master" (4:6–7).

God's question and warning seem to represent a divine effort to prompt Cain to talk about his anger and hurt. But Cain refuses to respond to God, nor does he express his feelings to his brother. Indeed, the next verse in the Bible ends midsentence: "Cain said to his brother Abel . . ."; we are never told *what* he said. Possibly nothing; Cain may well have been too angry to speak. Instead, the text continues: "When they were in the field, Cain set upon his brother Abel and killed him" (4:8).

Now God speaks to Cain a second time, and asks him, "Where is your brother Abel?"

Cain responds dismissively, "I do not know. Am I my brother's keeper?"

It is no exaggeration to say that much of the rest of the Bible constitutes an affirmative response to Cain's heartless question.

The Lord rails against Cain, "What have you done? Your brother's blood cries out to Me from the ground!"

The Hebrew word for blood that is used here, *d'mei,* is in the plural, so that the verse literally reads: "Your brother's *bloods . . .*" From this, the Talmud concludes that what cries out is not only Abel's blood, but that of all his future, never-to-be-born descendants. (We can say here that in comparable fashion, by the year 2040, almost all the Jews murdered in the Holocaust would have been dead in any event, but millions of their unborn descendants would have been alive.)

Although the Bible legislates a death sentence for murderers, God does not execute Cain. Perhaps the reason is that before this time no one had yet died. Thus, Cain might have been unaware that he was capable of killing someone. Therefore, although he was a killer, he did not premeditate murder, and so did not deserve capital punishment.

Instead, God tells Cain that he can no longer gain a livelihood as a farmer, for the earth, which opened its mouth to receive Abel's blood, will no longer yield its strength to Cain. God sentences him to be a ceaseless wanderer on the earth.

Cain's response is consistent with the arrogance he has earlier displayed. Not one word of remorse escapes his lips; instead, he complains: "My punishment is too great to bear!" He then says something that brings to mind a favorite expression of Isaac Bashevis Singer, the late Yiddish writer and Nobel Prize winner, "People who don't show pity to others, crave it for themselves." Thus, Cain, the murderer, now complains to God that "anyone who meets me may kill me."

God takes sufficient pity on Cain to pronounce a curse against any person who would slay him: "If anyone kills Cain, sevenfold vengeance shall be taken on him." He also puts a mark on Cain (this is generally assumed to be on his forehead, although the Bible does not so specify), so that everyone will recognize him and not abuse him.

When I learned this passage in elementary school (in Jewish day schools, Genesis is generally taught to seven- and eight-year-olds), one question preoccupied my fellow students and me, one to which I have still not heard a satisfying answer: If the only people alive then were Adam, Eve, and Cain, of whom was Cain so afraid? His statement, "Anyone who meets me may kill me," suggests a somewhat substantial population, a world in which not everyone would know Cain. Indeed, that is why God must give him a special mark.

The Bible provides no answer to this question, just as it doesn't tell us other facts, such as whom Cain later married. It's possible that although the Bible only records the creation of the world's first man and woman, God also created other human beings.

Adam soon has another child with Eve, thereby freeing the rest of humankind from the certainty that we all descend from a murderer. When the child is born, Eve names him Seth, explaining that "God has provided me with another offspring in place of Abel."

Meanwhile we learn little more about Cain other than that he settles in the land of Nod, has a son with his wife, and founds the world's first city, which he names Enoch after his son. Several generations later, another descendant, Lamech, is described by the Bible as having the same lovable personality as his ancestor. The first polygamist described in the Torah, Lamech brags to his two wives that he has "slain a man for wounding me, and a lad for bruising me" (4:23).

The downward moral spiral of humankind, beginning with the sin of Adam and Eve, and escalating with the murder of Abel and the killings committed by Lamech, soon grows greater. God feels like an unhappy parent, Creator of a creature who has free will and whom He cannot control. The level of God's disappointment can be gauged by the harsh words He speaks in in response to humankind's evil behavior (Genesis 6:7): "I will blot out from the earth the men whom I created . . . for I regret that I made them."

Only one thing stops God from doing so: Noah, a special, righteous man to whose life we now turn.

Source and further reading: The explanation that God was trying to prompt Cain to talk about his anger is suggested by psychologist Naomi Rosenblatt and Joshua Horwitz, *Wrestling with Angels*, pages 52–64.

4. Noah's Ark

GENESIS 6:11–8:22

The Bible now describes a new era, during which the world's moral deterioration has become so extreme that God concludes that He must eradicate humankind and start civilization anew. The Bible introduces Noah and describes him as a righteous man.* God appears to Noah and instructs him to make an ark of gopher wood, and to cover it with pitch. He is to make within it an opening for daylight, and to construct three levels or floors.

God confides to Noah His intention: Furious at how corrupt the earth is, He will flood the entire world till "everything on earth shall perish." When the Flood ends, the only creatures who will survive will be the fish in the water (obviously they will not drown), and all the inhabitants, both human and animal, on Noah's ark. Thus, in addition to his wife, three sons, and three daughters-in-law, Noah is to take on the ark one female and one male of every animal and bird, and seven each of certain types of "clean animals."

Saying nothing, Noah begins building the ark.†

*However, the text offers no specific instances of his goodness as it does, for instance, when introducing Moses, who is described as standing up on behalf of some young Midianite shepherdesses who are being bullied by male shepherds (see Exodus 2:16–17).
†Noah's silence, which contrasts with Abraham's lengthy, vociferous "negotiation" with God over His intention to destroy the evil cities of Sodom and Gomorrah (see Genesis 18:16–33), leads some Bible commentators to question how deeply Noah's streak of goodness runs. Indeed, since the huge ark takes so long to build, people may have inquired of Noah why he was

The Flood eventually comes; heavy rains fall continuously for forty days and nights. As the waters rise, the ark drifts from place to place. Soon, all human beings and animals outside the ark are dead. After many weeks of downpour, all the earth's mountains are covered, yet still the waters rise. No one can leave the boat, but no one goes hungry, presumably because Noah had stored away vast quantities of food.

Finally, after five months the waters begin to recede; by the seventh month, Noah's ark comes to rest on the top of Mount Ararat. (To this day, some amateur archaeologists claim to have spotted elements of the still-resting ark upon the mountain, which is in a remote region of Turkey.) However, it takes another three months until the mountaintops become visible.

Noah sends out a dove to see if the waters have receded enough for the ark's residents to disembark. But soon the dove returns, an indication that it can find no resting place. A week later, Noah again sends out the dove; that evening, the bird returns with a plucked-off olive leaf in its bill. Seven days after that, Noah sends the dove a third time; the bird doesn't return, a sign that there is now ample vegetation on the earth.

Soon thereafter, Noah, his family, and the animals disembark. God has created a situation similar to that of the Garden of Eden (although now there are four human couples instead of one).

Yet, as quickly becomes apparent (see next entry), the people through whom God has chosen to start all over are far from flawless.

A final note: When Noah emerges from the ark, he offers a sacrifice to God, choosing from the clean animals, which number at least seven. In response to the offering, God promises, "Never again will I doom the earth because of man, since the devisings of man's mind are evil from his youth" (8:21). God's reasoning has puzzled many Bible readers: A short term earlier He had destroyed the world *because* of human evil; now He announces that He will never destroy it again *because* of human evil.

My understanding of this is that God has at last made some peace with the fact of human evil; because human nature is so drawn to evil, God will not punish people so harshly. He therefore provides Noah with a sign that never again will the earth be destroyed by a flood; from now on rains will be followed by rainbows (Genesis

---

building such an enormous boat. And, if they did ask, one wonders what Noah answered.

9:12–17): "As long as the earth endures," God promises, "seedtime and harvest, cold and heat, summer and winter, day and night, shall not cease" (8:22).

Reflections: How righteous a man was Noah?—A talmudic dispute. In introducing Noah, the Bible describes him as "a righteous man, blameless in his generation" (6:9). The words "in his generation" seem superfluous; what do they add to what we already have been told?

Unwilling to accept the existence of superfluous words in a document they regard as divine, two Rabbis of the Talmud assert that these words convey important additional information about Noah, but disagree on the words' implications. Rabbi Yochanan argues that "in his generation" suggests that Noah should be regarded as righteous only by the standards of his particularly evil generation; had he lived in more normal times, he would have been regarded as morally average. Indeed, one could argue that, Noah's refusal to argue with God to save the world, and his later act of drunkenness (see next entry), call into question the depth of his righteousness.

Resh Lakish, Yochanan's rabbinic contemporary, takes the opposing view: If Noah grew up among such evil people and nonetheless is spoken of as righteous, how much greater would he have been had he been raised among moral people? His view of Noah, likely influenced by the fact that he too came from a "deprived" background, might well be psychologically more astute than that of Rabbi Yochanan. The Talmud offers alternate accounts of Resh Lakish's youth: In one version he was raised in a circus, in another, among a band of thieves. Resh Lakish, more than Rabbi Yochanan, well understood the difficulties entailed in overcoming an unsavory background. He was, therefore, more sympathetic to Noah, and rightly so, I believe.

How does the story of Noah and the Flood compare with other ancient flood stories? The existence of flood stories throughout ancient Near Eastern literature suggests of course the actual occurrence of a great primeval flood (archaeological evidence exists of a widespread inundation in the Near East, although there are no indications of one worldwide). The other flood stories bear some striking similarities to the story occurring in the Bible. To cite just one example, in the Babylonian Gilgamesh epic, Utnapishtim, the Babylonian Noah, speaks of sending out a dove that turned back because of lack of a resting place.

However, these other versions differ from the Bible's account in explaining both why the Flood occurred and why one man, or family, was saved. In the Mesopotamian accounts, either no reason is given for the deluge, or it is explained as the gods' angry response to the loud, bothersome noise made by humankind. Similarly, the hero's rescue is not attributed to his moral worthiness, but to the subterfuge of a particular god acting against the desire of the others (Nahum Sarna, *The JPS Torah Commentary: Genesis*, pages 48–49).

5. Ham's Sin and the Evil Caused by Drunkenness

GENESIS 9:20–27

The combination of Noah's drunkenness followed by his son Ham's vile disrespect toward him leads to one of the saddest incidents described in Genesis. It all begins when Noah and his family emerge from the ark after the flood, and Noah turns to farming. He plants a vineyard from which he produces his own wine. Shortly thereafter, he drinks of the wine and becomes drunk, stupefyingly drunk it would appear. What occurs next has been argued about by Bible commentators ever since. Noah uncovers himself within his tent, and his youngest son, Ham, "saw his father's nakedness and told his two brothers outside." The brothers, Shem and Japhet, walk backward into Noah's tent carrying a sheet, and lay it across their father, covering his nakedness without looking upon it themselves.

When Noah awakes from his stupor, "and learned what his youngest son had done to him," he curses Ham's son, Canaan, and condemns him and his descendants to serve his brothers and their descendants.

This passage is maddeningly obscure. First, why is Noah so enraged at Ham's act? Possibly, the words "saw his father's nakedness" are a euphemism for some perverse sexual act Ham performed on his drunken father (much later, Lot's two daughters get Lot into a drunken stupor during which they commit incest with him; Genesis 19:30–38). Supporting this interpretation is the fact that the Bible commonly uses the expression "to uncover someone's nakedness"— similar to, although not the same as, "saw his father's nakedness"—

as a euphemism for sexual relations (see, for example, Leviticus 18:6–19). If that is the case, Noah's wrath would be understandable.

On the other hand, the Bible's own words, and the reaction of Ham's two brothers, suggest that all Ham did was look upon his father's nakedness and perhaps mock it to his brothers. An intrusive, humiliating thing to do, certainly, but undeserving, it would seem, of the wrath it evokes.

The episode's second problematic feature is Noah's curse; he directs it, not against Ham, the son who uncovered his nakedness, but against Canaan. Why? We don't know, although in moments of rage people often say inappropriate things, as, for example, laying a curse on the descendants of the person at whom they are enraged. Noah's imprecation against Canaan is a particularly unfortunate one, guaranteed to provoke intrafamily hatreds for generations: "Cursed be Canaan, the lowest of slaves shall he be to his brothers." He then blesses his other two sons and concludes, "And let Canaan be a slave to them" (9:25, 27).

Canaan was the ancestor of the people who settled the land of Israel before the Israelites. It is presumably no coincidence that the Bible repeatedly denounces them for practicing sexual perversities (see, for example, Leviticus 18:23–30).

6. The Tower of Babel

GENESIS 11:1–9

The Tower of Babel story tells us something about human vanity and arrogance. More important, it also provides an answer to a seemingly unanswerable question: If all humankind descended from one couple, Adam and Eve, how did different nations and languages emerge? The Bible sets out to answer this question in the story of the Tower of Babel, the last Torah narrative to deal with the story of humankind as a whole (starting with chapter 12 of Genesis, the Torah becomes the story of Abraham and Sarah's family and the Israelite nation that descends from them).

At the beginning of Genesis 11, we learn that all humans live in close proximity to each other and speak a single language. Migrating from the east (the text does not record from where) to the Shinar valley in Babylonia, they develop a plan to build a brick tower "with its top in the sky, to make a name for ourselves; else we shall be scattered all over the world" (11:4).

Humans' desire to "make a name" for themselves—that is, to become famous, even immortal—represents a normal, although not always noble, expression of the human ego. But why do the people believe that if they don't build such a tower they will be scattered throughout the world? The Bible doesn't tell us.

God comes down from heaven to inspect the building project, and concludes, "If as one people with one language for all, this is how they have begun to act, then nothing they may propose to do will be out of their reach" (11:6). In other words, God sees dangers—albeit unspecified ones—to humankind's character by their having created this ancient superskyscraper. Unfortunately, this is as specific as the text becomes in detailing what the tower builders' sin was. The earlier sins committed in Genesis are explicit (Adam and Eve eat the divinely forbidden fruit of the "tree of knowledge"; Cain murders Abel; Noah's contemporaries are violent and lawless); here, the sin seems to be collective, overweening pride.

God decides to confound the builders' language "so that they shall not understand one another's speech." With this, the building of the tower comes to a halt; lacking a common language, the workers can no longer collaborate on the massive project. Shortly thereafter, they begin moving all over the world, probably with the few others who speak their language.

The tower is left uncompleted, while the city in which they had lived becomes known as Babel "because there the Lord confounded the speech of the whole earth" (11:9). The city's name has entered English as "babble"; indeed, after God confused the people's language, they experienced each other's speech as "mere babble."

7. The Patriarchs and Matriarchs: Abraham, Isaac, Jacob, Sarah, Rebecca, Leah, and Rachel

GENESIS, CHAPTERS 12–50

God's third attempt to influence humankind's ethical behavior begins with Abraham, the man whom Jewish tradition regards as the first Jew.

Prior to Abraham, God twice reveals Himself to all humankind in an attempt to direct them toward righteous behavior. First, He appears to Adam and Eve, who, while in paradise, defy His one prohibition that they not eat of "the tree of knowledge of good and evil" (see entry 2). Generations later, God spares Noah and his family from a massive flood. Through Noah, God tries anew to establish an ethical world. But the world soon becomes populated by people whose overweening ambitions drive them to erect the Tower of Babel; they hope to reach heaven to satisfy their own vanity. Once again, God is not satisfied with the outcome of His efforts.

But with Abraham, God apparently has given up the hope of changing all humankind at once. Rather, He decides to establish a model family, in the hope that it and its descendants ultimately will make God and His will known to the world.

Jewish tradition regards Abraham, his son Isaac, and his grandson Jacob as Judaism's founding fathers (identity at this time was determined by values, not blood; thus Jacob's twin brother, Esau, is not regarded as Jewish). For thousands of years, observant Jews have inaugurated the *Shmoneh Esray* prayer, the cornerstone of the three daily prayer services, with the invocation, "Blessed are You, Lord our God, and God of our Fathers, God of Abraham, God of Isaac, and God of Jacob."*

The three Patriarchs' spouses—respectively Sarah, Rebecca, Leah, and Rachel—become Judaism's founding Matriarchs. As will be ap-

---

*Commentators note that the word "God" precedes each Patriarch's name (as opposed to "God of Abraham, Isaac, and Jacob") to underscore that

parent in the following entries, these women are strong figures, willing to confront their husbands when they feel that their children's and other people's future is at stake. For example, after Sarah gives birth to Isaac, she orders Abraham to expel Ishmael, his son by her servant Hagar, from their house (Genesis 21:10). Abraham seems disinclined to accede to Sarah's demand, until God tells him, "Whatever Sarah tells you to do, do as she says" (Genesis 21:12). A generation later, Rebecca initiates the plot to deceive Isaac into giving his "innermost blessing" to Jacob, her favored child, rather than to Esau, Isaac's favorite.

Although the Bible makes no effort to hide the Patriarchs' and Matriarchs' human flaws, they remain to this day the heroic ancestors of the Jewish people. Their names, in Hebrew

> *Avraham* (Abraham; his original name was Abram, but God changes his name; Genesis 17:5)
>
> *Yitzchak* (Isaac)
>
> *Ya'akov* (Jacob)
>
> *Sarah* (Sarah; her original name was Sarai, but God changes her name; Genesis 17:15)
>
> *Rivka* (Rebecca)
>
> *Leah* (Leah)
>
> *Rakhel* (Rachel)

are among the most common names religious parents give their children, signifying the hope that their offspring will grow up to be committed Jews and progenitors of many future Jewish generations.

---

both Isaac and Jacob did not just accept their father's God, but evolved a personal relationship with Him, as described in this and the next entries.

8. God Chooses Abraham
GENESIS 12:1–9

Why does God choose Abraham? Oddly the Bible does not explain this, though if you attended a Jewish school as a child, you undoubtedly were taught the famous rabbinic *midrash* about Abraham, which tells that even as a young child he disbelieved in the powers of idols, and came to believe in one God Who rules the world.

According to this *midrash*, Terah, Abraham's father, is an idol worshiper; indeed, he owns a shop at which local residents purchase idols. One day, Terah leaves Abraham in charge of the store. Abraham, who has not previously expressed his skepticism about the idols to his father, smashes them all, except for the largest, in whose hand he places a large ax.

When Terah returns, he finds his store in chaos, and questions his son. Abraham explains that the large idol had become infuriated at the smaller ones, picked up an ax, and destroyed them all.

Enraged, Terah yells at his son, "Stop lying to me! You know that these idols can't walk or talk or move!"

"If they can't protect themselves," Abraham responds, "then why do you pray to them to protect you?"

How does Terah respond to this eminently sensible question? He takes Abraham to the local monarch to be burned, but God saves him.

Since there is no basis in the Bible for this story, why did the Rabbis transmit such a tale? I believe that they desired to explain what the Bible does not: why God chooses Abraham and endows him with a world-transforming mission.

Genesis 12:1 begins with God issuing an instruction to Abraham, who comes from Ur of the Chaldees (in modern-day Iraq): "Go forth from your native land and from your father's house to the land that I will show you." God promises to turn Abraham's descendants into a great nation (a promise that must have deeply touched Abraham, since his wife, Sarah, is infertile; Genesis 11:30), one through which all nations of the world shall be blessed.

The land to which God sends Abraham is Canaan; thus, the origins of the Hebrew people begin in exile. In Canaan God appears to Abraham and announces that "I will give this land to your offspring" (12:7).

Later, additional information is imparted that gives us a broader understanding of the moral/theological dimension of Abraham's mission. Shortly before destroying the cities of Sodom and Gomorrah, God confides to Abraham His intention to do so, since "I have singled him [Abraham] out, that he may instruct his children and his posterity to keep the way of the Lord by doing what is just and right" (Genesis 18:19).

This particularly significant verse expresses the idea that Abraham has been singled out for a special mission, to stand for justice. The label "Chosen People" has of course long been applied to the Jews, who are also known as "the children of Abraham." God's defining "the way of the Lord" as "doing what is just and right" underscores the Bible's primary message: that there is One Lord, and His major requirement of humankind is ethical behavior.

Abraham transmits his message to his son Isaac, who transmits it to Jacob, and he passes it on to his twelve sons, from whom the Israelite people descend. It has long been universally acknowledged that the concept of one God came to the world through the Jews, Abraham's descendants.*

Yet we are still left wondering: What is it about Abraham that impels God to choose him for this mission? In Moses' case, for example, the Bible relates three significant episodes prior to God's appointing him Israel's leader; all demonstrate his obsession with fighting injustice (see entry 31), a worthy occupation for one destined to be the Torah's greatest prophet. But about Abraham, we are told no such stories. All we know is that God saw something special within him and, as the historical record shows, God's instinct, needless to say, was very sound.

Sources and further readings: The *midrash* about Terah's idol shop can be found in *Tanna d'Bei Eliyahu,* pages 27–28, and *Genesis Rabbah* 38:13. An English language version, very similar but far more detailed than

---

*As theologian Louis Jacobs notes: "It becomes obvious that [regarding Jewish chosenness] we are not discussing a dogma incapable of verification but the recognition of sober historical fact. The world owes Israel the idea of the one God of righteousness and holiness. This is how God became known to mankind" (*A Jewish Theology,* p. 274).

the one I have recounted here, is found in Hayim Nahman Bialik and Yehoshua Hana Ravnitzky, *The Book of Legends*, pages 32–33.

9. When Abraham Lies to Save His Life

GENESIS 12:10–20; CHAPTER 20

Ask most people, even those who are familiar with the Bible, what are the first words the Bible attributes to Abraham, and you will probably draw a blank, or maybe a guess at some sort of affirmation of God. The surprising truth is that Abraham's first words are an instruction to his wife, Sarah, to tell a lie.

At the time, a famine is devastating Canaan, the land in which God has directed Abraham to settle. In order to obtain food, Abraham and Sarah are obliged to journey to Egypt (as his grandson Jacob and Jacob's sons are forced to do three generations later). As they near their destination, Abraham, suddenly overcome with fear, tells Sarah, "I know what a beautiful woman you are. If the Egyptians see you and think, 'She is his wife,' they will kill me and let you live. Say that you are my sister, that it may go well with me because of you and that I may remain alive thanks to you" (12:11–13).

Abraham's anticipation of how the Egyptians will react to his wife's looks proves justified. As soon as they enter Egypt, people notice her beauty. Soon, Pharaoh's attendants tell him about the new woman, who is taken into the king's palace. The Egyptian monarch expresses his gratitude to the woman's "brother" by giving Abraham a large bounty, including sheep, oxen, camels, and servants.

However, God protects Sarah by sending an unspecified plague upon Pharaoh and his court. Since the plague seems to have commenced immediately upon Sarah's arrival, Pharaoh assumes she is its cause. He summons Abraham and says, "What is this you have done to me! Why did you not tell me that she was your wife?" (12:18). The text does not tell us how Pharaoh deduced Abraham and Sarah's relationship. In all likelihood, after concluding that Sarah was the cause of the plague, he questioned her, and she acknowledged that Abraham was her husband. That her relationship with Pharaoh had already proceeded very far is suggested by two details: the lavish gifts he bestows on Abraham, and the angry rebuke he directs at the Patriarch: "Why did you say, 'She is my sister?' *so I took her as my wife*" (verse 19).

Pharaoh returns Sarah to Abraham, and orders his troops to send the couple away. He does not, however, reclaim the gifts he has given Abraham.

The story is puzzling, not least because of the fact that on some level Pharaoh is depicted as acting more nobly than Abraham. Of course, we do not know how he would have acted had Abraham told him from the beginning that Sarah was his wife. After the fact and after the plague, Pharaoh implies that he would never have taken the wife of another man, but it's not clear whether that would have been the case. Since few men would want to see their wives taken from them, we can only assume that Abraham had good reason to fear what would happen to him if people knew that Sarah was his wife.

Still, his behavior is disturbing. Shortly before this incident, God appeared to Abraham to inform him that "I will make of you a great nation. . . . I will bless those who bless you. . . . And all the families of the earth shall bless themselves by you" (Genesis 12:2–3). Did Abraham think that God would now desert him?

There is an alternate, though not very reassuring, explanation for Abraham's behavior: God's initial promise that he would make of Abraham a great nation seems to be directed to him alone; Sarah's name is not mentioned (although it is later), and in fact the Bible has already informed us that she is barren (Genesis 11:30). Thus, it is possible that Abraham believed that his descendants would issue from another woman than Sarah; therefore, even if she were destined to remain in Pharaoh's house, God's words to him could still be fulfilled.

This interpretation might strike one as the most logical explanation for Abraham's behavior, except for one not-so-small narrative detail: Eight chapters later, *after* God has told Abraham that the child who will carry on his mission will come from Sarah, Abraham tells Abimelech, king of Gerar, that Sarah is his sister. Like Pharaoh, Abimelech orders the woman brought to him. That night, God appears to the king in a dream and says, "You are to die because of the woman that you have taken, for she is a married woman" (Genesis 20:3).

In words reminiscent of Abraham's plea to God not to destroy Sodom and Gomorrah (Genesis 18:25), Abimelech protests to God, "O Lord, will You slay people even though innocent?" (20:4), and mentions the untruth that both Abraham and Sarah had told him ("She also said, 'He is my brother' ").

Abimelech summons Abraham and tells him that the possibility of committing adultery is something truly abhorrent to him: "What wrong have I done you that you should bring so great a guilt upon me and my kingdom?" (20:9).

Abraham justifies his behavior with an explanation that until now he has confined to Sarah: "I thought . . . surely there is no fear of God in this place, and they will kill me because of my wife" (20:11).* He also explains that his words, strictly speaking, weren't a lie. Sarah, we now learn, is Abraham's half sister; both he and she are the children of Terah, although they have different mothers (this is one of a number of instances in which the Patriarchs engage in behavior that later Torah law forbids; see Leviticus 18:9).

As was true in the earlier instance with Pharaoh, Abraham profits by this encounter when Abimelech sends him and Sarah off with cattle, servants, and even a thousand pieces of silver. Abraham is grateful to Abimelech, and prays to God to heal Abimelech, his wife, and his female servants so that they can bear children, "For the Lord had closed fast every womb of the household of Abimelech because of Sarah, the wife of Abraham" (20:17–18). This last detail in this, the Bible's first recorded prayer, is puzzling: The previous description gave the impression that the whole Sarah-Abimelech encounter had happened quickly, that the king's frightening dream had occurred shortly after Sarah had been brought to the king's house. The prayer, however, suggests that Sarah's presence may have been far longer, for it apparently provoked a bout of infertility within the palace.

One final point: How did Sarah feel about Abraham's stratagem? We have no way of knowing, although we do know that she went along with it by telling Abimelech that Abraham was her brother. But did Abraham's behavior upset her, particularly when she was taken away to Pharaoh's and Abimelech's courts?

While the Bible doesn't say, other episodes suggest that Sarah is not a shy, submissive wife. When she wants Abraham to do something, she is forthright in expressing her feelings. For example, when she wants Abraham to expel the concubine Hagar from their household along with Abraham's other son, Ishmael, she insists on his doing so, even though "the matter distressed Abraham greatly" (Genesis 21:11). Therefore, there are good grounds for assuming that

*This is the first time that the Bible associates a lack of belief in God with a lack of morality (see entry 153).

Sarah is capable of representing her own interests when she so wishes. Thus, her acquiescence in Abraham's request can only mean that she too feared for her husband's life if it became known that they were married, and she therefore willingly went along with her husband's scheme.

After learning a biblical story, people may ask, "What is the practical lesson (the *mussar haskel*) to be learned from this?" That it is occasionally permissible to lie? Definitely. That one should lie in the manner Abraham did, and expose one's spouse to adultery? That seems to me less certain, and indeed, the Bible's description of these events has provoked considerable discussion, and even criticism, among the traditional Bible commentators. The thirteenth-century Nachmanides (Ramban), whose commentary appears in standard Hebrew editions of the Torah, expresses unhappiness with Abraham's behavior: "Know that our father Abraham inadvertently committed a great sin in that he placed his virtuous wife in jeopardy of sin because of his fear of being killed." How would Nachmanides have counseled the Patriarch to act? "He should have trusted in God to save him, his wife and all he had, for God has the power to help and to save."

David Kimhi (Radak), another thirteenth-century biblical exegete, is more sympathetic to the Patriarch's dilemma. After first noting that Abraham should have remained where he was and suffered famine rather than endanger his wife, he justifies Abraham's behavior in Egypt on the grounds that the Patriarch chose the lesser of two evils. For had Abraham disclosed that Sarah was his wife, he would have been killed, and she condemned to a lifetime of degradation. However, his lie, although it might have forced Sarah to commit adultery, ensured that both she and Abraham stayed alive. In such a situation, Kimhi suggests, it would have been wrong for the Patriarch to rely on a divine miracle and tell the truth.

10. The Covenant Between God and Abraham

GENESIS, CHAPTER 15

Abraham, now seventy-five years old and still childless, is visited by God again. The Lord promises him a great reward for his loyalty. Strangely enough, this divine pledge seems to bring Abraham less reassurance than one might expect: "O Lord, God, what can You give me, seeing that I shall die childless, and the one in charge of my household is [my servant] Dammesek Eliezer" (15:2). To Abraham the only meaningful reward God can give him is a son.

God promises Abraham that he will yet have his own heir: "Look toward heaven and count the stars, if you are able to count them . . . so shall your offspring be" (15:5).

Finally assured that he will have a child, Abraham turns to the subject of God's other promise: "How shall I know that I am to possess [the land of Canaan]?"

God instructs Abraham to perform one of the strangest rituals described in the Bible, a ceremony that establishes God's covenant with Abraham and his descendants. He is to bring before God a three-year-old heifer, a she-goat, and a ram as well as a turtledove and two birds. He is then to gather the animals, cut them (with the exception of the bird) straight down the middle, and place each half opposite the other.

Abraham remains by the dead animals, driving away birds of prey, until he falls into a deep sleep. God again reveals Himself to Abraham, in a prophecy that speaks first of tragedy, then of triumph: Abraham's descendants will be enslaved for hundreds of years in a foreign land, but they ultimately will go free with great wealth. Abraham himself will lead a peaceful life and die at a ripe old age. And, in the distant future, the sins of Canaan's inhabitants will cause them to lose the land to Abraham's descendants.

Late that night, God concludes His covenant with Abraham. He sends a smoking oven and a flaming torch between the two halves of the animals, and again assures the childless Abraham that "to your offspring I give this land, from the river of Egypt to the great river, the river Euphrates."*

Note: The Hebrew word for covenant is *brit* (the Jewish organization B'nai B'rith means "children [or sons] of the covenant"), and "to make a covenant," *lichrot brit*, literally means "to cut a covenant," a reminder of the covenant Abraham carried out by cutting several animals in two.

11. Ishmael, Abraham's Firstborn

GENESIS, CHAPTER 16

When God first appears to Abraham and promises that "I will make of you a great nation," He makes no mention of Abraham's wife Sarah, and although she is infertile, Abraham does not ask God if the child will come from her. In fact, for many years after God's revelation, Sarah remains barren; this is the great tragedy of both her and her husband's life. Desperate, Sarah asks Abraham to take Hagar, her Egyptian maid, as a concubine;† "perhaps I shall have a son through her" (16:2).

Hagar becomes pregnant, and immediately her mistress is lowered in her eyes. Sarah responds by raging against her husband: "The wrong done me is your fault," a particularly irrational and unjustified outburst, given that it was Sarah who proposed that Abraham take Hagar as a concubine. Quite clearly, she is in pain; she has been incapable of providing her husband with an heir, and now her servant will do so.

Abraham tells Sarah, "Your maid is in your hands. Deal with her

*The modern state of Israel's borders are a fraction of this biblically ordained boundary. A somewhat different description of the land's ideal borders is found in Numbers 34:1–12 and Deuteronomy 1:7–8.

†*Isha*, the word I have translated as "concubine" also means "wife"; nevertheless, the fact that Hagar continues to be described as Sarah's servant, even after Abraham has relations with her, suggests that her status was that of a concubine, not a wife.

as you think right," a rather ungallant response, given that Hagar is pregnant with his child.

Sarah treats the Egyptian maid harshly—again, the Bible offers no details—and Hagar flees.

An angel appears to Hagar and instructs her to return home and submit to Sarah's harsh treatment. She is also assured that she will have descendants who will be too numerous to count (in this regard, the promise to Hagar is similar to that made to Abraham). Finally, the angel instructs Hagar to name the boy whom she will bear Ishmael (Hebrew for "God hears [your suffering]"). The angel then goes on to offer a peculiarly uncomplimentary description of Ishmael: "He shall be a wild man, his hand against everyone and everyone's hand against him" (16:12). Although most mothers might not be pleased by such a prophecy, Hagar is reassured. She returns home, and gives birth to a son. Abraham does name the boy Ishmael, which means that he and Sarah must have accepted Hagar's story about the revelation she had from God's angel.*

Initially, when Sarah proposed the liaison between Abraham and Hagar, she expressed the hope that she would be deeply involved in raising the latter's child ("I shall have a son through [Hagar]"). However, after Ishmael's birth, there is no indication that Sarah has any interest in the young boy. Apparently, the tension between the two women alienates Sarah not only from her servant, but also from her servant's offspring (although, of course, half of Ishmael's genetic makeup comes from Abraham).

Thirteen years pass; all we learn about Ishmael during this time is that Abraham circumcises him (Genesis 17:26; most Arabs, who regard themselves as Ishmael's descendants, still circumcise males at thirteen). Abraham has no more children with Hagar, so it is more than likely that their relationship ceased when she became pregnant with Ishmael. Nonetheless, it is clear that Abraham assumes that Ishmael will be his only offspring, for when God tells him that he is still going to have a child with Sarah, Abraham implores God, "If only Ishmael might live in Your presence!" (17:15–18). God assures Abraham that Ishmael will become the ancestor of a great nation, but that his covenant with Abraham will be carried on through the child he will have with Sarah (17:21).

---

*At some level, this revelation must have both inflamed Sarah against Hagar and alarmed her, that is, "If angels communicate with Hagar, perhaps I shouldn't mistreat her."

Finally, in the aftermath of a prophecy offered by three angels to Abraham that his wife Sarah will become a mother (Genesis 18:10), Sarah gives birth to Isaac. Having previously given up the hope of becoming a mother, she must now have intensely regretted having earlier encouraged Abraham to have a child with another woman. The next biblical mention of Ishmael is a sad one. On the day that Isaac is weaned, Abraham holds a great feast. Sarah's presumably elated mood becomes totally deflated the moment she sees Ishmael "playing" (with Isaac?). Perhaps the nature of his play is wild—the Bible doesn't tell us what he is doing—or perhaps Sarah just can't stand the thought that this boy is also regarded as Abraham's son, his firstborn no less. She confronts her husband and demands, "Cast out that slavewoman and her son, for the son of that slave shall not share in the inheritance with my son" (Genesis 21:10). Sarah's words are cruel; neither Hagar nor Ishmael is deemed worthy of having her or his name mentioned; they are reduced to being called the "slavewoman," and "the son of that slave."

Abraham is distressed. God, perhaps to Abraham's astonishment, sides with Sarah: "Whatever Sarah tells you, do as she says, for it is through Isaac that offspring shall be continued for you" (21:12). Perhaps the Lord feared the negative influence that Ishmael would exert on Isaac.

In one of the Bible's most heartrending descriptions, Abraham sends away Hagar and Ishmael with some food and water. Hagar soon uses up the water, leaves her son under a bush, walks a short distance away, says to herself, "Let me not look on as the child dies," and bursts into tears.

An angel again appears to Hagar and assures her that a great nation will issue from Ishmael. The angel leads her to a well, where she and Ishmael drink. Eventually, the young boy grows up and becomes an accomplished bowman. His mother also arranges a marriage for him with an Egyptian woman.

Isaac and Ishmael meet only once more in their lives, when they bury Abraham. They come together, perhaps mourn together for a few days, then never see each other again. Although this situation is clearly preferable to that which occurred between the world's first two brothers, when Cain murders Abel, still, such mutual alienation is sad.

God's promise to Hagar is fulfilled; a great nation, the Arabs, believe themselves to descend from Ishmael, and eventually they become far more numerous than the nation that proceeds from Isaac.

12. Abraham Argues with God

GENESIS 18:16–23

One of the most fascinating features of the Hebrew Bible is that
people argue with God when they feel He is acting unjustly. Job is
the most famous character to do so; the book that bears his name
consists largely of Job's repeated complaint that he is being afflicted
unfairly (a view that the book itself reinforces in chapters 1 and 2;
see entry 127). Much earlier, Moses argues strenuously with God
when He announces his intention to destroy the Israelites after their
sin with the Golden Calf (Exodus 32:31). The Psalmist voices a
protest more akin to that of Job, that God is allowing his believers
to be slaughtered like sheep (44:23).

Fittingly, the very first person to argue with God (except for
Cain's self-serving argument; Genesis 4:13) is Abraham, who is regarded as the first Jew. It is striking that he contends neither on
behalf of himself (as does Job), nor on behalf of his people (as does
Moses), but for the residents of Sodom and Gomorrah, whose sinning has provoked God's wrath.*

God seems to invite Abraham into a dialogue about the cities'
fates. After deciding that they deserve to be destroyed, God asks
Himself: "Shall I hide from Abraham what I am about to do . . . ?
For I have singled him out, that he may instruct his children and his
posterity to keep the way of the Lord by doing what is just and
right . . ." (Genesis 18:17, 19). In other words, God seems to be saying, "If My goal is that Abraham teach his descendants to do what
is just, I have to show him what it means to act justly."

Although we might expect a "pious" religious person to approve
of anything God intends ("Of course, Lord, they deserve to die"), or
remain silent (as does Noah; see Genesis 6:11–22), or just make an
appeal on behalf of his nephew Lot, Abraham's response is immediate
and confrontational: "Will You sweep away the innocent along with

---

*On the other hand, Abraham's arguing is not totally disinterested, given
that among the residents of Sodom is his beloved nephew Lot, on whose
behalf Abraham had earlier gone out in battle (Genesis 14:13–16).

the guilty? What if there should be fifty innocent [people] within the city; will You then wipe out the place and not forgive it for the sake of the innocent fifty who are in it? . . . Far be it from You! Shall not the Judge of all the earth deal justly?" (18:23–25).

From Abraham's three questions, it is clear that he already has understood justice to be an essential characteristic of God. Therefore, if God acts in a manner that is unjust, He is being un-Godly ("Far be it from You").

God seems fully willing to enter into negotiation with Abraham. He concedes the validity of Abraham's challenge: "If I find within the city of Sodom fifty innocent ones, I will forgive the whole place for their sake" (18:26).

Abraham is a persistent, determined negotiator. Having extracted from God a concession that Sodom will not be destroyed for the sake of fifty innocent residents, Abraham asks, "Will You destroy the whole city for lack of the five?" (that is, if there are only forty-five righteous people). God quickly concedes the argument, which emboldens Abraham to request that Sodom be spared for the sake of forty, thirty, twenty, and finally even ten innocent people.

Although Abraham argues vociferously with God, he still abides by certain ground rules. He addresses the Lord with befitting humility: "Here I venture to speak to my Lord, I who am but dust and ashes" (verse 27), and he expresses trust in God's sense of justice (he leaves it for God to discern if the requisite number of righteous people live within Sodom).

Is Abraham conducting his argument to save the innocent people or the guilty? The latter, it would seem. If Abraham's concern were to save the innocent, he would have challenged God differently: "Will You then sweep away the innocent along with the guilty? . . . *You must therefore lead the innocent people out to safety before You destroy the guilty.*" That is how Abraham should have argued if he feared that God was unfairly punishing innocent people.

Abraham's argument, however, is that God should spare the *guilty* for the sake of the *innocent*. Why?

Abraham knows that God has chosen him to teach certain truths to the world. Implicit in his mission is the realization that while many people often do not act justly, through Abraham and his descendants they might be influenced to change their behavior. As long as a requisite number of good people reside in a place, there is hope that they can influence and transform the evil ones.

It therefore makes sense for God to spare the guilty people of Sodom for the sake of fifty, forty-five, forty, thirty, twenty, even ten good people, since these people might change the others' behavior. For less than ten good people, however, God is not inclined to spare Sodom, nor is Abraham inclined to argue with Him. Why not? For good people to exert an influence, a certain "critical mass" is necessary. If this "critical mass" doesn't even equal the fingers of two hands, it becomes impossible for them to influence large numbers of bad people. Therefore, later Jewish law rules that if a person finds himself living in a city with almost no good people, he or she must leave immediately. The rationale is expressed in an old Jewish folktale told about Sodom:

A righteous man arrived in the city, and went about telling people to repent. The more he was ignored, the louder his calls for repentance grew.

One day, a young boy said to him, "Why do you continue yelling at people to change their behavior? You've been here a long time already, and you have affected no one."

"When I first arrived," the man responded, "I hoped that my yelling would change the people of Sodom. Now I yell so that the people of Sodom don't change me."

Source and further reading: The obligation to move out of an evil environment is recorded in Moses Maimonides' legal cole, the *Mishneh Torah:* "It is natural for a man's character and actions to be influenced by his friends and associates and for him to follow the local norms of behavior. . . . A person who lives in a place where the norms of behavior are evil and the inhabitants do not follow the straight path should move to a place where the people are righteous and follow the ways of the good" ("The Laws of Character Development," 6:1).

13. The Sinful Cities of Sodom and Gomorrah

GENESIS, CHAPTER 19

Although the Bible clearly states that Sodom and Gomorrah are exceptionally evil cities, it tells us few details of its residents' sins.

Within the text itself, we learn that they practiced homosexual rape and were extremely inhospitable (to say the least) to visitors.

Other oral traditions seem to have existed among the ancient Hebrews regarding Sodom's sins. Ezekiel speaks of her citizens' "haughtiness," and their refusal to help the poor and needy, a sin aggravated by the fact that the inhabitants were rich (Ezekiel 16: 49–50); the Torah likewise speaks of Sodom as being "like the garden of the Lord" [Genesis 13:10]). A lack of charitable behavior toward the poor, obnoxious in people of moderate means, is considered unforgivable in those who are rich.

God sends to Sodom two of the three divine messengers who had earlier visited Abraham (Genesis 18:2–10). When they arrive, Lot, Abraham's nephew and the city's one semirighteous resident, immediately invites them to his house. A gracious host, Lot prepares a feast for his guests.

But soon the Sodomites—"all the people to the last man," the text emphasizes (19:4)—gather round his house. They call out: "Where are the men who came to you last night? Bring them out to us, that we may be intimate with them" (19:5).

Lot steps outside, carefully closing the door behind him. "I beg you, my friends, do not commit such a wrong," he appeals to them, then he makes about the most vile offer recorded in the Bible: "Look, I have two daughters who have not known a man. Let me bring them out to you, and you may do to them as you please, but do not do anything to these men, since they have come under the shelter of my roof" (19:7–8).

One wonders if Lot shut the door behind him to keep the Sodomites from getting into his house, or to keep his daughters from hearing the proposal he was making. Among other things, his approach demonstrates that a desire to do good, although necessary, is insufficient; one also has to have some sort of philosophy defining goodness. Hospitality is a wonderful value, but to sacrifice your own children for the sake of guests hardly seems morally defensible. Since the Sodomites were interested in his male visitors, Lot could have offered himself; that might have been unwise, but at least it would have been more ethical than offering his daughters.

The Sodomites do not permit Lot's speech to deter them from their goal. They repudiate his offer and begin to assault him. The angels yank Lot back inside and strike the Sodomites with temporary blindness, "so that they were helpless to find the entrance."

The angels waste no more time in polite conversation. Informing Lot that they have come to destroy Sodom, they instruct him to tell this news to the members of his family not already with him. Lot seeks out his sons-in-law and tells them to leave, "for the Lord is about to destroy the city." The sons-in-law (they are married to other daughters of Lot; when he offers his two other daughters to the Sodomites, he emphasizes that they are virgins) laugh at him—they seem to think Lot is jesting, and they refuse to go. Their wives remain with them.

At dawn the angels urge Lot to leave immediately along with his wife and two remaining daughters, lest they be destroyed with the Sodomites. But Lot and his family delay, although the text provides no reason why.

One explanation might be out of concern for the daughters remaining in the city. Although Lot might not have been a protective father, he was sufficiently concerned about his daughters to try to convince their husbands to depart (Sodom was apparently so male dominated that Lot felt it only worthwhile to speak to his sons-in-law).

Pressed for time, the angels take Lot and his family by the hand, and lead them out of the city. "Flee for your life. Do not look behind you, nor stop anywhere in the Plain . . . lest you be swept away" (19:17). As Lot and his family flee, God rains down sulfurous fire upon Sodom and Gomorrah until the cities are annihilated.

There follows one of the best-known but most puzzling incidents in the Bible: "Lot's wife looked back, and she thereupon turned into a pillar of salt" (19:26). What a strange detail! To this day, visitors to Sodom are commonly shown a salt formation that tour guides assure them is the earthly remains of Mrs. Lot.

Why did she look back? Perhaps the best answer is offered by the novelist Rebecca Goldstein, who suggests that Lot's wife was looking back to see if her other daughters had followed at the last minute. For how could a mother, in the face of the tumultuous destruction of a city where some of her children live, not look back?

Ms. Goldstein's explanation makes more sense than any other I have heard. In addition, perhaps I feel the need to defend Mrs. Lot because her undignified punishment has made her the butt of many cruel witticisms and highly critical commentaries.

Lot and his two remaining daughters take up residence in the hills above the small nearby town of Zoar. Convinced that the entire world, except for them, has been destroyed, Lot's older daughter says to her younger sister: "Come, let us make our father drink wine, and let us lie with him, that we may maintain life through our father" (19:32). The first night, the daughters get Lot drunk, and the older one sleeps with him; the next night the younger does so. What level of drunkenness, I wonder, is necessary for a man not to know that he is having sexual relations with his own daughters? So immense, I guess, that it is hard to imagine Lot was really that drunk.

That these were Sodom's "best" citizens once again reveals the moral unworthiness of the city.

Lot's two acts of sexual intercourse result in both daughters becoming pregnant. The older gives birth to a son named Moab; the Bible informs us that the Moabites, one of ancient Israel's great enemies, descend from him. The younger delivers a son called Ben-ammi, the ancestor of the Ammonites, another adversary of ancient Israel. Needless to say, that the Bible depicts two of Israel's great foes as descending from an act of father-daughter incest is hardly a compliment.

Source and further reading: Rebecca Goldstein, "Looking Back at Lot's Wife," in Christina Buchmann and Celina Spiegel, editors, *Out of the Garden: Women Writers on the Bible,* pages 3–12.

14. The *Akedah*: The Near Sacrifice of Isaac

GENESIS, CHAPTER 22

In Western literature, the episode known in Hebrew as the *akedah* (the binding of Isaac) is usually referred to as "the sacrifice of Isaac." This mistranslation distorts the essence of the event, for at the story's end, Isaac is not sacrificed and God makes it clear that He *never* wants human beings to be sacrificed.

I suspect that Western literature, influenced by the Christian belief that God sacrificed His son for the sake of humankind, has tended to see the *akedah* as a foreshadowing of that later "sacrifice," but Jewish tradition regards it quite differently.

The story begins with an uncharacteristic, explanatory sentence: "Some time afterward, God put Abraham to the test" (22:1). My friend Israeli Bible scholar Professor Uriel Simon explains that informing the readers that this is a test gives them important information that is being withheld from Abraham. This is done, he argues, because without the explanation, the chapter will be too painful to read. By knowing in advance that what we are reading is only a test, we intuit that all will end happily.

The language with which God instructs Abraham to sacrifice Isaac is deliberately intended to magnify the pain the command raises: "Take your son, your favored one, whom you love, even Isaac, and go to the land of Moriah, and offer him there as a burnt offering on one of the heights which I will point out to you" (22:2).

More than a few commentators have expressed amazement at Abraham's silence in response to God's command. He has waited a lifetime for the son he is now told to kill, a son who God has promised will carry on his mission. Yet he says nothing, which is even more surprising considering that Abraham previously has not been silent when he disagreed with God. When the Lord informed him of His intention to destroy Sodom and Gomorrah, Abraham engaged God in a dispute and even challenged God's goodness: "Shall not the Judge of all the earth deal justly?" (18:25). Why then does Abraham remain silent when his son's life is imperiled?

When God confided to Abraham His intention to destroy Sodom and Gomorrah, He also confided a rationale for the destruction: The behavior of the citizens was so evil that they did not deserve to go on living. It was in response to this that Abraham framed his argument: "Perhaps there are fifty righteous people within the city; would You not save the city for the sake of the fifty righteous ones?" In other words, because God offered *His* rationale for destroying the two evil cities, Abraham could offer *a* reason that they should be spared.

But in the case of the *akedah,* God issues a command without an accompanying explanation. Abraham is left with the impression that even if he asked God why, the Lord would answer, "Because I so commanded." What could Abraham say then? God apparently gives Abraham no opening, no reason to believe that anything he might say would affect His decision.

The *akedah* generally provokes an intense moral conflict in modern readers. On the one hand, Jews and Christians see Abraham as the first Patriarch, a man to be admired and emulated. But how can moral people admire a man who is prepared to commit an act for which moral people might wish to see him executed, imprisoned for life, or consigned permanently to an asylum?

In actuality, the moral conflict is more apparent than real. Abraham's readiness to obey God's command shows him to be ethically deficient by later standards, but not by those of his age. True, God had revealed Himself to Abraham, but He had not made known to him the full ethical implications of monotheism. Since other contemporary religious believers sacrificed sons to their gods, God, in essence, was asking Abraham if he was as devoted to his God as the pagan idolaters were to theirs.

Abraham's willingness to sacrifice Isaac, therefore, shows the depth of his devotion to God. Only when God makes it clear that He doesn't want human sacrifice does Abraham learn how evil and immoral such behavior is. Thus, the modern reader can admire Abraham for his devotion without having to believe that his behavior is to be emulated. Presumably, had God appeared to Abraham a year after the event, and again ordered him to sacrifice Isaac, Abraham might have responded, "Shall not the Judge of all the earth deal justly?"

This, one of the Bible's most controversial chapters, deserves another look. Early on the morning following God's command, Abraham saddles his donkey and sets off with Isaac and two servants to the site God has designated. Why does the Bible record that Abraham departs from his house "early"? The traditional rabbinic explanation is that "pious people rush to perform a divine commandment" (Babylonian Talmud, *Pesachim* 4a). An alternate reason might be that Abraham wished to depart while Sarah was still sleeping; there is every indication within the text that Abraham never discusses with his wife the divine decree he intends to carry out.

The trip takes three days. Why so long? Most likely, to underscore the magnitude of the test. In a moment of religious enthusiasm, Abraham might readily fulfill the divine command. Now, however, he is forced to journey with Isaac a full seventy-two hours. When the sacrifice occurs, it will not be a spontaneous action; by imposing on Abraham a three-day trek, God is forcing him to act in a premeditated and deliberate way.

The text is terse. We are told nothing about the three-day journey, and no conversation between Abraham and Isaac is recorded. We can only imagine what the trip must have been like. One would guess that Isaac must feel excited; he is accompanying his father on an extended trip to offer God a sacrifice. Abraham, we can assume, is considerably more somber. When Isaac speaks to him, he must wonder: Are these the last words, the last thoughts, I will ever hear from my son?

Many questions must have plagued the Patriarch: Did I misunderstand God? If not, why could He possibly want such a sacrifice? If He does, why did He make me wait so long to have a child, all the while knowing that He would demand that I kill him?

In addition, we know that Sarah has a strong personality—in an earlier chapter, she forces Abraham to expel from their home Ishmael, his other son. Now, as Abraham proceeds toward the mountain, he must be suffering great trepidation, imagining what he will tell Sarah when he returns from the trip, alone.

Worst of all, Abraham's mind must constantly be focusing on the sacrifice itself. Isaac is his most beloved son. What will the boy think when he sees his father tie him to the altar, and raise a knife over his throat? That Isaac's last memory of life will be of being killed by his father must wrench Abraham's heart most of all.

When they finally arrive at the mountain site, Abraham instructs the servants to remain at its base. Still not wanting to alarm Isaac, he tells the men that he and Isaac will go up the mountain alone; there, they will worship, then, "*we* will return to you" (22:5).

Abraham places the wood for the burnt offering on Isaac's back, takes the firestone and knife in his own hands, and sets off with Isaac for their journey's final stage. In the midst of their climb, Isaac stops, puzzled. "Father," he asks, "here are the firestone and the wood, but where is the sheep for the burnt offering?"

Abraham responds, "God will see to the sheep for the burnt offering" (22:8).

That is the last dialogue the chapter records. When they arrive at the mountaintop, Abraham builds the altar, sets out the wood, and ties Isaac to the altar.

Does Isaac protest, try to flee, fight with his father, weep, or submit to God's will when Abraham explains that he is fulfilling a divine command? The text doesn't say. There is at least one reason to assume that Isaac acquiesces: His father is an old man; if Isaac did wish to resist him, it would be easy to do so.

Abraham is now ready to fulfill the divine command; he lifts his knife to slaughter Isaac.

An angel calls out to him: "Abraham, Abraham!"

The Patriarch stops and answers, "Here I am."

"Do not raise your hand against the boy, or do anything to him. For now I know that you fear God, since you have not withheld your son, your favored one, from Me" (22:12).

Presumably exultant, Abraham sees a ram caught in a nearby thicket, catches it, and offers the animal as a sacrifice instead.

The angel again calls out to Abraham, promising that as a reward for his behavior, his descendants will be as numerous as the stars in the heavens and the sands on the seashore.

Abraham returns to the bottom of the mountain, and he and his servants return to Beersheva, where Abraham remains.

In a stunning anticlimax, the Bible now informs us of a series of births in Abraham's extended family. The names given to the new-born children are among the ugliest in the Bible, lending the passage an almost humorous twist. Among his brother Nahor's sons are Buz, Hazo, Pildash, Jidlaph, Tebah, Gaham, and Tahash. Apparently, the point of this genealogical narrative is to mention the birth of yet another of Nahor's sons, Bethuel; the Bible tells us that he is the father of Rebecca (22:23), the woman who will marry Isaac.

A few verses earlier, we were concerned that Isaac was about to die, and Abraham's dynasty end. Now, immediately following the angel's pledge to Abraham about having numerous descendants, the Bible records the birth of Rebecca, the woman through whom Abraham and Isaac's line will continue.

This anticlimactic conclusion to the chapter deflects our attention from two characters in the *akedah* story. First, Isaac: What does he feel as he returns down the mountain with his father? What do they talk about on the journey home if indeed they travel home together (see 22:19)? Does he have trouble trusting his father after this incident? Or trusting God?

And then there is Sarah. The woman has waited almost her entire life to have a child, and Isaac's birth was her supreme joy. Yet, her name is not mentioned once in this chapter. How does she react when she hears what happened? Do Abraham and Isaac tell her, or do they make a pact to keep the incident secret?

Again, we do not know, although the late Rabbi Abraham Chen points out a peculiar, seldom noted detail in the text. When Abraham returns from the trip, the Bible notes that he stayed in Beersheva. Yet the second verse of the next chapter (Genesis 23:2) records that Sarah died in Kiryat Arba, and that Abraham came there to mourn for her. Although the text never explicitly says so, the implication is that Abraham and Sarah were living apart when she died. If so, did Sarah move away from him when she heard what Abraham had almost done?

Ultimately, Abraham was not asked to sacrifice his son, but did God's test cause him to sacrifice his wife?

Source and further reading: Rabbi Abraham Chen's suggestion that Sarah possibly separated from Abraham is cited in Herbert Weiner, 9½ *Mystics,* page 266. See also Søren Kierkegaard, *Fear and Trembling.*

15. The Cave of the Matriarchs and Patriarchs
(Me'arat ha-Machpela)

GENESIS, CHAPTER 23

Sarah's death at the age of 127 (she is the only woman in the Bible whose age at death is recorded) painfully drives home to Abraham his alien status in the land of Canaan. Despite God's promise that his descendants will eventually settle in and possess this land, Abraham has no place to bury his wife.

His concern palpable, Abraham rises from beside Sarah's death bed to meet with local Hebron residents, and asks them to sell him a burial site. What ensues epitomizes mideastern bargaining style.

The men whom Abraham approaches tell him that they will not hear of him paying money to bury his wife; they offer him free space in their own family cemeteries.

Abraham does not want Sarah buried on land owned by someone else (if he were later to have a falling-out with the owner of the land, that person might not permit him or other family members to be buried there or even to visit the site). Abraham asks his neighbors to intervene with a certain man named Ephron to urge him to sell Abraham "the cave of Machpela which he owns at the edge of his land." Abraham is not looking for any bargains: "Let him sell it to me, at full price."

Unbeknownst to Abraham, Ephron is part of the group to whom he is speaking. At first, he too offers the land as a gift, but it appears that this is just polite bargaining etiquette, for when Abraham again reiterates his desire to pay, Ephron asks for four hundred shekels of silver, an enormous price (although it is hard to draw monetary comparisons over centuries, it appears that a small plot of land, comparable in size to the Cave of the Machpela [Me'arat ha-Machpela], was sold for seventeen shekels circa 600 B.C.E.; Jeremiah 32:9).

Abraham accepts the price and immediately pays Ephron. He buries Sarah in the Cave of the Machpela: The Bible later records that Abraham, Isaac, Rebecca, and Leah were buried there as well (Genesis 49:30–31). The final words spoken by Jacob before he dies are a request that his sons "bury me with my fathers in the cave which is in the field of Ephron" (49:29; it's odd that Jacob calls it "the field of Ephron," since a full century has passed since Abraham bought it). The only Patriarch or Matriarch not buried in the Cave is Rachel, who died near Bethlehem and was buried there (Genesis 35:16–20).

The Cave of the Machpela is located in Hebron and remains a place of pilgrimage for Jews, Christians, and Muslims. In the Bible, this burial site on occasion united alienated brothers; there, Isaac and Ishmael (the respective progenitors of the Jewish and Arab people) came together to bury Abraham; likewise, Jacob and Esau met there to bury their father, Isaac.

The Cave's remarkable peacemaking powers seem to have waned in our century. Unfortunately, today, the Cave is often a scene of conflicts between Jews and Muslims who vie to pray there.

16. Isaac: The Man to Whom Things Happen

GENESIS, CHAPTERS 22, 24, AND 27

In the Jewish tradition, Isaac is regarded as a *tamim*, a good and gentle soul. Although he lacks the charisma of Abraham and the shrewdness of Jacob, he, assisted by his wife, Rebecca, guarantees the survival of Abraham's vision during an important, transitional generation. It is therefore quite interesting to note that though Isaac, the son of Israel's founder and the father of Jacob, the Bible's third Patriarch, plays a pivotal role in three major episodes of the Bible, his role is always passive.

The *akedah*, Abraham's near sacrifice of Isaac, is the event with which Isaac is most identified (see entry 14). Indeed, this childhood event might be related to his later passivity; the fact that he had almost been slaughtered by his father might have left scars that never fully healed. (The third major event of his life is the subject of the next entry.)

The second significant event in Isaac's life is the choosing of Rebecca to be his wife. He plays no role in this choice, although other biblical characters are actively involved in selecting their mates. Thus, Isaac's son Jacob marries Rachel, a woman with whom he falls deeply in love (see entry 19). Moses and David, to cite just two other major biblical characters, also choose their mates.

But Isaac's wife is chosen for him by Eliezer, his father's servant, who is acting at his father's behest. Abraham summons Eliezer (his name is not specifically mentioned in chapter 24, but based on the reference to him in Genesis 15:2, all biblical commentators assume he is the "servant" mentioned throughout this chapter) and tells him that he doesn't want Isaac to marry a Canaanite woman. He instructs Eliezer to go to the land of his [Abraham's] birth and there choose a bride for Isaac. Abraham never suggests that Isaac, a grown man of forty (Genesis 25:20), choose his own bride.

Deeply devoted to Abraham, Eliezer is nervous about his mission. His master has given him only a geographical guideline for choosing Isaac's spouse. When he arrives at the well outside the town of Nahor, he offers a prayer (this is only the second prayer offered in the Bible, and by a non-Hebrew at that!). He asks God to send him a sign by which he can choose an appropriate bride for Isaac: "Let the maiden to whom I say, 'Please lower your jar that I may drink,' and who replies, 'Drink, and I will also water your camels,' let her be the one whom You have decreed for Your servant Isaac" (24:14). It reflects Eliezer's good character that the sign he seeks is an ethical one.

Almost immediately, Rebecca, Abraham's niece through his brother Nahor, arrives at the well, a jar on her shoulder. After she fills it, Eliezer requests a sip. Rebecca lets him drink until his thirst is quenched, then says, "I will also draw for your camels, until they finish drinking" (no small task, given that thirsty camels are capable of drinking many gallons of water).

Concluding that Rebecca is God's answer to his prayer, Eliezer gives her a gold nose ring and two gold armbands, then asks her who she is and whether he can lodge with her family. When he learns that she is Abraham's niece, he is very pleased.

When Eliezer meets Rebecca's family, including her brother Laban, he tells them of the mission on which Abraham has dispatched him; he even relates the prayer he offered God and how Rebecca came by just after he finished. Finally, he requests the family's consent for Rebecca to marry Isaac, which they provide after first asking her.

Rebecca's decisive behavior marks her off as quite a different person from her future husband. She announces that despite her family's wish that she delay her departure, she will immediately accompany

Eliezer on his trip home (although given what we later learn of her brother Laban's seedy character, she might have been quite happy at this sudden opportunity to leave home), and shortly thereafter she marries Isaac.

The Bible's language—"Isaac then brought her into the tent of his mother Sarah, and he took Rebecca as his wife. Isaac loved her, and thus found comfort after his mother's death" (24:67)—conveys the sense that Rebecca serves as a kind of mother substitute for Isaac.

The three major episodes in which Isaac figures are not all the Bible tells us about him. On one occasion, he runs into the same dilemma that twice plagued his father: He arrives in a town where he fears the men will kill him in order to take his wife, a beautiful woman. Thus, he tells everyone that Rebecca is his sister (Genesis 26:7).

As a corollary to this story, we learn that Isaac's marriage to Rebecca seems to have been sensually fulfilling, for one day, Abimelech, the local king, looks out his palace window (probably the tallest building in town), and sees Isaac and Rebecca fondling one another. The king, who seems to have a strong moral sense, summons Isaac and attacks him for the lie he told: "One of the people might have lain with your wife and you would have brought guilt upon us." He issues an order that anyone who assaults Isaac or Rebecca will be put to death.

The Bible also indicates that Isaac had considerable business skills which, accompanied by the blessings God bestows on him, enabled him to become "very wealthy" (26:12). The local people grow envious of him, and maliciously stuff up with earth the wells that Abraham had once dug, in an effort to deprive Isaac's household and his flocks of water. Abimelech's earlier threat to kill anyone who molested Isaac proves hollow. Instead, he tells Isaac, "Go away from us, for you have become far too big for us." Only when Abimelech learns that Isaac continues to prosper even after he departs does he seek him out and propose a peace treaty. "We now see plainly that the Lord has been with you," this presumably pagan king says. Fearing that Isaac might have been offended by their last encounter, Abimelech sets out to reestablish good relations, to which Isaac agrees.

Wealthy as he becomes, even in his business dealings Isaac is decidedly nonaggressive. On two occasions, when his servants dig a well, and local herdsmen argue that the water is theirs, he moves on rather than argue with them. He rests only when he digs a well that provokes no disputes over water rights.

One reason Isaac might have led a more passive existence than Abraham and Jacob is because he encountered fewer life challenges than either of them. Bequeathed wealth by his father, he didn't have to struggle for money. He was also the only Patriarch who never left the land of Canaan. In contrast, his son Jacob matured during the years he had to live outside Canaan with his deceptive uncle Laban. Isaac, who suffered a trauma early in life, seems to have had a relatively calm life forever afterward. It is fitting, somehow, that he was the second Patriarch; it is hard to imagine him as the initiator of a dynasty.

17. Jacob and Esau

GENESIS, CHAPTERS 25 AND 27

Jacob Deceives His Father: "The Hands Are the Hands of Esau but the Voice Is the Voice of Jacob"

27:22

To any careful reader, it immediately becomes clear how many of the family problems that plagued Abraham and his descendants are ones with which we can identify today. One of the persistent conflicts that families face, and that occur repeatedly in the Bible, is parents expressing an undisguised preference for one child over another (see, for example, entry 22).

The third major event of Isaac's life, which occurs in his later years, revolves around a conflict in his feelings for his sons, Esau and Jacob; he and Rebecca each prefers a different son.

Isaac and Rebecca have been married many years before she becomes pregnant, with twins. Her pregnancy proves so painful that she cries out to God, "If so, why do I exist?" (i.e., "If I have to suffer like this, is it worth living?"). Unlike those of us who periodically pose such questions to the Almighty, Rebecca is given an immediate reply: "Two nations are in your womb, two separate peoples shall issue from your body. One people shall be mightier than the other, and the older shall serve the younger" (Genesis 25:23).

Indeed, the twins born shortly thereafter are markedly different. The older comes out red and hairy, and is named Esau; the younger emerges holding Esau's heel, and is called Jacob (in Hebrew, the name Ya'akov is etymologically related to *akev*, the word for "heel"). Esau grows up to be a skilled hunter, "a man of the outdoors," while Jacob, a mild man, generally stays at home.

Isaac favors Esau, for reasons that seem trivial, "because [Isaac] had a taste for game." Perhaps the physically robust and athletic Esau possesses precisely those traits that the largely passive Isaac (see preceding entry) himself desires.

Rebecca "favored Jacob," but the Bible does not tell us why. However, it is hard to imagine that she has not kept God's earlier prophecy firmly in mind.

The Bible recounts two episodes concerning the twins. In the first, Esau is described with contempt; in the second, he is dealt with more sympathetically.

Once, when Jacob is at home cooking a stew, Esau comes in from the field. Ravenously hungry, he sees what Jacob is preparing and cries out demandingly: "Give me some of that red stuff to gulp down, for I am famished."*

When Jacob replies, "First sell me your birthright," Esau expresses neither shock nor annoyance. He has convinced himself that his hunger is truly life-threatening: "I am at the point of death, so of what use is my birthright to me?"

Jacob proves quite wily. Aware that people in desperate straits are capable of making extravagant promises they later disavow, he offers Esau the food, but only on condition that he first swear to give up his birthright. Esau takes an oath to transfer it to Jacob, then gulps down a large meal. Clearly convinced that Esau's hunger was in no way life-threatening, the text concludes, "Thus did Esau spurn the birthright" (25:34).

The next time we meet the two brothers, the Bible's sympathies are less apparent.

---

*Literary scholar Robert Alter renders Esau's words even more graphically and vulgarly: "Let me cram my maw with this red-red [*ha-adom ha-adom hazeh*]." According to Alter, Esau is "too inarticulate to recall in his hunger or his sheer boorishness the ordinary Hebrew word *nazid*, 'stew.' "

Years have passed; Isaac is now old and blind. He summons Esau, his older son,* and tells him that he will soon die. He asks Esau to hunt some game and prepare for him a tasty dish, in return for which he will bestow upon Esau his "innermost blessing." The blessing to which Isaac is referring is very important and valuable, for this blessing was believed to determine the recipient's future destiny.

Esau must have been ecstatic at his father's words; he likely believed that receiving the blessing would undo the loss he had suffered by selling Jacob his birthright.

Rebecca overhears Isaac's conversation with Esau. As soon as Esau departs, she summons Jacob and tells him Isaac's plan, and offers her own: Jacob is immediately to slaughter two kids from the family's flock, and bring them to her. She will prepare just the sort of meal that Isaac loves, after which Jacob, not Esau, will receive the "innermost blessing."

Jacob objects, but on pragmatic, not moral, grounds. Esau is hairy, while he is smooth-skinned. The blind Isaac might touch him, deduce the deception, and curse instead of bless him (significantly, Jacob has no fear that Isaac will recognize him by his voice; perhaps because it resembles Esau's or maybe he is a good mimic). Rebecca refuses to be deterred. With the devotion long associated (particularly by Jewish comedians) with Jewish mothers, she says, "Your curse, my son, be upon me! Just do as I say . . ."†

Jacob brings the animals, and Rebecca prepares a favorite dish for her husband. Mindful of Jacob's earlier concern, she goes into Esau's room, takes his finest garment, and puts it on Jacob (that she dresses Jacob, a man who is certainly old enough to dress himself, suggests the depth of Jacob's nervousness and discomfort about carrying out this deception). Rebecca covers Jacob's hands and the hairless part

---

*Isaac does not know that Esau has sold his birthright, but the narrator does, which is why the text speaks of Esau as "the older son," and not as "the firstborn," a formal term carrying with it legal advantages.

†Rebecca's curse comes back to haunt her. Immediately after deceiving Isaac, Jacob is forced to flee his home, and no further encounter between him and his mother is recorded. A similar instance of a curse coming back to haunt the curser occurs years later when Jacob flees from his uncle Laban. His wife Rachel, Laban's daughter, steals her father's household idols. When Laban confronts Jacob and accuses him of the theft, Jacob, unaware of Rachel's action, imposes a curse of death upon whoever stole the idols. Laban searches and fails to find the idols (Genesis 31:30–35), but a short time later, Rachel dies while giving birth (35:16–19).

of his neck with the skins of the slaughtered animals. Then she sends him to his father.

When he enters Isaac's tent, Jacob utters only one word: "Father." Perhaps he is waiting to see if Isaac will call out, "What is it, *Jacob?*" in which case he will not go through with the deception. Instead, Isaac responds: "Yes, which of my sons are you?" Jacob, perhaps conscious of the reception he will receive from his mother if he doesn't follow through with her carefully orchestrated plot, tells his first lie: "I am Esau, your firstborn."* He tells Isaac that he has brought him the meal he requested. Fearing Esau's return, Jacob immediately adds the wish that his father bestow on him his "innermost blessing."

Isaac is puzzled that his son has returned so quickly with a prepared meal. We now see the fulfillment of the old proverb that "one lie drags another in its place," for Jacob is soon forced to tell additional lies to his father, even using God's name to support them. To Isaac's question "How did you succeed so quickly, my son?" he responds, "Because the Lord your God granted me good fortune" (Genesis 27:20).

Isaac is still unconvinced; from the little we know about Esau, invoking God's name would hardly spring instantly to his lips. Isaac urges Jacob to come forward; he wants to feel his son to see if it is really Esau. Jacob does as he asks, but Rebecca's ruse works; the young man feels like Esau. Isaac expresses his puzzlement, "The voice is the voice of Jacob, yet the hands are the hands of Esau."

Nonetheless, the hairy hands convince him, and he bestows the blessing on Jacob, but not before he elicits one more lie from his son. "Are you really my son Esau?" he asks, and Jacob answers, "Yes." Isaac then eats the food, drinks some wine (we can imagine Jacob's nervousness while his father eats, fearing all the while Esau's return), and calls his son to come and kiss him. Jacob does so, and the blind Isaac smells the garment Jacob is wearing and declares, "Ah, the smell of my son is like the smell of the fields that the Lord has blessed." He blesses Jacob that God should give him of the abundance of the land, and that others should serve him, including his brother (27:28–29).

*The unnecessary addition of "your firstborn" might convey Jacob's sense of bitterness about the exaggerated significance that has long been placed on which son is firstborn; like a child who would identify himself to his parent as "Brian, the doctor" in a household that put exaggerated stress upon professional attainment.

Jacob accepts the blessing, then immediately departs—just in time. Within minutes, Esau arrives, carrying a specially prepared dish for his father. But when he invites his father to partake of the food, Isaac asks, "Who are you?"

Esau must have thought that his father was becoming senile; nonetheless, he answers respectfully, "I am your son, Esau, your firstborn!"

Isaac trembles violently. "Who was it then," he asks, "that hunted game and brought it to me? . . . I ate of it before you came, and I blessed him; now he must remain blessed."

Esau bursts into wild and bitter sobbing. Unquestionably, this time the Bible's description of Esau's anguish is intended to evoke the reader's sympathy. On the previous occasion, Esau exaggerated his hunger, demanded food like a barbarian, and showed no understanding of his birthright's significance. But this time Esau's behavior has been appropriate. His father asks him to go hunting prior to receiving the blessing, and he does so. He doesn't address his father in a boorish manner, for example, by asking for the blessing before he hunts the game. Even now, despite the pain he is feeling, he speaks respectfully to his father and makes no angry accusations ("How could you not tell me apart from Jacob?"). All Esau can say to Isaac is "Bless me too, Father."

Instead of blessing him, however, Isaac speaks only of Jacob's deception. Infuriated, Esau hurls bitter accusations at his brother. Again he asks his father, "Have you not reserved even a single blessing for me?" (27:36).

Esau's question compels us to wonder what blessing, if any, Isaac had intended to bestow on Jacob. We will never know, for the blessing he now gives Esau is clearly intended for him: "Yet by your sword you shall live, and you shall serve your brother, but when you grow restive, you shall break his yoke from your neck" (27:40).

The Isaac whom we encounter here hardly comes across as a model parent. The Bible leaves us with the impression that he really had only one blessing prepared; he had prepared none for his younger son. Furthermore, when forced to improvise, Isaac bestows a blessing intended to encourage a permanent state of warfare between his two sons. What kind of parent wants that?

Biblical commentators have long struggled with this chapter. (Antisemites also have had a field day with it, seeing in Jacob the prototypical, wily, and scheming Jewish businessman.) Most commentators, Christian and Jewish, speak of Jacob in respectful terms; still, one would have to have a heart of stone to remain unmoved by Esau's pain, and to have no qualms about Jacob's lies.

Yet puzzlingly, almost all Bible commentators, in analyzing the episode's moral issues, focus almost exclusively on Jacob. They ignore the fact that the idea of deceiving Isaac is Rebecca's, and that it is she who plans the whole strategy.

An important issue that several commentators do address is whether Isaac is truly deceived by Jacob's behavior. Certainly, a literal reading of the text suggests that he is. When he initially suspects that the person confronting him might be Jacob, he goes so far as to feel his skin; only then is he sure that it is Esau. Also, his violent trembling when the real Esau comes into his tent indicates that he is shocked by what has happened.

But there also are grounds for believing that Isaac might not have been so unaware of what was happening. For one thing, blind though he is, there is no indication that Isaac suffers from any mental deterioration. How likely is it that a father, even a blind one, cannot differentiate one son from another (particularly when he only has two sons)?

There are stronger reasons to suspect that Isaac knows more than he reveals to Esau. If Jacob has secured Isaac's blessing under false pretenses, then why can't Isaac withdraw it? Are we to assume that this can never be done, that even if some servant of Isaac's had overheard him tell Esau to hunt some game for him and had then acted as Jacob did, that Isaac wouldn't have withdrawn the blessing from the servant?

Obviously, that can't be the case. Thus, Isaac *chooses* not to withdraw the blessing from Jacob.

Furthermore, if Isaac was aware that Jacob had fooled him, would he not have been furious with him? Yet the next time they meet, Isaac offers Jacob additional blessings with no hint of criticism. Thus, when Rebecca hears that the embittered Esau is intending to kill Jacob ("Let but the mourning period of my father come and I will kill my brother Jacob," 27:41), she goes to her husband. She doesn't want to tell Isaac what Esau has said; instead, she tells him that she wants Jacob to go away lest he intermarry with local, inappropriate, women, as did Esau: "If Jacob marries a Hittite woman like these . . . what good will life be to me?" (27:46).

Isaac summons Jacob, dispatches him to the house of Jacob's mother's family, and instructs him to take a wife from among the daughters of Laban, Rebecca's brother (to this day, Jewish law regards marriages between first cousins as permissible). He then blesses Jacob again, "May *El Shaddai* [a name of God] bless you, make you fertile and numerous, so that you become an assembly of peoples.

May He grant the blessing of Abraham to you and your offspring, that you may possess the land where you are sojourning, which God gave to Abraham" (Genesis 28:3–4). Both the tone and content of Isaac's words suggest not anger with Jacob but approval.

According to this explanation, Isaac at some unconscious level might have been aware that it was Jacob, not Esau, standing before him.

Psychologically, this makes much sense. Without question, Isaac preferred Esau; something about this son appealed to him. Isaac's favoritism was so strong that he couldn't hide it. Yet, at a less conscious level, Isaac realized that the great mission God had entrusted to his father, Abraham, and Abraham to him—to make God known to the world—could be carried on only through Jacob. He himself lacked the strength of character to deny the blessing to Esau, but when Jacob appeared, disguised as his brother, he went along with the deception, knowing that Jacob was worthier of the blessing. That is why he is able to greet him with affection at their next encounter, and send him off with a new blessing.

Reflections: How does the Bible regard Jacob's deception of his father? At the Jewish day school I attended as a child, we were taught that Jacob had acted appropriately. Esau was depicted as a terrible person (for example, we were taught a rabbinic tradition that Isaac had become blind from the incense used by Esau's wives when they offered idolatrous sacrifices). Isaac's preference for Esau was seen as so irrational that Rebecca and Jacob had to take preemptive action.

Indeed, this argument has some merit. Suppose a father has the power to bestow a life-transforming family mission on only one son, but for some perverse reason plans to bestow it on his least worthy child. In this instance, describing one son as less worthy is not just a subjective parental response. Rebecca knew—God had told her—which son was more worthy. Knowing what she did, should Rebecca (and Jacob) have gone along with Isaac's plan to bestow the blessing and the power that went with it on Esau? To do so would have constituted a betrayal of both their mission and their descendants. And, having acquired the birthright from Esau years earlier, Jacob had grounds for believing himself entitled to the blessing bestowed on the firstborn. One can certainly make a powerful case for the rightness of Jacob's behavior. Yet, a literary analysis of later episodes in Genesis strongly suggests a powerful undercurrent of biblical disapproval. During the remainder of his life, Jacob is paid back, measure for measure, for his deception. For example, he is able to fool the blind Isaac into thinking that he is

Esau. Years later, Jacob arranges with his uncle Laban to marry Laban's younger daughter, Rachel. On the wedding night, Laban sends Leah, his older daughter, into Jacob's tent (reminiscent of Rebecca sending Jacob into Isaac's tent). In a world without electricity, night's total darkness can render a person functionally blind. When Jacob awakes in the morning, he finds Leah next to him. The man who deceived his blind father now finds himself deceived by his uncle during his hours of "blindness."

When Jacob complains to Laban, his uncle responds: "It is not the practice in our place to marry off the younger before the older." In other words, "It is true that in your place such things are done, that the younger is given precedence over the firstborn, and his portion is taken away, and the younger is given the name of 'firstborn.' But such things are not done 'in our place to marry off the younger before the older.'" (Here, I am following the commentary of the sixteenth-century rabbi Eliezer Ashkenazi, author of *Ma'aseh Hashem*.)

This is not the only time that Jacob is painfully deceived. Many years later, his other sons gang up on Joseph, his favorite. They sell him into slavery after first removing the famous "coat of many colors" that Jacob has given him. They dip Joseph's coat in the blood of a slaughtered kid, which is reminiscent of the two kids with which Jacob deceived his father, then show Jacob the bloody garment. He who deceived his father now is deceived by his sons, in a manner that once again draws the reader's attention back to the initial act of deception.

Nehama Leibowitz, the great traditional Israeli Bible scholar and certainly no critic of Jacob, draws what I believe is an appropriate conclusion: "Sin and deceit, however justified, bring in their train ultimate punishment."

Esau in the Jewish tradition: The Book of Numbers describes an unnamed Sabbath desecrator who is executed by the Israelites (Numbers 15: 32–36). Many centuries later, Rabbi Akiva speculated on the basis of certain internal evidence (see Numbers 27:3) that he was a man named Zelophad. A contemporary called him to account: "Akiva, in either case you will have to justify yourself: if you are right, then you have revealed the identity of a man whom the Torah shielded; and if you are wrong, you are casting a stigma upon a righteous man" (Babylonian Talmud, *Shabbat* 96b).

This exquisite concern with not slandering the dead does not carry over into rabbinic speculations about Esau. I believe that the Rabbis were uneasy about the lies Jacob told his father, and so chose to justify him by defaming Esau; i.e., he was so terrible that Rebecca and Jacob were justified in doing anything to ensure that Esau not receive Isaac's blessing. Thus, while the Bible shows Esau as a flawed but far from terrible person, the Esau depicted in many rabbinic sources is unequivocally evil. To cite a few examples: In commenting on Esau's exhaustion when he sold the birthright, a talmudic passage claims that he committed five sins that day; he violated a betrothed maiden, murdered a person, denied God, rejected the notion of the resurrection of the dead, and spurned the birthright (Babylonian Talmud, *Bava Batra* 16b); these are much worse charges than Rabbi Akiva made against Zelophad, although Akiva had more textual basis for his accusation.

A *midrash* claims that Esau's evil nature was apparent even in the womb. Thus, whenever his mother, Rebecca, would pass by temples of idol worship, Esau eagerly would push inside her womb to come forth (*Genesis Rabbah* 63:6).

Another *midrash*, describing Esau's plan to kill Jacob after the death of Isaac, views Esau as a cynical plotter: "Said Esau, 'Cain was a fool for killing his brother Abel during his father's lifetime; he did not know that his father would procreate and beget Seth. I will not do so, but may the days of mourning for my father draw near, then I will kill my brother Jacob, and inherit his portion' " (while the desire to kill one's brother is of course a disgusting one, a close reading of the text suggests that Esau intended not to kill Jacob until after Isaac's death out of respect for his father, not out of a cynical desire to possess Isaac's entire estate).

The foregoing isn't the whole story. A rabbi as prominent as Simeon ben Gamliel, based on what the Torah actually says about Esau, views him as a model son who honored his father (*Deuteronomy Rabbah* 1:15). Still, it is hard to read the midrashic accounts of Esau without feeling that the Rabbis gave him a great deal less than the benefit of the doubt.

The noncommunicative marriage of Isaac and Rebecca: A reader senses that Isaac and Rebecca's marriage was far from perfect; they certainly did not communicate well. Thus, years earlier Rebecca had been bequeathed a divine prophecy that Jacob was destined to be the preeminent son, yet she apparently never shares this information with her husband, *even when she overhears him planning to bestow his innermost blessing on Esau.* Why? Most likely, Isaac's preference for Esau is so pronounced that she fears that he would not believe her; therefore, he must be tricked into "doing the right thing."

That Isaac speaks about bestowing the blessing only to Esau and doesn't tell Rebecca of his intentions also demonstrates the lack of communication in their marriage: It would be the equivalent of a man turning over a family business to one child, without speaking about the matter beforehand with his wife. On the other hand, Rebecca's preference for Jacob might have been so pronounced that Isaac wanted to bless Esau and confront Rebecca with a *fait accompli*. Unquestionably, the tensions between the twins parallel at least some of the tensions between the parents. Reading about how Rebecca confides in Jacob, one gets the impression that she feels closer to him—at least at that point in time—than she does to her husband. That is very sad, for the Bible had earlier spoken of Isaac's love for Rebecca (Genesis 24:67), while yet another passage—one that has few parallels in the Bible—describes the physical pleasure they took in each other (Genesis 26:8).

Sources: Nehama Leibowitz, *Studies in the Book of Genesis,* pages 317–324; I also found in Leibowitz the citation by Rabbi Eliezer Ashkenazi, page 323; Robert Alter, *The World of Biblical Literature,* page 93.

18. The Bible's First Dream: Jacob's Vision of a Ladder That Reaches Up to Heaven

GENESIS 28:10–22

When Jacob flees his father's house for that of his uncle Laban, his mood, we have reason to suspect, is fearful and depressed. True, Jacob had succeeded in deceiving his father into thinking he was Esau and thereby gaining the "innermost blessing" intended for his brother. However, at some level this must seem a Pyrrhic victory, for Esau has now resolved to kill him and so he must run for his life.

His first night on the run, Jacob stops in a field and goes to sleep, his head resting on a stone. One can imagine his dejection—this somewhat spoiled son of a loving mother now using a rock for a pillow. He has a vivid dream, the first dream recorded in the Bible.

Jacob sees a ladder set on the ground, its top reaching to the sky, and angels going up and down its rungs. Suddenly, the Lord is standing beside him, saying, "I am the Lord, the God of your father Abraham, and the God of Isaac; the ground on which you are lying I will give to you and to your offspring." God renews the promise that He had earlier made to Abraham: Jacob's descendants will be as numerous as the dust of the earth. Most important, God reassures this young man fearing for his life: "Remember, I am with you: I will protect you wherever you go and will bring you back to this land. I will not leave you until I have done what I promised you" (28:13–15).

Jacob awakes feeling greatly strengthened. "How awesome is this place. Surely God was in this place and I did not know it," he declares, and sets up the stone that served as his pillow as a pillar in honor of God.

Jacob, who earlier proved himself a tough negotiator with Esau, now makes a one-sided offer to God, without parallel in the Bible: "If God remains with me, if He protects me on this journey that I am making, and gives me bread to eat and clothing to wear, and if I return safe to my father's house, the Lord shall be my God" (28:20–21); the implication as to what will happen to his religious beliefs if these things do not come to pass is not spelled out. He also vows that if all these things happen, he will donate a tenth of his possessions to God (the notion of tithing is first mentioned in Genesis 14:20).

Unquestionably, Jacob's offer to God smacks of *chutzpah*. However, to his credit, when God does answer all of Jacob's prayers, he, in turn, fulfills his side of the bargain and devotes himself loyally to God.

19. Jacob, Rachel, and Leah: The Unhappy Triangle

GENESIS, CHAPTER 29

When Jacob arrived in Haran, birthplace of his mother and hometown of his uncle Laban, he must have been desperately lonely. He had spent nights sleeping outdoors, and in considerable fear, both of his rageful brother Esau and of wild animals.

Jacob heads immediately for Haran's well, the local gathering place (his mother undoubtedly had told him of how she had met Eliezer, Abraham's servant, at the well, and how this led to her marrying Isaac; see entry 16). He asks some shepherds gathered there if they know Laban, the son of Nahor. "Yes," they answer, "and there is his daughter Rachel, coming with the flock."

Jacob, the man who until now has been described in the most nonphysical of terms as a tent dweller, is so moved by the sight of his cousin that he singlehandedly rolls off a large stone covering the well, a task that normally requires the efforts of several men. He waters Rachel's flock, kisses her, and breaks into tears. A lonely man on the run, he has finally found a family again.

After he identifies himself to Rachel, she runs to summon her father. Although Laban later treats Jacob despicably, at this first meeting he is all unctious goodwill. He kisses and hugs his nephew, telling him, "You are truly my bone and flesh."

Jacob begins working for Laban. After a month's time, Laban asks him to name his wages. Jacob has already fallen in love with Rachel—she is "shapely and beautiful," as the text tells us—and he responds, "I will serve you seven years for your younger daughter in marriage." Laban expresses satisfaction with the proposed match.

The Bible's tone is uncharacteristically romantic in describing Jacob's feelings: "So Jacob served seven years for Rachel and they seemed to him but a few days because of his love for her" (29:20).

When the seven years end, Jacob reminds Laban that the time for the marriage has fallen due. The bride's father prepares a feast, but that night Laban brings Leah, not Rachel, to Jacob's tent. The darkness is total, Leah, we assume, is quiet and, as the Bible tersely put it, "When morning came, there was Leah."

Furious, Jacob confronts Laban: "What is this you have done to me? I was in your service for Rachel. Why did you deceive me?" (29:25).

Rather than apologizing, Laban offers a brief explanation, then makes an additional offer: "It is not the practice in our place to marry off the younger before the older. Wait until the bridal week of this one is over and we will give you that one too, provided you serve me another seven years."

This proposal has long been misunderstood by many Bible readers, who assume that Jacob had to work seven more years before he could marry Rachel. In actuality, he married her only one week after he wed Leah, but was then obligated to remain an additional seven years in service to Laban. Ever since, in Jewish tradition Laban has remained the personification of an evil and manipulative man.

The Bible provides no clue as to what Rachel was doing while her father and Leah arranged the deception of Jacob. We have every reason to believe that she fully reciprocated Jacob's love, and must have been desperate the night of their wedding; it is likely that Laban found some coercive means to keep her away. She probably learned of her father's plot at the last moment, but too late to warn Jacob.

Leah's role in the deception is not impressive. She remained with Jacob the whole night, most likely having sexual relations with him. She could have spoken up when she entered the tent, but she didn't. Perhaps she feared her father's wrath. What is more probable is that she loved Jacob and didn't want to pass up this opportunity to marry him. Perhaps Leah hoped that Jacob would fall in love with her, take her away from Haran, and eventually forget about Rachel. I doubt she realized that her father intended to offer Rachel to Jacob as well (later biblical law forbids a man from being married to two sisters simultaneously [Leviticus 18:18]; indeed, one of the best arguments for both the antiquity and the accuracy of this episode is that a later writer would not have depicted a biblical Patriarch as violating a later Torah law unless it were true).

Leah pays a high price for her role in this deception. She becomes an embittered, unloved woman. The Bible explicitly describes Jacob's feelings for his two wives: "He loved Rachel more than Leah." The problem apparently was worse than comparative degrees of love, for the Bible also tells us that "the Lord saw that Leah was unloved and

He opened her womb." Rachel, however, remains barren for many years.

Leah suffers terribly. When her first son is born, she names him Reuben, "For she declared, 'The Lord has seen my affliction,' " which also means, "Now my husband will love me." Apparently, her hope remains unfulfilled, for when her second son is born, she declares, "This is because the Lord heard that I was unloved and has given me this one also."

Upon the birth of her third son, the still hopeful Leah declares, "This time my husband will become attached to me, for I have borne him three sons." Her statements grow increasingly pathetic. She no longer hopes that her husband will love her for who she is, only because she has borne him three sons. Indeed, by the time her fourth son, Judah, is born, she is no longer speaking about love but proclaims, "This time I will praise the Lord."

The beloved yet barren Rachel perhaps is in no better emotional shape than her sister. Envious of the children Leah has borne, she confronts her husband: "Give me children, or I shall die" (Genesis 30:1).

Jacob, himself undoubtedly brokenhearted and most likely exasperated at Rachel's inability to conceive, turns on her wrathfully, asking, "Can I take the place of God, who has denied you fruit of the womb?"

"Each man kills the thing he loves," Oscar Wilde wrote thousands of years later. If all one knew of Jacob and Rachel's relationship was this single exchange, one would assume that their marriage was deeply unhappy. Numerous Bible commentators have remarked on the inappropriateness of Jacob's response; they compare his words with those of Elkanah, who, when he witnessed his wife weeping over her infertility, said, "Hannah, why do you weep? Why don't you eat, why do you feel bad? Am I not better to you than ten sons?" (I Samuel 1:8). Elkanah's words may not have fully consoled Hannah, who was desperate to have a child, but at least they conveyed love, not scorn or fury.

To appease Rachel, Jacob then acts as Abraham did: He has a child through his wife's maid, Bilhah. The results are far happier than was the case with Hagar, Sarah's maid (see entry 11; the sons born to Bilhah become progenitors of two of the Twelve Tribes). Leah, in turn, now insists that Jacob have children through her maid, Zilpah. The hapless Patriarch, who initially wanted one wife, now finds himself attached to four women.

After many years, Rachel finally becomes pregnant and gives birth to Joseph, Jacob's eleventh, but her first, son.

Throughout these years, Jacob has prospered as a raiser of livestock, but the income has gone largely into the hands of his father-in-law, Laban. Instead of receiving gratitude for his labors, Laban's sons claim that Jacob is stealing their family's wealth.

One night, the Lord tells Jacob that the time has come for him to return to his native land. After speaking with Leah and Rachel, who also express a desire to leave their father's house, he, they, their children, servants, and livestock set out for Canaan.

Much will happen before Jacob again reaches home, but one event casts a shadow over all the others. What should have been one of the happiest days of his life turns into what was probably the saddest; Rachel, in labor with her second child, Benjamin, dies in childbirth (Genesis 35:16–20). She is buried on the road, the only one of the Matriarchs or Patriarchs who is not buried in the Cave of the Machpela (see entry 15).

20. Jacob Becomes Israel

GENESIS 32:23–33

At times, God gives key biblical figures new names, particularly when the circumstances of their lives have altered. Thus, Abraham was known for most of his life as Abram, until God added the letter *hei* to his name as a sign that he "shall be the father of a multitude of nations" (Genesis 17:5).

However, no change has been as significant as that of Jacob, whose new name eventually became that of the entire Jewish people. And while Abraham was assigned a new name during a time of personal well-being, "Jacob" became "Israel" during a period when his and his family's lives were imperiled.

This whole episode hinges on an earlier episode in Jacob's life, when he deceived his father into granting him the firstborn-son blessing intended for Esau. From then on, his life seems anything but "blessed." While the Bible describes Abraham as "dying at a good ripe age, old and contented" (Genesis 25:8), and says of Isaac, "He was gathered to his kin in ripe old age" (Genesis 35:29), the elderly Jacob describes his life to the Egyptian pharaoh in these terms: "Few and hard have been the years of my life" (Genesis 47:9).

His hardships start immediately after receiving Isaac's blessing. Within days, Jacob is forced to flee his parents' home to escape Esau's murderous wrath. He arrives at the home of his uncle Laban, where he immediately falls in love with his beautiful cousin Rachel. He arranges to marry her, only to be deceived by his uncle and wed to Leah, Rachel's older sister. Although he eventually gains Rachel's hand in marriage, he remains in the employ of her treacherous father, a man who repeatedly attempts to defraud him.

Finally, he arranges to flee Laban's household, taking with him his family and possessions, only to learn that Esau is heading his way with four hundred men.

Twenty years have passed: Are Esau's intentions still murderous? He doesn't know, but Jacob has no reason to assume that his brother's rage has abated.

Although it is he who has acquired the birthright and the "innermost blessing" of his father, Jacob approaches his brother as if he were the younger and servile one. He sends messengers to Esau, instructing them to refer to him as "your servant Jacob." They are to tell Esau that "I send this message to my lord in the hope of gaining your favor" (32:4–6).

When Jacob learns that Esau has sent back no reply, and that he is continuing to march toward Jacob accompanied by troops, he is terrified. He divides his family and all his possessions into two camps, calculating that "if Esau comes to the one camp, and attacks it, the other camp may yet escape" (32:9).

He then turns to God in prayer, reminding the Lord that He had earlier promised to deal bountifully with him: "Deliver me, I pray, from the hand of my brother, from the hand of Esau; else . . . he may come and strike me down, mother and child alike" (32:12).

Jacob finally instructs his servants to prepare large numbers of domestic animals as gifts for Esau. The servants are to march ahead of Jacob and when they encounter Esau and are asked to identify themselves, to answer, "[the animals belong to] your servant Jacob; they are a gift sent to my lord Esau, and [Jacob] himself is right behind us." In this way, Jacob hopes that Esau will be well disposed toward him when they finally meet.

The son of the brilliant strategist Rebecca, Jacob apparently has become a shrewd strategist himself. In addition to prayers and gifts, he musters his forces, ready to do battle if necessary.

The night before the encounter with Esau may well have been the most frightening in Jacob's life. Will God keep His promise? Will Esau be propitiated by his gifts? If not, will Jacob's troops be able to successfully fend off Esau's four hundred men? Or will tomorrow be the last day of his and his family's life?

In the darkness, there occurs one of the most mysterious events in the Bible, an incident that establishes the name of the Jewish people.

Having sent his family and all his possessions across the water, Jacob remains alone on the other side. A supernatural but very tangible event occurs: A man attacks Jacob, who wrestles with him until almost the break of dawn. The attacker apparently had expected Jacob to be an easy victim; when he discovers that he cannot prevail, he wrenches Jacob's hip at the socket. Although in great pain, Jacob does not surrender.

The attacker grows desperate; apparently afraid of being seen, he appeals to Jacob, "Let me go, for dawn is breaking."

Jacob intuits the stranger to be a heavenly emissary, and responds, "I will not let you go unless you bless me."

"What is your name?" the man asks, and Jacob tells him.

The man replies, "Your name shall no longer be Jacob, but Israel, for you have striven with beings divine and human and have prevailed." (Yisra'el, the name he is given, means "God-wrestler.")

With understandable curiosity, Jacob inquires as to his attacker's name. "You must not know my name," the man answers and departs instantly.

Jacob immediately names the place of the encounter Pnei-el (the face of God) explaining, "I have seen a divine being face to face, yet my life has been preserved."

This strange encounter has affected Jewish life ever since. The alternate name of the Jewish people, Israel (or "children of Israel," in the Bible's language), has been in use ever since. While a relatively small percentage of contemporary Jews know that Israel means "to wrestle with God," the name has served more knowledgeable Jews as justification for arguing with God, which is a form of verbal wrestling (e.g., Book of Job, the Psalmist [44:24–25], and Habakkuk [1:2]).

In addition, the angel/man's dislocation of Jacob's hip socket becomes the basis for the dietary prohibition of eating the sciatic nerve on an animal's hip socket (see law number 3).

Despite the dislocated hip and a sleepless night, Jacob arises from this struggle reassured. Although the messengers he earlier dispatched to Esau brought back no words of reassurance, God has now given him a powerful message: If Jacob can prevail against a divine being, he has no reason to fear his own brother.

The next morning, Jacob chooses not to march behind his servants; instead, he runs ahead of his camp and bows low to the ground when he sees Esau.

This fierce man, the brother of whom Jacob has lived in terror for twenty years, turns out to be highly emotional and loving. He embraces Jacob, falls on his neck, and kisses him. The brothers weep, crying perhaps for the twenty years during which they have been estranged, and for the lifetime of alienation to which their parents' ill-disguised favoritism has helped condemn them.

Esau seems to harbor no ill will. When Jacob offers his gifts, Esau refuses them. "I have enough, my brother, let what you have remain yours" (33:9). One wonders when was the last time the two had ever addressed each other as brother.

Jacob now beseeches Esau to accept the gift. "For to see your face is like seeing the face of God, and you have received me favorably" (33:10).

Some commentators believe that Jacob's remarkable words are insincere, contending that he is willing to say anything simply to mollify Esau. Yet Jacob might well have been expressing how he truly felt. During his years away from home, he might have come to experience some guilt toward Esau. Though feeling justified in having gained the birthright and blessing, he may also have come to understand the pain that Esau has suffered. The gifts might well have been offered not to forestall war, but to produce a real peace.

Esau eventually accepts the gifts, but when he suggests that he and his troops march together alongside Jacob, the Patriarch demurs; his small children, he explains, cannot keep pace with Esau and his men (33:14).

Esau offers to have some of his men stay with Jacob's camp, but Jacob again refuses. Finally, Esau departs in one direction, Jacob in another. Jacob is relieved, for he has met the man he most feared and they have now parted on good terms.

The next time they meet is years later (when they come together to bury their father), which suggests that their reconciliation may have been somewhat superficial. Then again, as a later prophet taught, "Do not despise a day of small deeds" (Zechariah 4:10). Esau had once vowed that as soon as their father died, he would murder Jacob. Instead, the twins come together to bury Isaac, which demonstrates that some reconciliation has occurred. Some brothers have personalities so different that it is difficult for them to be close. Sometimes, the mere fact that they are not enemies is achievement enough.

21. The Rape of Dinah

GENESIS, CHAPTER 34

One might assume that Dinah, the lone daughter among Jacob's twelve sons, would have been the recipient of special attention and affection. If she was, the Bible gives no indication of it. Indeed, as my friend Dennis Prager notes, her birth, unlike that of each of her brothers, seems to have been treated as a nonevent. Thus, we are told the reason behind each of Jacob's sons' names. For example, "When Leah conceived again and bore Jacob a sixth son, Leah said, 'God has given me a choice gift; this time my husband will exalt me. . . .' So she named him Zebulun" (Genesis 30:19–20). In almost every instance the name chosen reflects a deep sense of gratitude to God. But in the case of Leah's final child, all we are told is that "lastly, [Leah] bore him a daughter, and named her Dinah" (30:21).

The only time we encounter Dinah after this muted birth announcement is when she becomes a young woman. She goes to visit the young women of the nearby Canaanite town of Shechem. There a man also named Shechem, the son of the town's chief, Hamor, rapes her.

Afterward, Shechem decides that he loves Dinah, and informs his father that he wishes to marry her. He clearly is not confident that Dinah reciprocates his feelings, for he keeps her under a kind of house arrest (34:26).

When Jacob hears that his daughter has been defiled, he says nothing; his sons are away in the field and, without them, he obviously feels too weak to confront Shechem's leading family. Then Hamor, along with his son, visits him, to request Dinah's hand in marriage formally. We are given no indication of how Jacob receives them; meanwhile, his sons arrive home, and they are of course furious at the violation of their sister.

Hamor now opens the marriage negotiations, but unfortunately he speaks in a manner that is unlikely to endear him to Jacob and his sons. Most important, neither he nor his son ever acknowledges—let alone apologizes for—what Shechem did to Dinah. From their subsequent behavior, one could deduce that they regard it as quite normal for a young man to rape a woman to whom he is attracted, and then, if he so wishes, marry her. Hamor now requests Jacob's consent to Dinah marrying Shechem; if the marriage takes place, he promises, then Jacob and his clan will be given grazing rights and permission to purchase land in the area.

When Hamor finishes, Shechem speaks up. He makes it clear that his desire for Dinah is deep, and that he will pay whatever bride-price Jacob requests.

The brothers respond with a counteroffer, although the Bible emphasizes that it is made with guile: "We cannot . . . give our sister to a man who is uncircumcised." It quickly becomes apparent that this is only part of the problem. For the marriage to occur, they explain, all the men of the city, not Shechem alone, must undergo circumcision. Then, Jacob's large clan will all be open to intermarrying with the people of Shechem.

Probably, Jacob's sons assume that their proposal will be rejected. For even if the suddenly lovestruck Shechem was willing to be circumcised, what are the chances that he would succeed in convincing all of Shechem's other adult males to undergo circumcision?

What, then, motivates the brothers to make this proposal? Simply, their desire to get their sister back. For all the friendly manner in which Hamor and Shechem are negotiating, the fact is that Dinah remains imprisoned in Shechem's house. This is why the brothers speak as if they are open to their sister's marriage to Shechem, but conclude their proposal by saying, "But if you will not listen to us and become circumcised, we will take our [sister] and go" (34:17).

Hamor and Shechem, however, accept the offer and return home, where they convince their fellow citizens to become circumcised. In speaking to them, Hamor appeals to their greed. True, we will have to circumcise ourselves if we wish to marry with Jacob's clan, but if we do, "their cattle and substance and all their beasts will be ours." It is not clear what Hamor has in mind, but it does sound as if some sort of plot is afoot by which Jacob and his sons will be dispossessed of their property. Another indication of Hamor's dishonorable intentions is that he omits mentioning the offer he made to Jacob, that he and his sons will be permitted to become landowners.

Yet, it seems unlikely that Hamor's appeal to greed alone would be sufficient to convince most male adults to become circumcised.

The fact that he was the city's chief, capable of punishing anyone who disobeyed him, likely had a great deal to do with the Shechemites' uniform decision to undergo circumcision.

Three days later, with the men of Shechem still weak and in pain, two of Dinah's brothers, Simeon and Levi—accompanied no doubt by their retainers—enter the city. They kill most of the town's males, then murder Shechem and Hamor, and finally rescue Dinah out of Shechem's house. Shortly thereafter, Jacob's other sons plunder the town because "their sister had been defiled."

At first, Jacob expresses no moral qualms about Simeon and Levi's behavior. He is angry at them not because they killed innocent townspeople, but because "you have brought trouble on me, making me odious among the inhabitants of the land . . . so that if they unite against me and attack me, I and my house will be destroyed" (34:30). The brothers are not impressed by Jacob's "wimpish" response: "Should our sister be treated like a whore?" they respond.

Decades later, it becomes apparent that Jacob's unhappiness over Simeon and Levi's action was motivated by more than pragmatism. Shortly before he dies, he blesses each of his sons. While the others are blessed individually, Simeon and Levi are spoken of as a pair, and Jacob refers to the incident at Shechem: "Their weapons are tools of lawlessness. . . . Cursed be their anger so fierce. And their wrath so relentless" (Genesis 49:5, 7).

One final issue: In noting that the brothers entered into the negotiations with Hamor and Shechem with guile, does the Bible mean to suggest that they intended all along to murder the men of Shechem? Not necessarily. Guile was required not to conceal murderous intentions but because, as Bible scholar Nahum Sarna points out, "The victim of the assault is still being held by the perpetrator, who has not even admitted to a crime, let alone expressed regret. There is no way that Dinah can be liberated by a tiny minority in the face of overwhelming odds—except by the exercise of cunning."

The brothers' reasoning in their negotiations with Hamor probably went as follows: Either he will reject our demand of circumcision and perhaps release Dinah, or he will accept it; if he does, we will enter the city while the men there are in a weakened state, incapable of fighting, and spirit Dinah away.

This was the likely intention of the other brothers, who did not anticipate the fierce and angry behavior of the fiercely angry Simeon and Levi. Unfortunately, anger, when unrestrained and unpunished, can turn in unexpected directions. The murderous rage that the brothers unleash against the citizens of Shechem will a short time later be directed at Joseph, their own sibling, who has provoked their ire (see Genesis 37:18).

Reflections: One thing that is striking and disturbing throughout this episode is Jacob's passive response to his daughter's rape. Many centuries later, King David responds with equally inappropriate passivity to the rape of his daughter Tamar, and, as in this case, killing results (see II Samuel, chapter 13, and entry 84).

Sources and further readings: Nahum Sarna, *The JPS Torah Commentary: Genesis,* pages 233–238; and Nehama Leibowitz, *Studies in the Book of Genesis,* pages 380–387.

22. The Young Joseph: Beloved Son, Hated Brother

GENESIS, CHAPTER 37

Of all Jacob's twelve sons, the Bible tells us he "loved Joseph best of all" (37:3). It is upon him that the Patriarch lavishes tremendous affection. Joseph is the firstborn son of Rachel, the only one of his four wives whom Jacob truly loved (Genesis 29:18; see also 29:30).

Jacob makes no effort to conceal his favoritism, causing painful envy among his sons and, ultimately, fierce enmity toward Joseph when he presents him with a special ornamental garment, a "coat of many colors." * The brothers become enraged: "And when his brothers saw that their father loved him more than any of his brothers, they hated him so that they could not speak a friendly word to him" (37:4). Anyone who has children should know the deep hostility

*Many centuries later, the talmudic Rabbis made caustic reference to this special garment: "A man should never single out one of his children for favored treatment, for because of two extra coins' worth of silk, which Jacob gave to Joseph and not to his other sons, Joseph's brothers became jealous of him, and one thing led to another until our ancestors became slaves in Egypt" (Babylonian Talmud, *Shabbat* 10b).

such blatant favoritism can cause, but Jacob seems oblivious or indifferent to the possibility of instigating fierce rivalry between Joseph
and his brothers.

Jacob also seems to have encouraged Joseph to tattle on his brothers, further inflaming their wrath. As the Bible tells us, "And Joseph
brought bad reports of [his brothers] to their father" (37:2).

Jacob is not the only one responsible for the animosity against
Joseph. The young Joseph—as distinct from the man into whom he
evolves—is no diplomat. He makes no effort to compensate for his
father's favoritism by showing his brothers that he is just "one of the
guys." Instead, he tells them of a dream he had: "There we were
binding sheaves in the field, when suddenly my sheaf stood up and
remained upright; then your sheaves gathered around and bowed
low to my sheaf." The brothers express understandable rage: "Do
you mean to reign over us?" Joseph seems oblivious to their reaction.
A short time later, he informs them of another dream: "The sun, the
moon, and eleven stars were bowing down to me." This time, even
Jacob becomes upset: "Are we to come, I and your mother and your
brothers, and bow low to you to the ground?" (37:5–10).

Some time later, the brothers go to Shechem to pasture their
flock. Jacob summons Joseph: "Go and see how your brothers are
and how the flocks are faring, and bring me back word." Apparently,
Jacob's favoritism includes exempting Joseph from the normal physical work in which his brothers are engaged (Joseph was no child at
this time; he was seventeen), which is why he is at home with his
father.

What is striking is Jacob's ignorance of the depth of ill will the
other brothers bear Joseph. Remember that the other brothers "could
not speak a friendly word to [Joseph]." How could Jacob fail to
notice this?

Joseph too seems oblivious to reality. Although his brothers have
made little effort to disguise their animosity toward him, he sets off
on the journey, wearing the very coat of many colors that has so
inflamed them. However, he does not find his brothers in Shechem.
A good son, he could have gone home at this point, but when an
unnamed man tells him that they have gone to the town of Dothan,
Joseph follows them there.

The brothers see him from afar, and say to one another: "Here
comes that dreamer! Come now, let us kill him and throw him into
one of the pits; and we can say, 'A savage beast devoured him.' We
shall see what comes of his dreams" (37:18–20).

Reuben, the oldest, is horrified by their talk. While most people would assume such threats are exaggerated (when a person says about someone he dislikes, "I could strangle him," you don't assume that he means it literally), Reuben takes their words very seriously. He doesn't try to dissuade them from doing any harm to Joseph— their anger appears too great to be open to such an appeal—but he suggests that they throw Joseph into a pit. That way, he will die without their having shed their brother's blood. In actuality, Reuben intends to return later and raise Joseph from the pit. The brothers make no response to Reuben's suggestion. But a few minutes later, when Joseph arrives, they strip off his hated coat of many colors, and throw him into an empty pit.

"Then they sat down to a meal" (37:25). There are few more damning lines in the Bible. These men have just thrown their brother into a pit, where they intend to leave him until he dies of hunger or thirst (the Bible emphasizes that the pit has no water). And what do they do then? Sit down to enjoy a meal.

Reuben, it seems, has temporarily left them. Thus, when they see a caravan of Ishmaelites drawing near, one of the brothers, Judah (perhaps thinking that Reuben really intends Joseph to die in the pit), offers a more self-interested suggestion: "What do we gain by killing our brother? . . . Come, let us sell him to the Ishmaelites, but let us not do away with him ourselves." The brothers agree.

At this point, the biblical narrative becomes somewhat confusing. The brothers seem to have temporarily moved away from the pit (perhaps their meal was being disturbed by anguished appeals from Joseph; see Genesis 42:21), for the next thing we know, a group of Midianite traders pass the pit, pull out Joseph, and then sell him to the Ishmaelites for twenty pieces of silver.

A short time later, Reuben returns to the pit, sees that it is empty, and tears his clothes in the manner of a mourner. "What am I to do?" he wails. (As the oldest, he is well aware that he will have to account for Joseph's disappearance to Jacob.)

Reuben's tears do not move his brothers. No one makes any effort to catch up with the slave traders and repurchase Joseph. Instead, they take the young man's hated coat, slaughter a kid, and dip the garment in its blood. They then take the coat to their father and ask him, in feigned ignorance, "We found this. Please examine it, is it your son's tunic or not?"

Jacob recognizes the coat. "My son's tunic! A savage beast devoured him! Joseph was torn by a beast!" In the entire Bible, no other character is depicted as mourning a death so deeply (37:34–35). First, Jacob lost Rachel, the one woman he loved. Now he has lost

Joseph, the son he most loved. All his children try to comfort him—
no doubt nervous all the while, that their foul deed will be uncovered—but Jacob can accept no consolation. The worst fate that can
befall a parent, losing a child, has befallen him. "I will go down
mourning to my son in Sheol"; in other words, "I will go to my death
in perpetual mourning."

Reflections: On sibling relationships in Genesis: Genesis repeatedly confirms
for us that love between siblings cannot be assumed. Cain, the first
human being born in history, murders his brother Abel. Jacob himself arouses the murderous wrath of his brother Esau, and has to flee
for his life. Here, Joseph's brothers first decide to murder him, then
to sell him into slavery. This is probably the most depressing episode
in Genesis.

Month after month, the brothers see their father in the deepest
of grief, yet none tries to retrace the steps of the Ishmaelite or
Midianite caravan: No one goes to Egypt to try to locate, and liberate, the brother they have sold. Perhaps they fear to do so; if
Joseph comes home and tells Jacob what happened, who knows what
their father will do? But it is more likely that they prefer to have
Joseph out of their lives, even at the cost of their father's perpetual
tears.

23. Tamar (and Judah): The Woman Who Disguised Herself as a Prostitute

GENESIS, CHAPTER 38

In one of the Bible's most remarkable stories, Judah, Jacob's fourth
son, and until now a rather undistinguished man, grows to greatness in the aftermath of his encounter with a "prostitute." The incident, occasioned by Tamar, Genesis's most unusual heroine,
begins with Judah's marriage to an unnamed Canaanite woman
with whom he has three sons. He marries off the oldest, Er, to a
woman named Tamar, but the son acts so wickedly—the Bible
does not specify what he does—that God causes him to die. In

accordance with the ancient tradition of "levirate marriage" (which commands that when a man dies childless, his brother must marry the widow, and their first child be accounted to the dead man, "that his name may not be blotted out in Israel"; see Deuteronomy 25:5–6), Judah quickly marries his second son, Onan, to Tamar. However, Onan has no desire to perpetuate his dead brother's memory; whenever he has intercourse with Tamar he withdraws prematurely and spills his seed on the ground. This infuriates God, who puts him to death as well.

Judah, who has little insight into his sons' characters (he may well have been an absentee father; the text records that his wife, not he, names their last two sons, and he is not even present when his third son is born; 38:4–5), apparently thinks it is Tamar, not God, who is somehow responsible for their deaths. Therefore, he withholds his third son, Shelah, from marrying her.

Tamar is in a quandary. Her two husbands having died rather quickly, she may well have developed a reputation for being a kind of toxic wife. Yet she is still a young woman, and the levirate tradition forbids her to marry anyone besides the very son whom Judah is withholding from her.

Some time later, Judah's wife dies. When the period of mourning ends, Judah and his friend Hirah set out for the city of Timnah, to be present at the shearing of Judah's sheep. When Tamar hears that her father-in-law is heading for Timnah, she takes off her widow's garments, covers her face with a veil, and sits down at the entrance to Enaim, a town on the road to Timnah.

When Judah sees her, he assumes that Tamar is a prostitute, for she has covered her face—apparently, this was a common practice among prostitutes—and he propositions her. It is revealing, and not particularly complimentary to Judah, that Tamar thinks that all she has to do is dress up as a prostitute to seduce him (indeed, the Bible might well have emphasized his wife's recent death to explain the alacrity with which he responds to Tamar). What is more peculiar, and reinforces the suspicion that Judah has devoted little attention to his family, is that he does not recognize Tamar's voice in the negotiations that ensue.

In response to her father-in-law's interest, Tamar asks him what he is willing to pay to sleep with her. Judah promises her a kid from his flock. Tamar agrees but insists that Judah entrust her with a pledge that she will return when she receives the kid. "What pledge should I give you?" Judah asks, and Tamar responds, "Your seal and your cord, and the staff that is in your hand." This was not a light request (the seal, for example, was a form of identification, a small stone with writing cut into it that could make an impression on a document); literary scholar Robert Alter notes that the contemporary equivalent would be a demand for one's major credit cards.

Judah gives Tamar what she requests, and they have sex. As soon as Judah leaves, Tamar returns to her parents' house and again puts on the garments of widowhood.

The following day, Judah sends his friend Hirah with the kid. But when Hirah comes to Enaim, he cannot find the prostitute; in fact, the townspeople tell him that they know of no prostitute who works at the city's entrance. Having made an honest effort to pay, Judah tells Hirah to forget the whole incident. "Otherwise, we will be laughed at."

Three months later, word is brought to Judah that Tamar is pregnant. Infuriated at her apparent act of betrayal, Judah sternly rules, "Bring her out, and let her be burned."

Before Tamar can be executed, she sends Judah the pledge he has given her, along with the message "It was the owner of these who made me pregnant. . . . Please recognize to whom these belong, the signet and the cord and the staff."

When Judah sees his pledge, he declares: "She is more in the right than I [alternatively, "more righteous than I"], since I did not give her to my son Shelah."

The execution, of course, is canceled, and Judah and Tamar never again are intimate.

Six months later Tamar gives birth to twin brothers (numerically, at least, replacing Judah's two dead sons). One, named Peretz, will become an ancestor of King David (Ruth 4:18).

In Jewish tradition, Tamar is regarded as a heroine, a fact underscored by the long-standing popularity of her name among Jewish women. That she is willing to feign being a prostitute in order to avoid a life of childlessness is not held against her. Furthermore, the Rabbis regard the delicate manner in which she makes Judah aware that he is the child's father as proof of her moral stature. Although facing a death sentence, she does not publicly humiliate her father-in-law.* Instead, she sends him, *and him alone,* his pledge, confident

---

*The Talmud deduces from Tamar's behavior the rather extreme, but ethically sensitive, conclusion that it is preferable for someone to let him- or herself be burned rather than publicly humiliate another person (Babylonian Talmud, *Bava Mezia* 59a).

that Judah's sense of justice will impel him to acknowledge his paternity.

As for Judah, *this incident may well be the turning point in his life.* Prior to it, Judah has done little to commend himself to posterity. True, he tries to dissuade his brothers from killing Joseph, but his proposal to sell Joseph into slavery hardly characterizes him as a great humanitarian (Genesis 37:27). Indeed, the Bible later legislates that selling a person into slavery is a capital offense (Deuteronomy 24:7). After the sale of Joseph, when Judah and his brothers deceive Jacob into believing that he has been killed by a beast, Judah witnesses his father's unending pain (see Genesis 37:34–35) *and does nothing.* He does not tell Jacob that he and his brothers have lied, that Joseph is alive, nor does he make an effort to go down to Egypt and find Joseph.

The early parts of this chapter likewise do not portray Judah in a praiseworthy light. That God finds his two oldest sons so evil as to be worthy of early death certainly does not reflect well on his parenting skills. And whereas Jacob mourns for the presumably dead Joseph "many days" (Genesis 37:34), the Bible does not record Judah as expressing any emotion upon the death of his sons. Furthermore, there is a hint of cruelty in the speed with which he is willing to put Tamar to death, particularly since it was he who had every intention of confining her to a life of celibacy and childlessness (his own behavior with Tamar suggests that he was unwilling to tolerate extended sexual frustration).

Yet Tamar's heroism—her willingness to risk her life to have a child—and her extraordinary graciousness in refraining from publicly humiliating him, seem to have transformed Judah. The man who coldly stood by while his father cried for his beloved son Joseph now becomes the family man par excellence. A few years later, it is Judah who guarantees to Jacob that he will protect his youngest brother, Benjamin, on their dangerous trip into Egypt (Genesis 43:3–10). Later, when Benjamin is threatened with being enslaved, it is Judah who steps forward and insists that he be enslaved instead (Genesis 44:33). It is this selfless act that causes Joseph to break down in tears, and finally and fully forgive his brothers.

The transformation of the cold, calculating Judah into an ethically passionate, loving, and responsible man helps account for the blessing Jacob later bestows on him, that he will become the leader of the family, and that rulers will descend from him (Genesis 49:8–10). And this transformation seems to have been due to one of the Bible's most unusual heroines, Tamar.

Reflections: In English, the word "onanism," derived from Onan, means masturbation. Because God put Onan to death, many people (particularly in premodern times) concluded that masturbation was a terrible crime, worthy of the most serious punishment. But even a casual reading of the text reveals that Onan's sin had nothing to do with masturbation, and everything to do with hatred for his brother, epitomized by Onan's unwillingness to perpetuate his dead brother's name. As my late friend Rabbi Wolfe Kelman explained, "It is the theme of brotherly hatred—Onan's refusal to perpetuate Er's name, and the sale into slavery of Joseph by his brothers—that links this chapter to the preceding one."

Sources and further readings: Robert Alter, *The Art of Biblical Narrative,* pages 3–11; David Gunn and Danna Fewell, *Narrative in the Hebrew Bible,* pages 34–45: Gunn and Fewell, who are rather harsh on Judah, find that his refusal to "know" Tamar after acknowledging her as righteous gives further evidence of his deficient character: "Judah did not know her when he sent her away to her father's house, and he did not know her when he lay with her. When he does come to know her, it is more than he cares to know, for she forced him to know himself" (page 44). Provocative as this reading is, the authors take no note of Judah's subsequent growth. The reason he refused to continue the relationship with Tamar is that now that his dead sons' names have been established, continuing a father-in-law–daughter-in-law relationship—even though his sons were dead—would amount to a kind of incest: Devora Steinmetz, *From Father to Son,* pages 45–49.

24. Joseph and Mrs. Potiphar

GENESIS, CHAPTER 39

The biblical narrative abounds in surprises. Thus, Joseph, raised in Jacob's house, seems incapable of achieving greatness in the orbit of his father. It is only when his brothers sell him into slavery that he starts to grow into a man of stature. But first, however, he must undergo repeated reversals of fortune.

His first experience of slavery is not so terrible. The Ishmaelite traders who acquire Joseph as a slave eventually bring him to Egypt, where they sell him to Potiphar, a high official in Pharaoh's court. The Bible repeatedly reiterates that the "Lord was with Joseph," so that he succeeds in every task his master assigns him.

In an action that anticipates Pharaoh's later elevation of Joseph, Potiphar appoints the young slave to be in charge of his household. Joseph is soon running everything—Potiphar "paid attention to nothing except the food that he ate" (39:6)—and his master's wealth grows quickly.

But while Potiphar is paying attention only to his meals, Mrs. Potiphar finds herself taken with the highly successful new slave her husband has acquired. Indeed, the contrast between her passive husband, whose interest extends only to his food, and the energetic and capable Joseph might have been one of the factors that attract her to the young slave. In addition, the Bible tells us that Joseph was "well built and handsome" (39:6).

Given her social superiority to, and her husband's ownership of, Joseph, Mrs. Potiphar feels no need for subtlety when approaching him: "Lie with me," she directs him.

"And Joseph refused," the Bible tells us. The Hebrew word for "refused" is *va-ye-ma-ain;* when it is chanted during the reading of the Torah, the reader uses a rare musical note, *shalshelet*—it occurs only three times in the Torah—that lasts about five seconds. In effect, the word is chanted thus: "And Joseph re-fu . . . s . . . s . . . ed," from which one might deduce that it was a real struggle for him to refuse her overtures. Nonetheless, what is clear is that this highly spoiled son of Jacob has evolved into a moral young man. Even as he wards off Mrs. Potiphar's efforts to sleep with him, Joseph tries not to insult her. Potiphar, he explains, has given all that he owns over into his hands, he "has withheld nothing from me except yourself, since you are his wife. How then could I do this most wicked thing, and sin before God?" (39:9). In the biblical view (see entry 162), adultery is a sin not only against one's spouse, but also against God, in whose presence the couple was married.

Joseph's high-minded argument makes little impression on his master's wife. Day after day, she coaxes the young slave to lie with her; day after day, he refuses.

Joseph must have been living in increasing terror. Like a black slave in the American South, he surely must have realized that only evil could come from this situation. If he slept with the woman and that fact became known, she would charge him with rape. And if he rejected her advances, she might grow angry and charge him with attempted rape.

The latter is what happens. One morning, Joseph shows up for work to find only Mrs. Potiphar present in the house. (The Bible doesn't indicate whether this was a chance occurrence or the result of her having dismissed the other servants.) She now tries a more direct approach, grabbing Joseph's coat and commanding him, "Lie with me."

Terrified, Joseph flees, his torn coat remaining in Mrs. Potiphar's hands. (This is not the first time a coat has gotten Joseph into trouble; see entry 22.)

Either in panic that Joseph will run to her husband, or out of humiliation and fury at his rejection of her overtures, Mrs. Potiphar immediately summons her servants and maligns Joseph. She tells them that he attacked her and that when she screamed, he fled, leaving his coat behind. The servants, some of whom undoubtedly resented Joseph's rapid rise to power, accept the story. Mrs. Potiphar now feels ready to present it to her husband.

What did Joseph do during this time? The Bible doesn't tell us, just as it doesn't inform us earlier about his activities during the hours his brothers imprisoned him in the deep, empty pit. He must have been terrified, particularly when he realized that he had left his coat behind. We can imagine him wandering about, a slave exiled in a foreign land, fearful to return to his master's house, but with nowhere else to go.

By the time Potiphar arrives home, his wife has refined her story. She starts by trying to manipulate her husband's guilt: "The Hebrew slave *whom you brought* into our house," she says, "came to have fun with me. But when I screamed at the top of my voice, he left his coat with me and fled outside" (39:17–18).

"And Potiphar was furious," the Bible records; he incarcerates Joseph in the royal prison.

With whom exactly was Potiphar furious? A simple reading of the text suggests that it was Joseph, of course. But I don't believe that for a moment. If Potiphar really believed that Joseph had tried to rape his wife, would he have been satisfied with imprisoning him? (Furthermore, the description of the prison in Genesis 40 makes it clear that it was not a particularly harsh prison.) Of course not! Throughout history, slaves accused of rape were killed; they were lucky if they were not tortured first.

Potiphar was furious, but at his wife, not Joseph. Furious because he must have known the kind of person to whom he was married, furious because she was attacking the one person who had truly enriched him, and furious because she had told everyone else in the house of her accusation. Doing so placed Potiphar in an untenable position; to ignore his wife's now widely known accusation would bring his family's name into disrepute.*

So, Potiphar places Joseph in prison, far from an ideal solution, but his only tenable compromise with his wife's evildoing. Joseph is confined in a *royal* prison, geographically nearer, if not in any other way, to the pharaoh of Egypt. Although the young man has no way of knowing it, the stage is being set for the eventual fulfillment of his two prophetic childhood dreams.

Reflections: In the Jewish tradition, certain figures have long been associated with special appellations. To this day, observant Jews refer to Moses as *Moshe Rabbenu* (Moshe, our teacher), and Abraham as *Avraham Avinu* (Abraham, our father). Joseph is widely known as *Yosef ha-Tzaddik* (Joseph, the righteous). Although the Rabbis never explain what specific behavior accounted for his being called "the righteous," Jewish commentators have always assumed that it was his repudiation of Mrs. Potiphar's adulterous advances. That this was the reason the Rabbis labeled Joseph a *tzaddik*—not because of his later direction of the Egyptian economy, which saved tens of thousands of people from starvation—indicates how difficult they believed it could be sometimes to avoid committing adultery.

---

*One of the great works of modern American literature, Harper Lee's *To Kill a Mockingbird*, describes a jury's conviction of an obviously innocent black man charged with rape. The behavior of the female accuser in the book is remarkably similar to that of Mrs. Potiphar, while the man's behavior parallels that of Joseph. Nonetheless, to have acquitted him, the bigoted all-white jury felt, would disparage all white women.

25. The Dreamer Becomes the Interpreter of Other Men's Dreams

GENESIS, CHAPTERS 40–41

The Lord who was with Joseph while he served in Potiphar's house remains with him in prison. Joseph finds favor in the chief jailer's eyes, and is soon put in charge of the other prisoners (yet another adumbration of the authority that Pharaoh eventually will grant him). As was the case with Potiphar, the jailer gives Joseph total independence in carrying out his responsibilities (Genesis 39:23).

A short time later, two members of Pharaoh's court, his cupbearer and baker, antagonize the Egyptian ruler. He orders them cast into the prison in which Joseph is confined.

One night, both men have highly evocative dreams. When Joseph sees them the following morning, they are distraught. Joseph asks them why, and they tell him about the dreams and how troubled they are at not knowing what they signify. Joseph humbly replies, "Surely God can interpret! Tell me [your dreams]" (40:8).

The chief cupbearer speaks first: "In my dream, there was a vine in front of me. On the vine were three branches. It had barely budded, when out came its blossoms, and its clusters ripened into grapes. Pharaoh's cup was in my hand, and I took the grapes, pressed them into Pharaoh's cup, and placed the cup in Pharaoh's hand."

Joseph responds immediately, with an intuitive understanding of each detail's significance: "The three branches are three days. In three days, Pharaoh will pardon you and restore you to your post; you will place Pharaoh's cup in his hand, as was your custom formerly when you were his cupbearer."

After sharing this happy prediction with the cupbearer, Joseph, for the first time, asks a favor: "But think of me when all is well with you again, and do me the kindness of mentioning me to Pharaoh, so as to free me from this place. For in truth, I was kidnapped from the land of the Hebrews; nor have I done anything that they should put me in the dungeon" (throughout his years in Egypt, Joseph never reveals what his brothers did to him; the truth that his own siblings were responsible for his being sold into slavery might well have been too humiliating to reveal).

Pharaoh's baker is encouraged by Joseph's optimistic interpretation of the cupbearer's dream, and tells about his own. He had dreamed that three baskets were on his head. The uppermost basket contained various delicacies for Pharaoh, but birds were eating out of it.

Joseph responds rather cold-bloodedly, informing the baker that "the three baskets are three days. In three days, Pharaoh will lift off your head and impale you upon a pole, and the birds will pick off your flesh."

Pharaoh's birthday occurs three days later, the only birthday mentioned in the Hebrew Bible. As part of the celebration, Pharaoh restores the cupbearer to his post and impales the baker, exactly as Joseph had predicted.

The one thing that does *not* follow is the cupbearer's fulfillment of Joseph's request: "Yet the chief cupbearer did not remember Joseph; he forgot him" (40:23). (The pattern of betrayal runs through the Joseph saga; first he is betrayed by his brothers, then by Mrs. Potiphar, now by the cupbearer.)

Two more years pass, during which Joseph must have wondered if he was destined to die as a prisoner in an Egyptian jail.

Then one night Pharaoh himself has a dream. As he is standing by the Nile, seven cows, handsome and sturdy, come up from the river and graze in the meadow. This pastoral scene ends in horror as seven ugly and gaunt cows come up behind the handsome ones and totally consume them.

Pharaoh awakens, then goes back to sleep, and has a second dream,* in which Pharaoh sees seven healthy ears of corn growing on a single stalk. Behind them sprout seven thin and scorched ears, which swallow up the healthy ones.

Pharaoh arises in the morning considerably agitated. He summons Egypt's leading magicians and wise men and confides to them his dreams, but no one can offer a satisfying interpretation.

Finally, the chief cupbearer speaks up. He seems a bit nervous; telling Pharaoh about Joseph means reminding the monarch that he had once found it necessary to imprison him. Nonetheless, the cupbearer overcomes his inhibitions and informs Pharaoh about the

---

*All six dreams in the Joseph sequence occur in pairs; his own dreams of future mastery over his family, the dreams of the two prisoners, and now Pharaoh's dreams. It was likely their parallel nature that convinced the dreamers of their significance.

dreams both he and the chief baker had: "A Hebrew youth was there with us . . . and when we told him our dreams, he interpreted them for us, telling each the meaning of his dream. And as he interpreted for us, so it came to pass; I was restored to my post, and the other was impaled" (Genesis 41:9–13).

Pharaoh promptly sends for Joseph. Pharaoh's messengers rush the young man from the prison, cut his hair, change his clothes, and bring him before the king. Pharaoh tells Joseph that he has heard about his unique ability to interpret dreams, to which Joseph humbly responds: "Not I! God will see to Pharaoh's welfare." It is striking that when Joseph makes reference to the God in Whom he believes, as he did previously with Mrs. Potiphar, the cupbearer, and the baker, no one asks him to clarify or explain anything further about God.

After Pharaoh recounts his dreams, Joseph responds immediately: "Pharaoh's dreams are one and the same: God has told Pharaoh what He is about to do. The seven healthy cows are seven years, and the seven healthy ears are seven years; it is the same dream. The seven lean and ugly cows that followed are seven years, as are also the seven empty ears scorched by the east wind; they are seven years of famine. . . . Immediately ahead are seven years of great abundance in all the land of Egypt. After them will come seven years of famine, and all the abundance in the land of Egypt will be forgotten. As the land is ravaged, no trace of the abundance will be left because of the severe famine. As for Pharaoh having had the same dream twice, it means that the matter has been determined by God and that God will soon carry it out" (41:25–32).

Joseph then advises Pharaoh to find a wise man to administer Egypt's affairs of state. Most important, this man should supervise the collection of an annual percentage of the food harvest to be set aside for the seven years of scarcity, "so that the land may not perish in the famine."

Pharaoh is not only attracted to Joseph, but to his God as well: "Could we find another like him, a man in whom is the spirit of God?" (41:38). This response is in marked contrast to his much later successor, who responds to Moses' request to give the Israelite slaves three days of respite to practice their religion: "Who is the Lord that I should heed him. . . . I do not know the Lord" (Exodus 5:2).

Pharaoh promptly appoints Joseph Egypt's second-in-command "only with respect to the throne shall I be superior to you" (41:40). He removes his signet ring and puts it in Joseph's hand, has Joseph dressed in fine linen robes (perhaps the first elegant clothes he has worn since his brothers ripped off his "coat of many colors"), and puts a gold chain around his neck. He also bestows a new name on Joseph, Zaphenath-paneah, which probably means, "God speaks; He lives," or "He who reveals that which is hidden."

In the rabbinic *midrash* there is an expression which has provided solace to suffering Jews for thousands of years: "Salvation can come in the twinkling of an eye." Joseph wakes up one morning, as he had for the preceding two years, as a falsely accused prisoner in an Egyptian jail. He goes to sleep that night, second in power only to Pharaoh; truly, Joseph's salvation comes "in the twinkling of an eye."

The seven years of abundance soon begin, just as Joseph had predicted, and of course are followed by seven years of famine. His interpretations of the cupbearer's and the baker's dreams have been fulfilled, and the interpretations of Pharaoh's dreams have also been realized. Only two dreams have yet to come true: Joseph's childhood visions.

Reflections: Chapter 40's final verse, "Yet the chief cupbearer did not remember Joseph; he forgot him," conveys an important lesson: Memory must be *active*, for unless one actively makes a point of remembering an event or a person, the information is apt to be forgotten. That is why later biblical verses repeatedly emphasize that the Israelites must remember their enslavement in Egypt, and not relate to others in the abominable manner in which they were treated. Without conscious efforts at remembering, the Israelites would become affluent, forget that they were descendants of slaves, and lose all sense of empathy with other people who suffer. This is exactly how the chief cupbearer acted: Once freed from prison and restored to his honored position, he neither desired to recall his unpleasant prison days, nor wished to help the young man who, like himself, had been imprisoned unjustly.

26. Joseph Tests His Brothers

GENESIS, CHAPTERS 42–45

Twenty-two years have passed since Joseph's brothers sold him into slavery and, except for the brief episode of Judah and Tamar, the Bible has focused exclusively on Joseph's experiences in Egypt.

Now we return to his family in Canaan. The very first verse in chapter 42 conveys the feeling that we have arrived in the middle of a conversation: "When Jacob saw that there were food rations . . . in Egypt, he said to his sons, 'Why do you keep looking at one another? Now I hear . . . that there are rations to be had in Egypt. Go down and procure rations for us there, that we may live and not die' " (42:1–2).

Ten of Jacob's twelve sons set out for Egypt, the same ten who sold Joseph into slavery. At the time the sale occurred, the youngest son, Benjamin, was very small and was staying at home with his father; now he is in his twenties. The only surviving child of the beloved Rachel, Benjamin has replaced Joseph in his father's affections, and remains at home with Jacob.

In Egypt Joseph has ultimate authority over the sale of the country's surplus food. He is present when his ten brothers arrive from Canaan, and their first act upon coming into his presence is noteworthy: "And Joseph's brothers came and bowed low to him, with their faces to the ground" (42:6), a fulfillment of the first of the dreams that Joseph had revealed to them shortly before they sold him (Genesis 37:6–7).

Joseph immediately recognizes his brothers, but they fail to identify him. At their last encounter, he was a smooth-faced teenager; now he is thirty-nine, dressed in garments appropriate to Egypt's second-highest official, and is speaking in Egyptian.

He greets his brothers with cold suspicion: "You are spies, you have come to see the land's weaknesses."

The brothers insist that they have only come to Egypt to procure food. They note that they are all sons of one man; would it make sense for their father to endanger so many sons on a spying expedition?

Unappeased, Joseph repeats his accusation. To a first-time reader of the biblical story, it appears as if Joseph intends to exact a brutal revenge on his brothers.

In the face of Joseph's accusations, the brothers start to reveal many details about themselves that they hope will assuage the Egyptian vizier's suspicions. They tell Joseph that their family originally consisted of twelve brothers (Dinah, the only sister, is apparently regarded as too unimportant to mention), but the youngest son is still at home with his father, while "one is no more."

Without revealing his own identity, Joseph has learned important information; his father and his brother Benjamin are still alive.

He proceeds to impose the first of several tests to which he will subject his brothers. All will be imprisoned save one, who will return to Canaan and come back with their youngest brother. If they do not agree to this test, Joseph will have no choice but to conclude that they are spies. The Bible does not tell us how the brothers react to this proposal, but the next thing that happens is that Joseph confines them in prison for three days.

Afterward, Joseph meets with them again, this time offering a more humane test. All the brothers will be released except one, who will remain incarcerated until the others return with their youngest sibling.

All this time, the brothers have been speaking to Joseph through an interpreter. After the interpreter leaves, the brothers start speaking among themselves, oblivious to Joseph's presence. One brother declares: "We are being punished on account of our brother, because we looked on at his anguish, yet paid no heed as he pleaded with us. That is why this distress has come upon us" (42:21). This is a fascinating detail, for in the Bible's initial description of the brothers' sale of Joseph, we never hear Joseph speak. Now it is revealed that he pleaded and begged for his life, and they ignored him.

Reuben speaks next, in an understandable, if unhelpful, I-told-you-so tone. "Did I not tell you, 'Do no wrong to the boy'? But you paid no heed. Now comes the reckoning for his blood."

As for Joseph? "He turned away from them and wept." Within these chapters, Joseph weeps more than any other biblical character. Clearly, he is moved by his brothers' words, but their expressions of contrition hardly constitute sufficient proof of their repentance. So he continues to test them.

He orders Simeon arrested and bound before their eyes. The text doesn't say why Simeon was chosen. It might be because Reuben, the oldest, had tried to save Joseph, and Joseph has no desire to punish him. Simeon, however, is the second-born. Alternatively, we know from the incident with Shechem (Genesis 34) that Simeon is capable of great violence. Is it far-fetched to speculate that this fierce brother might have been the one who proposed or argued most vehemently to kill Joseph?

The brothers start home, undoubtedly dejected. Soon, another surprise awaits them. When one of them opens a food sack acquired in Egypt, he finds the money they had paid for the grain mixed in with the food. Then they all find their money returned. Trembling, the brothers turn to one another, saying, "What is this that God has done to us?"

They return home and relate to Jacob all that has transpired, emphasizing that, unless they return to Egypt with Benjamin, Joseph will conclude that they are spies and will punish Simeon. Jacob responds with utter despair: "It is always me that you bereave. Joseph is no more and Simeon is no more, and now you would take away Benjamin." This outburst, "It is always me that *you* bereave," makes one wonder whether Jacob suspects that the brothers somehow share in the guilt for Joseph's fate. But Jacob's final words convey more of a note of self-pity than of accusation: "These things always happen to me!"

Reuben, desperate to take Benjamin with him to Egypt, steps forward with a proposal that can only further deepen Jacob's growing conviction that his sons are incompetent fools: "You may kill my two sons if I do not bring him back to you" (42:37). One only hopes that Reuben's sons and wife were not present to hear this statement of paternal devotion.

Needless to say, Jacob again refuses.

Soon the rations with which the brothers returned are entirely consumed. Feigning ignorance of their earlier discussion, Jacob instructs his sons to go to Egypt and purchase more food. Judah reminds him that without Benjamin accompanying them, there is no point in making the trip. "For the man said to us, 'Do not let me see your faces unless your brother is with you' " (43:5).

Again, Jacob scolds them for mentioning the existence of a younger brother to the Egyptian official.

Judah persists: "Send the boy in my care . . . that we may live and not die—you and we and our children." Unlike Reuben, who offered the lives of his two sons if Benjamin did not return to Jacob, Judah offers himself as a guarantee: "I myself will be surety for him; you may hold me responsible: if I do not bring him back to you and set him before you, I shall stand guilty before you forever" (43:8–9).

Because Judah's words impress Jacob in a way that Reuben's didn't, and because Jacob's extended family again is threatened with starvation, he consents to Benjamin accompanying them on the trip. He suggests only that the brothers bring the vizier gifts, including two that sound rather contemporary, "pistachio nuts and almonds" (43:11). He also advises them to bring double the money they had originally paid so that they can return the silver that was returned to them, perhaps inadvertently. Jacob speaks with the desperation of someone who is prepared to lose everything: "As for me, if I am to be bereaved, I shall be bereaved" (43:14).

The brothers return to Egypt, where to their shock they receive a warm welcome. Joseph's chief steward releases Simeon, and assures the brothers not to worry about the money found in their bags. He brings them into Joseph's house, where their donkeys are fed, they bathe, and are then informed that Joseph wishes them to dine with him.

A short time later, the brothers come before Joseph. He immediately recognizes Benjamin, and greets the young man with a blessing. Then Joseph rushes out of the room to shed tears that he no longer can contain. But he quickly regains control and returns for the meal.

To the brothers' astonishment, Joseph seats them in birth order. He also gives Benjamin a much larger portion than the others, most likely out of feelings of special love, but perhaps to observe how they react now to seeing one brother being favored.

The next morning, the brothers rise to leave, happy and certainly relieved. Unbeknownst to them, Joseph has instructed his steward to place his valuable silver cup in Benjamin's bag, for he has a second test in mind, one that will definitively prove if the brothers have truly repented of the evil they once did him.

Early in the morning, the brothers embark on their journey. Soon, however, Joseph's steward, accompanied by troops, overtakes them. "Why did you repay good with evil?" the steward asks them, as Joseph had instructed him. "[The silver cup] is the very one from which my master drinks, and which he uses for divination. It was a wicked thing for you to do!" (44:5).

Confident of their own honesty, the brothers respond, "Whichever of your servants with whom it is found shall die; the rest of us, moreover, shall become slaves to my lord."

"Only the one with whom it is found shall be my [meaning Joseph's] slave," the steward responds, "but the rest of you shall go free."

To heighten the suspense, the steward has the sacks examined in order, starting with the oldest brother. Therefore, by the time Benjamin's sack is reached, the brothers must have been certain that they would soon be on their way. But when Benjamin's sack is opened, *there* is the goblet. Like mourners, the other brothers rend their clothes and return, along with Benjamin and the steward, to the city.

There, Judah and all his other brothers throw themselves down on their knees before Joseph and reiterate their offer to become his slaves. Joseph represents himself as a just man: "Only he in whose possession the goblet was found shall be my slave; the rest of you go back in peace to your father."

Then Judah steps forward and asks permission to address Joseph. He proceeds to deliver one of the longest speeches recorded in the Torah. After reviewing all of the brothers' previous interactions with Joseph, he explains why it is impossible for him to return home without Benjamin: "Now, if I come to . . . my father and the boy is not with us . . . when he sees that the boy is not with us, he will die."

Judah also explains to Joseph the pledge he made to his father, and concludes: "Therefore, please let your servant remain as a slave to my lord instead of the boy, and let the boy go back with his brothers. For how can I go back to my father unless the boy is with me? Let me not be witness to the woe that would overtake my father" (44:33–34).

Many years earlier, Judah had been willing to sell a brother into slavery, and to endure years of seeing his father in perpetual woe. But that time is past. The Judah who had instigated the sale of Joseph has become a very different man.

The brothers have passed the test, and Joseph summons up his last measure of self-control and commands all his Egyptian attendants to leave the room. With no one else present, he reveals himself to his brothers, although his sobs are so loud that the Egyptians standing outside hear them.

As soon as everyone else has left the room, he cries out to his brothers: "I am Joseph! Is my father still alive?"

The brothers are so dumbfounded that they cannot speak.

Joseph invites them to draw near and when they do, speaks again: "I am Joseph your brother, whom you sold into slavery. Now, do not be distressed . . . because you sold me here; it was to save life that God sent me ahead of you." He instructs them to go home, then return to Egypt along with Jacob and all their families. Five more hard years of famine are still to come, he explains, but they will live in Goshen, a fertile region in Egypt.

It is clear now why Joseph has to be alone when he reveals himself to his brothers. What his brothers did to him was so shocking that if it became known to the Egyptians, they would be viewed as despicable and would likely be denied the right to settle in Egypt.

After he finishes speaking, he and his brothers kiss and weep together; "only then," the text tells us, "were his brothers able to talk with him." Eight chapters and twenty-two years earlier, the Torah had informed us that Joseph's brothers "hated him so [much] that they could not speak a friendly word to him" (Genesis 37:4). Now finally, after the kissing and weeping, are his brothers "able to talk with him."

In the thousands of years since the Torah was given, Judah's actions have served as the prototype of true repentance (in Hebrew, *teshuvah*). When a person has done an evil act, he should do all within his power to undo the evil. But even then how can a person know if he really has transformed himself? The twelfth-century philosopher Moses Maimonides notes that full repentance only comes about when a person is subjected to the same situation in which he once sinned, and does so no more. Judah, the brother who once advocated selling Joseph into slavery, now is prepared to become a slave in order to save another brother from the same fate. Judah's noble offer convinces Joseph that his test has gone far enough; because his brothers have truly changed, he can now reveal himself.

The Book of Genesis is filled with stories of fighting siblings. Cain murders Abel, and learns nothing. To God's question "Where is Abel your brother?" he replies contemptuously, "I don't know. Am I my brother's keeper?"

Ishmael and Isaac are separated at an early age, and come together again only to bury their father, Abraham. Certainly this is preferable to brothers killing each other, but it is a sad, deeply alienated relationship.

A generation later, Esau wishes to kill Jacob, who flees. For twenty years, the brothers have no contact. When Jacob learns that Esau and his soldiers are drawing near, he feels compelled to divide his camp in two: Thus, if Esau wipes out one camp, at least some people in the other camp will survive. However, when he sees Esau, the two brothers embrace and make peace. But they don't see each other again until their father dies. In other words, they "bury the hatchet," but each remembers where the hatchet is buried.

Finally, we come to the story of Joseph and his brothers. At one time, they couldn't speak a peaceable word to him. Joseph's brothers sell him into slavery and, as revealed by their later words to each other, are certain that he died. But when Joseph sees their moral transformation, he becomes reconciled with them, and they with him. In the deepest sense possible, Judah and the brothers have learned that the answer to Cain's question "Am I my brother's keeper?" is yes, yes, and again yes.

Reflections and sources: Many families are beset with tensions and conflicts that sometimes lead siblings, and parents and children, to stop speaking with each other. The cause of the fights is almost always far less ugly than brothers selling off one of their own into slavery. If Joseph and his brothers can reconcile and learn to communicate, the Bible is teaching us, why can't we?

Maimonides's statement on repentance is found in his *Mishneh Torah*, "Laws of Repentance," 2:1.

27. The Twelve Tribes

GENESIS, CHAPTERS 48–49

Jacob, the Bible's third Patriarch, who was renamed Israel after his struggle with the angel (Genesis 32:29), also is the leader from whose blessings and prophecies for his sons (and grandsons) come the twelve tribes. That is why the Israelite people become known as B'nai Yisra'el, the "children of Israel."

Shortly before his death in Egypt at the age of 147, Jacob summons his sons to hear his final "blessings," which in effect are reflections, compliments, criticisms, and prophecies (49:1ff.).

Addressing his children in the order of their birth, Jacob first speaks of Reuben, the "first of my vigor," and condemns him for having "mounted your father's bed," an allusion to his having slept with Bilhah (Genesis 35:22), one of the two concubine/wives Jacob acquired ("acquired" because Bilhah and Zilpah were given to him, respectively, by Rachel and Leah). Jacob denounces Reuben for having "brought disgrace" into his father's household.

Next, Jacob condemns Simeon and Levi for their unbridled, destructive rage, epitomized by their massacre of the people of Shechem (Genesis 34:25–26): "Cursed be their anger so fierce. . . . I will scatter them in Israel" (49:7). Indeed, when Israel later possesses Canaan, the descendants of Levi, called Levites, are given no tribal lands, but rather cities throughout the land, and earn their living working at the Temple and through performing other spiritual functions. Thus, in accordance with Jacob's words, they are scattered throughout Israel and do not dwell in proximity to Simeon. (The tribe of Simeon is granted its own territory.)

As for why a spiritual vocation is assigned to the descendants of so violent a man, the Levites are awarded this distinction in the aftermath of Israel's sin with the Golden Calf: They are the one tribe that remains loyal to God (Exodus 32:26), on this occasion using the fierce anger associated with their ancestor on behalf of a divinely approved goal.

Judah, the fourth son, is praised greatly and formally assigned a leadership role. Judah is the brother who spoke up before Joseph in Egypt and effected the reconciliation between Joseph and his brothers (Genesis 44:14–45:15): "The scepter shall not depart from Judah, nor the ruler's staff from between his feet" (49:10). Centuries later, when the Israelites possess Canaan, Judah becomes the largest tribe, occupying about half the land (like Alaska and Texas combined into one giant state). Later, in the aftermath of Solomon's death, ten tribes revolt and found the Kingdom of Israel, while Judah creates its own Kingdom, known as Judah, in conjunction with its tiny neighbor, Benjamin.

Jacob prophesies that Zebulun will live by the coast, and makes other predictions about the future dwelling places of his sons. Joseph is the only other son to receive as extended and complimentary a blessing as that bestowed on Judah: "The blessings of your father surpass the blessings of my ancestors. . . . May they rest on the head of Joseph" (49:26).

People often ask: Since Levi received no tribal inheritance, doesn't that mean that the land was divided into only eleven, not twelve, tribes?

Indeed, that would have been the case, but Jacob, instead of assigning a single tribe to Joseph, offers him two, named after Ephraim and Manasseh, Joseph's two sons. At around the same time that Jacob bestows his blessings on his male offspring, Joseph comes before his father with *his* two sons. At first, Jacob seems confused, asking Joseph, "Who are these?"*

When Joseph identifies the boys as his sons, Jacob summons them forward to be blessed. Jacob favors Ephraim, the younger boy, over Manasseh, his older brother: "He too shall become a people, and he too shall be great," Jacob reassures Joseph. "Yet his younger brother shall be greater than he" (48:19). The Bible does not inform us how this prediction, made in the presence of the two boys, affected relations between them.

Jacob also informs Joseph that "I give you one portion more than to your brothers," meaning that each of Joseph's sons will receive a tribal allotment. In effect, therefore, while disinheriting Reuben of the double portion normally allotted a firstborn son (such an allotment was formalized in later biblical law; Deuteronomy 21:17), Jacob "adopts" Joseph as his firstborn and gives him, through Ephraim and Manasseh, a double share of the inheritance.

Thus, it cannot be said that the twelve tribes were named solely for Jacob's sons, since Levi receives no tribal portion, and two tribes are named after Ephraim and Manasseh, Jacob's grandsons.

Note: To this day, the formula used by Jacob in blessing Joseph's sons, "By you shall Israel invoke blessing, saying, 'God make you like Ephraim and Manasseh,' " is the one with which Jewish parents bless their sons at the beginning of the Sabbath. Daughters are given the blessing "May God make you like Sarah, Rebecca, Rachel, and Leah."

---

*This bewilderment, along with the fact that Jacob's eyes are dim (48:10), reminds us of Isaac's confusion the day Jacob cajoled from him the blessing intended for Esau (see entry 17).

II. EXODUS

28. Pharaoh: History's First Antisemite

EXODUS 1:8–22

The speed of the Israelites' legal and economic decline during the reign of Pharaoh brings to mind the decline of their descendants in Germany some 3,500 years later. In 1932, German Jews were among the most affluent and professionally successful members of German society. A year later, Adolf Hitler came to power. Two years after that, German Jews were no longer citizens, and were forbidden to practice most professions. A few years later, the large majority of those who had not succeeded in fleeing Germany were murdered en masse.

Much, though by no means all, of what Hitler said about and did to the Jews is anticipated by Pharaoh, the first recorded Jew-hater in history.

A new pharaoh arose in Egypt, the Bible tells us, "who knew not Joseph." Since Joseph's role in Egyptian history had been so profound—he had saved Egypt from famine and financial collapse—great significance should be attached to the words "who knew not Joseph." If we could see into the future and learn that in 2060 a president would be elected in the United States "who knew not Abraham Lincoln," that statement alone would convey what an enormous and terrible change had come over the society.

Such is the case in Egypt. The new pharaoh surveys his society, and what troubles him? The presence of the Hebrews. It seems, however, that they are integrated into Egyptian society, for Pharaoh does not feel that he can proceed against them unilaterally. First, he must win the support of his people to carry out his program.

He starts his campaign with arguments that have been employed by bigots ever since: "The Israelite people are much too numerous for us" (1:9). Worse, they're a fifth column: "In the event of war, they will join our enemies in fighting against us . . ." (1:10).

And so Pharaoh appoints taskmasters over the Israelites. They are subjected to forced labor, building garrison cities for Pharaoh.

Because the Hebrew women are highly fertile, and their numbers increase, the oppression escalates. Pharaoh now embitters the Israelites' lives with more forced labor; in addition, they are now required to do fieldwork.

Still their numbers grow. Forced labor is no longer a sufficient resolution; only wholesale murder will dispose of the "Jewish problem." Pharaoh now launches a program to murder every male Hebrew baby (see next entry; in this regard, Hitler of course drew no distinction between the sexes).

Pharaoh ultimately fails in his plan to eliminate the Hebrews. But the pain he inflicts before he fails is massive and horrendous.

29. The Two Midwives and the World's First Recorded Act of Civil Disobedience

EXODUS 1:15–22

Pharaoh's initial impetus for enslaving and oppressing the Hebrews is to limit their growth. This scheme fails; as the Bible records, "The more they were oppressed, the more they increased and spread out, so that the [Egyptians] came to dread the Israelites" (1:12).

The Egyptian ruler decides on a more savage method to achieve his goal. He summons the two chief midwives working with the Hebrew women and instructs them to kill all boys born to them. Infant girls, he adds, are to be spared; presumably, in the absence of Hebrew males, they will marry Egyptians, assimilate, and so bring an end to the Hebrews.

The next verse (1:17) informs us that "the midwives, fearing God, did not do as the king of Egypt had told them; they let the boys live."

The midwives' refusal to obey Pharaoh's murderous edict on grounds of conscience constitutes history's first recorded act of civil disobedience. Most people who live under monarchic dictatorships (such as prevailed in ancient Egypt) or in totalitarian regimes (such as Nazi Germany or the Soviet Union) obey immoral laws, if for no other reason than fear of being executed. From whence then did the midwives derive the moral strength to disobey Pharaoh's decree?

The Bible tells us: They feared God. While the other inhabitants of Egypt feared Pharaoh more than anyone else, *the midwives' fear of God liberated them from the fear of the Egyptian tyrant.*

When Pharaoh learns that newborn male babies are still alive, he summons the midwives: "Why have you done this thing, letting the boys live?" he rails at them.

Although courageous enough to disobey Pharaoh's edict, the midwives have no wish to be martyrs. They tell Pharaoh a contrived story: They wished to carry out his decree but, unfortunately, "the Hebrew women are not like the Egyptian women: they are vigorous. Before the midwife can come to them, they have given birth" (1:19).

Their untruthful response contains an important lesson in biblical morality. Although a human being is obligated to resist a murderous order, she or he is not obligated to speak truthfully to a murderer, and die on account of this truthtelling. The Bible notes that God subsequently rewards the midwives for their courageous behavior, thereby indicating biblical approval both for their initial behavior as well as their untruthful response to Pharaoh.

Who are these heroic women? Are they themselves Hebrews? The Bible doesn't tell us. The Hebrew words used to describe them, *ha-meyaldot ha-ivriyot,* are ambiguous; they can be translated either as "the Hebrew midwives" (suggesting that they are Hebrews) or as "midwives to the Hebrews." For thousands of years, Jewish and non-Jewish scholars have argued about the women's ethnic identity. The first-century historian Josephus and the fifteenth-century biblical commentator Isaac Abravanel argue that they are non-Hebrews. Rashi, writing in the eleventh century and citing a view expressed in the Talmud (Babylonian Talmud, *Sotah* 11b), claims that the two women are none other than Yocheved and Miriam, respectively Moses' mother and sister.

Rashi's explanation, perhaps rooted in the belief that no non-Hebrews of the time would also be God-fearers, flies in the face of other information contained in the text. The Torah explicitly tells us the midwives' names: Shifra and Puah. If the heroines are Moses' mother and sister, why would the Bible conceal so important and praiseworthy a fact?

Common sense suggests that the midwives were non-Hebrews. If

Pharaoh wished to murder every male Hebrew baby, it is unlikely that he would have relied on Hebrews to implement his genocidal decree. Also, the way he questions the women when he learns that his order has not been fulfilled—"Why have you done this thing, letting the boys live?"—suggests that he is truly mystified by their behavior. He almost certainly would not have been so perplexed had he known the women were Hebrews.

Still, it is likely that the midwives were not Egyptians, for ruling people are rarely employed as midwives to a subservient group. (During the period of slavery in the United States, white Southern women did not serve as midwives to black slaves.) Rather, the midwives, whose names we now know to be Semitic, were probably members of another non-Hebrew, lower-class group residing in Egypt.

The lesson is clear: One does not have to be a Hebrew to fear God and to act morally. In a patriarchal and "tribalistic" world, the Bible holds up as models two heroic people who were female and most likely non-Hebrews.

Unfortunately, the midwives' courageous behavior only temporarily forestalls Pharaoh's genocidal plans. Turning now to the entire Egyptian people, he issues an order of extermination: "Every boy that is born you shall throw into the Nile" (1:22).

Reflections, source, and further reading: Nahum Sarna, *The JPS Torah Commentary: Exodus*, pages 6–8; Sarna notes the oddity of the Bible telling us the names of the midwives while omitting that of the reigning pharaoh: "In the biblical scale of values these lowly champions of morality assume far greater historic importance than do the all-powerful tyrants who ruled Egypt."

30. Moses: The Birth of the Bible's Greatest Hero

EXODUS 2:1–10

Had history proceeded logically, Moses would have died shortly after he was born. Pharaoh had given an order to drown all male Hebrew babies in the Nile at birth. Moses' mother, Yocheved, hides him for three months. When the baby can no longer be hidden, she puts him in a small wicker basket, caulks it, and places it in the reeds by the Nile. Logically, then an Egyptian soldier should have passed by, seen or heard the crying infant, and killed him. Undoubtedly, such had been the fate of numerous other Hebrew babies.

The person who finds the baby is a member of the royal family, one of Pharaoh's own daughters (Bible scholars generally trace the order to kill the babies to the reign of Ramses II, who also is known from Egyptian sources to have had fifty-nine daughters). She sends her servant to pick up the basket, and when she sees the crying infant inside, takes pity on him and decides to defy her father and save the baby.

Thus, remarkably, the greatest enemy of the Hebrews and their greatest friend are a father and daughter. What better illustrates the biblical view that what most matters about people is their values, not their blood.*

Miriam, Moses' sister, is watching Pharaoh's daughter from a distance. When she sees the woman's sympathetic response, she comes forward. A precocious child, Miriam approaches the princess. She doesn't beg that the child's life be spared, taking for granted that that is what the princess wants. Rather, she asks: "Shall I go and get you a Hebrew nurse to suckle the child for you?"

The princess assents and, almost immediately, arrangements are

---

*If one does not consider the Bible to be literally true, it is even more remarkable that the Israelites would have created a myth that their salvation came about through Pharaoh's daughter; it would be as if contemporary Jews believed that the Holocaust came to an end because of a child of Hitler.

concluded; Yocheved, Moses' mother, is hired to breast-feed her own son. Following the weaning, she is to bring the child to the palace, and the princess will adopt him.

Thus, Moses avoids two terrible fates, being murdered at birth or being raised as a slave. Instead, he grows up in the royal palace, where he develops a self-image unlike his Israelite compatriots'. He is a free man, and expects to be treated as one. Because he lacks a slave mentality, when he sees injustice he fights it (see next entry).

Reflections: Although the Bible is often accused, with some justification, of being patriarchal, this has more to do with its laws than its narratives. Thus for example, every significant hero in the story of Moses' early life is a woman. It is Moses' mother, not his father, who keeps him hidden and alive during the first months of his life, then prepares the basket in which to float him. It is Moses' sister, not his brother, who negotiates with the princess on his behalf (although to be fair, his brother Aaron was only three at the time; see Exodus 7:7). And it is Pharaoh's daughter, not his son, who takes pity on the infant (earlier, the two midwives were the only Egyptians to resist Pharaoh's genocidal plot against the Hebrews).

31. A Portrait of the Hero as a Young Man

EXODUS 2:11–22

We know nothing of the years that Moses spends in Pharaoh's court. Once his mother weans him and brings him to the palace to be raised by Pharaoh's daughter, many years pass before we hear of him again.

He next emerges as a young man, during three brief episodes that occur over a matter of days. Yet, because they are the only details the Bible provides us about Moses prior to God's choosing him to lead the Israelites, it is to these episodes that we must turn to understand the reason for God's choice.

First, we learn that when Moses grows up, he goes out to his kinsmen and sees their suffering. That he knows the Hebrew slaves are his "kinsmen" means that he realizes that he is not the biological child of the Egyptian princess, but an adopted son. The princess had instructed Moses' mother to keep the infant at home until he was weaned (a woman wishing to prolong this process could breast-feed a child until he was four or older), so Moses undoubtedly learned of his Hebrew identity from his mother.

Now, Moses leaves the palace to learn something about the conditions facing the people from whom he comes. What he sees shocks him; he witnesses an Egyptian (presumably an overseer, although the text does not say) beating a Hebrew. Moses is outraged, but acts with caution. He looks around, and when he sees no one else about, he strikes the Egyptian. Whether he intends to kill the man we do not know, but kill him he does. He then hides the body in the sand.

The next day, Moses again circulates among his fellow Hebrews. This time he witnesses two of them fighting, and one of them strikes the other. "Why do you strike your fellow?" he asks the offender.

The man retorts: "Who made you chief and ruler over us? Do you mean to kill me as you killed the Egyptian?"

Moses becomes frightened: His killing of the brutal taskmaster, an act he assumed had no witnesses, had been observed (of course, the one witness Moses did not take into account was the man being beaten). He realizes how quickly his action will become the subject of gossip; an Egyptian nobleman intervening on behalf of a beaten slave would certainly spark much comment among the other slaves. Nor could such information be kept hidden from the Egyptians. Once they discovered the body of their slain comrade, we can only imagine the brutal interrogation techniques they would inflict on any slaves found near the crime.

Indeed, Pharaoh soon learns that Moses is the culprit, and issues an order to have him executed. At first, this seems surprising; one might have thought that Moses, because of his close connection to an Egyptian princess, would be spared punishment for killing a "mere" overseer. But the fact that he identified with the Hebrews rather than the Egyptians marked Moses as a revolutionary and a traitor.

Moses flees Egypt. After several wearisome days of running, he finds himself beside a large well somewhere in the nearby land of Midian. At this point, Moses must be craving calm and peace. Instead, he finds himself immediately embroiled in yet another conflict. A local priest in Midian, a man known variously as Reuel and Jethro, has seven children, all daughters. When the girls come to the town's well to draw water for their father's flock, the local shepherds, who are bullies, drive them away. However, Moses rises to their defense and waters their flock.

When the girls return home, their surprised father asks: "How is it that you have come back so soon today?" (The shepherds' bullying must have been a common occurrence.) They tell their father about the "Egyptian" who helped them. Jethro is distressed that his daughters left their brave savior alone with the shepherds, and showed him no gratitude. He sends the girls back to the well to invite Moses home.

Moses accepts the invitation, and soon marries Tzipporah, one of Jethro's daughters. When she gives birth to a son, Moses names him Gershom (Hebrew for "a stranger there"), for he says, "I have been a stranger in a foreign land."

These episodes, which provide the only details we know about the young Moses, should be viewed as paradigmatic, revealing all that we need to know about a man qualified to be a leader and prophet. Most important, Moses comes across as a man obsessed with fighting injustice. When he sees a slave being cruelly mistreated, he acts to stop the mistreatment; indeed, he acts so decisively that the overseer will never again be able to mistreat any slave. A day later, when he sees two Hebrews fighting, he confronts the aggressor. Finally, he stands up on behalf of the mistreated daughters of the priest of Midian. True, their lives are not threatened, but they are being abused, and Moses finds this intolerable.

These stories also reveal Moses to have another trait indispensable in a leader: adaptability. A good leader utilizes different strategies to confront different provocations and injustices. When it is necessary to fight, he is willing to fight; when it is sufficient to talk, he is ready to talk; when it is necessary to stand up, he stands up.

These episodes also demonstrate prophetic greatness. If all we knew about Moses was the episode in which he confronted the Egyptian taskmaster, we would still not know enough about his character. Perhaps he was simply an ardent Hebrew "tribalist," outraged at the mistreatment of one of his people but not necessarily concerned with other instances of injustice. However in the final episode, he acts decisively when he sees non-Israelites mistreating other non-Israelites.

The Bible is teaching us that a true prophet of God is concerned with *all* types of injustice, not just that against his own people. That is why Moses intervenes when an Egyptian oppresses a Hebrew, when a Hebrew acts immorally, and when non-Hebrews oppress other non-Hebrews.

The very next time Moses appears in the Bible, the Lord summons him to return to Egypt and declare before Pharaoh: "Let my people go!" Apparently, these three events have been sufficient to convince God that He has found the right messenger to liberate His people from Egyptian bondage.

Reflections, sources, and further readings: My understanding of these three pivotal events has been deeply influenced by the great Israeli Bible scholar Nehama Leibowitz. She notes the remarkable impression conveyed by Moses' incessant battles against injustice: "A first win, as it were, proves little. Perhaps he was prompted by the incentive of recognition and reward. Only when repeated championing of justice brings no reward can we be convinced of the unselfishness of the deed. Perhaps Moses on the first and second occasion may have imagined that he would have earned the gratitude of his own folk, not their insults and threats, as he did. What is more, he had to run for his life from Pharaoh and go into exile. That was his only reward. Nevertheless, his first deed on arriving in the land of his forced exile after having risked his life to protect the defenseless was to repeat his action and champion the weak again" (see Leibowitz, *Studies in Shemot: The Book of Exodus*, pages 39–48; the above selection is on page 41).

Some readers are troubled that the Bible's greatest prophet inaugurated his career with a killing. But as Nahum Sarna notes, Moses was no indiscriminate aggressor: "The counter-assault was directed against the perpetrator of the atrocity, not indiscriminately aimed against anyone who is perceived to be a symbol of the coercive power of the state" (*Exploring Exodus: The Heritage of Biblical Israel*, page 34). Still, while Jewish Bible commentators overwhelmingly sympathize with Moses' act, one famous rabbinic *midrash* portrays God as condemning Moses for killing the Egyptian. This *midrash*, however, does not suggest what Moses should have done.

32. Moses, the Reluctant Leader

EXODUS, CHAPTERS 3–4

The Burning Bush

3:2–3

"I Shall Be What I Shall Be"

3:14

"A man makes plans and God laughs," an old Yiddish proverb teaches; in other words, a person schemes and strategizes, assuming that he is in control of events, all the while oblivious of the fate God has prepared for him. Thus, Moses, working as a shepherd in Midian, has no idea of the world-transforming role to which God intends to appoint him.

One day, as Moses tends his flocks, God confronts him, in the form of a fire shooting out of a thornbush; although ablaze, the bush remains intact. When Moses walks over to observe this phenomenon, God calls out to him from the bush: "Moses, Moses." He answers, "Here I am." God instructs him to remove his sandals because the place on which he is standing is holy.

God identifies Himself to the perplexed shepherd as the Lord of his father and of Abraham, Isaac, and Jacob (indicating that the Israelites had transmitted from generation to generation their family history and unique religious beliefs throughout their long sojourn in Egypt).

God quickly comes to the point: He has witnessed the suffering of His people in Egypt, and has decided to liberate them and bring them to Canaan, "a land flowing with milk and honey." He also has designated Moses to confront Pharaoh and lead the Hebrews out of Egypt.

During the remarkable dialogue that now ensues, Moses emerges as the most reluctant of leaders (perhaps his earlier attempts at combatting injustice have left him "gun-shy"). *Five times* he refuses God's

mission, offering arguments each time as to why he is an inappropriate choice.

Moses' first objection springs out of his humility (a later biblical
passage describes him as the most humble man of his age; Numbers
12:3): "Who am I," he asks God, "that I should go to Pharaoh and
lead the Israelites out of Egypt?"

God does not directly answer Moses but, rather, assures him that
He will be with him, implying that with God at his side Moses will
be able to overcome any obstacle.

Moses raises a second objection: He is lacking a clear designation
of God with which to approach the Israelites. For although God has
identified Himself as the God of the Patriarchs, what answer will
Moses give if the people challenge him and ask, " 'What is His name?'
What am I to tell them?"

God answers, " '*Ehyeh-asher-Ehyeh*'—I shall be what I shall be" [or
"I am that I am"]. Tell them, '*Ehyeh* sent me to you.' "

This enigmatic divine name is never again mentioned in the Torah, and during Moses' forty years as Israel's leader he never reveals
this name to the people. Contemporary Bible commentator Gunther
Plaut conjectures therefore that "the revelation was never meant for
the people at all, nor did Moses really inquire for the sake of the
people. *Moses had asked for himself, and the answer he receives is also meant
for him*" (*The Torah: A Modern Commentary*, pages 405–406).

What does this puzzling name of God mean? Countless biblical
exegetes have written hundreds of thousands of words trying to ex-
plicate God's three-word Hebrew name. The most likely interpretation is that the God of Abraham, Isaac, and Jacob reveals Himself
through His actions: "I shall be as I shall be" means therefore "I shall
be as I shall *act*" (in contradistinction to the "Unmoved Mover," Aristotle's description of God). In Exodus 33:19, God will similarly
describe Himself through His behavior, "I will be gracious to whom
I will be gracious, and show compassion to whom I will show compassion." Alternatively, God's name underscores that a true experience of the divine is very private; God will be what He will be *to
that person*. But He cannot be adequately described to others.

Having disposed of Moses' second objection, God prepares to
dispatch him on his mission. He is to go into Egypt, assemble the
Israelite elders, and inform them that the God of their fathers wishes
to liberate them and bring them into Canaan. He also tells Moses
that Pharaoh will not let the slaves leave willingly, although He does
not instruct him to share this information with the elders. This re-

fusal will provide God with an excuse to punish Pharaoh and the
Egyptians for the suffering they have inflicted on the Israelites.

Conscious of Moses' trepidations, God assures him that the elders
"will heed your message." Still not convinced, Moses raises a third
objection, his possible lack of credibility: "But suppose they will not
believe me, nor listen to my plea? For they may say, 'The Lord did
not appear to you.'"

God promises to demonstrate His power through three miracles.
He instructs Moses to throw to the ground the rod he is holding;
when Moses does so the rod turns into a snake. Then God tells him
to take hold of the snake by its tail, whereupon it reverts to being
a rod.

Next, He tells Moses to put his hand on his chest, then bring it
back out. When Moses does so, the hand has become leprous, as
white as snow. But a moment later, when he touches his chest again,
the hand is healthy once more.

Finally, God tells Moses of a third miracle he is to perform if the
people remain unconvinced by the first two. In anticipation of the
first plague that God will subsequently inflict on Egypt, He tells
Moses that he is to take water from the Nile and pour it on dry
land. The water, God assures Moses, will immediately turn into
blood.

Still reluctant, Moses offers a fourth objection, his personal lack
of eloquence and charisma: "I have never been an eloquent speaker,
neither in the past nor recently . . . I am slow of speech and tongue."

For thousands of years, Bible commentators have debated the precise meaning of these words. The most widely accepted explanation
is that Moses had a speech defect; he might even have been a stut-
terer. Proponents of this view note that God does not deny the truth
of Moses' objection, instead reassuring him he should not be afraid,
since, "I will assist you in speaking and will teach you what you are
to say." Too, Moses might have felt that he was an ineffective
speaker. Thus, during the three earlier episodes described above, he
is twice depicted taking successful action, killing the brutal Egyptian
overseer and defending Jethro's seven daughters against the Midianite bullies. But the one time he tries to resolve a conflict through
verbal persuasion, he fails (see Exodus 2:13–14).

Moses' objections having been uniformly demolished, he offers a
final demurral, perhaps motivated by a lack of self-confidence: "If
you please, Lord, send someone else."

At this point, God becomes furious. But even in His anger, He
does not deny that Moses' inability to speak in public is a problem.

He instructs Moses to go meet his brother Aaron (the first indication we have that Moses seems to have maintained some contact with his family): "I know that he is an eloquent speaker. . . . He shall speak to the people for you; he shall be your spokesman."

We have no way of knowing whether this final divine suggestion convinces Moses of his fitness to lead, but he does stop arguing. He returns to his father-in-law, Jethro, to whom he reveals nothing of his divine encounter and the grandiose mission he is now assuming. Instead, he states that he wishes to return to Egypt to learn if his family is still alive. Jethro sends Moses off with his blessings.

Moses' continued reluctance to become Israel's leader puzzles many Bible readers. It seems very strange that a religious figure would repeatedly argue with God and resist a divine command. Yet, in our own century, how many people—even if they felt personally instructed by God to do so—would have been willing to confront Adolf Hitler and say, "Let my people go! Shut down Auschwitz and Treblinka, or I will punish you and your people"?

Moses' concern about confronting Pharaoh might have been only part of the reason he tries to refuse God's command. His earlier encounter with the Israelite who sneered at him, "Who made you chief and ruler over us?" perhaps suggested that it would be no great joy to lead the Israelites (indeed, the Torah repeatedly documents their incessant caviling at Moses' leadership).

Hundreds of years after Moses, Jeremiah also complains to God about the unpleasantness of the prophetic vocation. "I have become a constant laughingstock. Everyone jeers at me." Jeremiah claims that at one point, he even resolved to prophesy no longer, "But [God's word] was like a raging fire in my heart, shut up in my bones; I could not hold it in, I was helpless" (Jeremiah 20:7, 9).

Although God overcomes each of Moses' objections, he has good reason to resist the life-transforming mission on which God now sends him. The rest of his life he is plagued by rebellions, doubts, and complaints from the people he serves; he seems to have little, if any, time to devote to his family; and, at the end of his life, he is denied the opportunity to march with the Israelites into their new homeland.

But painful as the choice might be for Moses, God surely knows the character of the man He is choosing. To this day, Moses remains the greatest leader, prophet, and personality in Jewish history.

Reflections, sources and further readings: The Rabbis of the Talmud tried to deduce religious significance from every detail of the biblical narrative. Thus, a *midrash* records that "a heathen asked Rabbi Joshua ben Korchah, 'Why did the Holy One see fit to speak to Moses out of a thornbush and not out of another kind of tree?' He replied, 'Had He spoken to Moses out of a carob tree or out of a sycamore tree, you would have asked me the same question, but to dismiss you with no reply is not right. So I will tell you: To teach you that no place on earth, not even a thornbush, is devoid of God's presence'" (*Exodus Rabbah* 2:5). Nahum Sarna notes that, with God's instruction to Moses to remove his sandals because he is standing on holy ground, "the idea of explicitly sacred space is encountered . . . for the first time. No such concept exists in Genesis [eds. note: although Genesis 28:17–22 implies such a thing] which features only sacred time— the Sabbath." On the other hand, the Bible does not accept the pagan notion that certain areas are *inherently* holy; the spot on which Moses is standing is holy only because God reveals Himself there. Similarly, when the Temple was in existence, the priests (*kohanim*) officiated there barefoot; to this day, those who descend from the priests remove their shoes before reciting the priestly blessing during the synagogue service (*The JPS Torah Commentary: Exodus*, page 15).

Moses' unwillingness to lead the Israelites certainly cannot be attributed to cowardice, for he refuses to employ the most logical argument for why he should not be sent into Egypt: He is under a death sentence there (Exodus 2:15); "Moses did not use personal safety as a reason to refuse God's command" (Nosson Scherman, *The Chumash: The Stone Edition*, page 303). Still, God does not expect people to rely on divine miracles in carrying out their daily affairs. Thus, after Moses accepts his mission, God tells him, "Go back to Egypt, for all the men who sought to kill you are dead" (Exodus 4:19).

33. "Let My People Go!"

EXODUS 5:1; 7:16, 26; 8:6; 9:1, 13; 10:3

"Let my people go!" the most dramatic words in Exodus—and the refrain in a well-known African-American spiritual—might well be the most famous political demand in history. With these four words (three in Hebrew, *shalach et ami*), Moses and Aaron repeatedly confront the Egyptian pharaoh, beginning with, "Thus says the Lord, the God of Israel, 'Let My people go so that they may celebrate a festival for Me in the wilderness" (5:1).

Pharaoh contemptuously dismisses the request: "Who is the Lord that I should heed Him and let Israel go?"

Fearful that Moses and Aaron's demand (the latter actually says the words) will spark the Israelite slaves to rebel, the Egyptian tyrant increases their daily work quota. Until now the slaves have been provided the straw out of which they fashion bricks; now they will be responsible for gathering it, while having to produce the same quota of bricks: "They are shirkers. That is why they cry, 'Let us go and sacrifice to our God,'" Pharaoh complains (Exodus 5:8).

Seeing the deteriorating condition of the slaves he intends to help, Moses wants to desist from his mission, but God does not allow him to. Again, He sends the two brothers to Pharaoh, with the same demand: "Let my people go that they may worship Me!" (7:16). Again, Pharaoh refuses. This time, Aaron, acting at God's behest, stretches his rod over the Nile and the other Egyptian bodies of water, turning them into blood.

During the 1960s, "Let my people go!" became the slogan of the international Soviet Jewry movement, which was created in large measure to win the right of emigration for Soviet Jews. In movement songs, Russia's Communist leaders were compared to Pharaoh.

The rationale for the political demand "Let my people go!" is reflected in a fourth Hebrew word, *ve-ye-av-duni*, "that they may worship Me." Moses' goal is not solely to win liberation from servitude, but also to enable the Hebrews to worship God. From the biblical perspective, freedom is not in and of itself a good. How one conducts oneself once one obtains it (is it used to obey the divine will?) determines whether or not freedom is really worthwhile.

34. The Ten Plagues

EXODUS 7:17–12:32

The Tenth Plague: The Killing of the Firstborn

EXODUS 12:29–30

Had God so willed it, He could have led the Israelite slaves out of Egypt without imposing any punishment on the Egyptians. Being all-powerful, God could have instructed Moses to lead the Israelites out while keeping the Egyptian army paralyzed.

This, however, is not the Lord's wish. Because the Egyptians had acted cruelly, God wishes to punish them. A nation that drowned newborn male infants in the Nile does not deserve to escape divine wrath. Indeed, the first plague strikes at the Nile—the scene of Egypt's cruelest crime against the Israelites—turning it into blood. Bible scholar Uriel Simon has noted to me the first plague's powerful symbolism. Undoubtedly, there were Egyptians who denied the evil their government was doing to the Israelites. Like nineteenth-century Southern slave owners who spoke of how slavery supposedly bene-fited "primitive" blacks, and who ignored or minimized the cruelties of many slave masters and the destruction of many black families, so there were Egyptians who ignored the evil done in their name. The first plague makes such denial impossible. For decades Israelite infants had disappeared in the Nile. Now the Nile turns to blood, "surfacing" the crimes committed there.

The first plague terrifies most Egyptians, but Pharaoh's heart hard-ens and he refuses to let the Israelites go. In short order, Egypt is afflicted with frogs, lice, swarms of insects (which, however, do not set foot in Goshen, the area where the slaves live), the death of Egyptian livestock, a plague of boils that afflict man and beast (no rationale is given for the suffering of the animals), a heavy downpour of hail, locusts, and three days of darkness so profound that "people could not see one another, and for three days no one could get up from where he was; but all the Israelites enjoyed light in their dwellings" (10:23).

Finally comes the tenth plague, the slaying of Egypt's firstborn sons. Both the first and tenth plagues bring to mind the Egyptians' murder of the Israelite babies. Because the Egyptians had killed the Israelites' sons (Exodus 1:22 emphasizes the whole society's involvement in the slayings), now their sons are condemned to die. The punishment is hard to understand, for God inflicts it on all firstborn males and not only on the children of the guilty (which in itself would raise moral questions): "Thus says the Lord: 'Towards midnight I will go forth among the Egyptians, and every first-born in the land of Egypt shall die, from the first-born of Pharaoh who sits on his throne to the first-born of the slave girl who is behind the millstones; and all the first-born of the cattle" (11:4–5).

The Israelites are instructed to slaughter a lamb (known since as the Paschal lamb), and to smear some of its blood on the doorposts of their dwellings: "And the blood on the houses in which you dwell shall be a sign for you; when I see the blood, I will pass over you so that no plague will destroy you when I strike the land of Egypt" (12:12).

That night, when the plague descends on Egypt, not a single Egyptian household is left unstricken (except, one assumes, for those that had no sons). For the last time, Pharaoh summons Moses and Aaron, and tells them, "Up, depart from among my people, you and the Israelites with you" (12:31). The Egyptians, who until now had blocked the slaves' attempts to leave, now hurry them along, and give them jewelry and other treasures, fearing that if the Israelites do not leave immediately, "We shall all be dead."

It is, of course, the tenth plague that once and for all evokes a fully affirmative response to Moses and Aaron's oft-repeated plea, "Let my people go!"

35. The Exodus

EXODUS 13:17–14:31

The Splitting of the "Red [Reed] Sea"

14:21–29

It's difficult to be wise or compromising when God hardens your heart, which is why Pharaoh enters history as the archetypical example of a "slow learner." Ten plagues, culminating in the death of Egypt's firstborn sons, prove insufficient to convince him that Israel's God is more powerful than he.

True, after the deaths of the firstborn, Pharaoh panics, summons Moses and Aaron, and orders them to leave Egypt at once along with the Israelite slaves. However, shortly after the plague ends, he and his advisers experience a change of heart: "What is this we have done, releasing Israel from our service?" (14:5). He orders some six hundred chariot drivers to chase after the departed slaves.

While such a suicidal plan is likely attributable to God's hardening of Pharaoh's heart (14:4, 9), the continuing obedience of his troops can only be attributed to a totalitarian mentality, a willingness to obey a superior's order, no matter how immoral or self-destructive.

The Israelites' mental condition also is not healthy. Centuries of servitude have wreaked havoc with their self-image. Upon seeing the pursuing Egyptian troops, they immediately forget God's awesome powers and instead experience a terrified response to their former masters: "Was it for lack of graves in Egypt that you brought us to die in the wilderness?" they cry to Moses. In a telling expression of the slave mentality, they claim that "it is better for us to serve the Egyptians than to die in the wilderness" (14:11–12). The possibility of a happier future doesn't seem to occur to them.

Although forty years of such complaining later will cause Moses to respond with rage, now he plays the role of a patient, comforting parent: "Have no fear. Stand by and witness the deliverance which the Lord will work for you today . . . The Lord will battle for you" (14:13–14).

Moses apparently then prays to God, for in the next verse God calls to him, "Why do you cry out to Me? Tell the Israelites to go forward" (14:15).

The Midrash, which conveys rabbinic teachings on the Torah, understands God's words as imparting an important lesson: When action needs to be taken, one should not "waste time" praying. God instructs Moses to lift his rod over the sea (the literal name of the sea, *yam suf*, means "sea of reeds," not "Red Sea"), causing it to split in two, leaving the middle dry.

Many people, under the impression that Moses lifts his rod and the sea immediately divides, see this as a virtually unparalleled supernatural miracle. But a reading of the text reveals that God wishes this particular event (as opposed, for example, to the tenth plague) to appear more natural than supernatural. The splitting of the sea does not occur instantaneously, but over the course of an entire night (a more immediate miracle is that God places "a pillar of cloud" between the Israelite and Egyptian camps, making it impossible for Pharaoh's troops to advance against the Hebrews). God causes an enormous wind to divide the sea in half by forcing the waters to both sides. Eventually, this enables the Israelites to cross over the dry land in the middle.

Because God has made the sea's splitting occur in a seemingly natural manner, Pharaoh and his troops, who are obsessed with overtaking the runaway slaves, fail to perceive the miracle occurring before their eyes (years later, the inability of someone who is obsessed to perceive the hand of God is similarly reflected in the tale of Balaam, who is too furious at his disobedient donkey to wonder at the peculiarity of the animal's talking; Numbers 22:28–35). The Egyptians follow the Israelites into the sea, but as soon as the Israelites finish crossing, God instructs Moses to extend his hands over the water. He does so, the waters quickly rush back in, and Pharaoh and all his troops drown.

Only now, when the Israelites see their oppressors dead, do they finally express faith in God and his servant Moses—a faith that lasts only until the next crisis confronts them.

36. Moses' and Miriam's Songs at the Sea

EXODUS 15:1–21

An ancient Jewish tradition teaches that when the pursuing Egyptian troops drowned in the Red Sea and the angels in heaven sang a song of praise to God, the Lord rejected their hymn: "My creatures are drowning, and you sing songs?" (Babylonian Talmud, *Sanhedrin* 39b).

Inappropriate though it might be for *angels* to rejoice at almost any human being's death, no such inhibitions necessarily apply to people. The Israelites greet their deliverance from their oppressors with a song of joy. The Sabbath on which this song is read in the synagogue is known as *Shabbat Shirah*, the Sabbath of Song. When *Shirat ha-Yam* ("the Song at the Sea") is chanted, the entire congregation stands (the only other time this occurs is during the recitation of the Ten Commandments). This Song at the Sea also has become part of an observant Jew's daily morning prayers.

Among its more famous verses is "This is my God and I will praise Him, the God of my father and I will exalt Him" (15:2). Novelist Herman Wouk selected "This is my God" for the title of his best-selling introduction to Judaism. The verse also underscores the dual nature of the relationship that people ideally should have with God. On the one hand, they should know the Lord as the "God of my father," but they should also identify God as "my God," a Lord with whom one has established a personal relationship.

After Moses concludes his song, his older sister, Miriam, takes a tambourine and leads the Israelite women in dance. The Bible records only one line of the poem Miriam chants, but it has become one of the Bible's best-known verses, "Sing to the Lord for he has triumphed gloriously. Horse and driver has he hurled into the sea" (15:21).

In referring to Miriam, the text speaks of her as "Miriam the prophetess, Aaron's sister" (15:20). Although the Bible does not reveal any specific prophecies granted by God to Miriam, she herself later declares that God has spoken through her (Numbers 12:2).

The Bible's description of Miriam as "Aaron's sister," though true, is peculiar, much like identifying the late Robert F. Kennedy as the younger brother of Joseph Kennedy, Jr., instead of his far more famous sibling, John F. Kennedy. Why the text associates Miriam with Aaron rather than Moses has puzzled many Bible commentators. Rashi, the classic eleventh-century exegete, conjectures that the text speaks of her in this manner to underscore that Miriam was a prophetess even before Moses' birth. Given, however, that Miriam was a young child when Moses was born, one wonders what divine prophecies were bequeathed to her at so tender an age.*

Note: The tradition of muting one's joy about the Egyptians' sufferings is maintained at the Passover Seder. When participants recite the Ten Plagues, they spill wine at the mention of each, a symbolic expression of the diminution of joy. However, appropriate as such behavior might be for the *descendants* of the ancient victims, there is no evidence that the enslaved Israelites expressed any sorrow at their tormentors' sufferings.

37. Manna: God's Heavenly Food

EXODUS 16:4–36

After the Israelites pass through the miraculously parted Red Sea, they join Moses and Miriam in singing ecstatic songs of praise to God. But their mood of exultation is short-lived; within days they become both thirsty and hungry, and begin grumbling against Moses. Matters are not helped when they find water in a place called *Marah* ("bitter") since it proves to be *very* bitter. In one of the Bible's less remembered miracles, God instructs Moses to throw a piece of wood into the water, whereupon the water immediately becomes sweet (Exodus 15:25).

A continuous miracle is required to feed the vast throngs of Israelites throughout their forty-year desert sojourn. After a nasty episode of widespread hunger, during which the people accuse Moses

*My friend Dr. Stephen Marmer notes that since Moses was gone from his parents' house from his infancy on, it makes sense to associate Miriam with Aaron since they grew up together.

and Aaron of bringing them into the wilderness to starve them to death (16:3), God promises Moses that "I will rain down bread for you from the sky, and the people shall go out and gather each day that day's portion" (16:4). God also promises to send down a double portion of food each Friday morning, so that the Israelites will not have to labor on the Sabbath.

The following morning, dew falls on the camp. When it lifts, there remains "a fine and flaky substance, as fine as frost on the ground" (16:14). The puzzled Israelites ask one another, *"Mahn-hu?"* ("What is it?"; apparently this becomes the basis for the word "manna"), and Moses informs them that it is the bread God has promised them.

From then on, manna falls daily until the Israelites enter Canaan and start to eat of the land's produce (Joshua 5:12).

Several miraculous elements are associated with the manna: First, it falls daily and without fail, except for the Sabbath, for forty years. Second, it provides each Israelite with precisely the amount of food he or she needs. Thus, those people who gather excessive amounts of manna find that the quantity contracts, while those "who had gathered little had no deficiency; they had gathered as much as they needed to eat" (16:18). Third, whereas excess manna normally spoiled overnight, becoming infested with maggots (16:20), the double portion bestowed on Friday remained fresh throughout the Sabbath.

According to the Bible, the manna looked like coriander seed, was white, and tasted like wafers in honey (16:31). The Israelites soon learn to prepare it in various ways, including boiling it and baking it into cakes.

Unfortunately, tasty though the manna might have been, the people's palates eventually grow tired of it. They soon begin to recall the more varied diet they consumed in Egypt: "If only we had meat to eat! We remember the fish that we used to eat free in Egypt, the cucumbers, the melons, the leeks. . . . Now our gullets are shriveled. There is nothing at all! Nothing but this manna to look to!" (Numbers 11:4–6).

This constant whining is the Israelites' least attractive trait. Although boredom with manna is understandable, still, one searches in vain for expressions of gratitude that they no longer are slaves and that, though wandering in the desert, they have sufficient food to eat.

The whining infuriates God, while Moses despairs of leading this nation of ingrates. He turns to God with one of the Bible's darkest prayers: "Kill me rather, I beg You, and let me see no more of my wretchedness" (Numbers 11:15).

An angry God allays the people's culinary boredom by raining down upon them vast quantities of quail, enough for them to "come out of your nostrils, and become loathsome to you" (Numbers 11:20).

And so He does. After that, we hear no more Israelite complaints about the monotony of the manna.

To this day, the miracle of the manna is commemorated in the weekly Friday evening and Sabbath lunch meals, which are traditionally inaugurated with two *hallot*, to commemorate the double portion rained down by God each Friday morning.

38. Amalek: Israel's Eternal Enemy

EXODUS 17:8–16; DEUTERONOMY 25:17–19

Amalek, a nomadic tribe living in the southern Negev, becomes the first nation to attack Israel in the desert. The tribe is unknown from nonbiblical sources. Amalek's attack is particularly vicious, proceeding from the rear, where the weakest Israelites—women, children, and the ill—are located.

God harshly condemns the Amalekites, perhaps because their preying on the people sets a precedent that encourages others to attack Israel. Surprisingly, the Bible's animosity for Amalek far surpasses that expressed for Egypt. Thus, one of the Torah's 613 commandments specifically prohibits Jews from hating Egyptians (Deuteronomy 23:8), while another enjoins them never to forget the Amalekite attack: "Remember what Amalek did to you. . . . Therefore . . . you shall blot out the memory of Amalek from under heaven. Do not forget" (Deuteronomy 25:17–19).

The Bible's severe language might prompt one to assume that the Amalekite attack inflicted massive casualties on the Israelites, but that is not the case. After Amalek's initial ambush, Moses instructs Joshua, his top aide, to lead troops in battle against them. In one of the

Torah's more unusual miracles, Moses watches the battle from atop a hill, and "Whenever Moses held up his hands [in which he held God's rod, thereby reminding the people of the plagues and the splitting of the Red Sea], Israel prevailed, but whenever he let down his hands, Amalek prevailed" (17:11). Moses eventually grows tired—he is over eighty—whereupon two men come to his side and support his arms aloft until the sun sets. By that time, Joshua has achieved an overwhelming victory.

Amalek is discussed twice in the Torah. The first time is in Exodus, where God undertakes personally to destroy Amalek: "I will utterly blot out the memory of Amalek under heaven"; indeed, Moses builds an altar and declares, "The Lord will be at war with Amalek throughout the ages" (Exodus 17:14, 16).

Had the continuing battle against Amalek been fought by God alone, it would not have raised moral difficulties. In Deuteronomy, however, the obligation to destroy Amalek devolves upon the Israelite people, who are told that once they've achieved mastery over Canaan and have vanquished their other foes, they are to "blot out the memory of Amalek" (Deuteronomy 25:19).

The deuteronomic teaching eventually gains dominance over that of Exodus. Hundreds of years later, when Saul becomes king, God declares through the prophet Samuel (I Samuel 15:2–3) that the time is ripe to fulfill the deuteronomic command. Saul battles with Amalek and kills many of their people, but spares Agag, the Amalekite king. As a punishment for the latter deed, Samuel tells Saul that he will lose the kingship, and proceeds to slay Agag himself.

Anyone reading about this incident could infer that Saul had killed every Amalekite except Agag. However, it is clear that many other Amalekites survive, for David attacks them (I Samuel 27:8), and their soldiers subsequently attack David's military camp (I Samuel 30:1–2).

Centuries later, a descendant of Amalek tries to murder all the Jews. The Book of Esther (3:1) records that Haman is an Agagite (a descendant of the king whom Saul initially spared). Because of this familial connection, the deuteronomic verses concerning Amalek are read every year in the synagogue on the Sabbath preceding Purim.

The Bible also condemns Amalek for lacking fear of God (Deuteronomy 25:18), yet neither this nor the tribe's being the first to attack Israel is sufficient to account for the Bible's unparalleled hatred for the Amalekites, who after all harmed Israel far less than did the Egyptians.

In Jewish life, Amalek is a term like "Nazi"; it evokes the deepest revulsion. Indeed, knowledgeable Jews who mention Hitler will often follow his name with the words *yemach shemo ve-zichro*—"may his name and memory be blotted out," precisely what the Israelites are commanded to do to Amalek.

39. Jethro: A Most Helpful Father-in-law

EXODUS, CHAPTER 18

Humor in many societies abounds in nasty jokes about in-laws. Moses, however, seems to have had a particularly warm spot in his heart for his father-in-law, Jethro. When word is brought to him that Jethro, Tzipporah (Moses' wife), and their two sons are arriving at Israel's desert campsite, Moses' excitement seems primarily focused on his father-in-law. He bows low when he sees Jethro, kisses him, and ushers him into his tent. Strangely, while the Bible luxuriates in the details of their discussion (Moses recounts to Jethro all that God had done to Pharaoh, and all the hardships in the desert), it doesn't mention any interaction between Moses and his wife and children.

Jethro is impressed by what Moses tells him, and the text also describes him as very respectful and admiring of the Israelite religion: "Now I know that the Lord is greater than all gods." He brings a sacrifice to God, whereupon Aaron and the elders participate with Moses and Jethro in a festive meal.

The Bible also depicts Jethro as wise and discerning. The next day, he witnesses Moses spending from morning until night adjudicating conflicts and giving people advice. Jethro is shocked. "Why do you act alone?" he asks Moses.

His son-in-law responds: "It is because the people come to me to inquire of God. When they have a dispute, it comes before me, and I decide between a man and his neighbor, and I make known the laws and teachings of God" (18:15–16).

Whether Jethro is the first person to realize how inefficient and self-destructive Moses' behavior is, or whether he is the first one who is not afraid to criticize him directly, we cannot know. But rebuke Moses he does: "The thing you are doing is not right. You will surely wear yourself out and the people as well, for the task is too heavy for you; you cannot do it alone." He suggests that Moses make known to the people God's revelations and the ways in which they should behave. Moses should select capable men, who fear God and who will spurn bribes, as chiefs of thousands (of families, not individuals), hundreds, fifties, and tens; "a hierarchy of judges," Bible commentator Gunther Plaut notes, "similar to the organization of an army." These people, Jethro suggests, can serve as judges of minor disputes, leaving the major cases to Moses. That way, neither Moses nor the people who now wait long hours to speak to him will be wearied.

Moses heeds his father-in-law. Thus, the system of justice established in the Torah is the legacy of Jethro, a man of the desert Kenite Tribe, and Moses' gentile father-in-law.

One further thought which I heard from Rabbi Jack Riemer: The episode with Jethro immediately follows the story of the Amalekite attack on Israel, as if to underscore a lesson to the Israelites: "Remember Amalek, but also remember that not all gentiles are Amalek. Look at Jethro!"

Jethro is also honored by having the Torah's most famous passage, the Ten Commandments, contained in the weekly Torah reading that bears his name.

40. The Covenant at Mount Sinai and the Giving of the Ten Commandments

EXODUS, CHAPTERS 19–20, 24

By the time the Israelites reach Mount Sinai (some seven weeks after the Exodus from Egypt), the first half of Moses' demand from Pharaoh, "Let my people go!" has clearly been fulfilled. Now, however, the time is ripe to fulfill the second clause: "That they may worship [literally, 'serve'] Me."

The revelation that ensues at Mount Sinai is unique in biblical history. Other revelations were made to individuals (to Noah [Genesis, chapter 9], and to Abraham [Genesis, chapter 15]), while this one is made before a whole people. Indeed, this is the only time in recorded human history that a people claimed that their God revealed Himself to all of them at once.

Thousands of years later, the Spanish-Jewish philosopher Judah Halevi argued that the revelation at Sinai, more than others the Bible describes, proves the historical truth of Judaism. Judaism, Halevi contended, began with a divine revelation before hundreds of thousands of people. Had the Jews standing at Mount Sinai not heard God's voice, they would never have accepted those Torah statements recording that they had heard it. Therefore, Jews trace their ancestry to people who personally experienced God's presence at Sinai.

Shortly before the Sinaitic revelation, God instructs Moses to tell the Israelites that they are His "treasured possession," and that they should be unto God "a kingdom of priests and a holy nation" (19:5–6).

When Moses informs the elders of God's words, they respond, "All that the Lord has spoken, we will do" (19:8).

Moses then warns the Israelites, on pain of death, not to approach the mountain too closely when God reveals Himself. Three days later, at dawn, there is an outburst of thunder and lightning, a dense cloud descends on the mountain, and a loud *shofar* (ram's horn) blast is heard. Following this, Moses leads the people to the foot of Mount Sinai.

God's glory is soon manifest on the mountain, and He declares before the Israelites the Ten Commandments. Jewish tradition claims that the Israelites hear only the first two commandments directly from God; terrified, they ask Moses to serve as an intermediary between them and the Lord. Moses subsequently hears the next eight commandments from God, and transmits them to the people. This explains why the first two commandments, those spoken by God to the people, are addressed in the first person (e.g., "I am the Lord your God . . ." [20:2–3]) while the last eight are in the third person (e.g., "The seventh day is a sabbath of *the Lord your God* . . ."); see chapter 20:5–17.

A separate discussion of each of the Ten Commandments is found in entries 156–165.

41. The Building of the Tabernacle

EXODUS, CHAPTERS 25–27, 30–31, 35–40

On Mount Sinai, God instructs Moses to erect a Tabernacle: "And let them make me a sanctuary,* that I may dwell in their midst" (25:8). God not only commands the building of such a sanctuary, but also designs it: "According to all that I show you concerning the pattern of the Tabernacle, and of all its furniture, so you shall make it" (25:9).

Among the Tabernacle's three areas is an outer court open to all, and a Holy Place restricted to the priests (in which twelve loaves of bread, representing the twelve tribes, are on permanent display). Its most sacred space is the Holy of Holies—inside which is a single object, the Ark containing the Ten Commandments—which was to be entered only by the High Priest on Yom Kippur, the holiest day in the biblical calendar.

The very detailed description both of the Tabernacle's contents and of the services to be performed there (see the Book of Exodus's final chapters and in Leviticus) is quite boring for most Bible readers. But as Rabbi Saul Berman suggests, one likely reason for the great detail[†] is to deter future priests from claiming divine sanction to solicit ever-increasing donations from the people to further beautify God's Tabernacle. By specifying precisely, in a document available to everyone, what God wants inside the Tabernacle, the Torah helps to forestall the possibility of future corruption.

In describing the Tabernacle, which was the forerunner of the *Beit ha-Mikdash*, the Torah specifies the garments to be worn by the

---

*The Hebrew word for sanctuary is *mikdash*. Centuries later, Solomon's Great Temple in Jerusalem was called the *Beit ha-Mikdash*, the "House of the Sanctuary."

†For example, "As for the tabernacle [referring in this instance to the smaller structure of the Holy of Holies within the Tabernacle], make of it ten strips of cloth; make these of fine twisted linen, of blue, purple and crimson yarns, with a design of cherubim worked into them. The length of each cloth shall be twenty-eight cubits, and the width of each cloth shall be four cubits . . ." (26:1–2).

priests working there, including the High Priest's *Urim* and *Tummim* (see next entry), through which he can make God's will known to the Israelites (28:15–30).

Although Torah law commands specific percentages of income to be given to the poor (Deuteronomy 26:12), it mandates only *voluntary* donations for the construction of the Tabernacle: "The Lord spoke to Moses saying: Tell the Israelite people to bring Me gifts; you shall accept gifts for Me from every person whose heart so moves him" (25:1–2).

Because God has no *need* of gifts, He wants those gifts offered Him proffered voluntarily. However, because the poor *do* need assistance, such help must be commanded and not be dependent on the voluntary contributions of more affluent people.

Further reading: Joshua Berman, *The Temple: Its Symbolism and Meaning.*

42. *Urim* and *Tummim*

EXODUS 28:15–30

To this day, no one knows precisely how the *Urim* and *Tummim* worked, but they were the divining devices by which designated priests in ancient Israel—usually but not always the High Priest—answered questions requiring divine responses.

In elaborate detail, the Torah describes the "breastplate of judgment" to be worn by Aaron, the first High Priest. It is composed of gold, blue, purple, and crimson yarn, and twelve different stones were mounted on the garment, corresponding to the Israelite tribes. Inside the "breastplate of judgment"—perhaps in a pouch—Aaron was to place the *Urim* and *Tummim* over his heart: "Thus Aaron shall carry the instrument of decision for the Israelites over his heart before the Lord at all times" (28:30).

Since the Torah provides no details about the functions of the *Urim* and *Tummim* (Leviticus 8:8 mentions them again but supplies no new information), we must assume the existence of an oral tradition—detailing how to use them—transmitted from the High Priest in each generation to his successor.

Most likely, the *Urim* and *Tummim* were stones that had upon them engraved signals signifying "yes" and "no," or "true" and "false." Some scholars conjecture that the High Priest would throw the stones like dice, and discern God's will in how they fell.

Josephus, the first-century Jewish historian, never saw the working of the *Urim* and *Tummim*, but recorded his understanding that the priest deciphered God's will through the flashing of the twelve stones on his breastplate.

The Bible periodically refers to the *Urim* and *Tummim*. When God instructs Moses to appoint Joshua as his successor, He tells him to invest Joshua "with some of your authority," and to instruct Joshua to consult with Elazar, Aaron's successor as High Priest, "who shall on his behalf seek the decision of the *Urim* before the Lord. By such instruction, they [i.e., the Israelites] shall go out [presumably in battle] and by such instruction they shall come in" (Numbers 27:18–21).

Apparently, Joshua utilized the *Urim* to identify Achan as the man who violated God's ban on stealing booty from Jericho. Joshua is somehow able to read the message of the *Urim* and *Tummim*, and he finds out that the thief comes from the tribe of Judah. Joshua then determines to what extended family he belongs, and ultimately he identifies him specifically as Achan. Achan immediately confesses (Joshua 7:14–20; interestingly, despite the text in Numbers, the text does not mention Joshua utilizing the services of a priest to read the *Urim*'s message).

King Saul seems to have consulted the *Urim* before pursuing the Philistines in battle. In contrast to Joshua's case, here a priest's involvement is mentioned. Thus, after Saul advocates pursuing the Philistines, a priest says, "Let us inquire of God."

"So Saul asked God, 'Shall I go down after the Philistines? Will you give them into Israel's hand?' But God did not answer him that day" (I Samuel 14:36–37).

The lack of divine response prompts Saul to assume that a great sin has been committed in the Israelite camp. By consulting with the *Urim* and *Tummim*, asking them several times to "cast a lot," he determines that the sinner is his own son Jonathan (I Samuel 14:38–42).

Saul immediately learns that Jonathan inadvertently violated his edict against eating food on the day of an earlier battle with the Philistines. The king wants to execute his son, but his officers, who recognize Jonathan as a true military hero, refuse to let him do so.

Some years later, when the *Urim* again fail to respond to a query of Saul—probably because by then God has withdrawn His favor from the king—he consults a medium to summon up the spirit of the dead prophet Samuel (see entry 78).

A final biblical reference to the *Urim* and *Tummim* dates from centuries later, to the time of Ezra and the return of the Jews to Israel after their exile to Babylon in 586 B.C.E. The Persians now control Israel, and a Persian governor orders the Jews to refrain from eating sacred food (permitted only to the priests) until the *Urim* and *Tummim* can be cast and used to determine which Jews are of priestly descent and therefore entitled to eat this food (Ezra 2:63).

Important during Israel's earliest history in discerning God's will, the *Urim* and *Tummim* become less significant during the time of the prophets, to whom the people are now expected to turn in order that they may learn God's will.

Source and further reading: A clear exposition of the *Urim* and *Tummim* is found in Lockyer, ed. *Nelson's Illustrated Bible Dictionary*, page 1083.

43. The Golden Calf

EXODUS, CHAPTER 32

"Whoever Is for God, Follow Me!"

32:26

"If only God would give me a clear sign of His existence. Like making a large deposit in my name in a Swiss bank account," quips comedian Woody Allen, the implication being that if only God would give him so clear a sign of His existence, Allen would never doubt the Lord's existence again.

The generation of Israelites in the desert had been given as clear a sign of God's existence as Allen demanded. They had seen God inflict the Ten Plagues on the Egyptians, had witnessed God splitting the Red Sea in two, thereby saving them from Egyptian troops that pursued them, and had been present at the revelation at Sinai.

How deep an impression did these miracles make on the Israelites' faith? Deep enough to last *less* than two months.

A few weeks after the splitting of the sea, Moses climbs Mount Sinai to commune with God. His visit lasts forty days, and the people conclude that Moses either is dead or has deserted them. Thus, they gather around Aaron, Moses' brother, and make this astonishing demand: "Come, make us a god who shall go before us, for that man Moses, who brought us from the land of Egypt, we do not know what has happened to him" (32:1).

What follows is the moral low point of Aaron's life. Whether he too fears that his brother is dead, or is simply afraid that the people will turn on him, he offers them no argument, instead suggesting: "Take off the gold rings that are on the ears of your wives, your sons and your daughters, and bring them to me" (32:2).

Those biblical commentators who are anxious to defend Aaron claim that he expected that his demand would prompt popular resistance and slow down the effort to build an idol. Perhaps Aaron hoped that by the time all the jewelry could be gathered, Moses would have returned.

If such was Aaron's reasoning, he erred. Very quickly, the people bring him an enormous supply of precious jewels, which Aaron takes and from which he forms a Golden Calf. Thereupon, the people exclaim: "This is your god, O Israel, who brought you out of the land of Egypt" (32:4).

It is impossible to know in what sense the people regarded the calf as a god. Their focus on finding a replacement not for God but for the missing Moses suggests that they might have seen the calf only as an intermediary between them and God (although the choice of an idolatrous intermediary to replace a human one indicates that at the very least they were constructing a "second degree" idol).

Aaron, perhaps anxious to avoid an even more immediate deterioration into idol worship, announces that "tomorrow shall be a festival of the Lord."

The following morning, people offer up sacrifices before the calf, have a big feast, "then [rise] to dance," which traditional commentators interpret to mean that they engage in an orgy.

Meanwhile, up on the mountain, the Lord informs Moses that the Israelites have constructed a Golden Calf, which they are worshiping. Enraged by the Israelites' ingratitude and treachery, God tells Moses: "I see that this is a stiff-necked people. Now, let me be, that My anger may blaze forth against them and that I may destroy them, and make of you a great nation" (32:9–10).

The ever-loyal leader, Moses employs several arguments to dissuade God from destroying the Israelites. He reminds God that the Israelites are "Your people," and that the only ones who would be happy to hear that they were annihilated would be the recently vanquished Egyptians. He adds that God had sworn to Abraham, Isaac, and Jacob that He would make their offspring as numerous as the stars and give them the land of Canaan as an eternal possession. To destroy the Israelites would thus be breaking a divine oath.

God renounces His intention to destroy the whole people, and instead sends Moses on his way, bearing the two tablets on which are inscribed the Ten Commandments, including the one banning idolatry.

Moses, accompanied by Joshua, descends toward the Israelite camp. When he sees the "calf and the dancing," he becomes enraged, and hurls down the tablets, which shatter at the foot of the mountain.

Terrified by Moses' appearance and by his rage, the people make no effort to resist him. Moses burns the Golden Calf in a fire so intense that it turns to powder, which he mixes with water. He then forces the Israelites to drink the potion (Bible commentator Gunther Plaut calls this "an immediate psychological punishment," comparable to "swallowing one's words").

Moses first directs his anger at Aaron, the man whom he thought he was leaving in charge: "What did this people do to you that you have brought such great sin upon them?" (32:21).

Aaron shifts all the blame onto the Israelites and onto fate by arguing that it is the Israelites who are bent on evil; furthermore, he is in no way responsible, since all he did was throw the gold into a fire "and out came this calf!"

This contention, somewhat less convincing than a child's claim that the family dog ate his homework, makes little impression on Moses. But he has no time to deal with Aaron, since anarchy now reigns in the Israelite camp. Indeed, the Torah pins the blame for this state of affairs on Aaron: "for Aaron had let them get out of control" (32:25).

Moses stands up in front of the disorderly, rebellious crowd and calls out: "Whoever is for God, follow me!" (32:26). The tribe of Levi rallies to him, and are subsequently rewarded by being named Israel's spiritual leaders.

Moses' instructions to the Levites are brief, and calculated to end the widespread sinning at once: Each man is to take a sword and kill anyone who has participated in the idolatrous orgy. The Levites follow Moses' command, slaying some three thousand people.

The next day, Moses tells the Israelites that although they have been guilty of a grievous sin, he will plead before God on their behalf. Moses then turns to God and inextricably ties his fate to that of the people whom he leads: "If You will forgive their sin [well and good]; but if not, erase me from the record which You have written" (32:32).

God assures Moses that He only wishes to punish those who have sinned. Almost immediately God unleashes a plague against those who had participated in the idol worship and who had not been killed by the Levites.

When the plague ends, God announces that, for the time being, He will not enter the Israelite camp for "if I were to go in your midst for one moment, I would destroy you" (33:5). Instead, God will dispatch an angel in lieu of Himself.

The expression "to worship the Golden Calf" has entered the English language as descriptive of those who worship money above all else. While those kinds of people deserve to be condemned, this was not the sin of the ancient Israelites. It was not money before which they offered sacrifices, but a very real, tangible idol.

III. LEVITICUS

44. Priests and Levites

When Israel entered Canaan, the land was divided among the Israelite tribes, with one exception: The members of the tribe of Levi received no territory. Instead, they were designated as the spiritual teachers and leaders of the other tribes, and were to be supported by a ten percent tax imposed on the other Israelites (Numbers 18:24; Deuteronomy 12:18–19 and 14:28–29). The tribes were also instructed to assign forty-eight cities throughout Israel for the Levites along with sufficient pasture for their cattle (Numbers 35:1–8; Joshua 21:1ff.).

The Bible attributes the Levites' special status to their behavior during the incident of the Golden Calf (see preceding entry). At a time when almost all of Israel had reverted to idolatry, and Moses issued his call for those who were on God's side to come forward, the Levites as a whole immediately responded to his plea (Exodus 32:26–28).

The Torah ruled that the religious service of Levites was to last either from age twenty-five (Numbers 8:24) or thirty (Numbers 4:35) to fifty, after which they entered a kind of semiretirement (Numbers 8:25–26). I Chronicles 23:24ff. records that King David subsequently lowered the age at which Levites began their responsibilities to twenty. In the post-Exilic period, during the time the Temple was standing, Levites provided musical accompaniment with song and instruments when sacrifices were offered.

A special subsection of Levites, the direct descendants of Aaron, Israel's first High Priest, were known as *kohanim* (priests), and it was they who were designated to officiate at the Temple and to offer sacrifices on Israel's behalf.

The Book of Deuteronomy assigns the *kohanim* additional duties: to judge difficult cases (17:8–9), regulate control of lepers (24:8), guard the Torah (17:18), and assist Moses in the ceremony of covenant renewal (27:9ff.).

While it has always been considered an enormous honor to be a *kohen*, the honor comes with several serious restrictions: The Bible forbids a priest to marry a divorcée (Leviticus 21:7),* and to come in contact with any corpse except that of a very near relative (Leviticus 21:1–4). Thus, priests were not permitted to attend funerals (except those of very near relatives) or visit cemeteries, laws that are still observed by Orthodox Jewish *kohanim*.

In traditional Ashkenazic Jewish congregations, *kohanim* bless the congregation on certain holidays (in many Sephardic congregations, they do so every Sabbath) with the "priestly blessing" recorded in the Book of Numbers. In Israel, many groups recite this blessing daily:

"The Lord spoke to Moses: 'Speak to Aaron and his sons: Thus shall you bless the people of Israel. Say to them:

'May the Lord bless you and protect you!

'May the Lord deal kindly and graciously with you!

'May the Lord bestow his favor upon you and grant you peace!' " (Numbers 6:22–26). Just prior to the *kohen*'s offering this blessing, the Levites present wash his hands.

Note: To this day, Jews with last names such as Levine, Levi, and Levinsky generally are descended from the tribe of Levi, while Jews named Cohen and Katz (an acronym meaning *kohen tzedek*, "a righteous priest") usually are *kohanim*.

Note: Although Jewish tradition holds that one can become a *kohen* only by being born to a father who is a *kohen*, a passage in II Samuel

---

*When divorce rates were low, this might not have been so marked a disadvantage. Today, however, with divorce rates high, an older, unmarried *kohen* can have difficulty finding an eligible woman. The law forbidding a *kohen* to marry a divorcée likewise includes his own wife whom he has divorced. The sole grounds for leniency in permitting a *kohen* to marry a divorcée is to disqualify his status as a *kohen*. Thus, if a person had been raised in an irreligious family, and knew himself to be a *kohen* only because his religiously nonobservant father had told him so, rabbis might rule that one should not accept testimony on a person's religious status from a nonobservant Jew, and invalidate the person as a *kohen*.

8:18 records that King David's sons were priests, even though David was the premier member of the tribe of Judah.

45. Nadav and Avihu's Sin and Punishment

LEVITICUS 10:1–7

The great tragedy of Aaron's life is the death, at the hands of God, of Nadav and Avihu, his two oldest sons.

The Bible offers the following rather terse description of the offense that prompted God's wrath: "Now Aaron's sons, Nadav and Avihu, each took his fire pan, put fire in it, and laid incense on it, and they offered the Lord *alien fire, which He had not enjoined upon them.* And fire came forth from the Lord and consumed them; thus they died at the instance of the Lord" (10:1–2).

Nadav and Avihu, priests like their father, Aaron, seem to have been offering a sacrifice of their own devising, not one that had previously been commanded. Commenting on the words "which He [God] had not enjoined upon them," Bible commentator Gunther Plaut observes, "The priestly ideal is one of conformity, not of innovation." Indeed, the "alien fire" of which the Bible speaks probably means that they did not draw from the flame on the altar, but made their own fire.

Immediately following their deaths, Moses attempts to comfort Aaron: "This is what the Lord meant when He said, 'Through those near to Me, I show Myself holy, and assert My authority before all the people'" (Leviticus 10:3).

The words Moses attributes to God are not found elsewhere in the Torah. Perhaps God had conveyed such a sentiment to Moses, and only now had the statement's meaning become clear to him. But clear though the words may have been to Moses, what do they mean, and why does Moses assume that these words will comfort his brother?

Most likely, Moses wishes to indicate that Nadav and Avihu have not been punished with death because they are terrible people, since, as a rule, only the worst people would be deserving of a death sentence. Rather, they have been punished because as "holy people" they were held accountable to higher standards than others. Ibn Ezra, the medieval Bible commentator, notes that God's words, "Through those near to Me, I show Myself holy," bring to mind the classic statement of Jewish chosenness cited in the Book of Amos: "You alone have I singled out of all the families of the earth—that is why I will call you to account for all your iniquities" (3:2).

Both holiness and chosenness confer upon their recipients special responsibilities, not special rights. As priests, Nadav and Avihu had special sacred responsibilities. Their job was to fulfill the laws of sacrifices as conveyed to them by Moses and their father. Their innovative offering—though maybe well intentioned—violated their responsibilities.

In response both to his sons' deaths and to Moses' words of consolation, Aaron remains silent. He utters no words of complaint against God, nor for that matter any words of acceptance (in contrast to Job, who, upon the deaths of his children, declares, "The Lord has given, and the Lord has taken away; blessed be the name of the Lord" [Job 1:21]).

Aaron's silence is likely due to shock and to fear of further angering God. Indeed, when God speaks to Aaron a short time later, it is to offer not consolation but a warning: "Drink no wine or other intoxicant, you or your sons with you [Aaron had two other, surviving sons] when you enter the Tent of Meeting, *that you may not die*" (10:9).

IV. NUMBERS

46. Miriam and Aaron Sin Against Moses

NUMBERS, CHAPTER 12

Miriam and Aaron are surely not the only sister and brother in history to be periodically annoyed by the great success of a younger sibling. Moses is the Bible's preeminent prophet; indeed, the Torah speaks of him as the greatest prophet who ever lived (Deuteronomy 34:10). For Miriam, who remembered Moses as a crying infant and who helped influence the Egyptian princess to save his life, his preeminent status must sometimes have been hard to accept.

The Bible describes a conversation between Miriam and Aaron in which they criticize Moses because of the Cushite woman he had married. Whether the woman in question is Moses' wife, Tzipporah, or a second wife he might have taken, we don't know, nor does the Torah seem to care. What matters is that Miriam and Aaron speak negatively about their brother.

A verse later, the conversation shifts to the real source of their discontent. Miriam and Aaron ask each other: "Has the Lord spoken only through Moses? Has He not spoken through us as well?" (Numbers 12:2). After all, they had on occasion acted as God's spokespeople: Miriam's Song at the Sea, and Aaron's speaking on behalf of the Israelites before Pharaoh. What seems to rankle them is that they are ranked as numbers two and three behind their brother.

God listens to their conversation (of course, God is able to hear every conversation, a fact that nonetheless inhibits few people from speaking unfairly about others), and the next verse makes it clear why He finds their words particularly offensive: "Now Moses was a very humble man, more so than any other man on earth" (12:3).

Moses, in other words, would be too humble to defend himself against his siblings' attacks; therefore, God feels that it is His responsibility to do so. God summons the three to the Tent of Meeting, where He appears in a cloud and instructs Aaron and Miriam to step forward. Although the text describes God as incensed (an anger that is reflected in the punishment Miriam soon suffers), His words sound more explanatory than furious. God explains what makes Moses different from prophets such as themselves: "When a prophet of the Lord arises among you, I make myself known to him in a vision. I speak with him in a dream [for example, God so appears to Jacob (Genesis 31:10–13), and later to Solomon (I Kings 3:5–14)]. Not so with my servant Moses.... With him I speak mouth to mouth, plainly and not in riddles.... How then did you not shrink from speaking against My servant Moses?" (Numbers 12:6–8). Having explained the nature of Moses' prophetic uniqueness, God departs.

As soon as He does, Miriam's body is stricken with flaky, snowy scales; it's some sort of horrific skin disease. It's unclear why she alone is afflicted and not Aaron; after all, both had spoken against Moses. The text's internal evidence does offer two suggestions that Miriam was the primary offender. First, the verb used to describe their initial comments is the feminine singular, *ve-teddaber* ("and she spoke"). Second, her name is given first, even though when Miriam and Aaron are mentioned together on other occasions, his name comes first.

Miriam's skin disease seems to leave her speechless; it is Aaron who approaches Moses on her behalf, asking him to help.*

Moses, the least petty of men, responds immediately to his sister's suffering. He cries out to God, and offers the shortest prayer in the Bible, *"El nah, refah na lah"* ("O Lord, please heal her" [12:13]).

However, God is not willing to let Miriam off the hook so quickly. He insists that she be shut out of the Israelite camp for seven days, and only then be readmitted (we do not know whether the skin disease is healed immediately or remains for seven days). God's rationale for punishing Miriam is particularly graphic: "If her father spat in her face, would she not bear her shame for seven days?

---

*Bible commentator Jacob Milgrom notes that the notion of soliciting prayerful intervention from the offended party occurs elsewhere in the Bible: "Abimelech is told that only Abraham, whose wife he has taken, can remove the plague (Genesis 20:7), and the friends who wronged Job must turn to him for their expiation (Job 42:7–8)." As Milgrom explains, "Moses' intercession has ironic implications. Only he whom Miriam and Aaron have wronged can help them."

Let her be shut out of the camp for seven days, and then let her be readmitted" (12:14).

Miriam's punishment suggests a biblical view that exalted and mighty figures are to be punished, just like everyone else, when they act badly. However, as befits her status, Miriam also is shown respect: During the seven days that she is shut outside the camp, the Israelites remain in place, not marching forward while Miriam is still apart from them.

Reflections: Does Aaron escape punishment entirely? Gunther Plaut argues that while Miriam is punished in her body, Aaron is punished mentally: "Aaron has pretended to be the equal of his younger brother, and now has to humble himself utterly, 'Oh, my lord,' he says to Moses and then begs his forgiveness and asks him to intercede with God. Humiliation is added to mental suffering. . . ." (Plaut, *The Torah: A Modern Commentary*, pages 1101–1102).

Sources: The analysis by Jacob Milgrom is found in his commentary in *The JPS Torah Commentary: Numbers*, page 97.

47. The Twelve Spies and the Generation of "Grasshoppers"

NUMBERS, CHAPTERS 13–14

A Land Flowing with Milk and Honey

13:27

"God made man out of nothing, but the nothingness shows through," wrote Paul Valéry, the twentieth-century French poet and essayist. This statement applies with considerable force to the generation of Israelites trekking through the desert. They rarely express appreciation to Moses, and routinely act as ingrates whenever a problem arises.

When the Israelites first exit Egypt and are pursued by Pharaoh's troops, they rant at Moses, and by implication at God: "Was it for lack of graves in Egypt that you brought us to die in the wilderness?" (Exodus 14:11). When there is a shortage of water, they complain, "Why did you make us leave Egypt to bring us to this wretched place . . . ?" (Numbers 20:5).

God generally responds to the people's complaints by providing them with whatever they need. On several occasions, however, their ingratitude makes Him very angry. The most famous such occurrence is the incident of the Golden Calf (see entry 43). A second such incident occurs some time later, after God instructs Moses to dispatch twelve spies, one from each tribe, to scout out the land of Canaan, which the Israelites are soon to enter.

Moses sends off the spies with a set of instructions and questions: "See what kind of country it is. Are the people who dwell in it strong or weak, few or many? Is the country in which they dwell good or bad? Are the towns they live in open or fortified? Is the soil rich or poor? . . . And take pains to bring back some of the fruit of the land" (13:17–20).

After spending forty days traveling all over Canaan, the spies return bearing an enormous bunch of grapes—symbolizing the land's fruitfulness—between two poles, then offer their observations to a large public gathering. They begin with a few words of praise, describing Canaan as indeed a land of "milk and honey" (13:27). They quickly add, however, that the people of Canaan are very powerful, and the cities are large and fortified. Although they don't explicitly say that the land is unconquerable, that is the implication.

Moses is silent, but Caleb, one of the twelve spies, attempts to neutralize his comrades' negativity: "Let us by all means go up, and we shall gain possession of [the land] for we shall surely overcome [the opposition]" (13:30).

Caleb's brave words provoke ten of the spies (only one other, Joshua, agrees with him) into expressing their opposition more intensely: "We cannot attack that people [the Canaanites] for [they are] stronger than we." The spies now cast off their previous verbal restraint, describing Canaan as a land "that devours its settlers," and depicting its inhabitants as giants: "We looked like grasshoppers to ourselves, and so we must have looked to them" (13:33).

If such terror has been evoked in tribal leaders, one can only imagine the effect these words had on the average Israelite. Panic breaks out among the people, who cry out to Moses and Aaron: "If only we had died in the land of Egypt . . . or if only we might die in this wilderness." As people in such an overwrought state are wont to do, they say increasingly foolish things: "It would be better for us to go back to Egypt!"

The panic soon threatens to turn into a full-scale rebellion. Moses and Aaron seem incapacitated; they fall on their faces but say nothing. Joshua, the one spy aligned with Caleb, and the man who will eventually succeed Moses, steps forth. Trying to appease the frightened mob, he reminds them that "if the Lord is pleased with us, He will bring us into that land, a land that flows with milk and honey, and give it to us" (14:8), and he urges them not to rebel against the Lord. But Joshua is confronting a hysterical mob, not reasonable men and women. Furious and defiant, the people pick up stones to throw at Moses, Aaron, and Joshua.

God now speaks to Moses, in pain and rage at the Israelites' ingratitude: "How long will they have no faith in Me despite all the signs that I have performed in their midst?" (14:11). He wants to destroy and disown all the people, except for Moses, Caleb, Joshua, and a few others. Moses, in a manner of speaking, appeals to God's "ego" in an effort to convince Him not to do so: "If then You slay this people . . . the nations that have heard of Your fame will say, 'It must be because the Lord was powerless to bring that people into the land which He had promised them on oath that He slaughtered them in the wilderness'" (14:15–16). Thus, Moses beseeches God to forgive the people for their lack of faith.

God accedes to this request, but rules that no one—except Caleb and Joshua—who had seen the miracles performed in Egypt will be permitted to enter Canaan.

God is still unappeased and instructs Moses to deliver the following message to the Israelites: "I will do to you just as you have urged Me. In this very wilderness shall your carcasses drop" (14:28–29).

When Moses repeats these words to the people, they are overcome with remorse and acknowledge their wrongdoing. Suddenly, they forget their previous fears and announce that they are ready to occupy Canaan immediately. Moses warns them not to do so because God will not help them, but the Israelites pay him no heed. They march ahead, only to be dealt a shattering blow by Canaanite and Amalekite forces.

In consonance with the biblical depiction of these early Israelites, the Jewish tradition regards the generation of the desert as a pathetic group. Reared as slaves, they retain throughout their lives a "slave mentality." When Egyptian troops, whom they greatly outnumber, pursue them, it never occurs to them to say, "Let's fight back!" Instead, they decry Moses' bringing them into the desert to die. When there are shortages of provisions, they don't think, "Is there anything we can do for ourselves?" Instead, like children, they turn on Moses and God and demand that they set everything right.*

Moses was different from the other Israelites, perhaps because he had been reared as an Egyptian prince; thus, he saw himself as a proud and free man, subservient only to God.

God's decree that the Israelites will remain in the desert until the generation of the Exodus die might not be motivated solely by a desire to punish them for lack of faith. God realizes that had this generation accompanied their children and grandchildren into Canaan, they would have acted as a demoralizing force. How could they do otherwise? For though their children view themselves as free men, the generation that came out of Egypt, including its leadership, see themselves as "grasshoppers." And so the Israelite entry into Canaan has to be postponed for forty years until this irresolute, self-deprecating group—the generation of the "grasshoppers"—passes from the scene.

48. Korah's Revolt Against Moses

NUMBERS 16:1–17:15

Korah, a populist demagogue, presents the most powerful challenge to Moses' leadership during the Israelites' long desert sojourn. Aligning himself with Datan and Abiram, and prominent members of the tribe of Reuben, he publicly confronts Moses and Aaron: "You have gone too far! For all the community are holy, all of them, and the Lord is in their midst! Why then do you raise yourselves above the Lord's congregation?" (16:3).

Korah belongs to the tribe of Levi and descends from so prominent a family that his own birth is recorded in the Bible (Exodus 6:21). Apparently, he is incensed at Moses' political and religious leadership and Aaron's control of the priestly functions. By speaking

*Indeed, as my friend David Szonyi notes, "In their dependency on God (for manna, etc.) and on Moses (for interceding with God), the people genuinely *are* in a childlike consummately dependent position."

of the entire community as being holy, Korah is clearly trying to widen support for his revolt, and there is every indication that he succeeds. Numbers 17:14 records that even after Korah's death, God punishes through plague an additional 14,700 people.

Moses responds to Korah's challenge by falling on his face, most likely in supplication to God. When he rises, he challenges his adversary to meet him the following morning in a contest before God. Korah and his followers, and Aaron and Moses, will each bring ritual fire pans and incense, and come before God at the Tent of Meeting; "then the man whom the Lord chooses [by accepting his pan], he shall be the holy one." Making no effort to disguise his fury, Moses denounces Korah for not being satisfied with his status as a Levite— the tribe that served as assistants to the priests—but for demanding the priesthood as well.

My friend Rabbi Leonid Feldman has noted an issue that few Bible commentators discuss: "When Korah publicly challenges and denounces Moses, one would think that the other Israelites would turn against him in rage, and would want to kill him for attacking their revered leader. The truth is, nobody utters a protest. The Israelites listen to Korah's challenge, then wait to hear Moses' response. For whatever reason, perhaps because he was so tough with them, the Israelites do not seem to have deeply loved Moses. They certainly weren't loyal to him."

After concluding his discussion with Korah, Moses turns to Korah's confederates, Datan and Abiram. He adopts a more conciliatory approach and summons them to a meeting at which their grievances can be discussed. However, both men refuse his summons—"We will not come"—then denounce him in terms reminiscent of Korah: "Is it not enough that you brought us from a land flowing with milk and honey to have us die in the wilderness, that you would also lord it over us?" (16:13).

Moses responds with anger, and asks God to ignore any sacrifices they offer Him (16:15). The whole Israelite enterprise is at stake, and he wishes to make sure that he wins.

The following morning, Moses and Aaron, fire pans in hand, confront the rebels in front of the Tent of Meeting. Certain that God will support him, Moses directs his words not to his enemies, but to the Israelites who come as spectators to the contest: "By this you shall know that it was the Lord who sent me to do all these things; that they are not of my own devising. If these men die as all men do . . . it was not the Lord who sent me. But if the Lord brings about something unheard-of, so that the ground opens its mouth and swallows them up . . . you shall know that these men have spurned the Lord" (16:28–30).

Immediately, the earth opens its mouth (as if the earth itself were pronouncing a judgment, notes Bible commentator Arnold Ehrlich) and swallows Korah and his supporters: "The earth closed over them and they vanished from the midst of the congregation" (16:33).

This dramatic punishment, however, does not end the revolt. The following morning, "the whole Israelite community" rails against Moses and Aaron, shouting, "You have brought death upon the Lord's people" (17:6).

Moses, presumably astounded at the widespread support for the rebellion—the text speaks after all of "the *whole* Israelite community"—says nothing. Along with Aaron, he goes into the Tent of Meeting, where an enraged Lord instructs him and Aaron to "remove yourselves from this community, that I may annihilate them in an instant" (17:10).

Moses, more loyal to the Israelites than they to him, urges Aaron to make a quick offering on the people's behalf. God accepts the offering but, as noted, sends a plague to punish 14,700 of Korah's remaining supporters.

Among those who survive the opening of the earth and the plague are members of Korah's family. Numbers 26:11 informs us that Korah's sons did not perish, presumably because they did not accompany their father. Thus, descendants of Korah are later listed as authors of eleven Psalms (42, 44–49, 84, 85, 87, and 88). Samuel, one of Israel's greatest prophets, also is descended from Korah (I Chronicles 6:18–22), a stunning detail, much like learning that a descendant of Benedict Arnold became a president of the United States.

Note: Hundreds of years after this incident, the prophet Elijah, perhaps guided by this biblical tale, issues a similar challenge to the priests of Baal. Elijah's goal is the same as Moses, to demonstrate before all the Israelites who really is God's authentic prophet (see entry 92).

49. Moses Strikes the Rock and Is Punished by God

NUMBERS, CHAPTER 20

One of the Book of Numbers' prominent themes is the Israelites' increasing discontent with Moses. Whenever there is a temporary lack of water or food, they complain that it would have been better had Moses let them remain in Egypt. When the spies return from their mission to Canaan and inform the people that the land is unconquerable, they turn against Moses in fury. And when Korah challenges Moses' right to lead them, the people wait for Moses and Korah to fight it out, rather than rally spontaneously to Moses' side.

Immediately after Miriam dies (20:1), with Moses very likely feeling depressed, a water shortage again occurs (20:2). Characteristically, the people turn on Moses and Aaron, asking bitterly, "Why did you make us leave Egypt to bring us to this wretched place?" (20:5).

Moses and Aaron do not respond but return to the Tent of Meeting, where they fall on their faces. One senses in their behavior the accumulation of almost forty years of weariness and a desire to be rid of this thankless responsibility.

Before they say anything, God speaks to Moses and orders him and Aaron to take the rod that was kept in the Holy of Holies, assemble the community, and command a large rock to yield water. God assures him that He will cause water to gush out.

Moses emerges from the tent with the rod, assembles the people in front of the rock, and says, "Listen, you rebels, shall we get water for you out of this rock?" Whereupon Moses raises his hand and strikes it with his rod. Water gushes forth in torrents sufficient to satisfy both the people's and their animals' thirst.

God immediately speaks to Moses and Aaron, imposing upon them about the most extreme punishment He can, short of execution: "Because you did not trust Me enough to affirm My sanctity in the sight of the Israelite people, therefore you shall not lead this congregation into the land that I have given them" (20:12).

In the thousands of years since this passage was written, students have argued about its meaning. By what measure was the sin committed by Moses, hitting the rock instead of speaking to it, so serious as to deserve such a severe punishment?

God's condemnation of Moses also seems to make no sense. His accusation that "you did not trust Me enough to affirm My sanctity in the sight of the Israelite people" sounds irrelevant. The Israelite people had not heard God instruct Moses to speak to the rock. When he hit it and water gushed out, this seemed to them like a miracle. Thus, although Moses might have disobeyed God's command, how did he not affirm God's sanctity before the Israelites?

Perhaps no contemporary Bible scholar has thought through the issue of Moses' sin and punishment more systematically than biblical commentator Jacob Milgrom. After reviewing all the previous analyses of Moses' sin, Milgrom concludes that he is certain of one thing: Moses was not punished because he struck the rock instead of speaking to it. To argue that this was the reason Moses was denied entry to Canaan is to depict God as cruel and unjust.

Rather, Moses' sin was what he said just before he struck the rock: "Shall *we* get water for you out of this rock?" When Moses made this statement, he was standing alongside Aaron in front of the entire Israelite community. His words, "Shall *we*," implied that he and Aaron were the authors of the miracle he was about to perform. His sin, then, was in not saying, "Shall *God* get water for you out of this rock?" but "Shall *we*."

There is virtually no more serious verbal gaffe Moses could have committed. His life's major task had been to teach the Israelites that there is one universal God Who rules the world, and that He is the only God to whom a person should pray, and Who can perform miracles. With this one sentence, uttered during a moment of anger, when many of us are apt to say foolish things, Moses suggested that he and Aaron too perform miracles. Had God allowed Moses to continue to lead the Israelites into Canaan, his ability to do so, at the age of 120, might again have appeared Godlike, and might have led the Israelites to worship Moses as a deity.

To keep monotheism pure, God had to make it clear to the Israelites that Moses and Aaron were mortal human beings. That is likely why Aaron dies almost immediately after this incident (20:25–29), and Moses a short time later.

Slips of the tongue are common, particularly when one is angry, and Moses certainly had reason to be in a foul mood on that particular day. Yet when one is a leader, slips of the tongue are not always forgivable. Moses' punishment was great, but the statement he made before the entire Israelite people could have undone all the good he had performed in his lifetime.

Was God's punishment harsh? Undoubtedly. Was God's punishment unfair? Apparently not.

Sources and further readings: Jacob Milgrom, *The JPS Torah Commentary: Numbers*, pages 163–167, and excursus 50, "Magic, Monotheism and the Sin of Moses," pages 448–456.

50. Balaam's Talking Donkey
NUMBERS, CHAPTERS 22–24

"How Goodly Are Your Tents, O Jacob, Your Dwellings, O Israel"
24:5

The non-Hebrew prophet Balaam has the unfortunate distinction of being known mainly because of his donkey.

His story begins when the nation of Moab hears about the approaching Israelite wanderers. Moab's leaders approach the chiefs of Midian to express the fear that the Israelites will pass through their territories and consume all their crops. Balak, Moab's king, dispatches messengers to Balaam, a well-known local prophet and commands him: "Come then, put a curse upon this people for me, since they are too numerous for me; perhaps I can thus defeat them, and drive them out of the land" (22:6). Balak concludes his message with an appeal to Balaam's ego: "For I know that he whom you bless is blessed indeed, and he whom you curse is cursed."

In one of the Bible's most remarkable passages, it soon becomes apparent that this non-Hebrew prophet believes in, *and communes with,* the universal God of the Bible. When the Moabite and Midianite messengers seek his assistance, he asks them to spend the night while he communicates with God.

God instructs him: "Do not go with them. You must not curse that people, for they are blessed" (22:12). So Balaam informs the messengers, who in turn relay the prophet's refusal to King Balak. While one would think that Balaam's refusal might cause Balak to consider entering into negotiations with the Israelites instead of fighting them, it only prompts him to send another, more distinguished, group of messengers to contract for Balaam's aid. This time, the king assumes that an appeal to Balaam's greed will prove efficacious: "I will reward you richly and I will do anything you ask of me. Only come and damn this people for me" (22:17).

Sounding like the most righteous prophet of Israel, Balaam responds: "Though Balak were to give me his house full of silver and gold, I could not do anything, big or little, contrary to the command of the Lord my God" (22:18). He again invites Balak's emissaries to remain overnight while he consults with the Lord.

This time, God tells Balaam that it is permitted for him to go with the messengers, but on the condition that "whatever I command you, that you shall do" (22:20).

Yet, it soon becomes evident that God is unhappy about Balaam's acceptance of Balak's offer. The next morning, Balaam saddles his donkey and sets off on his mission, accompanied by the Moabite dignitaries. Unseen by all is an angelic adversary traveling alongside them.

Shortly after they begin the journey, Balaam's donkey, and no one else, sees the angel standing in front of him with a sword drawn in his hand. The frightened donkey swerves to the side, going off the road into the fields. Balaam beats the donkey and turns her back in the direction of the road. Again, the donkey sees the angel and swerves, this time crushing Balaam's foot against a wall. Balaam hits the animal; the donkey, still conscious of an angel standing in front of her brandishing a sword, lies down on the road. The furious Balaam beats the poor creature with a stick.

"Then the Lord opened the donkey's mouth; 'What have I done to you that you have beaten me these three times?' " (22:28), she asks Balaam.

Consumed by his fury, Balaam does not even react to the mystery of his donkey being able to speak: "You have made a mockery of me. If I had a sword with me, I'd kill you," he rails at the creature.

The donkey now emerges as the voice of reason, reminding Balaam that the prophet has been riding upon her a long time. "Have I been in the habit of doing thus to you?"

Balaam answers, "No."

Finally, when God uncovers Balaam's eyes, he sees the angel in front of the donkey, his sword drawn. Balaam bows down, and the angel now speaks, sounding like a representative of the Society for the Prevention of Cruelty to Animals: "Why have you beaten your donkey these three times?" (22:32). He tells Balaam that the mission on which he is setting out is offensive to God. Indeed, Balaam should be grateful to the donkey, for had she not swerved but ridden straight ahead, "you are the one I should have killed."

After so startling an incident, the angel adds nothing to the message God had given Balaam the night before (perhaps the entire purpose of this encounter was to ensure that Balaam remember God's words to him): "You must say nothing except what I tell you" (22:35).

The donkey now fades from the scene, and Balaam continues his journey—only he proves to be no bargain to his royal employer. Each time Balaam is instructed to curse the Israelites, he sings their praises instead: "How can I damn whom God has not damned? . . . Who can count the dust of Jacob? . . . May I die the death of the upright, may my fate be like theirs!" (23:8, 10).

Balak is outraged. "What have you done to me? Here I brought you to damn my enemies, and instead you have blessed them" (23:11).

Balak drags Balaam to an outpost from which he can see a part of the Israelite camp, and commands him to damn them from there. What emerges from the prophet's mouth is hardly calculated to reassure the increasingly desperate Balak: "No harm is in sight for Jacob, no woe in view for Israel. The Lord their God is with them . . ." (23:21).

The desperate Balak is now willing to compromise. "Don't curse them and don't bless them" (23:25).

Balaam demurs. "But I told you: Whatever the Lord says, that I must do" (23:26).

Unwilling to admit defeat, Balak takes the prophet to yet another mountaintop, and again asks him to damn Israel. Instead, Balaam, looking down on the Israelite camp, utters words that have since entered the Jewish daily liturgy: "How goodly are your tents, O Jacob, your dwellings, O Israel" (*Ma tovu ohalecha, Ya'akov, mish-ke-no-techa, Yisra'el*).

The wrathful Balak dismisses Balaam and refuses to pay him anything. Balaam departs willingly, but not before uttering a fourth, final, prophecy in which he foretells Israel's eventual victory over Moab (24:15–24).

Balaam then sets out for home. Does he ride on the talking donkey that brought him there? We don't know. Having made her climactic appearance, Balaam's donkey disappears from the story. An old Jewish teaching claims that the creature died immediately after this episode, her life's mission having been fulfilled.

Balaam's donkey is one of two talking animals in the Bible, but the two are very different. The snake who speaks to Eve in the Garden of Eden is highly intelligent and evil; his goal is to convince Eve to disobey God. In contrast, Balaam's donkey is capable of seeing what a prophet engaged on an evil mission cannot see, an emissary of the Lord.

51. Pinchas's Zealousness

NUMBERS, CHAPTER 25

Having failed to triumph over the Israelites through Balaam's curses (see preceding entry), Moab's leaders conclude that the best way to defeat the Israelites is to alienate them from their God. They attempt to do so by sending beautiful Moabite and Midianite women into the Israelite camp, who offer their bodies in return for the Israelite men's souls. They expect that the men whom they seduce will offer sacrifices to the Moabite and Midianite gods. When many Israelite men do so, God becomes incensed. He tells Moses to seize hold of the Israelite ringleaders, and publicly execute them. Moses goes to the tribal judges* and instructs them: "Each of you slay those of his men who attach themselves to Baal-peor" (the Moabite deity; 25:5).

   At that very moment, while Moses and some faithful followers are weeping in front of the Tent of Meeting, an Israelite man walks by, proudly parading his Midianite consort. Pinchas, a grandson of Aaron, seizes a spear, follows the two into the tent where they go to couple, and stabs them both in the belly (possibly a euphemism for the genitals). We learn that the Israelite man is Zimri, a chief in

*Many translations of the Bible speak of these men as "tribal leaders," but the Hebrew word *shoftim* means "judges."

the tribe of Simeon; the Midianite woman is Cozbi, daughter of Zur, a prominent leader in Midian.

Pinchas's act causes God's anger to subside: "Pinchas . . . has turned back My wrath from the Israelites by displaying among them his passion for Me" (25:10). God then names Pinchas and his descendants to be Israel's leading priests.

How should modern readers regard Pinchas's vigilante act? Was it heroic and should it be emulated? Indeed, throughout history, more than a few extremists and assassins have cited Pinchas's act as justification for their own vigilantism.

Bible commentator Jacob Milgrom argues that although the Bible praises Pinchas, his behavior was never intended to serve as a model for anybody else's: "The Rabbis were uncomfortable with Pinchas' act. He set a dangerous precedent by taking the law into his own hands and slaying a man impulsively, in disregard of [the prescribed judicial procedure]. Some argued that Moses and the other leaders would have excommunicated him were it not for the divine decree declaring that Pinchas had acted on God's behalf (verses 12–13) . . . a recent commentator [B. H. Epstein, author of the *Torah Temimah*] remarks: 'Who can tell whether the perpetrator is not really prompted by some selfish motive, maintaining that he is doing it for the sake of God, when he has actually committed murder? That is why the sages wished to excommunicate Pinchas, had not the Holy Spirit testified that his zeal for God was genuine.'"

Source and further reading: Jacob Milgrom's comment is found in *The JPS Torah Commentary: Numbers,* page 215.

52. Zelophehad's Daughters: When Do Women Inherit?

NUMBERS 27:1–11; 36:1–12

About the only detail we know of Zelophehad's life is his death. He leaves behind five daughters, who come before Moses and other high officials at the Tent of Meeting. They speak of a sin for which their father died, never specifying what it was, then note that they will not receive any inheritance: "Let not our father's name be lost to the clan just because he had no son! Give us a holding among our father's kinsmen!" (27:3–4).

Unquestionably biased toward men, biblical laws of inheritance were not intended to hurt women, but to guarantee each tribe's territorial integrity. When the Israelites entered Canaan, the land was divided among the twelve tribes and property passed from fathers to sons.

Since married women lived in their husbands' tribes, the effect of daughters inheriting would be to confuse the tribal lands: Thus, if a woman from the tribe of Reuben married a man from Judah, and she inherited land from her father and bequeathed it to her children (whose tribal identity followed the father's tribe), the land would be irrevocably taken away from, say, Reuben and given to a member of Judah.

That seems to be why some of the tribal chiefs seek to nullify the daughters' appeal to Moses, complaining that if women inherit and marry men of other tribes, "their share will be cut off from our ancestral portion and be added to the portion of the tribe into which they marry. Thus, our allotted portion will be diminished" (36:3).

Caught between conflicting and compelling claims, Moses is bewildered. To deprive the young women of their father's inheritance is unjust, yet to let them inherit as males do will lead to the end of territorial sovereignty (which might not seem terribly important to us, but was critical to people at that time).

God speaks to Moses: "The plea of Zelophehad's daughters is just: you should give them a hereditary holding among their father's kinsmen: transfer their father's share to them" (27:7).

Moses follows God's ruling: However, to prevent tribal warfare, he restricts Zelophehad's daughters to marrying men of their own tribe (36:6). He also establishes the principle that when a man dies without sons, his daughters are entitled to inherit their father's land but *only* if they marry within their tribe: "Thus, no inheritance shall pass over from one tribe to another" (36:9).

Zelophehad's five daughters eventually marry first cousins, fellow members of the tribe of Manasseh. The Torah lists the five women's names, two of which are still used in modern Hebrew, Noa and Tirzah.

God's statement, "The plea of Zelophehad's daughters is just," has ever since helped to establish the legitimate legal claims of women.

Indeed, later Jewish law reflected rabbinic concern for the claims of unmarried daughters (unmarried women were regarded as among the most vulnerable members of society): "If a man died and left sons and daughters and the property was ample, the sons inherit and the daughters receive maintenance; but if the property was small, the daughters receive maintenance and the sons go begging" (Mishnah *Ketubot* 13:3). However, the Mishnah does incorporate the statement of later rabbis, who argued that the sons could protest, "Must I suffer because I am a male?" (Although daughters, deprived of inheritance, could easily pose the same question, "Must I suffer because I am female?")

Note: A biblical inheritance in which daughters share equally with sons: "Job expresses his respect for his daughters ... by providing them with property. Job, we are told, gave his daughters 'inheritance' [alternatively 'estates'] together with their brothers (Job 42:15). According to biblical law, only in the absence of male heirs were daughters permitted to receive their father's estate. Here, therefore, is a clear deviation from the law, for Job's daughters inherited, despite the fact that they have brothers" (Ilana Pardes, *Countertraditions in the Bible*, page 153).

53. Joshua Is Chosen to Succeed Moses

NUMBERS 27:12–23

God instructs Moses to climb to the top of Mount Abarim, where he can see the land of Canaan. See, but not enter, for "when you have seen it, you too shall be gathered to your kinsmen, just as your brother Aaron was" (27:13; Moses' death, however, doesn't occur until Deuteronomy 34, the Torah's final chapter).

An ever-faithful leader, Moses makes but one plea, that God appoint a successor to him "so that the Lord's community may not be like sheep that has no shepherd" (27:17).

God agrees, and instructs Moses to designate his assistant Joshua, son of Nun, to succeed him. Perhaps to preempt any possible coups or other disputes, the Lord insists that Joshua's leadership be affirmed at a public ceremony: "Have him stand before Elazar the priest and before the whole community, and commission him in their sight" (27:19). Joshua, Moses is told, is to work in cooperation with Elazar the priest, and to instruct him to consult the *Urim* and *Tummim* (see entry 42) when major decisions are to be made. Thus, political and religious leadership are to be shared.

Moses does as God commands, publicly laying his hands on Joshua's head so as to transmit his authority to his successor. *Semikha*, the Hebrew term for laying on of hands, is to this day the term for rabbinical ordination. Asking a person, "Do you have *semikha*?" is equal to inquiring, "Are you an ordained rabbi?" Today, however, the term is symbolic, since the laying on of hands does not generally accompany the investiture of modern rabbis.

54. Occupying Canaan and Dispossessing the Canaanites

NUMBERS, CHAPTER 33:50; CHAPTER 34

God's first efforts to reveal Himself to humankind (first to Adam and Eve, then to Noah and his sons) failed to achieve the intended result, the creation of a good and godly environment.

Fearing that the same might occur with the Israelites to whom He subsequently reveals Himself, God insists that when they enter Canaan they dispossess the Canaanites, whom the Bible condemns for practicing idolatry, child sacrifice, and incest and other forms of perverse sexuality (see Leviticus 18:21–25). The Israelites are enjoined to destroy all Canaanite idols—"You shall destroy all their figured objects; you shall destroy all their molten images, and you shall demolish all their cult places" (Numbers 33:53)—and the Canaanites as well.

Apparently, God wants Canaan to be the one place in the world consecrated exclusively to monotheism. If the Israelites do not undertake the harsh measures God orders, then "those whom you allow to remain shall be stings in your eyes and thorns in your side" (33:55).

When the Israelites enter Canaan, they war against some Canaanites, but do allow many residents to continue living there and practicing idolatry. Over the next few centuries, the Canaanites influence many Israelites to adopt their idolatrous practices, occasionally including even human sacrifice (II Kings 21:6). The Book of Judges describes how the Israelites "followed other gods from among the gods of the people around them, and bowed down to them. . . . They forsook the Lord and worshiped Baal . . ." (2:12–13).

After telling the people of God's command to dispossess the Canaanites, Moses details the borders of the land the Israelites are to occupy (chapter 34). The precise division of the land will be determined by lot, on a family-by-family basis.

Note: A description of the type of wars which the Israelites fought against the Canaanites, and a discussion of the moral problems in these episodes, are found in entry 61.

V. DEUTERONOMY

55. Moses' Final Speeches

THE BOOK OF DEUTERONOMY

The word "will" (as in "last will and testament") usually has an exclusively material connotation, how a person wants his financial assets to be divided when he dies. Jewish tradition knows of a second kind of will. Called in Hebrew a *tzava'a* (generally translated as "ethical will"), it expresses a person's wishes about how his descendants should conduct their lives after he or she dies.

The Book of Deuteronomy can be understood as Moses' ethical will, his final bequest to the Israelite people whom he has led for forty years.

Moses knows that his leadership and life are coming to an end; God has told him that the Israelites will soon cross over into Canaan, but that he, Moses, will not accompany them. At God's direction, Moses anoints Joshua to succeed him (see entry 53).

Before Moses gives up his duties, he delivers three final addresses to the Israelites, expressing in both precise and general terms the kind of lives he wishes them to lead.

The most famous segment of his orations occurs in Deuteronomy's sixth chapter, where Moses proclaims, *"Sh'ma Yis'rael*—Hear O Israel, the Lord is our God, the Lord is One," and follows this with an admonition to "love the Lord your God." Because Jewish tradition regards Moses as having been divinely inspired when he spoke these words, his directive to "love God" has long been understood as one of the Torah's 613 divinely ordained laws (see law number 418).

A central theme in these orations is the Torah's undying opposition to idolatry. God warns the people that "if you do forget the Lord your God and follow other gods to serve them or bow down to them, I warn you this day that you shall certainly perish" (8:19). According to Moses, the Israelites' right to possess Canaan depends upon their loyalty to God. If they betray God through acts of idolatry, they shall be ousted from the land "like the nations that the Lord will cause to perish before you, so shall you perish—because you did not heed the Lord your God" (8:20).

To forestall such deviations, Moses enjoins the Israelites not to intermarry with the seven nations inhabiting Canaan: "For they will turn your children away from Me to worship other gods, and the Lord's anger will blaze forth against you . . ." (7:4). Instead, he orders the people to destroy all the idolatrous temples and "consign their images to the fire" (7:5). In an idolatrous world, Moses, speaking at God's behest, seems desperate to carve out one small territory where monotheism can grow unmolested.

While religions usually promise their righteous adherents rewards in the "next world," Moses pledges both the Israelite nation and its individual members great rewards *in this world* if they but heed God's injunctions. Perhaps his most startling pledge is: "There shall be no sterile male or female among you . . ." (7:14). In the next verse, Moses also makes the remarkable promise that "the Lord will ward off from you all sickness."

Anticipating the fear the Israelites might experience upon entering Canaan and encountering its many residents, Moses reminds them that they have no reason to be afraid: "You have but to bear in mind what the Lord your God did to Pharaoh and all the Egyptians" (7:18). As long as the Israelites remain religiously loyal, God will do battle for them as he did against Pharaoh.

The mode of warfare Moses encourages is horrifying to modern ears; he advocates the vanquishing and total destruction of the Canaanite nations (7:24; see also 20:16). It is important to recall that that is how wars were fought in the ancient world (see entry 61). For example, the ninth-century B.C.E. Mesha Stone records the Moabite king's boast of murdering seven thousand Israelite men and women, and offering their bodies as sacrificial gifts to the god Ashtar-Chemosh.

In contrast to these stern words, what stands out most prominently in Moses' ethical will is his emphasis on carrying out the Torah's ethical commands. Thus, he repeats the Ten Commandments, with their insistence on the honoring of parents, and the prohibitions of murder, adultery, stealing, and coveting. The original version of the commandments cited in Exodus rooted the rationale for the Sabbath in imitation of God, who created the world in six days and then rested. But Moses roots the commandment in a recollection of how God freed the Israelites from Egyptian slavery: "Remember that you were a slave in the land of Egypt [and hence could not refrain from working one day each week] . . . : the Lord your God has commanded you to observe the Sabbath day" (5:15).

A loving father figure, Moses nevertheless does not conceal his fury at numerous Israelite transgressions against, and provocations of, God. Rabbi Irwin Kula has noted to me that although Numbers 20 explains God's refusal to permit Moses to enter Canaan as a punishment for Moses' own sin (see entry 49), in Deuteronomy Moses blames the Israelites for his fate: "Because of you, the Lord was incensed with me too, and he said: 'You shall not enter [Canaan] either'" (1:37).

Moses tells the people that their observance of the edicts he enjoins them to obey in his orations will make a profound impression on their gentile neighbors: "Observe them [i.e., the Torah's laws] faithfully, for that will be proof of your wisdom and discernment to other peoples, who on hearing of all these laws will say, 'Surely that great nation is a wise and discerning people'" (4:6). The great medieval philosopher Moses Maimonides understood this verse as meaning that Torah laws are rooted in reason. For if these laws were merely divine decrees without rationale, why would non-Israelites think that the Israelites are "wise and discerning" for observing them? Thus, although some later Jewish philosophers opposed the searching out of reasons for Torah laws, Maimonides rightly understood that Moses' words validated such an approach.

Moses also confronts the Israelites with a general admonition to "do what is good and right in the sight of God" (6:19), a directive that later Rabbis comprehended as instructing a person to act ethically, even when there was no specific ordinance to govern the situation at hand.

Moses' final orations, which take up virtually the entire Book of Deuteronomy, comprise an ethical will that has guided believers in the Bible ever since.

56. The Death of Moses

DEUTERONOMY, CHAPTER 34

"And No One Knows His Burial Place"

34:6

God had told Moses that his mission to lead the Israelites into Canaan would end with *their* entering, and *his* remaining outside, the land (see entry 49). Now, as Moses prepares to die, he climbs to the top of Mount Nebo (although he is 120 years old, Moses remains fully vigorous), some 2,643 feet above sea level, from where he gains a view of the land he will not be allowed to enter: "This is the land of which I swore to Abraham, Isaac, and Jacob, 'I will give it to your offspring,'" God tells him (34:4). Then, as if to forestall any last-minute appeals, God immediately adds, "I have let you see it with your own eyes, but you shall not cross there."

Immediately thereafter, Moses dies: the text implies that he dies on the mountain and is buried there, *by God*. Precisely where Moses is interred remains an eternal secret; "and no one knows his burial place to this day" (34:6).

Why such secrecy? Most probably because Moses' singular pre-eminence would have prompted some Israelites to start believing that he himself was a god. As Walter Kaufmann, the late professor of religion at Princeton, conjectured: "[Moses] went away to die alone, lest any man should know his grave to worship there or attach any value to his mortal body. Having seen Egypt, he knew . . . how prone men are to such superstitions. Going off to die alone, he might have left his people with the image of a mystery . . . with the thought that he did not die but went up to heaven—with the notion that he was immortal and divine. . . . Instead, he created an enduring image of humanity; he left his people with the thought that, being human and imperfect, he was not allowed to enter the promised land, but that he went up on the mountain to see it before he died. The Jews have been so faithful to his spirit that they have . . . never worshipped him. . . . What the Jews have presented to the world has not been Moses or any individual, but their ideas about God and man. It is a measure of Moses' greatness that one cannot but imagine that he would have approved wholeheartedly. It would have broken his heart if he had thought that his followers would build temples to him, make images of him, or elevate him into heaven. That he has never been deified [like Jesus or the Pharaoh of ancient Egypt] is one of the most significant facts about the ideas of God and man in the Old Testament."

Moses, as Kaufmann emphasizes, devoted his life to impressing upon the Hebrews the need to believe in one God. The very term by which the Torah refers to him, "the servant of God" (34:5), underscores his human nature. Because "no one knows his burial place to this day," Moses' grave could never become a shrine.

Like Aaron, his brother, Moses was mourned for thirty days (34:8), from which comes the Jewish tradition of observing intense grief for thirty days after the death of a close relative. This biblically based tradition has spread beyond the Jewish community: In the United States, deaths of great figures such as presidents and former presidents are commemorated by flying the flag at half-staff for thirty days.

The Torah provides a brief eulogy for Moses: "Never again did there arise in Israel a prophet like Moses—whom the Lord knew face to face" (34:10).

Operating from the premise that the entire Torah was dictated by God to Moses, Jewish commentators have long argued about who wrote the Torah's concluding verses (34:5–12), which describe Moses' death. Most significantly, how could he have written these lines, describing his own demise and the thirty days of mourning that followed it? Furthermore, if the words were written when he was already on the mountain, how could they have come into the possession of the Israelite community and become part of the Torah? In addition, the words "and no one knows his burial place to this day" sound as if they were written after, perhaps long after, the fact.

Nonetheless, some scholars maintain that Moses *did*, in fact, write these verses. God conveyed to him these words just before he left the Israelite community and climbed Mount Nebo. In these commentators' view, the occurrences at Mount Nebo were predestined; Moses was following an already completed script. The Israelites subsequently discovered the writing he had left behind in his tent, and thus learned how their leader had died.

Others argue that Moses wrote the entire Torah *except* for the last verses, which they claim were composed by Joshua, his chosen successor. It remains an open question how everything that happened on the mountain became known to Joshua. The only viable religious response is to say that it happened through prophecy.

Whatever the case, the Torah's eulogy, "Never again did there arise in Israel a prophet like Moses," is an apt assessment of the greatest figure of Jewish history.

THE EARLY
PROPHETS

JOSHUA

JUDGES

I AND II SAMUEL

I AND II KINGS

VI. JOSHUA

57. Joshua Sends Spies to Jericho

JOSHUA CHAPTER 2

Rahab: The Righteous Prostitute

During the Israelite sojourn in the desert, Joshua is one of the twelve spies recruited by Moses to survey Canaan so as to prepare for its conquest by the Israelites. However, ten of the spies—all but Joshua and Caleb—become petrified of the Canaanites and communicate their terror to their fellow Israelites (see entry 47).

Four decades later, the ten spies and all the terrified Israelites are dead. In a remarkable reversal of fortune, the new generation of Israelites raised in the desert inspire the same kind of terror among the Canaanites that the Canaanites had once evoked among Israel.

Joshua learns this when he dispatches two spies to Jericho, the first city he sets out to conquer in Canaan. The spies occupy a room in the house of a prostitute named Rahab. Word circulates of the Israelites' arrival, and Jericho's king orders Rahab to surrender the men. Instead, she hides them amid flax stalks on her roof, then "informs" the king's messengers that the men—whose nationality she claims not to have known—had left Jericho earlier that evening, just as the city's gates were closing. "Pursue them quickly, and you will be able to overtake them," she adds.

As the king's troops quickly mount their pointless pursuit, Rahab climbs her roof to Joshua's two spies. "I know that God has given you the land," she tells the men. She also informs them that all Jericho has heard about the splitting of the Red Sea and other wonders relating to the Israelites. "When we heard about it, we lost heart, and no man had any more spirit left because of you; for the Lord your God is the only God in heaven above and on earth below" (2:11).

Rahab, whose theological reflections hardly fit the image of a common prostitute, makes one important request of the spies; in return for hiding them, she and her extended family should be spared destruction when the Israelites conquer the city.

Grateful to Rahab for having saved their lives, the spies pledge to die in her place if the Israelites don't spare her and her family. They give the woman a sign to guarantee her safety: She is to tie a red thread in a window of her house, then make sure that her family remains in the house throughout the Israelite invasion. As long as the thread remains visible, everyone in the house will be safe (this brings to mind the blood that the Israelites were commanded to smear on their doorposts, a signal to God to pass over their houses and spare their firstborn sons from the tenth plague; see Exodus 12:22–23).

Rahab, whose house is built inside the city's thick walls, takes a rope and lowers the two men outside the city through a window to which she then attaches a red thread.

After hiding in the mountains for three days, the spies, witnessing the search party returning to Jericho, proceed on their way. Arriving safely at the Israelite camp, they bring Joshua the good news: "The Lord has delivered the whole land into our power; in fact, all the inhabitants of the land are quaking before us" (2:24).

When the Israelites conquer Jericho (see next entry), Joshua sends the spies to Rahab's house to save her family "as you swore to her."

Jewish tradition teaches that Rahab subsequently converted to Judaism and became the ancestress of no less than eight prophets, including Jeremiah (*Sifre Behaalotkha*). Believing in values more than in blood, the Rabbis had no trouble accepting that the preeminent prophet of the sixth century B.C.E.—and the author of the Books of Jeremiah and Lamentations—was the descendant of a former Canaanite prostitute.

58. "And the Walls Came Tumbling Down": Joshua and the Battle of Jericho

JOSHUA, CHAPTER 6

Joshua triumphs over many Canaanite cities, but no battle has taken greater hold of the popular imagination than his victory over Jericho. He enters the battle fully confident, God having told him earlier that He will deliver the city into the Israelites' hands. He instructs Joshua to have his troops march around the walled town once a day for six days. Seven priests are to march at their head, each carrying a *shofar* (ram's horn), and walking alongside the Ark, which contains the Ten Commandments. On the seventh day, the troops are to encircle Jericho seven times, after which the priests are to blow their horns, the troops to give a loud shout, and Jericho's thick walls will crumble.

Joshua transmits God's message to his soldiers, and instructs them to remain totally silent until he commands them to shout.

During each of the first six days of the siege, the soldiers march around the city once, then return to their camp. On the seventh day—according to Jewish tradition, it was the Sabbath—they circle Jericho seven times. The priests then blow on their *shofarot*, and Joshua calls out: "Shout, for God has given us the city!" He also warns the soldiers to take no booty from Jericho; all the city's possessions are to be consecrated to God (the Hebrew term for such a ban [consecration] is *herem*; see Deuteronomy 7:25–26), and given over to the temple treasury.

The soldiers let out a tremendous shout, the walls collapse, and the Israelites destroy the city and kill all its inhabitants except for Rahab and her family (see preceding entry). After hauling away the city's silver, gold, copper, and iron vessels to be stored in the Tent of Meeting, the soldiers set the city ablaze. Joshua then pronounces this oath: "Cursed by God be the man who shall undertake to fortify this city of Jericho; he shall lay its foundations at the cost of his first-born, and set up its gates at the cost of his youngest."*

---

*More than three centuries later, during the reign of King Ahab, Hiel of Beth-el rebuilt Jericho, and lost his firstborn and youngest sons in the pro-

Disturbing as is the depiction of the wholesale destruction of Jericho, the collapse of the city's walls has impressed biblical readers for thousands of years, particularly those most in need of God's help. For example, one of the most famous African-American spirituals composed during slavery proclaims: "Joshua fit [fought] the battle of Jericho, and the walls came tumbling down."

59. Achan's Theft

JOSHUA, CHAPTER 7

"All Israel are responsible for one another" is a famous talmudic maxim (Babylonian Talmud, *Shavuot* 39a). One meaning of this maxim, Jewish tradition teaches, is that one Jew's sins may cause others to suffer. A prooftext for this rabbinic belief is the incident of Achan, an Israelite soldier who fights in Jericho and who, despite Joshua's admonition to refrain from looting the city (see preceding entry), steals silver, gold, and a cloak, and hides them all in his tent.

Amid the chaos of battle, no one notices Achan's thievery, except God. He responds with fury, withdrawing His protection from the Israelite army. Thus, when an Israelite force follows their victory over Jericho with an attack on the city of Ai, the Israelites are routed and thirty-six soldiers die. Joshua and the elders rend their garments, and fall prostrate before God's Ark.

Joshua's words to God on this occasion bring to mind those uttered by the disgruntled Israelites in the desert: "Ah, Lord God . . . why did You lead this people across the Jordan only to deliver us to the hands of the Amorites, to be destroyed by them? If only we had been content to remain on the other side of the Jordan" (i.e., in the desert, 7:7).

God responds by informing Joshua of the violation of the *herem*, the ban on taking any possessions from Jericho. He says that His withdrawal of support from the Israelite army will continue until the

---

cess (I Kings 16:34). Subsequent to this, however, Jericho again became a vital and active town. Thus, II Kings 2:5 speaks of Jericho as a town in which prophets resided.

stolen property is confiscated, and instructs Joshua to bring together the Israelites on the following day and to conduct a kind of lottery, during which the guilty party will be exposed.

The following morning Joshua gathers the tribes. Using the *Urim* and *Tummim* (see entry 42), he first learns that the offender belongs to the tribe of Judah. Subsequent disclosures expose the offender as belonging to the clan of Zerah and the house of Zabdi. Finally, a man named Achan is exposed as the thief.

Achan quickly confesses his sin against God, and tells Joshua where the property is hidden. The stolen goods are brought to Joshua, who gathers the booty and also has Achan's family rounded up (since, presumably, they knew that he was hiding banned property in their tent).

"What calamity have you brought upon us!" Joshua declares. "The Lord will bring calamity upon you this day" (7:25).

Achan is pelted with stones, then burned with fire. He is buried under a large heap of stones (the text is ambiguous as to whether his family members are killed as well, but it seems more likely than not that they were).

Punishment during the age of Joshua was not dispensed with a gentle hand.

Note: What matters to the biblical author is fidelity to God, not ancestry: "Rahab [see entry 57] and the Gibeonites [see next entry] are outsiders who become insiders because they recognize Yahweh's power. Their counterparts are Achan and his family: By not recognizing Yahweh's holiness, these are insiders who become outsiders" (Danna Nolan Fewell, "Joshua," *The Women's Bible Commentary*, page 63).

How good people help their family and bad people hurt theirs: "[Achan] is the direct opposite of Rahab. Whereas Rahab, a Canaanite woman, saves her whole family, Achan, an Israelite man, is instrumental in destroying his" (Ibid., page 64).

60. The Gibeonite Surrender

JOSHUA, CHAPTER 9–10:21

The Sun Stands Still

10:12–14

The Israelite victories over Jericho and Ai succeed in unifying dozens of small Canaanite nations against them.

One small state, Gibeon (its central city is some six miles northwest of Jerusalem), refuses to join the Canaanite resistance, concluding that its only hope for survival is to make peace with Israel. Aware, however, that Joshua wishes to vanquish the Canaanite states rather than negotiate with them, the Gibeonites dispatch a delegation to meet him. The men load their donkeys with worn sacks, along with cracked and patched wineskins. They dress in tattered clothes and sandals, and carry dry, crumbly bread.

When the Gibeonite emissaries arrive at Joshua's camp, they represent themselves as having "come from a distant land," and request that Joshua and the Israelites conclude a peace treaty with them.

The first Israelites with whom the Gibeonite messengers negotiate don't inquire very carefully about the "distant land" from which the emissaries have come. When Joshua enters the discussion, however, he presses this point: "Who are you, and from where do you come?" (9:8).

"Your servants come from a very distant land," they tell him, "because of the fame of the Lord your God. For we have heard the report of Him, everything He did in Egypt." They tell Joshua that their elders dispatched them to meet with the Israelites and add, "We are your servants; now, make a treaty with us." The men point to their crumbly bread (insisting that it was fresh and warm when they left home), and worn clothes and sandals.

Something in the Gibeonite story should have rung false. Even had they heard about God's miraculous deliverance of the Israelites, why should that have motivated this distant people to offer themselves as Israel's servants?

Without consulting God, Joshua and the Israelites quickly conclude a peace treaty with the Gibeonites (9:15).

Three days later, they learn that Gibeon is a nearby neighbor. The Israelites do not launch an attack "for the leaders of the community had sworn to them by God, Lord of Israel" (9:18).

The question remains: Why did Joshua feel himself bound by a treaty extracted through fraud? The text doesn't offer a precise answer, although three leading medieval biblical exegetes—Rashi, Ralbag, and Abravanel—conjecture that violating an oath invoking God would desecrate God's name. Non-Hebrews, in other words, might hear that the Israelites had violated their oath—not knowing that it had been extracted through fraud—and conclude that both Israel and its God are tricksters.

The enraged Israelites, however, hardly let the Gibeonites off the hook. They turn them into servants, "hewers of wood and drawers of water" (9:23); Joshua also tells them that their servitude will last eternally (9:23).

The Gibeonites accept their condition uncomplainingly. However, when King Adoni-zedek of Jerusalem hears about the peace treaty, he becomes enraged at the Gibeonites, and quickly forms an alliance with four other monarchs to attack them.

The Gibeonites send an appeal to Joshua for help; he immediately proceeds to Gibeon with large numbers of troops.

The Canaanite armies panic when Joshua arrives, and he defeats them decisively. During this battle, the greatest miracle of his career occurs. In response to his prayer, God halts the sun from setting over Gibeon so that Joshua can complete his victory (10:12–13). "Never before or afterwards was there such a day when God obeyed a man, for God fought for Israel" (10:14), the Bible tells us.

Israel continued to observe its treaty with Gibeon for centuries. Some two hundred years later, when King Saul violated the treaty's conditions and killed an unspecified number of Gibeonites, God punished Israel with a famine. It ended only when David delivered seven of the king's descendants (Saul and three of his sons already were dead) to the Gibeonites to be executed and publicly impaled. Although the Gibeonites' demand that Saul's descendants be executed was in clear violation of the Torah law, "Parents may not be put to death for the crimes of their children, nor children for the crimes of their parents" (Deuteronomy 24:16), the Talmud justified David's acquiescence to the demand on the grounds that Saul's violation of the ancient treaty had caused God's name to be desecrated (Babylonian Talmud, *Yevamot* 79a). This view seems confirmed by the fact that only after Saul's descendants are executed do the rains resume, thus ending the famine (II Samuel 21:14).

61. Joshua and the Conquest of Canaan

THE BOOK OF JOSHUA

Joshua serves an extended apprenticeship to Moses (Exodus 24:13) before God singles him out to be his successor (Numbers 27:18).

He is anointed Israel's leader in time to bring the Israelites into the promised land, where he leads them in battle and conquers much of Canaan. Joshua is assigned to carry out God's disturbing command to wipe out those Canaanite nations that refuse to leave Israel: "You shall utterly destroy them [the Canaanites] . . . as the Lord your God commanded you, lest they lead you into doing all the abhorrent things that they have done for their gods and you stand guilty before the Lord your God" (Deuteronomy 20:17–18).

Not surprisingly, the Book of Joshua, filled as it is with bloody, ruthless battles, does not make for particularly pleasant reading. Here is the description of the conquest of Jericho: "They [the Israelites] exterminated everything in the city with the sword: man and woman, young and old, ox and sheep and ass" (6:21). Shortly thereafter, when the Israelites capture Ai, we are told that they struck down some twelve thousand people in one day, "the entire population of Ai . . . so that no one escaped or got away" (8:25 and 22). For good measure, Joshua lets Ai's king survive until the battle's end, whereupon he has him hanged (8:29).

The bloody fighting continues. When Joshua conquers Hazor, he "put to the sword every person in it. Not a soul survived, and Hazor itself was burned down" (11:11). Such a fate befell Canaanite city after city until "Joshua conquered the whole country . . . [and] assigned it to Israel to share according to their tribal divisions. And the land had rest from war" (11:23).

Chapter 12 lists by name thirty-one local kings whom Joshua defeated and dispossessed. In his later years, Joshua is informed by

God that there is more land that Israel still needs to conquer (13:1–2).

What can one say about Joshua's military ethics, and God's troubling commands?

For one thing, this is how wars were fought in the ancient world. As a recent book notes: "Ancient documents from Mesopotamia to Egypt abound in joyous references to annihilating neighbors—frequently the very same peoples the Bible mentions. For example, in the Amarna letters, the Amorites were said to be troublesome foes of the house of Egypt's Pharaoh and deserved annihilation. . . . Officials writing these letters [to Pharaoh] promised to bind all the Amorites: 'a chain of bronze exceedingly heavy shall shackle their feet . . . and [we shall] not leave one among them.' "

Most important, the reason that Joshua's and the Israelites' conduct so disturbs us is because the Bible itself has sensitized us to high standards of respect for human life, especially in its commands to love our neighbor and to love the stranger. As the late Princeton philosopher Walter Kaufmann wrote, "The reproach of callousness and insufficient social conscience can hardly be raised. Our social conscience comes largely from the religion of Moses." But, Kaufmann noted, "to find the spirit of the religion of the Old Testament in *Joshua* is like finding the distinctive genius of America in the men who slaughtered the Indians."

As I have written elsewhere, the Bible's disturbing ethics of warfare "can perhaps be best explained in terms of monotheism's struggle to survive. Monotheism started out as a minority movement with a different theology and ethical system than the rest of the world. It expanded and developed because it had one small corner in the world where it could grow unmolested. Had the Hebrews continued to reside amidst the pagan and child-sacrificing Canaanite culture, monotheism itself almost certainly would have died. That most likely explains the troubling ethics of warfare preached in the Bible."

The late Bible scholar Yehezkel Kaufmann similarly argues that only because of the wars Israel fought against Canaanite nations did "Israel . . . not assimilate into the indigenous population. . . . It provided Israel's new religious idea with an environment in which to grow free of the influence of a popular pagan culture."

Finally, despite the Bible's claim of Joshua's total victory over the Canaanites, it seems that many Canaanite nations and people survived (see, for example, Judges 1:27–33). Thus, the Book of Judges, which follows the Book of Joshua, records that the Israelites often adopted the religious practices of their Canaanite neighbors (2:11–12).

Sources: The comment about the cruel modes of ancient warfare is found in Eunice Riedel, Thomas Tracy, and Barbara Moskowitz, *The Book of the Bible,* page 40. Walter Kaufmann, *The Faith of a Heretic,* pages 260–261, and page 193. See also my *Jewish Literacy,* pages 69–70. The citation from Yehezkel Kaufmann comes from his *The Religion of Israel,* page 254.

VII. JUDGES

62. Deborah: Judge, Leader, and Prophet

JUDGES, CHAPTERS 4–5

In large measure, the fame of the Bible's most prominent women often derives from the even greater renown of the men to whom they are related. Sarah is far better known as Abraham's wife than is Abraham as Sarah's husband. The same applies to Rebecca (married to Isaac), to Rachel and Leah (wives to Jacob) and to Miriam (Moses' sister).

Deborah stands apart from this tradition. About her husband, Lapidot, all we know is his name, and even this fact is uncertain. Bible scholar Donna Nolan Fewell points out that *aishet lapidot*, which translates as "the wife of Lapidot" can also be rendered as "a woman of fire." Indeed, Deborah was.

The Bible never tells us how Deborah achieved her role as prophetess, judge, and leader of the Israelite people (circa 1100 B.C.E.), a particularly remarkable achievement given the patriarchal nature of ancient Israelite society. When we meet Deborah, she is already functioning as a judge, adjudicating disputes under a palm tree in the hill country of Ephraim (the tree becomes known as the "Palm of Deborah"; 4:5).

However, it quickly becomes apparent that she is far more than a local magistrate. When Deborah summons Barak, the foremost Israelite soldier of the age, he comes immediately. Deborah instructs Barak to assemble ten thousand troops and march on Mount Tabor, where he will confront and destroy Sisera, a renowned Canaanite general, and his army.

Barak must have been astounded by the audacity of Deborah's plan. The Israelites had suffered under the domination of Sisera's master, the Canaanite king Jabin, for some twenty years. Jabin's power was secured by a large army possessing nine hundred iron chariots, while the Israelites had none.

Nonetheless, so great is Deborah's prestige that Barak does not dispute her. He accepts her mandate with one condition: "If you will go with me, I will go; if not, I will not go" (4:8).

Deborah agrees to accompany Barak, but can't resist a jab at the sexism of the Israelite society: "Very well, I will go with you. However, there will be no glory for you in the course you are taking, for then the Lord will deliver Sisera into the hands of a woman" (4:9).

Deborah accompanies Barak as he musters the required troops, then goes with the Israelite forces as they march to Mount Tabor.

When Sisera hears that Barak and thousands of troops are approaching, he takes his army and its nine hundred chariots to confront them.

Deborah assures Barak that the Israelites have nothing to fear: "This is the day on which the Lord will deliver Sisera into your hands: the Lord is marching before you" (4:14).

Barak and his troops charge down the mountain while God unleashes a sudden torrential storm that causes Sisera's chariots to become bogged down in the mud. This unanticipated development throws the whole Canaanite army into panic, particularly the chariot drivers. The fleeing Canaanite troops are killed by the suddenly energized Israelite soldiers. In the ensuing chaos, Sisera abandons his chariot and flees.

He eventually makes it to the tent of Jael (pronounced Yah-el), a female Kenite, someone from a tribe that traces its descent to Moses' father-in-law (4:11). Jael's husband, Heber, is friendly with King Jabin; under the guise of friendship, Jael invites Sisera to seek refuge in her tent, where she feeds milk to the hungry and exhausted general. He, in turn, asks her to tell any inquiring Israelite troops that her tent is empty.

Yael waits until Sisera falls into a deep sleep, then takes a mallet and a tent pin and drives the pin through his skull.

Soon, Barak appears, in pursuit of Sisera, and Jael invites him inside: "Come, I will show you the man you are looking for" (4:22).

The victory at Mount Tabor presages the fall of King Jabin's domination over Israel. To commemorate this remarkable triumph, Deborah and Barak recite a poem, universally acknowledged as one of Hebrew literature's oldest works. One verse seems to reflect a surprising lack of modesty on the great judge's part: She speaks of how

Israel's fortunes had declined "until I, Deborah, arose; I arose, a mother in Israel" (5:7).*

As Deborah had warned Barak, much of the victory's glory attaches to Jael, spoken of in the poem as the "most blessed of women" (5:24).

The only unimpressive women referred to in the Deborah story are Sisera's mother and her attendants. At first, the poem depicts this mother sympathetically, peering through a window and wondering why her son and his troops are so late in returning from the battle. When a servant assures her that there is no reason for her to worry, that her son and his troops are undoubtedly dividing up the spoil, including "a womb, two wombs, per head, per hero" (5:30), Sisera's mother allows herself to be reassured by this image. How much sympathy can one have for a woman who joyfully imagines her son and his troops raping other women's daughters (how ironic, too, that Sisera meets his death at the hands of a woman).

The poem ends with a vengeful cry: "So may all your enemies perish, O Lord" (5:31).

As a prophet, judge, and leader, Deborah can be regarded as sort of a biblical Joan of Arc, although unlike the French heroine (who lived more than two millennia later and was burned at the stake), Deborah's life seems to have continued untroubled. The coda to her and Barak's poem informs us that "the land was tranquil for forty years."

Source: Danna Nolan Fewell, "Joshua," *The Women's Bible Commentary*, page 69.

---

*The Jewish Publication Society Bible translates the verse as "Until *you* arose, O Deborah . . . ," but the Hebrew, *ad she-kamti*, is stated in the first person singular and means, "Until *I* arose . . ." A talmudic text later criticized Deborah for this unseemly boastfulness (Babylonian Talmud, *Pesachim* 66b).

63. Gideon: The Man Who Would Not Be King

JUDGES, CHAPTERS 6–8

During their early years in Canaan, the Israelites often find themselves dominated and exploited by their neighbors. At some point during the twelfth century B.C.E., Midianite gangs start to swoop down on Israelite farms to destroy houses and steal produce and cattle. The marauders ride on camels, which had been domesticated only a short time earlier, and the Israelites, who have not yet domesticated camels, feel overwhelmed and terrified.

God sends an angel to Gideon, a member of the northern tribe of Manasseh. The young man is threshing wheat in the cramped space of a winepress so as to hide the grain from the Midianite troops. When the angel greets him in the name of God, Gideon responds in a manner that sounds somewhat like an anguished post-Holocaust Jew: "If God is with us, why has all this happened to us? Where are all His wonderful deeds about which our fathers have told us, declaring, 'Did not God take us out of Egypt'? But now, God has abandoned us, and delivered us into the hand of Midian" (6:13).

In the next verse, God speaks directly to him. He expresses no annoyance at the young man's challenging words, but also offers no response to Gideon's provocative questions. Instead, God commands Gideon to save Israel from Midian and promises to be with him.

Gideon brings the angel an offering, which includes a goat and some unleavened bread, and asks for a sign. The angel instructs Gideon to place the food on a stone, then sends a fire from the stone to consume it. Immediately afterward the angel disappears.

That night God speaks to Gideon again, instructing him to destroy the idolatrous altar of Baal in his father's house and to chop down the "sacred" pole (asherah) beside it. The altar must have been quite large, for Gideon takes with him ten of his servants to destroy it. They do so in the dark of night; Baal worship apparently is so popular that Gideon fears carrying out his attack in daylight.

Gideon's initiating his career with the destruction of his father's idols brings to mind one of the most famous *midrashim* (rabbinic tales and commentaries on the Torah) told about Abraham, whose father Terah owns an idol store. On one occasion, he asks his son to manage the store for a day. Abraham, who even as a young man disbelieves in idols, takes advantage of his father's absence to smash every idol but one with an ax, then places it in the hands of the surviving, and largest, idol. In response to his father's outraged query as to what has caused such destruction, Abraham responds that the large idol has destroyed all his smaller peers. Terah is not fooled: "Stop lying!" he yells at Abraham. "You know as well as I that these idols can't walk or do anything."

"If they can't save themselves, then how can you worship them?" Abraham responds. According to the rabbinic tale, Terah is not assuaged, and hands his son over to the local king to be burned as a heretic.

Gideon's father, Joash, however, demonstrates considerably greater familial loyalty. When the townspeople learn that it was Gideon who destroyed the altar, they demand that Joash hand him over to be executed. Although he is an idol worshiper like Terah, Joash does not want his son to die. He answers the would-be executioners with a logic reminiscent of Abraham's rejoinder to his father, "Do you have to fight for Baal or save him? . . . If he is a god, let him fight for himself." Gideon is saved, and from that day forward he becomes known as Jerubaal, Hebrew for "let Baal fight against him."

Shortly thereafter, God's spirit descends upon Gideon and he summons troops from three other tribes to fight Midian. Before the battle, Gideon, still unsure of God's commitment, asks for a sign. He places a woolen fleece on the threshing floor and asks that dew fall only on it while the surrounding earth remain dry. The next morning, he wrings out a bowlful of water from the sopping fleece, but the earth surrounding it remains unaffected. Still uncertain, Gideon now asks God to reverse the miracle, to make the earth wet while leaving the fleece dry. When God also performs this miracle, Gideon sets out to lead the Israelites in battle.

These wonders soon turn out to be the least of God's miracles. Although the Midianites have amassed 135,000 troops and Gideon only 32,000, the Lord tells him that he is overstaffed. If Israel routs the Midianites, they will not attribute it to God's intervention but, rather, will claim that "My own power has saved me."

God instructs Gideon to tell the 32,000 troops that "whoever is fearful and trembling, let him return home" (Deuteronomy 20:8 explicitly exempts "the fearful and disheartened," lest their fear cause their fellow soldiers' "hearts to melt"). Immediately, 22,000 troops leave.

The 13-to-1 advantage now enjoyed by Midian still strikes the Lord as insufficient; He wishes the Israelites to triumph by means that are so clearly miraculous that no natural explanation will suffice. He now instructs Gideon to lead his ten thousand thirsty troops down to the water. There, he is to separate those who lap water with their hands and then bring it to their mouths from those who kneel to drink.

The 300 troops who lap the water are retained for Gideon's army, while the remaining 9,700 are sent home. (Presumably, the "lappers," who keep their eyes focused in front even while drinking, are more trustworthy soldiers than those who get down on their knees and don't keep watch for the enemy.)

The Israelites now are outnumbered 450 to 1.

Gideon divides the remaining troops into three camps of one hundred soldiers each. He gives each soldier a *shofar* (literally a "ram's horn"), and a pottery jar into which a lit torch is placed; these are the only weapons the soldiers are to carry.

The Israelites surround the Midianites on three sides. At a pre-arranged signal during the middle of the night, the three hundred men blow their horns and smash their jars, revealing blazing torches all around the Midianite camp. The Midianite troops panic; in their terror, they strike out against each other, then flee. Tens of thousands of other Israelite troops now join Gideon in pursuing them; Gideon also invites Ephraim, a tribe he had not previously contacted, to join the battle.

After capturing and executing two Midianite princes, the Ephraim-ites come to Gideon carrying the dead men's heads, and utter an angry rebuke: " 'What have you done to us, not to call us when you went to fight against the Midianites?' "

Gideon proves to be as much a diplomat as a warrior: "What have I been able to do in comparison with you?" he asks the soldiers of Ephraim, then proceeds to offer lavish praise for their military prowess. His cajoling response immediately causes their anger to subside.*

Gideon pursues the battle until he fully vanquishes his Midianite foes. The Israelites are so grateful that they offer Gideon and his

---

*Several generations later, the far less diplomatic Jephtah responds to a similar, though more harshly worded, complaint from the men of Ephraim by slaughtering 42,000 members of that tribe (see Judges 12:1–6).

descendants the kingship. "Rule over us, you and your son and your grandson, for you have saved us from Midian" (8:22).

"I will not rule over you," Gideon responds, "and my son will not rule over you; the Lord will rule over you."

Had Gideon's story ended here, he would have entered biblical history as an unblemished hero, a man who fought at God's behest and wished no reward or glory for himself.

Unfortunately, this is not the end of the story. In lieu of kingship, Gideon requests that the people award him some of the gold booty captured in the war. He fashions the gold into an *ephod;* in the Torah, the *ephod* is the garment worn by the High Priest (Exodus 28:4–14; 39:2–7), but in Gideon's case it seems to refer to some sort of pagan image used for divination. Gideon installs it in his hometown, and although the text does not tell us precisely what outrage is performed with the *ephod,* we are informed that "all Israel prostituted themselves to it there, and it became a snare to Gideon and his family" (8:27).

Thus, the man who launched his career by destroying an altar of Baal concludes it by helping lead Israel back into idolatry.

Furthermore, despite having refused the offer of kingship, Gideon starts living like a monarch. While the Bible does not tell us precisely how many wives he took, the number must have been considerable, for they give birth to seventy sons. But even this is not sufficient for Gideon, who takes a concubine (apparently a Canaanite woman) from Shechem. He calls the son she bears him Abimelech, a Hebrew name meaning "My father is king." We have reason to believe, therefore, that the aging Gideon subsequently might have regretted his refusal to be king.

Although Gideon saves his people from the Midianites and brings them forty years of peace in the process, his moral impact proves negligible. As soon as he dies, the Israelites lapse back into worship of Baal.

Despite his later corruption, Gideon does, however, bequeath future generations that one marvelous verse which epitomizes a moral leader who is a true servant of God: "I will not rule over you, and my son will not rule over you; the Lord will rule over you."*

Sources and further readings: The *midrash* about Terah's idol shop can be found in *Tanna d'Bei Eliyahu,* pages 27–28, and *Genesis Rabbah* 38:13.

*Dr. Jeremiah Unterman has suggested to me that Gideon's influence may have been sufficiently powerful to prevent the rise of kingship in Israel until Saul.

An English-language version, very similar but far more detailed than the one recounted here, is found in Hayim Nahman Bialik and Yehoshua Hana Ravnitzky, *The Book of Legends*, pages 32–33.

64. Jotham: Author of the Bible's First Parable

JUDGES, CHAPTER 9

People who show no gratitude to God, the Bible believes, will likewise act as ingrates to their fellowmen. Thus, in the aftermath of Gideon's death, "the Israelites did not remember the Lord their God, who had saved them from all the enemies who surrounded them, nor did they remain loyal to the house of Jerubaal [Gideon] in return for all the good that he had done to Israel" (8:34–35).

Shortly after Gideon's death, Abimelech, Gideon's son by a concubine, seduces the citizens of his hometown, Shechem, into assisting him in a plot to murder Gideon's seventy other sons. The people of Shechem give Abimelech money to hire assassins, who murder all but one of Gideon's sons. Jotham, the lone survivor, saves himself by hiding.

The lords of Shechem and a neighboring city anoint Abimelech king (the Bible, however, regards Saul, who lives some hundred years later, as the first monarch, since he and his successor, David, are appointed by God).

When Jotham hears of Abimelech's investiture, he climbs on a ledge at the top of Mount Gerizim, overlooking Shechem, and delivers a speech to the city's citizens:

> The trees once went out to anoint a king over themselves. So they said to the olive tree, "Reign over us."
>
> The olive tree answered them, "Shall I stop producing my rich oil, through which God and men are honored, to go hold sway over the trees?"
>
> Then the trees said to the fig tree, "You come and reign over us."
>
> But the fig tree answered them, "Shall I stop producing my

sweetness, and my delicious fruit, to go hold sway over the trees?"

Then the trees said to the vine, "You come and reign over us."

But the vine said to them, "Shall I stop producing my wine, which causes God and men to rejoice, to go hold sway over the trees?"

So all the trees said to the bramble [a worthless tree, good only for catching fire and burning down other trees along with itself], "You come and reign over us."

And the bramble said to the trees, "If in good faith you are anointing me king over you, then come and take refuge in my shade [the bramble, of course, offers no shade]. But if not, let fire come out of the bramble, and devour the cedars of Lebanon" (9:8–15).

Jotham's attack on the notion of kingship is hardly subtle; only the most nonproductive—in fact, the most destructive—people want to rule over others. Jotham goes on to denounce the people of Shechem for helping to murder his sixty-nine brothers, then appointing their murderer as king. He curses Shechem and Abimelech, expressing the wish that a fire should issue from Abimelech and burn them, and that a fire should come from them and consume him.

As soon as he finishes, Jotham flees for his life; the biblical text never again mentions him. His parable, along with a later speech by the prophet Samuel (I Samuel 8:10–17), constitute the strongest antimonarchical statements in the Bible. Thousands of years later, Jotham's parable was cited by such students of the Bible as Oliver Cromwell and John Milton, who opposed the notion of "the divine right of kings."

Afterword: Jotham's curse is fulfilled. After three years of Abimelech's rule, the people of Shechem turn against him. He responds by razing the city, sowing it with salt, and murdering most of its residents. The surviving inhabitants flee to a nearby temple.

In an act eerily reminiscent of Jotham's parable, Abimelech takes an ax, cuts down a bundle of brushwood, and instructs his troops to do the same. He then sets the temple on fire, killing one thousand men and women.

A short time later, Abimelech leads his troops to put down a rebellion in the city of Thebez. The inhabitants flee to the city's tower. As Abimelech nears the tower to burn it down, a woman inside drops a millstone on his head, which crushes his skull. The near-dead Abimelech calls out to his armsbearer, "Draw your dagger and finish me off, so that people will not say of me, 'A woman killed him' " (9:54). Ironically, Abimelech's inglorious death is the aspect of his life that was most remembered (see II Samuel 11:21).

So dies the least worthy of Gideon's seventy-one sons.

65. Jephtah's Murderous Sacrifice

JUDGES, CHAPTERS 11–12:1–7

If there is one thing worse than being a fool, it might be being the child of one. This is the tragedy suffered by Jephtah's unnamed daughter.

To be sure, Jephtah's life is not an easy one. He is born to a prostitute, and a man named Gilead, in the region of the same name (within the tribe of Manasseh). As he grows up, his father's other children mock Jephtah's illegitimate status and drive him away, not wanting to share their father's estate with him.

Jephtah soon becomes leader of a gang—in the Bible's language, he gathers around himself "worthless men"—and apparently earns his living as a marauder. He also develops a reputation as a formidable fighter, for when the Ammonites make war against Israel, the elders of Gilead appeal to him to lead them in battle.

"But you hated me and drove me from my father's house," Jephtah responds with no small measure of bitterness. "Why are you coming to me now that you're in trouble?" (11:7).

The elders continue to plead with him; Jephtah finally consents to lead them in battle, on condition that he remain their permanent leader if he defeats the Ammonites. The elders agree.

After an unsuccessful diplomatic effort to make peace with Ammon, Jephtah leads an Israelite force into Ammonite territory. Just before the battle begins, he swears an oath to God: "If You deliver the children of Ammon into my hands, then whatever comes out of the doors of my house to meet me when I return safely from the Ammonites shall be God's, and I shall offer it as a burnt-offering" (11:30–31).

After leading the Israelites to victory, Jephtah returns home to be met by his daughter, his only child, who greets him with a celebratory dance. "Alas, daughter! You have brought me low; you have become my troubler," Jephtah responds, blaming the innocent girl for *his* mistake (11:35).

The young woman uncomplainingly accepts her fate. She requests only that Jephtah postpone sacrificing her for two months, while she goes into the forest with her friends; together, they bewail the fact that she will die childless. Her contempt for her father and his contemptible vow, although never openly expressed, seems apparent: The last thing she wants during the final weeks of her life is to be near the man whose foolishness has condemned her to death.

The most shocking aspect of this whole saga is what it reveals about the depraved level of Israelite morality at the time. One of the Torah's earliest teachings is that God abhors human sacrifice (Genesis, chapter 22), a point it repeatedly makes (Leviticus 18:21, 20:1–5; Deuteronomy 12:31, 18:10). Yet Jephtah and his fellow Israelites seem to think that an immoral vow takes precedence over innocent blood. Generations after Jephtah, King Saul also makes a murderous vow: If any soldier eats food on the day of a certain battle, he will be executed. His son Jonathan does not hear of his father's injunction and eats some honey. Saul wants to kill him, but the soldiers under his command refuse to let him do so (I Samuel 14:24–45). That Jephtah's fellow citizens allow him to sacrifice his daughter reflects almost as poorly on them as on him. To claim to believe in the God of the Torah, while simultaneously practicing human sacrifice, is absurd, akin to starting an organization composed of "Meat Eaters for Vegetarianism" (regarding Abraham's willingness to sacrifice Isaac, see entry 16).

A man capable of such cruelty toward his own child turns out to be equally cruel to the children of others. A fight erupts between Jephtah's supporters and the tribe of Ephraim (the Ephraimites are furious that Jephtah has not let them participate in the victory over Ammon, while he claims that he had asked for their help and they had refused). The text does not indicate who is in the right, but when a somewhat similar conflict arose between Gideon and the tribe of Ephraim, Gideon found the words with which to pacify them (Judges 8:1–2). Apparently, Jephtah, a man who had been scorned in his early years (11:2), does not deal well with criticism.

Jephtah and his troops overwhelm the Ephraimites. Instead of letting them escape, he stations forces at the fords of the Jordan who ask each fleeing soldier if he is from Ephraim. The soldiers understand that the inquiry is not motivated by goodwill; many answer no. Thereupon, Jephtah's wily soldiers ask them to pronounce the word *shibboleth* ("ear of wheat"). The Ephraimites have trouble with the *sh* sound and say *siboleth*. By the end of that day, 43,000 of their men have been murdered.

It is perhaps fitting that Jephtah, though a valiant fighter, seems to have died unmourned. The Bible informs us that he was buried somewhere in the towns of Gilead; no one seems terribly interested in his grave's precise location. How many people would wish to visit the grave of a man who had killed his own child?

Reflections: An alternative explanation of Jephtah's paternity: Generally, it is hard to know the identity of the father of a child born to a prostitute. While the Bible informs us that Jephtah's father was Gilead, that is also the name of a town and of a region. Thus, there might have been a certain ironic sensibility in so naming the father, comparable to saying, "And the father's name was New York"; in other words, any male in Gilead might have been Jephtah's father. Many of Gilead's citizens therefore might have mocked him, not just members of one family. If this was the case it would account for his bitter response when the elders of Gilead come to see him (see David Gunn and Danna Nolan Fewell, *Narrative in the Hebrew Bible*, page 114).

On Jephtah's vow: Jephtah and his fellow Israelites should have realized that a vow to violate Torah law is invalid and should not be fulfilled. It would be as if a person, in a moment of madness, declared: "I swear I'm going to kill you," repented of his words, but then declared that he was nonetheless obligated to carry them out. An illegitimate act is illegitimate; that one swore to carry it out is irrelevant.

66. Samson and Delilah

JUDGES, CHAPTERS 13–16

The name Samson has entered the English language as a synonym for someone of superhuman strength: With his bare hands, Samson kills a lion; with the jawbone of a donkey, he smites a thousand

Philistine soldiers; and across his shoulders he carries the mammoth gates that had marked the entrance to the city of Gaza.

While physical might is Samson's only impressive feature, the list of his less desirable traits and actions is long. Brutally honest about its heroes' foibles, the Bible is relentless in relating Samson's flaws. Most significantly, he makes no effort to control his massive sexual appetite, which seems confined to non-Israelite women. He likewise exerts no control over his fierce temper; when enraged, Samson displays no compunctions about attacking innocent people.

Aside from the Patriarch Isaac, Samson is the only biblical character whose conception is foretold by an angel. Rabbi Adin Steinsaltz, the Israeli scholar and talmudist, notes that "even Moses, Samuel, David and other great figures were not announced in this way to their parents." The angel who appears before Samson's unnamed mother informs her that she will soon conceive a son. She and her husband are to raise the boy as a *nazir* (see entry 190), a lifestyle that imposes on its practitioners the following prohibitions: drinking wine or any product of the vine, cutting one's hair, and touching any dead body, even that of a close relative.

The angel assures Samson's mother that if these conditions are met, her son will initiate Israel's deliverance from her Philistine oppressors, who have been ruling over Israel for forty years.

Of Samson's early years we know nothing. When we meet him, he is a young man bewitched by a beautiful Philistine girl from the nearby city of Timnat. He tells his parents to arrange a marriage with her.

Strained as political relations are between the Philistines and their Israelite subjects, intermarriage between the two peoples apparently is common. However, Samson's parents are upset that he does not choose a wife from among his own people. Under pressure from their headstrong son, however, they consent to the marriage.

While Samson is en route to his Philistine fiancée, a young lion roars at him. The "spirit of God" descends on the young man, and he rips the lion apart. Samson tells no one about the encounter, and hides the animal's carcass. Days later, returning home, he checks on the lion's body and finds that a swarm of bees—along with a large quantity of honey—is residing in the carcass. Samson takes some honey and eats it.

A short time later, during the marriage celebration, Samson makes a proposition to thirty Philistine guests: "I will ask you a riddle. If you can answer it within the seven days of the feast . . . then I will give you thirty sheets and thirty changes of garments. But if you cannot answer it, then you shall give me thirty sheets and thirty changes of garments." The guests accept the challenge, and he poses his riddle: "Out of the eater came food, and out of the strong came sweetness" (14:12–14).

After seventy-two frustrating hours, the Philistines realize that they will never solve the riddle. Several of the men approach Samson's bride, warning her that if she does not reveal the solution, they will burn down her and her father's house.

Had the young bride told Samson about the threat, much innocent blood would likely have been saved. Instead, she approaches her new husband with a subterfuge: "You really hate me and you don't love me! You proposed a riddle to my people, but you haven't told me the answer" (14:16).

Samson tries to assuage his wife's hurt, assuring her that he has told no one, including his parents, the solution to his puzzle.

Four days of nonstop crying, however, wear down his resistance. Finally, Samson confides to her the answer, only to have the words repeated just a few hours later by the Philistine wedding guests: "What is sweeter than honey? And what is stronger than a lion?"

"Had you not plowed with my heifer," the enraged, and suddenly poetic, Samson responds, "you would not have solved my riddle" (14:18).

This seemingly minor episode sets in inexorable motion Samson's ever-escalating life of violence. He pays off his debt by murdering thirty Philistine men, stripping off their garments and giving them to the men who "solved" his riddle.

Sometime later, Samson decides to rejoin his wife (the Bible does not explain why the Philistine authorities do not try to arrest him for the murders). But when he arrives at her house, he learns that his father-in-law, presuming that Samson has deserted her, has married her off to another.

In fury—not at his father-in-law, but at the Philistine guests who have provoked this situation—Samson decides to avenge himself on all Philistines. He catches three hundred foxes, ties two at a time together by their tails, places a lit torch between each pair, and sets the foxes loose in the middle of Philistine grainfields and orchards. A large harvest is destroyed.

When the Philistines learn who is responsible, they retaliate by burning Samson's father-in-law and former wife, the very fate the wife was hoping to avoid when she betrayed Samson's secret. (One of the motifs running through the Samson story is how innocent people are made to suffer for others' misdeeds.) The Philistines then pursue Samson.

His fellow Israelites are petrified when Philistine troops march into Judah to arrest Samson, and they make no effort to defend him. Instead, they march to the cave where he is hiding and tell him, "We have come to take you prisoner, and hand you over to the Philistines" (15:12).

Samson has no desire to battle his own people. He agrees to surrender on condition that his fellow Israelites not hurt him. They happily consent, tie Samson up with strong cords, and hand him over to the Philistines.

Seeing their great adversary bound, the Philistine troops charge at him. But the spirit of God again descends on Samson. He rips the ropes off his hands, picks up the fresh jawbone of a dead donkey, and fashions it into a weapon with which he kills a thousand Philistine soldiers.

As consumed as he is with hate for Philistine men is Samson overwhelmed with passion for Philistine women. We next find him in the Philistine city of Gaza, spending the night with a prostitute. When the Gazans learn who is visiting their town, they decide to burst into the woman's house at dawn;* presumably, after a long night of lovemaking, Samson will be exhausted.

However, he arises in the middle of the night, tears down the giant doors at the city's entrance, and carries them on his shoulders to a distant Israelite town.

Until now, Samson has proven himself untouchable. But then he falls in love with Delilah. The Bible never mentions her nationality, although given Samson's track record, she is almost certainly a Philistine.

Several Philistine chieftains approach Delilah with an offer: If she can "find out why he is so strong and how we can overcome him," they will pay her the large sum of 1,100 shekels each (a shekel is estimated to have been worth about 11.4 grams of silver).

Almost immediately, Delilah asks Samson the source of his strength. The strongman's initial instincts are self-protective, so he tells her a lie: "If I am tied up with seven moist cords which have not dried out, I will become weak like other men" (16:7).

The Philistine rulers bring Delilah the cords, then wait outside

---

*The Bible does not tell us if it is the prostitute who betrays him, although the two other Philistine women described in the story betray him.

Samson's door to ambush him. When he falls asleep, Delilah binds him with the ropes, then calls out, "The Philistines are upon you, Samson."

He immediately snaps off the cords; unfortunately, he never learns that Philistine troops are waiting outside and so continues to act lovingly toward Delilah.

Delilah asks him a second time the source of his strength; again, he makes up a fictitious story, and does so yet a third time.

Desperate for the reward, Delilah utilizes the same argument offered by his first wife: "How can you say you love me when you don't trust me?" (16:15).

Samson continues to refuse to reveal the secret of his strength, but she becomes unyielding. "She nagged him and pressed him every day with her remarks, until he wanted to die."

Finally, Samson confides the truth: "A razor has never touched my head, for I have been a Nazirite to God since I was in my mother's womb. If my hair were cut, my strength would leave me and I would become weak, like other men" (16:17).

Sensing that she has finally heard the truth, Delilah sends word to the Philistine rulers, "Come—this time he has confided in me."

The Philistines promptly arrive, bearing the silver shekels.

Delilah waits until Samson falls asleep with his head resting on her knees, then summons a man to cut off seven locks of hair on his head. "The Philistines are upon you," she cries out when the haircutter finishes. As he has done three times before, Samson jumps up, but this time his strength has deserted him.

The Philistines seize him and gouge out his eyes. They bind him in bronze fetters, then set him to work grinding grain in a prison in Gaza, the very city whose gate Samson had once carried on his shoulders.

Shortly thereafter, the Philistines organize a large celebration in honor of their god Dagon. They bring Samson from prison and parade him in front of the jeering crowd. When they finish displaying him, they leave him standing between two pillars.

During his torturous months in the Philistine prison, Samson's hair has grown, a phenomenon his captors have foolishly ignored. He wraps his arms around the pillars and prays, "O Lord God, please remember me and give me strength, just this once, God, so I will be able to take revenge on the Philistines if only for one of my two eyes" (16:28).

"Let me die with the Philistines," he calls out, pulling down the temple's pillars. The entire structure collapses on the three thousand worshipers of Dagon: "The slain he killed in his death outnumbered those he had killed during his lifetime."

Was the newly wealthy Delilah at the stadium? Was she one of those who were mocking Samson, and who died with him? The Bible doesn't say. With her betrayal of Samson, she is never again mentioned, although her name too has entered the vocabulary, as a codeword for a seductive and traitorous woman.

Samson, though entrusted by God with strength, is not endowed with wisdom. The last and most striking of Israel's fifteen judges, he represents the deterioration of an institution that had once numbered among its holders the heroic, and very wise, prophetess Deborah.

Reflections. The Samson story as a biblical attack on intermarriage: Bible scholar James Crenshaw argues that the Samson saga should be understood as an attack against the male Israelites' attraction to foreign women (generations after Samson, King Solomon married many foreign women, and they alienated him from devotion to God; see I Kings 11:3). Thus, the Bible juxtaposes Samson's mother, an ideal wife and mother, with three foreign women; the Philistine wife for whom Samson's attachment is apparently based on physical attraction alone, the harlot to whom he goes for sexual relief, and Delilah, a woman who epitomizes the dangers of unreciprocated love: "Samson's inability to emerge unscathed from such liaisons stood as a warning for lesser beings. The message could scarcely be missed; if the mighty Samson could not manage relationships with foreign women, how could ordinary Israelites succeed in such ventures?"

Sources and further readings: Adin Steinsaltz, *Biblical Images,* pages 123–133; Chaim Herzog, *Heroes of Israel,* pages 20–29; David Noel Freedman, editor, *Anchor Bible Dictionary,* volume 5, pages 950–954; the entry is by James Crenshaw.

67. "Each Man Did What Was Right in His Eyes": When Anarchy Prevailed in Israel

JUDGES, CHAPTERS 19–21

Nothing more powerfully conveys the Bible's abhorrence of anarchy than the episodes described in the last three chapters of Judges. The book's final verse—"In those days there was no king in Israel; everyone did as he pleased"—underscores the terrors that ensue when brute strength alone rules a society.

The biblical text never names the man and woman who trigger the bloody war that erupts between the tribes of Israel and the small tribe of Benjamin. Yet it devotes an inordinate amount of attention to this rather unimpressive couple. Identified only as a Levite, the man takes a concubine of the tribe of Judah. She has an affair, and eventually leaves the man and returns to her father's house in Bethlehem. The Levite waits four months, then visits her, hoping to win her back. The girl's father (the Bible speaks of him as the Levite's "father-in-law," although Judges 19:2 refers to the woman as a concubine) shows great affection for the man; the Levites are a prestigious tribe (see entry 44), and he is probably proud to have his daughter involved with a man of high social standing. Thus, it is quickly agreed that the woman will return home with the Levite.

The couple journey home accompanied by a servant and two laden donkeys. By evening, they find themselves in Jerusalem, then a Jebusite city known as Jebus. Feeling insecure in this non-Israelite city, the couple trek three miles north, to the Benjaminite city of Gibeah, where they head for the town square. However, Gibeah proves to be inhospitable; no one offers them lodging. At last, an old man—the Bible emphasizes that he is not a native of the city—invites them to his house.

What now ensues is a replay of the story of Sodom (see entry 13), only this time the villains are Hebrews. Surrounding the house, the townspeople call out to the old man: "Bring out the man who came to your house, that we may know him" (19:22). The modern reader should realize that "to know" in the Bible can also mean "to have sexual relations with." That this was definitely the Gibeans' intention is made clear by the following verse, in which the old man pleads with the townspeople not to commit such an abomination and outrage.

Unfortunately, the man's heroic plea is hardly evidence of unimpeachable moral character. "Look," he tells the people, "here are my virgin daughter and the man's concubine. I will bring them out; rape them, do to them as you please, but don't commit this abomination to this man!" (A similarly vile lack of paternal feeling was expressed by Lot; see Genesis 19:8.)

When the people ignore the old man's plea, the Levite takes decisive action: He pushes his concubine out the door.*

The people of Gibeah rape and otherwise torment the woman until dawn, then they release her. She staggers back to her "lover's" dwelling and collapses at the entrance.

The next verse begins, "Her master rose in the morning . . ." (19:27). This stunning detail reveals the depth of the Levite's evil. The woman he had shoved out the door was being raped, and how did he spend the night? Sleeping.

After dressing, the Levite opens the door and sees his concubine lying in front of the house. "Get up, let's go," he says to her, but there is no answer. He hoists the woman's lifeless body onto a donkey and proceeds home. Once there, he takes out a knife, cuts her into twelve pieces (Bible commentator Yaakov Elman points out that "even in death he refused her dignity"), one of which he sends to each tribe. When the other Israelites look at the severed limbs, and hear what happened, they declare this to be the most disgusting thing to have occurred among them during their entire history.

Within days a huge army is assembled; chapter 20, verse 2, speaks of a massing of 400,000 swordbearing soldiers. The Levite is summoned, and he reports what happened to his concubine, conveniently omitting the detail of his pushing her out the door.

The other tribes confront the Benjaminites with a demand: Turn over the guilty men of Gibeah to be executed. They refuse.

Twenty-six thousand men of Benjamin now gather to do battle. Among them are some seven hundred sharpshooters, men who can

---

*Is it any wonder that the woman had earlier left this man? Although the Bible doesn't tell us what possessed her to return home with him, we can imagine that when he arrived at her father's house, he expressed regret over former instances of bad behavior and promised that he would behave better in the future; like many abused women, she probably believed him.

throw stones with a sling with such accuracy that they can hit a hair.

At first, the Benjaminites prevail against the large force arrayed against them. On the first day of battle, some 22,000 soldiers from the other tribes are killed, the next day another 18,000 (the text doesn't inform us how many casualties the Benjaminites suffer but implies that they are very few). The Israelites are very discouraged until the High Priest, Pinchas, tells them that on the following day they will prevail.

Prevail they do. By the time the day ends, 25,100 of the 25,700 Benjaminite troops are dead. Their anger deepened by the losses sustained on the first two days of battle, the Israelite forces enter Gibeah, where they kill everyone they find and set the town on fire. (The 1922–1923 archaeological excavation at Tel el-Ful uncovered the remains of a village in the area of Gibeah that was completely destroyed by fire.) The troops then march through the rest of the small tribe of Benjamin, killing people and animals, then torching the cities.

The Bible now mentions a detail that was omitted earlier. When the original 400,000 troops were mustered, the people had taken a collective oath, "None of us will give his daughter in marriage to a Benjaminite" (21:1).

Now that the tribe of Benjamin has been almost fully destroyed— it would seem that only six hundred males are alive at the war's end—the rest of Israel suddenly feels regret: "God, Lord of Israel, why did this happen in Israel, that a tribe should be missing from Israel? . . . What can we do to provide wives for the survivors? For we have sworn by God not to give them our daughters in marriage!" (21:7).

For almost the first time in this terrible story, some people are actually concerned with acting decently. But the solution on which they decide shows the Israelites to be as morally obtuse as the old man who proposed having his own daughter raped in lieu of the Levite. The tribes decide to murder all the inhabitants of the city of Yavesh-Gilead, except for the virgins. The rationale? Yavesh-Gilead had contributed no troops to the battle against Benjamin; the rest of Israel earlier had sworn that all who did not join in the battle would be killed. So, with the exception of the four hundred virgins, everyone else in the city is murdered. The virgins, who had just had their parents and siblings murdered, are taken away to be married off to the surviving men of Benjamin.

Can this story become even more disgusting? Yes.

Four hundred women are not enough to supply every surviving Benjaminite with a wife. Truly concerned now with guaranteeing Benjamin's survival, the other tribes are in a quandary, since their oath not to give their daughters in marriage to a Benjaminite is still binding. They therefore advise the men of Benjamin on how to procure wives. They are to attend the annual festival for God in the city of Shilo. When the girls of Shilo come out to dance, each man should seize one maiden and carry her back to Benjaminite territory. So the men of Benjamin kidnap the women, bring them home, and start to rebuild their devastated homeland.

Thus, this horrific story ends. Within a century or two of their departure from Egypt, the Israelites have become as debased as the Canaanites who had previously inhabited the land. The covenant that God established with Abraham, which was later reconfirmed with Moses and the Israelites at Mount Sinai, has been shattered beyond recognition.

Never has the Israelite religion so clearly been in danger of dying. Something radical, it is clear, must occur if this fate is to be avoided. And something radical does occur. God sends a prophet, a man named Samuel. It is he who is charged with ensuring that Abraham and Moses' vision not be extinguished.

Source and further reading: Yaakov Elman, *The Living Nach,* pages 164–175.

VIII. I AND II SAMUEL

68. Hannah: The Woman Who Knew How to Pray

I SAMUEL, CHAPTERS 1–2

Although Hannah's husband, Elkanah, loves her deeply, she is miserable because she is barren. Both husband and wife know that Hannah is the infertile partner because Elkanah's second wife, Peninah, has had several children.

Aware that Elkanah strongly prefers Hannah, Peninah taunts her mercilessly, claiming that it is God who has closed her womb. The sensitive Hannah doesn't respond to her rival's taunts; instead, she weeps and stops eating.

Elkanah, who seems unaware of the depth of hostility between his wives, tries to assuage Hannah's pain: "Why do you weep? Why don't you eat? Why do you feel bad? Am I not better to you than ten sons?" (1:8).

I had always viewed Elkanah as the model of a compassionate, loving husband until my wife, Dvorah, provided a different perspective. She noted that even though his words were motivated by love, Elkanah's insistence that Hannah had *no* reason to feel badly—"Am I not better to you than ten sons?"—was insensitive.

During the family's annual visit to the sanctuary in Shilo, twenty miles north of Jerusalem, Hannah enters the temple during a quiet hour. "Bitter at heart . . . and weeping," she makes a vow: "O Lord of Hosts, if You will look upon the grief of Your maidservant and remember me . . . and give [me] a son, I will devote him to God all his life."

Hannah clearly has strength of character, perhaps too much, for she makes this oath, which determines her child's future, without consulting either her husband or Eli, the High Priest of Shilo (or, for that matter, without waiting for her son to grow up so she can discuss her plans with him). Concluding her prayer, she adds the final proviso that throughout her son's life, "a razor will never touch his head" (in other words, he will live as a *nazir*, a holy man; see entry 190).

The High Priest, Eli, is apparently the only other person present during Hannah's prayer. Because she prays quietly, with only her lips moving, Eli assumes her to be intoxicated and asks her angrily, "How long will you go around drunk? Sober up!"

"No, my lord," Hannah responds. "I am a troubled woman, I have drunk neither wine nor strong drink, but I have poured out my soul to God. . . . I prayed the whole time out of my overwhelming grief and vexation" (alternatively, "anger"; 1:15–16).

Eli does not ask about the nature of her prayer; perhaps ashamed at his unfair attack, he is evidently too embarrassed to probe. Instead, he sends Hannah home with a blessing: "Go in peace, and may the God of Israel grant the request you made of Him."

Hannah leaves the sanctuary. Whether because of Eli's blessing, the catharsis of having expressed her deepest feelings to God, or because she somehow intuits that her prayer will be answered, she no longer feels downcast. Instead, she returns home with her husband, soon thereafter becomes pregnant, and ultimately gives birth to a son, Samuel.

She keeps Samuel at home until he is weaned (probably about the age of three), then brings him to the temple in Shilo. She takes the boy to Eli, reminding the High Priest that "I am the woman who stood with you here, praying to God," and confides to him the vow she made that day, to dedicate the boy to a life of divine service.

She then leaves Samuel at Shilo to be raised under Eli's guidance. Within a few years, he becomes not only one of the Bible's youngest prophets but also one of its greatest (Psalm 99:6 suggests that he is comparable in certain respects to Moses and Aaron).

Blessed a second time by Eli, Hannah subsequently gives birth to five more children, three boys and two girls.

She also composes a second prayer, thanking God for Samuel's birth (2:1–10), thus revealing that she is not one of those who pray to God only when in need. While the earlier depiction of Hannah suggests her passivity in the face of Peninah's verbal attacks, she now declares, "I can now speak before my enemies."

The transformation in Hannah's mood after Samuel's birth might seem extreme only to those who have never known a once-infertile woman who became pregnant or adopted a child.

Reflections: Hannah's influence on Jewish prayer: Hannah's impact on Jewish religious life has been permanent. The Talmud notes that many important rulings about how to pray are based on the Bible's description of Hannah's prayer. From Hannah we learn that the *Amidah*, the prayer that remains the centerpiece of the thrice-daily Jewish prayer service, should be recited quietly but with moving lips. Based on Eli's comment that Hannah should not pray if she is drunk, Jewish law rules that a drunk person is forbidden to recite the *Amidah* (Babylonian Talmud, *Berakhot* 31a).

A prayer the Rabbis imagine Hannah praying: The barren Hannah's sorrowful plight stimulated the Rabbis' compassion. Although the Bible reveals the content of Hannah's prayer to God, the Rabbis added additional, poignant verses that they imagined Hannah saying: "Master of the Universe, nothing which You created in woman is superfluous. For what are these breasts you placed over my heart if not to nurse with? Give me a son to nurse!" (Babylonian Talmud, *Berakhot* 31b).

The pains of polygamy: Happy as Hannah's fate is after Samuel's birth, no biblical story so effectively conveys the terrible conflict and pain that occur in households where husbands had multiple wives.

On Elkanah's effort to console Hannah: A final thought about Elkanah's attempt to console Hannah. My explanation of his comment as well-intentioned but ultimately insensitive is only one way of understanding Elkanah's words. Another way is offered by Bible scholar Uri Simon who sees Elkanah's words as a model of how a husband should comfort his wife: "Notice the words of comfort that he uses. He says to her: 'Why do you weep? Why don't you eat? Why do you feel bad? Am I not better to you than ten sons?' Notice what he does not say. He does not say that he forgives her for not bringing him children. He does not say that because childbearing is not her only function in life. Instead, he speaks of how these children could someday bring her happiness and he promises to bring her that happiness himself, in their place. He focuses on *her* needs, not on his. That is what it means to really love a person. It means to feel her pain and to understand her needs and to speak to what really hurts her, as Elkanah did."

69. The Fall of the House of Eli

I SAMUEL 2:12–4:22

Eli, the High Priest at Shilo, was a good man with bad sons, a frequent phenomenon in the Bible. For example, of King David's first four sons, one was a rapist and two led revolts against him (see entry 84). Indeed, Samuel, who brought Eli a prophecy—more like a curse—from God concerning his sons, also reared evil children (I Samuel 8:3).

Eli's two sons were supposed to assist him at the temple, but their work turns out to be anything but spiritual. They take for themselves meat that is supposed to be sacrificed to God. When people resist giving them their portion of the sacrifices, they seize it by force; they also sleep with women who come to worship at the temple.

Eli is upset at reports about his sons' behavior, but is too old and weak to dismiss or disown them. Like countless parents before and since, he hopes to change them by appealing to their consciences. "Why do you do such things? No, my sons, it is not a good report I hear," he tells them in a masterful understatement. Absorbed in administering the temple's rituals, Eli has somehow come to believe that his sons' transgressions against God (stealing sacrifices intended for the Lord) are worse than their ethical offenses: "If one man sins against another, the judges judge him; but if a man sins against the Lord, who shall intercede for him?"

The pointed inquiries that Eli poses to his sons—"Why do you do such things?" "Who shall intercede for [you]?"—miss the mark. Such questions are appropriate for lads, not mature men. If they do not yet understand the horror of what they are doing, a few poignant expressions of pain from their aged father won't cause them to repent. Eli's sad words only indicate how out of touch he is with the children he has raised.

Soon, an unnamed prophet confronts Eli in the name of God, condemning him for honoring his sons more than the Lord, by permitting them to continue their sinful and criminal behavior at the temple. He promises terrible, seemingly eternal, punishment to the House of Eli: Both his sons will die on the same day, while none of his other descendants will live a long life (the eternal nature of the curse seems to constitute a violation of God's promise that He will punish no family members, no matter how evil their ancestors' crime, for more than four generations; see Exodus 20:5; also entry 157). Eli does not respond to the prophet's imprecation—what can he say?

Later, Samuel, who is presumably twelve or so and may be even younger, has his first revelation from God. Eli, who is almost blind, is asleep, while Samuel rests in a nearby room. God calls out to Samuel, and the boy answers, "I'm coming." He runs into Eli's room and says, "Here I am; you called me." Eli tells him that he didn't call him, and Samuel returns to bed. The same scene happens a second time, then a third. Eli understands that God has been calling Samuel, and says to him, "Go lie down. If you are called again, say, 'Speak, Lord, for Your servant is listening.'" Samuel returns to his bed and lies down.

When God calls him again, Samuel responds as Eli has instructed. God reveals to Samuel that He will soon bring a terrible punishment against Eli's family, "because his sons committed sacrilege, and he did not rebuke them." In great wrath, God also announces that "the iniquity of the house of Eli will never be expiated by sacrifice or offering" (3:14). (However, God does not say that the iniquity of Eli's house will *never* be atoned for by sincere repentance and change of behavior. He just specifies that ritual acts, such as bringing sacrifices, will not effect expiation.)

Understandably, Samuel has no desire to share this prophecy with Eli. The next morning, the old priest summons him. Understanding that the prophecy might have to do with him, and that Samuel might be afraid to tell it, he adopts a gruff manner that actually makes it easier for the young boy to reveal the prophecy God has imparted to him: "What did He say to you? Keep nothing from me. Thus and more may God do to you if you keep from me a single word of all that He said to you" (3:17).

When Samuel tells Eli everything, the old man responds, "He is the Lord; He will do what He deems right."

Some time later, the Israelites go out to battle against the Philistines, and suffer a grievous defeat. Troops are sent to Shilo, where Eli's two sons, Hofni and Phineas, have responsibility for the Ark of the Covenant of God (the holiest item in ancient Jewish life, it contains the Ten Commandments brought down by Moses at Sinai). The two men bring the Ark to the Israelite troops to accompany them in battle.

When the Philistines hear what has happened, their first reaction is terror. They have heard stories of how the God of Israel struck Egypt with plagues, and they fear that something similar will happen to them. Their commanders warn them that they had better fight or they will end up as the Israelites' slaves, just as the Israelites have until then been subservient to them. Aroused, the Philistines deliver a devastating defeat to the Israelites, killing thousands of soldiers, and Eli's two sons, and capturing the Ark.

Eli, by then ninety-eight years old, is sitting at the entrance to Shilo, in great anxiety, wondering what has befallen the Ark (he seems to have been most unhappy that it was taken to a battle). A survivor of the battle enters the city to break the horrible news: "The troops suffered a great slaughter. Your two sons, Hofni and Phineas, are dead, and the Ark of God has been captured." It is at the mention of the Ark's fate, not that of his sons, that Eli falls off the seat on which he is sitting, breaks his neck, and dies.

The family tragedy prophesied by God is now just beginning. Eli's daughter-in-law, Phineas's wife, is pregnant. When she hears about the Ark's capture and the deaths of her husband and father-in-law, she goes into premature labor. Her own physical condition quickly deteriorates. As she lies dying, the midwife tells her, "Do not be afraid for you have borne a son." With her last breath, the woman names him Ichabod ("without glory") for, as she explains, "The glory has departed from Israel."

During the coming years, under the leadership of Samuel and later of David, much of that glory will return.

70. Samuel: The Last of the Judges

I SAMUEL, CHAPTERS 1–16; 28:3–19

Judging from the evidence of Psalms, the prophet Samuel ranks alongside Moses: "Moses and Aaron among His priests, [and] Samuel, among those who call on His name—when they called to the Lord, He answered them" (99:6).

However, judging from the books named after him (I and II Samuel; only the first volume is set during Samuel's lifetime), it is hard to deduce what qualifies Samuel to be compared to Moses. Distinguished as he was, Samuel's accomplishments during his years as Israel's leader are not on a par with those of the preeminent figure of the Torah's last four books.

Samuel is the last of the non-monarchic rulers to guide the people during their first two centuries in Israel. He rises to prominence at a time of extraordinary moral debasement in the Israelite community. During a recent civil war, eleven of the tribes had killed almost everyone in the tribe of Benjamin. Benjamin, in turn, was no innocent victim. It had gone to war in defense of an act of gang rape and murder committed by some of its members, for which its leaders refused to punish the perpetrators (see entry 67). Furthermore, the Israelites' periodic reversions to idolatry—the avoidance of which was Israel's *raison d'être* for being assigned its own homeland—were common.

The Bible tells us of only one major incident that occurs during Samuel's years as judge and ruler. Suffering under Philistine domination, the Israelites yearn for political freedom. Samuel tells them how to obtain it: "You must remove the alien gods . . . from your midst, and direct your heart to the Lord and serve Him alone. Then He will deliver you from the hands of the Philistines" (I Samuel 7:3).

In a verse that recalls the speedy repentance with which the people of Nineveh responded to Jonah's prophetic admonition (Jonah 3:4–9), the Israelites immediately destroy the idols they had been worshiping alongside God, and serve the Lord alone.

Samuel decrees a kind of special Yom Kippur, a day of fasting and confession (7:5–6), during which the Philistines, who fear an insurrection, decide to launch a preemptive attack. Hearing of the Philistine plan, the Israelites are terrified. Samuel publicly offers a sacrifice on their behalf, after which God Himself goes out in battle against the Philistines and throws their troops into panic, so that Israelite troops chase and kill many of them. For many years after this battle, the Philistines stay out of Israelite territory, while Israel recovers the land that the Philistines had earlier taken from them.

Aside from this incident, Samuel seems to have spent his time going from town to town acting as judge (7:16), on one occasion even consulting with the young Saul about Saul's lost donkeys (I Samuel 9:1–20).

How then does one account for the great stature accorded Samuel in Psalms and in the Jewish tradition? His most important contribution is that he returned Israel to a pure monotheism, which followed the debased religion often practiced during the period of the judges. And, as shall be related in the next entries, Samuel, at God's behest, anointed Saul and David, Israel's first two kings.

71. "We Must Have a King over Us That We May Be Like All Other Nations"

I SAMUEL, CHAPTER 8

"A people that dwells apart, that is not reckoned among the nations"—so the Book of Numbers (23:9) describes the Israelites, a people that lives by a different code from that of others.

Few things more provoke a prophet's wrath than the Israelites' rationale for why they want a king: "that we may be like all other nations." Indeed, if not for those words, the people's request seems reasonable. Samuel, their prophetic leader, is growing old, and there are no other likely leaders on the horizon. Unfortunately, Samuel's sons have not inherited their father's sterling character; while acting as judges, both accept bribes and pervert justice (8:3).

The prophet is unhappy over the people's request for a king, but when he prays to God, the Lord tells him, "Heed the demand of the people in everything that they say to you. For it is not you they have rejected; it is Me they have rejected as their king" (i.e., why should they need a king since they already have one in God?; 8:7). The Lord goes on to instruct Samuel to warn the people about the negative aspects of kingship.

Still hoping that the people will rescind their request, Samuel delivers a lengthy warning on the evils of monarchy. He tells the people that the king will draft their sons for his own glory (to run in front of his chariots), or his own profit (to plow his fields). Their daughters will be taken to work as cooks and bakers. He'll tax the people and confiscate their land and give it to his aides. Ultimately, "you will become his slaves" (8:17). Monarchies have existed for thousands of years since Samuel's speech, but his talk remains one of the earliest, most penetrating, critiques of the injustices perpetrated by kings.

The people are undeterred by the prophet's words. "We must have a king over us, that we may be like all the other nations." Apparently, they wish primarily for a military leader who can lead them in war (8:20).

Samuel again consults God, who tells him, "Heed their demands and appoint a king for them." The prophet, displeased by the people's demand, seems displeased by God's response as well. He returns to the people and says nothing of what God has told him; instead, he instructs them, "All of you go home."

But while Samuel can hold out against the will of the people, he cannot long withstand God's command. A short time later, God instructs him to anoint Saul as king, and Samuel does so.

72. King Saul: Tragic Hero or Fool?

I SAMUEL 9:2–31:13

Greek literature conceived of a tragic hero as one who had many extraordinary qualities, but one fatal, hence tragic, flaw. By these standards, Saul, Israel's first king, was no tragic hero, for he had *several* serious flaws. First, he had a desperate, pathetic need to be liked by his subjects, a catastrophic trait for a leader who must sometimes make unpopular decisions. Saul also had a tendency to speak without thinking, occasionally making foolish, impulsive oaths, a trait which, we shall soon see, almost led him to kill his son Jonathan. Finally, when angry, Saul was capable of terrible vindictiveness.

Indeed, his bad qualities were such that it is difficult to remember that he enters Israelite history as a shy, handsome, likable, and courageous hero.

When the prophet Samuel, acting at God's behest, first informs Saul that he is to become king of Israel, the young man is astonished. "But I am only a Benjaminite, from the smallest of the tribes of Israel, and my clan is the least of all the clans of the tribe of Benjamin. Why do you say such things to me?" (9:21).

Samuel ignores his protestations, and privately anoints him with oil.

Soon after, the prophet convenes a large meeting of Israelites at which he publicly proclaims Saul their king. The new young monarch is terrified; when Samuel announces his name, he is nowhere to be found (the Bible speaks of him as "hiding among the baggage" [10:22]). Samuel finally presents the young man, who is taller than everyone else by a head, to the people, who shout, "Long live the king!" But some Israelites, unimpressed with the new monarch, ask, "How can this fellow save us?" Saul, the Bible tells us, heard their complaint, "but he pretended not to mind" (10:27).

Soon, however, Saul's bravery and decisiveness bring him to national prominence, when the city of Yavesh-Gilead is attacked by Ammon. Because the Israelites are weak at the time, the citizens of Yavesh-Gilead sue for peace, offering to become Ammon's servants. Nahash, Ammon's leader, answers their offer harshly: "I will make a pact with you on this condition, that everybody's right eye be gouged out; I will make this a humiliation for all Israel" (11:2).

The people of Yavesh-Gilead request seven days in which to consider this horrendous offer. During this time, they dispatch a messenger to Saul.

When Saul hears what Ammon intends to do to the people of Yavesh-Gilead, the spirit of God possesses him, and he becomes furious. He commands every available Israelite to follow him into battle, threatening to destroy all the cattle of anyone who does not do so. Some 330,000 men respond to his call, and inflict an overwhelming defeat on the Ammonites.

Saul quickly becomes so popular that some people approach Samuel and ask, "Who was it who said, 'Shall Saul be king over us?' Hand the men over and we will put them to death" (11:12).

At this early stage in his kingship, Saul is a merciful man: "No man shall be put to death this day! For this day the Lord has brought victory to Israel," he declares.

Confident now of the power and wisdom of their new monarch, the people hold a large celebration and reinaugurate Saul as king.

Unfortunately, Saul's happy days as king are of short duration. A short time later, he goes to battle against the Philistines, Israel's historic enemy and oppressor. They assemble a formidable army of foot soldiers, along with thirty thousand chariots and six thousand horsemen.

Facing such a force, Saul's troops start to panic and many flee, leaving the king in a quandary. A short time earlier, the prophet Samuel had instructed him to wait in the city of Gilgal for seven days before initiating battle. At that time, Samuel would appear, offer a sacrifice before God, and bless Saul's troops. But as the seven days end and Samuel does not come, Saul, anxious to forestall more desertions, offers a sacrifice himself.

Just as he finishes, he sees the furious prophet approaching him. Saul tries to justify his behavior, explaining that Samuel was late in coming and that he feared he would lose his army.

Samuel responds—to me it seems somewhat unfairly—without any sympathy. He tells Saul that the kingship will not endure in his family, and that God will "seek out a man after His own heart" (13:14).

The prophet immediately departs from the king's camp, while Saul continues with his battle plans against the Philistines. Perhaps thinking that he should do something "religious," in light of Samuel's angry words, Saul imposes a weird, foolish oath on his troops: "Cursed be the man who eats any food before night falls and I take revenge on my enemies" (14:24). One can imagine few more irresponsible restrictions to impose on a fighting army than to prohibit its troops from eating.

Saul's son, the courageous soldier Jonathan, who is absent when Saul pronounces this oath, eats some honey from a beehive and is rejuvenated by the food. Some troops see him eating and inform him of his father's oath, whereupon the forthright son declares: "My father has brought trouble on the people. See for yourselves how my eyes lit up when I tasted that bit of honey. If only the troops had eaten today of spoil captured from the enemy, the defeat of the Philistines would have been greater still" (14:29–30).

Saul's foolish vow has negative consequences. The troops become so famished that when they capture the Philistines' cattle, they slaughter the animals and eat the meat together with the blood, a violation of one of the Torah's oldest laws (Genesis 9:3–4).

Later, when Saul learns that his son Jonathan has violated his oath, albeit unknowingly, the king wants to execute him. What a sharp and sad contrast to the day he won his first great victory for Israel! Then, when some Israelites wished to kill the people who had earlier mocked him, he forbade them to do so. Today, however, he stands ready to kill his own son, the bravest soldier in his army. Fortunately, Saul's troops are outraged at the king's desire and refuse to allow him to kill Jonathan (14:45).

Sometime later, Saul violates Samuel's command, given in God's name, to destroy all the people of Amalek (see entry 38) and even their cattle. Saul captures Agag, the Amalekite king, and spares both him and the best of the cattle, with which he intends to reward his troops.

Furious, Samuel informs Saul, "Because you rejected the Lord's command, He has rejected you as king" (15:23). From that day on,

Samuel never sees Saul again (at least until the bizarre incident described in I Samuel, chapter 28, in which the dead prophet's apparition appears and speaks to Saul; see entry 78).

Eventually, Saul becomes pathologically jealous of David (see entry 74), who he suspects will succeed him as king. During the final years of his life, Saul expends most of his efforts trying to murder him. On one occasion, when he learns that the priests living in the city of Nob had given David a night's lodging (they had no idea that Saul regarded David as an enemy), he murders eighty-five of them (chapter 22).

By the end of his life, Saul is pathetic, and estranged from the people closest to him. Knowing that Jonathan, his oldest son, loves David and has tried to protect him from his father's murderous rage, Saul throws a spear at him, and denounces him with vile language (20:30–33). He also arranges the "marriage" of his daughter Michal to David, in truth hoping that the obscene dowry he demands of his would-be son-in-law—one hundred foreskins of Philistine soldiers—will lead to David's death in battle. Saul also accuses his closest advisers of having turned on him. Indeed, by the time Saul dies in a hopeless battle against the Philistines, one senses that death must come to him as a relief.

The conclusion? Saul's early heroism was far overshadowed by his later foolishness and evil. The most sympathetic thing one can say about the later Saul is that he was profoundly mentally disturbed. The text often refers to an "evil spirit" that would overcome him, and during which he would become both paranoiac and murderous. Did God afflict Saul with these "evil spirits," or was the king himself the victim of a chemical imbalance, the sort of affliction that could be helped with modern drugs? This might be the case, and while such an analysis might incline readers to view Saul with pity, it cannot erase from the historical record the many evil things he did (most notably, the murders of the people of Nob).

73. David and Goliath

I SAMUEL, CHAPTER 17

In a society that favored firstborn sons both legally and socially, David, the youngest of eight brothers, would seem to have started life with at least two strikes against him. He certainly does not get much respect from his older siblings.

At the time that he rises to prominence, Saul is Israel's king, and the Israelites are fighting one of their perennial battles against their Philistine oppressors. The two sides face off on adjacent hills in the territory of Judah, the tribe to which David's family belongs.

The Philistine army's most prominent soldier is the giant Goliath of Gath. The Bible describes him as standing some nine feet tall (at least that's how high he seems to the Israelites), and armed in impregnable, almost impossibly heavy armor (weighing 5,000 bronze shekels, or about 130 pounds).

Each morning he steps forth to challenge and taunt the Israelite troops: "Choose one of your men and let him come down against me. If he beats me in combat and kills me, we will become your slaves; but if I best him and kill him, you shall be our slaves and serve us" (17:8–9). Goliath then concludes his challenge: "Get me a man and let's fight it out!"

With not one of their soldiers ready to take on the giant, the Israelites become ever more terrified as for forty successive days Goliath issues his challenge.

Among the demoralized soldiers are David's three oldest brothers. One morning, Jesse, his father, dispatches him with generous supplies of food for his brothers and their officers. David, who is a shepherd, appoints someone to guard his flock, then sets out for the army camp. He arrives just in time to hear Goliath issuing his daily challenge, and to witness the Israelite troops standing nearest the Philistine giant flee in terror.

The young shepherd is unfazed. He asks some soldiers: "What will be done for the man who kills that Philistine and removes the disgrace from Israel?" (17:26). David is told that Goliath's slayer will be given King Saul's daughter in marriage, great riches, and an exemption from taxes.

Eliab, David's oldest brother, overhears the conversation and starts to berate him: "Why did you come down here, and with whom did you leave those few sheep in the wilderness? I know your impudence and impertinence; you came down to watch the fighting" (17:28).

Like many bullied younger brothers before and since, David responds in pained innocence: "What have I done now? I was only asking." As soon as Eliab turns away, David resumes grilling the troops about Goliath, and about the rewards that will accrue to the man who kills him.

Word is brought to King Saul that a soldier has appeared who seems willing to respond to Goliath's challenge. Saul's hopes are raised, but when David is brought before him, he is disheartened: "You cannot go to that Philistine and fight him; you are only a boy, and he has been a warrior from his youth" (17:33).

The king's words do not dissuade David, who tells Saul that during his years as a shepherd, he has fought off bears and lions that have attacked his sheep, and even has killed some of them with his own hands. Goliath, he assures the king, will fare no better than did these other predators: "The Lord who saved me from lion and bear will also save me from that Philistine" (17:34–37).

"Then go and may the Lord be with you," Saul blesses David. He offers the young warrior his own battle armor, but when David puts it on, he finds that it makes his movements awkward. He removes the armor, and goes forth to face Goliath with nothing more than a stick, a sling, and a few smooth stones.

Goliath, who has waited almost six weeks for an opponent, is infuriated at the sight of the youth now facing him. "Am I a dog that you come against me with sticks?" He promises David that his carcass will soon be feeding birds and beasts.

David responds with words that have long inspired believers in God when confronting powerful and evil forces: "You come against me with sword and spear and javelin; but I come against you in the name of the Lord of Hosts, the God of . . . Israel, whom you have defied. This very day the Lord will deliver you into my hands. I will kill you and cut off your head. . . . All the earth shall know that there is a God in Israel. And this whole assembly shall know that the Lord can give victory without sword or spear. For the battle is the Lord's, and He will deliver you into our hands" (17:45–47).

Goliath advances toward David, who slings a stone at the giant's forehead, one of the few exposed spots on his body. From the text's description, it is unclear if the stone penetrates Goliath's skull and kills him, or just knocks him unconscious. David, who lacks even a sword, runs over to Goliath (the giant's shieldbearer, mentioned in verses 7 and 41, seems to have fled), grasps his sword, and cuts off his head.

Witnessing their greatest hero killed by an unarmed Israelite youth, the Philistine troops flee in terror. The suddenly emboldened Israelites pursue and kill many of them.

David displays Goliath's head before King Saul, who shortly thereafter appoints him head of Israel's army. The former shepherd leads Israel's troops in many successful battles (the Bible doesn't mention if Eliab, and David's other brothers, fight under his command), and his valor and good looks (17:42) do not go unnoticed by Israel's women. When King Saul appears among them, they greet him with a song that chills the monarch's heart:

Saul has slain his thousands
David, his tens of thousands! (18:7)

"To David they have given tens of thousands and to me they have given thousands," the furious monarch thinks. "All that he lacks is the kingship!" (18:9).

Saul immediately turns on the young hero who saved his country from Goliath and, within a day, tries to murder David with a spear. The battle that now ensues between Saul and David (see next entry) lasts infinitely longer than that between David and Goliath, poisons both men's lives, and ends only with Saul's death.

Note: II Samuel 21:19 reports that during a fight between Israel and the Philistines, a soldier named Elchanan of Bethlehem killed a Philistine named Goliath the Gittite (the Goliath slain by David came from Gath). The following verse reports the killing of another Philistine giant in battle—a man with six fingers on each hand and six toes on each foot—by Shimei, David's nephew.

74. Saul's Longest Battle: His Maniacal War Against David

I SAMUEL, CHAPTERS 18–27, INTERMITTENT

[Rabbi Judah ben Tabbai, first century B.C.E.] said: If anyone had said to me before I entered high office, "Assume that office," my only wish would have been to hound him to death. Now that I have entered high office, if anyone were to tell me, "Give it up," I would pour a kettle of boiling water on his head. Because to high office it is hard to rise, yet . . . it is even harder to give it up. For so we find in the case of [King] Saul. When he was told, "Rise to kingship," Saul hid . . . (I Samuel 10:22); but when Saul was told, "Give up the kingship," he hunted after David [his designated successor] to kill him.

—*The Fathers According to Rabbi Nathan,* 10:3

When the prophet Samuel first informs Saul that he is to become king, the young man is amazed. He thinks the honor is highly inappropriate. "But I am only a Benjaminite, from the smallest of the tribes of Israel, and my clan is the least of all the clans of the tribe of Benjamin. Why do you say such things to me?" (I Samuel 9:21).

As the above rabbinic passage reminds us, when Samuel later readies himself to anoint Saul in front of the whole nation, the young man disappears and hides himself "among the baggage" (10:22).

Indeed, if there ever was a ruler whom one might expect to be willing to relinquish his position, it is Saul. But such is not the case. Rather, Saul grows to revel in the popularity and power inherent in monarchy. Perhaps equally important, he becomes enamored at the thought of establishing a dynasty.

Early in Saul's reign, he disobeys two of Samuel's commands (the second is transmitted as a command from God; see entry 72). Twice, the prophet tells Saul that, because of his acts of disobedience, God will take the kingship from him. Though well aware that he has been appointed king only because of God's word to Samuel, Saul does not resign. Instead, he clings to his position with an ever-growing obsession, that ultimately destroys his character and every relationship dear to him.

Samuel's prophecies evoke a terrible insecurity in Saul, which reaches paranoiac proportions shortly after David enters his camp. At first, when David establishes himself as a hero by killing Goliath (see preceding entry), the king rejoices in his accomplishments, until he hears a new song being sung by Israelite women: "Saul has slain his thousands, And David, his tens of thousands" (18:7).

"Saul was vexed," the Bible tells us; he thought to himself, "All that [David] lacks is the kingship."

The very next day, a black mood descends on the king; twice, he hurls his spear at David, but the young soldier whirls out of the weapon's way.

Remarkably, Saul and David continue to have a relationship after this event. Perhaps David attributes the spear throwing not to personal animosity, but to Saul's black mood; he would hardly be the first person who refuses to believe that someone whom he admires hates him. David's hope that Saul's attack was not intended personally must have seemed confirmed by the king's offer, shortly after the spear throwing, to have David marry his eldest daughter, Merab.

The only condition Saul places on the match is that David remain in the army. While David responds with humility—"What have I accomplished, that I should become Your Majesty's son-in-law?" (18:18)—Saul thinks, "[If he marries Merab], I will not have to get rid of him; [sooner or later] the Philistines will do it for me."

Saul by this time is clearly mentally unbalanced. Modern commentators might debate whether he was a manic-depressive, a paranoid schizophrenic, or had some other ailment, but all agree that he was not fully in his right senses, for a normal, loving father does not use his daughter as a pawn to have his son-in-law killed.

In any case, the wedding with Merab does not occur (perhaps, in a sane moment, Saul realizes the hideousness of what he is planning and marries Merab off to a man named Adriel). But Saul's maniacal hatred of David cannot be long suppressed. When he hears that his younger daughter, Michal, loves the young warrior, he is pleased. "I will give her to him," he thinks, "and she can serve as a snare for him, so that the Philistines may kill him" (18:21).

Saul now involves his unwitting courtiers in his plot, instructing them to tell David, supposedly on the sly, how much Saul desires him as a son-in-law. Unlike with Merab, this time Saul determines to demand from David a dowry that is so great—and so repulsive— that he will rid himself of the young man once and for all. The king instructs his courtiers to tell David that all he wants is the foreskins of one hundred enemy Philistine soldiers (the Philistines did not circumcise their males). Saul is certain that David will be dead long before he can kill the requisite number. Of course, he is wrong: David returns to him with *two* hundred foreskins and marries Michal.

"Hatred makes a straight line crooked," an old Hebrew proverb teaches. Because of his hatred, Saul can no longer think clearly, certainly not about David (the topic he seems to think about more than any other). The Bible informs us twice—after David successfully dodges Saul's spears and after he presents him with the two hundred Philistine foreskins—that Saul realizes that God is with David. Still, he continues in his efforts to kill David; he is like a crazed gambler who knows that the game has been fixed, yet insists on playing losing numbers.

It is soon difficult to know when Saul is speaking honestly or playing a role. For example, when Saul confides to Jonathan his intention to murder David, his horrified son defends David and accuses his father of wanting to spill innocent blood. Saul responds as if Jonathan's words have touched him deeply: "As God lives," he swears to Jonathan, "[David] will not die" (19:6).

Did Saul really have a change of heart or, realizing the depth of Jonathan's affection for David, did he just pretend, in the hope that Jonathan would not tell David of his intentions?

One thing is clear: Whether or not Saul's oath to Jonathan is sincere at the moment he makes it, is from David's perspective irrelevant. Within days Saul again tries to impale him with a spear, and David flees home to his wife, Michal. The king dispatches troops to the house who are told to kill David the following morning (the Bible does not tell us what rationale he offers his troops for murdering his greatest soldier. Perhaps they are simply corrupt men who will do anything the king bids them, or perhaps he has convinced them that David is planning a coup).

After becoming aware of her father's plot, Michal warns her husband: "If you do not escape tonight, you will be put to death tomorrow." Michal plots an escape for David that ever since has been the model for numerous prison escapes. She lowers him out a back window, then fashions a life-size dummy who wears a cloak and has goat hair atop its head, and which she lays on David's bed. When the troops arrive to take David, she tells them he is sick. They return to Saul with Michal's message. "Bring him to me," the crazed king says, "bed and all, that he may be put to death."

The troops return to the house, and discover the dummy; Michal's ruse has provided David with precious extra hours to escape.

Saul confronts his daughter: "Why did you play that trick on me and let my enemy get away safely?"

Michal realizes how demented her father is and that, if she tells him that she loves David, he might murder her. So she offers the lie that David had threatened her, saying, "Help me get away or I'll kill you" (19:17).

Michal's story is transparently false. If she was afraid that David would kill her, why did she tell the troops who came for him that he was in bed? He was in no position to harm her then, so she could have sent the troops upstairs to arrest him. On the other hand, if David already had escaped, then why didn't she inform the palace as soon as he had done so?

Shortly thereafter, and in defiance of the Ten Commandments' prohibition of adultery, Saul forces Michal into an adulterous relationship by marrying her off to another man (I Samuel 25:44). Perhaps he justifies this act on the grounds that a man who threatens to murder his wife should not be regarded as a husband.

Saul's attempts to murder David go on and on; they dominate the second half of First Samuel, and become the preeminent activity of his kingship. His obsession also poisons his family relationships. When he senses that his son Jonathan is trying to save David's life, he yells an obscure and obscene curse at him: "I know that you side with the son of Jesse [Saul cannot bring himself to say David's name]—to your shame, and to the shame of your mother's nakedness" (20:30).

When Jonathan again tries to defend David (he is clearly a less astute judge of his father than Michal is), Saul raises his sword against him.

The irony, of course, is that Saul is correct on one major issue; David is destined to succeed him as king. But so what? Had Saul acceded to God's initial decree that he no longer be king, he could have lived out his life in honor. As is apparent from David's behavior throughout Saul's vendetta against him, he always intended to treat Saul with respect. It is also clear that Jonathan has no great desire to be king, and is perfectly happy to serve as David's second-in-command.

Saul's pursuit of David soon transforms him from a tragic, but essentially decent, human being into an evil one who succeeds only in murdering his own conscience. Thus, when Saul hears that Achimelech, the High Priest of Nob, a city of priests, has provided David with some food and a night's lodging, he has the priest and his immediate and extended family arrested and brought before him, and accuses them all of a conspiracy. Achimelech, of course, denies the accusation; in fact, neither he nor anybody else in Nob even knows that Saul regards David as a traitor. But Saul now is beyond good and evil. He has everyone in Nob murdered, including eighty-five priests (22:16–19).

The Bible records one particularly telling detail: Saul insists that, in addition to slaying all the women and children in Nob, the oxen, donkeys, and sheep must be killed as well. Like the Nazis at Lidice, Czechoslovakia, he wants to exterminate the memory of this city. Years earlier, the "tender-hearted" Saul had refused to kill Agag, Amalek's murderous king, or to slaughter the Amalekite cattle. His cruelty to Nob, in contrast to his mercy to Amalek, caused the third-century rabbi Simeon ben Lakish to suggest that "whoever shows mercy to the cruel ultimately will be cruel to those deserving of mercy" (*Ecclesiastes Rabbah* 7:16).

The war against David continues. On two subsequent occasions, David has the opportunity to kill Saul. When he refuses to do so both times, Saul is stunned. On the first occasion, he thanks David for his graciousness, and even acknowledges that David will soon replace him as king (I Samuel 24:20). But within days, he is trying to kill David again (chapter 26).

Saul's crusade against David, the dominating passion of the last years of his life, ends only with his death. While one might have expected his demise to come at the hands of the man he so long has pursued, he kills himself rather than become a prisoner of the Philistines, to whom he has lost a battle. Of course, it is the Philistines, not David, who are the enemy—although for a long time he has ignored that fact—and it is they who are responsible for his death. As Saul witnesses his three sons die in battle (31:2), and realizes his own death is imminent, does he reflect for a moment on the self-destructive madness of his campaign against David?

If he does, he keeps such awareness to himself.

75. David and Jonathan: The Biblical Model of Friendship

I SAMUEL, CHAPTERS 18–20; 23:16–18; II SAMUEL, CHAPTER 1:11–27

"Love your neighbor as yourself," one of the Torah's most famous verses (Leviticus 19:18), is one of the hardest commandments to fulfill. However, the Bible tells us that Jonathan, King Saul's oldest son, befriended David "and loved him as himself" (18:3).

Jonathan is a man of generous disposition, the kind described in the expression "he would give you the shirt off his back." Indeed, Jonathan bestows on David his cloak, tunic, sword, bow, and belt (18:4).

Jonathan's friendship with David places him in unbearable tension with his father. Saul, perceiving David as the major threat to his kingship, wants him dead, and he is not shy about making his intentions known to those near him: "Saul urged his son Jonathan and all his courtiers to kill David . . . " (19:11).

Jonathan warns David of his father's intentions, and tells his friend that he will try to change his father's mind. He uses rational arguments to dissuade Saul, reminding him of the great things David has done on his behalf, most notably by slaying Goliath.

Saul responds as if Jonathan's arguments have convinced him: "As God lives, [David] will not die" (19:6). That Saul's words were meant seriously, not just as a pretense, is suggested by the fact that David comes to serve again in Saul's army.

Unfortunately, after a brief period of tranquillity, a black mood descends on Saul, and he renews his campaign to kill David more energetically than ever.

Jonathan, naively believing that he possesses more influence with his father than he does, tries to convince David that he has nothing to fear: "My father does nothing great or small without telling me," he tells him; since Saul has said nothing to Jonathan about killing David, that must mean that he is safe.

Far more realistic than his generous-hearted friend, David suggests that Saul has concealed his murderous intentions from his son, precisely because he knows how much Jonathan cares for him. He now asks Jonathan to become, in effect, his spy in Saul's court and inform him of the king's intentions, and Jonathan agrees. One senses Jonathan's awareness that the future belongs to David: "Do not ever fail to act kindly towards my house [i.e., descendants] forever, even after God has wiped all of David's enemies off the face of the earth" (20:15).

At dinner the next night, David is absent from the king's table (remarkably, he is still expected there). Saul says nothing, but on the following day, when David is again absent, the king asks, "Why didn't the son of Jesse [seemingly he can no longer bear to call David by name] come to the meal yesterday or today?" (20:27).

Jonathan fabricates a story that David had requested his permission to go to a family celebration, and that he had granted it.

In one of the Bible's most unusual and vivid denunciations, Saul rages at Jonathan: "I know that you side with the son of Jesse—to your shame, and the shame of your mother's nakedness" (20:30). He tells his son that he will never be king as long as David remains alive.

Jonathan refuses to back down. "Why should he be put to death? What has he done?" Saul now raises his spear to strike him.

Jonathan flees the table in rage. The next morning he rendezvous with David at a secret meeting place. Before Jonathan speaks, David deciphers from his friend's expression the awful news. For a long time, the two men say nothing; instead, they hug and weep together. Finally, Jonathan bids David to "go in peace. For we two have sworn to each other in the name of the Lord: 'May the Lord be [witness] between you and me, and between your offspring and mine, forever'" (20:42).

Saul's battle against David escalates. On one occasion, while David and his six hundred troops flee Saul and his army, Jonathan goes to find his friend. Although military might would seem to favor his father, Jonathan has no delusions about the future. He encourages his beleaguered friend, telling him, "Do not be afraid; the hand of my father Saul will never touch you." In a moving, and tragically unfulfilled prediction, he prophesies: "You are going to be king over Israel and I shall be second to you, and even my father Saul knows this" (23:17). The two make a pact that this prophecy should come to fruition.

Yet they never meet again. Sometime later, Saul goes off in hopeless battle against the Philistines, accompanied by Jonathan and two of his other sons (a fourth son, Ish-Boshet, doesn't participate in the fight). The night before the battle, the spirit of Samuel appears to Saul and prophesies that he and his sons will die the next day (28:19; see entry 78).*

Jonathan and two of his brothers are killed early in the fighting, and Saul eventually commits suicide to evade capture and torture at the Philistines' hands (see entry 79).

The grief voiced by David when he learns of Jonathan's death is profound, the deepest sorrow the Bible ever records him as expressing:

> I grieve for you, my brother Jonathan
> You were most dear to me.
> Your love was wonderful to me
> More than the love of women (II Samuel 1:26).

In this age of gay liberation, more than a few Bible readers have cited this verse to suggest the possibility of a homosexual relationship between David and Jonathan. This seems very unlikely given both the Bible's strong antihomosexual strictures (see Leviticus 18:22) and David's particularly extensive heterosexual liaisons (he had eight wives and at least eleven concubines during his life). What David likely meant was that Jonathan's love for him was more wonderful than that of women in the sense that it was so disinterested and platonic. Thus, Jonathan did not betray David to Saul, knowing full well that in the absence of David, he would be the one to succeed his father as king; instead, he risked death at Saul's hands to save David, which shows his to be an unselfish love. This is what it means to love one's neighbor as oneself, in the fulfillment of which Jonathan proves himself to be the Bible's most perfect practitioner.

---

*In the light of such a prediction, one might have thought that a loving father would try and dissuade his sons from accompanying him into battle (indeed, the one son who doesn't accompany him does not die). Unfortunately, there is little evidence that Saul is a loving father. The First Book of Samuel, chapter 14, verse 44, depicts him as trying to kill Jonathan for violating a foolish oath he had made and, as noted, chapter 20, verse 33, shows him raising his spear to strike Jonathan.

76. Michal: The Woman Who Loved Too Much

The great tragedy of Michal's life is not that she was never loved. She was, but by a man who was neither her father nor her husband.

Michal, the younger of King Saul's two daughters, has a distinction of which few biblical readers are aware: She is the only woman in the Hebrew Bible whose love for a man is recorded. The Bible relates several incidents of romantic love. We know that Isaac loved Rebecca, Jacob loved Rachel, and Samson loved Delilah. But in each case, except Michal's, love is described from the man's perspective.* Concerning Michal, the Bible tells us twice that she loved David, the young hero in her father's army (I Samuel 18:20, 28).

Unfortunately, at the time, her father is convinced that David will eventually usurp his throne. Saul thereupon embarks on a campaign to rid himself of David, and doesn't care whom he abuses in order to do so. He is pleased, the Bible tells us, when he learns that Michal is in love with David because he can utilize this love in his plan to get David killed. He therefore lets David know that nothing would make him happier than to have him become his son-in-law. To prove himself worthy of marrying into royalty, however, Saul requests that David bring him the foreskins of one hundred enemy Philistine troops.

We don't know what Michal thought of her father's dowry request. But Saul's intent was clear: If he forced David into a hundred one-on-one encounters, surely sooner or later he would be killed.

But God of course is on David's side, so that he soon brings Saul double the number of foreskins requested, and the marriage takes place.

Michal's love for David seems to have been deep; one senses from the biblical description the passion of first love. Yet she also appears to be a cooler, shrewder person than her older brother, Jonathan.

Both cared deeply for David. When Saul confided his hatred of

---

*The Song of Songs likewise describes love from a woman's perspective, although its main character, a shepherdess, is never named.

David to Jonathan, the young man defended David, thereby incurring his father's wrath (Saul raised a spear to strike him). Jonathan's feelings for his best friend were so deep he could not hide them.

Michal exerts greater control over her emotions. When her father angrily asks her why she helped David escape (see entry 74), she lies; she tells Saul that David had threatened to kill her if she didn't help him.

Saul now does something unprecedented in the Bible; he marries off his already-wed daughter to a man named Palti (I Samuel 25:44). Perhaps Saul hopes in this way to make it clear to all Israel that David is to be regarded as his enemy, not his son-in-law.

What a terrible scene must have transpired when Saul informed Michal that she was to be married to Palti. Because of the lie she had told her father, she was hardly in a position to tell him that she loved David. And what about the fact that such a bigamous marriage violated the Seventh Commandment, which bans adultery? If Michal, or anybody else, raised this objection, the Bible doesn't record it. Michal's plight is quite pitiable. She risked her father's wrath because she loved her husband. Now, not only is she forced to live without David, but she is compelled to marry another man.

It is impossible from the text to determine exactly how long her marriage to Palti lasts. Some years later, after Saul is killed, David becomes king of the tribe of Judah, while Michal's brother, Ish-Boshet, succeeds his father and reigns over the other tribes.

Ish-Boshet's grasp on the kingship is weak and becomes more so when Abner, his leading general, enters into secret negotiations with David. David tells Abner that he is happy to make a pact with him, but adds, "Do not appear before me unless you bring Michal daughter of Saul when you come before me" (II Samuel 3:13). While it would be nice to think that David has been pining away in rapturous love for Michal all these years, unfortunately, his motive seems to be political intrigue rather than romance. Notice that he *doesn't* say to Abner: "Do not appear before me unless you bring Michal, *my wife*"; rather, he refers to her as the *"daughter of Saul."* Michal's significance to him is that she is the former king's daughter. As David prepares to negotiate with Abner for the overthrow of Ish-Boshet, he wishes to have the previous king's daughter back in his palace, which will help legitimate his rule over all of Israel.

Simultaneous to this demand of Abner, David presents a similar demand to Ish-Boshet. Here, he does speak of Michal as his wife, though the rest of the message does not exactly exude romantic longing: "Give me my wife Michal, for whom I paid the bride-price of one hundred Philistine foreskins" (II Samuel 3:14). Ish-Boshet knows he is militarily much weaker than David, and scarcely in a position to resist David's demand.

So now Michal, again without being consulted, is taken from one husband and given to another. The Bible tells us only one detail about her second husband, Palti: He accompanied Michal on her journey back to David, "weeping as he followed her" (3:15). Finally, Abner orders him to turn back, which he does. From this short description, it seems that Palti loved Michal and was devastated to lose her.

What does Michal think of this arrangement? We have only one clue. Sometime later, David succeeds in bringing the Ark of the Lord (containing the original tablets of the Ten Commandments) to Jerusalem. This might well be the happiest day in his kingship; he has now brought the holiest possession of ancient Israel into the city he is establishing as Israel's capital.

David dances wildly with the people. "David whirled with all his might before the Lord" (II Samuel 6:14). The text tells us that Michal, looking out the palace window, sees her husband leaping and whirling, "and despised him for it." Later, when David returns home, Michal goes out to meet him and greets him with cold scorn: "Didn't the king of Israel do himself honor today—exposing himself today in the sight of the slavegirls . . . as one of the riffraff might expose himself?"

David responds to this verbal slap in the face with a verbal shot-to-the-heart: "It was before the Lord who chose me instead of your father and all his family, and appointed me ruler over the Lord's people Israel [that I danced]" (II Samuel 6:21). The chapter concludes with the verse "So to her dying day, Michal, daughter of Saul, had no children."

Bible commentators generally sympathize with David; many explain Michal's barrenness as divine punishment for her angry words to David. But in truth, if Michal's words were tactless, her husband's were cruel. There is no reason to assume that God chose to punish Michal. More likely, after this brutal exchange the two never again were intimate.

One wonders, when Michal went to sleep every night in the palace, was she thinking of David or of Palti, the only man who ever loved her?

77. Abigail: How David Meets His Wisest Wife

I SAMUEL, CHAPTER 25

During his years on the run from Saul, David loses one wife, Michal, whom Saul marries off to another man (see preceding entry) and acquires six more (II Samuel 3:2–5). The Bible, however, provides us details about only one, Abigail; she proves to be a highly independent, gracious, and shrewd woman.

When we first meet Abigail, she is married to Nabal. Her husband's name (Hebrew for "fool" or "scoundrel") is an immediate giveaway to his character. David and his troops had provided the wealthy Nabal's shepherds protection from thieves, no minor undertaking given that Nabal owned one thousand goats and three thousand sheep. Therefore, when David hears that Nabal is shearing his sheep, he sends some of his soldiers to request a gift. They do not specify its size, but simply ask that Nabal "give your servants and your son David whatever you can" (I Samuel 25:8).

Nabal treats David's soldiers as though they were emissaries from a Mafia leader, and contemptuously refuses their request; he also speaks of David as a slave in revolt against his master, King Saul (25:10).

When his troops inform David of Nabal's insult, he takes four hundred soldiers and sets out to attack him, ignobly intending to murder not only Nabal, but every male in his household (25:22).

Meanwhile, one of Nabal's workers, hearing his employer insulting David's soldiers, seeks out Abigail and informs her of her husband's behavior. He emphasizes how well David and his men had treated them, and that disaster is likely to result from Nabal's stinginess and abusive words.

In an action reminiscent of Jacob's appeasement of Esau (see entry 20), Abigail immediately assembles a generous gift offering, including a large quantity of bread, figs, and raisins as well as five prepared sheep. Saying nothing to her husband, she dispatches her heavily laden servants to David's camp, telling them that she will follow close behind.

En route, Abigail encounters David and his armed forces, and sets out to pacify him: "May my lord pay no attention to that wicked man Nabal. He is just like his name—his name is fool" (25:25). Abigail's statement strikingly equates foolishness with wickedness, a recognition of how often the two go hand in hand. The clear admiration for Abigail displayed in the text also suggests that biblical ethics do not require loyalty to an evil spouse.

A psychologically astute negotiator, Abigail appeals to David's sense of himself as a just person, urging him not to have on his conscience guilt arising from innocent bloodshed. Nabal might be evil, but the other people in his household whom David intends to kill are not.

She also understands how much her husband's contemptuous dismissal of David as Saul's slave has infuriated him. Abigail thus expresses her belief that David is God's choice to rule over Israel someday.

This wise woman more than succeeds in defusing David's rage. After blessing Abigail for her "good judgment," and for keeping him from killing all the men in Nabal's household, he accepts her gift.

Abigail returns home to find her husband in a drunken stupor. He has thrown a banquet to celebrate completing his sheepshearing and rejecting David's request. Abigail waits until the following morning, when he is sober, to tell him what she has done.

Apparently, Nabal had no grasp until now of how powerful David was—the Bible records that he had six hundred trained warriors under his command (25:12–13). When Abigail describes the danger into which he had thrust himself and his household, Nabal becomes terrified. His heart fails him, and he apparently has a stroke (that seems the most plausible explanation of the Bible's words: "he became like a stone"); within ten days, he is dead.

When David hears of Nabal's demise, he is happy that the man's end has come through God, not him. He is also pleased because Abigail has made a deep impression on him, so that he now dispatches servants to propose marriage on his behalf.

Abigail—who may have subscribed to the philosophy of a divorced and happily remarried friend of mine: "Better one for two than zero for one"—is delighted by David's offer. She wastes no time (apparently Abigail felt no need to go through a charade of mourning for Nabal), and sets out with five maids for David's camp, and then marries him.

Unfortunately, this is about the last we hear of her. A later text informs us that she gives birth to Chileab, the only one of David's first four sons who is not a scoundrel (his oldest son, Amnon, commits rape, while Absalom and Adonijah, his third and fourth male offspring, attempt coups against him; see entry 84). However, the Bible tells us nothing more about Chileab or about Abigail.

Still, Abigail endures as a biblical exemplar of a wise woman.

78. Saul Consults a Medium: The Necromancer of Endor

I SAMUEL, CHAPTER 28

The Bible is rarely charitable about people whose behavior it regards as evil. That is just one reason why chapter 28 of the First Book of Samuel is one of the Bible's most unusual chapters.

The Philistines have mustered their troops to go to war against Saul and the Israelites. The Israelite king perceives that the Philistine forces are superior to his and, in the days before the battle, seeks a sign from God—a dream, or a message from a prophet. But none is forthcoming.

He turns to his aides with a most unexpected request: "Find me a medium [a person who communes with the dead], and I shall inquire of her." The Torah long ago had forbidden such activity (Leviticus 19:31), and indeed Saul earlier had expelled all necromancers from Israel, apparently by threatening to execute those who remained.

His servants inform him of a medium in the town of Endor. That night, Saul disguises himself, takes two servants, goes to her, and says that he wants her to summon up a dead spirit. Fearing a trap, the woman responds, "Look, you know what Saul has done, how he has banned [the use of] ghosts . . . Why, then, do you entrap me to have me killed?"

Saul swears, "As God lives, you won't get into trouble over this."

The woman, still unaware of her visitor's identity, consents to the request. "Whom shall I bring up for you?"

"Bring up Samuel," Saul says.

When the woman sees the spirit of Samuel, she shrieks (an odd response for a medium, perhaps this was the first real ghost she had ever seen). With Samuel's appearance, she also deduces the identity of her "client."

With both Samuel and Saul, two dedicated enemies of necromancy, present, the woman is petrified. Saul, again reassuring her that she should not be afraid, asks her to describe what she sees.

"An old man is coming up, wearing a cloak," she responds. The cloak being Samuel's trademark garment, Saul is convinced of the spirit's identity and prostrates himself.

Samuel's spirit is angry (nothing new about that; during all of Samuel's and Saul's later encounters, the prophet is enraged): "Why have you disturbed me and brought me up?" he asks.

Saul tells Samuel that he is desperate for advice, for he needs to know what he should do vis-à-vis the Philistines.

Dispensing neither advice nor consolation, the prophet confirms for Saul every nightmare that the monarch has had: "God has torn the kingship away from you and given it to your comrade David. . . . God will also deliver Israel into the hands of the Philistines, and tomorrow you and your sons will be with me" (28:17–18). Terrified by Samuel's words, Saul throws himself again on the ground.

The medium, whom one would expect the Bible to depict unsympathetically, emerges as a woman of kind heart: "Please listen to me: Let me set before you a bit of food. Eat, and then you will have the strength to go on your way." Saul refuses. Desperate to entice him to eat, the woman slaughters a fatted calf for him, with no thought of payment. Saul finally eats and departs.

The story is enduringly significant because it is a prooftext for the biblical belief in life after death. The Hebrew Bible barely delves into the question of whether or not life in some form goes on when the body dies. Samuel's appearance to Saul, well after his death, is the Bible's most concrete affirmative response to this question.

Note: The rabbinic view of Saul's consulting a medium: Traditional Jewish scholars have long been horrified at Saul's violating Torah law by consulting a medium, and find absurd his oath to the woman: "As God lives, no punishment shall befall you because of this." Some 1,300 years after the event, Rabbi Simeon ben Lakish wrote: "[Saul] was like a woman with her lover who swore by the life of her husband. So, too, Saul inquired of a medium and swore by God" (*Leviticus Rabbah* 26:7).

79. The Death of Saul:
Is Suicide Ever Justified?

I SAMUEL, CHAPTER 31

By the time Philistine archers wounded Saul, he must have already lost much of his will to live. The night before this happened, Samuel's apparition had predicted his bloody demise (see preceding entry), and that morning three of his four sons had already been killed (the fourth, apparently, had not participated in the battle).

Saul pleads with his armsbearer to "draw your sword and stab me, lest the uncircumcised men come and stab me and make sport of me." The armsbearer refuses to obey Saul's command; he is too in awe of a king anointed at God's command to slay him. So, Saul plunges on his own sword, and dies.

Although Jewish tradition usually forbids suicide, Bible commentators, who have no scruples about criticizing Saul's other deeds, do not fault him for this act. They conclude that Saul was probably correct in assuming that the Philistines had every intention of tormenting him. Like all his countrymen, he was familiar with the fate that befell the captive Samson: First, the Philistines blinded him, then turned him into a mill slave, and finally forced him to dance before them at a public gathering convened to celebrate his capture (Judges 16:21, 25).

Upon finding Saul's body, the Philistines, unable to torment a living man, cut off his head, strip him of his armor, and impale his body, along with those of his sons, in a public square.

Although this is the end of Saul's life, it is not the story's conclusion. Because our image of King Saul has for so many chapters been determined by his ruthless pursuit of David, we have perhaps forgotten that there was once some good in this man. At the outset of his career, the citizens of Yavesh-Gilead were trapped by an Ammonite king who threatened to blind them all in their right eyes. Learning of their plight, Saul gathered an enormous army, and destroyed the Ammonite attackers. Now, long years have passed, yet "when the inhabitants of Yavesh-Gilead heard . . . what the Philistines had done to Saul, all their warriors arose and marched all night." Undeterred by fear of the Philistines, they took down the impaled bodies of Saul and his sons, and gave them a proper burial.

Although the last half of the First Book of Samuel details Saul's continuing lack of gratitude to David, it is moving that the book concludes with this remarkable act of gratitude.

Reflections: Is suicide ever justified?: On the basis of Saul's behavior, some rabbis have ruled that a person who knows he is about to be tortured and killed is permitted to commit suicide. Rabbi David Kimhi (circa 1160—circa 1235), a medieval biblical exegete known by the acronym Radak, comments: "Saul did not sin in killing himself . . . because he knew that in the end he was bound to die in that war. . . . It was, therefore, better for him to take his own life, rather than have the uncircumcised make sport with him" (commentary on I Samuel 31:4).

80. David Rules over Judah, Then All of Israel

II SAMUEL, CHAPTERS 2–5:5

When David kills Goliath (see entry 73) and becomes the leading soldier in Saul's army, he also emerges as the outstanding hero of his own tribe of Judah. Thus, when Saul dies in battle against the Philistines, Judah's leaders quickly anoint David king (2:4).*

Meanwhile, Abner, the commander of Saul's army, arranges to have Ish-Boshet, Saul's sole surviving son, made king over the other tribes (2:8–9).

The Bible describes a bizarre skirmish fought between David's troops, led by Joab (see entry 86), and those of Ish-Boshet, led by Abner. Instead of the two sides engaging in full-fledged battle,

---

*The Bible reports that David had previously been anointed by Samuel (I Samuel 16:12–13), but this was a private ceremony, performed in the presence of his family and unknown to others. That all his brothers knew about the ceremony also seems unlikely given the disrespectful manner in which Eliab, his oldest brother, subsequently treats him (I Samuel 17:28).

the two commanders arrange to have twelve soldiers from each side face off against each other. What the battle's purpose is, and what the consequences will be for the side that loses, are unclear. In any case, both sides lose, as the soldiers succeed in stabbing each other with their swords, so that all twenty-four men die (2:12–32).

This seems to have been only one among many ugly skirmishes in a continuing low-level civil war between the House of Saul and David. But as time went by, "David kept growing stronger, while the House of Saul grew weaker" (3:1).

The climactic act that leads to Ish-Boshet's collapse is Abner's defection to David, which is precipitated by Ish-Boshet's angry accusation that Abner has slept with one of Saul's concubines. Since a king's wife or concubine was permitted only to the king, sleeping with one of them constituted usurpation of the king's authority; therefore, Ish-Boshet is in effect accusing Abner of treason.

Abner, who neither confirms nor denies Ish-Boshet's accusation, reacts with fury: "Am I a dog's head from Judah?"*

Abner rages at what he regards as Ish-Boshet's ingratitude: "Here I have been loyally serving the house of your father Saul and his kinsfolk and friends, and I have not betrayed you into the hands of David, yet this day you reproach me over a woman" (these last words leave the impression that the accusation was very likely true). Further, he utters an oath that terrifies Ish-Boshet: "May God do this and more to Abner if I do not do for David as the Lord swore to him—to transfer the kingship from the House of Saul, and to establish the throne of David over Israel and Judah from Dan to Beersheva" (3:6–11).

These last words do, of course, express treasonous intentions toward Ish-Boshet, but the king is now far too frightened to confront Abner again.

Abner leaves his presence and enters into secret negotiations with David, to whom he offers to enlist the support of all Israel.

David expresses willingness to make a covenant with Abner, provided that he bring him Michal, Saul's daughter, to whom David had been married and whom Saul had given to another (see entry 76).

---

*That is, the lowest possible sort of person. Referring to someone as a Judahite—as if calling someone a "dog's head" was an insufficient insult—was, it would seem, the worst sort of opprobrium members of the Ten Tribes of Israel could heap on one another.

Sensing that the tide is turning in his favor, David also dispatches messengers to Ish-Boshet with the same demand: "Give me my wife Michal . . ." (3:14).

Anxious to avoid offering David a pretext for attacking him, the frightened Ish-Boshet sends troops to take Michal, his sister, from Paltiel, the man with whom she is living and to whom she is presumably married. The troops bring her to David, with Paltiel following much of the way, weeping over his loss of Michal (3:16; in I Samuel 25:44, he is called Palti).

Why, after so many years, is David suddenly concerned with regaining Michal as his wife? Most likely, David's move is strategic: He soon will be king over both Judah and Israel. Those Israelites still loyal to Saul will be more likely to accept his legitimacy if he is married to Saul's daughter.

Before Abner can fully commit Israel to supporting David, he is assassinated by Joab, David's leading general (for the reason for this murder, see entry 86, an act that is quickly followed by Ish-Boshet's murder by two of his own officers. The assassins bring Ish-Boshet's head to David, thinking that they will be rewarded. However, David, who does not want to be perceived as having gained power through the murder of Saul's sole surviving son (he doesn't simply want to rule over all Israel, he wants to be universally supported), immediately executes the assassins (4:12).

Shortly thereafter, representatives from the other tribes come to David in Hebron, Judah's capital city, and offer to make him their king. Now he is ruler over all of Israel, both the north and south (5:1–3).

David is thirty when he becomes king over Judah, and thirty-seven when he is anointed monarch over Israel, ruling over both kingdoms till his death at seventy.

81. Jerusalem Becomes Israel's Capital

II SAMUEL 5:6–9

In 1995–1996, the State of Israel, diaspora Jews, and many Christians throughout the world celebrated the three-thousandth anniversary of King David's establishment of Jerusalem as Israel's capital. Indeed, of all David's acts, this remains the one of most enduring significance.

Therefore, it comes as a bit of a shock to turn to the Bible and see that Jerusalem's capture and its establishment as Israel's capital occupies but four verses in the Second Book of Samuel.

When David becomes king, Jerusalem is not under the jurisdiction of any of the twelve tribes, although it falls within the tribal allotment of Benjamin. This fact makes it an attractive choice for a capital (in the same way that Washington, D.C., is not a part of any one state). Jerusalem has the additional advantages of being centrally located between Israel's north and south, and of being set on hills, which makes it easy to defend.

However, the city is not unoccupied. Its inhabitants, known as Jebusites, understandably have no desire to relinquish the city to David.

He dispatches his army, which easily overcomes Jebusite resistance, occupies the city (the part David occupied constitutes only a small part of present-day Jerusalem) and renames the town "City of David" (5:9), a name by which it has been referred to, along with "Jerusalem," ever since.

David soon brings the Ark of the Lord, containing the Ten Commandments, to Jerusalem, thus asserting the city's centrality in Israel's consciousness, and he builds a tabernacle for the Ark.

The king also has every intention of building the *Beit ha-Mikdash*, the Great Temple, in Jerusalem. However, the prophet Nathan dissuades him from this task, telling him that because of the extensive blood he has shed, the Temple's construction should be deferred until the time his son becomes king (I Chronicles 17:11–12).

That son, Solomon, does build the Temple, which further establishes Jerusalem as the Jewish people's holiest city, a status that the city has maintained for over three millennia.

82. David, Bathsheba, and Uriah: The Tragic Triangle

II SAMUEL, CHAPTER 11

Although Jewish tradition designates David, Israel's greatest king, as the ancestor of the Messiah, this does not mean that he is devoid of character flaws. None leads him into greater evil than his refusal to keep his sexual drives in check. David's violation of the Tenth Commandment, which forbids coveting one's neighbor's spouse, ultimately causes him to violate two far more serious transgressions: the prohibitions against adultery and murder.

Late one afternoon, while the Israelite troops are fighting in nearby Rabbah (in today's Jordan), David ascends to the roof of the royal palace, likely the tallest building in Jerusalem and erected on top of a hill, and sees a very beautiful woman bathing in a nearby house. David, who immediately makes inquiries about her, learns that her name is Bathsheba, and that she is married to Uriah the Hittite, an officer in his army.

Reading about David's inquiries, one assumes that he hopes to learn that the woman is single so that he can marry her. However, he is now so consumed with sexual desire that, even upon being informed that the woman is married, he dispatches messengers to fetch her. Bathsheba is brought to the palace, where she and David have sexual relations.

Although David has initiated the sin, Bathsheba does not come across as blameless. There is no indication that she says anything, or tells him that she does not want to commit adultery.

Bathsheba becomes pregnant, and sends word of this to David. The Bible also tells us that shortly before coming to the palace, she had purified herself after her period; thus, there is no question as to who the baby's father is.

David, who spent years on the run from King Saul and other foes, is not a man who easily panics. He orders Joab, commander of his army, to "send Uriah the Hittite to me."

When Uriah arrives, David engages him in a lengthy conversation. They discuss Joab, the mood of the troops, and the war's progress. Then he tells Uriah to return home and rest. Clearly David assumes that while at home, Uriah will make love to his wife; then, seven or so months later, when she gives birth, he will believe that the child was conceived on that occasion.

However, Uriah doesn't return home; instead, he spends the night at the entrance of the royal palace, in the company of other army officers.

The next morning, David summons Uriah and asks him, "You just came home from a journey; why didn't you go down to your house?"

Uriah is nothing if not noble: "My master Joab and Your Majesty's men are camped in the open; how can I go home and eat and drink and sleep with my wife? As the Lord lives and as you live, I will not do this" (11:11).

One can easily imagine the growing anxiety in the pit of David's stomach. He instructs Uriah to remain in Jerusalem for a second day, which the king spends eating and drinking with him; by evening Uriah is drunk. And, unfortunately for David, Uriah again spends the night at the palace.

Uriah's behavior seems perplexing. Is he truly a man of exemplary integrity who refuses to enjoy himself while his fellow troops are fighting? Or has he heard something? After all, it must strike him as odd that the king summons him to the palace, then spends an entire day entertaining him. Why is David doing this? he must be wondering. Furthermore, has somebody at the palace told Uriah something? It is possible. The biblical account suggests that David was not discreet when he slept with Bathsheba. First, he made inquiries about her, then had her brought to him by messengers. Certainly, there were people at the palace who could have informed Uriah of what had happened, had they wished to do so. The fact that Uriah does not return home even to greet his wife may even suggest that he feels a certain measure of alienation from or anger at her.

Still, in the absence of textual evidence to the contrary, one should presumably accept the reason the Bible suggests for Uriah's behavior: He possesses a rare nobility of character.

This very trait places King David in a serious quandary. Uriah's refusal to return home means that when Bathsheba gives birth, he will know that the child isn't his. Fearing her husband's rage, Bathsheba will probably confess who the father is. While Israel's king might be permitted many privileges, adultery isn't one of them. And when his top officers learn how he behaves while they are fighting on his behalf, they might mutiny. These are only some of the frightening scenarios that may well obsess David when he learns once again that Uriah has not returned to his home.

David now dispatches Uriah to the battlefront, along with a letter for Joab: "Place Uriah in the front line where the fighting is fiercest; then fall back so that he may be killed" (11:15).

The Bible provides us with few further details. How did Joab react when he opened the king's letter, with Uriah perhaps standing in front of him? What went through the general's mind? There is something sadistic in David having Uriah transmit the very missive that orders his own execution.

Joab acts quickly, and with greater *common* (though not *moral*) sense than David. Had he done precisely as the frightened and no longer clear-thinking king instructed him, the killing of Uriah could never have been kept a secret. Joab would have had to tell other officers to accompany Uriah to an exposed position, and then desert him. That Joab had wanted Uriah killed would then have become widely known. Instead, Joab dispatches Uriah, along with other troops, to a position where they confront able Ammonite warriors. They attack, and several officers, including Uriah, are killed. Joab's brutal shrewdness has ensured that David's scheme will remain a secret. It also means that David's adultery now has led not only to Uriah's death, but also to those of some of his other loyal officers.

Joab immediately sends a messenger with a full report of the battle to David. He specifically instructs the man to inform the king that "your servant Uriah the Hittite was among those killed."

The messenger describes the battle to David, informing him that several officers were killed, among them Uriah. Perhaps the most shocking detail in this entire episode is that David does not appear agitated when he learns of the unnecessary additional deaths. Indeed, so great is his moral corruption that he sends the messenger back to Joab with an extraordinarily cynical message: "Do not be distressed about this matter. The sword always takes its toll."

When Bathsheba hears of Uriah's death, she mourns him. Is her mourning sincere or just perfunctory? The Bible does not say. However, there is no indication that she knew then, or ever, that David had ordered her husband to be killed. To Bathsheba, Uriah's death may have seemed a coincidence, perhaps a fortuitous one.*

*Bible scholar Dr. Jeremiah Unterman, in a soon-to-be-published article, notes some striking similarities between the personalities of Bathsheba and Esther. At the beginning of their stories, both women accept their fates without a murmur (Bathsheba with David, Esther with Ahasuerus), while at

When her period of mourning ends—the Bible presumably is referring to the traditional week of mourning—David again has her
brought to the palace, this time to become his wife.

Situations like this undoubtedly happened often in the societies
surrounding the ancient Hebrews as well in modern civilizations.
What distinguishes the biblical narrative is the verse that follows the
news of David's marriage to Bathsheba: "But the Lord was displeased
with what David had done" (11:27).

A short time later, the Lord sends David a messenger, a prophet
by the name of Nathan.

Reflections: On David's complicated relations with women: In *Their Stories, Our
Stories,* a stimulating analysis of women in the Bible, Rose Sallberg
Kam proposes several provocative questions to her female readers:
"Michal lies to her father in order to protect David, Abigail thwarts
her husband's wishes in order to prevent bloodshed [I Samuel, chapter 25], and Bathsheba violates her own marriage vows at the king's
demand. What would you have done in their situations?" She also
asks: "All three of these women experience marriage to another man
besides David. On the basis of the clues given in the stories, which
marriage—Michal and Palti, Abigail and Nabal, Bathsheba and
Uriah—would you guess to have been the happiest, before David
disrupted it?" (page 127; editor's note: David did not disrupt Abigail's
marriage to Nabal; see entry 77).

Further reading: Meir Sternberg, *The Poetics of Biblical Narrative,* pages
186–219.

---

the end, when a life-threatening crisis erupts, both confront the king (see
entry 84 and entry 137).

83. Nathan Confronts David: "That Man Is You" (*Atta ha-ish*)

II SAMUEL, CHAPTER 12

The prophet Nathan seeks out David on the pretext of soliciting the king's advice on a minor, but disturbing, crime: "There were two men in the same city, one rich and one poor. The rich man had very large flocks and herds, but the poor man had only one little ewe lamb that he had bought. He tended it and it grew up together with him and his children: it used to share his morsel of bread, drink from his cup, and nestle in his bosom; it was like a daughter to him. One day, a traveler came to the rich man, but he was loath to take anything from his own flocks or herds to prepare a meal for the guest who had come to him; so he took the poor man's lamb and prepared it for the man who had come to him."

David flies into a rage: "As the Lord lives, the man who did this deserves to die."* Responds Nathan: "*Atta ha-ish*—That man is you." Speaking in the name of God, Nathan denounces David as a killer, an adulterer, and an ingrate to God: "It was I [i.e., God] who anointed you king over Israel, and it was I who rescued you from the hand of Saul. . . . Why then have you flouted the command of the Lord and done what displeases him? You have put Uriah the Hittite to the sword; you took his wife and made her your wife and had him killed by the sword of the Ammonites" (12:8–9).

Nathan emerges from this episode as the possessor of a rare skill, the ability to criticize another person (see Leviticus 19:17, and entry 181) in such a manner that the person recognizes his sin and does not become defensive or deny it.

As I have written in *Words That Hurt, Words That Heal*, had Nathan confronted David directly and denounced him for his adultery and murder, the king, like most of us, would likely have defended his behavior: "I didn't intend to commit adultery. Bathsheba is a very

*Since biblical law does not permit a person to be executed for the killing of an animal, David then rules that the rich man should have to pay four lambs to replace the one he killed (see Exodus 22:37).

pretty woman. I just wanted to speak with her, and then suddenly we were overcome with passion. When she sent me a note telling me she was pregnant, the last thing in the world I wanted was to have her husband killed. I summoned Uriah from the battlefield, then urged him to go home and spend the night with his wife; that way, when Bathsheba's pregnancy was revealed, he would have assumed the baby was his. But he refused to go home. He said it would be a betrayal of his army comrades for him to spend a night sleeping with his wife while they were still fighting. Twice I ordered him to go home, and both times he disobeyed me. Do you understand the position in which he put me? What happened was as much his fault as mine. He left me no choice. Had I done nothing, then he would have come back from the battle a few months later, found Bathsheba pregnant, and known that it couldn't be his child. Bathsheba would have been afraid of what he might do to her, so she would have told him that the baby was mine. And then he would have told all the other officers what had happened. Do you have any idea what that might have led to? The thought that I had slept with one of my men's wives while they were off fighting for me, even though it only happened this one time, might have caused them to mutiny. I am the king of Israel; the country's entire destiny rests on my shoulders. It was my duty to have Uriah killed, the country's survival depended on it."

Instead, the prophet Nathan presents David with a parable, and the king is forced to see his behavior reflected in someone else. By depersonalizing his critique, Nathan enables the king to see the issue's moral simplicity: He had stolen another man's wife just as the rich man had stolen the lamb the poor man loved. Once David had pronounced his verdict on the fictitious rich man, "The man who did this deserves to die!" and Nathan responded, "That man is you!" the king had no choice but to acknowledge the evil he had committed. Given his withering, and unintentional, *self*-condemnation, David is finally made to understand that all the tortured rationales in the world cannot wipe away his act of adultery and the innocent blood of Uriah.

Nonetheless, there remains a morally disturbing element both in Nathan's condemnation and in David's response. After denouncing the king's behavior, Nathan imposes a curse that is directed more toward David's family and descendants than toward the king himself: "Therefore the sword shall never depart from your house—because you spurned Me by taking the wife of Uriah the Hittite and making her your wife. Thus said the Lord: 'I will make a calamity rise against

you from within your own house; I will take your wives and give
them to another man before your very eyes and he shall sleep with
your wives under this very sun" (12:11).

One of the distinguishing features of Torah law is its categorical
repudiation of vicarious suffering, a characteristic feature of the societies that surrounded the ancient Hebrews. For example, the Code
of Hammurabi ruled that if a builder constructed a faulty building,
and it collapsed and killed the son or daughter of the building's
owner, then the punishment imposed on the builder was to have his
son or daughter executed. In contradistinction, the Bible rules, "A
person shall be put to death [and by implication, punished] only for
his own crime" (Deuteronomy 24:16). The upshot of Nathan's curse,
however, is that God will inflict punishment on David by having
another man defile his wives (a punishment that is fulfilled a few
years later when his rebellious son, Absalom, openly sleeps with ten
of David's concubines; see next entry). That such an act will also
humiliate David is true. But so what? Where is the justice in having
his wives and/or concubines suffer for his sin?*

Also disturbing is that although David accepts Nathan's condemnation, his response to the prophet is not entirely satisfying, at least
on moral grounds. "I stand guilty before the Lord," he says. But while
a person who has killed someone has assuredly sinned against God
(indeed, the Bible regards all sins as against God), the primary victim
is the person who died. Would it not have been better had David
said, "I stand guilty before Uriah and before the Lord"? David's admission of guilt somehow leaves the impression that he still thinks
his primary sin was his ingratitude toward the Lord.†

Nonetheless, Nathan is satisfied with David's statement of contrition; the king is told that he will not die, but that the child with
whom Bathsheba is pregnant will. (According to biblical law, that
child, the fruit of adulterous union, is a *mamzer*, a bastard and forbidden to marry any Israelite except another bastard (Deuteronomy
23:3; see entry 205).

This last prophecy of Nathan, perhaps because it will be fulfilled
so soon, hits David very hard. When the child is born, and imme-

---

*Bible scholar Dr. Jeremiah Unterman comments: "God, Who makes the
rules, can break the rules: God is above the law. We modern readers may
not like this, but the Bible doesn't have a problem with this."
†On the other hand, David's immediate admission of guilt contrasts favorably with Saul who, when castigated by the prophet Samuel for sinning,
starts making excuses.

diately becomes very ill, David—still hoping to influence God to save the child—fasts and prays nonstop for the child's recovery. His servants are concerned by his incessant praying and obvious depression, and try to get him to stand up and eat some food. David refuses. After seven days of illness, the child dies.

The servants, having witnessed David's extreme behavior during the infant's illness, fear to tell him of the child's death; they are apparently concerned that he will commit suicide (12:18). But when David sees his servants whispering among themselves, he deduces what has happened. "Is the child dead?" he asks them.

"Yes," they reply.

David takes a bath and changes into clean clothes. He then requests food. Astounded, his courtiers ask him, "Why have you acted in this manner? While the child was alive, you fasted and wept, but now that the child is dead, you rise and take food."

David—ever the realist, ever the survivor—tells them: "While the child was still alive, I fasted and wept because I thought, 'Who knows? The Lord may have pity on me, and the child may live.' But now that he is dead, why should I fast? Can I bring him back again? I shall go to him, but he will never come back to me" (12:22–23).

When Nathan originally confronts David, he denounces him in God's name for taking the wife of Uriah as his wife. One would have thought therefore that God condemned this union, since He decreed that the child of David and Bathsheba should die. However, subsequent to the infant's death, the marriage of David and Bathsheba seems to become blessed in God's eyes. Although David has no fewer than eight wives, and a minimum of eleven concubines, it is David and Bathsheba's next child, Solomon, who is chosen to succeed David as king.

84. One Rape, Two Rebellions: The Unhappy Relationship Between David and His Sons

Amnon and Tamar

II SAMUEL, CHAPTER 13

David and Absalom

II SAMUEL, CHAPTERS 14–19

The Revolt of Adonijah

I KINGS, CHAPTERS 1; 2:13–25

Nachas fun kinder, pleasure from children, is an oft-used Yiddish expression to describe the deepest satisfaction parents can experience. By this standard, David, the greatest of Jewish kings, does not fare well. Of the first four sons borne him, each by a different mother, one is a rapist, two lead revolts against him, and the fourth is mentioned only when he is born. The account of his relationships with three of these sons indicates that David, the wisest biblical military leader, is far less wise as a parent.

Amnon and Tamar (II Samuel, chapter 13)—The first thing we learn about Amnon, David's firstborn son and presumed successor, is that he develops an infatuation for his beautiful half sister, Tamar; "he became sick," the Bible tells us, in his desire for her, and confides to Jonadab, his wily first cousin, that "I am in love with Tamar." He also reveals despondently that she is totally inaccessible to him.

The cousin suggests to Amnon a way to overcome this problem: "Lie down in your bed and pretend you are sick. When your father comes to see you, say to him, 'Let my sister Tamar come and give me something to eat . . . and let her serve it to me'" (13:5).

Immediately, Amnon feigns illness. When his concerned father comes to see him, he utters the words suggested by his cousin. David dispatches Tamar to Amnon's house, where she bakes cakes for him. However, Amnon refuses to eat them; instead, he orders everyone but Tamar to leave the house, then insists that Tamar hand-feed him the food. When she comes near him, he grabs her and says, "Come lie with me, sister."

Tamar is horrified. "Don't, brother. Don't force me. Such things are not done in Israel!"

Amnon ignores her pleas and rapes her.

Verse 15 then makes it clear that Amnon's earlier protestations of love were simply lies, that what he had felt was no more than lust. As soon as his desire for Tamar is satiated, "Amnon loathed her greatly; indeed, his hatred for her was greater than the passion [literally 'love'] he had felt for her."

He orders Tamar to leave the house. When she begs him not to expel her, he summons a servant and orders him to "get that woman out of my presence, and bar the door behind her!" Tamar has now turned into "that woman," unworthy even of being called by name.

Tamar responds to being raped by acting like a mourner. She rends the multicolored robe she is wearing, pours ashes over her head, and stumbles away screaming.

When her brother Absalom sees her, he immediately deduces what has occurred. After urging her not to make the scandal public, he takes her into his house. She remains there, traumatized and broken.

When David hears what has happened, "he was very angry," yet *he does nothing*. Indeed, the ancient Septuagint translation of the Bible into Greek adds, "but he did not rebuke his son Amnon, for he favored him, since he was his firstborn." Absalom too says nothing "good or bad" to Amnon, but for a very different reason: "Absalom hated Amnon because he had violated his sister" (13:22).

Two years later, Absalom plans a big feast, to which he invites his father and all his brothers. David declines the invitation. But when Absalom tells David that he intends to invite Amnon as well, the king's suspicions seem to be aroused. He tells Absalom that there is no reason for Amnon to attend the party. However, when he keeps on insisting, David finally approves the invitation.

Just prior to the party, Absalom instructs his attendants, "Watch, and when Amnon is merry with wine and I tell you to strike down Amnon, kill him." So it is done. (There is a certain poetic justice in the way Absalom lures Amnon into a trap, just as Amnon had lured the unsuspecting Tamar.)*

After killing Amnon, Absalom, fearing his father's wrath, flees to the house of his maternal grandfather, king of the small monarchy of Geshur. David mourns a long time over Amnon (the Bible does not record if he does so over Tamar), then pines away for the absent Absalom.

Who knows, had David punished Amnon for the rape of Tamar or, at the very least, made it known that a rapist would not be allowed to succeed him as king, perhaps Absalom would not have carried out his act of vengeance.

David and Absalom (II Samuel, chapters 14–19)—David's top military commander, Joab, realizes that David desperately misses Absalom, yet cannot bring himself to summon the young man back from Geshur. After three years have passed, Joab arranges with a "wise woman" to approach the king with a pitiful story, and to then solicit his help.

The woman tells the king that she is a widow who had two sons, both young men. The boys had gotten into a terrible fight, and one had killed the other. Tragic as this was, her townspeople now demand that the living son be executed for the murder of his brother. If this were to happen, the woman cries out, "They would quench the last ember remaining to me, and leave my husband without name or remnant upon the earth."

David promises the woman that he will ensure that no evil befalls her son (14:1–11).

The grateful woman then requests permission to say one thing more: "In making this pronouncement, Your Majesty condemns himself in that Your Majesty does not bring back his own banished one."

The king, who immediately deduces that Joab is behind this scheme, is impressed by the woman's argument. He summons Joab and tells him, "Go and bring back my boy Absalom."

However, still furious at Absalom's killing of Amnon, David imposes a self-defeating condition upon the young prince's return: Absalom is to be permitted no contact with his father. For two years this absolute separation prevails.

*Dr. Michael Berger has noted to me several parallels between this story and stories in Genesis concerning Jacob's sons: The hatred for the person who has violated one's sister, and the luring of the rapist into a trap in order to kill him (see entry 21). In addition, Tamar, like Joseph, wears a multicolored robe (see entry 22).

The desperate Absalom appeals to Joab to intervene with his father the king, but the general, aware of David's attitude, refuses to respond to Absalom's requests for a meeting. Finally, the young prince dispatches his servants to set Joab's barley crop on fire. When the enraged Joab shows up at Absalom's door, the prince offers no apology. Instead, he just inundates him with complaints, most notably, "Why did I leave Geshur? I would be better off if I were still there" (14:32). Again, Absalom insists that Joab arrange a meeting between him and his father. The meeting occurs, and David kisses Absalom; it appears, however, that he has scant subsequent contact with the young prince. Apparently David, who could not bring himself to punish Amnon, now cannot bring himself fully to forgive Absalom.

Absalom himself is both a proud and unscrupulous person. These character deficiencies aside, he is an attractive man; the Bible declares that he is the best-looking man in Israel (14:25). He is particularly proud of his luxuriant hair, which he cuts but once a year; otherwise, it would grow too heavy.

Absalom also possesses great charm, a powerful asset in someone who is also very handsome. He starts spending a great deal of time at the Jerusalem city gate, where litigants who have cases to present before David enter the city. Absalom warns each petitioner to whom he speaks that although "your claim is right and just," the king will probably do nothing to help him. "If only I were appointed judge," he adds, ". . . and everyone with a legal dispute came before me, I would see that he received his due" (15:4).

Absalom is a shrewd populist. When a citizen leans forward to bow to him, Absalom extends his hand and kisses the person. Is it any wonder that, within a short time, "Absalom won away the hearts of the men of Israel" (15:6)?

During his years in Jerusalem, Absalom apparently cultivates relationships with other disgruntled subjects. When the time seems appropriate, he takes leave of his father and heads to Hebron along with two hundred armed men. Once there, he sends out messengers throughout the land to inform his co-conspirators that he has launched a revolt. Absalom's rebellion quickly gains strength; he even procures the services of Ahitophel, David's foremost adviser.

David seems to understand his son's character. He orders everyone around him in Jerusalem to flee "or none of us will escape [alive] from Absalom." David also asks that a few devoted supporters, among whom the most important is an adviser named Chushai, feign loyalty to Absalom, and keep David informed of all developments.

When Absalom and his troops arrive in Jerusalem, Ahitophel advises him to have intercourse with David's ten concubines, all of whom have remained behind to take care of the palace. In ancient times (and also more recently), having sexual relations with a king's consort was regarded as a treasonable attack against the monarch. Ahitophel counsels Absalom that such an act will convince all the "fence sitters" that the breach between him and his father is unbridgeable. Thus, those Israelites who have refused to support Absalom because they fear that David and he will reconcile, and they will then be regarded as traitors, now will be willing to publicly identify with him.

Ahitophel's advice appeals to Absalom. A tent is placed on the roof of David's palace, where Absalom sleeps with his father's concubines, a scandalous act that quickly becomes known throughout Israel (and thereby fulfills God's curse against David for his sin with Bathsheba; see II Samuel 12:11–12).

Ahitophel now suggests that Absalom immediately send troops to overthrow David. The king's disheartened state, Ahitophel counsels, will allow Absalom's troops to overwhelm David's and "kill the king alone." This advice "pleased Absalom" (17:4).

Ahitophel's advice is militarily sound, for Absalom has the upper hand. If his forces kill David, the young prince can immediately consolidate his power, while the small number of battle deaths will ensure that he will accumulate few enemies.

Had Absalom followed Ahitophel's advice, the whole course of Jewish history would have been altered. The Temple, built by David's son Solomon, would probably never have been erected. And the prophecy of a messiah descending from David through his son Solomon, which has played so significant a role in both Jewish and Christian history, would have long been forgotten.

At this turning point, Chushai, David's secret agent in Absalom's court, steps forward and convinces the prince that it would be catastrophic for him to attack David immediately. Using simple, powerful imagery, he describes David and his forces as courageous fighters who are "as desperate as a bear in the wild robbed of her cubs" (17:8). He notes that it would be naive to imagine that Absalom's hastily mustered troops would overwhelm David's veteran forces. Rather, Absalom should issue a military call to all the tribes of Israel, summoning a huge force to overwhelm David.

Seduced by Chushai's persuasive arguments (the text adds parenthetically that God has decreed that Absalom reject Ahitophel's sound advice; 17:14), Absalom decides to delay his pursuit of David.

Chushai dispatches messengers to David with the news; the king now has time to regroup his forces.

Aware that the only way the inexperienced Absalom can overwhelm David is to act immediately, and that the failure of Absalom's revolt will result in his execution for treason, Ahitophel returns home and hangs himself (17:23), one of the rare instances of suicide in the Hebrew Bible.*

Shortly thereafter, a climactic battle between David's and Absalom's forces is fought in the dense forest of Ephraim. David, standing watch as his troops march past him, orders his three leading generals, who are within earshot of the troops, to "deal gently with my boy Absalom, for my sake."

David's forces quickly overwhelm Absalom's. The young prince, fleeing on a mule, suddenly finds his hair caught in the tangled branches of a large oak tree. As the mule he is riding keeps on moving, Absalom continues to hang by his hair. One of David's men spots him and rushes to inform Joab of the young prince's location. The general rebukes the soldier for not killing Absalom, but he answers that he had heard David's appeal to treat Absalom gently.

Joab immediately sets out for the tree, throws three darts into Absalom's chest, then has ten other soldiers strike him until he dies. He and the troops then throw the body into a large pit and cover it with a heap of stones.

David's great joy at suppressing the threat to his kingship is overwhelmed by the news of Absalom's death. He staggers up the stairs of his house, moaning, "My son Absalom. O my son, my son Absalom! If only I had died instead of you! O Absalom, my son, my son!" (19:1).

There are few more pathetic passages in the Bible, nor many that illustrate more powerfully the irrational extent to which parents sometimes remain loyal to even the most hateful of their children. Absalom would have happily killed his father. Yet when he dies, David mourns him as if he were the most devoted and loving of children. "If only I had died instead of you" are the words he repeats over and over. Ironically, that is precisely the outcome Absalom also desired.

The revolt of Adonijah (I Kings, chapters 1; 2:13–25): With his older brothers Amnon and Absalom dead, Adonijah now believes that he is the rightful heir to the throne. He also appears to have been blessed with the same sweet character possessed by his older siblings.

---

*The other famous suicide is Saul, I Samuel 31:4–5; see also I Kings 16:18, which speaks of the self-induced death of Zimri, a king who ruled Israel for only seven days.

Thus, some years after the revolt of Absalom, with David old and somewhat enfeebled (in the words of the Bible, "and though they [his servants] covered him with blankets, he never felt warm"; 1:1), Adonijah goes about Jerusalem boasting, "I will be king."

David apparently bore some of the blame for Adonijah's arrogance, for the Bible notes, "His father had never scolded him, [and asked him], 'Why did you do that?' " In other words, David permitted Adonijah to go through life unchallenged and unreprimanded even when he behaved badly. It is difficult to imagine a more irresponsible way to raise a child.

As David's health deteriorates, Adonijah solicits and gains the support of his leading general, Joab, although Joab cannot bring over David's most loyal troops. Furthermore, the prophet Nathan refuses to side with Adonijah.

Adonijah decides to act preemptively and have himself declared king while his father is still alive. He makes an enormous coronation feast, to which he invites all his brother princes except for Solomon.

When Nathan is informed about the feast, he immediately seeks out Bathsheba, Solomon's mother. "Take my advice," he warns her, "so that you may save your life and the life of your son Solomon. Go immediately to King David and say to him, 'Did you not, O lord king, swear to your maidservant, "Your son Solomon shall succeed me as king, and he shall sit upon my throne"? Then why has Adonijah become king?' " (1:12–13). Nathan assures Bathsheba that he will enter as soon as she finishes speaking to confirm her words.

As Bathsheba prepared to speak with David, she must have been well aware of the mortal danger confronting her family: Since David had promised that Solomon would succeed him (a fact which Adonijah, who did not invite Solomon to his coronation feast, must have known), Adonijah's succession to the kingship would likely lead to Solomon's execution.

Bathsheba tells David everything that Nathan has instructed her to say, then appends an additional thought, intended to stir up in the sick and tired king his old sense of pride: "The eyes of all Israel are upon you, O lord king, to tell them who shall succeed my lord the king on the throne."

Before Bathsheba has finished, Nathan, as arranged, charges into the room. "At this very moment," he informs David, "[the other princes and army officers] are eating and drinking with [Adonijah] and they are shouting, 'Long live King Adonijah!' "

David then does something that no other king in Israel has done, either before or after him: He abdicates and orders his top aides to anoint Solomon publicly, sound the horn, and shout: "Long live King Solomon!" They are then to return Solomon to the palace and seat him upon David's throne.

Shortly thereafter, a priest named Jonathan bursts into Adonijah's party with the sobering news that David has made Solomon king and seated him on his own throne. Adonijah's support among the royal princes, though widespread, is very shallow. They flee the moment they hear Jonathan's report, not wanting to be implicated in their brother's rebellion.

Adonijah flees as well, to the local altar, whose horns he seizes.* In ancient times, it was believed that a temple was sacrosanct and could serve as a refuge (although biblical law also rules that a premeditated murderer who seeks refuge in an altar must be forcibly removed and executed; Exodus 21:14).

Solomon sends word through a messenger that Adonijah has nothing to fear: "If he behaves worthily, not a hair of his head shall fall to the ground; but if he is caught in any offense, he shall die" (1:52).

Once released, Adonijah pushes his luck. After David's death, he seeks out Bathsheba, asking her to serve as an intermediary to Solomon. He wants to marry Abishag, David's last, and very beautiful, concubine, and asks Bathsheba to secure Solomon's permission for him to do so.

When Bathsheba enters the palace, Solomon bows to her and has a throne placed alongside his. But as soon as she transmits Adonijah's request, Solomon grows incensed. "Why don't you just go ahead and request that he be made king?" he asks. Bathsheba apparently believes that Adonijah's request is motivated by love for Abishag, while Solomon sees it as an attempt to revive his rebellion. Why else would Adonijah request a royal concubine, knowing full well that the only person permitted to sleep with a king's concubine was the king's successor? (See, for example, II Samuel 16:21–23.) Solomon orders Adonijah's immediate execution.

The fate therefore of David's three beloved sons:

Amnon, the rapist whom David never punished, is murdered by his brother Absalom.

Absalom, with whom David can never effect a reconciliation, leads a bloody revolt against his father and is killed by Joab.

---

*The altar in ancient sanctuaries, and later in the Temple, had four projections, or horns (one in each corner), on which the sacrificed animal's blood was sprinkled (see Exodus 29:12).

Adonijah, whose evil behavior David has never challenged, leads an abortive revolt and is executed.

What of the remaining one of David's first four sons? His name was Chileab, and he was born second, after Amnon (II Samuel 3:3). The Bible tells us nothing about him, but the Rabbis, unwilling to accept that so many evil children could descend from Israel's greatest king, declares Chileab a saint, claiming that he was one of only four men in history (the others being Benjamin, Amram [Moses's father], and Jesse [David's father]) who were such righteous people that they would never have died were it not for the disobedience of Adam and Eve, which introduced mortality into the world (Babylonian Talmud, *Shabbat* 55b).

85. Sheva's Revolt Against David

II SAMUEL, CHAPTER 20

David has scarcely succeeded in suppressing Absalom's revolt when a man named Sheva, son of Bichri, launches another rebellion. He rouses support with the battle cry that "we have no part in David," by which he means that the king has favored his own native tribe, Judah, at the expense of the other tribes. His charge seems to have struck a raw nerve; the Bible reports that "all the men of Israel [i.e., the tribes other than Judah] left David and followed Sheva." David too seems to have been very concerned, for he confides to his military commander that "Sheva will cause us more trouble than Absalom."

In the end, the support for Sheva quickly dissipates. As the revolt collapses, he flees as far north as he can, ending up in a walled city called Abel.

David's soldiers prepare to batter down the town's walls when a clever woman inside the besieged city calls out to them: "Listen! Listen! Tell Joab [David's military commander] to come over here so I can talk to him."

When Joab approaches, the woman reproves him for wanting to destroy "a mother city in Israel."

Joab denies that he has any evil intentions against Abel. "Just hand over [the rebel Sheva] to us, and I will withdraw from the city." The woman promises to do so, gathers the rest of Abel's residents at a meeting, and arranges with them to cut off Sheva's head and throw it over the wall. Joab keeps his promise, and immediately withdraws his troops. Sheva's lack of resistance indicates that he must have escaped to Abel with almost no supporters.

The revolt is so quickly, almost effortlessly, suppressed that it would have remained of little significance but for an important talmudic discussion, which hinges on the behavior of the woman who arranged for Sheva's beheading.

The Talmud records the following discussion mandating how people should act whenever their lives can be saved only through indirectly taking another's life:

> A group of people are walking along a road when they are stopped by heathens, who say to them, "Give us one of you and we will kill him. If not, we will kill all of you."
>
> Let them all be killed and let them not surrender one soul from Israel. But if the heathens single out one name, as was the case with Sheva, son of Bichri, that person may be surrendered to them, so that the others may be saved.
>
> Rabbi Simeon ben Lakish said, "Only someone who is under a death sentence, the way Sheva son of Bichri was, may be turned over." But Rabbi Yochanan said, "Even someone who is not under sentence of death . . . [but any person whose name has been specified may be turned over]" (Palestinian Talmud, *Terumot* 8:10).

The only discrepancy in the talmudic discussion is that the people of Abel did not turn Sheva over to Joab's forces, they actually killed him. Nonetheless, according to the rabbinic view, the woman who arranged for Sheva's execution acted appropriately; as she reasoned, why should innocent people die defending the life of a traitor?*

Postscript: Unsuccessful as Sheva's revolt was, his cry "We have no part in David!" seems to have become a refrain among disgruntled members of other tribes who felt themselves unfairly dominated by David's tribe, Judah. Decades later, after King Solomon's death, a

---

*Alternatively, she reasoned as follows: If we turn him over, he dies, and if we don't turn him over, he *and* all of us will die; hence, in either case he will die, and there is no reason for us to share in his fate.

revolt against his son is initiated with the cry "What portion do we have in David? We have no share in the son of Jesse" (I Kings 12:16). This time the revolt succeeds, and ten of Israel's twelve tribes secede and form the kingdom of Israel (see entry 91).

86. Joab: David's Ruthless General

II SAMUEL, SCATTERED EPISODES THROUGHOUT THE BOOK; I KINGS 2:28–34

As capable as David is of ruthlessness in pursuing his political objectives, he comes across as a timid amateur in comparison with Joab, his chief of staff, and the most ruthless man in David's regime.

Although Joab is loyal to David, he is also a master at looking out for his own interests, and in brutally eliminating anyone who threatens them. During the years when David is king of Judah, and Ish-Boshet, Saul's son, rules over the other tribes, Joab encounters Abner, Ish-Boshet's commander-in-chief. After twelve troops on each side kill each other, a larger battle erupts. Asahel, Joab's younger brother, pursues Abner. The latter pleads with his pursuer for peace: "Turn away from me! Why should I strike you to the ground? How could I face your brother Joab?" (II Samuel 2:22). Asahel refuses to back away, and Abner, a superior fighter, kills him.

Some time later, Abner enters into secret negotiations with David to unseat Ish-Boshet and have David declared king over all Israel. Acting without David's knowledge, Joab deceives Abner into believing that he is being summoned to David's court for negotiations, then he stabs him to death. Joab's justification is that he is avenging the death of his brother Asahel, which he has neither a legal nor a moral right to do given that Abner killed Asahel in self-defense. What is more likely is that Joab murders Abner because he fears that David will install him as commander in chief over Joab.

David condemns Abner's murder, declaring: "Both I and my kingdom are forever innocent before God of the blood of Abner, son of Ner" (3:28). So why then does he not dismiss Joab? Because Joab is one of the few men David fears. As he explains: "Even though I have been anointed king, those men, the sons of Zeruiah [Joab's mother, and David's sister], are too strong for me" (3:39).

Impotent to stop Joab's evil doing, David lambastes his descendants, and curses them: They should suffer from various strange illnesses, be impoverished, and die by the sword (3:29–30).

Just as David fears Joab, Joab continues to fear that David will replace him. Years later, when Absalom's revolt against David fails and Joab becomes concerned, with good reason, that David will recruit Amasa, Absalom's commander, to take control of his army, Joab decides to eliminate Amasa. He reaches out to Amasa as if to embrace him, then spears him to death (20:9–10). Again, David does not dismiss Joab.

On another occasion, Joab participates, at David's command, in the greatest sin of the king's life. After David commits adultery with Bathsheba, and fears that Uriah, her husband, will find out, he dispatches a secret message to Joab ordering him to stage an unnecessary and dangerous battle so that Uriah will be killed. The wily commander, aware that the motive for a battle designed only to bring about Uriah's death will be transparent to his other troops, instead arranges for a number of soldiers to be killed, among them Uriah. Thus, several soldiers, including Uriah, die, without suspicion being aroused. However, the evil David initiates by killing one innocent man has now been magnified greatly by Joab.

Indeed, one suspects that one reason David might later have been loath to confront Joab is because of the incident with Uriah. It is hard to dismiss someone who can disclose so immoral an act that you have committed.

Not all of Joab's interactions with or for David are ugly. On one occasion, David's son Absalom is living in self-imposed exile in the nearby kingdom of Geshur, after having killed Amnon (his older half brother who had raped Tamar, Absalom's sister). David grieves over both the dead Amnon and over Absalom's absence from the palace; however, he cannot bring himself to invite Absalom back. Joab engineers a scheme which induces David to invite Absalom home (see entry 84).

Once back in Jerusalem, Absalom stages a revolt against David. On the day of the climactic battle, David appeals to Joab and his two other leading generals to "deal gently with my boy Absalom for my sake" (18:5).

However, when Absalom is caught, Joab throws three darts into his chest, then has ten of his armsbearers strike Absalom until he is dead (18:14–15). Having been the one who brought Absalom back into David's court, Joab perhaps felt Absalom's act of betrayal more acutely than the other members of the court.

There is reason to suspect that Joab succeeds in keeping his involvement in Absalom's death secret from David, for when the king later recounts Joab's evil deeds to Solomon (I Kings 2:5–6), his son and successor, he makes no mention of the killing of Absalom.

Although Absalom's revolt is successfully suppressed, David is incapacitated by grief when he learns of his death. Instead of celebrating the quashing of the rebellion, David's troops, witnessing their king's anguish, steal into town that day "like troops ashamed after running away in battle" (19:4).

Joab is the only one who is willing to confront the grief-stricken king: "Today you have humiliated all your followers, who this day saved your life [Absalom had intended to kill David] . . . by showing love for those who hate you, and hate for those who love you. For you have made clear today that the officers and men mean nothing to you" (19:6–7). By dint of his very forceful personality, Joab compels David to arise from his mourning and review his troops.

The Bible informs us of many of Joab's other accomplishments. He leads Israel in battle against Ammon (II Samuel, chapter 10), Edom, and the city of Rabbah. But the most important victory he achieves is in securing Jerusalem as Israel's capital (I Chronicles 11:4–6).

David's truest feelings about Joab, a man who was his compatriot for more than forty years, are revealed at the end of his life. Shortly before he dies, he summons Solomon and asks him to do several things he clearly wished he could have done himself. Reminding Solomon of Joab's unjustified murders of Abner and Amasa, he asks: "See that his white hair does not go down to Sheol in peace" (I Kings 2:6; i.e., that he does not die a peaceful death).

Soon enough, Joab provides Solomon with a pretext for killing him by conspiring against the new king, supporting Adonijah, an older son of David, in his bid for the monarchy. After Solomon has Adonijah executed, Joab flees to the Tent of the Lord, hoping that Solomon will treat the Tent as a sanctuary. The king orders his chief officer to kill Joab in the Tent, thereby "remov[ing] guilt from me and my father's house for the blood of the innocent that Joab has shed" (I Kings 2:31).

A man who lived by the sword, it somehow seems right that that is how Joab dies.

IX. I AND II KINGS

87. Solomon Becomes King

I KINGS, CHAPTERS 1–2

The Bible never tells us precisely how many sons David has from his eight wives. We know of Amnon, who rapes his half sister, Absalom, who leads a revolt against him, and Adonijah, who tries to become king while his father is still alive (see entry 84). Among his other sons, David comes to have a definite preference for Solomon; fearing that Adonijah might take power and murder Solomon, he resigns the kingship and immediately has Solomon anointed: "Take my loyal soldiers and have my son Solomon ride on my mule and bring him down to Gihon. Let the priest Zadok and the prophet Nathan anoint him there king over Israel, whereupon you shall sound the horn and shout, 'Long live King Solomon!' Then . . . let him come and sit on my throne. For he shall succeed me as king; I designate him to be ruler of Israel and Judah" (1:33–35).

Shortly before David dies, he advises Solomon on how he should act as king; this is the only recorded instance in the Bible of a king giving his son such advice.* He emphasizes that Solomon must be loyal to God, following all the regulations in the "teaching of Moses [i.e., the Torah], in order that you may succeed in whatever you undertake and wherever you turn." David promises that if Solomon and his descendants fully adhere to God's laws, then they will always rule as Israel's kings (I Kings 2:3–4).

This spiritual advice is followed by more practical counsel. David advises Solomon to eliminate Joab, his chief military officer (see

---

*Proverbs 31:1–9 records the advice offered the non-Israelite King Lemuel of Massa by his mother.

previous entry), and to find a pretext to eliminate Shimei, son of Gera, his old enemy (II Samuel 16:5–8). He also insists that Solomon show gratitude to the children of Barzillai, who helped David when he was fleeing from Absalom.

Having received his father's imprimatur, Solomon's regime is firmly, and immediately, established; he goes on to have the most peaceful and affluent reign of any of Israel's rulers.

88. The Wisdom of Solomon

I KINGS, CHAPTERS 3 AND 10

Shortly after Solomon becomes king, the Bible tells us, God appears to him in a dream and says, "Ask, what shall I grant you?"

"I am a young lad with no experience in leadership," Solomon responds. "Grant then your servant an understanding mind to judge your people, to distinguish between good and bad; for who can judge this vast people of yours?"

God is particularly pleased with Solomon's response. Because the young monarch asks not for long life, riches, or the deaths of his enemies, but for wisdom, God promises to grant him the wisest of minds as well as riches and glory.

Soon, Solomon is granted the opportunity to display his wisdom in public when two prostitutes come before him. The first relates that the two of them live together. A few days earlier each had given birth to a child. The second woman, though, had accidentally suffocated her child in the middle of the night by lying on him, whereupon she had then taken the living child from the first woman and substituted her dead child on the first woman's chest. When the first woman awoke in the morning to nurse the child, she saw that it was dead. When she looked more closely, she recognized that this was not the child she had borne.

The second woman disputes her. "No, the live one is my son, and the dead one is yours!" The first woman denies the claims of the second, and they continue to argue in front of the king.

In seeming despair at arriving at the truth, Solomon orders a servant, "Fetch me a sword." When it is brought, he announces his ruling: The live child is to be cut in two, so that each mother will receive half.

The first woman starts pleading with the king, "Please, my lord, give her the live child; only don't kill it!" The second insists, "It shall be neither yours nor mine; cut it in two." Solomon turns to the first woman and orders the second one: "Give the live child to her, and do not put it to death; she is its mother" (3:16–27).

This story spreads rapidly throughout the kingdom of Israel, and convinces Solomon's subjects that God has granted them a ruler who possesses the wisdom necessary to execute justice.

Solomon's reputation for wisdom soon spreads beyond Israel. Several years later, the queen of Sheba comes to visit, to learn if Solomon's wisdom is as great as she has heard. The queen apparently prepared for her visit. According to the Bible, "When she came to Solomon, she asked him all that she had in mind. Solomon had answers for all her questions; there was nothing that the king did not know, [nothing] to which he could not give her an answer" (10:3).

Unfortunately, the Bible does not detail either her questions or the king's responses. However, by the time the queen is ready to return to Sheba, she assures Solomon that what she heard from his lips has far surpassed the reports she had heard about his wisdom.

According to the Bible, Solomon writes 3,000 proverbs, and composes and writes 1,005 songs and poems. The original Renaissance man, he is capable of discoursing about trees, animals, and fish (I Kings 5:9–14).

Later Jewish tradition assigns to Solomon authorship of three biblical books. The Rabbis claim that as a young romantic man, he wrote the passionate love poem the Song of Songs. In his middle years, he composed the very measured and sensible Proverbs, while in his old age he wrote the world-weary and pessimistic Ecclesiastes.

To this day, the term "Solomonic" remains synonymous with wise.

89. The "Unwisdom" of Solomon

Although as a young man Solomon requests but one thing from God, "an understanding mind . . . to distinguish between good and bad," unfortunately, as he grows older, he loses his formerly unerring moral compass.

Solomon's decline seems to have started with his decision to enter into numerous "diplomatic marriages" with other kings' and princes' daughters. Although such marriages help procure peaceful relations with Israel's neighbors, they also bring into Jerusalem the thing God most opposes in Israel: idol worship.

To accommodate his wives' religious needs (the Bible speaks, one hopes hyperbolically, of seven hundred wives and three hundred concubines; see I Kings 11:3), Solomon erects temples at which they can worship their idols. One might have thought that this was intended to be a temporary measure, that a man possessing Solomon's wisdom would be capable of winning over his wives to his monotheistic beliefs. Unfortunately—and the Bible never explains how this happened—the elderly Solomon is more influenced by his wives than they by him: "In his old age, his wives turned away Solomon's heart after other gods." In one of the Bible's most shocking verses, we learn that this wisest of all Jewish kings, the man who built the Temple, became a follower of Ashtoreth, the goddess of the Phoenicians, and of Milcom, the god of the Ammonites (I Kings 11:4–5).

The young man who had once esteemed wisdom over money (see preceding entry) grows into a man who is overly fond of wealth: "All King Solomon's drinking cups were of gold, and all the utensils . . . were of pure gold; silver did not count for anything in Solomon's days" (I Kings 10:21). That Solomon drinks only from gold cups is not an impressive detail, certainly not in comparison to the lives of such biblical figures as Moses, Jeremiah, and Isaiah.

Solomon also ceases to be a wise ruler of men. He starts imposing high taxes on his subjects. To collect the taxes efficiently, he divides Israel into twelve administrative districts, each ruled by an officer appointed by him and each responsible for supplying one month of Solomon's annual budget. Given that Solomon maintains, to cite one example, forty thousand stalls for his horses, and twelve thousand horsemen (I Kings 5:6), there is reason to suspect that the taxes are onerous.

He also imposes forced labor on his subjects: Ten thousand men a month are sent to work in Lebanon; another seventy thousand porters and eighty thousand stone quarriers are assigned to labor in Israel. Perhaps Solomon believed that this was the only way the Temple and his other ambitious projects could be built; nonetheless, imposing forced labor on a people whose most significant historical memory was of being slaves in Egypt, could not have endeared him to his subjects.

The forty thousand horses, seven hundred wives, and numerous gold cups bring to mind the Torah's warning concerning kings: "Only he must not multiply horses for himself. . . . And he shall not multiply wives for himself, lest his heart turn away, nor shall he greatly multiply for himself silver and gold" (Deuteronomy 17:16–17).

Small wonder that by the time Solomon dies, he has ceased to be an admired monarch. His power and prestige spare him from being exposed to much of his subjects' rage, which in the end is focused on his arrogant, and far less wise, son, Rehoboam. Solomon's father, David, had spent forty years consolidating the Israelite empire. Within weeks of Solomon's death, that empire has been destroyed— permanently.

The truth is, the most important wisdom is the sort that God initially bestowed on Solomon, the ability to distinguish between good and evil. When the desire to draw on that wisdom is lost, of what benefit is the wise man to God or to his fellow humans?

90. The Building of the Temple (*Beit ha-Mikdash*) by King Solomon

I KINGS, CHAPTERS 5–9

The erection of a magnificent Temple, the *Beit ha-Mikdash*, in Jerusalem was the crowning achievement of King Solomon's reign. His father, King David, had wanted to build a great temple for God, to serve among other things as a permanent resting place for the Ark containing the Ten Commandments. A divine edict, however, had forbidden him to do so: "You will not build a house for My name, for you are a man of battles and have shed blood" (I Chronicles 28:3).

The Bible's description of Solomon's Temple suggests that it was 180 feet long, 90 feet wide, and 50 feet high. The king spared no expense in its construction; he ordered vast quantities of cedar from King Hiram of Tyre (I Kings 5:20–25), had huge blocks of the choicest stone quarried, and commanded that the building's foundation be laid with hewn stone.

To complete the massive project, he imposed forced labor on all his subjects, drafting people for work shifts lasting a month at a time. Some 3,300 officials were appointed to oversee the Temple's erection (5:27–30). Solomon assumed such heavy debts in building the Temple that he was forced to pay off King Hiram with twenty towns in the Galilee (I Kings 9:11).

Since the actual dimensions of the structure would not seem to have required such expenditures of money and work, one can assume that a large area near the Temple must have been built up as well.

When the Temple was completed, Solomon inaugurated it with prayer and sacrifice, even inviting non-Israelites to come and pray there. He urged God to pay particular heed to their prayers: "Thus all the peoples of the earth will know Your name and revere You, as does Your people Israel; and they will recognize that Your name is attached to this House that I have built" (I Kings 8:43).

Until the Babylonians destroyed the Temple some four hundred years later (587 B.C.E.), sacrifices were the dominant mode of divine service there; in fact, Jews were forbidden to offer them anywhere else.

Glorious and elaborate as the Temple was, its most important room contained almost no furniture. Known as the Holy of Holies (*Kodesh Kodashim*), it housed the two tablets of the Ten Commandments. Unfortunately, the tablets disappeared when the Babylonians destroyed the Temple, and during the Second Temple era (515 B.C.E. to 70 C.E.), the Holy of Holies was a small, entirely bare room. Once a year, on Yom Kippur, the High Priest would enter this room and pray to God on Israel's behalf. A remarkable monologue by a Hasidic rabbi in S. Anski's play *The Dybbuk* conveys a sense of what the Jewish throngs worshiping at the Temple must have experienced during this ceremony:

God's world is great and holy. The holiest land in the world is the land of Israel. In the land of Israel the holiest city is Jerusalem. In Jerusalem the holiest place was the Temple, and in the Temple the holiest spot was the Holy of Holies. . . . There are seventy peoples in the world. The holiest among these is the people of Israel. The holiest of the people of Israel is the tribe of Levi. In the tribe of Levi the holiest are the priests. Among the priests, the holiest was the High Priest. . . . There are 354 days in the [lunar] year. Among these, the holidays are holy. Higher than these is the holiness of the Sabbath. Among Sabbaths, the holiest is the Day of Atonement, the Sabbath of Sabbaths. . . . There are seventy languages in the world. The holiest is Hebrew. Holier than all else in this language is the holy Torah, and in the Torah the holiest part is the Ten Commandments. In the Ten Commandments the holiest of all words is the name of God. . . . And once during the year, at a certain hour, these four supreme sanctities of the world were joined with one another. That was on the Day of Atonement, when the High Priest would enter the Holy of Holies and there utter the name of God. And because this hour was beyond measure holy and awesome, it was the time of utmost peril not only for the High Priest but for the whole of Israel. For if in this hour there had, God forbid, entered the mind of the High Priest a false or sinful thought, the entire world would have been destroyed.

To this day, Orthodox Jews pray three times a day for the Temple's restoration and the reinstitution of the sacrifices offered there. During the centuries that the Muslims controlled Palestine and Jerusalem, two mosques, Al Aksa and the Dome of the Rock, were built on the site of the Jewish Temple (it was a common Islamic practice to build mosques on the sites of other people's holy places). Since any attempt to level these mosques would lead to an international Muslim holy war (jihad) against Israel, the Temple cannot be rebuilt in the foreseeable future.

Sources: James Harpur, editor, Great Events of Bible Times, pages 86–89. The scene from The Dybbuk is found in Joseph Landis, The Great Jewish Plays, pages 51–52.

91. The Two Jewish States: The Secession of the Northern Kingdom

I KINGS, CHAPTER 12

Had Rehoboam, Solomon's son, been wiser and kinder, the Jewish state established during the reigns of Saul and David would likely have remained unified. But Rehoboam was neither wise nor kind, and he was arrogant to boot.

When Solomon dies, the people of Israel are ready to support his son as king, but seek a few assurances: "Your father made our yoke heavy. Now lighten the harsh labor and the heavy yoke which your father laid on us, and we will serve you" (12:4).

The people are referring to the high taxes and forced labor that Solomon imposed on them to complete his building projects, including, of course, the Great Temple in Jerusalem.

Rehoboam asks the people to depart for three days, during which he will consider their request and then inform them of his decision.

The young monarch turns to the elders who had served Solomon. They advise him to react sympathetically to the demands: "If you respond to them with kind words, they will be your servants always."

Unfortunately, this is not the advice Rehoboam wishes to hear. So he turns to the young men with whom he has grown up, who, like him, have been born with silver spoons in their mouths. Like their friend the king, these young men are without compassion or empathy for commoners, and advise him to "say to [the Israelites], 'My little finger is thicker than my father's loins. My father imposed a heavy yoke on you, and I will add to your yoke; my father flogged you with whips, but I will flog you with scorpions'" (12:6–11; the scorpion was a particularly painful whip).

When the Israelites come before him, Rehoboam has sufficient sense not to boast about how his little finger is thicker than his father's loins, but that is the only sense he displays. In fact, he repeats verbatim the obnoxious words suggested to him by his young advisers.

Seeing the contempt in which their new king holds them, the people answer him:

> We have no portion in David,
> No share in Jesse's son!
> To your tents, O Israel! (12:16).

Rehoboam remains king over his native tribe of Judah and its tiny neighbor Benjamin, but the other tribes form their own kingdom, Israel, and appoint a man named Jeroboam as their king.

Rehoboam assembles a force of 180,000 troops to attack Israel and force its people to accept his kingship. But God sends him a message through a prophet named Shemaiah: "Thus says the Lord: You shall not set out to make war on your kinsmen the Israelites. Let every man return to his home, for this thing has been brought about by Me" (12:24). Finally aware of the valuelessness of the advice proffered by his arrogant young friends, Rehoboam heeds the prophet.

Meanwhile, Jeroboam, the newly anointed king of Israel, fears that if members of the Ten Tribes continue to offer sacrifices at the Temple in Jerusalem, "the heart of the people will turn back to their master [i.e., Rehoboam]" (12:27). He erects two new temples within the Ten Tribes' territory, one in Bethel, in the southern part of the kingdom, and one in Dan, in the far north. Inside these temples, he places golden calves (reminiscent of the one the Israelites had worshiped in the desert; see entry 43) and tells his subjects that they have no need to worship at the Jerusalem Temple, since "this is your god, O Israel, who brought you up from the land of Egypt" (12:28). Thus, within months of the establishment of the kingdom of Israel, the people are mired in the very kind of idolatry that, the Torah insists, Israel must reject.

The new state, composed of the Ten Tribes, exists for just over two centuries until its destruction by Assyria in 722 B.C.E. (see entry 97). It is ruled by nine different dynasties, most of which are evil and terminated through assassination.

The state of Judah exists until 587, when it is destroyed by King Nebuchadnezzar of Babylon. Although all its kings are descendants of David, many are evil and engage in murder and idolatry.

Might this national split have been avoided had Solomon managed to transmit some of his earlier wisdom (see entry 88) to Rehoboam? Very likely, yes.

92. Elijah's War Against Idolatry: The Killing of the Priests of Baal

I KINGS, CHAPTER 18

The prophet Elijah (in Hebrew, *Eliyahu ha-Navi*) is Judaism's greatest folk hero. Countless generations of Jewish children have waited expectantly at the Passover Seder for him to make a secret appearance to sip wine from the cup (*kos Eliyahu*) prepared for him. Jewish tradition also teaches that he appears at every circumcision, where a special chair (*kissei Eliyahu*) is set aside for him.

For well over two thousand years, Elijah has been the centerpiece of many folk tales, where he appears miraculously to save poor Jews and those threatened by antisemites. To this day, at the Sabbath's conclusion, Jews commonly sing about Elijah, who "should come speedily, in our days . . . along with the Messiah, son of David, to redeem us."

It comes as a shock, therefore, to turn to the biblical texts in which Elijah appears only to learn that the traditional kindly and lovable prophet bears no relationship to the Elijah of flesh and blood. The most furious and confrontational of the prophets, Elijah may well be the Bible's angriest figure.

The particular objects of Elijah's fury are King Ahab and his gentile, Baal-worshiping wife, Jezebel. The first known words the prophet speaks are a kind of curse directed toward the king, and the nation he is leading astray: "As the Lord lives, the God of Israel whom I serve, there will be no dew or rain except at my bidding" (I Kings 17:1).

As soon as Elijah delivers this message, God counsels him to hide from Ahab's wrath in a brook known as the Wadi Cherith, east of the Jordan River. There, the prophet drinks from the wadi, while God dispatches ravens to bring him daily portions of bread and meat.

The drought Elijah foretold comes to pass, and eventually the wadi dries up. God then instructs the prophet to go to the home of a certain widow, where he will be housed and fed. However, when Elijah encounters the woman and asks for bread, she tells him that she has no food; all she possesses is a handful of flour and a little oil. Elijah blesses her in God's name that "the jar of flour shall not give out and the jug of oil shall not fail until the day that the Lord sends rain upon the ground." From then on, the woman has sufficient food for herself, her son, and the prophet.

After three years of drought, God tells Elijah, "Go, appear before Ahab; then will I send rain upon the earth" (18:1). The Bible now mentions a startling detail, almost in passing. This evil king, Ahab—who "did more to vex the Lord, the God of Israel, than all the kings of Israel who preceded him" (I Kings 16:33)—maintains as his top aide a religious Jew named Obadiah. When Jezebel launches a campaign to murder all of Israel's prophets, Obadiah personally saves and feeds one hundred of them in two large caves.

Elijah encounters Obadiah before he can find Ahab, and tells him that he wishes to speak with the king. The royal aide is terrified; for three years, ever since Elijah told Ahab that there would be no rain, the king has been hunting for the prophet to kill him. The region's most powerful monarch, Ahab has demanded that the countries bordering Israel join in the search, compelling their monarchs to swear that they do not know his whereabouts. Now Obadiah fears that if he tells Ahab that he encountered Elijah but did not detain him, the king will execute him. Elijah swears to Obadiah in God's name that he will appear before Ahab that same day.

Obadiah informs the king of Elijah's whereabouts. As soon as Ahab sees the prophet, he declares: "Is that you, you troubler of Israel?" (18:17).

Elijah, a staunch advocate of "speaking truth to power," retorts: "It is not I who have brought trouble on Israel, but you and your father's house, by forsaking the commandments of the Lord and going after the [idolatrous] Baalim."

Elijah, fearing that Israel's future as a monotheistic nation is at stake, challenges Ahab to a remarkable competition: The king is to bring the 450 priests of Baal whom his wife has imported into Israel to confront Elijah at Mount Carmel in a contest to prove whose deity is more powerful. This would take place in the presence of tens of thousands of Israelites.

Desperate for the rain to fall again, Ahab agrees.

On the appointed day, Elijah steps in front of the huge crowd and asks: "How long will you keep hopping between two opinions? If the Lord is God, follow Him; and if Baal, follow him!" (18:20). The people remain silent.

Elijah then sets down the terms of the competition: He will stand on one side, the 450 priests of Baal on the other. Each side will sacrifice a bull and place the animal's remains on a wooden altar. The Baalite priests will invoke their god by name, and Elijah his, "and let us agree, the god who responds with fire, that one is God" (18:24).

The assembled Israelites and the priests accept Elijah's terms. The priests of Baal slaughter the bull, prepare the altar, and invoke Baal's name from morning till noon: "O Baal, answer us!" Receiving no response, they perform a hopping dance. Elijah mocks them: "Shout louder! . . . perhaps [your god] is asleep and will wake up" (18:27). Desperate to prove their god's power, the Baalite priests shout louder, then gash themselves with knives and spears. Soon their bodies are streaming with blood, but still there is no response.

Finally, Elijah steps forward. He builds an altar from twelve stones, corresponding to the number of Israelite tribes, then lays his slaughtered bull on the firewood. Three times, he summons bystanders to pour large buckets of water over the wood. Then, he prays to God: "O Lord, God of Abraham, Isaac and Israel! Let it be known today that You are God in Israel and that I am Your servant and that I have done all these things at Your bidding. Answer me, O Lord, answer me, that this people may know that You, O Lord, are God" (18:36–37).

Immediately, God sends down an intense fire, which consumes the offering, the wood, and even the stone altar. The people, prostrating themselves, cry out: "The Lord alone is God, the Lord alone is God!" (18:39).

Elijah commands the Israelites to seize the priests of Baal and kill all of them, which they do. He then tells Ahab that rain will soon fall. Seven times, Elijah dispatches his servant to the nearby sea to report if rain clouds can be seen. Repeatedly, the servant comes back and tells him, "There is nothing." However, the last time, he reports, "A cloud as small as a man's hand is rising in the west." Quickly, the sky turns black, and a torrential downpour ensues. Elijah runs in front of Ahab's chariot, all the way back to the monarch's winter palace in Jezreel.

In her biographical encyclopedia of biblical figures, Joan Comay concludes: "The confrontation on Mount Carmel ranks as the most dramatic moment in the centuries of struggle between Hebrew monotheism and the seductive pagan cults that constantly eroded it" (*Who's Who in the Bible*, page 113).

Yet as powerful as this encounter was—to this day, Jews conclude the Yom Kippur service by repeating seven times the words first recited by the Israelites at Mount Carmel, "The Lord alone is God" (*Adonai, hoo ha-Elohim*)—the competition's immediate repercussions are disappointing.

Remarkably, Ahab seems to have been totally unaffected by the miracles performed by God. When he arrives at the palace, the Bible suggests that all he does is tell his wife how Elijah had her 450 beloved priests killed. Furious, Jezebel sends the prophet this message: "Thus and more may the gods do if by this time tomorrow I have not made you like one of them" (I Kings 19:2).

And what of the contest's effects on the Israelites? Were they transformed? The internal evidence indicates that if an inner change occurred, it was hardly immediate. Thus, after receiving Jezebel's message, Elijah does not feel he can hide out with his fellow Israelites; rather, he has to flee for his life. He dismisses his servant, then heads alone into the desert.

Elijah's response when God asks him, "Why are you here?" likewise suggests that he feels the encounter has affected few people: ". . . for the Israelites have foresaken Your covenant, torn down Your altars. . . . I alone am left, and they are intent on taking my life" (19:10).

Is Elijah exaggerating when he says, "I alone am left"? Apparently so, for we know of Obadiah, Ahab's aide, who has risked his life to save a hundred prophets. God now tells Elijah that far more monotheists have survived; He speaks of seven thousand Israelites whose knees have not bent to Baal.

God instructs the embittered prophet to go to the nearby mountain of Horeb (Jewish tradition believes this to be Mount Sinai). The Lord sends a powerful, rock-shattering wind, but "the Lord was not in the wind." Next, the area is riven by an earthquake, "but the Lord was not in the earthquake," and after that comes a fire. Finally, God reveals Himself to Elijah with "a still small voice" (19:12), and instructs the prophet to leave the desert and return to his prophetic duties.

Reinvigorated, Elijah returns to civilization. Almost immediately, he comes across a young man named Elisha plowing in the fields, and throws his mantle over the youth's shoulders. Elijah, who until a few days earlier felt that he was the sole God-fearer left, now has recruited his first disciple and eventual successor.

Reflections: Why Elijah becomes the hero of Jewish folklore: The most satisfying explanation I've heard, suggested by my father, links the prophet Elijah's presence at both the Seder and circumcisions to the very fact of his anger, and was cited in *Jewish Literacy*: "In the immediate aftermath of Elijah's defeat of the priests of Baal, he flees from the enraged Jezebel into the desert, where he spends forty days in solitude. During this time, Elijah cries out angrily to God that 'the Israelites have forsaken your covenant and . . . I alone am left' (I Kings 19:14)—presumably meaning that he is the only Jew and only monotheist left on earth. God does not permit Elijah to wallow in self-righteousness: He gives him new tasks and sends him on his way. But perhaps here, in Elijah's exaggerated condemnation of every other Jew, is the kernel of the reason for his many reappearances. He who sees himself as the last Jew is fated to bear constant witness to the eternity of Israel, to be present when every male Jewish child enters the covenant, and when every Jewish family celebrates the Seder (to this day, circumcision and the Seder remain the most commonly observed Jewish rituals). Elijah stands in a long line of despairing Jews who erroneously have prophesied the end of the Jewish people" (page 88).

93. King Ahab and Navot's Vineyard

I KINGS, CHAPTER 21

"Have You Murdered and Also Inherited?"

21:19

If ever there was a king of Israel undeserving of a second chance, it was Ahab. After witnessing divine miracles at Mount Carmel (see preceding entry), he instigated his wife to continue her murderous campaign against the prophet Elijah.

Soon after, aided by advice from an unnamed prophet, Ahab inflicts a mighty defeat on the nearby kingdom of Aram, and shows surprising generosity to his defeated foes (I Kings 20:30–34). His own God and countrymen, however, are not the recipients of Ahab's kindness.

Adjacent to the king's winter palace in Jezreel is a beautiful vineyard owned by a man named Navot. Ahab requests Navot to cede him the land, offering him a choice of money or of a better vineyard.

Navot refuses; the land has been in his family's hands for a long time, perhaps since the Israelite settlement of Canaan. "The Lord forbid that I should give up to you what I have inherited from [my] fathers" (21:3).

Navot's rejection sends Ahab into a depression. He returns home, where he turns his face to the wall and refuses to eat.

Jezebel is shocked when she learns why her husband is upset. To her, the daughter of a tyrannical Phoenician monarch, it is inconceivable that a king's desire can be frustrated by a mere commoner. She rails at her husband: "Now is the time to show yourself king over Israel!" Sensing that Ahab is incapable of the decisive action necessary to secure the nearby field, she tells him, "I will get the vineyard of Navot the Jezreelite for you" (21:7).

The conscienceless Jezebel devises a plot that breaches three of the Ten Commandments. She starts with a violation of the prohibition against bearing false witness (the Ninth Commandment), by drafting a letter in her husband's name and using his seal and sends it to the most prominent officials in Jezreel: "Proclaim a fast and seat Navot at the front of the assembly. And seat two scoundrels opposite him, and let them testify against him: 'You have cursed God and the king.' Then take him out and stone him to death" (21:8–10).

Jezebel has now set the stage for violating the prohibition against murder (the Sixth Commandment). Jezreel's dignitaries meticulously follow the queen's orders. They proclaim a fast, convene an assembly, and seat Navot opposite two knaves, who testify, "Navot has cursed God and the king." Immediately convicted of blasphemy and treason, he is stoned to death.

Because people who are convicted of blasphemy and treason lose their estates as well as their lives, the queen rushes to her husband with the good news: "Come take possession of the vineyard of Navot . . . for Navot is no longer alive, he is dead" (21:16).

Gleefully violating the Eighth Commandment, which prohibits stealing, Ahab takes possession of the coveted vineyard (his violation of the Tenth Commandment, which prohibits coveting one's neighbor's possessions, is what precipitated Jezebel's and Ahab's violation of the other three).

God dispatches Elijah to the vineyard with a message for the king: "Have you murdered and also inherited? God says: 'Where the dogs licked Navot's blood, they will also lick your blood'" (21:19).

Elijah rushes to Navot's field, delivers God's message, then heaps additional curses on Ahab's descendants—"I will cut off every male in Israel belonging to Ahab"—and on his wife: "The dogs will devour Jezebel in the field of Jezreel" (21:23).

Terrified, Ahab believes that Elijah's words are truly divinely inspired. How else would the prophet know of Jezebel's plot against Navot? Like a mourner, Ahab rends his garments, and fasts. The shallowness and insincerity of his repentance, however, are reflected in that he retains possession of the stolen vineyard (II Kings 9:21 indicates that the field is passed on to Ahab's son, King Jehoram). Still, Ahab's act of abasement prompts God to postpone the eradication of his house to the time of his equally evil son.

Less hypocritical than her husband, Jezebel makes no pretense of repenting for Navot's murder. Unlike Elijah's prophecy concerning Ahab, his words predicting Jezebel's death are literally fulfilled. Many years after Ahab's death, a rebel leader, Jehu, stages a coup against Jehoram, Ahab's son. After killing Jehoram, Jehu orders his troops to seize Jezebel and toss her out a palace window. Badly injured by the fall, she is soon trampled by horses and dies. Jehu then sits down to a feast, after which he instructs his servants, "Attend to that cursed woman and bury her, for she was a king's daughter" (II Kings 9:34).

The soldiers go outside, but all they can locate are Jezebel's skull, feet, and hands; dogs have consumed the rest. Elijah's curse against Jezebel has apparently become widely known, for the soldiers report to Jehu: "It is just as the Lord spoke through His servant Elijah. . . . The dogs shall devour the flesh of Jezebel in the field [of Navot in] Jezreel" (II Kings 9:36).

Elijah's three-word condemnation of Ahab, *Ha-ratzakhta ve-gam yar-ashta?*—"Have you murdered and also inherited?"—remains perhaps the most powerful denunciation of an evil person in the entire Hebrew Bible.

94. Elijah Ascends to Heaven in a Chariot of Fire

II KINGS, CHAPTER 2

It is fitting that the departure from this life of Elijah, author of perhaps more miracles than any other biblical prophet, also occurs through a miracle.

The final day of Elijah's sojourn on earth seems to be known to many people, although the Bible does not tell us how. Everywhere he travels, accompanied by his disciple Elisha, people ask Elisha, "Do you know that God is taking your master away from you today?" He responds, "I know it too; be silent" (2:5).

Toward the day's end, Elijah and Elisha (prophets of the Northern Kingdom only) come to the Jordan River, where Elijah strikes the water with his cloak. The waters separate, and the men cross to the other side on dry land.

As they walk, Elijah says to Elisha, "Tell me what I can do for you before I am taken away from you."

Elisha is not hesitant. "Please give me a double portion of your spirit," he requests.

"You have asked a difficult thing," Elijah answers. "If you see me as I am being taken from you, this will be granted to you; if not, it will not" (2:9–10).

Suddenly, a fiery chariot, drawn by fiery horses, descends from the sky. Elijah is plucked away and ascends heavenward. His death never having been recorded, Elijah enters Jewish folk tradition, where he serves as the savior of poor and oppressed Jews, attends each Passover Seder and circumcision, and heralds the coming of the Messiah.

To his great relief, Elisha witnesses Elijah's ascent. Tearing his clothes in mourning, he picks up the cloak Elijah has dropped. Like his master, he strikes it against the water, and again the river parts.

Watching on the opposite side, Elijah's other disciples witness this miracle and declare: "Elijah's spirit now rests on Elisha" (2:15).

95. Elisha Cures Syrian General Na'aman, a Non-Israelite

II KINGS, CHAPTER 5

The Bible reports few contacts between Israelite prophets and non-Israelites (the one with the most far-reaching consequences is that of Jonah; see entry 118). One of the most unusual such meetings occurs between the prophet Elisha and the Syrian general Na'aman, an interaction that results in the latter's conversion to monotheism.

Na'aman, the powerful commander of Syria's army, "though a great warrior, was a leper" (5:1). During a raid against Israel, his troops capture a young Israelite woman who becomes a servant to his wife. She tells her mistress that if Na'aman would consult the prophet Elisha, he could be cured of his leprosy. When Na'aman tells his king of the girl's statement, the monarch promises to write his counterpart in Israel a letter on Na'aman's behalf.

Na'aman soon arrives at Israel's palace, carrying with him both gifts of silver and gold and the Syrian king's letter which states: "Now, when this letter reaches you, know that I have sent my courtier Na'aman to you, that you may cure him of his leprosy" (5:6).

Israel is militarily weaker than Syria, and the letter throws the Israelite king into a panic. He rends his clothes in the manner of a mourner, and expresses fear that since leprosy is incurable, the Syrian ruler is searching for a pretext to invade Israel.

Elisha, having heard what happened, sends a message to the king, telling him to send Na'aman, "and he will learn there is a prophet in Israel."

When Na'aman arrives at the prophet's house, Elisha sends a messenger out to him who instructs Na'aman to "go and bathe seven times in the Jordan, and your flesh shall be restored and you shall be clean" (5:10).

The message angers the general, for Na'aman had expected a miracle: Elisha perhaps would stand near him, invoke Israel's God by name, then wave his hand over the infected areas and cure them.

Instead, he is being dispatched to the Jordan, a shallow, unimpressive body of water: "Are not the Amanah and the Pharpar, the rivers of Damascus, better than all the waters of Israel? I could bathe in them and be clean" (5:12).

One of Na'aman's servants courageously confronts his master and with commonsense reasoning says: "Sir, if the prophet told you to do something difficult, would you not do it? How much more when he has only said to you, 'Bathe and be clean' " (5:13).

Na'aman allows himself to be convinced, and immerses himself in the Jordan. After his seventh dipping, his flesh becomes like that of a little boy, and his entire body is clear of leprosy.

The once furious general becomes an instant convert to the God of Israel. He comes before Elisha and declares: "Now I know that there is no God in the whole world except in Israel!" (5:15).

He presses Elisha to accept a gift, but the prophet refuses. Na'aman then requests permission to bring back to Syria two mule-loads of earth so that, while there, he can continue to pray on Israelite soil. Regarding himself now as a loyal follower of Israel's God, Na'aman asks for one dispensation: That when he accompanies the Syrian king to the idolatrous temple of Rimmon, he be permitted to bow down there with the king.

Although Elisha does not explicitly approve of such behavior, he apparently implies permission by telling Na'aman to "go in peace" (5:19).

When Na'aman leaves, Gehazi, Elisha's servant, rushes off to intercept him and to request, in his master's name, the reward that Elisha had earlier refused. Na'aman happily gives him a large quantity of silver and some new clothes.

But when Gehazi returns to Elisha's house, the prophet, who has divined his servant's behavior, is furious. In curing Na'aman, Elisha had intended to show the general the great power of Israel's God and, in his refusal to take a reward for the cure, the great goodness of Israelite religion. But now Gehazi's request for money has made it seem like Elisha is only a miracle worker out for a "quick buck."

Elisha curses Gehazi, bidding that he be afflicted with the very illness of which he has just cured Na'aman: "And as [Gehazi] left his presence, he was snow-white with leprosy" (5:27).

96. Jehu: From Righteous Assassin to Mass Killer

II KINGS, CHAPTERS 9–10

"The hand that strikes [even on behalf of a righteous cause] often loses its capacity for tender touches," the Russian poet Yevgeny Yevtushenko has said. Yevtushenko's statement seems to accurately describe the career of Jehu, an Israelite soldier who starts out as a righteous assassin, then becomes a somewhat indiscriminate killer.

Jehu is serving as commander-in-chief of Israel's army when a disciple of the prophet Elisha, acting at the prophet's command, anoints him at a military base. "I anoint you king over the people of the Lord, over Israel," announces the unnamed messenger. He goes on to instruct Jehu about his first order of business: "You should strike down the House of Ahab your master; thus I will avenge on Jezebel the blood of my servants" (9:6–7).*

Jehu returns to his officers and recounts all that has happened. The men sound a horn and proclaim, "Jehu is king."

While all this is transpiring, King Jehoram is in bed, recovering from wounds received in a recent battle with the Syrian army, while Ahaziah, Judah's king and Jehoram's nephew, is visiting him.

However, when Jehoram's servants report that Jehu has been seen racing toward the palace in a chariot, the king arises from his bed and goes to meet Jehu in what the Bible refers to as the field of Navot, which his father and mother had acquired through murder and thievery (see entry 93).

Concerned at his military commander's sudden appearance, Jehoram asks Jehu: "Is all well?" Jehu responds: "How can all be well as long as your mother Jezebel carries on her countless harlotries and sorceries?" (9:22).

---

*The king whom Jehu is ordered to kill is Jehoram (alternatively, Joram), the son of Ahab and the still-living Jezebel (see entry 92). "The blood of my servants" that he is being asked to avenge refers to the many Israelite prophets Jezebel had murdered during her husband's reign (I Kings 18:4, 13).

Jehoram shouts, "Treason!" and turns his horse to flee, but Jehu shoots him dead with an arrow and orders that his body be left in the field; Jehu also kills Ahaziah.

By the time Jehu reaches the palace, where Jezebel resides, the former queen has heard of the assassination. She puts on her makeup (yes, this detail is in the Bible [9:30]: "She painted her eyes with kohl and dressed her hair") and calls out through a palace window to Jehu: "Is all well, Zimri,* murderer of your master?"

Instead of responding to Jezebel's taunts, Jehu calls out to her servants: "Who is on my side? Who?" When two or three servants lean out the windows to signify support, he orders them to throw Jezebel out the window. The fall bloodies and badly wounds Jezebel, and nearby horses quickly trample her to death.

Jehu sits down to a feast, at the end of which he orders that Jezebel's body be buried, since "she was a king's daughter" (her father, Ethbaal, was king of Phoenicia). But all that can be found of Jezebel's body is her skull, feet, and hands; dogs have consumed the rest (as Elijah had predicted when Jezebel stole Navot's field; I Kings 21:23).

Jehu now proceeds against Ahab's descendants, who are potential claimants to the throne. He arranges for all seventy of them to be murdered by Ahab's former officials, the very people who have been charged with guarding them. Conscious of the political transformation that has occurred, the officials not only murder Ahab's descendants, but also cut off their heads and bring them to Jehu.

Acting as if he had no desire for such bloodletting, Jehu proceeds to murder the officials; thus, ridding Israel of all of Ahab's descendants and former high officers.

Jehu next murders forty-two relatives of King Ahaziah, who, unaware that the king has been killed, have arrived in Israel to visit him (there is no record of the kingdom of Judah reacting in any way

---

*A derogatory nickname, like calling someone Benedict Arnold. Zimri, a servant of King Elah, had murdered his master and proclaimed himself king. When Omri, Elah's commanding officer, heard of the assassination, he attacked the palace, which Zimri burned down with himself inside (I Kings 16:18). Zimri's reign as king lasted seven days, a fate Jezebel obviously wished for Jehu.

However, Jehu had two reasons to be optimistic that his future would be better than Zimri's: He was acting at a prophet's command, and he was already the commander-in-chief of the army; thus, he was in a far stronger position than Zimri had been to ward off attacks.

to Jehu's murder of Ahaziah; this in itself suggests that Ahaziah, also a descendant of Ahab, must have been a pretty evil person; see II Kings 8:27).

Pretending to be an idolater, Jehu next announces that he is hosting a large public sacrifice for Baal. Large numbers of Baal worshipers come, sufficient to fill up a Baalite temple from end to end. Jehu orders his troops to kill them all (10:25). After this deed, the soldiers turn the temple into a latrine.

God apparently approves of Jehu's actions, for He proclaims: "Because you have acted well and done what was pleasing to Me, having carried out all that I desire upon the House of Ahab, four generations of your descendants shall occupy the throne of Israel" (10:30; given the well-known Torah commandment prohibiting punishing children for a parent's offense [Deuteronomy 24:16], it is difficult to understand why God approves of the murder of Ahab's seventy descendants, some of whom apparently were quite young).

Jehu rules as king for twenty-two years, long enough for him to turn away from his formerly pure monotheism and become a worshiper of the golden calves at Israel's two main temples (10:29, 31).

Despite the Lord's earlier approval of Jehu's murders, the prophet Hosea denounces the king for his excessive bloodletting (Hosea 1:4). While his indictment is somewhat vague, the prophet likely was most offended by the murder of Ahab's advisers. Perhaps the fact that Jehu ended up an idolater suggests that his motive for the earlier killings was more power lust than devotion to God and monotheism.

97. How the Ten Lost Tribes Become Lost: The End of the Kingdom of Israel (722 B.C.E.)

II KINGS 18:9–12

The kingdom of Israel, composed of the ten northernmost tribes, was established in 931 B.C.E. after the death of King Solomon (see entry 91). It lasted for 209 very turbulent years, marked by numerous royal assassinations, repeated successions of new dynasties, and frequent reversions to idolatry.

Although Israel had periods of considerable military strength (e.g., during King Ahab's reign), it often fell under foreign domination. In the late eighth century B.C.E., Assyria ruled over Israel. But upon the death of Assyria's king, Tiglath-Pileser, in 727, Hoshea, the king of Israel rebelled.

The Assyrians responded with a siege of Israel that culminated with the kingdom's fall and the deportation of many of her inhabitants in 722. Years earlier, the prophet Isaiah had predicted that Assyria, "rod of [God's] anger," would punish Israel for her numerous sins (Isaiah 10:5).

Ever since Assyria dispersed Israel, the fate of the Ten Tribes has remained a mystery. Clearly, not *all* of the people assimilated into foreign nations and religions. Some fled to the still-surviving Jewish kingdom of Judah, and remained part of the Jewish people. However, the majority apparently did assimilate into the societies to which they were exiled.

Jewish folklorists have periodically conjectured that various nations might have their roots in the Ten Tribes. When a country has treated Jews well (for example, England after the 1917 issuance of the Balfour Declaration), some Jews have conjectured that its people are descended from the "lost tribes." Several decades ago, some scholars discovered striking similarities between the traditions of the Torah and of some North American Indian tribes (for example, some Native Americans used to observe a fall harvest holiday during which members built and lived in huts, a practice reminiscent of the biblical holiday of Sukkot; Leviticus 23:39–43), leading them to conjecture that these people descended from the Ten Tribes.

Prior to 722, each Israelite could identify him- or herself by the tribe from which he or she descended. From the Babylonian exile on, except for those who trace their ancestry to the tribe of Levi or to the *Kohanim* (a subgroup within Levi; see entry 125), all Jews are assumed to descend only from one tribe, Judah. Therefore, from the perspective of Jewish genealogy, the Ten Tribes are assumed to have vanished without a trace.

This dispersion, an event that occurred more than 2,700 years ago, remains repercussive in Jewish life. If not for this loss, the world's Jewish population, which now numbers fewer than three out of every one thousand people, would likely be two or three times as large (thirty to forty-five million people instead of fourteen million).

98. King Hezekiah's Illness (c. 701 B.C.E.)

II KINGS, CHAPTER 20

Israel's prophets generally delivered conditional warnings (*"If you continue to act in this way, this-and-this will occur, but if you change your behavior, such a fate might not befall you"*), not oracles (*"Such-and-such will happen no matter what you do"*). This is vividly illustrated by the experience of King Hezekiah, one of Judah's most righteous monarchs.

During his reign's middle years, the king falls desperately ill. The prophet Isaiah comes to him with a very dispiriting message: "Thus said the Lord: Set your affairs in order, for you are going to die; you will not get well" (20:1).

Normally, common sense and compassion would stop a person from delivering so discouraging a message; indeed, Isaiah's words alone could cause a person to lose all hope and die. Unfortunately, when dealing with a nation's leader, one must sometimes speak the harsh truth, since the leader must make preparations for his succession, which he would not do if he believed that he would soon recover.

Surprisingly, Isaiah's words, although phrased unconditionally, do not break Hezekiah's spirit. Immediately upon the prophet's departure, he turns to the wall, cries profusely, and prays to God: "Please, O Lord, remember how I have walked before You sincerely and wholeheartedly, and have done what is pleasing to You" (20:3).

Isaiah is still inside the royal court when God's word comes to him again, telling him to inform Hezekiah that the Lord has heard his prayer and seen his tears, "and I will add fifteen years to your life."

When Isaiah rushes to Hezekiah with the good news, the skeptical monarch asks, "What is the sign that the Lord will heal me . . . ?"

In an almost unprecedented act, Isaiah offers Hezekiah a choice of miracles. He asks the king if he would prefer to see the shadow on the sundial of Ahaz (a time-keeping device) advance or recede ten steps. Hezekiah answers: "It is easy for the shadow to lengthen ten steps, but not for the shadow to recede ten steps" (20:10). When Isaiah calls on God to make the shadow on the dial of Ahaz do so, it does and time "moves backward."

As predicted, Hezekiah lives another fifteen years, which proves fortuitous, given that Manasseh, the son who succeeds him, is among the most evil and idolatrous kings to rule over Judah (see next entry).

In the 2,700 years since Hezekiah lived, his story has emboldened many sick people. Even in the shadow of death, this story teaches that one must not lose hope. Prayer can still turn a decree of death into one of life.

Note 1: A second version of the story of Hezekiah's illness: Isaiah, chapter 38, also records the story of Hezekiah's illness and recovery, with several variations. Verse 8 tells us that God makes the shadow on the sundial of Ahaz recede, but no mention is made of the prophet asking Hezekiah to specify which miracle he would prefer. The thanksgiving that Hezekiah offers after his recovery (38:10–20) suggests that he prayed to God the entire night (38:13) before learning from Isaiah that his death would be postponed.

Note 2: The sundial of Ahaz: Nelson's Illustrated Bible Dictionary notes that the sundial of Ahaz "was probably not a small disk, as modern readers might suppose, but an escalating stairway on which the sun cast its shadow higher and higher during the day.... This stairway may have been constructed in such a way that a shadow cast by a stationary post or pillar climbed the stairs at the rate of one every half hour. The Greek historian Herodotus, writing several hundred years after Hezekiah, mentions the use among the Babylonians of a sundial marked off in this fashion.... The biblical writers identified this stairway with Ahaz, probably because it was constructed during his reign" (page 1016).

99. King Manasseh of Judah (687–642 B.C.E.): An Evil Man

II KINGS, CHAPTER 21; II CHRONICLES, CHAPTER 33

In contemporary American English, the word "successful" generally connotes wealth. If someone makes a great deal of money, we call such a person "successful," even if he has a miserably unsuccessful family life. If someone earns little money, we call him "unsuccessful," even if his life otherwise is beautiful.

By this standard, Manasseh, who ruled over Judah for fifty-five years, longer than any other biblical king, must be regarded as remarkably successful. Although he ruled under Assyrian domination, Judah was prosperous and at peace throughout his reign.

By the Bible's standards, however, Manasseh was anything but a success; indeed, the Bible regards him as the most evil Jewish king who ever reigned. Manasseh was not only evil himself, but also provoked evil in others: "Manasseh led them [the Jews] astray to do greater evil than the nations [i.e., the Canaanites] which the Lord had destroyed before the Israelites" (21:9).

For one thing, he was a thug: "Manasseh put so many innocent persons to death that he filled Jerusalem [with blood] from end to end" (21:16). He was pitiless even toward his own family and once sacrificed one of his sons in fire (21:6). An old Jewish tradition (Babylonian Talmud, *Yevamot* 49b) claims that he murdered the prophet Isaiah. The son of an ethical, God-fearing father, King Hezekiah, Manasseh rebuilt the pagan temples his father had destroyed, worshiped in them, and also put an idol into the Temple in Jerusalem.

While the Second Book of Kings, which tells Manasseh's story, has nothing good to say about him, the Second Book of Chronicles tells an interesting, if almost unbelievable, story about his final years. According to this account, God provoked the Assyrians to punish Manasseh (presumably because of his participation in an insurrection against them). They imprisoned him, bound him with bronze shackles, and took him to Babylon (II Chronicles 33:11). While in Babylon, Manasseh repented of his evil deeds, and turned to God in prayer. The Lord forgave him and restored him to Jerusalem, where he destroyed the idolatrous temples he had built and urged his subjects to return to God (II Chronicles 33:14, 16).

Frankly, this account sounds too good to be true. Before accepting it uncritically, one should remember that the Second Book of Kings, which tells the story of Manasseh's life *up to and including his death*, never suggests that his evil behavior improved. Had true repentance occurred, the author of the Second Book of Kings undoubtedly would have been delighted to relate that Judah's most evil king had eventually turned to God.

The account in II Chronicles is so bizarre that more than a few Bible scholars have conjectured that its author inserted the tale of Manasseh's repentance to account for the politically peaceful and materially prosperous nature of his reign. Otherwise, it seemed too unfair, too great a challenge to the author's notion of divine justice, that so evil a man could have led so "successful" a life.

For more sophisticated believers, the account in II Kings needs no emendation. That Manasseh was successful by nonbiblical criteria is sad but unsurprising. However, according to a "Higher Accounting," what is worth remembering about Manasseh is neither his wealth nor his fifty-five-year reign; only that he outdid "in wickedness all that the Amorites [the Canaanites] did before his time" (II Kings 21:11).

100. Josiah of Judah: The Reformer King (640–609 B.C.E.)

II KINGS, CHAPTERS 22–23; II CHRONICLES, CHAPTERS 34–35

The Jewish belief that the ultimate king, the Messiah, will descend from King David is a testament to Jews' belief both in David's greatness, as well as in the enduring nature of God's promise to him that "your throne shall be established forever" (II Samuel 7:16).

Unfortunately, David's greatness notwithstanding, most of the kings who descended from him (between 960 and 587 B.C.E.) were evil. The most notable, though not only, exception was Josiah, who restored to Judah some of the glory his illustrious ancestor, David, once had brought to all Israel. Indeed, the Bible declares Josiah the greatest king in biblical history in moral-religious terms: "There was no king like him before who turned back to the Lord with all his heart and soul and might, in full accord with the teaching of Moses; nor did any like him arise after him" (II Kings 23:25).

In light of such a testament, it is inspiring to learn that Josiah was the son of a morally debased father (King Amon) and grandfather (King Manasseh), even though it is depressing to know that he sired another evil man (Jehoiakim).

How did Josiah, coming from so corrupt a background, achieve such greatness? Apparently, as a result of family tragedies that would usually be regarded as catastrophic—the deaths of his grandfather and father while he was still a young boy. For Josiah these deaths were in fact highly beneficial, at least for his soul. After all, the Bible had condemned his grandfather Manasseh as the most evil king ever to reign in Israel (see preceding entry). Josiah's father, Amon, can be regarded as a good king *only* when compared to *his* father. When Josiah was six, Manasseh died; when he was eight, Amon was assassinated by court officials. When the plotters, who probably hoped to assume power, were themselves killed, the remaining court officials anointed Josiah king. Therefore, instead of growing up under his father's malevolent tutelage, he was evidently exposed to more benign influences (although we don't know precisely who they were).

The young man grows up to become something of a philosopher king. The Book of Chronicles tells us that at the age of sixteen, Josiah begins seeking God (II Chronicles 34:3) and by age twenty, he initiates his great work of religious reform. His first act is to have the Temple ritually cleaned (22:5). Josiah is not solely interested in ritual repentance, as evidenced by his concern that the carpenters and other laborers be paid fairly.

While the Temple is being cleaned out, Hilkiah, the High Priest, finds a scroll of the Torah, which expresses ideas unfamiliar to Jews of the time. The scroll is brought to the palace and read before Josiah, and "when the king heard [its] contents . . . he rent his clothes . . . [And he said] 'Great indeed must be the wrath of the Lord . . . because our fathers did not obey the words of this scroll to do all that has been prescribed for us'" (22:11).* The king then convenes

---

*When Hilkiah and others of the king's advisers consult with Huldah, a female prophetess (22:14), she assures them of the scroll's authenticity.

a public meeting of Judah's citizens and has the scroll read aloud to them.

Bible scholars have long argued about which Torah section was discovered in the Temple. The prevailing sentiment is that it was Deuteronomy, or parts of the Torah's fifth book, although Josiah's reforms suggest that many laws from the Torah's other books had also been forgotten.

Thus, we learn that *the Passover sacrifice, which was ordained in Exodus (12:1–11), had not been offered for centuries,* since before the period of the kings (II Kings 23:21–23).* That Passover, Josiah reinstitutes the sacrificial offering.

Based on the Torah scroll found in the Temple, Josiah initiates other reforms, among the most important being the destruction of idolatrous temples and idols throughout Judah. He also ends child sacrifice and male prostitution at the Temple. One biblical verse powerfully captures the mixture of prostitution and idolatry at the Temple: "He tore down the cubicles of the male prostitutes in the House of the Lord, at the place where the women wove coverings for [the goddess] Ashera" (II Kings 23:7).

Josiah's reforms last some twelve years until, in 609, he makes a fatal political miscalculation. King Necho of Egypt requests permission to march his troops peacefully through Judah to Carchemish, where he hopes to defeat the Babylonians. Necho repeatedly insists, even invoking God's name, that he will do Judah no harm. But Josiah refuses him permission to pass through Judah and goes out to do battle with him, at which point he is mortally wounded. His servants carry his body in a chariot from the battle site to Jerusalem, where he dies (II Chronicles 35:20–24).

Noble as Josiah was, his moral and spiritual revolution died with him.

Why did his extensive reforms make so little impact?

While she expresses admiration for Josiah's desire to act righteously, she claims that God has every intention of bringing about Judah's destruction as punishment for its numerous sins. But she prophesies that because of Josiah's moral worthiness, this destruction will be deferred until after his lifetime.

*Had only Deuteronomy, but not the Torah's other books, been lost, the people would still have known about the Passover sacrifice. That is why it seems that more of the Torah than just one book must have been rediscovered during Josiah's time.

In his commentary on the prophet Jeremiah, John Bright emphasizes two reasons:

—Josiah's reforms led to complacency. People believed that the
king's resanctification of the Temple would ensure that God would
always favor them.

—Although the reforms led to a turning away from idolatry, they
also resulted in an obsession more with ritual than morality,* at least
according to Jeremiah.

Jeremiah regarded Josiah as a righteous king, concerned with turning the nation toward good. Still, he viewed Josiah's reforms as but
a beginning; when the ruler died, the prophet became acutely conscious of the reforms' shallow impact on many of Judah's richest
citizens. Jeremiah believed that for many of them, rituals had become
a way of bribing God. He depicts God as asking, "What need have
I of frankincense that comes from Sheba, or fragrant cane from a
distant land?" (Jeremiah 6:20).

Apparently, then, Josiah's death quite literally demoralized the
nation, leading many to think that God, or the gods who controlled
the universe, had rejected him.

Preceded by an evil grandfather and father, Josiah is followed by
evil sons. He was a short burst of light, preceded and followed by
night.

Sources: John Bright, Anchor Bible, *Jeremiah*, page xlv. See also Richard
Victor Bergren, *The Prophets and the Law*, pages 182–183.

---

*This is still largely true. When we speak of someone becoming "religious,"
we assume that he or she has become ritually but not necessarily ethically
observant. According to the prophets, however, faith is primarily proven
through ethical behavior and the repudiation of idolatry. Almost all the
offenses denounced by the prophets are ethical in nature. Punctilious as
Josiah was in cleansing the Temple and Judah of idolatry, he was not
equally punctilious in cleansing his subjects of immoral practices.

101. Nebuchadnezzar and the Babylonian Siege of Jerusalem; The Temple Is Destroyed (587 B.C.E.)

II KINGS, CHAPTERS 24–25

Common sense dictates that if you decide to antagonize an opponent, you shouldn't pick on someone who is both stronger than you and particularly cruel. Unfortunately, the leaders of the commonwealth of Judah lacked common sense.

Judah *twice* chose to antagonize Nebuchadnezzar, the Babylonian king who ruled over the Jewish province for forty-three years, from 605–562 B.C.E.

The Judeans did not submit happily to being Nebuchadnezzar's vassals and, on two occasions, they revolted. The first time was in 598, under the leadership of King Jehoiakim (24:2). The revolt was suppressed, but soon renewed by Jehoiachin, the king's son and successor. This time, Nebuchadnezzar's troops imposed a severe punishment: Ten thousand of Judah's leading figures were exiled to Babylon (including commanders, soldiers, craftsmen, and smiths; 24:14). In addition, Nebuchadnezzar looted the Temple in Jerusalem, stripping it of its gold.

Nebuchadnezzar then appointed the twenty-one-year-old Zedekiah, Jehoiachin's uncle, to rule over the now-impoverished province ("Only the poorest in the land were left"; 24:14). In 587, almost ten years after becoming king, Zedekiah rebelled against Nebuchadnezzar. The strongest opponent of this suicidal revolt was the prophet Jeremiah, who came to be regarded by many of his fellow Judeans as a traitor (see entry 110). Some of Zedekiah's officers tried to murder Jeremiah, but an Ethiopian servant of the king saved the prophet; shortly thereafter he was summoned to a private audience with Zedekiah.

Speaking in God's name, Jeremiah tells the king that the only way he can save his and his family's lives, and spare Jerusalem from destruction, is by surrendering to Nebuchadnezzar (Jeremiah, chapter 38).

King Zedekiah's vague response to Jeremiah's advice leaves the impression that what really stops him from following the prophet's admonition is the fear that his army will overthrow him.

The revolt continues until Nebuchadnezzar unleashes the entire Babylonian army against Jerusalem. He imposes a siege on the city (its horrible effects are described in Lamentations; see entry 133) and after two and a half months, Jerusalem's walls are breached.

The Judean army deserts Jerusalem along with the king. Zedekiah is caught and brought before Nebuchadnezzar. Outraged at Judah's repeated revolts, the sadistic monarch has Zedekiah's sons murdered in front of him, then has him blinded so that the final sight he will carry with him till his death is the brutal death of his sons (II Kings 25:6–7).

Meanwhile, in Jerusalem Nebuzaradan, a general in Babylon's army, "burned the House of the Lord [the Temple], the king's palace, and all the houses of Jerusalem" (25:9). The soldiers carried off whatever Temple valuables that had not been stolen ten years earlier by Nebuchadnezzar—the bronze vessels, the remaining gold and silver, and even "the fire pans and sprinkling bowls" (25:13–17).

According to II Kings 25:8, the Temple's destruction began on the *seventh* day of the month of Av (which generally falls between mid-July and mid-August). Jeremiah (52:12) speaks, however, of the *Tenth* of Av, although Jewish law designates the *ninth* of Av as the fast day commemorating the Temple's destruction. Apparently, a tradition existed that the Temple was put to the torch on that day.

"Thus Judah was exiled from its land," the Second Book of Kings (25:21) notes. However, Nebuchadnezzar did make one concession to the tiny Jewish community remaining within Judah: He appointed a man named Gedaliah, a patriotic and religious Jew, to be Judah's governor (on Gedaliah's short term of office, see entry 103).

Nebuchadnezzar is remembered in the Western world for the hanging gardens he built atop his palace roof, which were regarded as one of the seven wonders of the ancient world. His standing in Jewish history is less illustrious, for he was the destroyer of Solomon's Temple, the greatest Israelite wonder of the ancient world.

102. The Babylonian Exile (587 B.C.E.)

Although Jewish tradition remembers the Babylonian Exile as a time of unending pain—"By the rivers of Babylon, there we sat, sat and wept, as we remembered Zion" (Psalm 137:1–5)—the meager historical data suggest that the Jews rapidly adjusted to, and even prospered, in Babylon.

In doing so, they were following the advice the prophet Jeremiah proffered in a public letter. Conscious that the Jews exiled to Babylon included the people who had instigated suicidal Judean revolts against Babylon's king Nebuchadnezzar, he urges the exiles "to seek the welfare of the city to which I [God] have exiled you, pray to the Lord on its behalf, for in its prosperity you shall prosper" (Jeremiah 29:7).

Jeremiah assures the exiles that hope is not lost; eventually, after seventy years, God will bring their descendants back to Israel (29:10). Meanwhile, however, the Jews are to eschew political/military attempts to regain Israel. Instead, they should "take wives and beget sons and daughters, and take wives for your sons, and give your daughters to husbands, that they may bear sons and daughters. Multiply there, do not decrease" (29:6).

Babylonia's Jews seem to have embraced the policy of normalcy advocated by Jeremiah. Ancient records note the involvement of Jews as builders and craftsmen in Babylon's royal buildings, while the Babylonian government apparently granted the Jews considerable autonomy in conducting their religious affairs.

There is striking empirical evidence of the Jews' successful acculturation to Babylonian society. In 539 B.C.E., King Cyrus of Persia defeats Babylon, and soon thereafter invites its Jewish residents to return to Israel. The large majority, like their diaspora descendants 2,500 years later when the modern State of Israel was established, decide to remain where they are. They opt instead to send money to help those Jews who do return (Ezra 1:4).

Some countries in which exiled Jews have lived have been horrible. It would seem that ancient Babylon was not one of them.

103. Gedaliah: The Last Jewish Governor of Judah (587–586 B.C.E.)

II KINGS 25:22–26; JEREMIAH 39:14 AND 40:5–41:18

Gedaliah was a man of "stout heart," to use a nineteenth-century expression. Unfortunately, his brain was of thinner dimensions; this was most unfortunate, since a shrewder ruler might have been able to keep the Jews from losing all power in their homeland.

Gedaliah came from an extraordinary family. His father, Ahikam, had conspired to keep Jeremiah alive at a time when the prophet Uriah (whose message was very similar to Jeremiah's) was murdered by command of King Jehoiakim (Jeremiah 26:20–24). Gedaliah's grandfather, Shaphan, was an official who helped King Josiah (reigned 640–609 B.C.E.) carry out his extraordinary religious and ethical reforms, including cleansing the Temple (II Kings 22:3–14).

At the lowest point in Judah's history, after the Babylonians had destroyed Jerusalem and burned down the Temple, the Babylonian king Nebuchadnezzar appointed Gedaliah as Judah's governor: He was empowered to rule over those Jews, generally the poorest segment of the population, whom Nebuchadnezzar had not exiled to Babylon. Because Jerusalem had been so devastated by the Babylonians, Gedaliah made his headquarters seven miles north of it, in the city of Mizpah.

Nebuchadnezzar also had the prophet Jeremiah, the fiercest Judean opponent of the revolt against Babylon, released from prison and entrusted to Gedaliah's protection (Jeremiah 39:11–14).

Jeremiah, who was perhaps Judah's most politically astute observer, was overjoyed at the appointment of Gedaliah as governor. If the Babylonian king was willing to appoint a Jew to this post, after having fought two Jewish revolts within eleven years, Jews could still have some input and influence in the running of their homeland. However, the prophet was not naive; he understood that the Babylonians would likely bestow little power on the Jew they appointed as governor. But it was better to have a Jew in this position—and one who was righteous—than a non–Israelite.

Aware of how intent the Babylonians were that the Jews not initiate a third revolt, Gedaliah tried to calm Judah's political atmo-
sphere by urging the people to "stay in the land and serve the king
of Babylon, and it will go well with you" (II Kings 25:24).

From the little we know of him, Gedaliah seems to have been a
moderate man of many virtues; insight, however, was not one of
them. An opponent of revolution and bloodshed, he naively under-
estimated the evils of which his fellow Jews were capable. Thus,
when Yochanan, son of Kareah, warned him of a plot by Ishmael—a
radical nationalist who regarded as a traitor any Jew that the Babylonians appointed to office—Gedaliah refused to believe that a fellow Jew would plot against him.

Yochanan, accompanied by other army troops, persisted and
shared with him accurate intelligence about Ishmael's intentions: "Do
you know that King Baalis of Ammon has sent Ishmael to kill you?"
Unfortunately, as the Book of Jeremiah records, "Gedaliah would not
believe them" (40:14).

Yochanan met secretly with Gedaliah at Mizpah, and begged him,
"Let me go and strike down Ishmael before anyone knows about it;
otherwise, he will kill you, and all the Judeans who have gathered
about you will be dispersed, and the remnant of Judah will perish."
But Gedaliah answered Yochanan: "Do not do such a thing: what
you are saying about Ishmael is not true" (40:13–16).

Gedaliah's estimation of Ishmael could not have been more wrong.
A few months later, Ishmael was invited to Gedaliah's headquarters
to share a meal. He came with ten men, and during the meal Ishmael
and his troops murdered Gedaliah and all those with him. They then
unleashed an orgy of violence against Gedaliah's supporters, dumped
their bodies into a giant cistern, and fled back to their patron, the
king of Ammon.

Yochanan, who had warned Gedaliah of Ishmael's treacherous intentions, fled with his troops to Egypt, convinced that the infuriated
Babylonians would wreak vengeance on any Jews remaining in Judah.
He took with him a protesting Jeremiah; the old prophet wished to
remain in Judah, and indeed prophesied that if the Jews remained
there, God would protect them (Jeremiah 42–43:7). The prophet's
words were ignored, and it was in Egypt that Jeremiah died.

Gedaliah's death, and the end of what little power the Jews still
had in Judah (Judah evidently lost all its separate identity following
the murder), have since been regarded by Jews as a tragedy. The
day of Gedaliah's death—which falls on the day after Rosh ha-
Shana, the Jewish New Year, is observed as a fast day.

THE LATER PROPHETS

ISAIAH

JEREMIAH

EZEKIEL

THE TWELVE MINOR PROPHETS

X. ISAIAH

104. Isaiah (8th Century B.C.E.): A Profile; "The Wolf Shall Dwell with the Lamb"

11:6

"Doing the right thing is generally the right thing to do," an old proverb declares. Basically, this is one of the messages Isaiah imparts to Ahaz, king of Judah, in 735 B.C.E. when Ahaz is pressured by Israel and Syria to join them in revolt against Assyria. Ahaz is shrewd enough to understand that such an alliance is insufficient to confront the Assyrian empire (it would be as if the small countries of Central America decided to unite in military confrontation against the United States), and he rejects their overtures. However, wishing to protect himself against these now-wrathful states, he decides to turn to Assyria for help, a move Isaiah opposes. Although Assyrian aid might help Judah win its short-term battle against Israel and Syria, it will also lead to its enslavement to Assyria.

The king ignores Isaiah's advice, and the prophet's prediction comes to pass.

This episode, drawn from Isaiah, chapter 7, defies the common image most people have of the biblical prophets as speaking only against idolatry and the nonoppression of the poor. As befits a man who was raised in affluent, sophisticated circles (Jewish tradition claims that he was a nephew of King Amaziah), Isaiah was worldly as well as pious, a man with a vision of both this world and the next.

Along with being politically astute, Isaiah is a deeply spiritual man who bequeaths to all generations an extraordinary, and in some ways baffling, account of a prophetic vision. In the year that King Uzziah died (740) he recounts a remarkable vision, one in which he sees himself as an earthly observer of God's heavenly council: "I beheld my Lord seated on a high and lofty throne. . . . Seraphs [angels] stood in attendance on Him. Each of them had six wings. . . ." (6:1–2). Isaiah hears the angels calling out to one another, "Holy, holy, holy! The Lord of Hosts! His presence fills the earth," words that have since been incorporated into the daily Jewish prayer service. He also describes himself hearing the Lord ask: "Whom shall I send? Who will go for us?" And he responds: "Here am I; send me" (6:8).

Unfortunately, the mission on which God sends Isaiah will not yield immediate success: The people will not repent. Thus, when the prophet inquires of God, "How long, my Lord [will my unhappy mission continue]?" God answers: "Till towns lie waste without inhabitants, and houses without people, and the ground lies waste and desolate" (6:11). However, God does assure Isaiah that a small remnant of the people will repent and survive (6:13).

Isaiah tells the Israelites that God is so upset with them because they have forgotten the primary mission with which they had been entrusted: to be obedient to God, whose major demand is ethical conduct. Thus, Isaiah's opening chapter summarizes the spiritual and moral offenses committed by the Israelites:

—Forsaking the Lord (1:4);

—Observing rituals while violating Judaism's ethics (1:11–15)— "Your hands are stained with blood";

—Israel's rulers are rogues, greedy for gifts and indifferent to the needs of orphans and widows (1:23).

Furious as Isaiah's indictment is, he still strives not to demoralize his listeners, assuring the Israelites that if they but "learn to do good, devote yourselves to justice; aid the wronged, uphold the rights of the orphans [and] defend the cause of the widow" (1:17), they can still reach an understanding with God: "Be your sins like crimson, they can turn snow-white" (1:18).

Along with his ethical teachings, Isaiah is associated in the Jewish tradition with the doctrine of the Messiah. He prophesies that there will arise a descendant of David ("a shoot shall grow out of the clan of Jesse," i.e., David's father; 11:1) upon whom the spirit of the Lord will alight, and who will usher in an age of justice during which "the wolf shall dwell with the lamb [and] the leopard lie down with the kid . . . with a little boy to lead them" (11:6). These words suggest a utopian age in which the desire for conquest, domination, and violence will end ("the lion, like the ox, shall eat straw"; 11:7). In such an idyllic world, the long-suffering Israelite people will be revered for their knowledge of God, and the gentile nations will seek their advice (11:10). Isaiah envisages the peoples of the world declaring: "Let us go up to the Mount of the Lord, to the House of the God of Jacob; that He may instruct us in His ways, and that we may walk in His paths. For instruction shall come forth from Zion, the word of the Lord from Jerusalem" (2:3).

In this messianic era, God will gather the remnants of dispersed Israel "from the four corners of the earth" (11:12), a prophecy often referred to since the State of Israel's creation in 1948, which has been followed by an ingathering of Jewish exiles from more than one hundred lands.

According to Isaiah, the messianic age will be characterized by a renunciation of war (see next entry). Instead, money spent on weaponry will be spent on growing food ("they shall beat their swords into plowshares").

Combining political shrewdness, ethical passion, spirituality, and poetic eloquence, Isaiah remains the prophet par excellence, a man who knew not only how to condemn injustice, but also how to inspire and console people.

105. "Nation Shall Not Lift Up Sword Against Nation, Neither Shall They Know War Anymore": Isaiah's Dream of World Peace

The numerous biblical descriptions of war sometimes seem to be approving of it. In one passage, the Lord is even described as a "Man of War" (Exodus 15:3). Yet few verses have so captured Bible readers' imaginations as Isaiah's prophecy of a future world in which human beings

> shall beat their swords into plowshares,
> And their spears into pruning hooks.
> Nation shall not lift up sword against nation,
> Neither shall they know war anymore (2:4).

The second half of the verse, "Nation shall not lift up sword against nation," is emblazoned on the Isaiah Wall, opposite the United Nations building in New York City.

Isaiah's hopes for a peaceful world do not reflect, as is commonly assumed, a pacifistic worldview. Unlike the twentieth-century Mahatma Gandhi, whose pacifism motivated him to advise the British army and people to stop fighting the Nazis,* Isaiah was much too obsessed with stopping injustice to believe that it was preferable for evil people to triumph without armed resistance. What the prophet hoped for was a world in which good itself triumphed, so that there would be no Hitlers, Nazis, or others who wished to destroy good people. He believed that such a world would come about only when the world's nations would look to the Lord's House (the Temple) in Jerusalem, and journey "to the House of the God of Jacob, that He may instruct us in His ways, and that we may walk in His paths" (2:3). When such an era comes, that is, when all people become ethical monotheists, then Isaiah's prophecies concerning universal peace will also come true.

Those who believe in just wars—indeed, particularly those who believe in just wars, but no other kind—find Isaiah's vision compelling. In *Winds of War*, Herman Wouk, a religious Jew and lifelong student of the Bible, has one of his characters speculate: "Oh, Lord, in a world so rich and lovely, why can your children find nothing better to do than to dig iron from the ground and work it into vast, grotesque engines for blowing each other up? . . . Is it because if my enemies make deadly engines then I must do it better or die? Maybe the vicious circle . . . will never end."

Isaiah's words remain a goad, a reminder that the goal to which mankind must aspire is universal peace. But such peace cannot come at once with a unilateral declaration of disarmament by good people; it must also be preceded by transformations in evil people as well. Otherwise, as Charles Pellegrino has written: "History teaches us

---

*At a time when Nazi Germany seemed poised to invade England, Gandhi offered the British the following advice: "I would like you to lay down the arms you have as being useless for saving you or humanity. You will invite Herr Hitler and Signor Mussolini to take what they want of the countries you call your possessions. . . . If these gentlemen choose to occupy your homes you will vacate them. If they do not give you free passage out, you will allow yourselves, man, woman and child, to be slaughtered, but you will refuse to owe allegiance to them" (*Non-Violence in Peace and War*).

that he who beats his sword into plowshares usually ends up plowing for those who kept their swords."

Until a transformed, messianic world is achieved, humankind probably should be guided by Ecclesiastes's nuanced advice: "[There is] a time for war, and a time for peace" (3:8).

Similarly, the prophet Joel, whose words are less widely known than Isaiah's and speaking of a world less serene than that foreseen by him, envisions a time when it will be necessary for good people to "beat your plowshares into swords, and your pruning hooks into spears" (Joel 4:10).

Source and further reading: Charles Pellegrino, *Return to Sodom and Gomorrah*, page 96; Pellegrino does not take credit for the quotation, but gives it an anonymous attribution. The quotation from Herman Wouk also is taken from Pellegrino's book.

106. "A Light unto the Nations"

BASED ON ISAIAH 49:6

An old Jewish source (Mishnah *Hagigah* 1:8) likens the numerous rabbinic laws of the Sabbath to a mountain suspended by a hair, a massive structure tied to a narrow base. The base referred to is the Torah's relatively few Sabbath laws.

Similarly, many Jewish theologians have created a large body of literature asserting that the Jewish people's mission is to act as "a light unto the nations." As powerful and well known as this expression is, most people are surprised to learn that the Hebrew Bible refers to such a mission only twice, both times in the Book of Isaiah.

The more important of these references suggests the idea's enormous significance: "I will also make you a light of nations, that My salvation may reach the ends of the earth" (49:6). Nothing could be more evocative of a universal mission than this mandate.

Although the phrase "light unto the nations" (*or la-goyim*) is not used outside Isaiah, the same idea seems to be underscored in the Torah law that commands Jews to sanctify God's name in the world (see entry 185), and to be a "kingdom of priests and a holy nation" (Exodus 19:6).

The Jewish people have carried out the command to be an *or la-goyim* with considerable success: Historians of religion have long acknowledged that the idea of One God has become known to humankind through the Jews.

107. On "Virgin Births" and "the Suffering Servant of God": The Different Ways in Which Jews and Fundamentalist Christians Read Isaiah

For fundamentalist Protestants, and for many other Christians as well (particularly in the past), what endows the Hebrew Bible with particular significance is its presumed prophecies about the coming of Jesus. For them the Book of Isaiah is deemed particularly important, since it is credited with two of the most significant such prophecies. Christian translators have generally rendered Isaiah 7:14—a prophecy that Isaiah makes to King Ahaz (circa 735 B.C.E.)—as follows: "Therefore, the Lord Himself shall give you a sign: behold a *virgin* shall conceive, and bear a son, and shall call his name Immanuel" (Hebrew for "God is with us"; Matthew 1:22–23 similarly translates this verse from Isaiah as "a *virgin* . . .").

For several reasons, Jews have never understood this passage as meaning what fundamentalist Christians claim it does. First, and most important, *almah*, which Christians have usually translated as "virgin," actually means "young woman." The Hebrew word for virgin is *betulah*. While a young woman may also be a virgin, if Isaiah intended to prophesy the miracle of a virgin giving birth, would he not, if for no other reason than to avoid ambiguity, have used the word *betulah*, since it has no meaning other than virgin?*

Second, the prophecy's context makes it clear that God was send-

*See, for example, Leviticus 21:3; Deuteronomy 22:19, 28; and Ezekiel 44:22.

ing a sign to King Ahaz, and was not speaking of a child who would be born more than seven centuries later (would you be convinced by a prophetic sign given in 2005 C.E. that would be fulfilled in 2705?). Thus, Isaiah tells Ahaz that *"the* young woman," not *"a* young woman," shall conceive, thus implying that he is alluding to a young woman known to the king. Probably, Isaiah is referring to Ahaz's young bride, the queen, and to a son who will be granted the couple as a kind of replacement for the little princes Ahaz had earlier sacrificed (II Chronicles 28:3). While one is free to question the justice of giving an infant to a man guilty of such horrific child abuse, Hezekiah, the child who shortly thereafter is born to the queen, is, unlike his father, loyal to the traditions of David (see entry 98).

Many Christians have also attached christological significance to Isaiah 53, which speaks of the "suffering servant of God." Christian exegetes have often interpreted this chapter as prophesying the mission of Jesus, whom they deem to be both a prophet *and* God, and whom they believe came to this earth to suffer a torturous, sacrificial death.

While it is true that Isaiah speaks of a suffering and despised "servant of God," the contention that he is speaking about Jesus is without foundation. "Servant of God" either refers to Isaiah himself, who like most of the prophets suffered for his service to the Lord, or to the collective Jewish people, who are referred to by the term "servant of God" nine times in earlier chapters of Isaiah (41:8, 9; 44:1, 2, 21, 26; 45:4; 48:20; 49:3). Traditional Jewish theology has generally understood chapter 53 as referring to the Jewish people's sufferings while trying to maintain their faith and make the idea of One God known to the world.

108. Does the Book of Isaiah Contain the Words of More Than One Prophet?

Traditional Jewish thought teaches that all sixty-six chapters of the Book of Isaiah were composed and uttered by the prophet Isaiah, son of Amoz, who lived in the eighth century B.C.E.

Yet already in the twelfth century C.E., the biblical exegete Abraham ibn Ezra, whose commentary is printed in most standard Hebrew editions of the Bible, challenged this belief. He argued with great cogency that chapters 1 to 39 were the writings of the eighth-century B.C.E. prophet. However, starting with chapter 40, ibn Ezra states, the book is the work of a prophet who lived some two hundred years later, after the Jews had been exiled from their homeland. This author wrote during the reign of Cyrus, the sixth-century king of Persia, who defeated the Babylonians and issued his edict permitting the Jews to return to Israel (see entry 142).

One detail in particular makes ibn Ezra's argument seem compelling: the fact that the prophet twice mentions King Cyrus by name (45:1: "Thus said the Lord to Cyrus, His anointed one," and 44:28, in which the prophet quotes God referring to Cyrus as "My shepherd"). The only way one can maintain that Isaiah wrote the whole book in the eighth century is to assume that he foretold that the Jews would be exiled from their homeland by the Babylonians, and then restored to Israel by a Persian king named Cyrus, *two hundred years before the events happened*. This belief effectively commits one to the view that human beings have no free will, since despite Isaiah's appeals to the Israelites of his time to change, he knew all along that they wouldn't change, that their descendants would be expelled, and that an unborn Persian king whose name he knew would one day restore their descendants to Israel. If history were so preordained, then, as the philosopher Maimonides asks, "How could God have commanded us through the prophets, 'Do this and do not do that, improve your ways, and do not follow your wicked impulses,' when, from the beginning of his existence, a person's [or, in this case, a nation's] destiny had already been decreed?" (*Mishneh Torah*, "Laws of Repentance," 5:4).

The late British Chief Rabbi, Joseph Hertz, offers yet another compelling and commonsensical argument for the later authorship of the second part of Isaiah: When the prophet refers to the exile of Israel and to King Cyrus, he never makes it sound like a prediction: "[These details] are everywhere assumed as facts known to the reader." Hertz, whose commentary reflects an Orthodox Jewish perspective, goes on to note that whether there is more than one prophet cited in Isaiah "can be considered dispassionately [since] it touches no dogma or any religious principle in Judaism."*

---

*What remains an open question is why the name of the author of Isaiah's latter chapters was lost, and how these chapters came to be incorporated into the earlier book.

Today, the large majority of Bible scholars assume that the Book of Isaiah starting with chapter 40 is the work of a second Isaiah, and some believe that the book's final chapters were written by yet a third prophet.

Unlike the words of moral condemnation with which the first Isaiah begins his book, the opening words of Second Isaiah (40:1–2) express consolation. They are read in the synagogue each year on the Sabbath following Tisha Be'Av, the fast day that commemorates the destruction of both Temples: "Comfort, oh comfort My people, says your God. Speak tenderly to Jerusalem, and declare to her that her term of service is over, that her iniquity is expiated. For she has received at the hand of the Lord, double for all her sins." After a long period during which numerous prophets condemned the Israelites for violations of the covenant, the prophet makes known that God still loves His people, and wishes to speak to them tender, forgiving, and loving words. (Hosea 14:5–9 and Amos 9:11–15 speak in a similar manner.) The Sabbath on which this chapter of Isaiah is read is known as Shabbat Nachamu, the Sabbath of Comfort.

Source: Joseph Hertz, *The Pentateuch and Haftorahs,* pages 941–942.

XI. JEREMIAH

109. The Loneliest Man of Faith

The prophet Jeremiah is probably the Hebrew Bible's loneliest and saddest figure. In general, biblical prophets led fairly unhappy and alienated lives, condemned by their profession to say the things their fellow citizens least wanted to hear. An old Yiddish curse summarizes their plight: "May you be the only wise man in a world of fools!" The depression to which this sort of isolation can lead lies at the root of Elijah's pitiful prayer to God: "Enough . . . Now, O Lord, take my life!" (I Kings 19:4).

Jeremiah can be singled out from this doleful group simply because we know the details of his desolation better than that of other prophets. Moses and David are the only other biblical figures whose experiences are described in such detail.

Jeremiah has a further, dubious, distinction: He is the only character in the Bible who is denied a family. Early in his career, God decrees that Jeremiah is to live alone: "The word of the Lord came to me. You are not to marry and not to have sons and daughters in this place" (16:1–2).

Many Bible scholars understand this singular command as motivated by God's desire that Jeremiah focus exclusively on carrying out His will (Christian exegetes, in particular, emphasize this, seeing in God's command a foreshadowing of Jesus' celibacy).

However, a close reading of the text suggests that Jeremiah might have been condemned to remain single because of the message he was destined to deliver. Immediately following God's prohibiting Jeremiah from having a family life, the Lord says to him: "For thus says the Lord concerning any sons and daughters that may be born in this place, and concerning the mothers who bear them, and concerning the fathers who beget them in this land: They shall die gruesome deaths, they shall not be lamented or buried. . . . They shall be consumed by the sword and by famine" (16:3–5).

Imagine that you bore such knowledge from God; would you want to bring children into the world? One also can assume that a man who went about making such pronouncements would hardly have struck most women as "good marriage material."

Strangely, the spiritual career of this man whose prophecies were so pessimistic (the English word "jeremiad," referring to mournful and angry statements, derives from his name) begins during a short, rare period of well-being within Judah's history, the reign of King Josiah (see entry 100).

Josiah was a reformer king who tried to eliminate idolatry from Israel and run the Jewish state according to Torah law. During the thirteenth year of his reign (627 B.C.E.), "the words of the Lord" came to Jeremiah, who was then probably about eighteen.

When God first appears to Jeremiah, He makes a remarkable statement, which suggests that a person's soul comes into existence *prior* to his or her birth: "Before I created you in the womb, I selected you. Before you were born, I consecrated you . . ." (1:5).

When God informs Jeremiah that He is appointing him to be a prophet, the young man demurs. Like Moses, who initially refused a similar offer from God (see entry 32), Jeremiah says he is unable to speak in public. God, however, gives Jeremiah no choice, telling him that He, God, will give him the message and the words that he needs.

Many years later, as the words Jeremiah feels condemned to speak grow ever harsher and bleaker, he notes how much he wishes to drop his prophetic vocation, and how hard he has tried: "I thought, 'I will not mention Him, no more will I speak in His name'" (20:9). But the prophet finds himself incapable of doing anything but speaking God's words; the message he preaches has become too deeply internalized. Having spent his whole adult life denouncing evil and foolishness, he cannot suddenly stop: "[God's] word was like a raging fire in my heart . . . I could not hold it in, I was helpless" (20:9).

This very helplessness intensifies Jeremiah's intense bitterness at the life to which God has appointed him. With the possible exception of Jonah (see entry 118), no other prophet seems as unhappy with the divine mission imposed upon him:

Cursed be the day that I was born.
Let not the day be blessed when my mother bore me!
Cursed be the man who brought my father the news,
And said, "A boy is born to you" (20:14–15).

In his overflowing bitterness, Jeremiah damns the man who brought news of his birth for not killing him in his mother's womb: "Let him hear shrieks in the morning and battle shouts at noontide, because he did not kill me before birth" (20:16–17). In one of the most wrenching speeches in the Bible, he concludes:

Why did I ever issue from the womb,
To see misery and woe,
To spend all my days in shame (20:18).

One more reason for Jeremiah's utter dejection is that he had the misfortune of seeing his prophecies of destruction come true. While most other prophets warned of a great catastrophe *if* the people did not turn from evil to good, Jeremiah actually witnessed Jerusalem's and the Temple's destruction.

Jeremiah might at least have had the gratification of being able to say, "I told you so," but that would not have been true to his nature. After all, he was not a mere oracle, indifferent to the fate of those about whom he was prophesying. A legitimate critic reproaches out of love, not vindictiveness. Jeremiah's loneliness and sadness were intense because he cared so greatly about the very people who were rejecting him and his message.

How startling then to learn that, at the very end of Jeremiah's life, he became a prophet of hope. As to how that happened, see entry 111.

110. Was Jeremiah a Traitor?

When a nation is at war, its citizens usually regard active and vociferous opponents of the war as traitors. Sometimes, when the war is obviously justified—as in the case of America's declaration of war after the Japanese attack on Pearl Harbor—such an assessment is correct. Unfortunately, however, the tendency to tar opponents of a war as betrayers exists even when it is unjustified. Thus, it was Jeremiah's misfortune to oppose a futile war in which his nation was engaged, and consequently to be treated as a traitor.

During the last years of the First Jewish Commonwealth (circa 600 B.C.E.), Jeremiah advocates that the Jews submit to their Babylonian rulers. However, the prevailing sentiment within Judah is to throw off Babylonia's yoke. When Jehoiakim, Judah's king, launches a military revolt against Babylonia, Jeremiah tells the people that God wants them to be defeated as punishment for their evil behavior and refusal to repent; their only hope for avoiding total destruction is to surrender.

Jeremiah does not express this thought in private conversations with friends. Wishing to influence his fellow Jews, he repeatedly offers his ideas in public speeches. Soon, most of his fellow Judeans regard him as a traitor—in effect, an ally of Babylon. Peshur, a priest and officer at the Temple, has the prophet flogged and put in the stocks (20:1–2).*

Jeremiah is not easily cowed. Shortly after being released, he prophesies that Peshur will be exiled to Babylon, where he will die (20:6).

Jeremiah's fellow townspeople in Anatot, the city where he was born and raised, warn him that they will kill him if he continues prophesying. Others wish to cut out his tongue.

A short time later, after King Jehoiakim orders his arrest (36:26), the prophet, along with his assistant Baruch (the scribe who wrote down Jeremiah's words), goes into hiding.

Jehoiakim's revolt is quickly put down (598), and many of Judah's

---

*The meaning of the Hebrew word that is translated as "stocks" is unclear; it might mean prison.

leading officials, including the king, are exiled to Babylon (the king's son, Jehoiachin, rules for three months, then is deposed by Nebuchadnezzar, king of Babylon). Zedekiah, the former king's uncle, is appointed as monarch. Eleven years later, in 587, Zedekiah, a confused man influenced by militant officers, inaugurates yet a second rebellion.

Jeremiah opposes this revolt as strenuously as he opposed the first. Zedekiah's officials, acting on their own, not on the king's command, take Jeremiah to a royal prison compound, dump him in a deep, muddy pit, and leave him to die.

An Ethiopian servant of the king tells him what has been done to Jeremiah, and requests permission to free him. The king accedes, and Jeremiah is raised from the pit, but remains confined to the prison grounds.

But when the Judean military situation seriously deteriorates, King Zedekiah summons Jeremiah to a meeting. "I want to ask you something," he tells the prophet. "Don't conceal anything from me" (38:14).

Jeremiah responds: "If I tell you, you'll surely kill me, and if I give you advice, you won't listen to me."

Zedekiah swears in God's name that he will not harm, or allow others to harm, Jeremiah because of anything he says.

Speaking in God's name, Jeremiah tells Zedekiah to surrender to Babylon. If he does, his life will be spared, and Jerusalem will not be destroyed. But if he continues the revolt, the Babylonians will burn down the city and take him hostage.

When Jeremiah finishes his speech, Zedekiah orders him, on pain of death, to keep the contents of their conversation secret. The king apparently fears that if his army officers learn that he has sought Jeremiah's counsel, they will mutiny. He instructs Jeremiah to tell whoever learns of the meeting and questions him about it that he had simply pleaded with the king not to send him back to prison. Jeremiah abides by this command and is returned to prison, where he remains until the day the Babylonians capture Jerusalem.

King Zedekiah must have quickly regretted his refusal to follow Jeremiah's advice, for the prophet's somber predictions quickly come to pass. The Babylonians occupy and destroy Jerusalem, the Temple, and the kingdom of Judah. (Archaeological evidence reveals that all of Judah's fortified towns were razed to the ground and left desolate for generations.) The king himself flees Jerusalem, is caught, and forced to witness the execution of his two sons, before being blinded and taken off to Babylon as a hostage.

*   *   *

Was Jeremiah, then, a traitor or a patriot?

Only those who believe in "my country right or wrong," and justify whatever wrong their country is doing, can regard Jeremiah as a traitor. Indeed, while many of Jeremiah's contemporaries so perceived him, Jews started viewing him quite differently after the revolt against Babylon failed; shortly thereafter, Jeremiah came to be regarded—and has been regarded ever since—as a hero and lover of his people. As a matter of fact, most Bible readers view those who labeled Jeremiah a traitor—King Jehoiakim, the priest Peshur, and the officials of King Zedekiah who threw Jeremiah into a muddy pit—as villains, fools, or a combination of both.

In his monumental nineteenth-century history of the Jews, Heinrich Graetz asks the following provocative question: Why is it that Jeremiah, who advocated surrender to the Babylonians, is considered by later Jewish generations to be a Jewish patriot, while the historian Josephus Flavius, who advocated Judean surrender to the Romans (in the revolt of 66–70 C.E.), and even cited Jeremiah's words, is still viewed with suspicion?

Graetz responds that Jews regard Jeremiah as a loyal Jew because when he urged surrender, he spoke from within Jerusalem, while Josephus spoke from the Romans' camp.* In other words, the Jews came to accept and cherish Jeremiah because they sensed in him a righteous advocate: He spoke, not to advance a personal agenda, but because he felt compelled to warn his fellow Jews of the suicidal nature of their revolt. Josephus might well have been correct in urging surrender—indeed, I believe he was, given that the revolt against Rome was as suicidally hopeless as that against Babylon. But Jews sensed that he did not speak from the Romans' camp only to preserve his life, but because he had come to identify with Rome, as much, perhaps more, as he did with his fellow Jews.

---

*To be fair, had Josephus tried to deliver his message inside Jerusalem, the rebels would have immediately killed him. The rebels against Rome were far less tolerant of dissent than were those against Babylon, most of whom were content to let Jeremiah languish in prison.

111. Prophet of Hope and an Early Zionist

JEREMIAH 32:6–15 AND CHAPTER 33

The true prophet is in conflict with his times. When things are going well *materially*, he notes what is wrong *morally*. In the Bible's view, false prophets, such as Hananiah (Jeremiah, chapter 28), tell the people optimistic lies rather than the hard truths that they need to hear.

For almost all of his forty-year career, Jeremiah tells the Israelites what they would rather not hear, most notably that God spurns sacrifices unaccompanied by ethical behavior, and that Judah's revolt against Babylon will fail and lead to the country's destruction.

Most Israelites regard him as a despair-ridden crank, for they are certain that their sacrifices before God will ensure their and the Temple's safety and guarantee a successful revolt.

When it finally becomes evident that Babylon's army will defeat Judah, the people grow despondent. Then Jeremiah, the prophet of despair, suddenly becomes a prophet of hope. As the Jews go into exile, he buys land in Israel from Hanamel, his cousin from his hometown of Anatot, making certain that a deed is written and signed.

Jeremiah instructs Baruch, his secretary and scribe, to put the deed into an earthen jar so that it may last a long time: "For thus said the Lord of Hosts, the God of Israel: 'Houses, field and vineyards shall again be purchased in this land'" (32:6–15).

In retrospect, given the well-known return of the Jews to Israel, Jeremiah's prophecy may seem obvious, but at the time that he uttered it, we know of no exiled people who had ever regained their homeland.

Similarly, as the Judeans survey the ravaged Jerusalem (archeological evidence indicates that the Babylonian army utterly destroyed the holy city), Jeremiah offers an optimistic vision of the city's future: "Thus said the Lord: 'Again there shall be heard in this place which you say is ruined . . . in the towns of Judah and the streets of Jerusalem that are desolate . . . the sound of mirth and gladness, the voice of bridegroom and bride. . . . For I will restore the fortunes of the land as of old,' said the Lord" (33:10–11).*

Jeremiah also promises the disheartened Judeans that God will always be open to restoring them to their land if they only return in repentance to Him (33:9). Thus, during these darkest hours of the people's exile, the prophet instructs them to set up markers to remind them how to find their way back to Israel (31:21).

Jeremiah, the prophet of gloom, proved correct in predicting Judah's destruction if it pursued its suicidal revolt against Babylon. He was equally prescient when he became a prophet of hope; within less than seventy years of his prophecies, the Israelites had begun to return to their land, while the Babylonian empire that had destroyed their state was destroyed by Persia.

Reflections: Jeremiah's inspirational letter to the exiled Jews residing in Babylon: Dr. Jeremiah Unterman has observed to me that the letter Jeremiah dispatched to the Jewish exiles was as influential a document as any of his other prophecies, and helped motivate the despondent, exiled Jews to get on with their lives. In this letter (see 29:1–28), Jeremiah cautioned the Jews to "seek the welfare of the city to which I [God] have exiled you. . . . For in its prosperity you will prosper." He urged the disheartened exile not to wallow in despair; rather, they should "build houses . . . plant gardens and eat their fruit. Take wives and beget sons and daughters." He further urged the people to pray to God; Unterman speculates that this demand of Jeremiah might have stimulated the creation of synagogues.

Jeremiah's impact on later biblical writers and on the Jewish people: Jeremiah's prophecies of hope are cited repeatedly in later biblical books (Daniel 9:2; II Chronicles 36:21–23; Ezra 1:1–3). These prophecies gave the Jewish people encouragement to maintain their faith until they were redeemed, and returned to Israel, under the Persians. In contrast, the Ten Lost Tribes had no prophetic tradition of hope, and disappeared from history (see entry 91).

*These words are recited during the Jewish wedding ceremony.

112. Ethics as God's Central Demand

JEREMIAH, CHAPTER 7, 9:22–23

In apparent opposition to most Israelites of his day, Jeremiah insists that God's *central* demand of people is ethical behavior:

> Thus says the Lord:
> Let not the wise man glory in his wisdom;
> Let not the strong man glory in his strength;
> Let not the rich man glory in his riches.
> But only in this should one glory:
> In his earnest devotion to Me.
> For I, the Lord, act with kindness,
> Justice, and equity in the world;
> For in these I delight—declares the Lord (9:22–23).

In these two verses, Jeremiah negates three evils that are still common:

—self-sufficient intellectualism ("Let not the wise man glory in his wisdom"),

—power that does not regard itself as responsible to a higher cause ("Let not the strong man glory in his strength"), and

—self-congratulatory materialism ("Let not the rich man glory in his riches").

In what then does God delight? "Kindness, justice, and equity."

Jeremiah delivers his message about the supremacy of ethics at the Jerusalem Temple. In his view, the Temple goers are practicing a form of idolatry. While self-acknowledged idolators believe that they can gain the gods' favor by sacrificing their sons, the Judeans feel that they can do so by sacrificing animals. Although less immoral than human sacrifice, the principle—the belief that God can be bribed—is the same.

Jeremiah argues that the only "bribe" acceptable to God is justice—not to oppress the stranger, the orphan, and the widow (7:6). Righteous behavior toward society's most vulnerable members is the prerequisite for the Israelites' remaining in Israel: "Then only will I let you dwell in this place, in the land that I gave to your brothers for all time" (7:7).

Jeremiah's contemporaries apparently believed that as long as they brought sacrifices, God would forgive their cruel behavior and sins, and protect them from their enemies. This belief was abhorrent to the prophet. Instead of praising the Israelites for bringing sacrifices, Jeremiah denounces them for violating five of the Ten Commandments: "Will you steal [number 8], and murder [6] and commit adultery [7] and swear falsely [9] and sacrifice to Baal and follow other gods [2] . . . and then come and stand before Me in this House which bears My name and say, 'We are safe'? [Safe] to do all these abhorrent things!" (7:9–10).

For Jeremiah the popular belief that the essence of religion is ritual observance is a lie. His contemporaries might equate devotion to God with offering sacrifices, but Jeremiah reminds the Temple goers that on the day God revealed Himself at Sinai, He made no mention of sacrifices; instead, He gave Israel the Ten Commandments, whose provisions they are violating.

According to Jeremiah, only two things can save the Judeans from divine punishment: the observance of God's ethical commands, accompanied by the categorical repudiation of idolatry: "If you do not shed the blood of the innocent . . . if you do not follow other gods . . ." (7:6).

Speaking in God's name, then, the prophet insists on the supremacy of ethics and monotheism. Together the two comprise ethical monotheism, the Bible's most important contribution to human thought and history.

XII. EZEKIEL

113. The Valley of the Dry Bones

37:1–14

Although he is as stark a pessimist as his older contemporary Jeremiah (see entry 109), the prophet Ezekiel bequeaths to Israel one of its most enduring images of hope.

As a young man, Ezekiel serves as a priest in the Temple. In 598 B.C.E., when the Babylonians first occupy Jerusalem, Ezekiel is exiled to Babylon with several thousand other prominent Jews, and he becomes the first prophet to live outside the land. From Babylon, he prophesies that Jerusalem will be destroyed, as indeed it is in 587.

After the destruction, Ezekiel predicts that the Jews will return to their homeland. Throughout the book, Ezekiel has numerous fantastic visions detailing Israel's future: On one occasion, a divine guide gives him a personal, extraordinarily detailed tour of the new Temple that will be rebuilt on the site of the destroyed one (chapters 40–43).

Ezekiel's most famous vision is a metaphor for the revival of the seemingly "dead" Jewish people. According to Ezekiel, God sets him down in a valley filled with lifeless bones, which have been in the hot sun so long that the flesh has been stripped from them. God asks: "O mortal, can these bones live again?" (37:3).

"Only You know," Ezekiel replies, whereupon God orders him to prophesy to the bones: "O dry bones, hear the word of the Lord. . . . I will cause breath to enter into you and you shall live again."

As Ezekiel pronounces these words, the bones stir and begin to come together. Flesh grows on them, and soon the bones form into bodies, but there is no breath in them. God instructs Ezekiel: "Say to the breath, thus said the Lord God: 'Come, O Breath, from the four winds, and breathe into these slain, that they may live again."

Breath now enters into the corpses, which stand on their feet, constituting a vast multitude. And God tells Ezekiel: "O mortal, these bones are the whole House of Israel. They say, 'Our bones are dried up, our hope is gone; we are doomed.'" God then instructs Ezekiel to prophesy to the House of Israel: "Thus said the Lord God: I am going to open your graves and lift you out of the graves, O My people, and bring you to the land of Israel. . . . I will put My breath into you and you shall live again, and I will set you upon your own soil."

Many Jews have seen in the creation of the State of Israel, which came about only three years after the end of the Holocaust, the seeming fulfillment of Ezekiel's rather bizarre 2,600-year-old vision. Throughout Jewish history, this prophecy also has been cited as proof that God someday will resurrect the dead.

Ezekiel's image of a dried-up, exiled, and hopeless Jewish people coming back to life in their homeland makes him as much a prophet of the twentieth century C.E. as of the sixth century B.C.E.

Reflections: On a prophet's moral obligation to warn people away from evil behavior: In one of Ezekiel's most powerful images, he speaks of God as appointing him a watchman for the House of Israel, "and when you hear a word from My mouth, you must warn them for Me. If I say to a wicked man, 'You shall die,' and you do not warn him— you do not speak to the wicked man of his wicked course in order to save his life—he, the wicked man, shall die for his iniquity, but I will require a reckoning for his blood from you'" (3:16–18).

XIII. THE TWELVE MINOR PROPHETS

114. Why "Minor" Does Not Mean "Insignificant"

In Aramaic, the term for the Twelve Minor Prophets is *trei asar,* which simply means "twelve." This is a preferable name for these books, since the word "minor" seems to connote something unimportant. If one tells someone that she should read one of the "minor prophets," she might well respond, "Why bother?"

Almost certainly, whoever first designated these short books as "minor prophets" did not intend to reduce them to insignificance. It is just that unlike the major prophets, Isaiah, Jeremiah, and Ezekiel (consisting of sixty-six, fifty-two, and forty-eight chapters respectively), who left behind large bodies of writings, the twelve produced much shorter records of their prophecies. In fact, the entire legacy left by Obadiah consists of only twenty-one verses, comprising a single chapter.

Still, some of these books are anything but minor (perhaps a better name for them might be the "Twelve Brief Prophets"). I venture to guess that larger numbers of Bible readers have read and been influenced by the Book of Jonah than have read the far longer Ezekiel.

In the Book of Amos is found one of the most important statements about Jewish chosenness (see entry 117), while the prophet Micah beautifully expresses the essence of what God demands of humankind (see entry 119). Through wrenching personal example, Hosea offers an illustration of the depth of God's love for his erring people (see entry 115).

Since Hosea, Amos, Jonah, and Micah are discussed in separate entries, what follows is a brief description of the other eight prophets presented in this series of books.

Joel
Obadiah
Nahum
Habakkuk
Zephaniah
Haggai
Zachariah
Malachi

Joel: The only biographical detail we have about Joel is the name
of his father, Pethuel (1:1). The detailed references within the book
to agriculture suggest that he might have been a farmer (1:7,
10–12).

Since Joel makes no mention of the Judean or Israelite kings who
lived during his time, it is difficult to date the period during which
he prophesied. He describes a terrible plague of locusts that has
recently swept over the land and destroyed so much foliage and
crops that Judah's people and animals face starvation (chapter 1).

However, Joel's real intent in describing the plague is to warn of
the much greater devastation that will be wrought on God's Day of
Judgment, the sufferings of which can only be averted if the people
"turn back to Me [God] with all your hearts." Joel promises that if
this desired repentance occurs, then "Judah shall abide forever, and
Jerusalem from generation to generation" (4:20).

Among the book's most famous verses are Joel's appeal to the
people to "rend your hearts rather than your garments" (2:13; the
essence of repentance is internal transformation, not the performance
of external rituals). He also admonishes the people to go to war
when necessary: "Beat your plowshares into swords, and your pruning hooks into spears" (4:10).

Obadiah: If you ever want to brag that you know an entire biblical
book by heart, choose Obadiah, the work of a Judean prophet; as
noted, his entire recorded corpus of writings occupies but one chapter. It is uncertain exactly when Obadiah lived, but it was clearly
during a period when the nearby kingdom of Edom was oppressing
Judah.

Obadiah promises that God will wreak vengeance against the
Edomites—"I will make you least among nations" (1:2)—in repay-
ment for the cruelties they have inflicted on Israel (1:10).
Although the prophet speaks as if he were addressing the Edom-

ites directly, it is more likely that he is delivering the prophecy inside Judah.

In a prophecy that brings to mind the Jews' return to Israel in the twentieth century, Obadiah speaks of the Israelites as regaining their land from "those who dispossessed them" (1:17; see also 1:19–20).

Nahum: Nahum is another prophet about whom we know little. He is identified by the city from which he comes, Elkosh (1:1), but since this place is not mentioned elsewhere in the Bible, it is difficult to place the prophet within a broader context.

The book's three chapters deal with one theme: the prediction of the imminent fall of Nineveh, the capital and symbol of Assyria (as Washington can be spoken of as symbolic of the United States). In fact, Assyria was invaded by the Babylonian King Nabopolassar in 612 B.C.E. and fell three years later. Earlier, during its more than century-long domination of the ancient Near East, it had vanquished the Ten Tribes (722 B.C.E.) and exiled its inhabitants. Nineveh also was the city that responded so powerfully to Jonah's call to repent (see entry 118).

Nahum identifies God as one "who takes vengeance on His enemies [and] rages against His foes" (1:2). Although slow to anger, God, once aroused, punishes those deserving punishment. Thus, Nineveh, "city of crime, utterly treacherous, full of violence, where killing never stops" (3:1), will soon be punished by the Lord (3:5).

Nahum's intense furious language, directed against a society that had inflicted much suffering on the Ten Tribes, brings to mind the vengeful language of Psalm 137, verse 8 (ironically that verse is directed against the Babylonians who, shortly after Nahum's prophecy, were "the rods of God's anger" against the Assyrians; see entry 125).

Habakkuk: Another prophet about whom we know nothing save his name, Habakkuk is among those biblical characters who question God's justice* and seeming absence from human affairs:

> How long, O Lord, will I cry out
> and You not listen
> Shall I shout to You violence
> And You not save? (1:2).

---

*Other examples include Abraham (Genesis 18:25), the Psalmist (44:25), and Job (scattered references throughout the book; see entry 127).

Habakkuk is particularly upset with the rising power of Babylon, which threatens Judah (Babylon defeated Assyria in 612 B.C.E., which suggests that Habakkuk must have prophesied around this time): "Why do You . . . stand by idle, while the one in the wrong devours the one in the right?" (1:13).

The prophet notes that God has promised him that Babylon itself eventually will be punished.

Among the book's most enduring influential verses is Habakkuk's prophecy of a future day when "the earth will be filled with the knowledge of the glory of the Lord, as the waters cover the sea" (2:14; see Isaiah 11:9). The Babylonian Talmud (*Makkot* 24a) cites the prophet's statement that the "righteous shall live by his faith" (2:4) as a one-sentence summary of all the Torah's commandments. Chapter 3 is a stirring song describing nature as standing in awe of God as He comes to rescue his people.

Zephaniah: This prophet, who lived in Judah in the seventh century B.C.E., before the fall of Judah, had a distinguished lineage. His great-great-grandfather was Hezekiah, a particularly righteous king of Judah. Since Zephaniah was a relative of the king, he probably lived in Jerusalem.

Zephaniah prophesied during the reign of King Josiah (640–609 B.C.E.), who in 621 initiated many important reforms to raise the spiritual and ethical level of Judah. Zephaniah's condemnations of Judean idol worshiping, as well as his insistence that it was not enough to observe ritual laws but that one must also seek righteousness (2:3), suggest that his prophecies preceded these reforms.

He predicts that God will punish Judah for its wickedness, and that idolators will be judged severely on the forthcoming "day of the Lord." Yet, following the reckoning, Israel's foes will be swept away (3:15), Jerusalem will have no reason again to fear attack (3:16), and God will soothe His Chosen People with love (3:17); on that day, the Lord will gather them and bring them home (3:20).

Haggai, Zechariah, and Malachi: The Babylonian Talmud (*Yoma* 9b) groups these three together. It refers to them as the Bible's last prophets, after whom the Holy Spirit ceased to function in Israel.

Haggai lived during the period when Jews had started to return to Israel from the Babylonian exile, about 539 B.C.E.; a short time later, some Jews began rebuilding the Temple.

The builders soon became discouraged and stopped working; in 520, Haggai, in conjunction with the prophet Zechariah (see Ezra

5:1), began actively to encourage, in God's name, the completion of the Temple. Haggai assures the Jews that this Temple's glory will exceed that of Solomon's (2:9). The prophet's inspiring words apparently made an impact, and the Temple was completed in 515.

The latter sections of Zechariah (chapters 9–14) are filled with esoteric prophetic visions, including what has become the well-known prophecy of the Messiah's arrival:

". . . your king is coming to you.
He is victorious, triumphant
yet humble, riding on a donkey . . ." (9:9).

Zechariah prophesies that the Messiah will banish the "warrior's bow" (bring about universal peace), and be acknowledged as a world leader. He also is author of one of the Bible's most famous verses, one that has long inspired persecuted people: "Not by might, nor by power, but by My spirit—said the Lord" (4:6).

Concerning Malachi, the last of the twelve prophets, we are not even certain of his name; Malachi means "my messenger"; so it might have been a symbol to signify a messenger of God.

The Book of Malachi is best known for its concluding two verses in which, for the first time, the prophet Elijah is identified as the one who will herald the coming of the Messiah: "Lo, I will send the prophet Elijah to you before the coming of the awesome, fearful day of the Lord" (3:23).

And what is the primary task Elijah will need to accomplish to pave the way for the Messiah's coming? "He shall reconcile parents with their children and children with their parents," a well-needed reminder that tensions between parents and children are a problem older even than the prophet Malachi, who is presumed to have spoken these words about 450.

In addition, one of Malachi's most famous verses conveys why the belief in One God should and must lead to the brotherhood of humankind: "Have we not all one Father? Did not one God create us? Why do we break faith with one another . . . ?" (2:10).

With Malachi, the age of the prophets comes to an end. From now on, Israel's leaders will have to rely on God's previously enunciated words, written in the Torah and in the writings of the prophets, in their efforts to decipher His will. Humankind is now on its own, with only the written records of God's will, not direct revelation, to guide it.

115. Hosea: The Prophet Betrayed by His Wife (c. 755–715 B.C.E.)

THE BOOK OF HOSEA

A person who has never been sick might well grow up to be unsympathetic to those who suffer from illness. Similarly, a person in a happy marriage might find it difficult to relate to someone who remains in a marriage after a spouse has repeatedly betrayed him (or her). Such an acquaintance would probably advise the betrayed individual to divorce: end of issue.

To ensure that there is at least one Israelite who fully understands the pain and betrayal God feels because of the Israelites' repeated reversions to idolatry, the Lord makes an unprecedented demand of the prophet Hosea: "Go and get yourself a wife of whoredom and children of whoredom" (1:2).

Given that these are God's first words to Hosea, the prophet must surely have been shaken; indeed, he must have wondered if it was truly the Lord who was addressing him. But Hosea soon becomes convinced that that is the case, and he marries a woman named Gomer. The text never specifies whether she was a prostitute or just promiscuous, but clearly she was not a monogamist.

Hosea and Gomer live together for several years, during which she gives birth to three children, two boys and a girl. Hosea curses these poor children, particularly the last two, with perhaps the most unpleasant symbolic names in the Bible. The first son he calls Jezreel, a name that reflects God's promise to "break the bow of Israel in the Valley of Jezreel" (that is, to end the monarchy and the nation of Israel).

The second child, the daughter, is named Lo-ruhamah, "Not pitied," indicating that God will no longer pity and forgive the Israelites for their sins.

The third is named Lo-ammi, "Not my people," signifying God's rejection of Israel.

Hosea experiences repeated shame because of his enduring love for Gomer; time after time, he takes her back. On one occasion, he seems to have been forced to buy her at a slave market or redeem her from a master (3:2).

Painful as Hosea's sufferings are, they sensitize rather than embitter him, and broaden his perspective. Because he never stops loving Gomer, he comes to identify with God's pain in having been repeatedly rejected and betrayed by Israel, a people whom He still loves. The prophet sees parallels between God's sufferings and his: As Israel often took the gold and silver with which the Lord had blessed them to worship Baal, so Gomer used the jewelry and clothes Hosea had given her, to seduce other men. And, just as God reclaims Israel after her betrayals, so does Hosea keep taking Gomer back.

When Hosea redeems Gomer from the slave market, he brings her home and tells her that she must now go for a long time without having sexual relations with anyone, including him. In comparable manner, Hosea prophesies that Israel, too, must endure for many days without a king and officials, and without sacrifices: "Afterward, the Israelites will turn back and will seek the Lord their God and David their king—and they will thrill over the Lord and over His bounty in the days to come" (3:5).

One of Hosea's great contributions is his invention of the husband/wife metaphor for the God/Israel relationship. The text repeatedly alternates between the story of Hosea and his faithless wife and that of God and his faithless people, between painful reflections on the acts of betrayal and blissful hopes for a future reconciliation. Eventually, both visions converge as the prophet imagines the day when God will say to the Israelites, symbolized by Lo-ammi (the third child, whose name means "Not my people"): " 'You are my people,' and [they] will respond, " '[You are] my God' " (2:25).

We never learn whether Gomer, the compulsive adulteress, finally becomes loyal to her ever-loving husband. We can only hope, just as God does, that she stays faithful to Hosea and the Israelite people to their Lord.

Hosea ranks as among the Bible's most daring books. Traditional Jewish law forbids a cuckolded man from acting as Hosea did, and taking back an adulterous wife (see also Jeremiah 3:1). However, such a legal restriction would probably have meant little to Hosea. His love had no pride; furthermore, it was only through its unconditional nature that he hoped to transform his erring wife.

In the history of theology, such unconditional love has come to be associated far more with Christianity than with Judaism.

Therefore, it is bracing for Jews to learn that they too had a prophet whose unconditional love encompassed a nonstop betrayer and sinner.

116. Amos: "Let Justice Well Up Like Water, Righteousness Like a Mighty Stream"

5:24

Amos, who is the first of the later, or literary, prophets—his book, however, does not appear first—inaugurates a new stage in Jewish religious development. Desirous of ensuring that their message and teachings not die with them, the later prophets, or possibly their students, preserved their writings in separate books that came to be called by each one's name (unlike earlier prophets, such as Moses, Nathan, and Elijah, whose prophecies are recorded in books that form part of the general history of ancient Israel). Although we have no way of knowing the efficacy of Amos's message in his own time, that tens of millions of people continue to read and be affected by his words almost three millennia after they were written attests to how important this development was for the history of humankind.

Amos, who seems to have prophesied from about 775 to 750 B.C.E., came from Tekoah, a small city about twelve miles from Jerusalem, where he worked as a cattle breeder. He lived during an affluent period in the history of both Judah and Israel, the roots of which preceded him. In 805, Assyria had crushed Syria, Israel's historic enemy, so decisively that both Jewish states had little to fear from Syria for a long time. Then, from 782 to 745, Assyria was governed by a series of weak kings, who largely left the Mediterranean area alone.

During this period, the kingdom of Israel extended its boundaries, retook border cities that Syria had captured earlier (II Kings 13:25), and took control over the trade routes that ran through the country.

A wealthy class emerged. Amos 3:15 speaks of people living in winter and summer homes, decorated with expensive furniture. The prophet's description conveys a sense of decadent affluence:

They lie on ivory beds
Lolling on their couches
Feasting on lambs from the flock . . .
They drink straight from the wine bowls
And anoint themselves with the choicest oils . . .
But they are not concerned with the ruin of Joseph (i.e., their
fellow Israelites; the largest tribe in Israel was named for
Ephraim, a son of Joseph) (Amos 6:4–6).

As Amos points out repeatedly, the poorer classes do not share in
the new wealth. Thus, while archaeological evidence from the tenth
century B.C.E. indicates that the Israelite houses were similar in size,
by Amos's time, there were stark contrasts between the elaborate
homes of the wealthy and the small quarters of the poor. What was
worse, small farmers were dispossessed to make room for large estates
(recalling the story of Ahab and Jezebel's confiscation of Navot's
vineyard; see entry 93), and many are reduced to living as virtual
serfs.

This marks the first time in Israelite history that a society with
sharp class divisions emerges. What further enrages Amos is the
claim of the affluent that wealth, in and of itself, demonstrates that
God approves of them and their behavior.

The rich class alone does not propagate this evil theology, for, as
Amos charges, the priests at the Bethel temple corrupt the Israelite
religion by encouraging their followers to bring elaborate gifts to
the Temple. They act as if God is a pagan deity who can be bought
with sacrifices. Amos 4:4 speaks of morning sacrifices and tithes,
thank offerings and free-will offerings, all of which enrich the priests,
in return for which they do not question their patrons' immoral treatment of the poor.*

---

*In his classic study of Amos's confrontation with the priests, the late Sha-
lom Spiegel explains how the priests came to espouse the belief that sacrifices are more important to God than helping the poor: "Certainly what
we owe to creatures can never compare to what we owe to the Creator. If
neglect of man be sin, neglect of God is sacrilege." Furthermore, the priests
could argue that even were they to take all the gold and silver from the
temples and give it to the poor, what effect would that have in the long
run? The Bible itself teaches that "the poor will never cease out of the land"
(Deuteronomy 15:11). Soon, there would be new poor people and decrepit
temples.

According to Amos, the perversion of Judaism's values goes further yet. At that time, even many prophets could be bought, which is why he takes no pride in being called a prophet: "I am not a prophet nor a child [alternatively, "disciple"] of a prophet. I am a cattle breeder and tender of sycamore trees" (Amos 7:14).

Ignoring the High Priest Amaziah's suggestion that he leave Bethel and prophesy in Judah, Amos continues to deliver his message at the Bethel temple, where he accuses the affluent worshipers of several offenses:

1. *Exploitation of the poor*

While the wealthy people claim to show respect to God by bringing sacrifices, they continually violate the most basic laws of the biblical covenant. For example, Deuteronomy 15:7–8 instructs that if a man becomes impoverished, "you shall not harden your heart . . . you shall lend him sufficient for his needs." Instead of the wealthy following this command, debtors are being sold as slaves: "They have sold for silver those whose cause was just, and the needy for a pair of sandals" (Amos 2:6).

Similarly, Exodus 22:25–26 commands that if a creditor takes a debtor's night garment as a pledge, he has to return it every evening: "It is his garment for his skin, in what shall he sleep?" Since the procedure is so cumbersome, it is likely that the Torah's intention was to discourage taking pledges of clothing from the poor in the first place. Yet Amos 2:8, which describes vile acts going on at the Temple, writes: "They recline by every altar on garments taken in pledge."

2. *Business dishonesty*

Amos condemns the rapacious mind-set of the nouveau riche: "Listen to this, you who devour the needy, annihilating the poor of the land, saying, 'If only the new moon were over, so that we could sell grain, the Sabbath, so that we could offer wheat for sale, using an *ephah* [a measure] that is too small, and a *shekel* that is too big, tilting a dishonest scale, and selling grain refuse as grain . . . The Lord swears . . . 'I will never forget any of these doings'" (8:4–7).

Abraham Joshua Heschel, the great twentieth-century Jewish theologian and author of *The Prophets*, notes that "the juxtaposition of observing the laws of the Sabbath, while waiting for the day to come to an end [so that one can deal] deceitfully with false balances strikes home a melancholy irony, easily lost on the modern reader. Man is waiting for the day of sanctity to come to an end so that cheating and exploitation can be resumed. This is a stunning condemnation."

Amos also alludes to sexual decadence: "Father and son go to the same girl, and thereby profane my Holy name" (2:7).

Had Amos been more timid, he might have remained in Tekoah and issued polemics denouncing the perverse priorities of the Israelites at Bethel. But he doesn't. Instead, he delivers his message before throngs of worshipers who have gathered there.

A shrewd rhetorician, Amos opens his talk with a denunciation of the moral evils committed by the nations that surround Israel. The Philistines, referred to here by their capital city, Gaza, are condemned for selling a captive people into slavery to make money (1:6), while the Ammonites are denounced for ripping open the stomachs of pregnant women in Gilead while annexing a strip of territory there (1:13). Syria, Tyre, Edom, and Moab are condemned as well.

Amos's denunciation of these acts in God's name reveals the Lord of Israel to be One who is concerned with the righteousness of all people, and Who is angered far more by ethical than ritual transgressions. As the late Israeli Bible scholar Yehezkel Kaufmann noted, the nations of the world are punished for gross moral offenses, not idolatry.

By beginning with these denunciations, Amos establishes his credentials. No one can accuse him of being a self-hating Israelite (in 2:4–5, he likewise discusses Judean sins).

But the crowds' appreciation of Amos's castigations of their enemies must have turned to anger when his poetry is directed at them.

First, as noted earlier, he denounces the mistreatment of the poor (2:6–8), then he attacks the idea that because Israel is God's Chosen People, they will go unpunished for their sins (see next entry).

Amos expresses particular contempt for ritual observance unaccompanied by ethical behavior. Speaking in God's name, he declares:

I loathe, I spurn your festivals,
I am not appeased by your solemn assemblies
If you offer Me burnt offering or your meal offerings
I will not accept them
I will pay no heed to your gifts of fatlings (5:21–22).

This is what God wants from His people:

But let justice well up like water,
Righteousness like a mighty stream (5:24).

Amos announces that if Israelite society is unjust, even the mightiest army will not save it from destruction. Standing in the Temple courtyard, he prophesies:

"The shrines of Isaac shall be laid waste, and the sanctuaries of Israel reduced to ruin, and I will turn upon the House of Jeroboam* with the sword" (7:9).

These words prove so intolerable that the High Priest Amaziah sends a message to the king: "Amos is conspiring against you within the house of Israel. The country cannot endure the things he is saying" (7:10–11).

Amaziah turns to Amos: "Seer, off with you to the land of Judah. . . . But don't ever prophesy again at Bethel. For it is a king's sanctuary and a royal palace."

The High Priest, who has chosen to expel the messenger without considering the possible truthfulness of the message, is informed by Amos of the price that he and Israel will pay for ignoring God's words: Amaziah will die in exile, his family will be destroyed, and the Ten Tribes of Israel will be expelled from their land (7:17).

At this point, Amos apparently is deported.†

Amos's insistence that justice is the most important value, and that chosenness confers additional obligations, not superior rights, are his most important contributions to biblical theology. Perhaps equally significant was his decision—or that of his students—to record his prophecies; because Amos and his successors wrote down their words, they have been able to influence every generation since.

---

*Jeroboam II, the then-reigning king of Israel (793–753 B.C.E.), should not be confused with the earlier Jeroboam, Israel's first king; see entry 91.
†Shalom Spiegel notes: "In justice to the ancients, however, we must not lose sight of the amazing freedom of speech in the northern kingdom of Israel. After all, Amos was not burned at the stake . . . nor even condemned to drink the cup of hemlock by an enraged citizenry. He was permitted

Does Amos's denunciation of his contemporaries reveal the ancient Israelites to have been unusually wicked? Amos and most other prophets depict the Israelites very critically—the English-Jewish writer Israel Zangwill once said, only half humorously, that they were among the world's first antisemites. Indeed, some medieval Christian theologians quoted the prophets to show the Jews' supposedly eternally evil nature.

Such an attitude is naive; it is analogous to a future historian concluding that the Soviet Union was a morally superior and happier society than the United States, as "proven" by the low level of antigovernment protests recorded in *Pravda* in contrast to the much higher level of reportage of anti-government protests in the United States as recorded in *The New York Times.*

Yet, from Amos's orations, it appears that the sins committed by Israel's neighbors—mass murder, exiling of other people, a total lack of pity for others (1:3–2:3)—are worse than those attributed to Israel. Israel is reproved at greater length, not because it is worse, but because it is accountable to higher standards (3:2).

Ultimately, what most makes the ancient Israelites different from their neighbors is that they canonized their critics; they took writings that criticized them in strong terms and turned them into holy books that would be studied by Jews throughout history.

As far as I know, this is something no other nation or religion has done.

Were the ideas of Amos and the other prophets original? Many students of biblical criticism have argued that the teachings of men such as Amos, Hosea, Isaiah, and Micah, that morality is God's supreme command, were original. According to these critics, who believe in a moral evolution that is parallel to Darwinian physical evolution, the Torah was concerned with ritual ordinances and uprooting idolatry, while the literary prophets developed the notion that moral behavior is God's central demand.

The late Princeton University philosopher Walter Kaufmann has effectively demolished the contention that the ethics taught by the prophets did not derive from the Torah: "We are asked in effect to believe that, in the eighth century, Amos and Hosea, independent of each other and without the least awareness of their originality—

---

peaceably to repair to his native Tekoah where he wrote his book . . . [which] ultimately [became] a part of the most widely read book in civilization."

came up all at once with the same moral demands. These were ech-
oed almost immediately by Isaiah and Micah who, rather oddly, also
seemed to think their people had long been told what they were
reminding them of, and that it was truly shameful and inexcusable
that Israel should have forgotten, or rather failed to live up to, these
ancient standards."

Sources: Abraham Joshua Heschel, *The Prophets;* Theodore Friedman,
editor, *The Teacher's Resource Guide for the Rabbi's Bible,* page 109, describes the archaeological evidence for the disparity between rich
and poor homes in eighth-century B.C.E. Israel; Shalom Spiegel,
"Amos vs. Amaziah," in Judah Goldin, editor, *The Jewish Expression,*
pages 38–65. The statement concerning free speech in ancient Israel
is on page 47; Yehezkel Kaufmann, *The Religion of Israel,* page 364;
and Walter Kaufmann, *Religions in Four Dimensions,* page 45.

117. Amos: "You Alone Have I Singled Out of All the Families of the Earth—That Is Why I Will Call You to Account for All Your Iniquities"

3:2

Amos and the Meaning of Jewish Chosenness

Although it is not intended to do so, the doctrine of chosenness can lead some people to believe that they are superior to others and/or more beloved by God. Amos apparently feared that many of his Israelite contemporaries so regarded themselves; thus, he felt the need to explain the true implications of chosenness. The fact that "you alone have I [God] singled out of all the families of the earth" endows Israel not with a superior status, but with a greater responsibility: "That is why I will call you to account for all your iniquities."

In similar manner, parents might love children equally but not treat them equally. For example, they might punish a fifteen-year-old child for an offense for which the child's younger sibling will go unpunished. Why? The older child is held to a higher standard; more has been explained to him or her, and therefore that child should know better. So, too, because of the divine revelation God has granted Israel, He holds them accountable to a higher standard of moral behavior.

Unfortunately, throughout history, the temptation to view chosenness as a dispensation, rather than as a summons to a higher standard of behavior, has been pronounced. As noted later (see entry 119), Martin Luther asserted that those who believe Jesus to be God will go to heaven, even if they have committed murders, while those who do not affirm Jesus' divinity will spend eternity in hell, even if they are righteous people, indeed, even if they are the victims of those murderers who are believers. In his view, apparently, Amos should be rewritten to read: "You alone have I singled out of all the families of the earth—that is why I will *not* call you to account for all your iniquities."

A similar conviction that chosenness allows the chosen to practice an inferior morality seems to have been held by Arnuad-Amalric, legate of Pope Innocent III and commander of the Crusader army in 1209 C.E. that murdered 15,000 Frenchmen in Béziers in pursuit of some 220 supposed heretics in the city. Legend has it that when the Crusaders asked his advice as to whom they should kill (since they could not distinguish the good from the wicked), Arnaud-Amalric responded: "Kill them all! God will recognize his own" (in other words, the concept of being chosen did not obligate the Crusaders to refrain from murdering innocent people; see Otto Friedrich, *The End of the World*, pages 76–78).

In recent times, those Jews who hailed Baruch Goldstein's February 1994 murder of twenty-nine Arabs praying at a Hebron mosque likewise seem to believe that the prophet Amos spoke falsely, as do Muslim religious leaders who have supported Ayatollah Khomeini, Hamas, and other proponents of Islamic terrorism.

Amos also argues that chosenness does not mean that God loves Israel more than He loves other people:

> To Me, O Israelites, you are just like the Ethiopians, declares the Lord (9:7).

God loves all His children, not only Israel, but also the Ethiopians. Nor do I believe that it was by chance that Amos compared Israel to Ethiopia. Given that racism probably has existed throughout history, one can imagine the multitude at the Israelite temple in Bethel murmuring, "Imagine comparing us to a group of Ethiopians—saying that God loves them as much as He loves us."

That of course is precisely what Amos *is* saying: that God loves all human beings equally, since they are all created "in His image."

118. Jonah and the Whale

THE BOOK OF JONAH

The entire Book of Jonah consists of but forty-eight verses, yet it contains many of the Bible's most remarkable teachings. How unfortunate, therefore, that most people know only one thing about this book, that Jonah was swallowed by a whale. This is almost definitely wrong and is, anyway, one of the story's least important elements.

The first thing we learn about Jonah is that he is something of an Israelite chauvinist and, like many extreme nationalists, an angry man. That is why he is upset when God tells him to go to the large non-Jewish city of Nineveh, "and proclaim judgment upon it, for their wickedness has come before Me" (1:2).

Jonah does something unprecedented for a prophet: He flees from God, going to Jaffa, where he boards a ship heading for Tarshish (likely in Spain), which is in the opposite direction from Nineveh.

Why does Jonah flee? If indeed he is a chauvinist, shouldn't he rejoice at God's message? After all, the Lord is angry at Nineveh's wickedness, and wants Jonah to pronounce judgment on the city.

However, Jonah understands that if God had simply wanted to destroy Nineveh, an act that he, Jonah, would have happily approved, He would have told Jonah to prophesy, while still in Israel, Nineveh's imminent demise. That God wants him to carry the divine message to Nineveh can only mean that the Lord hopes that Jonah's words will provoke the people there to repent, something he does not wish to see happen.

That is why Jonah flees. But how can anyone, let alone a prophet, believe that a person can escape God's presence? Jonah learns that he can't.

The Lord sends a terrible storm, which threatens to destroy the ship on which he has left. The petrified sailors pray to their gods and dump the vessel's cargo overboard.

As the storm rages, Jonah remains belowdecks, sleeping. The ship's captain rouses him: "How can you be sleeping so soundly? Up, call upon your god! Perhaps the god will be kind to us and we will not perish" (1:6). What an irony! A heathen sailor has to instruct an Israelite prophet to pray.

On deck, the petrified sailors cast lots to determine who is responsible for the calamitous storm. The text, which speaks of the sailors casting "lots," implies that the "choice" may have fallen several times on Jonah (1:7).

The sailors surround the prophet and ask him: "Tell us, you who have brought this misfortune upon us, what is your business? Where have you come from? What is your country, and of what people are you?" (1:8).

Four questions are posed to Jonah, but he answers only one: "I am a Hebrew, I worship the Lord, the God of Heaven, who made both sea and land" (1:9). His final words are of course meant to underscore that the storm has indeed been sent by his God.

When Jonah tells the terrified sailors that he is fleeing from God, they ask him, "What must we do to you to make the sea calm around us?" Jonah instructs them to throw him overboard, after which the sea will become calm.

Rejecting Jonah's suggestion, the sailors row with all their strength toward land, but their labors are in vain; even as they row, the waters surrounding them rise higher and higher.

On this and several other occasions, the Bible depicts the book's non-Israelite characters as being highly moral; here, they do all that is within their power to save Jonah. Their behavior contrasts starkly with that of the prophet, who has demonstrated no concern for non-Israelite lives. First, he flees God because he doesn't want to save Nineveh from destruction, and then he sleeps through the ship's likely destruction, unconcerned that the storm will kill many people aside from himself.

Only after the sailors' efforts to reach shore have failed do they decide to heave Jonah overboard. But first they turn to his God in prayer: "Oh, please, Lord, do not let us perish on account of this man's life! Do not hold us guilty of killing an innocent man!" (1:14).

As soon as Jonah is tossed into the water, the sea calms. The awed sailors offer God a sacrifice, and make vows before Him. Another irony! Even when fleeing his prophetic mission, Jonah is responsible for bringing heathen sailors to belief in God.

God sends an unidentified "huge fish" to swallow Jonah, and he resides in its belly for three days. The Bible never tells us the fish's species. The popular assumption that it is a whale is an example of Bible readers filling in narrative gaps, similar to the belief that the forbidden fruit that Adam and Eve ate was an apple. However, we do know that there is no way a person can be swallowed by a whale without being destroyed in the process.

Inside the fish, Jonah, shocked to realize that God has saved him, offers a prayer of thanksgiving; God, in turn, then commands the fish to spit him out onto dry land.

Once again, God commands Jonah to proclaim His message to the people of Nineveh. He now sets out for the city and upon arriving begins walking about, proclaiming, "Forty days more and Nineveh will be destroyed!" (3:4).

The Bible doesn't tell us much about the city's people, only that, believing Jonah's words to be true, they proclaim a fast and don sackcloth. Nineveh's king hears of Jonah's prophecy, and declares a fast that is binding on beasts as well as human beings. In an unintentionally humorous copyist's error, the text suggests that the king enjoins the beasts to cry out to God along with the human beings (3:8).

Seeing the actions of Nineveh's inhabitants, God renounces the punishment He had intended for them. What determines God's decision to remit judgment is His realization that the people "were turning back from their evil ways" (3:10). This emphasis on ethical behavior is characteristic of the Hebrew Bible. Had the story of Jonah appeared in the New Testament or the Islamic Quran, the people's repentance would probably have been proven by a conversion to Christianity or Islam. In the Hebrew Bible, particularly in the case of non-Hebrews, repentance is proven by an ethical and behavioral, rather than a theological and ritual, transformation. As the Talmud comments, "The verse does not read: 'And God saw their sackcloth and their fasting,' but 'God saw what they did, how they were turning back from their evil ways' " (Babylonian Talmud, *Ta'anit* 16a).

Unlike prophets such as Moses and Jeremiah, who become angry when their listeners ignore their words, Jonah becomes furious when the people of Nineveh heed his. Because Nineveh was the major city of Assyria, historic enemy of Israel (in 722 B.C.E., after the period in which the Bible claims the Book of Jonah was written, Assyria destroyed the Northern Kingdom of Israel and deported its inhabitants), Jonah had hoped to see Nineveh punished.

Eventually, Jonah becomes so unhappy about God's mercy on Nineveh that he prays to God to kill him.

The Lord ignores his irascible prophet: "Are you that deeply grieved?" He asks him (4:4).

The weary Jonah doesn't bother to respond; instead, he wanders out of the city and erects a small shelter. God causes a vine to grow quickly over Jonah's head and provide him with shade. Jonah is happy about the plant but, the following dawn, God sends a worm to chew the vine and kill it, so that the morning's burning sun blazes down on Jonah. The heat makes him faint, and he again prays for death.

"Are you so deeply grieved about the plant?" God asks him.

"Yes," Jonah replies, "so deeply that I want to die."

God responds: "You cared about the plant, which you did not work for and which you did not grow, which appeared overnight and perished overnight. And should I not care about Nineveh, that great city, in which there are more than a hundred and twenty thousand persons who do not yet know their right hand from their left [i.e., small children], and many beasts as well?" (4:10–11).

With these words, the Book of Jonah ends, but it has provided important teachings to Jews and all Bible readers ever since. Among its important themes is the idea of a Jewish mission to the world. Ultimately, and against his will, Jonah preaches about God and his moral message to the world, and his message influences people for good. That is one reason why on Yom Kippur, the Jewish people's holiest day, this short book is read in its entirety during the afternoon *Mincha* service.

In addition, the Book of Jonah underscores God's love for all human beings; at the end, He speaks of the people of Nineveh as his children, just as God speaks in other passages of the Israelites. And for those Israelites who might feel that they are the ethical superiors of their gentile neighbors, the Book of Jonah holds out a surprising lesson. The very model that is offered Jews on Yom Kippur of how to repent is based on the behavior of the gentiles of Nineveh.

The Book of Jonah also teaches a lesson that human beings have found difficult to incorporate since the time of Adam and Eve (see Genesis 3:8): One cannot hide, or flee, from God.

Reflections: Jonah is one of my favorite biblical books, and over the years I have read many commentaries and essays on it. Here are selections from just a few contemporary Jewish thinkers.

On Jonah as archetypical of the Jewish mission: "Jonah's task is to bring God's word to the Gentiles . . . without ceasing to be Jewish" (Elie Wiesel, *Five Biblical Portraits,* page 129).

On why the Book of Jonah is read on Yom Kippur: "The lesson in Jonah is that nothing is . . . sealed. God's will itself may change. Even

though punishment has been programmed, it may be cancelled ...
every human being is granted one more opportunity to start his life
all over again" (ibid., page 151).

*Literary devices by which the Bible shows how fleeing from God leads man
into descent:* "Instead of heeding the divine call to *arise* and go to
Nineveh (1:2) ... Jonah rather *goes down* to Jaffa, *goes down* to the
ship, and finally *goes down* to the innermost part of the ship. Fleeing
from God is a continuous state of descent" (David Shapiro, *Studies in
Jewish Thought,* Volume I, page 236).

On the repentance of the people of Nineveh: "In its comprehensive combination of fasting, praying and turning away from evil, the repentance of the people of Nineveh can be considered a model of what
repentance is to be" (Uriel Simon, "The Book of Jonah: Its Structure
and Significance," in *Sefer Yitzhak Aryeh Zeligman* [Hebrew], page 291).

119. Micah: The Three Things God Requires of People

MICAH 6:8

The determination of what the essence of something consists of,
particularly a religious or philosophical system, fascinates many people because once that essence is identified, it is far easier to establish
priorities. In its absence, all of God's laws, for example, would seem
to be of equal importance, and one would have no guideline by
which to observe when two laws conflict.*

Various religious traditions and thinkers have isolated different
essences as being most significant to God. The Protestant founder
and religious reformer Martin Luther believed that what mattered
most to God was faith (in God and in Jesus Christ as God's son).

---

*For example, Jewish law mandates both fasting on Yom Kippur, and the
saving of innocent life. Which of these laws takes precedence when fasting
will endanger an ill person's life? Jewish law concludes that the saving of
innocent life takes precedence; consequently, a severely ill person is *required*
to eat on Yom Kippur.

To Luther, faith in Jesus was so central a command that others receded before it in significance: "It is sufficient [to attain salvation] that we recognize through the wealth of God's glory the lamb who bears the sins of the world; from this, sin does not sever us, even if thousands, thousands, of times in one day we should fornicate or murder" (letter to Philip Melanchthon, Luther's friend and close associate, August 1, 1521).

In Luther's view, a murderer who has faith in Jesus is fulfilling the most important of his obligations to God; his act or acts of murder, though morally abhorrent, need not sever him from God's glory. However, a person who does not have faith in Jesus, but who lives a moral life, *will* be severed from God's glory (i.e., will not be saved in the hereafter).

Martin Luther's understanding of God's will differs markedly from that of Micah, one of the earliest literary prophets.* In an effort to convey to his fellow Israelites in simple, direct terms the sort of life God expects them to lead, Micah speaks of three essences:

He has told you, O man, what is good,
And what the Lord requires of you:
Only to do justice,
And to love goodness
And to walk modestly with your God (6:8).

The insistence on justice follows from the Torah's admonition, "Justice, justice you shall pursue" (Deuteronomy 16:20). *Tzedek,* the Hebrew for "justice," is the root of the word *tzedaka,* which is translated as "charity," but which literally is a derivative of "justice" (from the biblical perspective one who does not give *tzedaka* is not merely uncharitable, but unjust).

Micah's injunction "to love goodness" recalls Deuteronomy 6:18, "Do what is right and good in the sight of the Lord," and Proverbs 2:20, "So follow the way of the good, and keep to the paths of the just."

That God's primary concerns are justice and goodness also is emphasized by the prophet Jeremiah:

*The term "literary prophets" refers to those who left behind written records of their teachings, unlike the earlier prophets, such as Elijah, who left behind no such writings. Micah, a younger contemporary of Isaiah, prophesied in the last half of the eighth century B.C.E..

But *only in this* should one glory:
In his earnest devotion to Me.
For I the Lord act with *kindness,*
Justice and equity in the world;
For in these I delight—declares the Lord (Jeremiah 9:23).

In other words, to prove one's devotion to God one must act kindly, justly and equitably.

Micah's final demand is "to walk modestly with your God": The sort of faith that leads one to believe that he or she knows exactly what God requires in every situation can make a person arrogant. This passage demands humility of believers.

The pursuit of justice, an obsession with doing good deeds, and humility, these are what constitute for Micah a godly person. As Rabbi Hillel (first century B.C.E.) remarks after offering a similar ethical statement of Judaism's essence: "All the rest is commentary" (Babylonian Talmud, *Shabbat* 31a).

Reflections: Micah's universalism: In chapter 4, verse 5, Micah expresses a remarkable statement of universalism and tolerance: "For let all people walk everyone in the name of his god, and we will walk in the name of the Lord our God for ever and ever."

Source: The extract from Luther's letter to Melanchthon is printed in Walter Kaufmann, *Religions in Four Dimensions,* page 156.

THE WRITINGS

PSALMS

PROVERBS

JOB

THE FIVE SCROLLS

DANIEL

EZRA AND NEHEMIAH

I AND II CHRONICLES

XIV. PSALMS

120. An Introduction

The Book of Psalms has 150 chapters, more than any other book in the Bible. It contains the Bible's longest chapter (119, which has 176 verses) as well as its shortest (117, with but two verses). Psalms serves as the "backbone" of the Hebrew *siddur* (prayerbook). For example, the traditional Friday evening Sabbath service starts with six psalms (95–99 and 29), representing the six days that have passed since the end of the preceding Sabbath. Psalm 145, known by Jews as *Ashrei* ("happy"—the *ashrei* verse itself is found in 84:5), is recited thrice daily during the morning and afternoon prayer services. The *Hallel* prayer, recited on most Jewish holidays and the beginning of each month (Rosh Chodesh), comprises Psalms 113–118. Because of the Book of Psalms' omnipresence throughout the various prayer services, most observant Jews know many of its verses by heart.

The Book of Psalms attributes the authorship of many of the psalms to King David, the warrior-king who was also a poet. Many of David's psalms follow a petitionary format, soliciting God's help during times of hardship. For example, Psalm 3, which begins, "A psalm of David when he fled from his son, Absalom," expresses the Psalmist's plea: "Rise, O Lord! Deliver me, O my God!" (3:8).

At the Temple, some psalms were recited with musical accompaniment. For example, Psalm 4 begins with an instruction to the musical leader: "For the leader, with instrumental music."

A common theme expressed in the Book of Psalms is the request that God involve Himself more actively in fighting evil people, particularly Israel's enemies:

O God, do not be silent;
do not hold aloof;
do not be quiet, O God!
For your enemies rage . . .
They plot craftily against your people. . . .
They say, "Let us wipe them out as a nation;
Israel's name will be mentioned no more" (83:2–5).

Because of the large number of psalms, I have chosen five that are representative; they run the gamut of religious emotions expressed in these immortal creations.

121. Psalm 1: "Happy Is the Man Who Has Not Followed the Advice of the Wicked"

1:1

Unlike many later psalms, the first one focuses more on the differences between good and bad people than on God.

However, rather than starting with a description of what a good person *does*, Psalm 1 describes what a good person *avoids*— most notably, association with the wicked. The Talmud later elaborated on this theme: "Keep far away from an evil neighbor, and don't become friendly with the wicked" (*Ethics of the Fathers* 1:7). The assumption underlying this teaching is that bad companions generally assert a stronger influence than do good ones (in today's terms, one more often hears of teenagers who are persuaded to take drugs by their peers than of drug addicts who go cold turkey because of their friends' influence). Similarly, the Psalmist praises a person who avoids asking for advice from those who are wicked.

Significantly, this psalm doesn't speak of a person who avoids associating with the wicked as "good," or "wise," although such terms surely apply; rather, it refers to such a person as "happy" (alternatively, "satisfied," or "happy with oneself"). One who avoids dealings with immoral people, and thereby avoids the troubles such involvements entail, will end up a happier person.

Along with enjoining one to avoid evil people, the Psalmist urges staying clear of scoffers, people who mock everything and for whom nothing is holy. Oscar Wilde, the brilliant playwright and, strangely enough, quite a scoffer himself, defined a cynic as "a person who knows the price of everything and the value of nothing."

With what does a happy and, by implication, good person occupy himself? The study of Torah, "the teaching of the Lord."

Such a person becomes, in words that have long been popularized in an African-American spiritual, "Like a tree planted by the water" (literally, "a tree planted beside streams of water"). The Psalmist specifies a fruit-bearing tree, one that has substance, not just beauty, to offer the world (1:3).

Describing how the world *should* work, the Psalmist compares the wicked to chaff blown away by the wind. And like chaff, the wicked cannot long survive; rather, it is the righteous who, cherished by God, endure while "the way of the wicked is doomed" (1:6).

Although this verse conveys Judaism's view of the fate of the wicked in the next world, it is not clear that the wicked are necessarily "doomed" in this world. It is, however, a noble hope. Later Jewish tradition taught that the doom of the wicked need not mean their death, perhaps only the "death" of their wickedness. A famous talmudic passage teaches: "There were some criminals in Rabbi Meir's neighborhood who caused him much trouble, and he prayed that they should die. His wife Beruriah said to him: 'What are you thinking?' [or How could you possibly believe that such a prayer is even allowed?]. Do you justify it on the basis of the verse [in Psalms 104:35], 'May sinners disappear from the earth, and the wicked be no more'? But the word that you take to mean 'sinners' [in Hebrew, *ho-tim*] can also be read as 'sins' [*hatta-im;* "Let *sins* disappear from the earth"]. Furthermore, look at the end of the verse, 'and the wicked be no more.' Once the sins will cease, there will no longer be wicked men! Rather pray that they repent, and there will be no more wicked people around.' Rabbi Meir did pray for them, and the criminals repented" (Babylonian Talmud, *Berakhot* 10a).

122. Psalm 15: "Lord, Who May Sojourn in Your Tent, Who May Dwell on Your Holy Mountain?"

15:1

Proverbs 31:10 initiates a description of an ideal woman with the question: "A woman of valor, who can find?" (see entry 126). In comparable manner, Psalm 15 begins a description of an exemplary person by asking who is worthy of dwelling in God's presence.

The psalm answers this question by listing eleven attributes that characterize a righteous person.

The first traits are worthy, rather general, personal attributes:

1. He who lives without blame;
2. who does righteous acts; and
3. who speaks the truth in his heart.

Jewish sources understand "who speaks the truth in his heart" as referring to a person who follows the truth even when it is known only to him or her and is disadvantageous. Some commentaries cite the example of Rabbi Safra, a Babylonian Jew who lived in the early centuries of the Common Era. One day, while reciting the *Sh'ma* prayer ("Hear, O Israel"), a man entered the rabbi's office and made an offer for an item the rabbi was selling. Not wishing to interrupt his prayers, Rabbi Safra said nothing. The would-be buyer interpreted the silence as rejection, and raised his offer several times. When Rabbi Safra finished praying, he explained why he had been silent, and he accepted the original bid, noting that when he first heard it, he knew that he would be willing to sell the item at that price.

Nahum Sarna, author of *On the Book of Psalms*, notes that the Psalmist next cites items that "are not essential attributes of character, but rather [the avoidance of] specific, sometime offenses":

4. who has had no slander upon his tongue (alternatively, "whose tongue speaks no deceit");
5. who has not done harm to his fellow;
6. or borne reproach for [his acts toward] his neighbor.

Trait 4 brings to mind Leviticus 19:16: "Do not go about as a talebearer...." In enjoining human beings not to spread negative gossip, the Torah makes a demand that is particularly difficult for most people to fulfill. Yet it is impossible to be a good human being if you do not watch what you say, since so much pain and damage are inflicted by ill-considered and unfair words.

The meaning of attribute 6 is somewhat unclear; perhaps it refers to one who acts so justly toward his neighbors that he or she never deserves to be reproached by them.

The next three traits, as Sarna notes, deal "with the character and reputation of one's associates":

7. for whom a contemptible person is abhorrent;
8. who honors those who fear the Lord;
9. who stands by his oath even when it is to his disadvantage.

Attribute 7 reminds us that a good person is not a Milquetoast, someone who is equally nice to good and bad people. Saul Bellow has written that "a person is only as good as what he loves." Thus, a good person finds evil people contemptible; even if he acts kindly toward them, perhaps in the hope of influencing them, he never rationalizes or justifies their evil acts.

Why is the Psalmist so concerned that one have contempt for those who are contemptible? Because otherwise one may be taken in by a bad person's external charm and be influenced by his or her behavior. "Woe to the evil man, and woe to his neighbor," the Talmud warns (Babylonian Talmud, *Sukkah* 56b).

Attributes 8 and 9 emphasize that the good man honors those who fear God, and stands by his word, even when fulfilling it can be costly.

Sarna observes that the final two virtues—

10. who has never lent money for interest;
11. or accepted a bribe against the innocent—

"are paired because they are two facets of a single grave offense— the misuse of assets." The first prohibits profiting from society's most vulnerable members (the Torah's concern in prohibiting interest is to protect those who need money for such necessities as food, clothing, and housing; see entry 206), while attribute 11 refers to not corrupting the judicial system.

Being cruel to the poor violates the oft-repeated biblical injunction to be generous to widows and orphans (see entry 171).

Indeed, the Torah claims that God will personally wreak vengeance against those who mistreat such people: "I will put you to the sword, and your own wives shall become widows and your children orphans" (Exodus 22:23).

As for attribute 11, one of the greatest evils that can overtake a society is the corruption of its judicial system. When this occurs, a victim of injustice has no place to go to seek redress. Thus, the Bible regards both those who offer and those who accept bribes as the "lowest of the low."

A talmudic tale relates that Rabban Gamliel, president of the Sanhedrin, the ancient Jewish high court, used to weep when reading Psalm 15; he was overwhelmed by thoughts of how hard it is to fulfill all its ethical demands. He was right; nonetheless, reading and rereading this Psalm—it's not a bad idea to start one's day by reading Psalm 15—may well evoke the kind of introspection that influences one to act virtuously, kindly, and courageously.

Source and further reading: My understanding of this psalm owes much to Nahum Sarna, *On the Book of Psalms,* pages 98–121. Sarna makes an interesting observation about the puzzling opening verse, which speaks of sojourning in God's tent: "To call the great Temple in Jerusalem, built of stone, a 'tent'—in Hebrew *ohel*—might seem odd, but this designation occurs several times in the Bible, always in poetic texts. It harks back to pre-Solomonic times, when the religious center of Israel was indeed a tent, beginning with the construction of the mobile Tabernacle in the course of the wilderness wanderings" (page 108).

123. Psalm 23: "The Lord Is My Shepherd"

23:1

Because Psalm 23 is so well known, more than a few Jews from assimilated backgrounds have confided to me that they had always thought it came from the New Testament. Perhaps this is because this psalm is among the most familiar among Christians, since it expresses a very intimate relationship between believers and God, Who is likened to a shepherd just as Jesus compares himself to one in the New Testament: "I am the good shepherd" (John 10:11).

Shepherds occupy a privileged place in the Hebrew Bible, and many foremost biblical characters herd sheep: Rachel (Genesis 29:9), Moses (Exodus 3:1), the young David (I Samuel 17:15), and the prophet Amos (1:1).

A famous rabbinic *midrash* teaches that it was Moses' behavior toward his flock that convinced God to appoint him as Israel's leader: "[When Moses shepherded the flocks of Jethro], he used to stop the bigger sheep from grazing before the smaller ones, and let the smaller ones loose first to feed on the tender grass; then he would let the older sheep loose to feed on the grass of average quality; lastly he let the strong ones loose to feed on the toughest. God said, 'Let . . . him who knows how to shepherd the flock, each according to its strength, come and lead my people' " (*Exodus Rabbah* 2:2).

Psalm 23 describes God as the Psalmist's shepherd. Though many English renditions of the opening words of the psalm exist, none has penetrated people's hearts more powerfully than the King James version: "The Lord is my shepherd, I shall not want." The Psalmist goes on to depict God as the source of all goodness; He leads one to water, symbolic of the fulfillment of one's material needs, and guides His followers in the right moral direction.

Most important, during life's darkest hours, "though I walk through the valley of the shadow of death," the believer remains serene: "I fear no evil, for You are with me" (23:4).

An upright person, who is at peace with his or her conscience and senses God's presence, never feels fully alone. During much of the late 1970s and 1980s, Natan Sharansky, the prominent Soviet-Jewish dissident who suffered long incarceration in Soviet prison camps ("the valley of the shadow of death"), kept with him at all times and as his most prized possession, a small Hebrew volume of Psalms that had been given him by his wife. Later, after his release, he entitled his memoirs *Fear No Evil*.

Psalm 23 has long been a particular favorite of people who are suffering or who are pursued by evil forces. Although the odds (in the case of illness) or forces arrayed against them may be great (in Sharansky's case, it was the whole apparatus of the Soviet government), the believer in God sees the Lord as the protecting, and comforting, shepherd who will keep him or her safe.

The hope is that God will help one in this world ("Only goodness and steadfast love shall pursue me all the days of my life"), and that this experience will be preparatory to an eternal union between the believer and God: "And I shall dwell in the house of the Lord forever."

Because of its insistence on a believer's eternal repose with God, Psalm 23 is frequently recited at funerals.

124. Psalm 44: "Why Do You Hide Your Face, Ignoring Our Affliction and Distress?"

44:25

No psalm, or other biblical chapter for that matter, speaks as powerfully to many post-Holocaust Jews as Psalm 44, a pain- and rage-filled complaint against God for His seeming noninvolvement in this world.

It starts by reminding God that He had once been an active participant in Israel's history: "Our fathers have told us the deeds You performed in their time, in days of old" (44:2). God is reminded how He had once planted Israel in Canaan in the face of opposition and, how, with God at their side, the children of Israel overcame their foes:

Unfortunately, it seems as if such days are past:

Yet you have rejected and disgraced us;
You do not go with our armies.
You make us retreat before our foe;
our enemies plunder us at will (44:10–11).

Whereas the prophetic writings often proclaim that God has been loyal to Israel but that its people have betrayed God, the anguished Psalmist claims that the opposite has now occurred:

All this has come upon us,
yet we have not forgotten You . . .
though You cast us, crushed into a desolate place [literally,
   "where the sea monster is"]
and covered us with deep darkness (44:18, 20).

Why does Israel suffer such persecution from her adversaries? The Psalmist believes that Israel is hated because it serves as witness to God: "It is for Your sake that we are slain all day long, that we are regarded as sheep to be slaughtered" (44:23).

This image of Jews as sheep has long both roused and pained the Jewish soul. When the poet Abba Kovner launched his appeal to the Jews of Vilna to revolt against the Nazi slaughter (January 1, 1942), he wrote: "We will not be led like sheep to the slaughter. . . . Brothers! It is better to die fighting like free men than to live at the mercy of the murderers. Arise! Arise [and fight] with your last breath!"

Unfortunately, the expression "like sheep to the slaughter" later was used by some to disparage those Jews who perished in the Holocaust without revolting. Yoel Palgi, a Palestinian Jew who parachuted into Hungary in 1944 to try to instigate Jewish resistance, notes that when he returned to Palestine after the war, he went to a veterans' club where he encountered the following reaction: "Everywhere I turned, the question was fired at me: why did the Jews not rebel? Why did they go like lambs to the slaughter? Suddenly I realized that we were ashamed of those who were tortured, shot, burned. . . . Unconsciously, we have accepted the Nazi view that the Jews were subhuman. . . . History is playing a bitter joke on us: have we not ourselves put the six million on trial?"

Palgi's defense of the Holocaust victims was true to the Psalmist's vision. When speaking of Jews going as "sheep to be slaughtered," the Psalmist does not feel that the victims have done anything for which they need feel ashamed or need apologize; rather, it is God who should be ashamed. For it is He, the Psalmist believes, who has acted wrongly: "Why do you sleep, O Lord? Awaken, do not reject us forever!" (44:24).*

The Holocaust was a humiliation for God's chosen people, leaving loyal Jews with the question the Psalmist asks of his seemingly disloyal God: "Why do You hide Your face, ignoring our afflictions and distress?" (44:25).

In the final verse, the Psalmist, still trusting in God's love, seems to feel that if he can only find the right words, God can be motivated to act: "Arise and help us, redeem us, as befits Your faithfulness" (44:27).

Most psalms exalt God's glory and try to motivate readers to draw closer to Him; they repeatedly express trust in God. But occasionally, just occasionally, when a religious person is overwhelmed by evil forces, he or she is motivated to ask God why He doesn't protect those people who have been loyal to Him, and who are suffering because of that very loyalty.

Psalm 44 has nothing to do with atheists who deny God because of evils such as the Holocaust. Rather, it is an anguished cry of a fervent believer, a person who feels abandoned by the One Who claims to love him, and who is confident that if God only wished to act, He could easily stop the evil and return humankind to a state of well-being.

125. Psalm 137: "If I Forget You, O Jerusalem, Let My Right Hand Wither"

137:5

Although Jewish tradition attributes authorship of the psalms to King David, no one assumes that he composed the 137th psalm, which describes events that occurred more than four centuries after his reign.

*Dr. Jeremiah Unterman has pointed out to me that the very notion that God sleeps is an attack—i.e., "Are You a pagan deity who needs to sleep?" (see, for example, I Kings 18:27)—and is intended to spur God to action.

The scene of Psalm 137 is Babylon, some years after the Babylonians had destroyed Judah and the Temple in Jerusalem, and exiled
many of Judah's inhabitants to Babylon. The Psalmist writes:

> By the rivers of Babylon,
> There we sat,
> sat and wept,
> as we remembered Zion (1:1).

The Psalmist speaks of Babylonians who taunt the exiled Jews with
requests for songs they used to sing during their happier days in
Jerusalem. "How can we sing a song of the Lord in an alien land?"
the Jews respond, then they recite an oath that has since become
part of the consciousness of all committed Jews:

> If I forget you, O Jerusalem,
> let my right hand wither;
> let my tongue stick to my palate
> if I cease to think of you,
> If I do not keep Jerusalem in memory,
> even at my happiest hour (137:5).

The final clause is understood today as lying behind the well-
known custom of shattering a glass at the conclusion of a Jewish
wedding ceremony. Since marriage constitutes one of the "happiest
hour[s]" in a couple's life, Jewish tradition mandates that a glass be
shattered to remind the celebrants that the Jerusalem Temple (the
most tangible symbol of the city's glory) has still not been rebuilt.

In 1903, at the Sixth Zionist Congress, when Theodor Herzl proposed that the delegates consider a part of Uganda instead of Israel
as the Jews' temporary homeland, he was denounced by many for
betraying Zionism's dream. Stung by the accusation, Herzl mounted
the podium and recited: "If I forget you, O Jerusalem . . ."*

The psalm's conclusion is jolting. In the next-to-last verse, a curse
is called down on "Babylon, you predator," and "a blessing on him

---

*More recently, the late Menachem Begin offered a variation of this verse
to underscore the centrality of the Holocaust in contemporary Jewish consciousness: "If I forget the extermination of the Jews, may my right hand
wither, may my tongue stick to my palate if I cease to think of you, if I
do not keep the extermination of the Jews in memory even at my happiest
hour" (cited in Tom Segev, *The Seventh Million*, page 216).

who repays you in kind for what you have inflicted on us." Had the psalm concluded with this general, unspecified call for revenge, it would have shocked no one. But the Psalmist then details the specific act that he would like to see repaid in kind to the Babylonians: "a blessing on him who seizes your babies and dashes them against the rocks" (137:8).

Since Jewish law forbids punishing children for their parents' sins (Deuteronomy 24:16), this final verse violates the Torah's ethical norms. Rather, one should regard it as the anguished, rageful cry of an impotent victim who is powerless to hurt his oppressor with deeds, and therefore discharges his rage with words. Unlike the rest of the psalm, the last verse is rarely, if ever, cited. It is the earlier verse, "If I forget you, O Jerusalem," that has made this psalm so memorable and often quoted.

XV. PROVERBS

126. "A Woman of Valor Who Shall Find?"

31:10

Trying to summarize the Book of Proverbs, which contains over one thousand sayings, is like attempting to summarize a book of quotations; the material is too varied to lend itself to concise description. Among its subjects are the importance of obeying parents (1:8), avoiding bad companions (1:10–19; 4:14–19), not committing adultery (5:3–4, 20–22), being honest in business (3:28), doing kind deeds (3:27), and not being lazy (6:6–11).

Proverbs is obsessed with the subject of wisdom, what it is and how to acquire it. The author feels that to become wise, one must first acknowledge God: "The fear of the Lord is the beginning of knowledge" (1:7; see entry 153 for a discussion of fear, as opposed to the love, of God).

Since according to Jewish tradition the Torah is the wisest book ever written, many proverbs extol its wisdom. One verse, "She [the Torah] is a tree of life [*etz chayyim*] to them that hold her, and happy are those who hold her fast" (3:18), is recited during the Sabbath morning and festival synagogue services while the Torah is being returned to the Ark.

The opening words of this book, "The proverbs of Solomon, son of David, king of Israel," along with I Kings 5:12, which teaches that Solomon "spoke 3,000 proverbs," accounts for the book's long-standing attribution to the tenth-century-B.C.E. monarch. Yet evidence suggests that Solomon did not write all the proverbs.* For

---

*Chapters 10:1 and 25:1 refer specifically to proverbs authored by Solomon, suggesting that other parts of the book might not have been written by him. In addition, chapters 25–28, although attributed to Solomon, are

example, chapter 30, which contains a moving prayer to God asking that one's basic financial needs be met (verse 8), is attributed to a man named Agur, while the opening verses, and perhaps the whole of chapter 31, are attributed to the mother of a King Lemuel of Massa.

Unfortunately, Proverbs also contains my least favorite verses in the Bible, an admonition to parents to beat their children: ". . . if you beat him [i.e., your son] with a rod, he will not die. Beat him with a rod and you will save him from the grave" (23:13–14).

Many biblical verses have motivated human beings toward noble behavior. Think of "Love your neighbor as yourself" (Leviticus 19:18) and Micah's advice to "do justice and love mercy and to walk modestly with your God" (6:8). Verses 13 and 14 have the dubious distinction of inspiring people to display cruelty, and toward whom? Their own children, the very people who presumably most trust them.

Even more unfortunately, the author repeats this advice: "He who spares the rod hates his son, but he who loves him disciplines him early" (13:24).

Like adults, children need discipline, but the equation of discipline with beating is an example of very bad advice in a good book. In these two verses, morality is turned upside down: People who don't beat their children are made to appear unloving, while those who do beat them (some of whom, one must assume, are sadists) are rewarded by being told that this proves that they are loving parents.

Proverbs' concluding poem is as far from the spirit of these verses as possible. It is a love poem describing an ideal woman, which many traditional Jewish males recite to their wives at the beginning of the Sabbath. In recent years, it has also become customary at some modern Orthodox Jewish weddings for the groom to chant these verses from chapter 31 to his bride.

The poem starts with a rhetorical question: "A woman of valor who shall find?" and then goes on to describe the manifold traits characterizing such a woman.

The valorous woman is first characterized by her goodness to her husband: "She is good to him, never bad"; he, in turn, totally trusts her.

She also takes care of all her family's needs: "She rises while it is still night, and supplies provisions for her household" (31:15).

---

said to have been written down during King Hezekiah's reign, more than two hundred years after Solomon; see 25:1.

Unlike the stereotypical stay-at-home wife as the preferred model of womanhood, the woman of valor is a businesswoman, who "makes cloth and sells it, and offers [for sale] a girdle to the merchant" (31:24). In addition, she is:

wise—"Her mouth is full of wisdom" (31:26);
kind—"Her tongue with kindly teaching" (31:26);
generous—"She gives generously to the poor" (31:20);
hard-working—"Her lamp never goes out at night" (31:18);
a good manager—"She oversees the activities of her household" (31:27);
contented—"Her children make her happy" (31:28); and
lauded—"Her husband praises her" (31:28).

Beauty can deceive, and ultimately it is illusory (there are no eighty-year-old Miss Americas), but the woman of valor has the most important trait of all, fear of God, which guides all aspects of her life.

So flawless is the woman of valor that she brings to mind a sentiment expressed by Robert Schumann, the former French foreign minister, who quipped that as a young man he "vowed never to marry until I found the ideal woman. Well, I found her—but alas, she was waiting for the ideal man."

Indeed, one might well speculate what traits would characterize a man worthy of this woman of valor. Psalm 15 would seem to be a good starting place for such a search (see entry 122).

XVI. JOB

127. When God Gives Power to Satan: The Unhappy Test of Job

JOB, CHAPTERS 1–2

"The Lord Has Given and the Lord Has Taken Away; Blessed Be the Name of the Lord"

1:21

Almost all the Bible's noble characters have long been honored by having children named for them. Names such as Abraham, Isaac, Jacob, Moses, David, Sarah, Rebecca, Rachel, Miriam, and Deborah have been for many generations among the most common Jewish names, and they are popular among Christians as well.

There is only one biblical hero for whom, I believe, no child has ever been named: Job. His life is so tragic that no parents have ever wished to associate their offspring with so horrific a fate.

The Book of Job opens with a description of its leading character that is exceedingly complimentary. Job, we are told, is blameless and upright, a man who fears God and shuns evil. He also lives a blessed life, possessing extraordinary wealth and a large, healthy family, consisting of seven sons and three daughters.

With all that, Job does not take God or his good fortune for granted. After his children have a party, he offers sacrifices on their behalf. Like many parents before and since, Job wonders what might have transpired at the party: "Perhaps," he worries, "my children have

sinned and blasphemed God in their thoughts" (1:5). (Were Job living today, he likely would have expressed some other fears as well.)

Two scenes in the book's opening two chapters are set in heaven
and, oddly enough, God is depicted in these scenes in a less complimentary light than Job. The Lord is portrayed as speaking with
Satan (literally "the accuser," who here makes one of his rare ap-
pearances in the Hebrew Bible). When Satan tells God that he has
been roaming the earth, God asks him, "Have you noticed my servant Job? There is none like him on earth, a blameless and upright
man who fears God and shuns evil."

Satan mocks God for being naive. Of course, Job is pious: Has
not God generously rewarded him for his good deeds and religiosity?
Who, Satan challenges God, would not be pious in the face of so
generous a payoff? But just take away from Job all that he has, and
he "will surely blaspheme You to Your face" (1:11).

God consents to the test, and appoints Satan to administer it. He
only denies him the right to physically harm Job.

Satan immediately arranges to have all of Job's wealth and possessions destroyed, then sends a hurricanelike wind to destroy the
house in which his children are gathered. All ten of them die.

Job still does not blaspheme, proving Satan wrong and God right.
Instead, he bequeaths to later generations a statement of faith that
mourning believers in their anguish have recited for thousands of
years: "The Lord has given and the Lord has taken away; blessed be
the name of the Lord" (1:21).

Satan won't admit defeat. Shockingly, God goes along with him
and allows the cruel wager to continue. The only limit He places
this time is on Job's life itself: "See, he is in your power, only spare
his life" (2:6). Undaunted by this restriction, Satan inflicts terrible
boils on Job. The poor man sits in ashes and scratches himself with
a potsherd. "Curse God and die!" Job's wife rails at him. But he
remains steadfast in his faith, more loyal to God than God has been
to him. "Should we accept only good from God and not accept evil?"
(2:10).

Job's torments continue.

Is it any wonder that one view expressed in the Talmud is that
the entire Book of Job is a parable: "Job never was, he never existed,"
the third-century rabbi Resh Lakish declares (Babylonian Talmud,
Bava Bathra 15a). Resh Lakish, I am convinced, was trying to protect
God's good name. A god who would make such a wager with Satan
might indeed be all-powerful, but He would neither be good nor
morally worthy of being worshiped.

For post-Holocaust readers of Job, who are well aware of what it means to subject the bodies of good people to the power of Satan and his human disciples, the talmudic teaching that Job never existed offers a great consolation. By telling us that the whole book is a parable, the Talmud frees us to study the arguments raised by Job's wife, his friends, Job himself, and God without feeling overwhelmed by anger at God.

A final point: Although Job's sufferings might provoke anger at God, the challenge Satan raises before God may still contain some legitimacy. Job's love of God, as described at the book's beginning, might really have been utilitarian; he loves God because God has been good to him. But as Bible scholar Moshe Greenberg notes: "A pious man whose life has always been placid can never know whether his faith in God is more than an interested bargain—a convenience that has worked to his benefit—unless it is tested by events. . . ." In words that are chilling but difficult to refute, Greenberg concludes: "The terrible paradox is that no righteous man can measure his love of God unless he suffers a fate befitting the wicked."

Reflections, source, and further reading: Moshe Greenberg, "Reflections on Job's Theology," in *The Book of Job,* pages xvii–xxiii; the quotation cited is from page xviii. Greenberg proceeds to argue that, at some level, it is healthy for a person's spiritual well-being to know that his or her devotion to God is disinterested; hence, the logic of God's acquiesence to Satan's test. Scandalous as the depiction of God in the book's prologue is, Greenberg argues that it also is necessary because: "Without the prologue we should lack the essential knowledge that Job's misfortune really made no sense; without the prologue the . . . arguments [later offered by Job's friends; see next entry] that misfortune indicates sin would be plausible, and Job's resistance to them liable to be construed as moral arrogance. . . . The author [of Job] must convince his readers that Job's self-estimation [that he has done no evil worthy of the sufferings he is undergoing] is correct, and that therefore his view of moral disorder in God's management of the world is warranted" (pages xvii–xviii).

128. "With Friends Like This"— The Friends of Job

When we first meet Eliphaz, Bildad, and Zophar, Job's three friends, they seem wonderfully sympathetic. Hearing of their old companion's sufferings, they journey together to console and comfort him. When they see how miserable he is—the friends barely recognize him at first—they break into loud weeping and tear their garments. For a full week, they sit on the ground with Job but remain silent; they realize that he is not ready to speak and so they wait for him to speak first.

Once they start responding to Job's comments, however, the friends quickly seem far less impressive. The view of God and of suffering that they express is so primitive that God Himself becomes angry at their defense of Him.

The first to speak is Eliphaz. Offended by Job's lament that he regrets having been born, he challenges Job to reflect rather on his responsibility for the horrors that have befallen him: "Remember, no man ever perished being innocent" (4:7), he chides him.

Job refuses to submit to Eliphaz's indictment, insisting that he has committed no sins worthy of the punishment he is now suffering. This defense enrages the second friend, Bildad: "How long will you speak such things? Your utterances are a mighty wind! Will God pervert the right? Will the Almighty pervert justice?" In his anger, Bildad makes no effort to control his tongue; his indictment includes what, for Job, must have been the most painful aspect of his sufferings: "If your sons sinned against Him, He dispatched them for their transgression" (8:2–4).

A week earlier, these men had arrived to console their suffering friend. Now they are telling him that both he and his children deserved their fate.

Tempting as it is to dismiss Job's friends as simply vicious—yet also naive in their very narrow conception of why people suffer— the truth is they must have been terrified. If such suffering could come upon Job, the friends likely reasoned, it could similarly befall us—unless, Job is being punished for specific sins.

That is why Job's refusal to acknowledge his sins so angers his friends. It threatens them. If what Job is saying is true, that he has not committed any great evil, then their lives and happiness are at as great a risk as his. They desperately need to believe that Job has done some great wickedness, so that they can say or conclude, "Now we know why this has happened to him. But we, we haven't done anything like that. So we are safe."

Zophar, Job's third friend, takes the others' approach a step further, contending that God has punished Job less than his sins deserve (11:6).

Finally, a fourth friend appears. Younger than the others, Elihu is angry both at Job (for considering himself in the right against God) and at the three friends for not answering Job appropriately (32:2–3). Yet his arguments add little that is new to those that have already been advanced. Once again, Job is accused of mouthing "empty words" and of "piling up words without knowledge" (35:16).

By the book's end, it turns out that it is Job's pious friends, not he, who have provoked God's fury: "I am incensed at you and your two friends," God tells Eliphaz, "for you have not spoken the truth about Me as did my servant Job." In the friends' lame efforts to "protect" God's name against Job's accusations of injustice, they have libeled Job. God orders the three men (Elihu is not mentioned in this scene) to offer sacrifices in atonement for their sin, and to beseech Job, the victim of their cruel tongues, to pray on their behalf. The men do so, Job prays for them, and they are forgiven (42:7ff.).

The lesson the Bible intends to convey is about as subtle as a knock on the head. When others suffer, the goal of a friend must be to do all in his or her power to ameliorate the suffering. It is forbidden to increase the tormented person's suffering by insisting that the sufferer deserves his or her fate.

The expression "Job's friends" is not meant as praise; rather, it brings to mind the rhetorical question "With friends like this, who needs enemies?"

Reflections: On trying to explain another person's sufferings: The sin committed by Job's friends—trying to explain the reason for *someone else's* suffering—is a danger inherent to theodicy, which is the branch of theology that tries to explain why a good God allows evil. In their attempts to justify God's ways to humans, practitioners of theodicy frequently blame people for their sufferings. For example, some contemporary Jewish fundamentalists have sought to blame the Holocaust on Jewish irreligiosity in pre–World War II Europe. Rabbi

Irving Greenberg has rightly responded to these modern versions of Job's friends: "Now that [the victims of the Holocaust] have been cruelly tortured and killed, boiled into soap, their hair made into pillows, and their bones into fertilizer, their unknown graves and the very fact of their death denied to them [by Holocaust deniers], the theologian would inflict on them the only indignity left: that is, insistence that it was done because of their sins" ("Cloud of Smoke, Pillar of Fire: Judaism, Christianity and Modernity After the Holocaust," in Eva Fleischner, editor, *Auschwitz: Beginning of a New Era?*, page 25).

129. "Out of the Whirlwind": God Answers Job

JOB, CHAPTERS 38–41

The Book of Job, which describes its protagonist who is afflicted with the most terrible suffering as the most righteous of men, raises to an intense and painful level the problem of why a just God allows human suffering.

Throughout the book, the question that Job repeatedly asks, and which God never answers, is: Why has such evil befallen me? When the Lord does finally respond to Job "out of the whirlwind," it is with His own rhetorical questions:

> Where were you when I established the world?
> Tell me, if you know so much,
> Who drafted its dimension? Do you know? . . .
> Did you ever command forth a morning? . . . (38:4–5, 12).

How can one explain God's response? God never tells Job why he, or any human being, suffers. God is God is basically what He says, and who are we to assume that we can understand everything? Who "established the world," human beings or God? As a medieval Hebrew proverb teaches, "If I knew God, I'd be God."

Admittedly, that may not be the response we, or Job, hoped for, but *what* answer would we desire? If God is God and humans are humans, is there any other possible answer than the one Job receives?

God concludes with the challenge: "Will the contender with God yield?" (40:2).

And Job, who throughout the book has sought a divine response, no longer has questions and challenges for God: "I am small, how can I answer You? My hand I lay on my mouth" (40:4).

Perhaps the Book of Job's most important teaching is that the "why" of human suffering is, and always will be, beyond human knowledge or understanding.

XVII. THE FIVE SCROLLS

130. The Three Peculiar Heroines of the Five Scrolls: Esther, Ruth, and the Shepherdess

Aside from the five books of the Torah, the Five Scrolls are the only biblical works that are read in their entirety during the synagogue service each year: the Song of Songs on Passover, Ruth on Shavuot (the spring holiday celebrating the giving of the Torah), Lamentations on the fast day of the Ninth of Av (commemorating the destruction of both Temples), Ecclesiastes on Sukkot (the fall harvest holidays during which the huts known as Sukkot are built), and Esther on Purim.

By ordaining the annual reading of these books, the Rabbis clearly wished all Jews to become fully conversant with them. Two of the books, Ecclesiastes and Lamentations, have no story line: The former is a philosophical rumination on the futility of most of humankind's endeavors (see entry 134); the latter is a lament, attributed to the prophet Jeremiah, over the fall of Jerusalem and the Temple in 587 B.C.E. (see entry 133).

The other three scrolls contain characters, but what is remarkable, given the centrality of males in most biblical narratives, is that their leading, and most heroic, figures are women. And although the Bible is usually regarded as advocating very traditional roles for women, these books' heroines are very untraditional women.

The Book of Esther tells the story of a Persian-Jewish woman who wins a beauty contest, and marries a non-Jewish king. While such a marriage offends traditional Jewish sensibilities, Esther utilizes her new position to save the Jewish people from Haman's genocidal plot (see entry 137).

The Book of Ruth relates how a Moabite woman (Moab was a

despised neighbor of Israel) accepts Israel's religion, and is deemed so virtuous that the Bible traces the future Messiah's descent to her— quite an honor to bestow on a convert! Clearly, Ruth's behavior matters more to the biblical author than does her ancestry (see entry 132).

Then again, some of Ruth's behavior must have startled traditional sensibilities. At a certain point in the story, it becomes clear to Ruth, and to her friend and mother-in-law Naomi, that Boaz would make a suitable new husband for her. Unfortunately, Boaz does not seem particularly aware of Ruth's desire. So she slips into his tent at night and lies down at his feet to seek his protection (3:9). Ruth quickly convinces the obviously smitten Boaz that he should marry her.

Traditional societies prefer women to wait until the man whom they desire pursues them. However, this wouldn't have helped Ruth, who was very willing to act boldly to get the man she wanted.

The unnamed shepherdess of the Song of Songs has no problem describing, in vivid, sensual imagery, her feelings for the man she loves: "My beloved is mine, and I am his . . . Upon my couch at night, I sought the one I love" (2:16; 3:1; see next entry).

Defying the traditional view that women should be passive and stay at home, these three biblical heroines also remind us not to stereotype people by the few facts we might know about them ("She's intermarried" or "She's a convert"), but to judge them by how they act. By that standard, all three women are exemplary.

131. Song of Songs: The Bible's Love Poem

No biblical book is so vividly sensual as Song of Songs, a love poem attributed in the book's opening verse to King Solomon (1:1). It begins with a passionate description of the most common expression of love: "Oh, give me of the kisses of your mouth, for your love is more delightful than wine" (1:2). Surprisingly, given that many of us have been conditioned to think of women in ancient times as generally prudish, it is a woman, not a man, who speaks these words.

The speaker, in whose voice Solomon has written the opening verses, tells us little about herself, only that she is dark-skinned from working in the fields, and quite pretty (1:5–6).

The text quickly shifts to the voice of the shepherd whom the young maiden loves. He speaks of his beloved with poetic exuberance: "Like a lily among thorns, so is my darling among the maidens" (2:2).

The text shifts back and forth between the two lovers: "Like an apple tree among trees of the forest, so is my beloved among the youths. I delight to sit in his shade, and his fruit is sweet to my mouth" (2:3). "I am my beloved's and my beloved is mine . . . ," the young woman later declares (6:3), words often recited by today's Jewish brides at weddings.

The young man describes the charms of his beloved with poetic details: "Your eyes are like doves. . . . Your hair is like a flock of doves. . . . Your lips are like a crimson thread. . . . Your breasts are like two fawns, twins of a gazelle. . . . Every part of you is fair, my darling. There is no blemish in you" (4:1–7).

The shepherdess is equally rapturous in praising her lover: "My beloved is clear-skinned and ruddy, preeminent among ten thousand. His head is finest gold, his locks are curled and black as a raven. . . . His legs are like marble pillars. . . . His mouth is delicious, and all of him is delightful" (4:1–16).

In the first century C.E., some Rabbis argued against including Song of Songs in the biblical canon. In their view, its vivid descriptions of erotic love made the book anything but a holy text. Less than a century later, Rabbi Akiva denied that the inclusion of Song of Songs in the Bible could ever have been debated since its sanctity was so obvious: "All the writings [in the Bible] are holy, but Song of Songs is the Holy of Holies" (Mishnah *Yadayim* 3:5).

Rabbi Akiva notwithstanding, the article on Song of Songs in the *Encyclopedia Judaica* (15:143–152) clearly suggests its unusual character: "The Song of Songs is unique in the Bible, for nowhere else within it can be found such a sustained paean to the warmth of love between man and woman. It is completely occupied with that one theme. No morals are drawn: no prophetic preachments are made. God receives no mention, and theological concerns are never discussed. While the Book of Esther also fails to mention God, an unmistakable spirit of nationalism permeates its pages; but the Song of Songs lacks even this theme."

The Rabbis of the Talmud claimed that Song of Songs is allegorical in nature, that it presents a model of love between a man and a woman to explain that between God and the Jewish people. However, the use of such a model suggests the very high regard in which the Bible holds male-female love and sexuality.

132. Ruth, Naomi, and Boaz: The Bible's Happiest Triangle

THE BOOK OF RUTH

"Your People Shall Be My People, Your God Shall Be My God"

1:16

There are two models of friendship in the Hebrew Bible, one male, the other female. The male model, David and Jonathan, is a friendship that begins happily and ends with Jonathan's tragic death in battle against the Philistines (see entry 75). The female model, the friendship of Ruth and Naomi, originates in sorrow: When we first encounter Ruth, her husband, Naomi's son, has recently died. Yet the two women's friendship deepens throughout the suffering that they endure, and the book ends on as joyful a note as any in the Bible.

One of the most romantic and happiest stories, the Book of Ruth is also characterized by a spirit of universalism, in which a person's value is measured by deeds, not ancestry.

In the opening verse, we learn that this story occurred during the time of the judges—the twelfth and eleventh centuries B.C.E. A famine has struck Israel, and Naomi and her husband, Elimelech, along with their two sons, leave their hometown of Bethlehem (in the tribe of Judah) for the nearby gentile nation of Moab.

In Moab, Elimelech dies, and the two sons eventually take Moabite wives, Orpah and Ruth. After ten years of marriage, both young men die (the Bible does not tell us the cause); Naomi has now lost her entire immediate family.

She soon hears that the famine has subsided in Israel, and she decides to return home. Her devoted daughters-in-law leave with her, but Naomi tries to discourage them from accompanying her to Israel. Because both women are young (likely in their mid- to late twenties), Naomi blesses them with the wish that they return home and find new husbands. The two women insist on remaining with her, but after Naomi reiterates her appeal, Orpah kisses her and bids her farewell.*

Naomi urges Ruth to return with Orpah but she, in one of the Bible's most moving passages, refuses: "Do not urge me to leave you, to turn back and not follow you. For wherever you go, I will go; wherever you lodge, I will lodge; your people shall be my people, your God shall be my God" (1:16).

In the thousands of years since Ruth spoke these words, no one has better defined the combination of peoplehood and religion that characterizes Judaism: "Your people shall be my people" ("I wish to join the Jewish nation"), "Your God shall be my God" ("I wish to accept the Jewish religion").

Shortly thereafter, at the beginning of the barley harvest, Naomi and Ruth arrive in Bethlehem. Although the text never details the

---

*Although subsequent Jewish law ruled that marriages between Jews and non-Jews were invalid (i.e., if such a marriage is terminated, there is no requirement for a *get*, a Jewish divorce), the text speaks of Orpah and Ruth as Naomi's daughters-in-law, and of Naomi as their mother-in-law, indicating an acknowledgment of these intermarriages.

women's economic circumstances, they apparently are penniless. Within days of their arrival, Ruth goes into the fields to glean some barley behind the reapers.*

Ruth goes to a field belonging to Boaz, a relative of Elimelech, her deceased father-in-law. When Boaz learns that the young Moabite woman gleaning in his field accompanied Naomi back from Moab, he goes to her and requests that she "work" exclusively in his field. In a society in which an unmarried foreign woman could easily feel vulnerable and defenseless, Boaz assures her that "I have ordered the men not to molest you" (2:9).†

Boaz then gives Ruth a delicacy, roasted grain; before she leaves, he instructs his workers to leave behind large quantities of food for her to take home (2:15–16).

Naomi is delighted when Ruth tells her of the fortunate experience she has had at Boaz's farm. Given Boaz's kinship to Elimelech, one wonders why Naomi didn't from the first suggest to Ruth to go there? Perhaps she feared that Boaz would be antagonistic, instead of friendly, to a Moabite woman who had intermarried with his relative.

Naomi then tells Ruth of the man's relationship to her late husband, and contrives a plan to bring about Boaz's marriage to Ruth. Knowing that at the height of the harvest, Boaz and his employees work far into the night, then go to sleep in tents set up in the field (which also deters marauders from stealing the harvest), Naomi instructs Ruth to bathe herself and dress up, then go to the place where Boaz is sleeping and lie down at his feet.

Ruth does as her mother-in-law instructs her. In the middle of the night, a startled Boaz wakes up to find a woman, whom he cannot recognize in the darkness, at his feet. "Who are you?" he asks.

"I am your handmaid, Ruth. Spread your robe over your handmaid, for you are a redeeming kinsman" (3:9).

These last words are a reference to an ancient biblical law, which directed that when a man died childless, his brother was to marry

---

*Leviticus 19:9–10 legislates that when a farmer harvests his crop, he is not to reap "all the way to the edges of the field," i.e., and gather all the fallen grain or fruit; these are to be left "for the poor and the stranger." Thus, Ruth was acting in accordance with biblical law in following behind the reapers and gathering whatever was left behind.

†The perennial nature of sexual harassment is reflected both in Boaz's instruction to his employees, and in the advice Naomi later offers Ruth: "It is best, my daughter, that you go out with his [Boaz's] girls, and not be annoyed in some other field" (2:22).

the widow. The first son born of this union was regarded as if he was born to the deceased, and ultimately received his estate, so that the dead man's line was not cut off (Deuteronomy 25:5–10).

Yet, in fact, Boaz was not a brother of Ruth's dead husband but apparently a cousin (the nature of the relationship is not specified). He may not even have been a first cousin, for Boaz immediately informs Ruth that before he can marry her as a "redeeming kinsman," he must first clear matters with another, closer, relative of her late husband.*

The Bible does not inform us of the age of any of the book's characters, but Boaz apparently is significantly older than Ruth, and he is very touched by her wish to marry him: "Your latest deed of loyalty is greater than the first, in that you have not turned to younger men, whether poor or rich" (3:10). He invites Ruth to stay with him until morning, and she remains at his feet. Anxious, however, to protect the reputation of the woman he hopes soon to marry, and his own reputation, Boaz has her leave before the sun rises.

The Ruth story strikingly reveals how accepting the early Israelites were of intermarriage (as long as it was not with one of Canaan's seven resident nations; see Deuteronomy 7:1–4). The fact that Boaz's cousin had married this non-Israelite woman† and had died childless did not in his eyes free him or his cousin's other relatives from acting as "redeeming kinsmen."

The following morning, Boaz seeks out the other potential redeemer, in the presence of ten witnesses. He tells the man that he can redeem Elimelech's and his two sons' land, but only if he takes Ruth as a wife, "so as to perpetuate the name of the deceased upon his estate" (4:5). The man is interested in the estate, but not in marrying Ruth (particularly since the son to whom she might one day give birth will acquire the estate and will further inherit from him), and he asks Boaz to act as redeemer instead.

Boaz marries Ruth, who soon gives birth to a boy named Obed, who becomes the grandfather of King David. Since Jewish tradition

---

*Although the statute in Deuteronomy never suggests that the law of "redeeming kinsman" applies to anyone other than a brother, both Ruth's statement and Boaz's reaction tell us that some Israelites extended this law to include cousins.

†That Ruth had not converted to Judaism during the time she had been married is proven by the fact that Naomi felt justified in urging her and Orpah to return to Moab and find new husbands.

claims that the Messiah will descend from David, this means that the Messiah will be a direct descendant of Ruth, a Moabite convert to Judaism.

133. Lamentations: A Lament over Jerusalem's Destruction

The Book of Lamentations is what its name implies, moaning, pain-ridden poetic dirges over Jerusalem and Judah's destruction by the Babylonian army in 587 B.C.E. (see entry 102).

Jewish tradition attributes its authorship to the prophet Jeremiah, who spent most of his career urging his fellow Jews to repent of the sins that would bring about their nation's destruction (see entry 110).

If the work was indeed authored by Jeremiah, he describes Judah's destruction without reverting to any "I told you so's." Instead, he speaks in anguish, referring to Judah and Jerusalem as if they were living entities: "Bitterly, she weeps in the night, her cheeks wet with tears" (1:2). He personalizes Jerusalem's disgrace, describing how her enemies now jeer at her. However, the author does not blame God for acting unjustly: "The Lord is in the right, for I have disobeyed Him" (1:18).

Nonetheless, a hint of bitterness toward God for abandoning His people surfaces periodically: "The Lord has acted like a foe" (2:5); "He has stripped his Booth [the Temple] like a garden" (2:6).

The author also speaks of the terrible sufferings inflicted on Judah's most innocent victims: "As babes and sucklings languish in the squares of the city, they keep asking their mothers, 'Where is bread and wine?' . . . as their life runs out in their mothers' bosoms" (2:11–12). He notes that "little children beg for bread; none gives them a morsel" (4:4).

In some of the Bible's most horrific passages, we learn that star-vation has led to cannibalism: "Alas, women eat their own fruit, their new-born babes" (2:20); "With their own hands, tenderhearted women have cooked their children; such became their fare, in the disaster of my poor people" (4:10).

Only the belief that God's kindness has not permanently ended, and that His mercies can still be renewed (3:22–23), gives the author hope. He therefore urges the people to examine their ways, "turn back to the Lord," and confess their sins (3:40–41).

This prophetic lament over Judah's fate concludes with a challenge to God: "Why have You forgotten us utterly?" (5:20), and an appeal to the Lord to take back His people and to "renew our days as of old!" (5:21). The book's final verse, "For truly, You have rejected us, bitterly raged against us" (5:22), is so dejected that the Rabbis, not wishing to end a biblical book with such gloomy words, insisted on following this verse with a repetition of the verse preceding it, "Take us back, O Lord, to Yourself, and let us come back; Renew our days as of old!"

Note: One of Lamentations' enigmatic verses reads: "They that are slain with the sword are better than they that are slain through hunger" (4:9). The author is not saying that those that are slain with the sword are "better off" than those slain by hunger (presumably because death from a sword comes quickly, while death from starvation is protracted), but that somehow those slain with the sword are "better people" than those who die from hunger.

Life sometimes serves as a commentary on otherwise inexplicable biblical texts. The Hasidic *rebbe* and Holocaust survivor Israel Spira, the Grand Rabbi of Bluzhov, claims that only in the Nazi work camp of Janowska did he come to understand this passage. Imprisoned with him and thousands of other Jews were young twin brothers, whose family were among the rabbi's followers. The three helped each other whenever possible.

One day, when the camp inmates were taken to work, Rabbi Spira, one of the twins, and a third inmate were told to remain behind to clean the barracks. During the day, a German guard sadistically shot the twin in one leg, ordered him to stand, then shot him in the other leg, ordered him to stand again, and when he couldn't, emptied his revolver into the young boy. Rabbi Spira and the other inmate were instructed to carry the dead boy over to the pile of corpses that accumulated daily at the camp. While carrying him, the rabbi shed tears; he later recalled that one thought dominated him:

How will he tell the other twin about his brother's death? How will he break the terrible news to one of two souls that were so close to each other?

"Tell him that his twin brother is very sick," the other Jew advised the rabbi.

Evening came. The inmates returned to camp. "Chaim'l, your brother is very sick, his life is in danger. It is quite possible that he is no longer alive," said the Rabbi of Bluzhov, trying to avoid the boy's eyes.

The brother began to cry. "Woe unto me! What am I going to do now?"

The rabbi tried to comfort the boy, but he refused to be comforted. "Today was his turn to watch over the bread. I left all the bread with him, now I don't have a single piece of bread left."

The rabbi was shocked but continued his ruse, saying that the other twin had sent him Chaim'l's share. With a trembling hand, he took from under his coat a small piece of bread which was his ration for the day and gave it to the boy. Chaim'l glanced at the small piece of bread and said, "It's missing a few grams. The piece I left with him was a much larger one."

"I was hungry and ate some of it. Tomorrow I will give you the rest of the bread," replied the Rabbi of Bluzhov.

When Rabbi Israel Spira finished telling the story [in 1976, more than thirty years after the event] he said, "Only on that day in Janowska did I understand the verse in the Scriptures, 'They that are slain with the sword are better than they that are slain with hunger' "—Yaffa Eliach, *Hasidic Tales of the Holocaust,* pages 153–155.

134. Ecclesiastes: "Vanity of Vanities, All Is Vanity"

1:2

"A Time for War and a Time for Peace"

3:8

If Job and Lamentations are the Bible's saddest books, Ecclesiastes is its most pessimistic. From the outset, the author makes no effort to conceal his belief that life is futile. Indeed, the book's most famous verse, "Vanity of vanities, all is vanity," is rendered more accurately, if less poetically, in the modern Jewish Publication Society translation: "Utter futility! All is futile!"

Instead of believing that civilization will someday advance, the author believes that humans, like animals, live cyclically: "One generation goes, another comes, but the earth remains the same forever" (1:4). The future holds no excitement, since "only that shall happen which has happened, only that occur which has occurred" (1:9).

Ecclesiastes's author describes himself as a son of King David and himself a king, which led the Rabbis to ascribe the book's authorship to Solomon—the book was written, they believed, during Solomon's final years—which is why they incorporated this otherwise rather irreligious work into the Hebrew Bible. However, few contemporary Bible scholars believe Ecclesiastes to have been authored by Solomon. Most significantly, the book's speaker uses words that were unknown in Solomon's time. For example, *pardes*, a Persian word meaning both "grove" and "paradise" probably became known to the Jews no earlier than the sixth century B.C.E., four hundred years *after* Solomon, yet the word appears in the book (2:5).

Ecclesiastes portrays himself as a world-weary old man who has had the best, in terms of wealth and wisdom, that this world can offer ("I further amassed silver and gold and treasures of kings and provinces. . . . Thus, I gained more wealth than anyone before me in Jerusalem . . . ; 2:8–9). Yet he concludes that human efforts are pointless, because the same fate, death, awaits both the fool and the wise man, "to what advantage, then, have I been wise?" (2:15).

In as unidealistic a passage as one can imagine in the Bible, the author concludes: "There is nothing worthwhile for a man but to eat and drink and enjoy pleasure" (2:24).

While even devoutly religious people can empathize with the author's melancholy tone—what sensitive person is not periodically haunted by a sense of weariness and futility?—the book's most disturbing feature, at least to most people of religious sensibilities, is its rejection of a belief both in an afterlife and in reward and punishment. The God of whom Ecclesiastes speaks is morally indifferent: "For the same fate is in store for all: for the righteous and for the wicked, for the good and pure and for the impure, for him who sacrifices and for him who does not. . . . That is the sad thing about all that goes on under the sun; that the same fate is in store for all" (9:2–3).* Of course, that fate is death, following which Ecclesiastes insists that there is no action, reasoning, or learning (9:10).

Fortunately, the book is not entirely a diatribe on the futility of human efforts; it also contains some wise advice, much of which one finds quoted in later Jewish moralistic writings. Thus, the author reminds his readers that "a good name is better than fragrant oil," although even in this case he can't resist concluding with the gloomy thought "and the day of death than the day of birth" (7:1). It must have been "real fun" to have this morose preacher as a guest at a party celebrating a baby's birth.

Prudently, Ecclesiastes reminds his readers to be cautious with their words, since "it is better not to vow at all than to vow and not fulfill" (5:4). The author reserves special contempt for people who devote all their efforts to amassing wealth: "As a man came out of his mother's womb, so must he depart at last, naked as he came. He can take nothing of his wealth with him" (5:14). He conveys a very contemporary-sounding sense of dismay with the administration of criminal justice: "And here is another frustration: the fact that the sentence imposed for evil deeds is not executed swiftly, which is why men are emboldened to do evil" (8:10–11).

Chapter 3 contains Ecclesiastes's most famous passage, which became popularized during the 1960s in a song sung by the English rock group The Byrds. It is a brilliant statement of moderation, and

---

*Substitute the name Anne Frank for the word "righteous," and that of Adolf Hitler for "wicked," and the disturbing nature of this verse becomes even more apparent.

a recognition that different times and circumstances call forth different responses:

> To everything there is a season
> And a time for every purpose under heaven.
> A time to be born and a time to die.
> A time to plant and a time to pluck up that which is planted.
> A time to kill and a time to heal.
> A time to tear down and a time to build up.
> A time to weep and a time to laugh. . . .
> A time to keep silent and a time to speak.
> A time to love and a time to hate.
> A time for war and a time for peace (3:1–8).

In addition to their belief that Ecclesiastes was authored by King Solomon, the Rabbis also canonized this controversial work because of the pious tone of the final verse, which defies the rhetoric of the rest of the book: "The sum of the matter, when all is said and done, revere God and observe His commandments, for that is the whole duty of man" (12:13).

I sometimes wonder if by attributing the authorship of Ecclesiastes to Solomon, the Rabbis were exacting a gentle revenge on the ancient Jewish monarch. For while Jewish tradition regards him as the wisest man who ever lived, the Bible makes it very clear that in his final years Solomon became a bit of a fool, and an arrogant one at that (see entry 89). Thus, in attributing Ecclesiastes to Solomon's last years, perhaps the Rabbis were delivering a hidden, if ironic, assessment of their true feelings about this work's value.

135. Vashti: An Early Feminist

ESTHER, CHAPTER 1

Whereas Esther and Mordechai are heroes in the Jews' life-and-death struggle against the wicked Haman's plot to murder every Jew, Queen Vashti is an unsuccessful heroine in an early struggle for women's dignity.

Her husband, King Ahasuerus, a singularly unimpressive man, is a heavy and unpleasant drinker. During the third year of his reign, he hosts a massive party in Shushan, Persia's capital, which lasts half a year and is followed by a weeklong concluding celebration. Guests are plied with vast quantities of liquor ("royal wine in abundance"; 1:7), and the king, along with numerous subjects, becomes drunk ("merry with wine" is how the Bible euphemistically describes him; 1:10).

While in an inebriated state, he orders several aides to bring Queen Vashti, then hosting her own party for women, so that her beauty can be publicly displayed to his subjects. The text does not state whether the king intends to display Vashti in the nude, but its emphasis on Ahasuerus's drunkenness when he summons Vashti suggests that his intentions might well be less than honorable.

This, apparently, is what Vashti assumes, for she refuses Ahasuerus's summons. If the king's intent were only to show everyone her beautiful face—the Bible states that Vashti was "fair to look at"—her refusal would be difficult to understand. Certainly, she must have realized what a great risk she was incurring by disobeying a royal decree. If, however, the king wished to display her in the nude, Vashti's refusal is understandable. Perhaps she hoped that when he came out of his drunken stupor he would forget about her refusal, or let the whole matter pass.

In any case, the Bible never informs us of Vashti's thoughts. We only know that she refuses the royal summons, and the king is furious with her. Seven top Persian princes are asked to suggest an appropriate punishment for Vashti (1:15).

One, Memucan, condemns the queen's behavior in the strongest possible terms: "Vashti the queen has not done wrong to the king only, but . . . to all the peoples who are in all the provinces of King Ahasuerus. For this deed of the queen will be made known to all women, so as to make their husbands contemptible in their eyes [and the women will all refuse to obey their husband's orders]" (1:16–17).

Memucan suggests that Queen Vashti immediately be deposed, and that her royal estate be confiscated and "given to one better than she" (1:19). If this is done, then all wives throughout the empire "shall give honor to their husbands."

Ahasuerus, pleased by this suggestion, carries it out and has letters published in each language spoken by his subjects, ordaining "that every man should bear rule in his own house" (1:22).

We never again hear about Vashti, although the capricious way in which Ahasuerus allows one of his princes to convince him to punish her anticipates the ease with which he is later persuaded by Haman to sign an order mandating the murder of every Jew within Persia. Vashti thus is the first victim of this foolish and cruel drunk.

Reflections: Dr. Jeremiah Unterman has noted to me the absurd irony of Ahasuerus, a king who needs a royal commission to decide what to do with his wife but who will soon let a whole people be consigned to slaughter (see next entry) without even investigating the matter.

136. Haman, the Antisemite

ESTHER, CHAPTERS 3–9

So quintessentially evil is Haman that it comes as little surprise to learn that the Bible traces his descent to Amalek, the people whom God regards as the most hateful nation on earth (see entry 38).

When we are first introduced to Haman (3:1), we learn that he descends from Agag, a murderous Amalekite king executed hundreds of years earlier by the prophet Samuel. Haman, the Bible tells us, has just become King Ahasuerus's most powerful adviser.

Wherever Haman goes, all the people bow, for so the king has commanded, except for Mordechai, a Jewish resident of Shushan, who does not bow or show Haman reverence. The king's servants are shocked by this behavior, and ask Mordechai why he transgresses the king's command. All that Mordechai offers by way of answer is that he is a Jew.

Ever since, Bible students have debated the rationale behind Mordechai's refusal to bow to Haman. The answer that he gives, that he is a Jew, suggests to many that Mordechai considered it wrong to bow to any human being because it would be a form of idolatry. The problem with this explanation is that there is no indication that Mordechai refrained from bowing to King Ahasuerus and indeed, Jewish law never forbade bowing to a king or other authority figure—particularly when such a refusal would endanger one's life—as long as it was clear that the person was not being worshiped as a divinity. Such was certainly the case with Haman. Nobody, Haman included, claimed that Haman was a god; indeed, he derived his right to be bowed to *solely* by order of the king.

Why then did Mordechai act so provocatively toward Haman? The answer might lie in the very sentence in which the Bible informs us that Haman is a descendant of King Agag of Amalek. That Haman continues to claim such descent some five hundred years after Agag's reign must mean that he closely identifies with his ancestor, a great enemy of the Jews. Imagine that five hundred years from today, a man went about proudly identifying himself as a direct descendant of Adolf Eichmann. Although Eichmann would be long dead, Jews would react with enormous dislike to such a man. Therefore, when Mordechai explained to others that he would not bow down to Haman because he, Mordechai, was a Jew, he was not making a theological statement but a nationalistic point: i.e., as a Jew, he would not bow down to a man who claimed descent from a great enemy of his people. The king's servants understand Mordechai's behavior, for as soon as he tells them that he isn't bowing down, they ask no more questions; they only watch, curiously, to see if he will get away with such disobedience.

He doesn't. Mordechai's behavior enrages Haman. Well aware that his ancestor Agag died at the hands of the Jews (just as the future descendants of Eichmann will know that he was executed by the Jewish state), he decides to wreak vengeance on Mordechai and all the Jews.

Haman comes before King Ahasuerus, and tells him, "There is a certain people scattered abroad and dispersed among the people in all the provinces of your kingdom; and their laws are different from all people, nor do they keep the king's laws; therefore, it is of no benefit to the king to tolerate them. If it please the king, let it be written that they may be destroyed . . ." (3:8–9).

Fearing that such an appeal will not be sufficient to incite Ahasuerus to genocide, Haman adds a bonus to sweeten the deal: If Ahasuerus gives him permission to murder the Jews, he will pay the king 10,000 talents of silver (each talent weighed about 75.5 pounds).

Haman's depiction of the Jews is of course a lie. Although it is true that they have their own set of laws, there is no indication that they disobey the king's ordinances. Lies though they be, Haman's words have influenced antisemites ever since. It is a mainstay of antisemitic propaganda that Jews are an international people ("scattered among the people") who have no national loyalties except to themselves, and who cheat, steal, and otherwise disobey the laws of the people among whom they live.

Haman's suggestion does not upset Ahasuerus. He takes off his ring, gives it to Haman, and tells him: "[the Jews] are yours, to do with as you please" (3:11).

Confident even before the meeting of his ability to influence Ahasuerus, Haman has already cast a lot and has chosen Adar, almost a full year away, as the month in which to murder the Jews. After he receives the royal ring—which gives him authority to issue decrees in the king's name—Haman orders scribes to write and dispatch letters throughout the kingdom authorizing the destruction of the Jews and the confiscation of their property on the thirteenth day of the month of Adar (3:13).

Haman's and the king's first act immediately after the orders are dispatched is to sit down and share a few drinks (3:15). Indeed, Ahasuerus is the alcoholic par excellence of the Bible.

Mordechai's worst fear, the damage that an antisemitic chief of state can do to the Jewish people, has now been realized. He rends his clothes, and walks through the streets of Shushan as a mourner. So do Jews throughout the Persian empire, since they know that they have less than a year till the order of genocide is to be carried out.

Mordechai sees but one hope for averting the decree. Secreted inside Ahasuerus's palace is his cousin Esther, a Jewish queen who, at Mordechai's suggestion, has kept her religious and national identity a secret. We know from the earlier incident of Vashti (see preceding entry) that Persian society, at least according to this book, seems to regard women, even queens, as playthings, worthy of little more than being publicly displayed; hence, it is not surprising that Esther has not heard about the bargain struck between Haman and her husband. Mordechai, however, sends word to her of Haman's plot, and urges her to intervene with the king.

After much discussion (see next entry), Esther consents. She soon proves to be as powerful a plotter as her adversary. At first, unaware of whether her husband is an antisemite or just an unwitting accomplice to Haman's plan, she invites both men to a party. There, the king acts with great love and affection to her, instructing her to make whatever request she wishes of him, "even up to half the kingdom" (5:6).

His devotion should be reassuring to Esther, but as the king still does not know that she is Jewish, she remains uncertain whether or not he is an antisemite. Instead of immediately asking him to reverse the genocidal decree, her only request is that Ahasuerus and Haman come back the following evening for a second party.

That night, Ahasuerus suffers from insomnia (6:1; one senses that this insomnia is divinely ordained, although God's name never appears in the Book of Esther), and summons a servant to read to him from the chronicles recording the history of his reign. The pages the servant reads to Ahasuerus concern an earlier plot to murder him, a plot that Mordechai had brought to the royal police's attention (2:21–23). The king asks: "What honor or advancement has been conferred on Mordechai for this?" (6:3) and learns that Mordechai has never been rewarded.

By now it is morning, and at just this moment Haman is entering the king's court to secure his permission to hang Mordechai on a seventy-five-foot-high gallows that he has built. Before Haman can speak, the king asks him: "What should be done for a man whom the king wishes to honor?"

Certain that the request can refer to no one but himself ("To whom would the king delight to do honor more than to myself" [6:6]), Haman suggests that the man be clothed in royal garments, then seated on a royal horse with a royal crown placed on his head. He should then be led throughout Shushan by one of the king's highest officials, who will proclaim before all the spectators: "Thus shall be done to the man whom the king delights to honor."

In one of the Bible's happiest reversals of fortune, Ahasuerus responds, "Make haste . . . and do so to Mordechai the Jew" (6:10).

There is great significance in Ahasuerus referring to Mordechai as "the Jew." For one, it suggests that he likely has no recollection of the power he gave Haman to murder the Jews (for all we know, Haman might have waited for a moment when Ahasuerus was drunk to spring the plot upon him). Second, if anyone brought Ahasuerus's words back to Esther, she would now know that the king bore her people no animosity; the only significant antisemite at the court is Haman.*

After finishing his rounds with Mordechai, Haman rushes home to prepare for the evening feast with the king and Esther. But when he tells Zeresh, his wife, what happened that day, she says, "If Mor-

---

*It is interesting to speculate about Haman's mind-set as he drives Mordechai around Shushan. He had entered the court that morning ready to initiate his anti-Jewish plot with the hanging of Mordechai; now he must be experiencing some anxiety that something seems to be going terribly wrong.

dechai be of the seed of the Jews, then you shall not prevail against him, but you shall surely fall before him" (6:13).

Zeresh's reference to the Jews is peculiar. Didn't she know about her husband's antisemitic plot beforehand? Why didn't she speak up then? We will never know, for Haman offers her no answer. Instead, even as they speak, officers come from the king's court to escort Haman to the party.

Esther, now confident that the king bears her people no hatred, waits once more for the predictable Ahasuerus to ask: "What is your petition, Queen Esther, and it shall be granted you, and what is your request, and it shall be performed, even to half the kingdom?" (7:2).

Esther answers: "If I have found favor in your sight, O king, and if it please the king, let my life be given me . . . and my people . . . ; for we are sold, I and my people, to be destroyed, to be slain, and to be annihilated" (7:3–4).

Ahasuerus, previously quite happy to consent to the murder of innocent (but abstract) people, is now furious: "Who is he, and where is he, that presumes to do so?" (7:5).

"The adversary and enemy is this wicked Haman," Esther responds.

One wonders at what point during Esther's speech Haman begins to sense the direction in which her words are leading. What other people, after all, had been sold to be annihilated? In addition, after his unpleasant day of leading Mordechai around on a horse, and after hearing his wife's prophecy, Haman might well have been feeling a frightening sense of inevitability.

As soon as Ahasuerus learns the identity of Esther's enemy, he bolts the room in fury, only to return a few minutes later to see Haman astride Esther's bed importuning the queen to save his life. Ahasuerus chooses to interpret Haman's behavior as an assault on Esther: "Will he even assault the queen in my own presence?" (7:8).

Harbonah, a previously unmentioned royal aide, steps forward and tells the king of the seventy-five-foot gallows Haman had prepared for Mordechai. And the king says, "Hang him there."

Haman is hanged; a short time later, his ten sons, probably participants in their father's plot, are hanged as well. The Book of Esther then describes the holiday of Purim, which Mordechai ordained should be observed in commemoration of the Jews' miraculous deliverance from their foes. Indeed, the book's ending is so satisfying that it prompted a Yiddish wit to coin a cynical summary of Jewish history: "So many Hamans and only one Purim."

137. Esther: The Beauty Queen Who Saves the Jewish People

ESTHER, CHAPTERS 2–10

"Who Knows Whether You Have Come to Your Royal Position for Just Such a Time as This?"

4–14

Esther is one of the Bible's unlikeliest heroines, a Jewish girl who wins a beauty contest and marries a non-Jewish king, then saves the Jewish people from destruction.

It all begins when the alcoholic King Ahasuerus throws a drinking party for his friends and subjects, then summons his queen, Vashti, to make an appearance. She refuses to come, and is expelled from her royal position (see entry 135).

A short time later, the king, ruler over some 127 provinces, calls for a national beauty contest. Beautiful virgins are transported to the capital city of Shushan to be inspected by the king. Among the women brought before Ahasuerus is Esther, a beautiful Jewish girl and an orphan. She has been raised by her older cousin, Mordechai,* who advises her to tell no one inside the palace about her religion or her people. Ahasuerus selects Esther as his bride, not knowing therefore that she is Jewish. A short time later, when Haman, his foremost adviser, suggests to him a plot to murder a "certain people" in the Persian empire (we, the readers, know it's the Jews), Ahasuerus agrees. He doesn't even ask the name of the people Haman intends to wipe out.

When Mordechai hears of Haman's plot, he informs Esther and

---

*That Esther was Mordechai's cousin, and not his niece, as is commonly thought, is indicated in 2:7. Mordechai was older than Esther and had adopted her when her parents died (2:7)

instructs her to go to the king to plead with him to revoke the decree. Esther's first response is not to get involved. She explains to Mordechai that on pain of death no one, herself included, can enter the king's inner court without being summoned.

Mordechai rebuffs Esther's excuse with words that ever since have summoned people to act courageously: "Do not think in your heart that you shall escape in the king's house any more than all the other Jews. For if you remain silent at this time, then relief and deliverance shall arise to the Jews from elsewhere; but you and your father's house shall perish: And who knows whether you have not come to your royal position for just such a time as this?" (4:13–14).

Mordechai's words melt Esther's heart. She tells him to gather all the Jews in Shushan, and have them fast and pray for her for three days, after which she will go into the king's court; "and if I perish, I perish."

"So Mordechai went his way, and did according to all that Esther commanded him" (4:17), a relatively rare biblical instance in which a man follows a woman's commands.*

Esther proves to be a singularly shrewd strategist. As explained in the preceding entry, she holds two parties for Ahasuerus and Haman. During the first party, she learns that the king is still deeply in love with her; then between the first and second party, she learns that the king has no antisemitic animus, and that the plot to murder all the Jews is due solely to Haman's machinations. At the second party, she reveals Haman's plot to the king, who immediately has Haman executed.

The Jews would seem at this point to be saved, only now Esther learns that things are not so simple. When she asks Ahasuerus to annul Haman's genocidal decree, which has already been dispatched to Persia's 127 provinces, the king tells her that that is impossible. By a strange quirk of Persian law, a royal decree, once issued, is irrevocable. Instead, Ahasuerus gives Esther control of Haman's estate (8:1), and instructs her to have new orders sent out to the 127 provinces: The Jews are given permission to arm themselves and attack any of their enemies, to kill them and take possession of their property. The issuance of these orders is soon followed by news of the Jews prevailing against their foes, aided by Ahasuerus's royal officials (9:2–4).

The Bible's most fairy-tale–like narrative, the book ends with the

*See entry 11, where Abraham is told to follow Sarah, and entry 62 which describes how Barak followed Deborah.

sense that Esther lived happily ever after, although one must wonder how happy a woman could be married to a dunce like Ahasuerus.

One of the deeper meanings of the story is that the Jewish people should be careful before they write off any of their members. Esther would certainly have seemed an unlikely savior of her people. She appears to have come from an assimilated background; her name derives from the name for an idolatrous goddess, Astar. Furthermore, she married a non-Jew and kept her own Jewish identity secret. Yet, when the crisis came, Esther was willing to risk her life for her people, and becomes one of their most famous heroines.

138. Mordechai: The Model of a Diaspora Jewish Leader

ESTHER, CHAPTERS 2–10

Clever, astute, and proud, Mordechai is one of the Bible's most enduring heroes. Unlike David and Solomon, whose actions take place within a sovereign Jewish state, Mordechai serves as a model to diaspora Jews, whose decisions must take into account their minority status.

The Bible tells us few details about Mordechai. We learn that he is descended from Jews who were exiled from Israel when the land was conquered by the Babylonians (587 B.C.E.). In Persia he has raised his beautiful younger cousin, the orphan Esther; when she is summoned to King Ahasuerus's court to be considered as a possible wife for the king, Mordechai advises her to conceal her Jewish origins.

Once Esther is taken away to the king's court, Mordechai can communicate to her only through messengers. He himself spends much time at the court; during this period, he overhears two of the king's aides, Bigtan and Teresh, plotting to overthrow the king. Mordechai has the information conveyed to Esther, who in turn conveys to the king, in Mordechai's name, news of the plot. The story is investigated, the plot is found to be true, and both conspirators are hanged (2:21–23).

Although Mordechai had instructed Esther to conceal her origins, he makes sure to emphasize his own Jewishness when news of the plot is reported to the king (see 6:10). We do not know if the king is informed at the time that the man who saved him is a Jew, but this information is certainly known to the royal official in charge of maintaining the court records.

The next action by Mordechai to be reported is a provocative one. Unlike everyone else in Shushan, he refuses to bow down to Haman, the king's newly appointed highest official. Mordechai's refusal is likely rooted in his animosity toward Haman's Amalekite origins, an ancestry in which Haman seems to take great pride (see entry 136). In other words, Mordechai perceives Haman to be a great enemy of his people, and for this reason refuses to honor him with a bow.

The wrathful Haman decides to wreak a terrible vengeance on Mordechai and all the Jews, and launches a plot to murder them. He offers Ahasuerus an enormous bribe to back his plot, and the king agrees.

Word quickly spreads of Haman's scheme, and Mordechai sends word of it to Esther, asking her to intervene with the king. Esther refuses, fearing that such intervention will lead to her own execution, but Mordechai convinces her (in one of the Bible's most moving appeals; see 4:13–14) to risk her life and stand up for her people.

Intelligent as Mordechai is, the ingenious plot by which Esther turns Ahasuerus against Haman seems to be exclusively of her own devising. While all this is going on, Mordechai remains outside the palace, leading Shushan's Jews in a fast on Esther's behalf.

The Bible gives sparse details when describing Mordechai and Haman's one sustained interaction. In the very midst of Esther's efforts to thwart Haman's plans, Ahasuerus experiences severe insomnia one night. He summons an officer to read to him from the official chronicles of his reign, and the officer reads the story of how Mordechai thwarted a plot to assassinate him. When Ahasuerus learns that Mordechai has never been rewarded, he orders Haman, his highest official, to lead a royally clad Mordechai around Shushan on a horse, proclaiming, "Thus shall be done to the man whom the king delights to honor" (6:11).

The Bible gives us no information about Mordechai's emotional state during this ceremony, but as this event happens during Esther's desperate attempt to thwart Haman's plot, Mordechai must have finally sensed that the tide was turning against Haman.

Within twenty-four hours, Haman is executed. Esther, who has now publicly acknowledged her Jewishness, is free to tell the king that Mordechai is her relative. The king, in sudden need of a new prime minister, appoints Mordechai to the post. Within a few months, Mordechai directs a military campaign against all of Haman's surviving allies within the Persian empire. Only after they have been eliminated, does he settle back to help Ahasuerus rule over Persia (chapters 9–10).

The Book of Esther informs us that it was Mordechai who established the holiday of Purim, to commemorate the destruction of Haman and of his plot to annihilate the Jews (9:20–23).

Within the Jewish psyche, Mordechai occupies a place similar to Joseph, a Hebrew who achieves high power under a non-Israelite king and who remains totally loyal to his people—"seeking the good of his people" is how the Bible describes Mordechai (10:3).

Note: Who was Ahasuerus? Bible scholars generally identify King Ahasuerus with the Persian king Xerxes I (486–465 B.C.E.), son of Darius I, although no historical document has yet emerged that identifies any Jewish prime minister serving under Xerxes.

XVIII. DANIEL

139. Shadrach, Meshach, and Abednego Are Thrown into Nebuchadnezzar's Furnace

DANIEL, CHAPTERS 1 AND 3

After King Nebuchadnezzar suppressed the first Judean revolt in 597 B.C.E., he deported to Babylon many of the province's leading citizens. There, the Babylonians selected some of the most intelligent Judean youths—"of royal descent and of the nobility—youths without blemish, handsome, proficient in all wisdom . . . and capable of serving in the royal palace" (1:3–4)—to serve in Babylon's government. Among those chosen are Daniel, and three friends, Hananiah, Mishael, and Azariah.

The Babylonians bestow Babylonian names on their Judean employees. Daniel is called Belteshazzar, while the three other youths are named, respectively, Shadrach, Meshach, and Abednego.

Resolving to adhere to the Bible's dietary laws, the four refuse to partake of the palace fare, which is filled with forbidden meats, and adhere to a vegetarian diet instead. Although the chief officer at the palace fears that the boys' physical condition will compare unfavorably with those on the richer diet, "when the ten days were over, they looked better and healthier than the youths who were eating of the king's food" (1:15; this might be the earliest instance in any literature to extol the health advantages of a vegetarian diet, although Dr. Jeremiah Unterman has suggested to me that, more likely, the text's author intended to emphasize that the young men were favored by God).

Nebuchadnezzar subsequently erects an enormous statue of gold, and orders, "Whoever will not fall down and worship [it] shall at once be thrown into a burning fiery furnace" (3:6). All of his subjects bow down. But certain Babylonians, envious of the high position achieved by the king's Israelite advisers, inform him that "there are certain Jews whom you appointed to administer the province of Babylon, Shadrach, Meshach and Abednego; these men pay no heed to you, O king; they do not serve your god or worship the statue of gold that you have set up" (3:12).

Nebuchadnezzar immediately summons the three men, and asks if the report brought him is true. The men do not cower before the now raging king: "For if it must be so, our God whom we serve is able to save us from the burning fiery furnace, and He will save us from your power, O king. But even if He does not, be it known to you, O king, that we will not serve your god or worship the statue of gold that you have set up" (3:17–18).

Nebuchadnezzar becomes so enraged that his face contorts, and he commands his officers to tie up the three young men, and to throw them into the fiery furnace. The furnace is heated to such excess that the soldiers who carry the three men to it are themselves killed when a "tongue of flame" leaps out at them. Inside the furnace, however, the three suffer no harm.

Now yet another miracle confounds Nebuchadnezzar. He turns to his companions and asks: "Did we not throw three men, bound into the fire?"

"Surely, O king," they respond.

"But I see four men walking about unbound and unharmed in the fire and the fourth looks like a divine being" (3:24–25).

The Bible never tells us who this fourth being is or what makes him look divine, but Nebuchadnezzar immediately has the three men released from the furnace, and blesses their God, who sent an angel to save them. Suddenly sounding like the most pious of believers, Nebuchadnezzar extols the men who "flouted the king's decree at the risk of their lives rather than serve or worship any god but their own God" (3:28).

A few moments earlier, Nebuchadnezzar had wanted to burn the men for worshiping the God of Israel, now he commands that anyone who blasphemes Israel's God "shall be torn limb from limb, and his house confiscated," because "there is no other God who is able to save in this way" (3:29).

Nebuchadnezzar's transformation has long struck me as one of the least impressive repentances in history.

140. Daniel Reads the Handwriting on the Wall

DANIEL, CHAPTER 5

When King Belshazzar, son of Nebuchadnezzar, throws a banquet for his hundred leading nobles, the drinking quickly gets out of hand. The inebriated king orders that the gold and silver cups that his father had stolen from Solomon's Temple be brought out, and he has drinks served in them. Adding insult to injury, the king, his nobles, and their consorts and concubines drink from the holy vessels, and then praise "the gods of gold and silver, bronze, iron, wood and stone" (5:4).

At this moment, a large unattached finger appears and writes unintelligible words on the wall opposite where the king is sitting. Belshazzar watches in terror as the finger writes.

The king's knees knock together, and he summons diviners and exorcists to the palace, promising a high government position to anyone who can decipher the message.

No one can do it. The queen arrives at the banquet hall, and reminds her husband of Daniel, a man whose wisdom his father, Nebuchadnezzar, had trusted.

Daniel is brought before Belshazzar, who offers him purple (i.e., royal) garments, a gold chain to place around his neck, and a position as one of the country's three top officials if he can explain the writing on the wall.

Daniel is unimpressed, telling the king: "You may keep your gifts for yourself and give your presents to others . . ." (5:17). And he denounces the king for the gross disrespect he has displayed to God by drinking liquor from the Temple's holy vessels, then praising the idolatrous gods he and his people worship (5:23). Finally, he proceeds to read the writing on the wall: *Mene Mene Tekel Upharsin.* "And this is its meaning: *Mene*—God has numbered [the days of] your kingdom and brought it to an end; *Tekel*—you have been weighed in the balance and found waiting; [*Upharsin* he now reads as] *Peres*—your kingdom has been divided and given to the Medes and Persians" (5:25–28).*

---

*This whole episode reads like a mirror image of the Joseph story (see entry 25), in which an alarmed pharaoh can receive no adequate expla-

Terrified and distraught as Belshazzar must have been, he remains faithful to his offer. Daniel is clothed in purple, a gold chain is hung around his neck, and his leadership position is confirmed.

However, the story concludes with a stunning one-verse coda: "That very night, Belshazzar, the Chaldean [Babylonian], king was killed," while the following verse tells us that Darius the Mede (most likely Cyrus of Persia) becomes the new ruler (5:30–6:1).

141. Daniel in the Lions' Den

DANIEL, CHAPTER 6

After Darius the Mede, probably an alternative name for King Cyrus of Persia, defeats the Babylonian empire, he appoints Daniel to serve as one of his three highest officials. Daniel quickly emerges as the king's favorite, and the other ministers and court officials, jealous of Daniel's status, search for ways to reduce his standing at the court. However, since Daniel is extremely wise and impeccably honest, they are forced to conclude: "We are not going to find any fault with this Daniel, unless we find something against him in connection with the laws of his God" (6:6).

Daniel's rivals soon devise a plot that takes advantage of an idiosyncratic feature of Persian law, the king's inability to abrogate a law he has signed. They approach Darius and suggest that a royal ban "be issued under sanction of an oath that whoever shall address a petition to any god or man, beside you, O king, during the next thirty days, shall be thrown into a lions' den. So issue the ban, O king, and put it in writing so that it be unalterable as a law of the Medes and Persians that may not be abrogated" (6:8–9).

---

nation from his diviners for a disturbing set of dreams he has had. Pharaoh is advised to summon an intelligent young Hebrew, Joseph, and ask him to interpret the dreams. Joseph offers Pharaoh an interpretation of how he can avert a disaster and bring prosperity to his land. Here, Daniel explains to Belshazzar that his kingdom will fall very soon, and that there is nothing he can do to avert this fate.

Darius signs the ban into law, while Daniel, although he is aware of the new decree, continues praying to God three times a day in the direction of Jerusalem.

The ministers, who have passed this decree solely to harm Daniel, charge into his house, where they find him "petitioning his God in supplication." They immediately go to Darius and ask, in feigned innocence, about the status of the new law he signed. Darius replies, "The order stands firm, as a law of the Medes and Persians that may not be abrogated" (6:13). They then tell him of Daniel's thrice daily violation of the law.

Darius, who loves and esteems Daniel, is distressed and spends the whole day trying to find a pretext by which he can circumvent the law, but he fails to do so.*

As Daniel is arrested, taken to the lions' den, and cast inside, the king expresses to him the wish that "your God, whom you serve so regularly, will deliver you" (6:17). When the king finishes speaking, Daniel's enemies place a rock over the den's mouth.

Strangely, the Bible's attention now focuses on Darius rather than Daniel. The king spends the night sleepless and fasting. At the break of dawn, he rushes to the den and calls out to Daniel: "Was the God whom you served so regularly able to deliver you from the lions?" To the king's immense relief, Daniel responds that God sent him an angel "who shut the mouths of the lions so that they did not injure me, inasmuch as I was found innocent by Him, nor have I, O king, done you any injury" (6:23).

The ecstatic Darius has Daniel removed from the den, then orders that Daniel's enemies be thrown there in his stead. The hungry lions, having spent the entire night frustrated by the angel, quickly devour them.†

---

*This bizarre feature of Persian law also appears prominently in the Book of Esther. King Ahasuerus, influenced by Haman, permits an order to be issued in his name decreeing the murder of all Jews in the Persian empire. A short time later, he concludes that the law is wrong, but there is nothing he can do about it, since "an edict that has been written in the king's name, and sealed with the king's signet, may not be revoked" (Esther 8:8). Instead, Ahasuerus issues a new decree, authorizing the Jews to kill anyone who tries to harm them. Its wording makes it clear that the king's sympathies lie solely with the Jews, not with their opponents.

†A disturbing feature of Darius's revenge is that he has the wives and children of Daniel's opponents thrown into the den along with them, an act that the Torah, although apparently not Persian law, forbids: "Parents shall not be put to death for children, nor children be put to death for parents:

Daniel's emergence from the lions' den makes a deep impression on Darius, who issues a statement acknowledging the greatness of the living God "of Daniel" (6:27). Daniel continues as Darius's chief adviser, although the Bible does not inform us whether under his guidance the king subsequently exercises greater caution before signing unalterable decrees.

Note: If the theory that Darius and Cyrus are one and the same is correct, then chapter 6, verse 28, must be rendered as "Thus Daniel prospered during the reign of Darius, namely the reign of Cyrus the Persian."

---

a person shall be put to death only for his own crime" (Deuteronomy 24:16; the final clause of the verse implies that spouses are not to be punished for each other's offenses).

XIX. EZRA AND NEHEMIAH

142. Cyrus the Great, King of Persia (559–530 B.C.E.)

EZRA 1:1–4

Although the Hebrew Bible largely deals with the story of the Israelite people and religion, its first and last characters are not Hebrews. Adam and Eve, the first human beings, have no religious identity, while Cyrus, the Bible's last character, is a Persian king (II Chronicles 36:22–23).

Called "the Great" because he rules over what was then the largest empire in history, Cyrus is certainly one of the outstanding heroes of biblical history. A tolerant man, he permits the peoples he captures to remain in their homelands (the Babylonians preferred to exile people) and to continue practicing their religious and other ancestral traditions. He also returns to their homelands those exiled by the Babylonians.

In 539 B.C.E., Cyrus defeats Babylon and soon thereafter issues a declaration to the Jewish exiles living there: "Thus says King Cyrus of Persia: 'The Lord God of heaven has given me all the kingdoms of the earth; and He has charged me with building Him a House in Jerusalem, which is in Judah. Any one of you of all His people, the Lord his God be with him, and let him go up!'" (II Chronicles 36:23; this is the Bible's final verse). Although most Jews stay where they are, it is estimated that some forty thousand subsequently migrate to Israel.

The Book of Ezra, which records a fuller version of Cyrus's decree (1:2–4), mentions a clause that makes Cyrus sound like a modern-day organizer for the United Jewish Appeal, in which he instructs those Jews who do not return to Jerusalem to contribute silver, gold, goods, and livestock to those who do.

He also permits the Jewish returnees to take with them the sacred vessels Nebuchadnezzar and his troops had stolen from the Jerusalem Temple and placed within Babylonian temples. Under the direction of Sheshbazzar, who is appointed Judah's governor by Cyrus (Ezra 1:8), the Jews bring back a total of 5,400 gold and silver vessels.

Cyrus also seems to have instructed the people of Sidon and Tyre to sell the Jews the cedarwood necessary for constructing their Second Temple (Ezra 3:7).

In language unprecedented in the Bible for describing non-Hebrew kings, the prophet Isaiah speaks of Cyrus as God's "shepherd" (44:28), and calls him God's "anointed" (45:1; the word "anointed," *meshicho*, as in "messiah"). Although Cyrus probably regarded himself as an independent Persian king, both Ezra (1:1) and II Chronicles (36:22) speak of him as having been sent by God to fulfill Jeremiah's prophecy that God would one day bring the Jews back to their land (Jeremiah 29:10).

143. Ezra and the Jewish Restoration to the Land of Israel

EZRA, CHAPTERS 7–10

The book named for Ezra the scribe has only ten chapters, and remarkably, Ezra makes his first appearance only in the seventh. The first six chapters detail the tribulations of the Jews who returned to Israel after King Cyrus of Persia's decree (538 B.C.E.) that the Jews, exiled to Babylon in 587, could return home.

When the returning Jews begin erecting a Temple to replace the destroyed Temple of Solomon, they encounter stiff opposition from the Samaritans and other non-Israelite residents in Israel. Attempts are made by these people to convince Judea's Persian rulers that the Jews are plotting a rebellion. Only in 515, under the inspiration of Haggai and Zechariah, the Bible's final two prophets (see entry 115) is the Temple completed.

The text now "fast-forwards" some sixty years to the reign of King Artaxerxes of Persia.* Although we never learn how Ezra, a Torah scholar and a priest who traced his descent to Aaron (7:5), established a relationship with the Persian king, the Bible quotes the letter of authorization that Artaxerxes gives Ezra, which empowers him to go to Jerusalem and set up a theocratic state: "For you are commissioned by the king and his seven advisers to regulate Judaism and Jerusalem according to the laws of your God . . ." (7:14). Artaxerxes explicitly permits Ezra to execute, imprison, flog, or confiscate the property of those who disobey the Torah's laws. Ezra also secures a royal tax exemption for the priests and all those who work at the Temple. The Bible never explains why a Persian king wishes to help establish a Jewish theocracy in Israel.

With the royal authorization in hand, Ezra sets out from Babylon (mainly in modern-day Iraq) in 458 B.C.E. for Israel. Fearful of making an unfavorable impression on Artaxerxes, Ezra and his entourage go alone: "I was ashamed to ask the king for soldiers and horsemen to protect us against any enemy on the way, since we had told the king, 'The benevolent care of our God is for all who seek him' " (8:22).

As detailed in the next entry, Ezra devotes his earliest efforts to combating intermarriage between the Israelites and the people among whom they live. However, he might well be most famous for an act described in the Book of Nehemiah, which follows the Book of Ezra. Subsequent to having ordered Israelite men to separate themselves from their non-Israelite wives, Ezra convenes a mass celebration of Rosh ha-Shana, the Jewish New Year, at the Jerusalem Temple, and he reads to the people from a Torah scroll (Nehemiah 8:1–3).

Apparently, most Jews no longer know Hebrew, so that as Ezra reads, an interpreter simultaneously translates into Aramaic, the language then spoken in Israel. The people, conscious of their manifold religious violations, weep as they hear the Torah's ordinances. However, Ezra and the religious functionaries with him tell them: "This day is holy to the Lord your God; you must not mourn or weep" (Nehemiah 8:9).

Jewish ignorance of biblical regulations seems to have become widespread; many are no longer familiar with the holiday of Sukkot (8:14), during which the Torah instructs people to set up booths

---

*Almost definitely Artaxerxes I, who ruled 465–425, and not Artaxerxes II, his grandson, who ruled 404–358.

and to eat and live in them for a week (Leviticus 23:42). That year, throughout the weeklong holiday, Ezra continues to read aloud from the Torah.

After the holiday, the people gather again and, acting under the Levites' inspiration, pledge not to let their children intermarry (10:31), not to do business on the Sabbath (10:32), to observe the laws of the Sabbatical year (see entry 187), and to support the Temple (10:33–40).

The Talmud regards Ezra as one of the Bible's preeminent heroes: "Ezra would have been worthy of receiving the Torah for Israel had not Moses preceded him" (Babylonia Talmud *Sanhedrin* 21b). For one thing, his public reading of the Torah helped democratize Judaism's holiest document, making it as much the possession of the common laborer as of the priest. For another, although his insistence on dissolving intermarriages was harsh, without it the Jewish community would likely have assimilated and adopted the lifestyles of their pagan neighbors.*

144. Ezra's War on Intermarriage

EZRA, CHAPTERS 9–10

The Jewish community residing in fifth-century-B.C.E. Israel is small, and its survival is by no means guaranteed. Thus, Ezra is distraught when he arrives in Israel only to learn that large numbers of Israelites, among them religious leaders ("priests and Levites"; 9:1), have intermarried with local non-Jewish and, usually, idolatrous residents. (The account given in the Book of Ezra leaves the impression that it is overwhelmingly Jewish men who are taking non-Jewish spouses.)

Ezra reacts like a mourner to the news of widespread intermarriage by rending his garments; he even tears hair out of his head (9:3). He then turns to God in desperate prayer: "O my God, I am too ashamed and mortified to lift my face to You, O my God, for our

---

*Given that in the fifth century B.C.E. the Jews were the world's only believers in one God, their disappearance would have meant the end of monotheism.

iniquities are overwhelming and our guilt has grown as high as heaven" (9:6).

While his language can be construed as racist—he says that "the holy seed has become intermingled with the peoples of the land" (9:2)—he repeatedly emphasizes the religious and moral, not the genetic, implications of intermarriage: "Shall we once again violate Your commandments by intermarrying with these people who follow such abhorrent practices?" (9:14; see also 9:1; the text does not however specify the abhorrent rituals in which the Jews' neighbors engage).

Even as Ezra is praying and confessing Israel's sins before God, many Israelites, headed by a man named Shecaniah, gather around him. Shecaniah urges Ezra to establish a covenant between Israel and God in which the Israelite men agree "to expel all these women and those who have been born to them" (10:3).

Soon, Ezra issues a proclamation throughout Judah summoning all Jews to an assembly in Jerusalem. To ensure widespread attendance, he announces that "anyone who [does] not come in three days [will], by decision of the officers and elders, have his property confiscated and himself excluded from the congregation of the returning exiles" (10:8).

The threat works: Three days later, an enormous convocation of Jews gathers at the Temple. Ezra stands up and orders the attendees "to separate yourselves from the peoples of the land and from the foreign women" (10:11).

The Israelites beg Ezra to grant them some time, because this is not "the work of a day or two" (10:13). A procedure is worked out under which Jewish men with foreign wives appear before local judges. The text implies that within a few months, Ezra and his assistants "were done with all the men who had brought home foreign women" (10:17).

The Bible then lists dozens of names of priestly families in which such intermarriages occurred (10:18–43); it is suggested, but not explicitly stated, that all these men expelled their wives and children.

Had the rates of intermarriage continued unabated, it is quite possible that the Jewish community in Israel would have ceased to exist. Still, one has to have a heart of stone to read these chapters and not feel the pain the expelled wives and children must have experienced.

What is puzzling is that neither Ezra nor any other Israelite men raise the possibility of converting the wives and children. Despite the biblical model of Ruth (see entry 132), it seems that the larger Jewish community had not yet accepted the idea of conversion to Judaism. How unfortunate!

145. Nehemiah and the Jewish Restoration to Israel

THE BOOK OF NEHEMIAH

Nehemiah had a prestigious, if dangerous, job at the court of the Persian king Artaxerxes: He was the king's cupbearer. One of his duties was to be the first person to taste the king's food to ensure that it was not poisoned. Such a position guaranteed that Nehemiah saw the king often.

A loyal Jew, he is overcome with grief when he meets with visitors from Israel, who come to the king's palace in Susa (alternatively known as Shushan, Susa lies in southwestern Iran), and tell him of the dire circumstances of the Jewish community in Israel. Jerusalem's walls are in terrible disrepair, its gates have been destroyed by fire, and its Jewish residents subject to attacks from hostile neighbors.

Nehemiah cries at the unhappy report, and prays to God to show compassion to His persecuted people.

Some time later, while Nehemiah is serving the king wine, Artaxerxes asks him: "How is it that you look bad, though you are not ill? It must be bad thoughts" (2:2). Although frightened that the king might be displeased with him, he nevertheless answers forthrightly: "How should I not look bad when the city of the graveyard of my ancestors lies in ruins, and its gates have been consumed by fire?"

The king asks how he can be of assistance, and Nehemiah requests that he be dispatched to Israel and given the authority to rebuild Jerusalem. Artaxerxes grants permission, and sends army officers and cavalry to accompany him.

Once in Jerusalem, Nehemiah surveys the city and quickly concludes that, without a strong defense strategy, the Jews will live in a permanent state of disgrace, subject to humiliating attacks. Thus, he makes rebuilding Jerusalem's walls his first priority (2:17).

Nehemiah's efforts to strengthen Jerusalem's defenses soon provoke the Jews' enemies. News is brought him of a plot his foes are concocting: "Before they know or see it, we shall be in among them and kill them, and put a stop to the work" (4:5).

The militarily astute Nehemiah divides his workers into two groups, one devoted exclusively to building the walls, while the other holds "lances, and shields, bows and arms" to ward off attacks (4:10). Nehemiah completes the job in fifty-two days (6:15).

Having dealt with the major external threat to Israel's survival, he now turns to an internal Jewish problem, the wealthy class's mistreatment of the poor. "After pondering the matter carefully" (5:7), he convenes a meeting with the nobles, and reproaches them for their unforgiving attitude on loans made to their poorer brethren; some nobles have even sold debtors into slavery. Nehemiah argues that such behavior is not only heartless, it also constitutes a gross "desecration of God's name" (see entry 185): "You ought to act in a God-fearing way so as not to give our enemies . . . room to reproach us" (5:9).

Announcing that he is willing to forgo his own claims against certain poor people [perhaps tenant farmers], he urges everyone present to "give back at once their fields, their vineyards, their olive trees, and their homes and [abandon] the claims . . ." (5:11). The nobles agree to do so, whereupon Nehemiah summons priests and has the nobles swear in their presence to forgo their claims.

The themes that preoccupy Ezra, intermarriage and Sabbath observance, concern Nehemiah as well. Thus, he orders Jerusalem closed on the Sabbath, so that no goods can be brought into the city on the holy day (13:19).

Like Ezra, he pushes for the dissolution of intermarriages, citing the biblical law forbidding Ammonites and Moabites from entering the congregation of Israel. He claims that when he reminded Israel of this prohibition, "they separated all the alien admixture from Israel" (13:3). However, the Book of Nehemiah omits one very significant exemption: Jewish law does allow Ammonite and Moabite women to become Jews. This is evidenced by Ruth, a Moabite woman who embraces the Israelite religion and people, and becomes the great-grandmother of King David (see entry 132).

Although the Bible attributes the story of Ruth to the time of the judges, seven hundred years or so before Nehemiah, some scholars speculate that the book named after her might have been written during or around the period of Ezra and Nehemiah, in protest against a growing chauvinistic tendency within Judaism evidenced by a refusal to countenance the possibility of non-Jews becoming Jews. Indeed, the belief that King David, and through him the Messiah, was descended from a Moabite woman certainly seems counter to the spirit of men such as Nehemiah (13:1–3).

Throughout the book named for him, Nehemiah speaks as one who has a deeply personal relationship with God. Thus, when he writes of how he purged the Temple of perverse pagan practices, he concludes: "O my God, remember it to my credit" (13:31).

Note: On Nehemiah's leadership style: Although the Bible speaks of Solomon as the wisest man of his age, Nehemiah seems to have learned from Solomon's mistakes how *not* to rule. Chapter 13, verse 26, condemns Solomon for sinning through his many marriages to non-Israelite women, while Nehemiah fights against intermarriage; also, Solomon's imposing of high taxes on the Israelites to pay for his building projects spawned enormous resentments that resulted in a revolt against his son within weeks of his death. Nehemiah, however, keeps taxes low so as not to lay heavy, infuriating burdens on the people (5:15–18).

XX. I AND II CHRONICLES: THE BIBLE'S FINAL BOOKS

If you think you have a high threshold of boredom, begin reading through I Chronicles and see how far you can get. If you make it through the first nine chapters, congratulations. A typical passage of this listing of genealogies reads: "Canaan begot Sidon, his first-born, and Heth, and the Jebusites, the Amorites, the Girgashites, the Hivites, the Arkites, the Sinites, the Arvadites, the Zemarites, and the Hamathites" (I Chronicles 1:13–16).

However, starting with chapter 10, Chronicles becomes a historical account of King David and the royal dynasty he established. The narrator starts with the death of Saul, Israel's first king, followed by all Israel's appeal to David to become its monarch (I Chronicles 11:1; the Books of Samuel commence with the story of Samuel, then proceed to Saul, and only then do they cover the story of David and his descendants).

The material covered in Chronicles is generally the same as that recounted in the books of Samuel and Kings, extending from the reign of David (circa 1000 B.C.E.) to Cyrus's decree authorizing the Jews to return to Israel from exile (538). Changes, however, are introduced that reflect the narrator's particular religious orientation.

For example, in the Second Book of Samuel (24:1) God, angry at Israel, incites David to commit a sin so that God will have an excuse to punish the people. Understanding that this story casts the Lord in a rather unpleasant light, the author of Chronicles alters the account and has Satan, not God, inciting David to sin (I Chronicles 21:1).

The narrator also protects the good name of David. Thus, David's sin with Bathsheba, an event that is so central in II Samuel (see entry 82), goes unmentioned. Attention is focused rather on David's organization of the kingdom.

Chronicles introduces some new material about David. For example, we are informed that David intended to build a great Temple for God (which was later built by his son Solomon) but was told by the prophet Nathan not to do so because of the blood he had shed in battle (I Chronicles 28:3). While I Kings 5:17 mentions in passing David's desire to build the Temple, in II Chronicles his role in the Temple's creation is greatly enhanced.

As was the case with David, the author of Chronicles chooses to disregard the unflattering details about Solomon that the author of Kings mentioned. Thus, the First Book of Kings, while glorifying Solomon's early years, describes the great failings that characterized the king's later years, most notably his decline in religiosity (see entry 89). The account in Chronicles speaks only of Solomon's glorious deeds.

After Solomon's death, the kingdom of Israel split in two; the ten northern tribes formed the kingdom of Israel, while the kingdom of Judah continued to be ruled by the descendants of David and Solomon. Although the former kingdom existed for over two hundred years, until the Assyrians destroyed it in 722 B.C.E., Chronicles' author is quite uninterested in the northern kingdom. His concern is almost exclusively with the House of David, which he, and Jewish tradition, regard as the only legitimate royal household. Thus, II Chronicles 13 depicts Judean King Abijah as climbing to the top of a mountain in the hill country of Ephraim, and there berating the Israelites for rejecting the House of David: "Surely you know that the Lord God gave David kingship over Israel, forever, to him and his sons . . ." (verse 5). He goes on to accuse the Israelites of "opposing the kingdom of the Lord" (verse 8).

Consistent with his pious approach, the author of Chronicles devotes most of his attention to Judah's righteous kings (Asa, Jehoshaphat, Hezekiah, and Josiah). Writing of the wicked King Manasseh, whose reign lasted fifty-five years, he adds a detail found nowhere in the Book of Kings—that Manasseh, in his later years, repented of all his evil deeds (II Chronicles 33:12–13). Manasseh's earlier evil had been so great (see entry 99) that it is hard to believe in the sincerity of his atonement. One suspects that the Chronicler wanted to believe in it as a way of accounting for the king's long and materially successful reign.

The Talmud credits Ezra (see entry 143) as Chronicles' main author, and assumes that Nehemiah (see entry 145) made some additions. Originally, the two books of Chronicles were one long volume that was later divided into two (as was the case with the two books of Samuel and Kings).

The pious history conveyed in Chronicles, with its elimination of unflattering details about kings David and Solomon, makes the narrative much flatter and may account for I and II Chronicles being the least read of the Bible's historical books.

Sources: Geoffrey Wigoder, editor, *Illustrated Dictionary and Concordance of the Bible,* pages 230–233; Louis Jacobs, *The Jewish Religion,* pages 80–81.

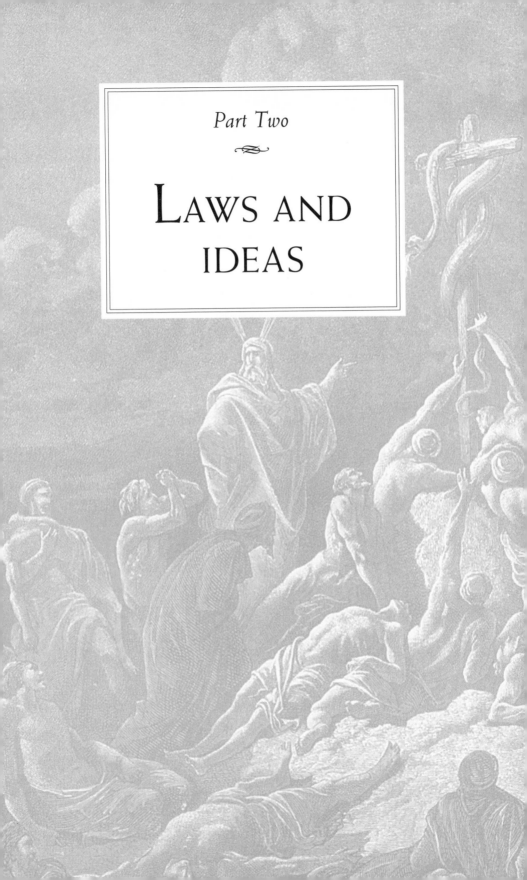

Part Two

LAWS AND IDEAS

XXI. GENESIS

146. What Does It Mean That Human Beings Were Created "in God's Image"?

GENESIS 1:27

Adam and Eve, unlike the beings created before them, are created "in God's image." Jewish tradition has never understood this biblical phrase to mean that God, like human beings, has a body and that humankind has physical traits in common with Him. Rather, what people share with God, but not with the animal kingdom, is an awareness of good and evil.

True, people sometimes use the words "good" and "evil" when speaking of animals, but these words are not intended literally. A dog trained by anti-Nazi partisans to attack Nazis was no more making a moral choice to do good than a German shepherd trained to attack concentration camp inmates was making an immoral choice to commit evil. When applied to animals, the word "good" usually is nothing more than a synonym for "obedient."

Because people are created "in God's image," the biblical view is that they have a higher intrinsic worth than animals. However, they are not divine. For though they share with God a knowledge of right and wrong, they have in common with animals many bodily needs and urges. Thus, human beings combine aspects of both God and animals, though they have one significant advantage over the latter: The fact that they are created "in God's image" provides them with the potential to overcome evil urges and impulses.

From the biblical perspective, it would seem that a human being who does not know right from wrong, or who is incapable of resisting the impulse to do evil, cannot be regarded as being "in God's image" in the same sense in which moral human beings can be so regarded.

Reflections: Two second-century rabbinic commentaries on humankind's creation in God's image: "Rabbi Akiva used to say: 'Beloved is man for he was created in God's image. Still greater was the love shown him in that it was made known to him that he was created in God's image. For it is written, "For in His [God's] image did God make humankind" ' " (Genesis 9:6; *Ethics of the Fathers* 3:14).

" 'Love your neighbor as yourself' (Leviticus 19:18): Rabbi Akiva said: 'This is the major principle of the Torah.' Ben Azzai said: 'The verse, "When God created man, He made him in the likeness of God" (Genesis 5:1) utters a principle even greater: You must not say, "since I have been humiliated, let my fellow man also be humiliated; since I have been cursed, let my neighbor also be cursed." For, as Rabbi Tanhuma pointed out, "If you act in this manner, realize who it is that you are willing to have humiliated, him whom God made 'in the likeness of God' " ' " (Palestinian Talmud, *Nedarim* 9:4; see also *Genesis Rabbah* 24:7).

147. "Be Fruitful and Multiply"

GENESIS 1:28

Jewish tradition regards God's charge to Adam and Eve, "Be fruitful and multiply," as the first of the Torah's 613 commandments.

While the injunction, when read in context, sounds more like a blessing than a command, Jewish tradition understands the verse as mandating marriage and procreation. A chapter later, Genesis 2:24 proclaims: "Therefore shall a man leave his father and mother and cling to his wife, so that they become one flesh."

Although God's words seem to be directed toward both Adam and Eve, Jewish law rules that the obligation to procreate devolves only upon the man. *Meshech Hokhma*, a biblical commentary by Rabbi Meir Simcha of Dvinsk (1843–1926), explains: "The Torah freed the woman from the religious obligation to 'be fruitful and multiply' [because] . . . the woman endangers her life in pregnancy and childbirth [and hence cannot be obligated to have children]. . . . But for the sake of the preservation of the species God so formed woman's nature that her yearning to have children is stronger than the man's" (commentary on Genesis 9:1).

The freeing of women from the obligation to procreate implies that, according to rabbinic law, only they can ever practice birth control. Thus, although most Orthodox rabbis severely restrict the right to practice birth control, in those instances where they permit it, only the woman is allowed to practice contraception. Non-Orthodox rabbis generally leave decisions concerning birth control to the couple's discretion.

Although males are considered responsible for observing Jewish law starting at age thirteen (*Bar Mitzvah*), the talmudic Rabbis ruled that the obligation to procreate (restricted to people who are married) becomes mandatory only at age eighteen.

The Bible itself never addresses the question of how many children one is required to have to fulfill this commandment. The Talmud's prevailing view, as articulated by Rabbi Hillel, is two, one child of each sex; in other words a couple are obligated to replace themselves (*Mishnah Yevamot* 6:6).

The biblical view might be more lenient than Hillel's, since it seems to acknowledge that two children, even though of the same sex, fulfill the divine injunction. Thus, Isaac has two sons (Jacob and Esau) but no daughters, and there is no indication that he is deficient for this reason. Likewise, Moses has two children, both sons.

Further reading: David Feldman, *Birth Control in Jewish Law.*

148. Human Nature: "The Tendency of Man's Heart Is Towards Evil from His Youth"

GENESIS 8:21

A common, perhaps prevailing, notion in the Western world—at least since the time of Rousseau and the Enlightenment—is that human beings are born good. Those who hold to this notion believe that evil emanates from society, which corrupts humankind's essential good nature.

The quite different biblical view sees human beings as born morally neutral, with strong tendencies toward evil. Nowhere is this expressed more emphatically than in Genesis 8:21, in which God says, "The tendency of man's heart is towards evil from his youth."

Often misunderstood, this verse has nothing in common with the Christian doctrine of Original Sin, which views people as eternally tainted by Adam and Eve's sin in the Garden of Eden. This taint, most Christian teachers have long taught, can only be removed through baptism (in the absence of baptism, many fundamentalist Protestants teach, a person will be damned for eternity). Thus, Original Sin is unrelated to human behavior, since a totally moral person who has not been baptized will nonetheless be regarded by God as damned.

In contrast, the Hebrew Bible's view is rooted in an assessment of human nature. Evil does not come from forces *outside* human beings, as many secular thinkers believe, but from *within* them. People aren't sinners because Adam and Eve sinned; rather, *we* sin as they did.

Biblical narrative repeatedly reenforces this point. Cain, the first child born to the first couple, murders his brother. He is not motivated to do so by society's corrupting influences, but he murders Abel because he doesn't control his envy and his rage (see entry 3). Later, during Noah's time, people sin and engage in violence; it is this behavior that prompts God's negative assessment of human nature.

The Bible's unsentimental perspective is also reflected in the Torah's extensive body of laws. In general, the more optimistic one's assessment of human nature, the less one is inclined to impose extensive legislation. Thus, anarchism, the nineteenth-century philosophical and political movement, believed in humankind's natural decency and consequently opposed centralized government, police forces, and almost all state regulations. Basic to biblical jurisprudence, however, is the assumption that a state must have police and judges (Deuteronomy 16:18; lawyers are not mentioned). Furthermore, if people are naturally generous and good, as many contemporary secularists believe, there would be little reason for the Bible to promulgate laws directed to individuals, such as requiring them to donate a significant percentage of their income to charity. Wouldn't they give that much, perhaps even more, without such laws?

In contrast to the anarchic and Enlightenment worldviews, the extensive nature of the Bible's ethical legislation is probably based on the belief that without such laws, many, if not most, people will act much less decently.

149. The Noahide Laws

GENESIS 9:3–17

The most famous biblical revelation is the one that God makes on Mount Sinai (Exodus, chapter 20), but that is not His first revelation of law to humanity. Thousands of years earlier, just after God sends a flood that destroys the world but spares Noah and his family, He reveals to Noah a number of laws that are intended to maintain the world's moral equilibrium.

Like Adam and Eve, Noah and his sons are first instructed to "be fruitful and multiply" (9:1), which makes great sense given that the world's population is hovering at just a little above zero. God then gives humankind permission to eat meat (9:3), an option that had been denied Adam and Eve (1:29).

However, humans are prohibited from consuming blood (9:4). Bible scholar Jacob Milgrom, noting that such a prohibition did not exist among any of ancient Israel's neighbors (indeed, many of them consumed blood), concludes: "Man has a right to nourishment, not to life. Hence the blood, which is the symbol of life, must be drained, returned to the universe, to God."

Genesis 9:6 instructs that murderers are to be executed: "Whoever sheds the blood of man, by man shall his blood be shed" (see next entry).

God concludes his covenant with Noah and his family by swearing never again to destroy the world. The rainbow will serve as a reminder both to God and to human beings of this new divine covenant with the world.

Later Jewish tradition, building on God's first covenant with humankind, enumerates seven laws designated as binding on *b'nai Noach*, the "children of Noah" (non-Jews; Jews are regarded as the "children of Abraham," although Muslims, of course, also consider themselves descended from Abraham through his son Ishmael).

The seven Noahide laws forbid:

1. denying God (as, for example, through idolatry)
2. blaspheming God
3. murdering
4. engaging in incestuous, adulterous, bestial, or homosexual relationships
5. stealing
6. eating a limb torn from a living animal (in biblical times, some people did this in order to keep the rest of the animal fresh for later consumption).

They also mandate:

7. establishing courts to ensure obedience to the other six laws (Babylonian Talmud, *Sanhedrin* 56a).

In *Crime and Human Nature*, an overview of the causes of crime, the authors note that "certain acts are regarded as wrong by every society, preliterate as well as literate; that among these 'universal crimes' are murder, theft, robbery and incest"—among the key acts forbidden by the Noahide laws.

Sources and further readings: Jacob Milgrom, commentary on *Leviticus*, volume 1, Anchor Bible Series, pages 704–713; also, "The Biblical Diet Laws as an Ethical System"; James Wilson and Richard Herrnstein, *Crime and Human Nature*, page 22.

150. "Whoever Sheds the Blood of Man"

GENESIS 9:6

On Murderers and the Death Sentence

The biblical belief that murderers deserve to be executed is so fundamental that it is legislated long before God's covenant with Abraham; thus, the law mandating the death sentence for those who shed innocent blood is directed not only toward Israelites but all mankind.

After the Flood with which God devastates the world, God makes a covenant with Noah: Never again will He wreak such havoc on mankind. In return, Noah and his descendants are to be bound by certain moral standards, whose goal is to ensure that never again will humankind become so wicked that God will be tempted to destroy them (see preceding entry). Within this context, God issues the injunction that "whoever sheds the blood of man, by man shall his blood be shed, for in His [God's] image, did God make humankind."*

Executing murderers is so basic a cornerstone of biblical justice that it is the only law repeated in every one of the Torah's five books.

Exodus 21:12 rules: "He who fatally strikes a person shall be put to death." The Bible intends this punishment only for *premeditated* murderers, as is clear from the following verse: "If he [the killer] did not do it by design, but it came about by an act of God, I will assign you a place to which he can flee."†

Another law stated in Exodus closed off a loophole by which murderers in Phoenicia and Syria (and later in Greece and Rome) could escape or postpone punishment. Chapter 21 verse 14 decrees: "When a man schemes against another and kills him treacherously,

---

*Because man is the only creature made "in God's image" (the meaning of this term is discussed in entry 146), murderers are considered to have also committed a serious transgression against God.

†The "place to which he can flee" is described by later biblical legislation as one of the "cities of refuge" (see entry 195).

you shall take him from My very altar to be put to death." In other, non-Israelite societies, the altar of a temple was regarded as providing absolute security to fugitives, including those who were guilty of premeditated murder. Biblical law finds this notion repugnant. During the reign of Solomon, the renegade general Joab tries to evade punishment by grasping the horns of an altar. In compliance with the law in Exodus, Solomon instructs his leading general to kill Joab on the spot, justifying the execution by noting "the blood of the innocent that Joab has shed" (I Kings 2:28–34). From the Bible's perspective, permitting a murderer to evade punishment by clinging to God's altar would, in a sense, involve God in an ex post facto alliance with the murderer.

The third book of the Torah, Leviticus, reconfirms the ruling in Exodus: "Whoever takes the life of any human being shall be put to death" (24:17). It also legislates the death sentence for parents who sacrifice their children to the idolatrous god Molech (20:2). Because such sacrifices are considered premeditated murders, the only equitable punishment for them is death.

Numbers, the Torah's fourth book, says this about the treatment of murderers: "Anyone, however, who strikes another with an iron object so that death results is a murderer; the murderer must be put to death" (35:16ff.). Subsequent verses (35:22ff.) reiterate that when the killing is unintentional or unpremeditated, the killer is to be provided with a city of refuge to which he can flee from the "avenger of blood."

In modern times, campaigners against the death penalty have often propagated the myth that capital punishment was the original, most primitive punishment inflicted on murderers. Therefore, lesser punishments for those who murder reflect a more advanced society and culture. However, the opposite appears to be true. The societies that surrounded the ancient Hebrews, some of whose legislation is older than that recorded in the Torah, offered murderers alternatives to the death penalty. For example, a victim's family was permitted to accept money from the murderer in return for absolution. It is in repudiation of this practice that the Torah rules: "You may not accept ransom for the life of a murderer who is guilty of a capital crime; he must be put to death" (Numbers 35:31).* This ruling re-

*Moses Maimonides, the twelfth-century codifier of Jewish law, explains the Bible's rationale: "The soul of the victim is not the property of [his family members] but the property of God"; *Mishneh Torah*, "Laws of Murder and Preservation of Life," 1:4).

flects the biblical belief in one standard of justice; permitting the murderer to escape punishment by paying a bribe would grant a grotesque advantage to wealthy killers. To this day, affluent murderers almost always escape full punishment for their crimes; the Bible regards this as unconscionable.*

Deuteronomy, the Torah's fifth and final book, rules that if a *premeditated* murderer tries to claim asylum in one of the cities of refuge, he should be expelled and executed: "Do not look on him with pity. Thus you will purge Israel of the blood of the innocent . . ." (19:11–13). In one instance of attempted "judicial murder," the Torah likewise legislates a death sentence: where witnesses falsely testify that a person has committed a capital crime. Such an abuse of the legal system is regarded as so perilous that the Torah rules, "You shall do to him as he schemed to do to his brother . . ." (Deuteronomy 19:19).

What accounts for the Torah's unwavering commitment to executing premeditated murderers? First, ". . . and you shall burn the evil out from your midst" (Deuteronomy 19:19 and 24:7). Because the Bible regards innocent life as being of *infinite* value, one who murders an innocent person has committed an *infinite* evil. Therefore, any lesser punishment than death would not fit the crime.

In addition, the Bible wants murderers executed "so that others will hear and be afraid, and such evil things will not again be done in your midst" (Deuteronomy 19:20). Relying on common sense, the Bible assumes that the threat of death can and will deter at least some murderers from killing.

Finally, the Bible believes that innocent blood cries out to God from the earth (Genesis 4:10).[†] A society that lets premeditated murderers live—let alone paroles them from prison, as commonly occurs today—is, from the Bible's perspective a polluted culture, for "blood pollutes the land, and the land can have no expiation for blood that is shed on it, except by the blood of him who sheds it" (Numbers 35:33).

---

*In its concern for equality under the law, the Bible also rules—in a piece of legislation that I believe is unparalleled in any society, ancient or premodern—that anyone who beats a slave to death is to be executed (Exodus 21:20).

[†]Cain was not executed for killing his brother Abel probably because he did not know his blows could cause death; no human being before Abel had died.

Out of concern that innocent people not be killed, the Torah places a major restriction on imposing the death sentence: A murderer could be executed only if there were two witnesses to the crime (Deuteronomy 17:6). This explains the relative infrequency with which capital punishment was administered; most murders are not committed in the presence of witnesses, particularly if the murderer knows that in their absence he cannot be executed. The Torah's insistence on two witnesses is likely due to the fact that in biblical times all evidence, other than that supplied by witnesses, was circumstantial. In those days, nothing was known about fingerprints or DNA data.

Because murder is the ultimate crime, the Bible insists that it deserves the ultimate punishment.

151. Circumcision

GENESIS 17:1–27

Along with the prohibition of eating pig, circumcision is one of the most widely known Jewish rituals, among non-Jews as well as Jews. Unlike almost all other biblical laws, which the Torah traces to the time of Moses, it is commanded much earlier, during the time of Abraham, Israel's founding Patriarch.

Abraham is ninety-nine when God instructs him to circumcise himself and all other males who live with him, including his thirteen-year-old son Ishmael and his servants. God emphasizes that this ordinance is binding forever, and that circumcision is "the sign of the covenant" between Abraham (and his descendants) and God.

Circumcision, the removal of the foreskin of the penis, was widely practiced among many of ancient Israel's neighbors, including the Canaanites and the Egyptians. However, it was generally performed as a puberty rite on twelve-year-old boys, indicating their initiation into adulthood. God, however, ordains that Abraham's descendants be circumcised eight days after birth. So basic is this law to future Israelite identity that any uncircumcised male "shall be cut off from his kin; he has broken [God's] covenant" (Genesis 17:14).*

Why does God choose circumcision as the visible sign of His covenant with Israelite men (no physical sign of covenant is mandated for women)? The Bible offers no explanation; however, it is likely that imposing the sign of the covenant on the penis—that most anarchic and hardest-to-control male organ—is a powerful symbolic way for a boy or man to express his willingness to subjugate himself to God's will.

In early Jewish history, men were expected personally to circumcise their sons. Subsequently, circumcision began to be performed by a person who was specially trained to carry out this procedure, a *mohel*.

The technical name for the ritual is *brit milah* (the covenant of circumcision). In Jewish tradition, the child is formally named at the circumcision ceremony; traditional Jews don't reveal what the child's name will be until it is announced at the ceremony.

So basic has circumcision been to Jewish identity that the seventeenth-century philosopher Baruch Spinoza argued that as long as Jews practice circumcision they will remain a separate people. Some early radical leaders of nineteenth-century German Reform Judaism tried to eliminate the ritual, regarding it as a "barbaric rite," but most Reform Jews wished to maintain this tradition. Indeed, a tradition dating back to Abraham, and the only specific ritual (aside from animal sacrifice) that the Bible records the first Patriarch as performing, cannot be easily dismissed.

There are a number of later references to circumcision in the Bible. One occurs in one of the Torah's most mysterious passages. After God selects Moses to lead the Israelites from Egypt, He commands him to return to Egypt. En route, "the Lord encountered [Moses] and sought to kill him" (Exodus 4:24). Tzipporah, Moses' wife, immediately takes a flint knife, cuts off their son's foreskin, and touches Moses with it; whereupon, it seems, Moses makes an immediate recovery.

This cryptic tale's meaning is unclear, although most Jewish commentators interpret the passage as signifying that God intended to punish Moses for not having taken care to circumcise his son.

---

*This does not mean, as some people mistakenly believe, that an uncircumcised male is regarded as a non-Jew—any child born to a Jewish mother is Jewish—but that such a person, in effect, has cut his ties with the Jewish community.

The Israelites did not circumcise their newborn sons during their forty-year desert sojourn, probably because such a procedure might have been life-threatening for a group of nomadic wanderers. Once the Israelites entered Canaan, Joshua arranged for all uncircumcised males to be circumcised (Joshua 5:2–3).

The ancient Israelites regarded uncircumcised men, such as their Philistine neighbors, with contempt, calling them *arelim* ("uncircumcised"); I Samuel 17:26, 36).

At the beginning of the Common Era, a divisive dispute over circumcision, which Jewish law also demands of all male converts to Judaism, was one of the decisive issues that led to the permanent split between Judaism and Christianity. As a Jew, Jesus was circumcised at eight days (Luke 2:21); his early followers believed that all of his male adherents had to bear the sign of the covenant.* However, the early Christian leader Paul declared that circumcision no longer was obligatory, which made it easier, and certainly less painful, to become a Christian than to become a Jew (Romans 2:26–29).† After Paul's ruling, Christianity ceased to be a sect within Judaism, and became a separate religion.

152. Multiple Wives: The Conflicting Views of Biblical Law and Biblical Narrative

SCATTERED EPISODES IN THE BOOKS OF GENESIS, DEUTERONOMY,
JUDGES, I AND II SAMUEL, AND I KINGS

Biblical law permits a man to have more than one wife (Deuteronomy 21:17); indeed, many of the Bible's most prominent figures (e.g., Abraham, Jacob, David, and Solomon) practiced polygamy. Since

*Thus, Jesus' Judean disciples taught: "Unless you are circumcised according to the custom of Moses, you cannot be saved" (Acts 15:2).
†See also Romans 4:9–12, Galatians 2:3, and most significantly Galatians 5:2, 6: "Listen! I, Paul, am telling you that if you let yourselves be circumcised, Christ will be of no benefit to you. . . . For, in Christ Jesus neither circumcision nor uncircumcision counts for anything. . . ."

polygamy was permitted throughout the ancient Near East, this should come as no surprise. What is significant, however, is that biblical *narrative*, in opposition to biblical *law*, depicts multiple marriages as almost always leading to multiple miseries.

Abraham takes a concubine-wife because of his wife Sarah's barrenness. Indeed, it is at Sarah's insistence that he takes her servant Hagar as a wife, for, as Sarah tells him: "Perhaps I shall have a son through her" (Genesis 16:2). When Hagar becomes pregnant, she starts treating Sarah with contempt. Sarah blames Abraham for Hagar's arrogance and Abraham, wishing to avoid marital conflict, tells his wife to treat Hagar as she wishes. Sarah treats Hagar harshly, impelling her to flee. Later, Hagar returns and provides Abraham with his first child, a boy named Ishmael.

Sarah's wish that "I shall have a son through her" is not fulfilled; there is no mention of any relationship, let alone maternal feelings, between Sarah and Ishmael. Some years later, Sarah finally gives birth to her own son, whereupon she forces Abraham to expel Hagar and Ishmael. Sarah speaks of Hagar in the most contemptuous of tones: "Cast out that slave-woman and her son, for the son of that slave shall not share in the inheritance with my son Isaac" (Genesis 21:10; see entry 11).

Abraham's grandson Jacob might well have preferred to be a monogamist, for he was passionately in love with his cousin Rachel. Yet he was tricked into taking more than one wife, and the miseries generated in this polygamous household ultimately led to his descendants' exile and enslavement in Egypt.

As a young man, Jacob falls in love with Rachel and arranges with his uncle Laban to marry her. But Laban, not willing to permit Rachel to marry before her older sister, Leah, substitutes a heavily veiled Leah during the marriage ceremony. The deception works; it does not seem, though, that Laban did Leah any favor. Jacob insists on marrying Rachel as well (later biblical law forbade a man from being married to two sisters simultaneously or successively unless one sister had died; Leviticus 18:18), and "he loved Rachel more than Leah" (Genesis 29:30). This likely is an understatement, since the next verse tells us that Leah was "unloved."

However, as if through divine compensation, Leah gives birth to many children, while Rachel remains barren for many years. When she finally gives birth to Joseph, he becomes Jacob's beloved son, preferred over those borne by Leah (and by Rachel's and Leah's maidservants, whom he has also taken as concubine/wives). Jacob's undisguised favoritism for Rachel, and then for Joseph, is the original reason for the other brothers' hatred for Joseph, which causes them to sell him into Egyptian slavery. The origins of this enmity once again lie in polygamy.

While there is little that any law can do to protect an unloved wife, biblical legislation does protect her offspring: "If a man has two wives, one loved and the other unloved, and both the loved and unloved have borne him sons, but the first-born is the son of the unloved one, [then], when he wills his property to his sons, he may not treat as first-born [firstborn sons were given a larger percentage of the inheritance] the son of the loved one in disregard of the son of the unloved one who is older . . . the birthright is his due" (Deuteronomy 21:15–17).

In the post-Torah age, polygamy continues to generate many of the Bible's most famous family tragedies. We are never told how many wives the judge Gideon took, but they are enough to produce seventy sons. He also has a concubine, through whom he has yet another child, Abimelech. Gideon does not seem to have established fraternal love among his offspring. After his death, Abimelech murders sixty-nine of his brothers; the youngest, Jotham, escapes (Judges 8:30–31; 9:5).

The Bible also tells us about Elkanah, a man who has two wives; Hannah is barren, while Peninah is quite fertile. Their house is not a happy one; her "rival"—as the Bible labels Peninah—taunts Hannah with the claim that "the Lord had closed her womb." Peninah's cruelty is likely motivated by feelings of being unloved; the text tells us that Hannah is Elkanah's "favorite." Hannah, the beloved wife, is also miserable; Peninah's taunting causes her to weep and lose her appetite (I Samuel 1:4–7).

The Bible tells us the names of eight of David's wives, and this does not include an additional eleven concubines (I Samuel 18:27; 25:42–43; II Samuel 3:2–5; 11:27; 15:16). The usual pattern of fraternal hatred prevails among the numerous offspring. David's third son, Absalom, kills his oldest brother, Amnon, and subsequently launches a revolt against his father. The fourth son, Adonijah, tries to launch a coup while David is still alive in order to prevent Solomon, a younger half brother, from becoming king (see entry 84). When Solomon does ascend to the throne, he subsequently suspects Adonijah of still harboring royal aspirations, and has him executed (I Kings 2:24–25).

No biblical figure is credited with taking more wives than Solomon; he has seven hundred wives and three hundred concubines

(I Kings 11:3.* Although Torah law had never placed a formal limit on the number of wives a man was permitted, it had specifically warned concerning a king: "And he shall not have many wives, lest his heart go astray . . ." (Deuteronomy 17:17).

In his later years, Solomon's many wives turn his heart away from God; the best that can be said of the monarch is that he becomes equivocal in his monotheism (I Kings 11:4–5).

Are there *any* happy polygamous marriages described in the Bible? No, although sometimes we are given no information about a marriage, so we have no way of knowing whether or not it was happy (for example, see Lamech, the Bible's first polygamist [Genesis 4:19, 23]).

In those instances, however, where the text does supply details about a polygamous marriage, it either is miserable for at least one partner (Hagar and Leah), creates hatred between the children (Joseph and his brothers, David's sons), or wreaks havoc with the husband's character (Solomon).

There is yet one further indication that the Bible's preference is for "one man, one wife." When God creates the world, he populates it with only two people, one of each sex; He could have given Adam a second wife but doesn't. Furthermore, the Bible's very first reference to marriage presupposes a state of monogamy: "Therefore shall a man leave his father and mother and cling to his wife, so that they become one flesh" (Genesis 2:24).

Why, then, does the Bible permit polygamy?

The nature of biblical law generally is evolutionary rather than revolutionary (except when it comes to uprooting idolatry, with which the Bible refuses to brook any compromise). To have categorically outlawed multiple marriages in a world where they were widely practiced would most likely have led to an increase in adulterous affairs, or to affairs with unmarried women to whom the men would have no obligations. Better, therefore, for a man to have several wives, to each of whom he has legal obligations.

However, by depicting in considerable detail the misery generated within these marriages, biblical narrative makes it clear that it is far better for a man to have only one wife. As we shall see in other

---

*Many of the marriages were intermarriages, undertaken to secure good relations with the nations from which these women came. However, the text does emphasize that Solomon loved many of these foreign wives (I Kings 11:2).

instances (e.g., the laws favoring the firstborn son versus the narratives favoring the younger sons; see entry 201), biblical narrative ultimately influences Jewish life more than biblical law. The Talmud, compiled during the early centuries of the Common Era, lists well over one thousand rabbis. We know of none who practiced polygamy. During the tenth century, a rabbinic ban was issued outlawing polygamy for all Jews living in Europe. There is little question that the rabbis felt their act was in consonance with the Bible's ethical spirit. This ban, uniformly accepted in Jewish life today, represents perhaps the most dramatic victory of biblical narrative over biblical law.

XXII. EXODUS

153. Fear of God

EXODUS 1:17; LEVITICUS 19:14, 32; 25:36, 43; DEUTERONOMY 6:13; 10:20

The commandment to love God may occasionally be difficult to fulfill, but it is among the Bible's least controversial laws. The admonition to *fear* God, on the other hand, antagonizes many people, bringing to mind primitive images of religion, accompanied by threats of punishment and damnation.

In fact, fear of God in the Torah is intended to achieve two effects:

—to prevent people from fearing human beings more than God;

—to promote ethical and compassionate treatment of society's weakest members.

The Bible understands fear of God to be liberating. Exodus 1:15 records the Egyptian pharaoh's decree to murder all male Hebrew infants at birth by ordering attending midwives to kill them. The two leading midwives, Shifra and Puah, thwart Pharaoh's plan by allowing the babies to live.

What motivates these women to risk their lives by disobeying a royal decree? The Bible writes: "The midwives, *fearing God*, did not do as the king of Egypt had told them; they let the boys live" (Exodus 1:17).

The frustrated pharaoh then commands all the Egyptian people to participate in his murderous plan. Unlike the midwives, who are more in awe of God than of Pharaoh, the rest of the Egyptians fear Pharaoh more than God and follow his orders.

The liberating effect of fear of God has often been manifested in twentieth-century totalitarian societies (both Nazi and Communist), in which a disproportionate percentage of political dissenters have been God-fearers. People who don't believe in or fear God are far less likely to risk their lives—the most valuable possession they have—to defy the regime and help others. In contrast, true fearers of God, such as the midwives, recognize that obedience to God's will is more important than anything, including life.

Fear of God also motivates ethical treatment of the vulnerable, the very people whom one would otherwise have no reason to fear. Thus, Leviticus 19:14 ordains: "Don't put a stumbling block in front of a blind man, but you shall fear God."

Most people, even those with sadistic inclinations, would be cautious about tripping a person who can see. Knowing who hurt him or her, the victim might exact vengeance or summon a stronger relative or friend to do so. Harming a blind person, however, would seem to be risk-free, since the victim would have no way of knowing the perpetrator's identity. Hence, the Bible's appeal, "but you shall fear God." God will always know who performed the malicious act, and He might well choose to exact vengeance. As in protecting the blind, the words "but you shall fear God" are added on several other occasions to verses that mandate the just treatment of vulnerable people:

"You shall honor the old *and you shall fear God*" (Leviticus 19:32).

"Take no interest [from one who has become impoverished] *but you shall fear God*" (Leviticus 25:36).

"You shall not rule over [your servant] ruthlessly, *but you shall fear God*" (Leviticus 25:43).

One major lesson the twentieth century teaches us is that one should particularly fear those who fear not God. A common characteristic of this century's three most murderous leaders—Hitler, Stalin, and Mao—has been contempt for the notion of a God who punishes evil behavior. Few people are more dangerous than those who combine passionate hatreds with a lack of belief in a God whose primary demand of human beings is ethical behavior.*

*Regarding another twentieth-century tyrant, the Ayatollah Khomeini of Iran, who *did* believe in, and presumably feared, God, the problem was that he apparently did not believe in a God who judged people by ethical standards. Indeed, to Khomeini, a person's ethics seem to have been irrelevant, a fact that enabled him to murder without compunction highly ethical members of the Baha'i religion, a faith that Khomeini and other Muslim fundamentalists viewed as a heresy against Islam. Although the Bible was unrelentingly negative against faiths it called idolatrous, it almost always

154. God Hardens Pharaoh's Heart: Does the Bible Believe in Free Will?

EXODUS 4:21, AND THROUGHOUT THE STORY OF THE TEN PLAGUES

Throughout the account of the Ten Plagues, the Bible repeatedly reiterates that God "hardens" and/or "strengthens" Pharaoh's heart so that he refuses to let the Israelite slaves leave, thereby giving God an excuse to keep punishing him and the Egyptians. Not surprisingly, the biblical admission that it is God who hardens Pharaoh's heart strikes many readers as unfair. Why punish Pharaoh for refusing to release the Israelite slaves, when it is God who stops him from doing so?

Criticized though God may be for denying Pharaoh free will, few readers realize that had God *not* hardened Pharaoh's heart, the Egyptian monarch also would have been denied free will. Thus, had God permitted Pharaoh to respond naturally to the Ten Plagues, Pharaoh would likely have released the Hebrews as soon as the Nile turned to blood, and certainly when Egypt became overrun with frogs. But it is naive to claim that such a liberation would have resulted from a free-will decision on the Egyptian monarch's part; it's like saying that a man who signed a contract with a gun pointed to his head made a free-will decision to sign the contract.

Clearly, God felt that Pharaoh and the Egyptian people deserved to suffer for the centuries of slavery they had imposed on the Israelites. To have allowed the Egyptians to free the Israelites after one or two plagues would have constituted insufficient punishment. Thus, God strengthened Pharaoh's heart, making him fearless before physical perils that would terrify anyone else. However, there is no evidence that Pharaoh was denied the opportunity of acknowledging the evil that he had done, and freeing the Israelites—*not out of terror*—but out of recognition of the sin that he and his people had committed against them. Such recognition Pharaoh refused to make.

---

emphasized the *immorality* that resulted from idolatry (e.g., child sacrifice), rather than its heretical nature.

155. The Ten Commandments: An Introduction

EXODUS 20:1–14; DEUTERONOMY 5:6–18

The Ten Commandments, the most famous document in the Hebrew Bible, is generally regarded, along with monotheism, as the Bible's most important contribution to Western civilization. Yet, over the course of many years, during which I have given numerous lectures dealing with the Ten Commandments, I have often asked audiences how many of them can name all ten. Rarely do more than fifteen percent raise their hands, although a majority claim they can name at least five.

When I ask people to start enumerating the commandments, I find that many people err; for example, people often believe that "Love your neighbor as yourself" is one of the Ten Commandments. It isn't. On the other hand, relatively few recall that two of the commandments relate to speech; the Third, which prohibits carrying God's name in vain, and the Ninth, which outlaws perjury.

Here then are the Ten Commandments:

1. I am the Lord your God.
2. You shall worship no other gods besides Me.
3. You shall not carry God's name in vain.
4. Remember the Sabbath day to make it holy.
5. Honor your father and mother.
6. You shall not murder.
7. You shall not commit adultery.
8. You shall not steal.
9. You shall not bear false witness against your neighbor.
10. You shall not covet your neighbor's house: you shall not covet your neighbor's wife . . . or anything that is your neighbor's.

The lack of a clear directive in the First Commandment (most Jewish sources regard it as an adjuration to believe in God; see next entry) is responsible for the different enumerations that the Ten Commandments have been assigned. The one here is the Jewish listing, but the Roman Catholic Church considers that Commandments 1 and 2 are together the First Commandment ("I am the Lord your God," and "You shall worship no other gods besides Me") and divides the Tenth Commandment in two: Commandment 9 is "You shall not covet your neighbor's house," and 10 is "You shall not covet your neighbor's wife."

Why is it, many Bible students have wondered, that the first two commandments are formulated in the first person ("*I* am the Lord . . .), while the remaining eight are given in the second person (the Third Commandment does not read, "Do not carry *My* name in vain," but rather speaks of "*God's* name"). The Bible itself provides no answer, but the rabbinic explanation is that God Himself announced the first two commandments to the Israelites gathered around Mount Sinai. However, the people were petrified at being addressed directly by God, and beseeched Moses to serve as the intermediary between them and God; hence, the last eight commandments are announced by Moses.*

The Bible teaches that Moses wrote the Ten Commandments on two tablets. Over the centuries, this division has evoked many creative and insightful commentaries on the contents of each tablet.

Traditional Jewish teachings distinguish the tablets as follows: Part 1 consists of laws regulating relationships between people and God,

---

*A striking feature of the Ten Commandments is the lack of judicial penalties associated with their violation. True, God promises to personally punish violators of Commandments 2 and 3 (see entry 157), but this itself is distinctive from most biblical legislation, the violation of which is followed by a judicial punishment (for example, murderers are to be executed, and thieves ordered to pay a hundred percent fine). Bible scholar Moshe Weinfeld argues that the Ten Commandments had a more elevated purpose than merely designating the permitted, the forbidden, and the obligatory: "These commandments are . . . rather a formulation of condition for membership in the community. Anyone who does not observe these commandments excludes himself from the community of the faithful. . . . The definition of laws and punishments is given in various legal codes, but this is not the concern of the Decalogue, which simply sets forth God's demands of His people." From this perspective, then, the Ten Commandments are more like the Declaration of Independence, in which listing a punishment for anyone who refuses to accept the principle that "all men are created equal" would be inappropriate; the rest of the Torah's legislation, however, is more similar to that of the Constitution.

part 2 legislates between people. The Fifth Commandment, mandating honor of parents, is regarded as the link between the two parts; parents are human beings, but they are to be treated with a greater respect than other people; because of parents' role in creating us, the respect we owe them is in some ways akin to the respect accorded God.

Contemporary Bible scholar Nehama Leibowitz offers a provocative analysis of the progression of the laws. Building from the observation that people generally associate worship of God with internal feelings and beliefs, Leibowitz notes that this is precisely what the first two commandments are concerned with (belief in God and nonbelief in idols). The Third Commandment is more active in tone, addressing the faculty of speech (not to carry God's name in vain), and the Fourth Commandment expresses itself in terms of action (observing the Sabbath). Thus, although religious truths are initially expressed through thought, the goal is to actualize them in deed.

When it comes to ethics, the tendency is to assume that all that matters is right behavior. Commandments 5 through 8, therefore, mandate ethical deeds (honor of parents, and prohibitions against murder, adultery, and stealing). The Ninth Commandment outlaws an act of speech (perjury), while the Tenth Commandment addresses a forbidden emotion, coveting a neighbor's property or spouse. In other words, the last six commandments start by dealing with actions, but make it clear that the goal of transforming people's external behavior is ultimately to transform their inner selves.

Sources and further readings: Nehama Leibowitz's analysis of the progression of the Ten Commandments is found in her *Studies in Shemot: The Book of Exodus,* Vol. 1, page 343. Her analyses of Commandments 1, 2, 3, 9, and 10 appear on pages 303–351; a compilation of rabbinic commentaries on the Ten Commandments is contained in Dr. Menachem M. Kasher's *Encyclopedia of Biblical Interpretation: Exodus:* Vol. 9; Moshe Weinfeld's point about the lack of designated punishments is found in his commentary, *Deuteronomy 1–11,* page 248. His extensive discussion of the Ten Commandments is found on pages 242–327.

156. The First Commandment: Monotheism

"I Am the Lord Your God Who Brought You Out of the Land of Egypt, Out of the House of Bondage"

EXODUS 20:2

A well-known talmudic tradition records that the Torah contains 613 commandments (Babylonian Talmud, *Makkot* 23b–24a; a listing of those commandments is found in Part III of this book). Yet it's not always clear which verses are commandments. Thus, if a group were to sit down and read the Torah straight through, each person trying to compile a list of *the* 613 commandments, all the lists would be largely similar but not identical.

For example, is there a commandment to believe in God?

Maimonides, the foremost medieval philosopher and codifier of Jewish law, considers the commandment to believe in God as preeminent among the 613; preeminent because all the other commandments derive from God and would not exist without Him. Because there is no verse stating explicitly, "You are commanded to believe in God," Maimonides bases this obligation on the Ten Commandments' first verse: "I am the Lord your God who brought you out of the land of Egypt, out of the house of bondage." According to Maimonides, this verse constitutes the First Commandment; implicit in it is a command to believe that there is One God.

As Maimonides writes in his *Book of the Commandments,* commandment 1, "The first commandment is that He commanded us to believe in the Deity, that is, that we believe that there is a cause and a motive force behind all existing things. This idea is expressed in the statement 'I am the Lord your God.'"

Two other medieval philosophers, Hasdai ibn Crescas and Don Isaac Abravanel, argue that there can be no such commandment, for if you believe in God, it is because you believe in Him, not because you are commanded to do so. And if you don't believe in God, then *who* is commanding you?

Ibn Crescas's and Abravanel's argument seems more rationally compelling than that of Maimonides. Also, a linguistic reason exists for asserting that there is no commandment to believe in God. The Hebrew word for commandment, *mitzvah*, has the plural *mitzvot*. Thus, the Ten Commandments should be called in Hebrew *Aseret ha-Mitzvot*, but are not. Rather, they are called *Aseret ha-Dibrot*, the "Ten Statements," the reason being that the verses open with a statement, followed by nine commandments. If one accepts this explanation, then the opening verse is not intended to command belief in God, but to establish what God has done for the Israelites, and His right therefore to issue commands to them: "Because I was the one who liberated you from slavery, I therefore have the right to command you to honor your parents, observe the Sabbath, not murder, etc."

Still, most Jewish scholars side with Maimonides, and regard the Ten Commandments' first verse as prescribing belief in God.

The deity in whom the Jews are told to believe is markedly different from Aristotle's "Unmoved Mover," a god who does not act although its existence causes other actions to take place. The Bible's God, in contrast, intervenes in history; thus, the First Commandment emphasizes God's role in freeing the Jews from Egypt.

The Bible also reveals to humankind a universal God. People in the ancient world usually believed in local deities, who supposedly ruled over the society in which they were worshiped. If someone moved elsewhere, he was expected to pray to the gods of the community into which he had moved. But the Torah's God rules everywhere; indeed, the opening chapter of Genesis portrays Him as creating the world.

The God of the Hebrew Bible has two significant traits. He is One, and His primary demand of people is ethical behavior. When the later prophets summarize what God wants of humankind, they invariably place primary emphasis on moral behavior. For example, one of the earliest of the literary prophets, Micah (eighth century B.C.E.), states:

> He [i.e., God] has told you, O man, what
> is good, and what the Lord requires of you:
> Only to do justice,
> to love goodness,
> and to walk modestly with your God (6:8).

Jeremiah, in the sixth century B.C.E., likewise presumes God's obsession with the ethical: "For I the Lord act with kindness, justice, and equity in the world; for in these I delight" (9:23).

Judaism's greatest sages believed that the Torah command to "love your neighbor as yourself" (Leviticus 19:18) constituted, alongside affirmation of God, "the major principle of the Torah" (Palestinian Talmud, *Nedarim* 9:4).

These two ideas, that the world is ruled by One, Universal God, whose primary demand of human beings is ethical conduct, are together known as ethical monotheism, and comprise Judaism's major intellectual and spiritual contribution to the world.

Sources and further readings: Israeli Bible scholar Nehama Leibowitz presents a thorough analysis of the First Commandment in which she discusses at length the views of Maimonides, ibn Crescas, and Abravanel (see *Studies in Shemot: The Book of Exodus,* Vol. 1, pages 303–314). Regarding the verse's closing words, ". . . who brought you out of the land of Egypt, out of the house of bondage," Leibowitz summarizes an insight by Benno Jacob, a twentieth-century German-Jewish Bible scholar: The land of Egypt was the center of ancient culture, famed for its pyramids, art, and wise men. But for the Israelites it was nothing more than "the house of bondage." According to Jacob's interpretation, those words are intended to convey that "if a land of culture has no room for freedom, then the servant of God renounces [such] culture."

Thus, the reason the Torah places such emphasis on Egypt being a "house of bondage" is because later generations are apt to look back on such ancient Egyptian accomplishments as the building of the pyramids without taking into account the moral price paid for those accomplishments: the thousands of slaves who were worked to death in erecting those architectural marvels. This verse reminds us that Egypt's massive artistic achievements were built on human slavery and misery.

157. The Second Commandment: Against Idolatry

EXODUS 20:3–6

"You Shall Have No Other Gods Beside Me"

EXODUS 20:3

The Second Commandment states that it is not sufficient to affirm the One God of the Torah; one must also repudiate the other, idolatrous, gods. "You shall not bow down to them or serve them," the Torah commands (20:5); it likewise forbids making sculptures or images that could be worshiped.

God promises to punish those who violate this command: "For I the Lord your God am an impassioned God, visiting the guilt of the fathers upon the children, upon the third and fourth generation of those who reject Me" (20:5). This verse has long offended many people's sense of justice; indeed, it apparently flies in the face of a later biblical commandment: "Fathers shall not be put to death for sins of sons, nor sons for sins of their fathers" (Deuteronomy 24:16). Does God permit Himself a standard of behavior that He specifically forbids to human beings?

Jewish tradition has long understood "visiting the guilt of the fathers upon the children" as meaning that God will punish only those who *persist* in committing the same evils as did their parents and other ancestors. Thus, the Book of Numbers (chapter 16) tells the story of Korah, a first cousin of Moses and Aaron (Exodus 6:21), who leads a rebellion against their leadership. God intervenes, and has the land open up and swallow Korah and his followers—but not those members of his family who did not participate in the revolt. I Chronicles 6:18–22 records that Samuel, whom Jewish tradition regards as second only to Moses in prophetic stature, was a direct descendant of Korah.

If the correct meaning of the verse is that God does not punish righteous children for their parents' evil acts, an ethical dilemma still remains: Is God just in intensifying the punishment inflicted on evil children because of what their parents did? On one level, this seems unfair; after all, evil people's children are reared in an environment that is more likely to lead them to evil behavior. The Bible seems to feel that rather than serving as an excuse, their parents' evil behavior should shock the children and cause them to turn to good. Angry as most Jews might be when they encounter an antisemite, most will be even more enraged if they learn that the antisemite is German and a descendant of an S.S. officer. As one whose ancestors helped murder six million Jews, such a German who continues to affirm his ancestors' evil behavior would be regarded by most people and, as this verse makes clear, by God Himself, as more worthy of punishment.

Far less frequently cited is the verse that follows the one just cited, which states that God's love is hundreds of times stronger than His wrath: "[But I will show] kindness to the thousandth generation of those who love Me and keep My commandments" (20:6). This divine affirmation is the basis for many Jewish prayers, in which worshipers affirm their descent from Abraham, Isaac, and Jacob, hoping thereby to remind God of their ancestral merit.

Reflections: Given that idol worship is no longer practiced, does the Second Commandment have any contemporary applicability?

From Judaism's perspective, idolatry occurs when one holds any value (for instance, nationalism) higher than God. Thus, a person who, on the basis of "my country right or wrong," performs acts that God designates as wrong is an idolater; his behavior makes it clear that he regards his country's demand to do evil as more binding than God's demand to do good. Such a person's claim to worship God—an assertion that was actually made by some S.S. officers who worked in concentration camps—is plainly false; the person is an idolater, not a follower of God.

158. The Third Commandment:
"You Shall Not Carry the Name of the Lord
Your God in Vain"

EXODUS 20:7

This verse is often translated as "You shall not take God's name in vain." As a child, I was taught that this meant that it was forbidden to use the Lord's name in a curse (saying "Goddamn"); also, that God's name should not be pronounced except in the context of prayer. Thus, instead of saying "Adonai," observant Jews are taught to say "Adoshem" in nonliturgical settings.

Some people believe that the Third Commandment refers as well to the writing of God's name. Many religious Jews will not spell out God's name even in English; instead they write G-d (perhaps out of concern that the paper on which God's name is written will be thrown out).

The verse's second half adds that "the Lord will not clear one who carries His name in vain." No such severe admonition is added to the other commandments, including those prohibiting murder, thievery, and adultery. Even as a child, I felt it strange that God should express such strong negative feelings only toward those who violated this particular commandment. Why such anger at a human being using His actual name, even if it is unnecessary?

When the Hebrew is translated literally, as has been done here (a translation I first heard from Dennis Prager), the commandment yields the meaning: "You shall not carry the name of the Lord your God in vain." What is forbidden, therefore, is something altogether different from that implied by the commandment's usual translation.

People often "carry" and cite God's name when they promote a cause. If the cause they promote is just and righteous (for example, Martin Luther King's battle against racial injustice), then they are "carrying" God's name in truth, and are to be commended. But if they "carry" God's name in promotion of a cause that is evil (e.g., the medieval crusaders who murdered innocent people in the name of God, or members of racist organizations such as the Ku Klux Klan that claim that what they do is God's will), then they violate the Third Commandment.

It now becomes clear why God expresses such hostility to anyone who violates this law, for this is *the* one commandment the abrogation of which causes God to suffer. If a person acts in a disreputable manner, that individual brings him- or herself alone into disrepute. But if one acts in a disreputable manner while claiming to be acting in the name of God, such a person alienates people not only from himself, but from God as well. Which is why God, the victim of this transgression, promises personally to punish its violator.

Reflections: Alienating people from God is one of the few sins for which it is impossible to repent fully, since there is no way one can know all the people whom one has affected. Therefore, extreme caution must be exercised before performing any act, particularly a controversial or questionable one, in the name of God.

159. The Fourth Commandment

EXODUS 20:8–11

"Remember the Sabbath Day to Make It Holy"

EXODUS 20:8

Ask most people to give the rationale for the Fourth Commandment, and you will be told that the Bible instituted the Sabbath to provide human beings with a day of rest. From this perspective, the truly important days are the six productive weekdays ("Six days a week shall you labor"); the Sabbath, however, is merely a day off, whose goal is to help people renew their strength so that they can function more effectively on the other six days.

However, the Ten Commandments' rationale for the Sabbath is to make one day a week holy, not promote rest. As Rabbi Saul Berman has said, "There is more to Shabbat than not working just as there is more to peace than not fighting." Therefore, the Sabbath is clearly not an adjunct to the six weekdays, but is in some respects far more important than they are. Indeed, in the creation story, the seventh day is the only day that God sanctifies (Genesis 2:3).

The Sabbath is one of the Bible's revolutionary innovations. We know of no society prior to the Torah that mandated a day on which human beings were to refrain from their normal labor. Indeed, ancient societies tended to regard people as worthwhile only while they were working. Leading Roman thinkers ridiculed the Sabbath, citing it as proof of Jewish laziness. Seneca, the first-century Roman Stoic, wrote, "To spend every seventh day without doing anything means to lose a seventh part of life, besides suffering loss in pressing matters from such idleness." (The less courteous Plutarch regarded the Sabbath as one of the Jews' "sordid habits," while the antisemitic Tacitus saw it as another of the Jews' "sinister and shameful" customs.) In the ancient world, the Bible's struggle to establish the principle that human beings have value even when not producing was a difficult one.

The Sabbath commandment also applied to slaves, and even to animals: "Six days shall you labor and do all your work. But the seventh day is a sabbath of the Lord your God; you shall not do any work, you, your son or daughter, your male or female slave, or your cattle, or the stranger who is within your settlement" (20:9–10).

In the United States, as recently as the late 1800s, workers in the steel mills of Homestead, Pennsylvania, were expected to work twelve hours a day, seven days a week, 363 days a year (they were off on Christmas and July 4). Over three thousand years ago, the Ten Commandments forbade treating animals in the manner that workers were permitted to be treated just a century ago.

The Ten Commandments offer two rationales for why the seventh day is to be special. "For in six days, the Lord made heaven and earth and sea, and all that is in them, and He rested on the seventh day; therefore, the Lord blessed the sabbath day and hallowed it" (20:11). Thus, the Sabbath is intended to remind us that God created the world; we refrain from creativity and labor on that day as God did.

A second version of the Ten Commandments appears in Deuteronomy. Although the legal content is identical to the Exodus version, some commandments are worded differently. In reference to the Sabbath, Moses speaks not of God's creation of the world, but of the day's ethical underpinnings: "so that your male and female slave may rest as you do. Remember that you were a slave in the land of Egypt and the Lord your God freed you from there with a mighty hand and outstretched arm; therefore, the Lord your God has commanded you to observe the sabbath day" (Deuteronomy 5:14–15).

Throughout history, slaves were generally required to work seven days a week. The Bible finds this morally unacceptable, for it reduces life to only labor. A person who observes the Sabbath never works more than six days consecutively, while a slave may go for hundreds or thousands of days without an opportunity to rest and renew him- or herself (see Exodus 23:12).

Although the Sabbath's importance is suggested by its being the only ritual law in the Ten Commandments, there is little specific Sabbath legislation in the Bible. Exodus 34:21 emphasizes the inviolable nature of the Sabbath prohibition of work: "You shall cease from labor even at plowing time and harvest time," even though farmers often feel compelled to work seven days a week during this season.

During their forty years of wandering, the Israelites daily gathered manna, the food God dispensed during their sojourn in the desert. Exodus 16:5ff. explains that every Friday, God provided the people a double portion, so that they would not have to gather it on the Sabbath; the implication being that one should not do such work on the Sabbath.

Exodus 35:3 forbids kindling fire on the Sabbath. Exodus 16:29, if taken literally, decrees that everyone should stay at home on the Sabbath: "Let everyone remain where he is; let no man leave his place on the Sabbath." Rabbinic Judaism never took this provision literally; indeed, the very next verse suggests a more symbolic interpretation: "So the people remained inactive on the seventh day" (Exodus 16:30). Therefore, verse 29 is understood as meaning not that people have to remain in their houses on the Sabbath but that they should not take a trip outside the city limits.

The Torah itself makes no reference to buying and selling on the Sabbath, although the prophet Nehemiah (13:15–22) speaks of commercial activities being forbidden on that day.

In a burst of messianic enthusiasm, Isaiah tells of the end of days when "sabbath after sabbath, all flesh shall come to worship Me, said the Lord" (66:23).

To this day, a commitment to Sabbath observance (though levels of observance differ) characterizes all Jewish religious denominations: How could it not, given its central role in the Ten Com-

mandments? Indeed, no Jewish community has survived more than
a few generations without observance of the Sabbath. As Ahad
Ha'am, the early Zionist philosopher, taught, "More than Israel has
kept the Sabbath, the Sabbath has kept Israel."

160. The Fifth Commandment:
"Honor Your Father and Your Mother"

EXODUS 20:12

When I was growing up, I took it for granted that a religion would
emphasize the parent-child relationship in its first legal document.
Religions, after all, have long served as society's main family-support
system. Only much later did I come to realize how unusual it is for
a religion to emphasize children's devotion to parents in its first legal
document. New religions usually want to alienate children from parents. When one thinks of cults, one of the first associations is the
attempt to drive a wedge between parents and children. Christianity,
ever since it became an established religion, has always been extremely supportive of the family. Nevertheless, in its first generation,
as reflected in the teachings the gospels attribute to Jesus, one finds
considerable ambivalence toward the family. In Luke 14:26, Jesus
says, "No one can come to me without hating his own father,
mother, sister and brother," while in Matthew 8:22, he advises a
young man to forgo attending his father's funeral, and to follow him
instead.

The Ten Commandments' emphasis on honoring one's parents is,
therefore, striking.

A parallel to the Fifth Commandment is found in Leviticus 19:3:
"Let each man have awe [alternatively, fear] of his mother and father."

There has been considerable discussion among Jewish biblical exegetes about why the father comes first in the Fifth Commandment
("Honor your father and mother"), while the mother comes first in
that concerning awe. The general consensus is that the wording is
intended to safeguard the parent who is in the weaker position. Thus,

because children are more apt to feel awe or fear of their fathers, the Bible mentions the mother first. When it comes to honor, children are more apt to show affection for their mothers (as I once heard someone say, when was the last time you heard a star athlete being interviewed after a game sending love to his dad?); therefore, the father is mentioned first.

Yet the Bible does not command one to love one's parents. The reason cannot be that the Bible believes it is inappropriate to command love. After all, other verses command people to love God (Deuteronomy 6:5), their neighbors (Leviticus 19:18), and the stranger (Leviticus 19:34). Love of parents is not commanded either because it is subsumed under love of neighbor or because, in so intimate a relationship, it is pointless to command love. Either the child feels love or he or she doesn't.

But whereas a child who loves his or her mother and father will probably honor and revere that parent in any case, this law is intended to give guidelines to children who are not feeling loving toward their parents. Even so, the Fifth Commandment emphasizes that certain minimum standards of behavior apply: Children are obligated to show honor and awe.

Punishments are threatened against those who violate the Second or Third commandment, but the Fifth Commandment promises a reward: "that you may long endure on the land which the Lord your God is giving you." The promised reward is not parallel in structure to the earlier threatened punishments, in which the violator is told that God will exact a punishment from him or possibly from his descendants. Here, the Israelites are *collectively* told that observance of this law will lead to their long sojourn on the land God has given them.

The implication is clear: A society in which children do not honor their parents will rapidly lose the means through which the society's culture, religion, and ethics can be transmitted, and thus will soon disintegrate.

Other biblical laws emphasize the need for children not to show their parents disrespect; for example, the Torah mandates that it is a capital offense to strike a parent (thereby inflicting a wound serious enough to draw blood) or curse them in the name of God (Exodus 21:15, 17; however, we have no indication that such a punishment was ever carried out).

Virtually every generation of parents seems to believe that children are showing parents less respect than they did. My mother, Helen Telushkin, used to bemoan the fact that she was part of the last generation in history that was expected to show respect to its parents; alas, she became a mother during the first generation in which children were no longer expected to treat their parents with respect.

In actuality, parent-child tensions are age old; given human nature, how could they not be? In a passage with a contemporary ring, Genesis notes that Esau married two women whom his parents thought inappropriate, "and they were a source of bitterness to Isaac and Rebecca" (26:35; strangely enough, one of the women had what subsequently became a quintessentially Jewish name, Judith, in Hebrew *Yehudit*).

A stronger indication of the long-standing nature of parent-child tensions is articulated by the prophet Malachi. Speaking of the future messianic days, he envisions God sending Elijah, whose miraculous task will be to "reconcile parents with children and children with their parents" (3:24). If parents and children were getting along as well as romanticizers of the past would have us believe, God would not have had to assign such a task to Elijah. The reconciliation's significance is suggested by the verse's end, in which God promises that if it does not occur, He will "strike the whole land with utter destruction."

In the Jewish tradition, honor for parents is reflected in the fact that they are the only relatives whose death prompts a full year of mourning; upon the deaths of a spouse, sibling, or child, the legal period designated for grief is only a month. Since the death of a spouse or of a child is more emotionally devastating for most adults than that of a parent, how does one explain this? One factor is gratitude. Children owe their lives to their parents, and not only in the sense of being born. As essayist and talk-show host Dennis Prager has noted, only because of their parents' constant, watchful concern do children grow up, one hopes, with all their limbs intact, or grow up at all. Just the day before I wrote these words, my two-year-old son slipped in a pool; his head was submerged in water when I plucked him out.

A second possible reason for the prolonged period of mourning for parents is that they are, by definition, singular; a child has only one mother and one father.

The Torah does not set down specific guidelines on what it means to show parents "honor" and "awe." In explicating the commands concerning parents, the Talmud comes up with the following: "Honor means that a child must give him [his father, here representative of both parents] food and drink, clothe and cover him, and lead him in and out [when the parents are old and need a helping hand].... Revere means that a child must neither stand nor sit in his [parents'] place, nor contradict his words, nor tip the scale against him [by siding with his parents' opponents in a dispute" (Babylonian Talmud, *Kiddushin* 31b). However, the Rabbis rule that a parent is permitted to forgo his or her honor, and permit a child to dispute with the parent and to contradict his or her words.

A close-knit family structure, which has characterized the Jewish community throughout its history, reflects the significance Jews have long attached to the Fifth Commandment.

161. The Sixth Commandment: "You Shall Not Murder"

EXODUS 20:13

The King James version, along with many other English renditions of the Bible, translates this verse as "You shall not kill." However, Hebrew has a word for kill, *haroq*, and this is not the term used in the Sixth Commandment. Instead, the Bible uses *ratzakh*, "to murder" (the commandment itself reads *Lo tirtzakh*). This distinction is by no means pedantic. If the commandment had read, "You shall not kill," it would have suggested that all killing is illegal, including that in self-defense. Indeed, certain religious groups such as the Jehovah's Witnesses take this position, and insist that their members refuse army service (during World War II, in Germany Jehovah's Witnesses refused to fight for the Nazis while their American coreligionists refused to fight against them).

Reading the Hebrew Bible in its entirety reveals that the verse could not possibly mean "you shall not kill." For one thing, the Torah legislates the permissibility of killing in self-defense. Exodus 22:1 rules that if a thief tunnels into a person's house at night, it can be assumed that he is prepared to kill the householder; therefore, if the householder kills the intruder, "there is no bloodguilt in his case" (on the other hand, if the householder has good reason to believe that the thief doesn't represent a mortal threat, he is forbidden to kill him; see Exodus 22:2).

The Bible also mandates that the ancient Israelites go to war to conquer the land of Canaan. In addition, each of the Torah's five books commands that anyone who has committed premeditated homicide must be executed (see entry 150).

What the Sixth Commandment does prohibit is *murder*, killing someone who has committed no offense for which he or she deserves to die. Clearly, most killings are also murders, since most people who are killed do not deserve to die. Yet the King James rendition of this commandment has, from the Jewish perspective, led to considerable moral confusion. For ten years, my friend Dennis Prager served as moderator of *Religion on the Line*, a Los Angeles–based radio program whose weekly panelists included a minister, priest, and rabbi. Prager often asked participating clergy whether they could respect a person who, for reasons of conscience, would have refused to kill Adolf Hitler *during* World War II. Almost without exception, Christian clergy, who have been raised to believe that the Sixth Commandment means "you shall not kill," responded that they could, although they acknowledged that not killing Hitler would have enabled him to continue murdering millions of innocent people. From the Hebrew Bible's perspective, stopping a killer, even at the cost of his life, is mandated by yet another biblical law: "Do not stand by while your brother's blood is shed" (Leviticus 19:16; see entry 179). A person who can stop a killer, and doesn't, therefore bears some moral responsibility for the killer's future victims.

162. The Seventh Commandment: "You Shall Not Commit Adultery"

EXODUS 20:13

The Bible's definition of adultery is not the same as that used in contemporary society. According to biblical law, whether or not adultery has occurred depends exclusively on the woman's marital status. A married woman who has sexual relations with anyone other than her husband is regarded as having committed adultery, as is her lover. But an unmarried woman who has sex with a married man has not committed adultery, nor has her lover. Sexist as it may sound, biblical law permits men to have more than one wife; thus, having sex with a woman other than one's wife is not viewed—at least legally—as a betrayal of one's spouse. However, since a woman is forbidden to have more than one husband, sex with someone other than her spouse is always regarded as a betrayal.

In the ancient world, in which the biblical definition of adultery was similar to that of other societies, adultery was generally considered to be a crime against the husband alone. He thus had the right to either insist upon punishment for the adulterous couple, or to forgive them. In the biblical view, adultery is also regarded as a crime against God; therefore, it is not within the province of the cuckolded spouse to forgive the betrayal. According to rabbinic law, if a woman commits adultery, she is subsequently forbidden both to her husband and to her lover (on the other hand, David marries Bathsheba with whom he had an earlier adulterous relationship [see entry 82], and Hosea takes back a wife who has betrayed him [see entry 115]).

163. The Eighth Commandment: "You Shall Not Steal"

EXODUS 20:13

This commandment is straightforward: It is forbidden to take something belonging to another without permission.

Subsumed under the prohibition of stealing is kidnapping (rabbinic Judaism regards kidnapping as the act forbidden in this commandment, while ordinary stealing is forbidden by the other biblical verses cited in this entry). In the ancient world, this was generally done not for ransom but to sell the kidnapped person into slavery. The Bible regards it as a capital offense: "He who kidnaps a man—

whether he has sold him or is still holding him—shall be put to death" (Exodus 21:15).

Regarding other forms of stealing, the Bible generally mandates that a captured thief return double the value of what he has stolen (Exodus 22:3). If the thief lacks the means to do so, he is required to work off the payment in servitude, although no matter how valuable the objects stolen, the servitude is never to exceed six years. Harsh as forced labor might sound to contemporary ears, it guaranteed that the thief's victims at least would receive restitution for what was taken from them. This rarely happens today, when captured thieves are imprisoned and aren't even required as a condition of parole to make restitution.

The Torah, which was legislating for an agricultural society, imposes more severe punishment on someone who steals domestic animals: "When a man steals an ox or a sheep, and slaughters it or sells it, he shall pay five oxen for the ox and four sheep for the sheep" (Exodus 21:37).

The "Holiness" chapter of Leviticus (chapter 19), which reiterates the laws of the Ten Commandments, offers the following series of injunctions, to serve as an expansion upon the tersely worded Eighth Commandment: "You shall not steal; you shall not deal deceitfully or falsely with one another. . . . You shall not defraud your neighbor. You shall not commit robbery. . . ." (Leviticus 19:11, 13).

164. The Ninth Commandment: "You Shall Not Bear False Witness Against Your Neighbor"

EXODUS 20:13

Many of the Torah's laws concern the judiciary, reflecting an intuitive understanding that judicial immorality or inequity will quickly contaminate the rest of society. To cite one example, justices are strongly admonished to rule on the basis of equity alone, and neither to favor the rich nor pity the poor (Leviticus 19:15; pity and compassion for the poor are of course mandatory, but *only outside the courtroom*). In its specific prohibition of perjury, the Ninth Commandment addresses not only the judiciary but every Israelite. The Bible, it is true, contains a number of statements prohibiting lying; for example, "Keep yourself far away from falsehood" (Exodus 23:7), and "Do not deceive and do not lie to one another" (Leviticus 19:11). But biblical ethics never regarded all lying as forbidden (for example, God instructs the prophet Samuel to lie to King Saul rather than tell a truth that will prompt the king to attempt to kill him; I Samuel 16:1–3).

However, in the courtroom, where an individual has sworn in the name of God not to lie, all deviations from the truth are prohibited. The Bible sees this as so vital to societal functioning that it imposes a law without parallel in biblical legislation. Instead of designating a set punishment for perjury, Deuteronomy rules that the punishment depends on the damage the lying witnesses intended to inflict on the person against whom they were testifying: "And you shall do to them as they plotted to do" (Deuteronomy 19:19). Thus, if lying witnesses intended to win an award of one thousand dollars against a man, their punishment is to pay their intended victim a thousand dollars. On the other hand, if their testimony could have resulted in another person's execution, the witnesses themselves are executed. That perjuring witnesses should be punished with the evil they attempted to inflict on another seems so equitable that one wonders if secular society might not profit from adopting this bit of biblical legislation.

165. The Tenth Commandment: "You Shall Not Covet Your Neighbor's House: You Shall Not Covet Your Neighbor's Wife, or His Male or Female Slave, or His Ox or His Donkey, or Anything That Is Your Neighbor's"

EXODUS 20:14

The commandment against coveting, while not unique, is atypical of biblical legislation, which usually is directed against actions, not thoughts. However, coveting is understood as so dangerous a type of thought that it will lead inexorably to evil action.

Although one might assume that the ban on coveting would most likely be violated by the poor (after all, they have so much to covet), later biblical stories show this commandment as being violated by two kings; in both instances, coveting leads to far worse misdeeds.

The Second Book of Samuel, chapter 11, depicts King David desiring Bathsheba, Uriah's wife. He quickly progresses from coveting to adultery, summoning Bathsheba to the royal palace and sleeping with her. When she becomes pregnant, and David realizes that the scandal cannot be hushed up (see the discussion in entry 82), he arranges to have Uriah killed.

A century later, King Ahab covets a field adjacent to the royal estates that has belonged for many generations to the family of a man named Navot, who refuses the king's offer to buy it. (Israelite law seems to have protected a commoner's right to refuse such a royal offer.) Ahab returns to his palace deeply upset. His wife, the Baal-worshiping queen Jezebel, arranges to acquire the field for him. After she sends two men to testify falsely that Navot had spoken blasphemously and treasonously against God and the king, Navot is executed and his property is confiscated by the state (a common punishment inflicted on traitors). Jezebel then turns the land over to her husband.

What starts with a violation of the ban on coveting soon leads to the violation of the Ninth Commandment (prohibiting perjury), the Sixth (prohibiting murder), and the Eighth (prohibiting stealing).

How then can someone safeguard him- or herself from such a powerful temptation? By keeping two things in mind:

First, it is not wrong to want more than you have. What is wrong is to want it at your neighbor's expense. There's no evil in desiring a Jaguar, only in wanting the one belonging to the person next door. Anyone who sincerely tries to practice the command to "Love your neighbor as yourself," will feel uncomfortable coveting that which belongs to someone else.

Second, the medieval Bible commentator Abraham ibn Ezra offers advice on how to internalize the commandment. Writing in the thirteenth century, in the context of a feudal society, he notes that a common man will not covet the queen, who is so removed from him socially that it will never enter the man's head that he might take her away from the king. Ibn Ezra counsels that God has instructed us that our neighbor's wife is as forbidden to us as is the queen. Just as the common man will not spend hours fantasizing how he will win over the queen, so too must we not spend wasted hours imagining how we will win over our neighbor's spouse. That person is forbidden to us. End of issue.

166. Slavery in the Bible

SCATTERED REFERENCES IN EXODUS, CHAPTER 21, AND THROUGHOUT
THE TORAH

"If slavery is not wrong, nothing is wrong," declared American President Abraham Lincoln. Unfortunately, the Hebrew Bible, radical and uncompromising in its battle against idolatry, was evolutionary rather than revolutionary in its rulings regarding slavery. Thus, although the Book of Exodus is in large measure an antislavery polemic—the Egyptian people suffer ten horrific plagues as punishment for enslaving the Hebrews—the Bible did permit slavery in the society the Israelites established in Canaan.

To be sure, the biblical laws mandated a more humane form of slavery than that practiced in other contemporaneous societies. For example, a master who beat his slave to death was himself punished with death (Exodus 21:20ff.); this was a powerful statement of the belief that, *in God's eyes*, slaves are as important as masters. Unfortunately, the humanitarian thrust behind this law was largely undermined by the added provision that if the beaten slave did not die immediately, but lingered for two days or longer before succumbing, the master was not punished, "for he is his [master's] property." The reference to a human being as "property" is jarring.

The humanitarian inclination again comes to the fore in the ruling that a master who causes his slave to lose a limb, or even just a tooth, is obligated to free him (Exodus 21:26), a ruling that once more emphasizes the slave's humanity. But if a slave is gored to death by another man's ox, it is the slave's owner who receives the thirty-shekel fine (Exodus 21:32)—thirty shekels being the average price for a slave—which yet again emphasizes that the slave is property, more akin to animal than human being.

Perhaps the most unusually liberal law concerning slaves is found in Deuteronomy 23:16, which prohibits returning a runaway slave to his master, it being assumed that a slave fled his master because he suffered, and must therefore be granted refuge. It was of course this biblical law that Chief Justice Taney violated in the United States Supreme Court's infamous 1857 Dred Scott decision, in which Taney led the court in its ruling that a slave who had been taken to a free state could subsequently, and against his will, be returned to slavery. Taney's contempt for the Bible was likewise evident in his statement that "black people have no rights which a white man need to respect," a frank repudiation of the rights of a slave that the Bible enjoins masters to respect.

In the modern world, application of this deuteronomic law would encompass granting political asylum to refugees from totalitarian states, since many residents of such societies lead lives akin to slaves.

Concerning the Bible's overall attitude toward slavery, it should be emphasized that, although permitted, no law more powerfully indicates the Bible's fundamental opposition to slavery than the mandatory death sentence for anyone who kidnaps and sells a person into slavery (Exodus 21:16).

Biblical law distinguishes two forms of slavery, that of gentiles and that of Hebrews.

Gentile slaves were generally acquired through warfare, and were considered the property of whoever had spared their lives (Numbers

31:26; Deuteronomy 20:10–14). Non-Hebrew slaves also could be purchased (Exodus 12:44; Leviticus 22:11; 25:44–45). Furthermore, children born to gentile slaves became the property of the master; gentile slaves served in perpetuity, and could be passed on to one's descendants (Leviticus 25:44–46).

Male gentile slaves were circumcised, and the Sabbath and festival laws applied to both male and female slaves. Thus, the fourth of the Ten Commandments, which mandates the Sabbath, prohibits a master from employing a slave for work on the Sabbath (Exodus 20:10). I am not familiar with any other legal system that legislated a weekly rest day for slaves.

Hebrew slaves occupied a superior position to gentile slaves. Most important, they did not serve for life; the maximum period of enslavement was six years. A person could become a slave in several ways. If he committed a robbery, and lacked the means to return to his victim the stolen goods plus the hundred percent fine imposed on thieves, he could be sold into slavery to pay off his debt. In addition, if a person owed heavy debts, he could sell himself into slavery, and the money paid him could be used to discharge his obligations.

A Hebrew slave's master had the right to pair him off with a female gentile slave, and then keep any children they had as slaves. In a law that I, for one, find painful to read, the Torah rules that when a Hebrew slave's six years of slavery are up, "the wife and children shall belong to the master" and "he shall go out by himself" (Exodus 21:4). As they say in Yiddish, *"Oi vey."**

Several other provisions safeguarded the rights of a Hebrew slave. The master was forbidden to rule over him harshly (Leviticus 25:39; Deuteronomy 15:14). Furthermore, the slave had to be treated on a level of relative equality to his master. Basing its ruling on a biblical

---

*This provision seems so cruel that Rashi, the great medieval biblical exegete, argues that the Torah only permitted a master to pair off a Hebrew slave who was already married. Because the Torah did not wish a Hebrew to remain in slavery beyond six years, it assumed that a slave who had a family outside of slavery would immediately gravitate to that family when his term of service was complete. If, however, his slave family was his only family, then he would be inclined to want to remain a slave, which is why Rashi argues that it was forbidden to pair off an unmarried Hebrew slave. However, the wording of Exodus 21:5, "But if the slave shall say, 'I love my master, my wife and my children—I do not wish to go free,'" suggests that this family might well be his only family.

text, the Talmud says that if the master slept on a bed with pillows, the slave had to be given an equally comfortable bed (Babylonian Talmud, *Kiddushin* 20a). If the master had but one pillow, he had to give it to his slave. Indeed, laws protecting the Hebrew slave were so far-reaching that the Talmud later concluded that one who acquires a Hebrew slave has acquired a master (Babylonian Talmud, *Kiddushin* 20a).

Although slavery as practiced in the United States violated many of the Bible's norms (e.g., Southern law did not free a slave whose limb had been destroyed by a master, or whose tooth the master had knocked out; it did not punish the murder of a slave with death—in most instances, no punishment at all was rendered—and it violated the biblical ordinance granting freedom to runaway slaves), the fact that the Bible allowed it enabled many nineteenth-century clerical charlatans to argue that God approved of slavery as practiced in the United States.

It is important to note, however, that the abolitionists—whose reading of the Bible's intent was closer to the truth than that of their proslavery adversaries—were generally deeply religious students of the Bible.

There is one final biblical ruling which stands in the sharpest possible contrast to slavery as practiced in the United States. At the termination of the Hebrew slaves' six years of service, the Bible rules: "When you set him free, do not let him go empty-handed: Furnish him out of the flock, threshing floor, and vat with which the Lord has blessed you" (Deuteronomy 15:13–14).

167. A Husband's Obligations to His Wife

EXODUS 21:10

The Bible never describes a wedding ceremony (the Jewish marriage ceremony practiced today was formulated by the Rabbis of the Talmud), although it assumes that people will marry: "Therefore shall a man leave his father and mother and cling to his wife [the word for 'woman' and for 'wife' is the same in Hebrew] so that they become one flesh" (Genesis 2:24).

The Bible presumes that it is the man who proposes marriage, and therefore details—from the male's perspective—the obligations a man assumes upon marrying a woman. Written in the context of a society that permitted multiple wives and concubines, the Torah specifies three obligations of a husband to his wife: to provide her with proper clothing, sufficient food, and regular sexual relations (Exodus 21:10).

While the first two requirements should come as no surprise, most Bible readers are startled by the third. The concern with guaranteeing the wife's sexual relations is likely rooted in two considerations: First, it was assumed that women are generally shyer than men in expressing their sexual needs. It was possible, thus, for a sexually indifferent male to torment (consciously or not) a wife with prolonged periods of abstinence (talmudic law subsequently ruled that withholding sex from one's spouse out of anger for more than a few weeks was grounds for divorce). Second, the obligation of regular sexual relations protected less-favored wives in a society that permitted polygamy. If a man took a second, younger wife, this law made it impossible for him to ignore his older, and perhaps physically less attractive, spouse.

The Bible does not specify how often a man is commanded to have sexual relations with his wife, although later rabbinic law mandated a minimum of once a week for Torah scholars, preferably on Friday night, and more often for men whose work did not entail extensive travel and was regarded as less taxing than Torah study. In more recent years, the late rabbinic scholar Rabbi Moshe Feinstein suggested that, in such a society as the United States that is far more interested in sexual fulfillment, the minimum for Torah scholars should be raised to twice weekly.

168. The Bible on Kidnapping

EXODUS 21:16; LEVITICUS 25:42

Kidnapping, one of the most abhorrent crimes and every parent's nightmare, is generally carried out for ransom; the perpetrator holds the victim captive until a specified sum of money is paid. Often, to ensure that they cannot be traced, kidnappers murder the victim whether or not the ransom has been handed over. Bruno Hauptmann, America's most famous kidnapper, killed Charles Lindbergh's son almost immediately after stealing him, then went on to extract a $50,000 ransom from the devastated, still hopeful parents.

The Bible knows nothing of such motives for kidnapping. In ancient times, people kidnapped others with the expectation of selling their victims into slavery. Kidnappers so regularly acted with this purpose in mind that the Bible takes it for granted that this was the criminal's intention, even if the kidnapper when caught was still holding his victim: "He who kidnaps a man [any human being]—whether he has sold him or is still holding him—shall be put to death" (Exodus 21:16).

Nineteenth-century Southern, and some Northern, clergy often defended the enslavement of blacks in America on the grounds that the Bible permitted slavery. But given that the Hebrew Bible legislated that kidnapping a person and selling him into slavery was a capital crime, and given that slaves in America either had been kidnapped and sold into slavery or were descended from people who had suffered this fate, obviously the Bible could only have condemned slavery as practiced in the United States.

Because kidnapping is one of the most vile of crimes, the Bible deems it worthy of the harshest punishment.

169. "An Eye for an Eye": Vengeance or Justice?

EXODUS 21:24

It seems odd that "an eye for an eye," a basic principle of biblical justice, has become one of the Bible's most controversial verses, and is often cited by critics of "Old Testament" morality as an example of an inferior and barbaric standard of behavior.

In fact, "an eye for an eye" not only mandated punishing a person who maimed another, but also *limited* the retribution which could be inflicted. The verse meant that it was forbidden to take "two eyes for an eye," or for that matter inflict an injury on the offender's relative.* This might seem obvious, but in the ancient world in which the Torah was written, punishment was often imposed on the offender's near kin. The Babylonian Code of Hammurabi ruled that if a builder erected a house for a client, and it collapsed and killed the owner's daughter, the builder's daughter was to be executed (Law 229).† Because Babylonian society considered children as possessions of their parents, rather than as independent human beings, this ruling made sense: By building a faulty house, the builder caused damage to the owner's property (his daughter); in turn, he must be deprived of a comparably valuable piece of property.

Christian critics of "an eye for an eye" often contrast the Hebrew Bible's supposedly vengeful standard with the New Testament's forgiving statement attributed to Jesus: "You have learnt how it was said: 'An eye for an eye and a tooth for a tooth.' But I say this to you: offer the wicked man no resistance. On the contrary, if anyone hits you on the right cheek, offer him the other as well. If a man takes you to law [i.e., court] and would have your tunic, let him have your cloak as well" (Matthew 5:38–40).

The Hebrew Bible was clearly trying to establish a legal standard of justice, while Jesus was voicing a *personal* (and potentially anarchic) view of how a saintly individual should act. Probably for this reason, this teaching has had no impact on legislation in Christian societies. *No Christian society in history* has ever mandated that good people must offer wicked people no resistance; indeed, in contemporary America, fundamentalist Christians have committed themselves very actively to resisting those people and policies they regard as evil. Nor has any Christian society mandated that defendants sued in court settle by giving the plaintiff more than that for which he or she has asked (in line with Jesus' words, "If a man takes you to law and would have your tunic, let him have your cloak as well").

Why then did Jesus make such a statement, the effect of which would be to have people relinquish control of this world to the most wicked?

It is possible that Jesus' approach to this world was so otherworldly that he did not regard it as terrible to lose a tooth or an eye; therefore, he was willing to forgive a person who maliciously

---

*Consider how many Jews were murdered throughout history on the premise that they were descended from "Christ-killers" and therefore worthy of death.
†Jewish law also differed from Hammurabi's Code in that it *never* legislated execution for someone who killed another person accidentally.

took one or the other. On the other hand, when dealing with an issue that Jesus regarded as of paramount importance, people's acceptance of him as a spiritual master, he was quite unforgiving: "But the one who disowns me in the presence of men, I will disown in the presence of my Father in heaven" (Matthew 10:33). Thus, while advocating that those who slap or maim (modern counterparts would be wife-beaters and muggers) should not be punished, Jesus wished God to disown people who rejected him, an attitude that sounds suspiciously similar to "an eye for an eye."

I have yet to hear a morally convincing argument as to why people who *intentionally* blind others should retain the right to go on seeing. However, based on the earliest known Jewish legal records, Jewish courts did *not* blind those who deprived others of sight; instead, offenders were forced to pay financial compensation.

The reason for not enforcing "an eye for an eye" was rooted in the biblical concept of justice, which demanded that punishment be commensurate with the deed, but not exceed it: "Now if you assume that actual retaliation is intended, it could sometimes happen that both eye and life would be taken [in payment for the eye], as, for instance, if the offender died as he was being blinded" (Babylonian Talmud, *Bava Kamma* 84a).*

Thus, although morally speaking, a person who intentionally blinds another deserves to be blinded, in practice, Jewish courts demanded that the offender make financial compensation instead, lest the court commit the greater injustice of killing as well as blinding the assailant.

"An eye for an eye," therefore, establishes two biblical principles of justice: Evil must be punished, and punishment must be proportionate to, and not exceed, the offense.

---

*Ironically, as my friend Daniel Taub notes, "This was the very logic used to defeat Shylock in *The Merchant of Venice*."

170. Penalties for Stealing

EXODUS 21:37, 22:6; DEUTERONOMY 21:37

In contemporary society, victims of robberies rarely recover their stolen possessions. When the thief is caught, he or she usually has spent the money or disposed of the stolen item. The thief might be tried and sent to prison, but American law does not compel him to restore what he has stolen before he can be released from jail. As a matter of fact, when released he is generally regarded as having completed his punishment. If he then gets a job and starts working, his salary is not garnisheed to provide restitution to his victims. Thus, the thief's punishment rarely helps the victim.

The Bible's primary concern, however, is with aiding the victim. The first demand it makes of a thief is that he return the stolen goods to the victim. In addition, the thief is punished with a hundred percent fine, payable to the victim, not the state (Exodus 22:3). If the thief has spent the proceeds, and lacks the funds to reimburse his victim, he is sold into slavery for a maximum period of six years; he can either be put to work for his victim until such time as the debt is paid off, or sold to another and the price paid given to the thief's victim.

Biblical law places restraints on the owner of such slaves, with the result that their slaves' status was more akin to that of "domestic servant" (see entry 166). Most important, this form of servitude ensured that a thief's victim was compensated for his or her losses.

In certain instances, thieves were punished with more than a hundred percent fine. Just as in the nineteenth-century American West, horse thieves were punished more severely than other robbers (depriving a person of a horse, the most important mode of conveyance, could cause great personal suffering), the Torah imposed a stricter punishment on those who stole oxen and sheep, the two most important animals in the Israelite agricultural economy. The punishment is stated thus: "He shall pay five oxen for the ox" and "four sheep for the sheep" (Exodus 21:37)

In contrast to the mores of other societies in the ancient Middle East the Hebrew Bible regards property and human life as utterly incommensurate. Horrible as stealing is, thievery is never punished with death (the one exception being a kidnapper who sells a person into slavery; Exodus 21:16), a punishment that Hammurabi's and other codes inflicted on certain types of thieves (such as looters at a fire), and one that was inflicted in England *on nonviolent* thieves as recently as two hundred years ago. Biblical law likewise has no parallel to Islamic legislation practiced in Saudi Arabia to this day, which prescribes amputation of a thief's hand.

It is evident that biblical law is primarily concerned *not* with punishment of the thief, but with gaining restitution for the victim. The 100 percent, 300 percent, and 400 percent fines were intended both to compensate the victim for some of the anguish he or she suffered, and to discourage the thief from stealing again. In the absence of such a fine (suppose the thief were only required to return what he had stolen), the law would in no way deter thieves: At worst, they would be required to give back what they stole. If, however, they were not caught, then they would keep the fruits of their crime. So why then not steal?

Source: Moshe Greenberg, "Some Postulates of Biblical Criminal Law."

171. "You Shall Not Ill-treat Any Widow or Orphan"

EXODUS 22:21

In male-dominated societies, such as existed when the Torah was written, no people were as vulnerable as widows or orphans. Both lacked male protectors, and an orphan lacked a female protector as well (it is likely that the Bible regarded a fatherless child as an orphan as well).

To compensate for this deficiency, God declares Himself to be such people's protector: "If you do mistreat them, I will heed their outcry as they cry out to Me, and My anger shall blaze forth." God goes on to promise the most terrible of punishments for those who mistreat widows and orphans: "And I will put you to the sword, and your own wives shall become widows and your children orphans" (Exodus 22:22–23).

Later, when the Bible ordains that a tithe be given to the poor, it specifies "the orphan and the widow" (Deuteronomy 26:12) as among its recipients.

It would be nice to report that God's threat alone sufficed to deter people from taking advantage of society's most vulnerable members, but unfortunately the world has never lacked for bullies, and who are more logical victims of such people than orphans and widows?

Second Kings, chapter 4, tells of a poor woman whose husband has died, leaving her in debt. She seeks out the prophet Elisha, to complain that one of her husband's creditors is coming over to seize her two children as slaves. Fortunately, the prophet, through a miracle, provides the widow with the means to pay off her debt. However, most widows and orphans had no access to miracle-workers, and many suffered terrible privations.

The recurrent insistence in the Bible's later books on the necessity of treating orphans and widows kindly indicates how often they must have been mistreated. Isaiah instructs Jews to "uphold the rights of the orphan, defend the cause of the widow" (1:17); Jeremiah reminds the people of the need to "not oppress the . . . orphan and the widow" (7:6); Job establishes his credentials as a righteous person when he recalls the time when he had money, and would save "the orphan who had none to help him. . . . [and] gladdened the heart of the widow" (29:12–13).

Although God's warning did not deter all evil people, the command to help widows and orphans profoundly affected the way Jewish communities, and individual Jews, have treated them and continue to do so. Moses Maimonides, perhaps the most influential codifier of Jewish law, wrote: "One must always speak to them [widows and orphans] tenderly. One must show them unwavering courtesy; not hurt them physically with hard toil, or wound their feelings with harsh speech. One must take greater care of their property and money than of one's own. Whoever irritates them, provokes them to anger, pains them, tyrannizes over them, or causes them loss of money, is guilty of a transgression" (*Mishneh Torah*, "Laws of Character Development and Ethical Conduct" 6:10).

A final question remains: Powerful as is God's threat personally to bring about the death of anyone who mistreats orphans and widows, there is no evidence that such punishment has systematically been imposed on such people. How can one explain this? It remains an open question.

XXIII. LEVITICUS

172. Sacrifices

THE BOOK OF LEVITICUS, INTERMITTENT

For ancient Jews, animal sacrifices were what prayer services are to their modern descendants, the most popular expression of divine worship. Well over one hundred of the Torah's 613 laws deal with sacrifices.

Moses Maimonides, the greatest medieval Jewish philosopher, believed that animal sacrifices were instituted to wean people from the ancient and horrific practice of offering humans to the gods. In fact, when God stopped Abraham from sacrificing his son Isaac (Genesis 22:11–13), the Patriarch immediately substituted a ram for his son (see entry 14).

In offering God an animal sacrifice, Abraham was hardly innovative. Earlier biblical narratives inform us that Abel sacrificed an animal to God (Genesis 4:4), and that Noah's first act upon leaving the Ark was to sacrifice several animals and birds (Genesis 8:20).

The most famous biblically ordained sacrifice was that offered on Passover. Known as the Paschal lamb, it commemorated God's deliverance of the Jews from Egyptian slavery. In the post-Torah age, at Passover a Jew would bring a lamb to the Temple (*Beit Ha-Mikdash*) in Jerusalem and present it to a priest, who would slaughter the animal, sprinkle its blood upon the altar, and burn its entrails and fat. The remainder would be returned to the donor, who would take back the meat to his family. A *seder* would be prepared, at which the family would eat the lamb along with *matzah* (unleavened bread), bitter herbs, and other foods, and the meal would be accompanied by recountings of the Exodus from Egypt. The roasted shank bone that Jews still place on the Passover *seder* plate commemorates this Paschal lamb.

Once King Solomon built the First Temple in Jerusalem (about 950 B.C.E.), it was legislated that sacrifices were to be offered only there. The *kohanim* (priests), a subgroup within the tribe of Levi, were responsible for this ritual (see entry 44).

Some sacrifices were brought every morning and afternoon. To this day, the religious services held at these times (*shacharit* and *mincha*) commemorate these daily Temple offerings. Because during the time of the Great Temple, the afternoon sacrifice was offered at about 12:30 P.M., Jewish law forbids praying *mincha* before then. Other sacrifices were offered by those wishing to atone for violations of Torah laws; a third kind was gift offerings to God.

In general, some parts of the sacrificed animal were reserved for the priests to eat; others were returned to the donor who brought the sacrifice. In another kind of sacrifice, however, the animal was completely burned; this came to be known in English as a "holocaust" (in Hebrew, *olah*).

Only kosher, domesticated, and non–meat-eating animals—cattle, sheep, goats, and certain designated herbivorous birds—could be used for sacrifices. The talmudic Rabbis explained: "The bull flees from the lion, the sheep from the wolf, the goat from the tiger. Said the Holy One, blessed be He, 'You shall not bring before Me such as pursue, but only such as are pursued' " (*Leviticus Rabbah*, 27). By law, the sacrificed animals had to be without blemish (Leviticus 3:6, and 22:17–25).

Besides animals, people brought offerings of their first fruits, wheat, and barley to the Temple.

Most biblical legislation concerning sacrifices is found in Leviticus, the Torah's third book. Among those enumerated are the peace offerings (chapter 3), sin offerings (chapter 4), guilt offerings (5:14–26), meal offerings (chapter 2 and 6:7–16), and thanksgiving offerings (7:11–15).

When the Second Temple was destroyed in 70 C.E., many Jews despaired of ever gaining forgiveness for their sins, since there now was no place where they could offer sacrifices. Yet, after the Temple's destruction, Rabbi Yochanan ben Zakkai revolutionized Jewish thinking with his pronouncement that acts of loving-kindness now superseded sacrifices as the preferred way of attaining God's forgiveness. In addition, the Talmud later taught that "studying of Torah is a greater act than bringing daily sacrifices" (Babylonian Talmud, *Megillah* 3b). Indeed, from Judaism's perspective, Christianity's emphasis on the atoning sacrifice and blood of Jesus is regarded as a throwback to human sacrifice.

173. The Dietary Laws

LEVITICUS, CHAPTER 11; DEUTERONOMY 14:4–21

The Torah's oldest dietary law precedes the beginnings of the Israelite people. When Noah and his descendants are given permission to eat meat,* God specifically forbids them to consume the blood of the animals which they eat (Genesis 9:4). As the Torah later explains, "the blood is the life" (Leviticus 17:14) and therefore must be treated with respect. Later, when the Torah repeats this prohibition for the Israelites (Leviticus 17:10–14), it instructs them to drain the blood from any meat they consume.

Some Bible scholars speculate that the blood prohibition reflected an ancient Near Eastern taboo. Professor Jacob Milgrom investigated attitudes about consuming blood among peoples who lived in the ancient Middle East and discovered that "surprisingly, none of Israel's neighbors possessed this absolute and universally-binding blood prohibition. Blood is everywhere [else] partaken of as food. . . . [But in the Bible's view] man has a right to nourishment, not to life. Hence the blood, which is the symbol of life, must be drained, returned to the universe, to God."

It has been conjectured that the lower incidence of violence among Jews in all societies for which we have adequate statistical records might be partly traceable to their never consuming blood and to their draining it, two practices that were antithetical to bloodthirst.

The Torah permits the consumption only of land animals that have cloven hooves and that regurgitate their food. The most commonly eaten kosher animals are the cow and the lamb.

Permitted fish are those with both fins and scales (Leviticus

*Adam and Eve had been restricted to a vegetarian diet (Genesis 1:29).

11:9–12; Deuteronomy 14:9–10); the Torah provides no explanation for this specification. All shellfish are forbidden, so that many of the most popular fish, such as shrimp and lobster, are *treif* (unkosher).

Among birds, only those that Jewish tradition specifically enumerates as kosher are permitted, including chicken, turkey, and duck (instead of listing permitted birds, Leviticus 11:13–19 and Deuteronomy 14:12–18 enumerate a large number of forbidden birds).

All the permitted animals and birds are herbivorous. Thus, birds that prey on other birds are unkosher, as are all meat-eating animals. The Talmud notes that one sign of a forbidden bird is that it possesses a talon to kill.

In three separate places, the Torah legislates: "You shall not seethe a kid in its mother's milk" (Exodus 23:19, 34:26; Deuteronomy 14:21). Jewish law deduced from the law's threefold repetition that it is also forbidden to prepare milk and meat products together, eat them during the same meal, or derive benefit from them (by selling them).

Despite the common misconception that the Torah laws governing *kashrut* are largely determined by considerations of health and/or taboo, the Torah provides a rationale for its dietary laws, repeatedly associating them with holiness (see, for example, Leviticus 11:44–45, and Deuteronomy 14:21).

Further reading: Jacob Milgrom, *Leviticus 1–16,* Anchor Bible Series, pages 713–737.

174. Sexual Offenses in the Bible

LEVITICUS, CHAPTERS 18 AND 20:10–21

The Bible is straightforward in its treatment of sexual matters. When it discusses marriage, it speaks of a man "[clinging] to his wife, so that they become one flesh" (Genesis 2:24). It is hard to imagine a more graphic way to depict the ideal of marital sexuality. The Bible is equally frank in depicting the sexuality of many of its most significant figures. After Jacob has worked seven years in order to pay the dowry price for Rachel, he goes to Laban, Rachel's father, and tells him: "Give me my wife, for my time is fulfilled, that I may sleep with her" ((Genesis 29:21).

Later Bible readers may have been shocked by the directness of Jacob's request—I suspect that few men would appreciate being so spoken to by their daughters' fiancés—but there is no indication that Laban or the Bible disapproved of it.

Many centuries later, the biblical Song of Songs describes in passionate, sensual images the feelings between a young shepherdess and her lover.

But liberal as the Bible is in its approval of permitted sexual relations, it imposes numerous restrictions on other types of sexual behavior. Many of these prohibitions appear in Leviticus, chapter 18.

The chapter opens with a denunciation of sexual deviancy in Israel's two closest neighbors, Egypt and Canaan. From records external to the Bible, we know that marriage between brothers and sisters was commonly practiced in the Egyptian royal family (although incest was forbidden to "commoners"). The biblical laws forbid incest on pain of death: "None of you shall come near anyone of his own flesh to uncover nakedness" (18:6). The prohibition is extended to include nonblood relatives (e.g., a stepmother, even in an instance where the father has died [18:8]; a man also is forbidden to marry the widow of his uncle or son).

In addition, the Bible outlaws marrying a half sister. Of course, Abraham had done so when he married Sarah (Genesis 20:12), although this occurred long before Torah law forbade such a union. Strangely enough, there is no specific law outlawing father-daughter relations, although an explicit one forbids relations between a grandfather and granddaughter, and in language that makes it clear that all such incest is forbidden ("The nakedness of your son's daughter, or of your daughter's daughter—do not uncover their nakedness; for their nakedness is yours" [Leviticus 18:10]).

Verse 18 prohibits marrying one's wife's sister—including the sister of a divorced wife—during the wife's lifetime.* The Bible does not explain the rationale for this law, which was likely intended to discourage a man who was attracted to his sister-in-law from divorcing his wife and marrying her. If the wife died, however, such

*Jacob, of course, was simultaneously married to two sisters, but as he lived prior to the giving of the Torah, he obviously was not bound by this restriction.

a marriage was permitted; indeed, Jewish tradition encouraged it, out of the belief that an aunt would likely make the best stepmother to the orphaned children.

Biblical law does not regard the marriage of first cousins as incest. In Jewish life, such marriages were long encouraged and, until recently, widely practiced (though not among contemporary Jews).

Biblical law forbids the marriage of an aunt and a nephew, but not of an uncle and a niece. Amram, Moses' father, was married to his father's sister, Yocheved (Exodus 6:20), although this, too, occurred before Torah law was promulgated.

Other sexual activities forbidden in Leviticus 18:

—intercourse with a woman during her period (18:19; see also Leviticus 15:19);

—adultery (18:20), although its more famous prohibition is the seventh of the Ten Commandments;

—homosexuality (18:22); and

—bestiality (18:23).

The Bible is emphatic in its insistence that widespread violation of its sexual norms will lead to national catastrophe: "Do not defile yourselves in any of those ways, for it is by such that the nations which I am casting out before you defiled themselves. Thus the land became defiled; and I called it to account for its iniquity, and the land spewed out its inhabitants" (18:24–25).

175. "You Shall Be Holy"

LEVITICUS 19:2

Leviticus 19 contains the Torah's richest collection of ethical injunctions. The medieval *Sefer ha-Hinnuch* (*Book of Education*), a compilation of and commentary on the Torah's 613 commandments, traces 48 of the commandments (almost eight percent) to this thirty-seven–verse chapter.

The chapter opens with a general injunction: "You shall be holy, for I the Lord God am holy." As the context makes clear, this commandment is addressed to all Israelites. For perhaps the first time in recorded history, an entire nation, not just a spiritual or intellectual elite, is summoned to a life of sanctity.

"Every man is called upon to make something of himself," commented the late Walter Kaufmann, professor of religion and philosophy at Princeton University. *"Perhaps this was the most revolutionary idea of world history"* (emphasis added). As Kaufmann notes, if this last assertion sounds overstated, it is only because the Hebrew Bible's impact on Western society has been so great that such a call "may appear to be a commonplace; elsewhere, for example, in Egypt, not only in Moses' time but also in . . . ours, one can appreciate the revolutionary impact of these words."

Although Leviticus 19:2 does not specify how one achieves holiness, the entire chapter suggests that one does so by performing numerous ethical and ritual commands that help one achieve a state of sanctity.

The seemingly vague injunction "Be holy" stands in contrast to the more detailed manner in which most biblical commandments are phrased. The thirteenth-century Bible scholar Moses Nachmanides—to whom Jewish sources refer by the acronym Ramban—understands this law as serving as a moral check on legalistic, but otherwise amoral, Israelites. As Ramban notes, it is possible technically to observe most of the Torah's commandments, but still be a repulsive human being, or what he calls "a scoundrel with the full permission of the Torah." Thus, one could observe the Torah's edicts regarding permitted and forbidden foods—laws themselves rooted in the injunction to be holy (see Leviticus 11:44–45)—but eat gluttonously. Similarly, a person can drink liquor or conduct his business affairs in a way that breaks no Jewish laws but still is unholy. According to Ramban, a general injunction mandating holiness was therefore necessary, for even in areas where there is no specific biblical legislation, a person should not feel free from all restraints. This injunction obligates one to search out the specific behavior that seems most ethically and spiritually proper and elevating.

The Talmud expresses a similar notion: "Sanctify yourself through that which is permitted to you" (Babylonian Talmud, *Yevamot* 20a). In this way, no matter what the activity in which a person is engaged, he must ask himself whether he is fulfilling the biblical command "You shall be holy."

A note about Leviticus 19: Many laws recorded in Leviticus 19 are either set down elsewhere (e.g., observance of the Sabbath, verse 3) or are similar to statutes found in other places (thus, verse 3 also legislates awe of parents, closely paralleling Exodus 20:12, "Honor your father and mother"). Since I generally have written about a law when it makes its first, or otherwise primary, appearance, many ethical injunctions recorded in Leviticus 19 are discussed in earlier chapters.

In addition, although the command to "be holy" does not occur anywhere else in the Torah, it recalls God's command to the Israelites in Exodus: "And you shall be unto me a kingdom of priests, and a holy nation" (19:6).

Sources and further readings: Walter Kaufmann, *Religions in Four Dimensions,* pages 25–29, discusses the implication of the injunction to be holy within the context of a comparative analysis of ancient Israelite and Egyptian worldviews; a full translation of Ramban's commentary on Leviticus 19:2 is found in Louis Jacobs, *Jewish Biblical Exegesis,* pages 57–60; the *Sefer ha-Hinnuch,* the compilation and commentary on the Torah's 613 commandments, has been translated into English by Charles Wengrov, and is published in a five-volume edition by Feldheim Publishers, New York.

176. To Pay the Wages of a Laborer Promptly

LEVITICUS 19:13; DEUTERONOMY 24:15

A day laborer is to be paid by the end of the day during which he does his or her work; "the wages of a laborer shall not remain with you until morning" (Leviticus 19:13). In modern terms, this law encompasses domestic workers and handymen.

The Torah returns to this theme in Deuteronomy, although there the law is phrased in positive terms: "You must pay him his wages on the same day, before the sun sets, for he is needy and urgently depends on it" (Deuteronomy 24:15). The deuteronomic formulation specifies that it applies to Hebrews and non-Hebrews alike (verse 14).

However, the law does not apply to a permanent employee, with whom one is permitted to arrange payment on any mutually agreeable basis, nor does it apply to a contractor, whom one is obliged to pay upon a job's completion.

The focus is on day laborers because they are generally the poorest members of society; thus, the Torah's words: "For he is needy and urgently depends on it." Because of the widespread proclivity to abuse society's poorest, most vulnerable members, the Torah adds the threat that if one exploits a worker, "he will cry to the Lord against you, and you will incur guilt" (Deuteronomy 24:15).

With empathy the Talmud also decries the cruelty of delaying payment to workers: "Why did this worker climb the ladder [to build a house], suspend himself from a tree [to pick fruit], and risk death? Was it not for his wages?" (Babylonian Talmud, *Bava Mezia* 112a).

Although post-Torah biblical books seldom legislate law, they do provide much moral guidance. For example, in an obvious expansion on this law, Proverbs 3:28 teaches: "Do not say to your fellow, 'Come back again, I'll give it [the wages] to you tomorrow,' when you have it with you."

If someone is short of funds and cannot pay a day worker on time, he or she is obliged to tell the worker in advance; unless an acceptable alternative payment plan has been worked out, the biblical obligation to compensate the worker on time appears to be absolute.

177. "You Shall Not Curse the Deaf or Place a Stumbling Block Before the Blind"

LEVITICUS 19:14

Obviously, these two laws prohibit cruel practical jokes. People sometimes ridicule deaf people or say mean things about them in their presence, thereby taking vicious advantage of their handicap.

Even crueler are those who satisfy sadistic impulses by tripping the blind. In appending the words "you shall fear your God," the Torah underscores that, although the deaf person will not know he was insulted, nor the blind person who hurt him, God does know. Thus, although you have no reason to fear the deaf or blind person, the fear of God should deter you from acting in such a manner (see entry 153).*

These two biblical laws, so specific in their original context, were subsequently given broader application in Jewish law. Thus, the injunction against cursing the deaf is understood as applying to insulting anyone not present, or anyone who is in effect deaf to what you are saying. Similarly, the injunction against placing a stumbling block before the blind is interpreted as prohibiting taking advantage of anyone who is "blind" in the matter at hand. If people ask your advice on a matter on which you have more information than they do, don't take advantage of their "blindness" by giving them bad advice that will cause them to suffer. Also, if a person has an addiction, don't take advantage of the individual's weakness. I recall reading about a prominent baseball player, a recovering alcoholic, who attended a party where somebody who was aware of his condition gave him a drink of orange juice spiked with liquor. Since an alcoholic who consumes even a small quantity of liquor will often be stimulated to drink much more, the person who played this joke was in violation of one of the Torah's most unusual laws, "Don't place a stumbling block in front of a blind man."

178. "Do Not Go About as a Talebearer Among Your People"

LEVITICUS 19:16

While Western society generally regards telling an ugly, but true, story about another person as morally permissible, biblical law regards such gossip as forbidden. The reason can be found in the law that is stated only two verses later, in Leviticus 19:18: "Love your neighbor as yourself." To love someone as yourself means to treat him as you wish to be treated. For instance, if you had done something that would be embarrassing if it became known to others (and

*Deuteronomy 27:18 returns to this theme, proclaiming a curse against one "who misdirects a blind man on his way."

which of us hasn't?), you would hope that anyone who learned about this episode would keep it quiet. Similarly, you are obligated not to spread information that will embarrass others.

This law alerts us to the cruel acts often committed by the tongue. As I have observed in my book *Words That Hurt, Words That Heal,* "Unless you or someone dear to you have been the victims of terrible physical violence, chances are the worst pains you have suffered in life have come from words used cruelly, from outbursts of anger, excessive criticism, sarcasm, gossip, and rumors."

179. "Do Not Stand By While Your Neighbor's Blood Is Shed"

LEVITICUS 19:16

Contemporary American law is rights-, rather than obligation-, oriented. For example, if you could easily save a child who is drowning, but instead stand by and watch it drown, you have violated no American law. Under biblical law, however, you have committed a serious crime.

Later Jewish legal codes give numerous examples of how the commandment "Do not stand by while your neighbor's blood is shed" can be fulfilled or violated. The Talmud rules that "if one sees someone drowning, mauled by beasts or attacked by robbers one is obligated to save him . . ." (although you are not *required* to do so if your own life is put at serious risk). On the same page, the Talmud cites this law as the basis for ruling that if one person pursues another to kill him, "the pursued person must be saved even at the cost of the pursuer's life . . ." (Babylonian Talmud, *Sanhedrin* 73a).

The sixteenth-century *Shulkhan Arukh,* the standard code of Jewish law, rules: "He [or she] who hears heathens or informers plotting to harm a person is obliged to inform the intended victim. If he is able to appease the perpetrator and deter him from the act, but does not do so, he has violated the law 'Do not stand by while your neighbor's blood is shed' " (*Hoshen Mishpat* 426:1).

Another rabbinical source cites this ordinance as the basis for ruling that "if you are in a position to offer testimony on someone's behalf, you are not permitted to remain silent" (*Sifre Leviticus*, commenting on this verse).

Reflections: On a societal level, this law suggests that a country is forbidden to ignore the fate of innocent people being murdered in another country. Indeed, this ordinance would seem to serve as an implicit protest against a society becoming isolationist and arguing that it bears no moral responsibility for what goes on elsewhere, particularly if it is in a position to help protect victims from their oppressors. To be neutral in the battle between the firemen and the fire—to borrow a phrase from Abba Eban, Israel's former foreign minister—is to side with the fire. Thus, the Allies' refusal to bomb the train tracks leading to Auschwitz during the summer of 1944, when they had uncontested air superiority over the region of Poland in which Auschwitz was located, in effect passively aided the Nazi "Final Solution" against the Jews.

180. "Do Not Hate Your Brother in Your Heart"

LEVITICUS 19:17

One of the relatively few biblical laws addressed to our hearts, this commandment obliges us to confront a person who has provoked our enmity. Without such confrontation, the hatred usually festers and grows.

The Second Book of Samuel tells us that Absalom hated his half brother Amnon (with good reason, since Amnon had raped Tamar, Absalom's sister and Amnon's half sister; see entry 84). The hatred was so deep that "Absalom didn't utter a word to Amnon, good or bad . . ." (II Samuel, 13:22).

After two years of repressed but growing anger, Absalom arranged with his servants to murder Amnon (verses 28–29).

"Hatred makes a straight line crooked," an old Jewish proverb teaches. When you hate a person, you can't think clearly about him or her; instead, you interpret all the person's behavior in a manner that will justify and deepen your hatred. Thus, except for rare reasons of extreme provocation, there is a need to speak to the source of your enmity. As long as you remain on some sort of speaking terms with the person, the hatred you bear is less likely to fester and explode.

181. "Reprove Your Kinsman and Incur No Guilt Because of Him"

LEVITICUS 19:17

If you see someone doing something immoral, this law obligates you to criticize the person, and try to influence him to alter his behavior. For example, if you see parents acting cruelly to a child, and believe that there is a chance your words can influence them to act more kindly and fairly, you are obliged to speak up. If you don't, then, as the commandment's second clause suggests, you bear some of the guilt for their continuing bad behavior.

For many of us, this is a particularly hard law to fulfill, either because we are too shy to intervene in other people's affairs, worry about sounding self-righteous, or fear being dismissed as busybodies (as a child, I remember being embarrassed when my mother would intervene if she saw children fighting). This biblical law, however, obliges us to overcome our inhibitions, and speak up. If someone you know is drunk and about to start driving, you are obliged to try to stop him. If you make no effort to do so, you bear some of the moral guilt for the deaths and other sufferings that may ensue.

Later Jewish sources offer an alternative explanation of the law's second clause. If you reprove someone who is doing something wrong, the Rabbis teach, you are performing a morally upright act. However, don't taint this act by humiliating the person whom you are reproving, since by doing so you are sinning and incurring "guilt because of him."

Why is this so? In truth, many of us become self-righteous and cruel when criticizing others. Humiliating another person is itself a sin; furthermore, if your goal is to dissuade the person you criticize from committing a wrongful act, humiliating him or her more likely will stimulate anger and defensiveness rather than cause the person to change.

Moses Maimonides, the great twelfth-century philosopher and codifier of Jewish law, offered some very helpful advice on how to administer a rebuke: "He who rebukes another, whether for offenses against the rebuker himself or for sins against God, should administer the rebuke in private, speak to the offender gently and tenderly, and point out that he is only speaking for the wrongdoer's own good. . . . One is obligated to continue admonishing until the sinner assaults the admonisher and says to him, 'I refuse to listen' " (*Mishneh Torah*, "Laws Concerning Character Development and Ethical Conduct," 6:7).

182. "Do Not Take Revenge or Bear a Grudge Against a Member of Your People"

LEVITICUS 19:18

The two injunctions contained in this verse represent a radical effort to reshape human behavior. It is natural for most people to want to injure those who have wronged them and to remain angry at people who have hurt them. But the Torah insists that we restrain both impulses.

Significant as these laws are—they form the first half of the verse which goes on to legislate, "Love your neighbor as yourself"—the Torah offers little concrete guidance on how they should be carried out. What is clear is that they are addressed to individuals, not to the state (which, when punishing criminals, is considered to be carrying out justice, not revenge).

Many centuries after these laws were first promulgated, the Talmud offered this illustration to explain the difference between not taking revenge and not bearing a grudge: "What is revenge and what is bearing a grudge? If A says to B, 'Lend me your sickle,' and B says,

'No,' and the next day, B says to A, 'Lend me your ax,' and A replies, 'I will not, just as you refused to lend me your sickle,' that is revenge [and is forbidden by the Torah].

"And what is bearing a grudge? If A says to B, 'Lend me your ax,' and B says, 'No,' and the next day B says to A, 'Lend me your garment,' and A replies, 'Here it is. I am not like you, who would not lend me what I asked for,' that is bearing a grudge" (Babylonian Talmud, *Yoma* 23a).

After many years of meditating on the difficulty of carrying out these formidable commands, I have concluded that if every member of a family were to retaliate against and/or mention every slight committed by a spouse, child, or parent, the family would soon disintegrate. Thus, the Torah seems to be telling us that we should broaden the definition of family to include the entire Jewish community.

But as I have written elsewhere, "I know of no Jewish source that delineates how often one is obligated to fulfill this Torah commandment vis-à-vis the same person. Thus, if even after the above incident, B continues to refuse to lend A what he or she needs, is A obligated to continue lending items to B without making a comment?" I don't know, but somehow that doesn't seem right (*Jewish Wisdom*, page 177).

183. "Love Your Neighbor as Yourself, I Am God"

LEVITICUS 19:18

Since love is demonstrated through deeds, this law implies that we must act in the same loving manner toward others as we want them to act toward us. This is the first time that this injunction, the basis of the Golden Rule, is recorded in world literature.

In citing this teaching, people generally omit the verse's final words, "I am God." These words serve a very important function, emphasizing that "because I am God who created both you and your neighbor, I have the right to instruct both of you on how to act."

"Love your neighbor as yourself" makes sense only within a religious context. Without God, all that exists in the world is the physical; from where then would come the basis for legislating moral
obligations? The inability to derive moral obligations without a meta-
physical basis has been a bedrock problem confronting all atheistic
philosophical systems. As Bertrand Russell, perhaps the twentieth-
century's most eloquent atheistic philosopher, wrote: "I cannot see
how to refute the argument for the subjectivity of all ethical values,
but I refuse to accept that the only thing wrong with wanton cruelty is
that I don't like it." Unfortunately, over many decades of writing, Russell was never able to formulate a stronger critique of "wanton cruelty"
than that he didn't like it. Even more unfortunately, there are many
people who do like it, a factor which helps account for this century's
Nazi and Communist horrors.

Significantly, the biblical verse does not read: "Love all humanity
as yourself," but it specifically speaks of one's neighbor. After all, it
is easier to engage in lofty statements about humankind than to show
loving behavior to the person next door, who might be a rather
flawed creature. Then again most of us are quite flawed as well; as
the eighteenth-century founder of Hasidism, Israel Ba'al Shem Tov,
taught, "Just as we love ourselves despite the faults we know we have,
so should we love our neighbors despite the faults we see in them."

Although the Torah promulgates its commandments without specifying that some laws are more significant than others, Jewish teachers have long understood this injunction as being of particular
significance. The second-century rabbi Akiva, one of the Talmud's
pivotal figures, taught, " 'Love your neighbor as yourself'—this is the
major principle of the Torah" (Palestinian Talmud, *Nedarim* 9:4).
More than a century earlier, Rabbi Hillel, desiring to give practical
advice on how to carry out this law, taught, "What is hateful unto
you, don't do unto your neighbor." He underscored the law's ultimate
significance by adding, "The rest [of the Torah] is a commentary
[on how to fulfill this law]" (Babylonian Talmud, *Shabbat* 31a).

184. "You Shall Love [the Stranger] as Yourself"

LEVITICUS 19:34; DEUTERONOMY 10:18–19

Ask people to enumerate the three biblical commandments ordaining love, and many will quickly come up with "Love your neighbor as yourself" (Leviticus 19:18), and "You shall love the Lord your God" (Deuteronomy 6:5). Far fewer, my experience has shown, are aware of a third such commandment: "The stranger who resides with you shall be to you as one of your citizens; you shall love him as yourself, for you were strangers in the land of Egypt: I the Lord am your God" (Leviticus 19:34).

This might well be the most extraordinary commandment in the entire Torah. In a world that was even more chauvinistic than our own, the Torah mandates that the Israelite people love peaceful non-Israelites living among them *no less than they love themselves* (obviously the law does not refer to *enemies* living among the Israelites, since other biblical verses command the Israelites to fight against their adversaries).

The German-Jewish philosopher Hermann Cohen (1842–1918) rightly identifies this law as the beginning of what is known as "ethical monotheism": "The stranger was to be protected, although he was not a member of one's family, clan, religion, community or people; simply because he was a human being. *In the stranger, therefore, man discovered the idea of humanity.*"

The Hebrew for "stranger" is *ger*. During the talmudic era, more than a thousand years after the time of Moses, this word acquired a second meaning, "convert" (i.e., a stranger who converts to Judaism). In the Talmud, some Rabbis argue that the biblical provisions concerning the *ger*, to love him (or her) and to treat him with full equality under the law, are intended to apply only to a "stranger" who converts to Judaism. However, such a view clearly contradicts the Torah, as proven by Leviticus 19:34, which, in addition to commanding love of the stranger, provides a rationale for this commandment: because "you were strangers in the land of Egypt" (and know, therefore, what it means to be a stranger and to be mistreated). If the biblical meaning of *ger* were "convert," then this verse would acquire an altogether different and absurd meaning: "You shall love the convert as yourself because you were converts in the land of Egypt." The Israelites were converts? To what? The religion of Egypt? And if so, why should that affect how they treat converts to Judaism?

The admirable desire of some talmudic Rabbis to raise the esteem Jews felt toward converts (apparently, there were some intolerant, perhaps racist, Jews who regarded converts as inferior and loved them less than other Jews) unfortunately led them to denigrate the status of gentiles living among the Israelites. However, the Torah desired to elevate the status of such people, and it identifies the stranger as a class of people—indeed, the only such class—whom God Himself loves (Deuteronomy 10:18).

185. Sanctifying, and Not Desecrating, God's Name: "You Shall Not Profane My Holy Name That I May Be Sanctified in the Midst of the Israelite People"

LEVITICUS 22:32

The mission of chosenness imposes on Jews the responsibility to make known both to non-believing Jews and to gentiles that there is One God, that His primary demand is ethical behavior, and that all humankind should worship Him. However, knowledge of this One God alone will not necessarily cause people to change their behavior.

What is more apt to influence their actions are the actions of those who teach them that there is One God. If these people are exceptionally kind, honest, and generous, then others are likely to be impressed with their claim that the source of their goodness is the God in whom they believe. But if they are perceived as sly, fanatical, and cruel, then others will probably assume that a belief in God leads to these unattractive traits, and will refuse to consider the possibility that their beliefs about God are true.

Therefore, sanctifying God's name (*kiddush ha-Shem*) means acting in a way that evokes love and admiration for the Lord. The Torah teaches that one should first try to impress fellow Israelites, in line with the admonition "that I may be sanctified in the midst of the Israelite people." The Talmud notes, "If a person studies Bible and Mishnah . . . and is honest in his business dealings, and speaks gently to people, what do people say about him? 'Happy is the father who taught him Torah. Happy is the teacher who taught him Torah. Woe unto those who haven't learned Torah. This man studied Torah; see how noble his ways are, how good his actions'" (Babylonian Talmud, *Yoma* 86a).

As regards the non-Jewish world, Torah study is unlikely to make a positive impression unless it prompts ethical behavior. The impression made on non-Jews by the way Jews behave is the subject of a story in the Palestinian Talmud (*Bava Mezia* 2:5):

> Rabbi Samuel . . . went to Rome. The Empress lost a bracelet and he happened to find it. A proclamation was issued throughout the land that if anyone returned it within thirty days, he would receive such-and-such a reward but if, after thirty days, he did not do so, he would lose his head. He did not return it within the thirty days but thereafter.
>
> She said to him: "Were you not in the province?"
>
> He replied: "Yes, I was here."
>
> She said: "But did you not hear the proclamation?"
>
> "I heard it," said he.
>
> "What did it say?" she asked.
>
> He replied: "If anyone returns it within thirty days, he will receive such-and-such a reward, but if he returns it after thirty days, he will lose his head."
>
> She said: "In that case, why did you not return it within the thirty days."
>
> He said: "Because I did not want anyone to say that I returned it out of fear of you, whereas, in fact, I returned it out of fear of the All-merciful."
>
> She said to him: "Blessed is the God of the Jews."

Conversely, when Jews, particularly religious ones, act badly, it alienates people from God. The murder of Israeli Prime Minister

Yitzhak Rabin by a ritually observant Jew in 1995 prompted some Israelis and others throughout the world to perceive Jewish religiosity as fanatical and cruel, and as a force for evil rather than good. This is similar to the way in which many ethical people responded to the evils committed in Islam's and God's name by the late Ayatollah Khomeini, Iran's ruler.

Jewish law eventually came to regard desecrating God's name, and thereby alienating people from God, as one of the very few unforgivable offenses (see also the discussion of the Third Commandment, entry 158).

186. Holy Days

LEVITICUS, CHAPTER 23

Important as holidays are in biblical religion, the only one mentioned in the Ten Commandments is the Sabbath. While additional holidays are mentioned in different contexts in the Torah, Leviticus 23 summarizes the Bible's holy days.

The chapter starts with a reminder to observe the Sabbath: "For six days labor may be done, and the seventh day is a day of complete rest, a holy convocation, you shall not do any work" (23:3).

Passover, which remains to this day the most widely observed holiday among Jews, is the next holiday mentioned. Leviticus does not call it *Pesach* (Passover); instead, it speaks of the "festival of matzot," designating the festival by the food with which it is most associated.

The text then speaks of the Omer, the forty-nine days that are counted daily, starting with the second night of Passover. On the fiftieth day, the holiday of Shavuot (Weeks) is observed. While the Torah associates this holiday with the end of the harvest, Jewish tradition primarily associates Shavuot with the giving of the Ten Commandments and the Torah at Mount Sinai.

The text then turns to Rosh ha-Shana, the New Year, mentioning the *shofar*, the ram's horn that is to be blown on this day, and which Jewish tradition credits with the ability to arouse people to repent.

Following Rosh ha-Shana comes Yom Kippur, a day of complete

rest from work on which the Israelites are commanded to "afflict" themselves. Jewish tradition understands "afflict" as an admonition to refrain from eating, drinking, bathing, wearing leather shoes, and engaging in sexual relations. The Bible describes Yom Kippur as a "Day of Atonement to provide you atonement before the Lord your God" (23:28). The day is so significant that it is described as a "Sabbath of Sabbaths" (23:32). The Torah decrees that "any soul who will do any work on this very day, I will destroy that soul from among its people" (23:29).

Just five days after Yom Kippur comes Sukkot, a harvest festival during which the Israelites are commanded to dwell in temporary booths (*sukkot*). Today, however, while many Jews build *sukkot*, few actually dwell in them throughout the weeklong holiday; instead they eat their meals in the *sukkah*, but sleep in their homes.

On the eighth day after the beginning of Sukkot, the Bible ordains the holiday of Shemini Atzeret, at which time the Israelites were expected to assemble at the Sanctuary, and rededicate themselves to the service of God and the study of Torah.

These are the only holidays the Torah ordains. Modern Jews observe many additional festivals, commemorating events that occurred subsequent to the giving of the Torah (for example, Purim, Hannuka, and Israeli Independence Day).

187. Jubilee and Sabbatical Years

LEVITICUS 25:8–24

In its insistence that human beings have a right to own land and property, the Bible's worldview seems closer to a capitalist than socialist vision. The capitalism it endorses, however, comes with some strict limits. In an effort to avoid the development of a permanent underclass, the Torah legislates some unusual and, it would seem, seldom enforced laws. For example: "Every seventh year you shall practice remission [i.e., forgiveness] of debts" (Deuteronomy 15:1–2). The intent here is to ensure that a temporary state of impoverishment not turn into a permanent one.

Every fiftieth year, in a recurring cycle that Jewish tradition traces to the world's creation, all property was to be restored to its original owner, and Hebrew slaves were to be emancipated. Thus, when the Israelites entered Canaan, the land was divided among the tribes; within each tribe, every family was given a share. If a tribal member sold his land because of economic need, it reverted to that individual or to his descendants during the Jubilee year.

The Hebrew word *yovel* (from which "Jubilee" derives) means "ram's horn," since a ram's horn was sounded near the year's inception (Leviticus 25:9).

Unfortunately, utopian legislation has a way of being ignored. The Talmud declares that the Jubilee year was not observed throughout the period of the Second Temple, attributing this to the fact that most Jews no longer lived in Israel. However, there is no evidence that it was observed before this time, even during periods when almost all Jews *did* reside there. Certainly, the prophets' complaints about rich people's mistreatment of the poor do not leave the impression that land was returned to the poor every Jubilee year.

The Sabbatical year is to be observed in recurring seven-year cycles. During this year, fields are to be left unplanted and, during the Sabbatical year for debts, debtors are released from their obligations. Because people were reluctant to loan money to poor people, particularly as a Sabbatical year approached, later Jewish law created a legal fiction known as a *prosbul*, by which debts were transferred to a court by the creditor simply telling the court that they were authorized to collect his debt. Since the debts owed a court were not canceled in the seventh year, they continued to be collectible by the court even after the Sabbatical year was over. The court, in turn, gave the money to the creditor.

Hillel, the first-century B.C.E. sage who instituted the *prosbul*, claimed that his motivation was not to help affluent people collect their money, but to ensure that everyone would be motivated to lend money to the poor (see Deuteronomy 15:9–10).

The Sabbatical law regulating that fields lie fallow every seventh year is still applicable. In Israel many rigorously Orthodox Jews observe this regulation throughout the Sabbatical year (the next one falls in 2000/2001), and they purchase produce only from Arab farmers. Other Orthodox Jews resort to a legal fiction and "sell" the land of Israel to a gentile before the Sabbatical year commences.

188. Charity

LEVITICUS 25:35–37; DEUTERONOMY 15:7–8

Since this world is not utopia, the Bible presumes that poverty is a perennial problem: "For there will never cease to be needy people in your land, which is why I command you: open your hands to the poor and needy" (Deuteronomy 15:11).

Such generosity is primarily intended to help a poor person work his way out of poverty. The twelfth-century sage and philosopher Moses Maimonides specified eight degrees of charitable giving, the highest of which is to assist a poor person "by providing him with a gift or a loan, or by entering into a partnership with him, or helping him find work; in a word, by putting him where he can dispense with other people's aid" (*Mishneh Torah*, "Laws Concerning Gifts to the Poor," 10:7).

Maimonides based this interpretation on Leviticus 25:35–37, which declares: "When your brother Israelite is reduced to poverty and cannot support himself in the community [literally, 'and his hand falls'], you shall uphold him as you would a resident stranger. ... You shall not charge him interest on a loan ... ," and on Deuteronomy 15:7–8: "If, however, there is a needy person among you ... do not harden your heart and shut your hand against your needy kinsman. Rather you must open your hand and lend him sufficient for whatever he needs." To this day, biblical law obligates one to make interest-free loans to people in need, and it is common to find Free Loan societies (*Gemilut Hesed*) in the Orthodox community.

Regarding the most immediate need of the truly poor, food, Leviticus 19 (the "holiness" chapter) rules: "When you reap the harvest of your land, you shall not reap all the way to the edges of your field, or gather the gleanings of your harvest. You shall not pick your vineyard bare, or gather the fallen fruit of your vineyard; you shall leave them for the poor and the stranger ..." (verses 9–10).

So important did rabbinic Judaism regard the obligation of dispensing charity that the Talmud declared: "Charity is equal in importance to all the other commandments combined" (Babylonian Talmud, *Bava Bathra* 9a).

Note: For a description of how these laws operated in daily life, see the Book of Ruth, chapter 2.

XXIV. NUMBERS

189. *Sotah:* The Ordeal of a Suspected Adulteress

NUMBERS 5:1–31

The most peculiar judicial procedure legislated in the Torah concerns the *sotah,* a woman suspected by her husband of having committed adultery. The husband is instructed to bring his wife before a priest (perhaps this procedure was intended to stop him from wreaking private vengeance). The priest summoned the woman forward, to stand before God; then he took some sacred water, mixed it with earth from the floor of the tabernacle, and bared the woman's head (married women kept their hair covered, a practice still observed by Orthodox Jews), an act intended to shame her. The priest then delivered the following adjuration: "If no man has lain with you . . . while married to your husband, be immune to harm from this water of bitterness. . . . [But] if a man other than your husband has had carnal relations with you . . . may the Lord make you a curse . . . among your people as the Lord causes your thigh to sag and your belly to distend" (5:19–21).*

After the priest had finished, the woman was instructed to say, "Amen, amen."

The priest wrote down the curse, then rubbed the words in the "water of bitterness" until they dissolved in the water. He then gave the woman this concoction to drink. If she was guilty, the water

---

*Bible scholar Jacob Milgrom suggests that the word "thigh" is a euphemism for the procreative organs, thus indicating an inability to have children. Milgrom also argues that, by prescribing this procedure, this ordeal served to prevent the "lynching" of women suspected of adultery.

would cause her belly to distend and her thigh to sag. If innocent, she would remain unharmed.

No similar "ordeal" was imposed on a husband suspected of adultery (the biblical definition of adultery differs from the contemporary one, which holds adultery to have occurred if either partner in a marriage has sex with anyone other than their spouse. According to the Bible, a married man who slept with an unmarried woman had not committed adultery; if a man, married or not, slept with a married woman, he had; the Bible's rationale for this definition is explained in entry 162). However, during the talmudic era, the Rabbis ruled that since so many men had committed adultery, it was unfair to impose this procedure on women suspected of adultery.

Even before they ended the *sotah's* ordeal, the talmudic Rabbis had already tried to limit the instances in which it could be imposed. Though the biblical text suggests that any suspicious husband could force his wife to undergo the ordeal, the Talmud ruled that in order for it to take place a man had first to warn his wife, in the presence of two witnesses, against spending any time alone with the person he suspected was her lover (Mishnah, *Sotah* 1:2). Only if she ignored his warning could he insist on her undergoing this ordeal.

190. The Nazirite

NUMBERS 6:1–21

For many people, increased religiosity correlates with an increase in the number of objects and activities one forbids oneself. Thus, among many religions, holy people are expected to refrain from sexual activity.

Jewish ideology is generally unsympathetic to asceticism; a famous talmudic admonition declares: "In the future, a man will have to give an accounting before heaven for every good thing his eyes saw, but of which he did not eat" (Palestinian Talmud, *Kiddushin* 4:12). Nonetheless, aware of asceticism's attraction to some, biblical law made provision for those who felt a religious need to deny themselves.

Such a person is referred to in the Torah as a *nazir*. The Bible speaks of a man or woman taking a Nazirite vow "to set himself apart for the

Lord." A Nazirite is subject to the following (and in comparison with other religious traditions rather moderate) restrictions:

—not to drink wine or grape juice; nor to eat fresh or dried grapes. The prohibition of wine was likely intended "to guard the Nazirite from being controlled by any spirit other than God's" (Lockyer, ed., *Nelson's Illustrated Bible Dictionary*, page 749);

—not to cut his hair, and to let it grow untrimmed, a public sign of his consecration to God;

—to have no contact with a corpse, including that of his father or mother.

As a rule, one remained a Nazirite for a set period. The Torah doesn't specify how long the period was, though it clearly did not wish a person to become a perpetual *nazir*. At the conclusion of the *nazir*'s term, he was instructed to bring an offering to the Temple. Significantly, the priest was instructed to bring a *sin* offering on the *nazir*'s behalf (6:16), an indication that the Bible seems to have permitted Nazirite activity as a concession to human nature, but disapproved of it. The priest brought a burnt offering as well, after which the Nazirite cut off his hair and burned it at the altar. After that, the Bible notes, "the Nazirite may drink wine" (6:20).

The Bible's most famous Nazirite is Samson, whose mother pledged him to a permanent Nazirite lifestyle even before he was born. Nonetheless, if the goal of being a *nazir* is to refrain from ungodly activities, the process failed in Samson's case. During his years of being a *nazir*, he engaged in promiscuous sex with gentile prostitutes, and conducted his life in a decidedly unholy manner. He clung to at least one Nazirite prohibition wholeheartedly, the ban on shaving one's hair; eventually, he confided to Delilah, his final lover, that if his hair was cut, he would lose all his strength (see entry 66). Delilah immediately proceeded to cut Samson's hair and career short.

Although the term *nazir* is not mentioned, I Samuel 1:11 implies that the prophet Samuel might have been a *nazir*, too.

In modern times, Rabbi David Cohen, a foremost disciple of Chief Rabbi Abraham Isaac Kook of Palestine, accepted the Nazirite restrictions on himself, and he became known as "the Nazir." Although he was a holy and profound thinker, Rabbi Cohen's singular act does not seem to have sparked imitators.

Several talmudic dictums suggest normative Judaism's general objection to Nazirite asceticism:

"It is not enough what the Torah has forbidden you, but you wish to forbid yourself more things?" (Palestinian Talmud, *Nedarim* 9:1).

"Sanctify yourself through that which is permitted you" (Babylonian Talmud, *Yevamot* 20a).

191. The Priestly Benediction
(*Birkat Kohanim*)

NUMBERS 6:22–27

The most famous blessing bestowed in the Torah is the one Aaron and his priestly successors are instructed to bestow on the Jewish people:

"The Lord spoke to Moses: Speak to Aaron and his sons: Thus, shall you bless the people of Israel. Say to them:

'May the Lord bless you and protect you!

'May the Lord deal kindly [literally, "illuminate His countenance for you"] and graciously with you!

'May the Lord bestow His favor upon you and grant you peace!' "

This blessing still forms a regular part of the Jewish liturgy. On certain holidays, the priests present in the congregation* go to the front of the synagogue and call out this blessing to the congregation. While the benediction is being recited, it is forbidden for people to look upon the priests; God's glory is assumed to be manifest at that moment, something that is forbidden for human beings to witness.

When reciting the blessing, the priests remove their shoes as did their ancestors in the Temple (recalling God's words at His first revelation to Moses: "Remove the sandals from your feet, for the place on which you stand is holy ground"; Exodus 3:5).

Priests, however, are not the only Jews who recite this blessing. Many rabbis so bless their congregations at the conclusion of services. Also, this priestly blessing is recited by parents to their children at the onset of the Sabbath.

Reflections: In his commentary on Numbers, Jacob Milgrom notes that although there is but one Hebrew word meaning "to bless," *berekh*, it can have different meanings. When a blessing is uttered by God, it

---

*The only way to become a priest—in Hebrew, a *kohen*—is to be descended from a father who is a *kohen* (see also entry 44).

is a decree. Thus, in Genesis 17:16, God reveals to Abraham, "I will bless [your wife Sarah]; indeed, I will give you a son by her. I will bless her so that she will give rise to nations. . . ."

When uttered by a human being, a blessing is a prayer. The sole exception is in Genesis 27:34–38, where it is assumed that Isaac's blessing of his son will—like a blessing bestowed by God—necessarily be fulfilled.

Dr. Jeremiah Unterman has pointed out to me the mathematical progression in the three lines of the priestly blessing. In Hebrew, the first line contains three words and fifteen letters, the second line five words and twenty letters, and the third line seven words and twenty-five letters. Unterman concludes: "The progression indicates the symbolic nature of the blessing—growth to better things."

Source: Jacob Milgrom, *The JPS Torah Commentary: Numbers,* pages 360–362.

192. *Tzitzit*—The Law of Fringes

NUMBERS 15:38–40

"Speak to the Israelite People and Instruct Them to Make for Themselves Fringes on the Corners of Their Garments Throughout the Ages"

NUMBERS 15:38

At one time, it was common in the United States for a person who was fearful of forgetting an errand to tie a string around his finger. Throughout the day, whenever he saw the string, he would be reminded of the errand.

Tzitzit, the ritual fringes which the Bible ordains must be worn at the corners of one's garment, are a sort of ethical string-around-the-finger. That this is the rationale behind *tzitzit* is reflected in the verses

in which they are ordained: "The Lord said to Moses: 'Speak to the Israelite people and instruct them to make for themselves fringes on the
corners of their garments throughout the ages; let them attach a cord
of blue to the fringe at each corner. That shall be your fringe; *look at it
and recall all the commandments of the Lord and observe them,* so that you do not
follow your heart and eyes in your lustful urge" (15:38–39).

That a major goal of these fringes is to curb "lustful urge[s]" is
likewise reflected in a talmudic story about a yeshiva student who is
particularly scrupulous in wearing *tzitzit*. The young man hears of an
exceptionally beautiful, and expensive, harlot in a far-off land. He
sends the payment required to sleep with her, then journeys to meet
the woman. When he sees the harlot, he is overwhelmed by her
beauty but, when he starts to undress, the fringes fly up in the air
and slap him across the face. Realizing the incongruity of his going
to a prostitute, the young man sits down on the floor in the style of
a mourner. The prostitute comes down from her bed, sits down
opposite him, and queries him as to the fault he has seen in her that
has caused him to turn away. The young man assures her that he
finds her beautiful, but explains to her about *tzitzit*. Amazed and
impressed by the power of this ritual to overcome sexual lust, the
prostitute follows the young man back to Jerusalem, where she converts to Judaism and marries him (Babylonian Talmud, *Menachot* 44a).

It is not coincidental that the Talmud specifically emphasized the
power of *tzitzit* to help a person resist an inappropriate sexual liaison.
Numbers 15:39, which almost always is rendered in a sanitized translation, literally reads: ". . . Look at it [the fringe] and recall all the
commandments of the Lord and observe them, so that you do not
follow your heart and eyes *after which you go whoring*" [in Hebrew,
zonim acha-rei-hem]."

Orthodox Jews understand the law of *tzitzit* as mandating men to
wear a fringed garment throughout the day; they don a four-
cornered garment *(arba kanfot)*, composed of a square piece of cloth
with fringes at each corner and a hole in the middle that allows it
to be slipped over the head. The garment is worn under the shirt,
although many Orthodox Jews let the fringes hang outside the shirt
so that they are visible.

Male Jews of all denominations—and now some women—fulfill
this biblical injunction during morning prayer services by wearing a
tallit, a large cloth with fringes at the four corners.

As for the biblical provision that the garment contain "a cord of
blue" at each corner, this law apparently was observed for centuries.
The blue dye came from a type of snail that eventually became

extinct (perhaps a surge in the Jewish population was responsible for this): The Rabbis ruled that the obligation to have a blue thread was therefore suspended.

In modern times, one Hasidic dynasty claimed to have found the supposedly extinct snail that generated the required dye, and reinstituted the blue thread. This practice, however, has remained rather on the fringes of contemporary Jewish life.

Why a blue thread? The Torah doesn't say, although Bible scholar Jacob Milgrom conjectures that the blue dye was expensive and associated with royalty (hence "royal blue"). By insisting that every Jewish male wear at least some blue, biblical law enabled even poor Jewish men to feel special.

If the goal of *tzitzit* is to remind all Jews to observe God's laws, then why is the commandment restricted to males? Indeed, the Torah does not mandate such a restriction (it speaks of it as obligatory for the "Israelite people"). However, by the time of the Talmud, the Rabbis ruled that *tzitzit* are not obligatory for women. Perhaps the rationale was that women were more homebound than men, and thus less likely to come into contact with the sort of temptations that *tzitzit* were intended to guard against (in addition, the wearing of *tzitzit* was only mandated during the day, when they could be seen, and women were generally exempt from fulfilling such time-bound commandments [Babylonian Talmud, *Menachot* 43a]). In the modern world, however, the rationale for women wearing *tzitzit* would seem to be as binding as the one for men: to recall the commandments of God "so that you do not follow your heart and eyes after which you go whoring."

193. The Red Heifer

NUMBERS 19:1–21

According to Jewish tradition, King Solomon, the wisest of mortals, could understand and explain just about all the laws of the Torah. But even Solomon was "stumped" by the Torah law legislating that an unblemished red heifer, upon which no yoke had been laid, should be brought to the High Priest and burned. The cow's ashes were then retained to be used in the cleansings of Israelites who had become ritually impure.

The Bible legislates that a person who touches a human corpse is ritually unclean for seven days. During this time, he or she is forbidden to enter the Tabernacle and, in later times, the Jerusalem Temple. During the seven days, a ritually clean person takes ashes from the red heifer, mixes them with fresh water, and sprinkles the ashes on the unclean person on the third and seventh day of impurity. After the second sprinkling, the unclean person washes his clothes, bathes in water, and at nightfall again becomes ritually clean. A person who is not sprinkled with the red heifer's ashes remains permanently impure.

Another strange feature of this law is that the person who handles the ashes himself becomes impure for one day. Thus, the ashes make the impure pure, and the pure impure.

When a gentile asked Rabbi Yochanan ben Zakkai the reason for the law of the Red Heifer, he fended off the questioner with a far-fetched rationale, then admitted to his disciples that he did not understand the Bible's reasoning: "As you live, the corpse does not defile, nor does the [mixture of ashes and] water cleanse. The truth is that the rite of the Red Heifer is a decree of the King who is King of Kings. The Holy One said: 'I have set down a statute. I have issued a decree. You are not permitted to transgress My decree.' [As it is written,] 'This is a statute of the Torah commanded by God'" (Numbers 19:2; *Tanchuma B*, Chukat # 26).

Reflections: How the law of the Red Heifer still affects Jewish life: "These ashes are no longer available and since, according to Maimonides, the site of the Temple still enjoys its sanctity and since everyone has come into contact with a corpse or with one who has, Orthodox Jews, nowadays, do not enter the Temple site and a notice appears at the entrance to warn them off" (Louis Jacobs, *The Jewish Religion: A Companion*, page 415).

194. Fulfilling a Vow

NUMBERS 30:3; DEUTERONOMY 23:23–24

The requirement that a person carry out his promises is a cornerstone of biblical morality: "If a man makes a vow to the Lord or takes an oath imposing an obligation on himself, he shall not breach his pledge, he must carry out all that has crossed his lips" (Numbers 30:3). By insisting on the binding nature of pledges, the Bible intends to influence people to be very cautious before undertaking a vow: "Whereas you incur no guilt if you refrain from vowing, you must fulfill what has crossed your lips and perform what you have voluntarily vowed . . . having made the promise with your own mouth" (Deuteronomy 23:23–24).

To modern ears, the Bible's concern with fulfilling one's word sounds almost quaint. Today, people commonly utter oaths, even when they have no intention of carrying them out. Think how often you hear someone say, "I swear to God that . . ." followed by a promise of action ("I'm never going to do that again!") that he or she has no serious intention of fulfilling.

In conformity with the Torah, the Psalmist teaches that a righteous person "stands by his oath even when it is to his disadvantage" (15:4). Jewish commentators understood this to mean that if during a moment of enthusiasm one announces a pledge to donate a large sum to a charity and subsequently regrets doing so, he or she is still obliged to give the promised amount of money.

A charitable contribution is, in fact, the subject of the very first vow the Bible records, one offered by Jacob. Fleeing for his life from his brother Esau, he pledges to God that if he returns home safely, "of all that You give me, I will set aside a tenth for you" (Genesis 28:22; this, and Genesis 14:20 are the Bible's first mention of tithing).

Some vows (e.g., "I swear I'm going to kill whoever did that") should of course not be fulfilled. This may seem obvious, but it wasn't to Jephtah, an early military leader who led his fellow Israelites in a massive victory over Ammon. Shortly before the battle began, he vowed that if God granted Israel victory in battle, then, upon his return home, he would offer as a sacrifice to God the first living thing to come out of his house (Judges 11:31).

The rash Jephtah undoubtedly expected an animal to emerge first; instead his daughter did, and he felt obliged to sacrifice her. Doing so was an act of murder, since a basic principle of Jewish jurisprudence is that a vow to break a biblical law (such as the ban on human sacrifice) is invalid and should never be implemented.

"Think before you speak," the advice parents often give children, is totally consistent with biblical ethics regarding words and vows. By obligating people to fulfill noncriminal vows, the Bible intended to force them to consider carefully the implication of their vows before they utter them. (Proverbs 20:25 teaches: "It is a snare for a man to pledge a sacred gift rashly, and to give thought to his vows only after they have been made.")

The Torah rules that the vow of a young woman living at home can be countermanded by her father. But if the father hears of her vow and offers no objection, then the vow is binding. Likewise with a married woman: "If her husband restrains her on the day that he learns of [her vow] he thereby annuls her vow . . . and the Lord will forgive her" (Numbers 30:9). If he says nothing, the vow remains in force.

Although there clearly seems to be a patronizing element in this law, I'm quite certain that more than a few men who have made rash oaths would have been pleased had the Torah permitted their mothers or wives to veto them.

As for divorced and widowed women, no man can annul their vows, which thus are as binding as oaths taken by men. But Jewish law does incorporate procedures to allow people escape clauses from highly inconvenient vows (see laws 406–407).

195. Cities of Refuge

NUMBERS 35:12–36:13

The Torah, even while advocating that premeditated murderers be put to death (see Genesis 9:6, Exodus 21:12–14), was equally con-

cerned that *involuntary* manslayers be spared death. To ensure that
the victim's enraged relatives did not exact a blood vengeance, six
cities of refuge were to be set aside in Israel "to which a manslayer
who has killed a person unintentionally may flee" (Numbers 35:12;
see also Deuteronomy 4:41–43 and Joshua 20:7–8).

The Torah carefully establishes criteria for judging whether a
homicide was voluntary or involuntary. For example, if one hits another with a stone tool that can cause death, and death does result,
the slayer cannot claim that the death was accidental; because he
used a weapon capable of causing death, he is seen as "a murderer
[who] must be put to death" (35:17).

The negligent manslayer is, for example, one who inadvertently
drops a heavy stone on another (perhaps through carelessness). In
modern terms, a heedless or drunk driver who runs over and kills a
pedestrian would fit into this category.

The Torah is concerned both about protecting the negligent manslayer from death, and about ensuring that he is punished. The city
of refuge serves both purposes. Provided that the manslayer remains
within the city limits, the victim's relatives are forbidden to wreak
vengeance; if they do, they will be punished as premeditated murderers. On the other hand, if the manslayer leaves the city of refuge,
the victim's closest relatives (known in Hebrew by the term *go'el ha-
dam*, the "blood avenger") are permitted to kill him.

The Torah legislates that the manslayer "must remain inside the
city of refuge until the death of the High Priest; after [his] death
. . . , the manslayer may return to his land holding" (35:28).

What is the logic behind this seemingly arbitrary period of punishment? It appears to contain a tit-for-tat element. The manslayer
acted with disregard for other people's lives (pushing someone without considering the consequences [35:22], or handling rocks without
being careful). Thus, there is a certain poetic justice in having his
needs treated arbitrarily. Upon entering the city of refuge, the manslayer has no way of knowing how long he will have to remain there.
If the High Priest lives for a long time, the sentence could be
lengthy; or conversely, it could be short. Thus, as Bible scholar Jacob
Milgrom writes: ". . . the punishment is made to fit the crime; the
deliberate homicide is deliberately put to death; the involuntary
homicide who took life by chance must await the chance of the
High Priest's death in order to be released from the asylum city."*

*The Mishnah, the standard work of the Oral Law, which was written about
200 C.E., records that the High Priest's mother would personally bring food

Within a city of refuge, the manslayer is permitted to work at his profession and bring his family to live with him. The sole restriction is geographical: He cannot venture outside the city.

Once the involuntary slayer is released from the city of refuge, the blood avenger is forbidden to take revenge; if he does so, he is regarded like any other premeditated killer and is punished accordingly.

While generally regarded as an outmoded feature of biblical legislation, the cities of refuge suggest an interesting way for punishing nonviolent criminals. Confining such people alongside violent criminals often subjects nonviolent offenders to violence, rape, and, at the very least, to exceedingly undesirable influences. In addition, separating nonviolent offenders from their families sometimes imposes an unnecessary hardship on the families. Thus, the cities of refuge constitute a piece of criminal legislation that penologists might consider reintroducing into modern law.

---

and clothing to the residents of the cities of refuge in the hope that they would not pray for her son's death (Mishnah, Makkot 2:6).

XXV. DEUTERONOMY

196. *Sh'ma Yisra'el*: The Jewish Credo

DEUTERONOMY 6:4–9

The Commandment to Love God

6:5

The Commandment to Teach Torah to One's Children

6:7

Tefillin

6:8

Mezuzah

6:9

Six simple words, "*Sh'ma Yisra'el, Adonai Eloheinu, Adonai Echad*—Hear, O Israel, the Lord Is Our God, the Lord Alone" [alternatively, "the Lord Is One" or "the Lord Is Unique"]—summarize monotheism's essential ethical and philosophical revolution. The nation of Israel proclaims, first to itself, then to the world, that it worships One Universal God. If God alone is God, then worship of anything other than God, be it a fertility or nature deity, the nation-state, or money, is idolatry.

The five verses that follow the *Sh'ma*, which constitute its first paragraph (paragraphs 2 and 3 are made up of Deuteronomy 11:13–21 and Numbers 15:37–41), are part of the daily prayer service, and contain basic theological and ritual ordinances intended to deepen the Israelites' commitment to monotheism.

Love of God—The first verse reads: "You shall love the Lord your God with all your heart and with all your soul and with all your might" (6:5).

In a world in which people feared gods—how could they not, given that these gods demanded human sacrifice?—it was unique to have a religion that demanded that one love God. Indeed, as Dennis Prager has noted, the fact that God wants to be loved, and not just feared, makes Him lovable (on fear of God, see entry 153).

The Talmud, which takes care to concretize even abstract laws such as love, defines every element in the preceding verse. Concerning the words "You shall love the Lord your God," the talmudic Rabbis comment, "[This means that you should] cause God to become loved through you. One who studies the Law, serves Torah scholars, is honest in his dealings and speaks gently with people, what do people say of him? 'This man who studies Torah—how pleasant are his ways, how becoming are his deeds'" (Babylonian Talmud, *Yoma* 86a). In other words, love of God is expressed through study of His Torah, and through honest and kind treatment of the human beings He has created "in His image."

On "with all your heart," the Rabbis note: "With both of your inclinations, the good and the evil" (Babylonian Talmud, *Berachot* 54a). The evil inclination (in Hebrew, *yetzer ha-ra*) refers to aggressive (including sexual) desires. Thus, if one has a desire to be famous, one should try to satisfy that desire through ethical acts that will bring one renown. Although the yearning for fame emanates more from selfish than altruistic motives, whoever satisfies this desire through doing great good (e.g., a wealthy person who donates money to a charity to put up a building that will be named for him) has marshaled his or her "evil desire" in the service of God.

"With all your soul" is understood as meaning that one should be willing to die rather than betray God. That is why Jewish martyrs, who often accepted torture and execution rather than conversion to another religion, recited the *Sh'ma* just before they were murdered. The second-century rabbi Akiva was the most famous Jewish martyr to die with the *Sh'ma* on his lips.

"With all your might" is interpreted by the Rabbis as meaning with all one's wealth. One shows love of one's Creator by a willingness to dispense charity. Jewish sources regard a person who is unwilling to dispense money to help others as something of an idolator, since his worship of money takes precedence over his worship of the God who commands him to share with others some of that money.

Studying Torah—"And you shall teach them [the words of Torah] to your children, and you shall speak about them when sitting in your house, when walking on the way, when lying down and when rising up" (6:7).

Although the Torah never explicitly says, "This commandment is more significant than that,"* the ordinance that a person must teach Torah to his children came to be understood as one of the Torah's preeminent commandments. To study Judaism is a moral imperative, because to be good one has to know what one's duties are and what goodness entails (e.g., Lot thought he was acting morally when he offered two of his daughters to be raped by a mob, in lieu of two visitors to his house; Genesis 19:7–8), and this requires study.

We know of Jewish communal ordinances dating back to at least talmudic times requiring that children be educated. At a time when few gentiles were literate, Jewish law demanded that even the poor be given the opportunity to study. The prooftext on which this commitment rested is the *Sh'ma's* command "And you shall teach it to your children. . . ."

This verse is also understood as mandating that one should engage in Torah study at least twice daily; in the morning ("when you rise up") and in the evening ("when you lie down").

Tefillin—"And you shall bind them as a sign upon your hands and they shall be a frontlet between your eyes" (6:8).

In Jewish tradition this verse is understood as mandating that men don *tefillin*,† small black boxes containing verses from the Torah. Men are supposed to wear one box on one arm and another on the head every weekday (but not on the Sabbath and on most other holidays). My friend Dr. Stephen Marmer suggests that *tefillin* thus influences both how we see the world ("between your eyes") and how we act ("upon your hands").

---

*The greater seriousness of one commandment over another can sometimes be gauged by comparing the relative punishment exacted for each one's violation.
†I refrain from using the English word "phylacteries," since I have yet to find a person who knows the word "phylacteries" who doesn't also know *tefillin*. As a rule, anyone who says "phylacteries" does not wear them: I have heard many Jews say, "I put on *tefillin* this morning"; I have yet to hear anyone say, "I put on phylacteries this morning."

Mezuzah—"And you shall write them on the doorposts of your house and on your gates" (6:9).

Jews are commanded to affix on the doorposts of their homes a *mezuzah,* a small box containing the Torah verses in which this verse appears as well as related verses. The goal of the *mezuzah* is to transform the house of the person who puts it up. Prior to a Jew leaving the house, the *mezuzah* is intended to remind one how to act in the outside world; seeing the *mezuzah* before one enters the house suggests how one should act at home.

The recitation of the *Sh'ma,* then, reminds us of our omnipresent duties to God: to love God, to study His Torah, to don *tefillin* in the morning, and to make our house a place in which God and Torah are venerated.

Reading: Dennis Prager, "Is God Loveable?" in *Think a Second Time,* pages 244–246.

197. To Neither Add nor Detract from the Torah's Laws

DEUTERONOMY 13:1

Torah law is sometimes startling in its insistence on banning subtle as well as obvious injustices. Leviticus 19:15 outlaws the indisputable evil of a judge "showing deference to the rich," but likewise forbids a justice to "favor the poor."* For the Torah, the "bottom line" admonition to judges is that "you shall not render an unfair decision . . . [but you shall] judge your neighbor fairly" (Leviticus 19:15).

A similarly subtle balancing is at work in the deuteronomic prohibition "Be careful to observe only that which I [God] enjoin upon

---

*It is hard to imagine that judges in other societies were reminded not to unfairly favor the poor.

you; neither add to nor take away from it" (13:1; see also Deuteronomy 4:2).

That the Israelites are warned not to *diminish* the laws God commanded them is obvious; the Lord would hardly want to see Israelites neglecting ordinances such as the Sabbath, respect for the aged, or love of one's neighbor. Surprising, however, is the Torah's insistence that legislators not add laws, a prohibition that flies in the face of the common human tendency to regard the observance of ever more statutes as evidence of greater piety.

Later rabbinic authorities, who did add extra ordinances to those already legislated in the Torah, felt compelled to justify doing so with two rationales: First, gratitude to God necessitated establishing additional holidays (e.g., Purim and Hannuka) to express appreciation for God's delivering His people from post-Torah dangers. Second, additional regulations were needed to guard against the possible violation of Torah laws. The rabbinic term for such prophylactic legislation is "fence." As a fence makes a field more difficult to enter and thereby safeguards it from being violated, "legal fences" safeguard the law. For example, since the Torah forbids a man from having sexual relations with his wife during her monthly period, the Rabbis also forbade all expressions of physical affection during this time as well, on the assumption that such behavior might lead a couple to violate the biblical injunction.

The Rabbis understood their right to extend Jewish law as rooted in another piece of deuteronomic legislation. Deuteronomy 17:9–10 rules that when a baffling legal case arises, Israelites are to appear before the magistrates and "when they announce to you the verdict in the case, you shall carry out the verdict that is announced to you . . . , observing scrupulously all their [the leaders of the age] injunctions to you."

This verse notwithstanding, more than a few Jews have expressed concern that the tendency to define religiosity by "more" led the Rabbis to be more vigorous in enforcing Deuteronomy's second clause, which urges one not to diminish the law, than its first clause, which cautions against adding to the law.

Sources: Moses Maimonides elaborates on the permissibility of establishing such "fences" in the *Guide of the Perplexed* 3:41. He notes that it is permissible to add on laws as long as one makes it clear that these laws have been added on, and are not Torah laws.

198. "Justice, Justice, You Shall Pursue"

DEUTERONOMY 16:20

As a rule, the Bible obligates people to observe a commandment only when the appropriate opportunity arises. For example, the To-rah decrees that one show respect for old people by rising in their presence (Leviticus 19:32); however, a person is not commanded to go about trying to find elderly people so that he or she can fulfill this commandment.

However, Deuteronomy 16:20's "Justice, justice, you shall pursue" suggests that the Torah is mandating a particular aggressiveness in performing this commandment. "Pursuing" justice implies that one should become personally involved when hearing about an injustice that one is capable of ameliorating.

This law is directed with particular emphasis to judges, who are instructed to be guided in the courtroom by considerations of justice, not compassion. Thus, "You shall not render an unfair decision: do not favor the poor nor show deference to the rich; judge your kins-man fairly" (Leviticus 19:15). The eleventh-century Bible commen-tator Rashi offers the traditional Jewish understanding of this verse: " 'Do not favor the poor.' [What does this mean?] You shall not say, 'This is a poor man, and the rich man in any case is obliged to help support him. Therefore, I will rule in the poor man's favor and he will thereby obtain some support in a respectable fashion.' 'Or show deference to the rich.' [What does this mean?] You shall not say, 'This is a rich man, or a man of noble descent, how can I shame him or be witness to his shame?' . . . It is for this reason that the Torah states, 'nor show deference to the rich.' "

A concern with enforcing standards of justice likewise is behind the ordinance "Magistrates and officers [shotrim, the word for officers, means "police" in modern Hebrew] shall you appoint in all your cities" (Deuteronomy 16:18). In biblical times, three, twenty-three, or seventy-one judges, depending on a case's severity, adjudicated both disputes and criminal violations. In serious criminal cases, some judges were appointed to seek out all potentially exonerating evi-dence; others, all incriminating evidence. Each group then presented what they had learned before the other judges, who decided the case. Thus, judges in ancient Israel fulfilled the role practiced today by lawyers and juries. Unlike in contemporary society, unanimity was not required to reach a judgment of guilt or innocence.

Because administering justice often requires courage, the Torah demands of judges: "You shall not tremble before any man" (Deuteronomy 1:17).

The command to pursue and practice justice does not devolve solely on judges; individual Israelites are instructed to accord justice even to their enemies. Although biblical law never subscribed to Jesus' statement in the New Testament to "love your enemies" (Matthew 5:44), it did command just treatment of them: "If you encounter an ox of your enemy or his donkey wandering, you shall return it to him repeatedly [if necessary]. If you see your enemy's donkey lying down under its burden, and would refrain from raising it, you must nevertheless raise it with him" (Exodus 23:5).

This obsession with justice also permeates the Torah's narrative sections. When Abraham believes God might be acting unjustly, he challenges the Lord: "Shall not the Judge of all the earth deal justly?" (Genesis 18:25; see entry 12). The most frequently quoted verse of the prophet Amos is an appeal to his fellow Israelites to act justly: "Let justice well up as waters and righteousness as a mighty stream" (5:24; see entry 116).

The repetition of the word "justice" likewise suggests that one must pursue justice in a just manner, that is, a just end must be pursued through just means.

199. The Biblical View of Kingship

DEUTERONOMY 17:14–20

Several passages throughout the Hebrew Bible reflect profound ambivalence on the institution of monarchy. Early in Israelite history, in Canaan two prominent leaders oppose the very idea of kingship.

When the people approach Gideon, a successful warrior and leader, and ask him to become their king, he dismisses the request as a repudiation of God: "I will not rule over you, and my son will not rule over you; the Lord will rule over you" (Judges 8:23; see also entry 63).

Several generations later, the prophet and judge Samuel also understands the people's rationale for wanting a king, "that we may be like all other nations" (I Samuel 8:5), as repudiating divine authority. Indeed, God tells Samuel, who feels personally slighted by the Israelites' desire for a new leader: "For it is not you they have rejected; it is Me they have rejected as their king" (8:7). Nonetheless, God instructs Samuel to appoint a king, conditioning his right to rule on absolute obedience to the Lord.

An earlier reference to kingship occurs in Deuteronomy 17. While the Israelites are still wandering in the desert, the institution of monarchy is anticipated and, although spoken of neither positively nor negatively, is hedged with many restrictions. Thus, the very rationale the people later offer Samuel for wanting a king, and which so irritated him, is foreseen as normative in Deuteronomy: "If, after you have entered the land that the Lord your God has given you, and occupied it and settled in it, you decide, 'I will set a king over me, *as do all the nations about me,'* you shall be free to set a king over yourself, one chosen by the Lord your God" (Deuteronomy 17:14–15).

Along with insisting that the king be chosen by God, the Torah hedges his appointment with restrictions and warnings. First, he must be an Israelite, not a foreigner (comparable to the constitutional requirement that the president of the United States be a native-born American). Israelite kingship begins sometime before 1000 B.C.E., when Saul is appointed king, and lasts until 587, when the Babylonians depose Zedekiah, Judah's final king, and no king was a non-Israelite.*

Other Deuteronomic restrictions on monarchs are famous largely because of their violations by Solomon, long regarded as one of Israel's preeminent kings. The text rules that the king is not to accumulate, or direct his people to go down to Egypt to acquire, a large number of horses (17:16). First Kings, chapter 5, verse 7, reports, however, that Solomon maintained no less than forty thousand stalls for his horses.

---

*On the other hand, Israelite identity, unlike later Jewish identity, seems to have been determined by the father, not the mother. Thus, King Ahaziah was the son of the Israelite king Ahab and his Phoenician queen Jezebel. Although Ahaziah was a disgusting ruler, Elijah denounces him for being an evil king, not for being a non-Israelite ruler; II Kings, chapter 1.

Similarly, the monarch is not to take many wives, "lest his heart go astray" (17:17). In I Kings 11:3 Solomon is reported as having seven hundred wives and three hundred concubines, some of whom did indeed lead him astray (see 1 Kings 11:4–5, and entry 89).

Finally, the king is forbidden to amass excessive amounts of silver and gold; I Kings 10:21 informs us that "all King Solomon's drinking cups were of gold, and all the utensils . . . were of pure gold. . . ."

Perhaps most important, the Bible prescribes a positive commandment for the king. Upon assuming office, he must personally write, or hire someone to do so, a scroll of the Torah, which is to be kept near him at all times. The law's goal is to remind the monarch that he is not the maker of Israelite laws, but the enforcer of God's laws and subject to those laws like every other Israelite. (A parallel would be if an American president, upon inauguration, was asked to personally write, or to have written for him, a copy of the Constitution.)

In short, the biblical view of kingship is ambivalent, approving of the institution of monarchy when a king sees himself as fully bound by the laws of the Torah, but apparently doubtful that such an idyllic state can occur easily. Despite all these doubts, the Bible does portray God as proclaiming that all true kings must descend from the House of David (II Samuel 7:16).

200. *Ba'al Tashchit*: The Biblical Law That Forbids Gratuitous Destruction

DEUTERONOMY 20:19

"When you besiege a city . . . you shall not destroy its [fruit] trees. . . . You shall eat of them, do not cut them down; for man's life depends on the trees of the field" (Deuteronomy 20:19).

The Bible has considerable respect for the environment, particularly for trees; indeed, a famous biblical verse speaks of the Torah as an *etz hayyim* ("tree of life"—Proverbs 3:18). The biblical injunction outlawing gratuitous destruction of trees was eventually broadened to forbid *all* acts of gratuitous destruction. In the twelfth century, Moses Maimonides ruled: "Not only one who cuts down fruit trees, but also one who [purposely and impulsively] smashes household goods, tears clothes, demolishes a building, stops up a spring, or destroys food, violates the [above] command, 'You shall not destroy. . . .' "

Rabbinic elaborations, assembled in the Midrash, condemn both gratuitous destruction and environmental carelessness: "When God created Adam, He led him around the Garden of Eden and said to him: 'Behold my works! See how beautiful they are, how excellent! All that I have created, for your sake did I create it. See to it that you do not spoil and destroy my world; for if you do, there will be no one to repair it after you' " (*Ecclesiastes Rabbah* 7:13).

Another *midrash*, noting that God demanded that the Tabernacle be constructed from the non–fruit-bearing acacia tree (Exodus 36:20), deduces that "God set an example for all time, that when a man is about to build his house from a fruit-producing tree, he should be reminded: If, when the supreme King of kings commanded the Temple to be erected, His instructions were to use only such trees as are not fruit bearing—even though all things belong to Him—how much more should this be so in your case?" (*Exodus Rabbah* 35:2).

Later Jewish law outlaws *pointless* destruction, but permits cutting down fruit trees that harm more valuable plants, damage another's property, and/or if their wood becomes more valuable than the fruit they produce (Moses Maimonides, *Mishneh Torah*, "Laws of Kings," 6:8–9).

Yet some contemporary radical proponents of ecology, in their insistence that almost all diverse life forms—trees, animals, and human beings—possess equal value, seem to espouse what the Bible views as paganism. This worldview is often shaped by the notion that God is within nature; thus, the natural world itself is holy. As Rabbi Norman Lamm notes, the biblical view is different: "The God of the Bible is beyond, not within, nature: 'In the beginning, God created heaven and earth' " (Genesis 1:1).

Ecological sensitivity should not blur the distinction between human beings and the rest of God's creation. This is underscored by God's first words to Adam, commanding him to "fill the earth and master it; and rule the fish of the sea, the birds of the sky and all the living things that creep on the earth" (Genesis 1:28). From the Bible's perspective, then, making use of an animal is permitted, while abusing it is not.

Source: Norman Lamm, "Ecology in Jewish Law and Theology," pages 162–185.

201. Firstborn Sons: The Conflict Between Biblical Law and Biblical Narrative

DEUTERONOMY 21:15, 17, AND SCATTERED REFERENCES
THROUGHOUT THE TORAH

Throughout most of recorded history, firstborn sons have enjoyed enormous advantages, with respect to power within the family and by inheritance. Biblical *law*, as opposed to biblical *narrative*, continues this tradition. Thus, firstborn sons are given a double share of an inheritance (Deuteronomy 21:17). If a man had two sons, the first-born received two thirds; if he had four sons, his estate was divided into fifths, and the firstborn took two shares (in biblical times, un-married daughters had to be supported by their father or brothers; they inherited only if their father had no sons [see entry 52]). In later times, the Bible tells us, King Jehoshaphat had many sons, "but he gave the kingdom to Jehoram because he was the first-born" (II Chronicles 21:3).

Thus, one might expect most, if not all, male heroes in the Bible to be firstborn sons.

In fact, the opposite is the case. Few things are more striking than the biblical narrative's preference for younger sons. Of Abraham's two sons, Ishmael is older by thirteen years, but there is never any question that Abraham's monotheistic mission will be carried on through his younger child, Isaac. Isaac, in turn, has twin sons. Esau technically became the firstborn by emerging from Rebecca's womb minutes ahead of Jacob. Yet it is the latter who is deemed the one worthy to carry on his family's mission.

In the next generation, Jacob has twelve sons. The oldest, Reuben, outrages Jacob by sleeping with one of his wives (Genesis 49:4), whereupon Jacob removes his right of primogeniture and bestows it on Joseph, his *eleventh* son (by adopting Joseph's two sons [Genesis 48:5], Jacob in effect gives Joseph a double share of his inheritance).

By the law of averages, a few firstborn sons should have been some of the Bible's great figures, but it didn't happen. Aaron had many commendable traits, but the outstanding figure of the Torah's last four books is his younger brother, Moses (also, Aaron is the second child born to his parents; he has an older sister, Miriam).

David, Israel's greatest king, is the youngest of eight sons. He, too, has many sons, but all that we know about Amnon, his firstborn, is that he is a rapist. David ultimately entrusts the kingship to the wise, but much younger, Solomon.

Can the preeminence of younger sons be simply a coincidence, or is the biblical narrative registering a protest against a world in which firstborn sons are given preeminence for no reason other than their birth order? Such seems to be the case. Human beings, the Bible seems to be teaching us, should be judged according to their accomplishments, not on the chronological order in which they are born.

In this regard, biblical narrative eventually predominates over biblical law. For centuries, the large majority of Jews, in preparing their wills, have ignored the Torah's insistence on giving a double portion to the firstborn (so as not to explicitly violate the biblical law, among some Orthodox Jews today, the firstborn sons are expected to renounce any special rights in the inheritance.

As in the case of polygamy, it is clear that although the Bible occasionally acquiesces in a deeply rooted tradition (such as favoring the firstborn), when it finds such a tradition to be morally dubious, it finds a way to make its disapproval known.*

---

*Analogously, when the United States was established, slavery was permitted, but the Declaration of Independence's insistence that "all men are created equal" eventually helped undermine slavery.

202. Biblical Laws Concerning the Humane Treatment of Animals

DEUTERONOMY 22:6–7, 10; 25:4; AND ELSEWHERE.

In one well-known biblical tale, the kind treatment of animals is regarded as a singularly important gauge of character. In Genesis 24, Abraham instructs his servant Eliezer (see entry 16) to find a wife for his son Isaac, without providing him with any guidelines on what moral qualities he should seek in her.

Eliezer proceeds to the city of Nahor and goes to the well where local women come to draw water. He prays to God for a sign: "Let the maiden to whom I say, 'Please, lower your jar that I may drink,' and who replies, 'Drink, and I will also water your camels,' let her be the one whom you have decreed for Your servant Isaac" (Genesis 24:14).

Almost immediately, the tender-hearted Rebecca passes by; she not only gives Eliezer water, but adds, "I will also draw for your camels, until they finish drinking" (verse 19). A short while later, Rebecca marries Isaac and becomes the Bible's second Matriarch.

In another biblical narrative, the prophet Nathan confronts King David, after the king has committed adultery, and relates the parable of the poor man with one little lamb: "He tended it and it grew up together with him and his children; it used to share his morsel of bread, drink from his cup, and nestle in his bosom; it was like a daughter to him" (II Samuel 12:3). When David hears that the poor man's wealthy neighbor has killed the animal to provide a meal for a guest, he flies into a rage and declares that the wealthy man "deserves to die." David immediately adds that he has no intention of executing the animal's killer, but intends to exact a heavy fine from him (verses 5–6; see Exodus 21:37).

David's response is consonant with biblical teachings about animals. Because animals, like human beings, are created by God, they deserve to be treated with tenderness and concern. But because animals, unlike human beings, are not created in the "image of God" (see entry 146), they are considered less valuable than human beings. Thus, a person is not to be executed for killing an animal.

The extensive biblical teachings concerning the kind treatment of animals are generally skipped over by most Bible readers. Ask people which of the Ten Commandments concerns itself with animals, and you will generally draw a blank. Nonetheless, the Fourth Commandment, legislating the Sabbath, rules that "the seventh day is a sabbath of the Lord your God; you shall not do any work, you, your son or daughter, your male or female slave, or your *cattle*" (Exodus 20:10). In the ancient world, no other society legislated a rest day for servants, let alone for animals.

The Bible seems to have viewed vegetarianism as the ideal way for people to live. When Adam and Eve are created and placed in the Garden of Eden, they are told to restrict their diet to fruits and vegetables (Genesis 1:29). Verse 30 suggests that God also expected all other creatures to be herbivorous as well. Thousands of years later, Isaiah, in prophesying a messianic age, likewise assumes it will be herbivorous: "The wolf shall dwell with the lamb, the leopard lies down with the kid. And the lion, like the ox, shall eat straw" (Isaiah 11:6, 8).

The Bible never explains why, but after the world turns evil, and God destroys all of humankind except for Noah and his family, He permits human beings to eat meat: "Every creature that lives shall be yours to eat . . ." (Genesis 9:3. Later, severe restrictions limited the animals Israel could eat; see entry 173).

Despite this permission to kill animals, the Torah enacts several other laws to encourage people to treat them kindly.

"If along the road, you come upon a bird's nest . . . with fledglings or eggs, and the mother sitting over the fledglings or eggs, do not take the mother together with her young. Let the mother [fly away] and only [then] take the young" (Deuteronomy 22:6–7). Since animals have maternal feelings, it is cruel to take the young in the presence of its parent. A similar concern for animals' feelings is found in Leviticus: "No animal . . . shall be slaughtered on the same day with its young" (Leviticus 22:28).

Because the ancient Israelites primarily worked in agriculture, other Torah ordinances are concerned with the proper treatment of animals laboring in the field: "You shall not plow with an ox and mule harnessed together" (Deuteronomy 22:10). This law focuses on protecting the mule, which, weaker than the ox, will not be able to keep pace with it and will suffer thereby. Another biblical law expresses concern for the ox: "You shall not muzzle an ox while it is threshing" (Deuteronomy 25:4). Before modern technology, an animal would be tied to a central post and be made to walk in circles treading the corn. The Torah regards muzzling an animal that is working for you, thus preventing it from eating any of the food it is threshing, as a kind of torture.

The Torah also expresses concern that enmity between people not lead to animals' suffering: "When you encounter your enemy's ox or ass wandering, you must take it back to him" (Exodus 23:4). People who hate one another sometimes will harm each other's animals. Not only does the Torah forbid such obviously evil behavior, but it also legislates that one must overcome one's evil impulse and return the animal to one's enemy. In similar spirit, the next verse rules: "When you see the donkey of your enemy lying under its burden, and would refrain from raising it, you must nevertheless raise it with him." You might have a good reason for disliking someone, but why should an overburdened animal suffer because of it?

"You save man and beast," the Psalmist declares (36:7), while the final verse of the Book of Jonah depicts God as worrying greatly both over the tens of thousands of people in the sinful city of Nineveh, and the animals residing there (4:11).

A key doctrine of biblical morality is the concept of *imitatio dei* (imitating God). Thus, if God is loving and caring for animals, human beings are obligated to be so as well.

203. On Building a Safe Roof

DEUTERONOMY 22:8

Most people associate biblical law primarily with rituals. Few are aware that one of the Torah's 613 laws obligates homeowners to make sure that their roofs are safe. Deuteronomy 22:8 rules: "When you build a new house, you shall make a parapet for your roof, so that you do not bring bloodguilt on your house if anyone should fall from it."

Contemporary building codes often also obligate the construction of such parapets, although I'm unaware of other ancient legal codes that do. The Bible's reasoning, "so that you do not bring bloodguilt

on your house," suggests that this law should be broadened to prohibit having anything dangerous in your house. On the basis of this
verse, the Talmud rules that "a person should not raise a vicious dog
or keep a rickety ladder in his house" (Babylonian Talmud, *Ketubot*
41b). Post-talmudic Jewish law ruled that if you dig a pit or well on
your property, you either have to make a railing around it, or cover
it so that no one falls in (*Shulkhan Arukh, Hoshen Mishpat* 427:7).

Thus, modern Jews, and Christians as well, who build a railing
around their swimming pools to protect young children from falling
in, also are fulfilling a biblical law.

204. *Shatnez*

DEUTERONOMY 22:11

Shatnez, the biblical law that forbids wearing a garment containing a
mixture of linen and wool, is generally regarded as the quintessential
example of a law for which there is no rational explanation. The
Bible offers no reason for this ordinance. It speaks of *shatnez* first in
Leviticus 19:19, in the verse following "Love your neighbor as yourself," where the prohibition is stated vaguely: "You shall not put on
cloth from a mixture of two kinds of material." Deuteronomy 22:11,
which specifies "You shall not wear cloth combining wool and linen,"
is understood to be an elaboration of the earlier verse.

Few non-Orthodox Jews are aware how punctilious their coreligionists are in observing this biblical law. A company called Shatnez
Laboratories, located in Brooklyn, New York, checks woolen garments to make sure that no linen has been mixed in.

Large stores that have an observant Jewish clientele are well aware
of this regulation. Some years ago, I bought a suit at Barney's, the
large Manhattan clothing store. The salesman, an African American,
noticing my yarmulke, asked me, "Do you want the suit checked for
shatnez?" When I said yes, he took out a preprinted sticker and inserted it inside the suit's external breast pocket. "We have people
who come in regularly to check for *shatnez*," he explained.

205.　Problematic Laws: Regarding Bastards

DEUTERONOMY 23:3

and Rape

DEUTERONOMY 22:25

There is but one exception to the Torah law that forbids punishing children for their parents' sins (Deuteronomy 24:16): When a man and woman commit adultery or incest, a child that results from their union is deemed a *mamzer* (bastard), and forbidden to marry any Israelite except for another *mamzer*. The Torah enjoins that the curse of bastardy is passed on to any child a *mamzer* might sire: "none of his [a *mamzer's*] descendants, even to the tenth generation, shall be admitted into the congregation of the Lord" (Deuteronomy 23:3).*

Because the word "bastard" in English generally refers to any child resulting from a premarital or extramarital relationship, many people erroneously assume that *mamzer* connotes the same thing. That is not the case; in Jewish life, a child resulting from a premarital relationship is not considered either a "bastard" or "illegitimate." As for the offspring of an extramarital relationship, biblical law determines whether or not adultery has occurred according to the woman's marital status. A married woman who has sexual relations with any man other than her husband is guilty of adultery, as is her paramour, and the child she bears is a *mamzer* (so, too, is the offspring of an incestuous union). However, since biblical law permits polygamy—thereby establishing the principle that a married man can have relations with more than one woman—a sexual act between a married man and an unmarried woman is not considered adulterous.†
Therefore, the child of such a union is not designated a "bastard."

*Postbiblical Jewish law permits a *mamzer* to marry a convert, but since the children of such a union also will bear the scar of *mamzerut*, this would be a very undesirable match for a proselyte to make.
†Postbiblical Jewish law forbids such behavior, but does not deem it a violation of the Seventh Commandment ban on adultery.

The problem of *mamzerut* continues to bedevil modern Jewish law. When a couple divorce, biblical law mandates that a man give his wife a *get*, a religious bill of divorce (Deuteronomy 24:1; see entry 207). If he does not, and if for example the couple only secure a civil divorce, Jewish law regards them as still married. Thus, a woman who remarries without obtaining a *get* has the status of an adulteress, and the children produced through her second union are *mamzerim*.

Because the law of *mamzerut* is so unbending and destructive of the *mamzer's* quality of life, rabbis have exercised extraordinary ingenuity throughout the generations to avoid inflicting this status on anyone. In cases such as the one where a woman has remarried without securing a Jewish divorce, rabbis will often strive to find a technicality by which they can annul the woman's first marriage* (as noted, the children of this first marriage would not bear the scar of bastardy if their parents' marriage was annulled).

In another remarkable effort to avoid inflicting the status of *mamzer* on a child—and the status of adulteress on the child's mother—the *Shulkhan Arukh* (the sixteenth-century Code of Jewish Law) ruled that if a woman gave birth to a child up to a full year after her husband had gone off to sea, one must assume that she had a very long pregnancy (*Even ha-Ezer* 4:14). As Rabbi Michael Gold has observed: "[The Rabbis] were willing to ignore biological facts to avoid ending the marriage and imposing the stigma of 'bastard' on the newly born child."†

Why does the Bible punish the *child* of an adulterous or incestuous union?‡ Years of reflection have led me to conclude that the Torah,

---

*For example, if the witnesses that were necessary to establish the legitimacy of a Jewish wedding were nonobservant Jews, the rabbis might rule that their testimony as to the marriage's validity is unacceptable before a religious court. In the absence of valid witnesses, no marriage ever occurred, and the relationship's dissolution thus requires no Jewish divorce.

†The Rabbis also refrained from inquiring too closely about a person's past. In a gloss of Rabbi Moses Isserles to the *Shulkhan Arukh*, the author concludes: "If one who is unfit [i.e., a *mamzer*] has become mixed in a particular family, then once [he or she] has become mixed [he or she] has become mixed and whoever knows of the disqualification is not permitted to disclose it and must leave well alone since all families in which there has been an admixture [of *mamzerut*] will become pure in the future" (*Even ha-Ezer* 2:15; according to the Talmud, when the Messiah comes, the taint of *mamzerut* will be removed).

‡In theory, the adulterous couple were subject to the death penalty, but

understanding how difficult it is for many people to keep the Seventh Commandment, "You shall not commit adultery," decreed the law of *mamzerut* as a warning to a would-be adulterous couple: "You want one another so badly, that's your sin, but know that any child you conceive will be cursed till the day of its death." That knowledge, the Torah hoped, would give potential adulterers the strength to resist giving in to temptation.

Torah law is much less severe regarding rape than modern sensibilities would expect. Although the Torah never adopted the sexist view that a sexually abused woman was in some way "asking for it," it also did not impose a particularly harsh punishment on the rapist. If the violated woman was unmarried, the perpetrator could be forced to pay a bride fee and be ordered to marry the woman without the right to divorce her (Deuteronomy 22:28–29). Of course, the woman could refuse to marry her rapist, in which case he would still have to pay the bridal fee. In addition, if during the rape he struck her, he was obligated to make payments for the pain and damage he inflicted (see, for example, Exodus 21:18–19).

The presumed rationale for the Torah's ruling was concern for the future of the attacked woman. In a society that so valued virginity, a raped woman, although not responsible for her condition, would probably have found it very difficult, if not impossible, to arrange another marriage. Thus, the Torah offered her the option of compelling her rapist to marry her.

The Bible itself provides internal evidence that raped women's families regarded the crime with considerably less equanimity than is suggested by the ruling in Deuteronomy. Genesis 34 describes the rape of Dinah, daughter of the Patriarch Jacob, by a man named Shechem. His father tries to negotiate a settlement with Jacob along the lines suggested in Deuteronomy: Shechem will marry Dinah and pay any bride-price that Jacob and his family demand. Jacob's sons pretend to accept the offer, but shortly thereafter kill both Shechem and his father (see entry 21).

Centuries later, Absalom, a son of David, reacts to the rape of his sister, Tamar, by murdering the rapist, his half brother Amnon (II Samuel, chapter 13; see entry 84).

All the cases cited here refer to the rape of an unmarried woman;

---

the Rabbis instituted stringent procedures that made it virtually impossible to inflict capital punishment.

that of a married woman, or of a woman formally betrothed, is punishable by death (Deuteronomy 22:25).

206. The Prohibition of Charging Interest

DEUTERONOMY 23:20–21

One of the most enduring negative stereotypes of medieval Jews is as usurers, people who charged exorbitant interest rates to those who borrowed money. The most famous example of a usurer is Shakespeare's fictional Shylock, the villain of *The Merchant of Venice* (to make matters worse, Shakespeare depicts Shylock as wanting his interest paid in a pound of flesh).

The Torah forbids Israelites to charge interest on loans to fellow Israelites, while permitting them to take interest on loans to foreigners (23:20–21). This double standard was probably a response to the surrounding non-Israelite societies, which permitted charging interest to Israelites, and to everybody else.

The categorical prohibition against charging interest to fellow Israelites made moral sense within the agricultural society for which the Torah was legislating. Such a society was characterized by extensive barter, while money often was needed for emergencies. The Torah therefore forbade charging interest on money that a person might require to purchase food, clothing, and other life necessities.

As the economy in which Jews lived grew more urban, the blanket prohibition on interest stifled economic development. Granted, a good-natured individual might make an interest-free loan to a poor man, but why should he lend his money interest-free to someone who intended to use it to open a business and profit thereby?

Desirous as some Rabbis might have been of finding a way to permit the charging of interest on a business loan, they could not simply abrogate a Torah law. Instead, they developed a legal fiction, known in Aramaic as a *heter iska* (literally, "permission to do business"), under which a person who loans another money to open a business becomes in effect a silent partner, and receives a fixed annual payment, including a profit on his loan whether or not the business is profitable.

However, when people needed money to purchase necessities, the biblical prohibition against charging interest remained in force. Throughout history, Jewish communities have set up Free-Loan Societies to lend funds to those in dire need, in keeping with the Torah's command: "If your brother, being in straits, comes under your authority . . . do not exact from him advanced or accrued interest, but fear your God . . ." (Leviticus 25:35–36).

Although the Bible permits a lender to demand collateral on a loan, it places several restrictions on what he or she can do to obtain it as well as the use to which it is put: "When you make a loan of any sort to your neighbor, you must not enter his house to seize his pledge. You must remain outside, while the man to whom you made the loan brings the pledge out to you. If he is a needy man, you shall not go to sleep in his pledge [i.e., a needy person might have nothing more valuable than garments to offer as collateral]. You must return the pledge to him at sundown, that he may sleep in his garment and bless you . . ." (Deuteronomy 24:10–13).

Thus, biblical morality would be highly supportive of American laws that restrict debt collectors from harassing people who are late in repaying.

As regards Jewish moneylenders in the Middle Ages, some historians have speculated that the grave animosity they provoked was a major cause of medieval antisemitism. This view, however, seems naive. It presumes that Jews were active, well-accepted members of European society until they collectively began to practice moneylending, whereupon antisemitism erupted. In fact, Jews were generally hated, and barred from most other professions; they were forced to become moneylenders, a profession the Church forbade to Catholics. Jewish moneylending exacerbated, but did not cause, antisemitism. Furthermore, there is no record of a Jewish moneylender ever demanding payment in flesh; this was an evil image bequeathed to the Western world by William Shakespeare.

207. Divorce

DEUTERONOMY 24:1

The Bible assumes that it is the man who initiates the marriage ("A man takes a wife . . ." [24:1]). In consequence, if there is to be a divorce, it must also be initiated by the man. Unlike societies that permitted a man to divorce a woman by oral declaration alone (in Muslim societies into this century, a man could do so by declaring to his wife three times, "I divorce thee"), the Bible required him to "write her a bill of divorcement" (later known as a *get*). The insistence on a legal document was probably intended to make divorce more difficult to obtain, and also gave the ex-wife proof of her unmarried status if she wished to remarry.

The Bible is unclear as to what constitutes appropriate grounds for divorce. The text, as written in the modern Jewish Publication Society translation of the Torah—in conformity with the Talmud's majority view—suggests that a man can divorce a woman for any reason whatsoever: "A man takes a wife and possesses her. She fails to please him because he finds something obnoxious about her, and he writes her a bill of divorcement, and sends her away from his home" (24:1).

Ervah, the word translated as "obnoxious," derives from the same root as *arayot*, suggesting the alternative translation "sexually improper." Indeed, this understanding of the verse underlay Rabbi Shammai's ruling that adultery was the sole grounds for divorce (Mishnah *Gittin* 9:10; the majority view, which translates *ervah* as "obnoxious," is that a man can divorce his wife for any reason).

The Bible's favoring of the husband in the laws of divorce troubled sensitive rabbinic scholars throughout the ages. Jewish law eventually ruled that although only a man could initiate a divorce (fair or unfair, the Rabbis did not feel they could overturn a biblical law), a woman could not be forced to *accept* a *get* against her will. Thus, today Jewish law permits divorce, *for any reason whatsoever*, as long as it is by mutual consent.

Postbiblical Jewish law also ruled that if a man mistreated his wife, and a rabbinic court ordered him to grant her a divorce, he was required to do so. If he refused, the court was empowered to whip him until he either died (in which case, the woman was freed to remarry by virtue of becoming a widow) or authorized the issuance of a *get*. In contemporary Israel, the one society where matters of marriage and divorce are exclusively determined by Jewish law, whipping is forbidden, but recalcitrant husbands are sometimes imprisoned until they grant a divorce.*

208. To Walk in God's Ways

DEUTERONOMY 28:9

The Bible regards human beings as distinctive because they alone are created "in God's image," a characteristic that endows human life with an inherent sanctity. Having been created "in God's image," people are expected to try to imitate God's actions. Such behavior is commonly known by the Latin term *imitatio dei* (imitating God), an idea derived from Deuteronomy 28:9: "The Lord will establish you as his holy people, as he has sworn to you, if you shall keep the commandments of the Lord your God, *and walk in His ways.*"

The Rabbis point to several instances in the Torah of divine behavior that human beings are expected to emulate. For example, because God is depicted as clothing the naked—"And the Lord God made garments of skin for Adam and his wife, and clothed them" (Genesis 3:21)—human beings should do likewise and provide clothing for the poor.

Because God visited the sick—"The Lord appeared to [Abraham] by the terebinths of Mamre" (immediately following Abraham's circumcision at the age of ninety-nine; Genesis 18:1)—we should visit and comfort the sick. This important commandment acquired a spe-

---

*Unfortunately, both in Israel and the diaspora, the problem of husbands who refuse to grant a *get* (and, to a lesser extent, of wives who refuse to accept one) continues to bedevil Jewish life, and leads to much misery. A woman who does not receive a *get* from a man whom she wishes to divorce is known as an *agunah*, a chained woman, for she is "chained" to a marriage from which she seeks to be freed.

cial Hebrew name, *bikur holim* (visiting the sick). Within Orthodox Jewish communities, one often finds *Bikur Holim* societies whose members make regular visits to hospitals, where they often see patients who have no other visitors.

Because God buried the dead—"He buried [Moses] in the valley of Moab" (Deuteronomy 34:6)—one should help bury the dead, particularly the poor, on whose behalf money must be collected to purchase a plot.

The Rabbis regard burial as the highest ethical act because it is done without any expectation that the "recipient" will repay the good deed (in Hebrew, *chesed shel emet*, a true act of loving-kindness). Likewise it is the highest form of imitation of God, since all of God's acts are done without expectation, or need, of repayment.

"To walk in His ways" means to ask oneself before performing a deed: "Is this what God would want me to do? Is this the Godly way to act?"

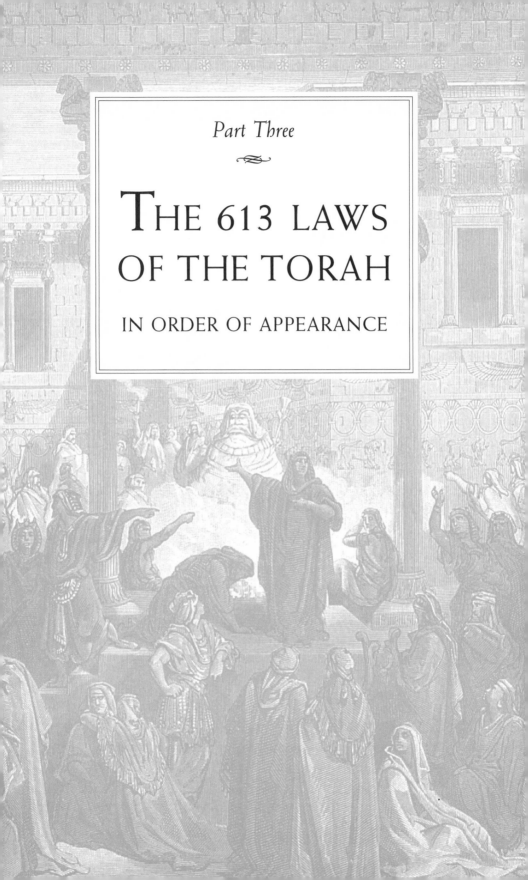

Part Three

THE 613 LAWS OF THE TORAH

IN ORDER OF APPEARANCE

The Jewish teaching that the Torah enumerates 613 commandments does not in fact appear anywhere in the Bible. It is recorded in the Talmud: "Rabbi Simlai stated: 613 commandments (*mitzvot*) were told to Moses; 365 prohibitions corresponding to the number of days in the solar year, and 248 positive commandments corresponding to the number of organs and limbs in the human body" (Babylonian Talmud, *Makkot* 23b). However, the Talmud never specifies exactly what the 613 *mitzvot* are.

Many medieval Jewish scholars did attempt to enumerate them. Two such works which are still widely studied are Moses Maimonides's twelfth-century *Sefer ha-Mitzvot* (*The Book of the Commandments*), and Rabbi Aaron haLevi of Barcelona's thirteenth-century *Sefer ha-Hinnuch* (*The Book of Education*).

Since Rabbi haLevi based his rendering of the commandments on Maimonides, their enumeration in these books is the same, although the books' structures are different. Maimonides divided his listing into positive commandments (e.g., "Remember the Sabbath day to make it holy") and negative ones ("You shall not murder"). In addition, he gathered topically related commandments and arranged them in a logical progression. For example, in Maimonides's *Sefer ha-Mitzvot*, the prohibition against working on the Sabbath (Exodus 20:10), is followed by the prohibition against journeying on the Sabbath (Exodus 16:29), although in the Torah the latter prohibition precedes the former.

In contrast, the *Sefer ha-Hinnuch* enumerates the commandments in the order of their appearance, so that those Jews who study the weekly Torah portion can easily study the specific commandments listed in that week's portion. Like Maimonides, Aaron haLevi transmitted the rabbinic understanding of the Torah's laws, which does not always correspond to the verses' literal meaning. For example, Deuteronomy 24:16 commands: "Parents shall not be put to death for children, nor children be put to death for parents; a person shall be put to death only for his own sins." Maimonides and Aaron haLevi, in consonance with the Talmud, interpret this as legislating that people shall not be put to death based on the testimony of close relatives (i.e., as if the verse read, "Parents shall not be put to death on the basis of the testimony of their children . . ."). Obviously, the Talmud did not make up such an interpretation but was relying on an orally transmitted teaching that this was the law this verse intended to convey.

The Bible makes it clear that earlier Jews had understood the verse's literal meaning as its primary one. The Second Book of Kings (14:5–6) records that King Amaziah executed his father's murderers "but he did not put to death the children of the assassins, in accordance with what is written in the Book of the Teaching of Moses, where the Lord commanded: 'Parents shall not be put to death for children, nor children be put to death for parents; a person shall be put to death only for his own crime.' "

Usually, but not always, I have explained the verses in accordance with the teachings of Maimonides and Rabbi Aaron haLevi; in any case, the talmudic understanding of the Torah's laws generally does follow the simple meaning of the text.

For those wishing to study the 613 commandments in greater detail than is offered here, both Maimonides's and Rabbi Aaron haLevi's works have been translated into English—see the Bibliography. In addition, several shorter books provide an overview of the commandments; two I have consulted are Rabbi Abraham Chill, *The Mitzvot: The Commandments and their Rationale*, and Rabbi A. Y. Kahan, *The Taryag Mitzvos.**

About a century ago, the Chaffetz Chaim, the great Eastern European rabbinic sage, compiled his *Sefer ha-Mitzvot ha-Katzar (The Short Book of the Commandments)* in which he set down only those commandments that still are applicable (hundreds of the commandments are concerned with sacrifices and impurity, and cannot currently be

---

Taryag mitzvos means "the 613 commandments." In Hebrew, letters represent numbers (i.e., *aleph* is one, *bet* is two), so that the four Hebrew letters that comprise *taryag* equal 613 (*taf* is four hundred, *resh*, two hundred *yud*, ten, and *gimmel*, three).

practiced). According to his compilation, slightly fewer than 300 of the 613 laws still can be practiced.

GENESIS

1. The obligation for human beings to procreate (Genesis 1:28): "And God said to them: 'Be fertile and increase, fill the earth and master it. . . .'" (for a discussion of this commandment, see entry 2).
2. The commandment of circumcision (Genesis 17:10): "Every male among you shall be circumcised" (see entry 151).
3. The prohibition against eating an animal's thigh muscle (Genesis 32:33): "Therefore, the children of Israel to this day do not eat the thigh muscle that is on the socket of the hip [i.e., the sciatic nerve], since Jacob's hip socket was wrenched at the thigh muscle" (when he fought with the angel; see entry 60). The thigh muscle includes the area known as the "sirloin." Rabbinical law prohibited eating the peroneal as well as the sciatic nerve.

EXODUS

4. The obligation to sanctify the new moon each month (Exodus 12:2): "This month shall mark for you the beginning of the months; it shall be the first of the months of the year for you." The month referred to is Nissan, during which the Israelites were liberated from Egypt. Jewish tradition understands this verse as mandating the sanctification of each new Hebrew month, which is celebrated as the minor holiday of *Rosh Chodesh*.
5. The slaughtering and preparing of the Paschal lamb (Exodus 12:6): "And all the assembled congregation of the Israelites shall slaughter it [i.e., the Paschal lamb] at twilight."
6. The obligation to participate in the eating of the Paschal lamb (in modern terms, this means participating in a Passover Seder; Exodus 12:8): "They shall eat the flesh [of the Paschal lamb] that same night." The verse mentions that the lamb should be eaten with "unleavened bread and with bitter herbs."
7. The prohibition against eating the Passover lamb raw or boiled; it must be roasted (Exodus 12:9): "Do not eat any of it raw, or cooked in any way with water, but roasted . . . over the fire."
8. The prohibition against leaving remains from the Paschal lamb (Exodus 12:10): "You shall not leave any of it over until morning; if any of it is left until morning, you shall burn it."

9. The requirement to remove *chametz* (leavened food) from one's possession before the beginning of Passover (Exodus 12:15): "You shall remove leaven from your houses."

10. The obligation to eat matzah (unleavened bread) during Passover (Exodus 12:18): "In the first month [i.e., Nissan] from the fourteenth day of the month at evening, you shall eat unleavened bread until the twenty-first day of the month at evening." Rabbinic Judaism understands this law as mandating the eating of matzah on the first day of Passover (and on the first two days in the diaspora), i.e., although one is forbidden to eat leavened products during all of Passover, one is required to eat *matzah* only on the first day of Passover.

11. The prohibition against having any *chametz* in one's possession throughout Passover (Exodus 12:19): "No leaven shall be found in your houses for seven days."

12. The prohibition against eating any food containing *chametz* during Passover (Exodus 12:20): "You shall eat nothing leavened; in all your settlements you shall eat unleavened bread."

13–14. The forbidding of certain individuals to eat the Paschal lamb (Exodus 12:43, 45): "No foreigner shall eat of it. . . . No . . . hired servant [i.e., a non-Israelite hired servant] shall eat of it." However, ". . . any slave a man has bought may eat of it once he has been circumcised" (Exodus 12:44).

15. The prohibition against removing any part of the Paschal lamb from the house in which it first was eaten (Exodus 12:46): "It shall be eaten in one house: you shall not take any of the flesh outside the house."

16. The prohibition against breaking any of the Paschal sacrifice's bones (Exodus 12:46): "Nor shall you break a bone of it."

17. The stricture against an uncircumcised man eating the Paschal lamb (Exodus 12:48): "But no uncircumcised person may eat of it" (this would include an uncircumcised Israelite).

18. The commandment to sanctify the firstborn of all human beings and of those animals that were eligible to be sacrificed (Exodus 13:2): "Consecrate to Me every firstborn; man and beast, the first issue of every womb among the Israelites is Mine" (see also Numbers 18:15, 17; Deuteronomy 12:17; 15:19). The firstborn animal was presented to the priest. If found to be without blemish, it was offered as a sacrifice, and the priest could eat the portions that remained. If blemished, the priest could sell the animal or eat it himself. In a practice which is known as *pidyon ha-ben* (redeeming of a son), and which is still observed (see commandment number 392), a firstborn male child is presented to a priest thirty-one days after birth and redeemed with five pieces of silver, or something of equal value.

19. The prohibition against eating any *chametz* (leavened food) during Passover (Exodus 13:3): "And Moses said to the people: 'Remember this day, on which you went free from Egypt, the house of bondage, how the Lord freed you from it with a mighty hand: no leavened bread [*chametz*] shall be eaten." There is a very subtle difference between this ordinance and number 12, which sounds remarkably similar. Jewish tradition understands the earlier commandment as forbidding the eating of food items containing *any chametz at all*, while this commandment is understood as forbidding the consumption of those foods that are *primarily chametz*.

20. The stricture against *chametz* being seen in any Israelite dwelling during Passover (Exodus 13:7): "Throughout the seven days [of Passover] . . . no leavened bread shall be found with you, and no leaven shall be found in all your territory." This commandment is similar to number 11, but the emphasis here on having no *chametz* "in all your territory" makes this more a national imperative, as opposed to number 11, which places primary stress on the elimination of *chametz* from individual houses.

21. The obligation to tell one's child the story of the liberation from Egypt (Exodus 13:8): "And you shall explain to your son on that day, 'It is because of what the Lord did for me when I went free from Egypt.'" This commandment remains key to the Passover Seder, and, perhaps because of its centrality, more Jews participate in a Seder than in any other recurring Jewish ritual.

22. The requirement to redeem a firstborn donkey (Exodus 13:13): "But every firstling donkey you shall redeem with a sheep." The donkey is the only unkosher animal for which the Torah required redemption by a priest. The owner would give the priest either a sheep or the donkey's value in money. Firstborn donkeys of Levites and priests did not require redemption.

23. The obligation to break the neck of a firstborn donkey that is not redeemed (Exodus 13:13): "If you do not redeem it [see above commandment], you must break its neck."

24. The prohibition against walking beyond permitted limits on the Sabbath (Exodus 16:29): "Let every man remain where he is [on the Sabbath]: let no man leave his place on the seventh day." Jewish law understood this as forbidding walking more than about a half-mile outside city limits on the Sabbath; walks within these boundaries were permitted.

25. The commandment that one believe in God (Exodus 20:2): "I am the Lord your God who brought you out of the land of Egypt, out of the house of bondage." Most traditional Jewish commentators understand this as a command to believe in God, and count it as the first of the Ten Commandments. However, other scholars disagree, arguing that it is impossible to mandate belief (see entry 156). Their enumeration of the 613 commandments would therefore be slightly different from this enumeration.

26. The prohibition against worshiping as divine anything other than God (Exodus 20:3): "You shall have no other gods beside Me" (see entry 157).

27. The stricture against making a graven image (Exodus 20:4): "You shall not make for yourself a sculptured image [to be worshiped as a god]" (see entry 157).

28. The prohibition against bowing down to worship an idol (Exodus 20:5): "You shall not bow to them [i.e., idols]."

29. The stricture against worshiping an idol in the usual ways its adherents do (Exodus 20:5): "Or serve them [i.e., an idol]."

30. The prohibition against uttering God's name for a vain or immoral purpose (Exodus 20:7): "You shall not carry the name of the Lord your God in vain" (see entry 158).

31. The obligation to hallow the Sabbath by maintaining its holiness (Exodus 20:8): "Remember the Sabbath day to keep it holy" (see entry 159).

32. The prohibition against working on the Sabbath (Exodus 20:10): "But the seventh day is a sabbath of the Lord your God: you shall not do any work—you, your son or daughter, your male or female slave, or your cattle, or the stranger who is within your settlements" (see entry 159).

33. The obligation to honor one's parents (Exodus 20:12): "Honor your father and mother" (see entry 160).

34. The prohibition against murder (Exodus 20:13): "You shall not murder" (see entry 161).

35. The stricture against adultery (Exodus 20:13): "You shall not commit adultery" (the biblical definition of which differs from the word's contemporary meaning; see entry 162).

36. The prohibition against theft (Exodus 20:13): "You shall not steal" (see entry 163). Rabbinic Judaism understood this prohibition as specifically directed against kidnapping.

37. The prohibition against giving false testimony (Exodus 20:13): "You shall not bear false witness against your neighbor" (see entry 164).

38. The prohibition against coveting a neighbor's property or spouse (Exodus 20:14): "You shall not covet your neighbor's house: you shall not covet your neighbor's wife, or his male or female slave, or his ox or his donkey, or anything that is your neighbor's" (see entry 165).

39. The prohibition against making idolatrous images (Exodus 20:20): "You shall not make any gods of silver, nor shall you make for yourselves any gods of gold."

40. The prohibition against constructing an altar of hewn stones (Exodus 20:22): "And if you make for Me an altar of stones, do not build it of hewn stones; for by wielding your tool upon them, you have profaned them." Jewish sources understand this as prohibiting the use of iron tools when constructing the Temple, since iron is used for making weapons. Thus, only stones that already were smooth were permitted (see Abraham Chill, *The Mitzvot*, page 57).

41. The obligation to approach God's altar with small, dignified steps, lest one's genitals be exposed (Exodus 20:23): "Do not ascend My altar by steps, that your nakedness may not be exposed upon it."

42. The obligation of an owner of a Hebrew slave to free the slave after a maximum of six years (Exodus 21:2): "When you acquire a Hebrew slave, he shall serve six years; in the seventh year, he shall go free without payment" (for a discussion of the status of Hebrew and non-Hebrew servants, see entry 166).

43–44. A master's obligations concerning female Hebrew slaves (Exodus 21:8): "Her master should provisionally designate her as his bride, and if she is not pleasing to him, he must let her be redeemed [i.e., freed through payment by her relatives]." According to Jewish tradition, the master, upon acquiring the slave, signifies his honorable intentions by declaring, "You are my designated bride" (see Babylonian Talmud, *Kiddushin* 19a, and Maimonides, *Mishneh Torah*, "The Laws of Slaves," 4:7).

45. The prohibition against a master selling a female Hebrew slave whom he decides not to marry (Exodus 21:8): "He shall not have the right to sell her to outsiders, since he broke faith with her [i.e., by not marrying her]." Jewish tradition understands this as an absolute prohibition against a master selling a female Hebrew slave, whether to non-Israelites or Israelites (see commandment number 43), since it would dishonor and humiliate the woman to be "passed" from owner to owner.

46. The specified rights of a wife (Exodus 21:9): "He must not withhold . . . her food, her clothing, or her conjugal [sexual] rights." (For a discussion of what the Torah obligates a husband to do for his wife, see entry 167.)

47. The obligation to execute a murderer (Exodus 21:12): "He who fatally strikes a man shall be put to death" (other Torah verses make it clear that such punishment applies only to one who *premeditatedly* kills another; see entry 161).

48. The prohibition against hitting one's parents (Exodus 21:15): "He who strikes his father or mother shall be put to death." Jewish tradition understood this commandment as having been violated only if one struck a parent hard enough to draw blood. There is no record of someone actually being executed for this offense.

49. The specification of fines for those who physically harm others (Exodus 21:18–19): "When men quarrel and one strikes the other with stone or fist, and he does not die but has to take to his bed—if he then gets up and walks outdoors upon his staff, the assailant shall go unpunished, except that he must pay for his loss of work and complete cure." The last two words (*rapo ye-rapay* in Hebrew) suggest a biblical presumption that injured or sick people will be treated by physicians.

50. The mandating of capital punishment for those who murder slaves (Exodus 21:20): "When a man strikes his slave, male or female, with a rod, and he dies there and then, he must be avenged (*nakom ye-nakem*)." Traditional Jewish sources understand *nakom ye-nakem* as requiring the murderer's execution.

51. The action to be taken when one's animal kills a person (Exodus 21:28): "When an ox gores a man or a woman to death, the ox shall be stoned and its flesh shall not be eaten, but the owner of the ox is not to be punished." This applies only when the ox has not previously gored a person. However, if it has killed previously (at least twice before, according to the rabbinic understanding), and the owner, though warned, failed to guard it, then, morally speaking, he too deserves to die, although he can avoid capital punishment with the payment of a stiff fine (see 21:29–30).

52. The prohibition against eating the meat of an ox executed for killing a person (Exodus 21:28): ". . . and its flesh shall not be eaten" (see preceding commandment).

53. The obligation of one who dug or uncovered a pit and left it uncovered to pay damages for any ensuing injuries (Exodus 21:33–34): "When a man opens a pit, or digs a pit and does not cover it, and an ox or donkey falls into it, the one responsible for the pit must make restitution; he shall pay the price to the owner but shall keep the dead animal."

54. The mandating of a special, onerous fine on thieves who steal oxen or sheep (Exodus 21:37): "When a man steals an ox or a sheep, and slaughters it or sells it, he shall pay five oxen for the ox, and four sheep for the sheep." Generally, a thief was required to pay a hundred percent fine for stolen goods, but this far higher fine was imposed to discourage the stealing of the animals most required by farmers. The law is comparable to the laws in the nineteenth-century American West that made the stealing of a horse a far more serious offense than the theft of other animals.

55. The commandment to hold a person financially responsible for the damage caused by his or her livestock (Exodus 22:4): "When a man lets his livestock loose to graze in another's land, and so allows a field or a vineyard to be grazed bare, he must make restitution for the impairment of that field or vineyard."

56. The commandment to hold a person financially responsible for the damage caused by a fire he or she has started (Exodus 22:5): "When a fire is started and spreads to thorns, so that stacked, standing or growing grain is consumed, he who started the fire must make restitution."

57. The specifying of responsibilities for one who is the guardian of another's property (Exodus 22:6): "When a man gives money or goods to another for safekeeping, and they are stolen from the man's house, if the thief is caught, he [i.e., the thief] shall pay double. If the thief is not caught, the owner of the house [in which the goods were being guarded; i.e., the guardian] shall testify before God that he has not laid hands on the other's property." Jewish tradition understands this as applying to one who is guarding an object free of charge. However, if one is paid to be a guardian, he or she is responsible to make restitution if it is stolen (see commandment number 59).

58. The obligation of judges to adjudicate cases between plaintiffs and defendants (Exodus 22:8): "In all charges of dishonesty . . . the case of both parties shall come before the judges; he whom the judges declare guilty shall pay double to the other." Although the verse speaks of the case coming "before God" (*ha-elohim*), Jewish tradition understands this as meaning that it shall be decided before a human court: By declaring righteous judgment, judges are assumed to be carrying out God's will.

59. The specification of damages against one who is entrusted with guarding an animal and is unable, or fails, to do so (Exodus 22:9–12; see commandment number 57): "When a man gives to another a donkey, an ox, a sheep, or any other animal to guard, and it dies or is injured or is carried off, with no witness about, an oath before the Lord shall decide between the two of them that the one [i.e., the guard] has not laid hands on the property of the other; the owner must acquiesce, and no restitution shall be made. But if [the animal] was stolen from him, he shall make restitution to its owner. If it was torn by beasts, he shall bring it as evidence; he need not replace what has been torn by beasts." Jewish tradition understands this as referring to the case of a guardian who was paid for his or her services and thus is held responsible if the animal is stolen.

60. The obligations devolving on one who borrows an animal from another (Exodus 22:13): "When a man borrows [an animal] from another and it dies or is injured, he must make restitution." Since the animal presumably is borrowed for work, if it dies while doing normal (not overly strenuous) work, Jewish law frees the borrower from having to make restitution; otherwise, he or she is responsible for any injury the animal suffers.

61. The punishment imposed on one who seduces a virgin (Exodus 22:15–16): "If a man seduces a virgin for whom the bride-price has not been paid, and lies with her, he must make her his wife by payment of a bride-price. If her father refuses to give her to him, he must still weigh out silver in accordance with the bride-price for virgins." Jewish tradition understands this as applying only to a virgin who is a minor. In ancient societies, a non-virgin would have found it very difficult to marry. This likely is the reason the seducer is obliged to marry her.

62. The prohibition of witchcraft (Exodus 22:17): "You shall not let live a sorceress." A male sorcerer also was subject to the death penalty (Leviticus 20:27). In Everett Fox's recent translation and commentary on the Torah, he notes: "Magic as such was forbidden all over the Bible, as an attempt to manipulate God's world behind His back, as it were" (*The Five Books of Moses*, p. 381).

63–64. Two prohibitions against oppressing or wronging a stranger (Exodus 22:20): "You shall not wrong a stranger or oppress him, for you were strangers in the land of Egypt." The Jewish tradition understood "wrong[ing]" as hurting someone with words, and "oppress[ing]" as doing so monetarily. Since people are more prone to do such things to foreigners than natives, the text reminds Israelites not to mistreat others; they should know from their experience in Egypt how vulnerable one is when a stranger and how horrible it is to be exploited (see entry 184).

In the Talmud, the biblical word for stranger, *ger*, denotes "convert" (and continues to have this meaning to this day) and the Torah verses protecting strangers were reinterpreted as referring to converts to Judaism. However, it is clear from the rationale that the Torah provides for this commandment, "for you were strangers in the land of Egypt," that it was speaking here about the protection of strangers, i.e., non-Hebrews (alternatively, if the word *ger* in the Torah meant "convert" the verse would make no sense, "for you were converts in the land of Egypt").

65. The prohibition against oppressing a widow or orphan (Exodus 22:21): "You shall not ill-treat any widow or orphan" (regarding the particularly harsh punishment God will inflict on one who violates this commandment, see entry 171).

66. The obligation to lend money interest-free to those in need (Exodus 22:24): "If you lend money . . . to the poor among you, do not act toward them as a creditor: exact no interest from them" (see entry 206).

67. The prohibition against dunning a poor person unable to repay his or her debt (Exodus 22:24–26): "Do not act toward them [i.e., to poor people to whom you have lent money] as a creditor. . . . If you take your [poor] neighbor's garment in pledge, you must return it to him before the sun sets; it is his only clothing, the sole covering for his skin. In what else shall he sleep? Therefore, if he cries out to Me, I will pay heed, for I am compassionate."

68. The prohibition against helping a borrower or a lender transact an interest-bearing loan (Exodus 22:24): "Exact no interest from them." Jewish law cites this verse as the basis for ruling that one is forbidden to serve as a witness or write a contract for such a transpages action (see entry 206).

69–70. The prohibition against cursing God (Exodus 22:27): "You shall not revile God." The *Sefer ha-Hinnuch* understands this verse as containing two prohibitions: against cursing God and against cursing a judge, since he is understood as acting in God's stead (see commandment number 58).

71. The prohibition against cursing the leader of one's nation (Exodus 22:27): "Nor put a curse upon a chieftain among your people."

72. The obligation to make proper payment of tithes and other dues (Exodus 22:28): "Do not delay your offerings of newly ripened produce and your agricultural offerings." The Torah saw fit to impose several taxes on the ancient Israelites, including *bikkurim*, "first fruits," which were given to the priest at the Temple, and the *terumah gedolah*, "approximately two percent of the harvest, to be presented to the priest in the Temple" (Abraham Chill, *The Mitzvot*, p. 90).

73. The prohibition against eating the meat of an animal killed by other animals (Exodus 22:30): "You must not eat flesh torn by beasts in the field; you shall cast it to the dogs."

74. The commandment not to spread false rumors (Exodus 23:1): "You must not carry false rumors."

75. The prohibition against helping a guilty man gain acquittal (Exodus 23:1): "You shall not join hands with the guilty to act as a malicious witness." In his Torah commentary, Rabbi Joseph Hertz interprets this verse as meaning, "Do not make common cause with the guilty person to give evidence which will bring about his acquittal."

76. The stricture against joining with a majority to do wrong (Exodus 23:2): "Do not follow the majority to do evil."

77. The prohibition against perverting testimony (Exodus 23:2): "You shall not give perverse testimony in a trial so as to pervert it in favor of the mighty. . . ."

78. The commandment to follow the majority decision in legal cases (Exodus 23:2): ". . . a case must be decided on the basis of the majority." This is one way of understanding the last three words of the verse (*aharei rabim le-hatot*), although in context the last part of the verse might be read as "Do not speak up in a trial, leaning toward the majority to pervert justice" (see Rabbi Aryeh Kaplan, *The Living Torah*, page 371).

79. The requirement that a judge not permit pity for a poor man to affect his rulings (Exodus 23:3): "Nor shall you show deference to a poor man in his dispute." Outside the courtroom, there is room for compassion; inside, impartiality must prevail (see entry 198).

80. The obligation to help another person, including one's enemy, to unload a burden from his or her animal (Exodus 23:5): "When you see the donkey of your enemy lying under its burden and would refrain from raising it, you must nevertheless raise it with him." The fact that you dislike someone does not entitle you to ignore his or her animal's sufferings. A third-century rabbinic *midrash* illustrates how observing this law can transform one's relationship with one's antagonist:

> Rabbi Alexandri said: Two donkey drivers who hated each other were walking on a road when the donkey of one lay down under its burden. His companion saw it, and at first he passed on. But then he reflected: Is it not written in the Torah, "If you see your enemy's donkey lying down under its burden . . . ?" So he returned, lent a hand, and helped his enemy in loading and un-

loading. He began talking to his enemy: "Release a bit here, pull up over there, unload over here." Thus peace came about between them, so that the driver of the overloaded donkey said, "Did I not suppose that he hated me? But look how compassionate he has been." By and by, the two entered an inn, ate and drank together, and became fast friends. [What caused them to make peace and to become good friends? Because one of them kept what is written in the Torah]. *Tanhuma, Mishpatim* #1; with minor variations, I have followed the translation of William Braude in Hayim Nahman Bialik and Yehoshua Ravnitzky, eds., *The Book of Legends (Sefer Ha-Aggadah)*, page 459.

81. A prohibition forbidding judges to discriminate against a poor person in a judicial proceeding (Exodus 23:6): "You shall not subvert the rights of your needy in their disputes." The Rabbis extend this law to include a prohibition against discriminating even against a known sinner, one who is, so to speak, poor in good deeds.

82. The obligation to take particular care in capital cases not to execute an innocent person (Exodus 23:7): "Do not bring death on those who are innocent and in the right, for I will not acquit the wrongdoer."

83. The prohibition against judges taking bribes (Exodus 23:8): "Do not take bribes, for bribes blind the clear-sighted."

84. The commandment to let the land lie fallow every seventh year (Exodus 23:10–11): "Six years you shall sow your land and gather in its yield. But in the seventh you shall let it rest and lie fallow. Let the needy among your people eat of it, and what they leave let the wild beasts eat. You shall do the same with your vineyards and your olive groves" (see entry 187).

85. The mandate to rest on the Sabbath, and to allow both people and animals who work for you to do so as well (Exodus 23:12): "On the seventh day, you shall cease from labor, in order that your ox and your ass may rest, and that your bondmen and the stranger may be refreshed."

86. The prohibition against mentioning (i.e., invoking) false gods (Exodus 23:13): "Make no mention of the name of another god; it should not be heard on your lips."

87. The prohibition against leading Israelites into idolatry (Exodus 23:13). This is how Jewish tradition understands the second half of the verse quoted in the preceding commandment.

88. The commandment to celebrate the three holidays of Pesach (Passover), Shavuot (Weeks), and Sukkot (Booths) (Exodus 23:14):

"Three times a year you shall hold a festival for Me." Subsequent verses go on to describe these holidays, then conclude, "Three times a year all your males shall appear before the Sovereign, the Lord" (23:17). Because of this verse, these holidays became known as the *shloshet regalim* (the three pilgrimage holidays), during which Israelites were supposed to go up to Jerusalem to offer sacrifices to God.

89. The prohibition against slaughtering the Paschal lamb on Passover Eve while one still has *chametz* (leavened products) in one's possession. Jewish tradition bases this law on Exodus 23:18: "You shall not offer the blood of My sacrifice with anything leavened." Following the rabbinic understanding of this verse, Rabbi Aryeh Kaplan translates it: "Do not sacrifice the blood of My [Passover] sacrifice in the presence of leavened bread" (*The Living Torah*, page 373).

90. The prohibition against waiting until morning to offer the parts of the Paschal lamb that are to be sacrificed on the altar (Exodus 23:18): ". . . and the fat of My festal offering shall not be left lying until morning." If they are, these parts become ritually unacceptable.

91. The commandment to bring the harvest's first fruits to the sanctuary (Exodus 23:19): "The choice first fruits of your soil you shall bring to the house of the Lord your God." Jewish tradition understands this as referring to the seven fruits that characterize the Land of Israel (Deuteronomy 8:8): wheat, barley, vines, figs, pomegranates, olives, and date honey. A farmer was supposed to bring at least one sixtieth of his first fruits as an offering to the priests.

92. The prohibition against cooking animal meat with milk (Exodus 23:19): "You shall not boil a kid in its mother's milk." This verse occurs twice elsewhere in the Torah (Exodus 34:26 and Deuteronomy 14:21). Jewish law draws different legal implications from each occurrence (prohibitions against eating milk and meat together, and against making a profit from selling such an admixture to a non-Israelite).

93. The stricture against making a treaty with the seven idolatrous nations resident in Canaan (Exodus 23:32): "You shall make no covenant with them and their gods."

94. The commandment against allowing idolaters to settle in Israel (Exodus 23:33): "They [i.e., idolaters, see preceding commandment] shall not remain in your land, lest they cause you to sin against Me; for you will serve their gods—and I will prove a snare to you."

95. The requirement that the people build a sanctuary for God (Exodus 25:8): "And let them make Me a sanctuary that I may dwell among them." During the Israelites' years in the desert, they built a

mobile sanctuary for God. Jewish tradition regards the Temple in Jerusalem built by King Solomon (see entry 90) as the fulfillment of this command.

96. The commandment to leave in their rings the poles supporting the ark (Exodus 25:15): "The poles shall remain in the rings of the ark: they shall not be removed from it." The ark, which contained the Ten Commandments, was the holiest object in ancient Jewish life. The medieval *Sefer ha-Hinnuch* explains the rationale behind this seemingly obscure piece of legislation: "We were commanded not to remove the poles of the ark from it, for fear that we might need to go with the ark out to some place swiftly, and perhaps, amid the anxiety and haste, we will not check well if its poles are as strong as necessary, and then, Heaven forfend, it may fall from their [i.e., those who are carrying it] hands."

97. The requirement that the priests always display the showbread at the sanctuary (Exodus 25:30): "It is on this table that showbread shall be placed before Me at all times."

98. The commandment to kindle a lamp (*menorah*) in the sanctuary (Exodus 27:20–21): "You shall further instruct the Israelites to bring you clear oil of beaten olives for lighting, for kindling lamps regularly. Aaron and his sons shall set them up in the Tent of Meeting . . . [to burn] from evening to morning before the Lord. It shall be a due from the Israelites for all time, throughout the ages."

99. The specification of special garments to be worn by the priests (Exodus 28:4–5): "These are the vestments they are to make: a breastpiece, an *ephod* [vest], a robe, a fringed tunic, a headdress and a sash. They shall make those sacral vestments for your brother Aaron and his sons, for priestly service for Me." According to Jewish law, an ordinary priest wore four garments when performing his priestly services, a special shirt, pants, belt, and turban. In addition to these four garments, the High Priest also wore a special robe, vest, breastplate, and headdress.

100. The commandment that the High Priest's breastpiece should not come loose from his *ephod* (Exodus 28:28): "The breastpiece shall be held in place by a cord of blue from its rings to the rings of the *ephod*, so that the breastpiece rests on the decorated band and does not come loose from the *ephod*." Because the breastpiece contained the Tetragrammaton (four-letter, most holy name of God), great care was taken that it not fall to the ground.

101. The requirement to include a binding in the opening (for the head) of the High Priest's robe to prevent tearing (Exodus 28:32):

"The opening for the head [in the High Priest's robe] shall be in the middle of it; the opening shall have a binding of woven work round about . . . so that it does not tear."

102. The prohibition against others' eating the special food set aside for the priests (Exodus 29:32–33): "And Aaron and his sons shall eat the flesh of the rams, and the bread that is in the basket, at the entrance of the Tent of Meeting. These things . . . may not be eaten by a layman, for they are holy."

103. The commandment that the priests burn aromatic incense at the sanctuary (Exodus 30:7): "On it, Aaron shall burn aromatic incense: he shall burn it every morning when he tends the lamps."

104. The prohibition against offering sacrifices on the sanctuary's altar of gold (see Exodus 30:3 and 30:9): "You shall not offer alien incense on it, or a burnt offering or a meal offering; neither shall you pour a libation on it."

105. The requirement that every Israelite give a half-shekel (most probably equal to about 88 grams of silver) annually to support the sanctuary (Exodus 30:13): "This is what everyone who is entered in the records shall pay: a half-shekel by the sanctuary weight . . . a half-shekel as an offering to the Lord." The intention behind this universal tax seems to have been to give all Israelite families an equal "stake" in those sacrifices offered on behalf of the entire people.

106. The requirement that priests wash their hands and feet when ministering at the sanctuary (Exodus 30:19–21): "And let Aaron and his sons wash their hands and feet [in water drawn] from it [i.e., a laver of copper]. When they enter the Tent of Meeting they shall wash . . . their hands and feet. . . . It shall be a law for all time for them . . . throughout the ages."

107. The commandment to anoint the High Priest with specially prepared oil (Exodus 30:25, 26, 30): "Make of this a sacred anointing oil, a compound of ingredients expertly blended, to serve as sacred anointing oil. With it anoint . . . Aaron and his sons, consecrating them to serve Me as priests."

108. The prohibition against using this special anointing oil on someone other than a High Priest (Exodus 30:32): "It must not be rubbed on any [other] person's body."

109. The stricture against replicating the anointing oil described in the Torah (Exodus 30:32): "You must not make anything like it in the same proportions; it is sacred, to be held sacred by you."

110. The prohibition against using for private purposes the formula described in the Torah to make ritual incense (Exodus 30:37): "But

when you make this incense, you must not make any in the same proportions for yourselves."

111. The stricture against eating or drinking food or liquor that had been offered before an idol. This law was based on Exodus 34:15: "You must not make a covenant with the inhabitants of the land, for they will lust after their gods and sacrifice to their gods and invite you, and you will eat of their sacrifices."

112. The prohibition against laboring on the Sabbath even during plowing and harvesting times (Exodus 34:21): ". . . on the seventh day you shall cease from labor; you shall cease from labor even at plowing time and harvest time." The Rabbis understood this verse as prohibiting plowing and harvesting during the *shmittah*, the sabbatical year.

113. The stricture against eating milk and meat together (Exodus 34:26): "You shall not boil a kid in its mother's milk (see explanation of commandment number 92). This became the basis of a central component of *kashrut* (Jewish dietary laws), the separating of meat and milk food.

114. The prohibition against making a fire on the Sabbath (Exodus 35:13): "You shall kindle no fire throughout your settlements on the sabbath day."

LEVITICUS

115. The specification of the burnt-offering sacrifice known as *olah* (Leviticus 1:3): "If his offering is an *olah* from the herd, he shall make his offering a male animal without blemish. He shall bring it to the entrance of the Tent of Meeting, for acceptance in his behalf before the Lord."

116. The commandment to bring the meal offering known as *mincha* (Leviticus 2:1–3): "When a person presents an offering of meal to the Lord, his offering must consist of the best grade of wheat meal. On it, he shall pour oil, and place frankincense. He shall bring it to the priests who are Aaron's descendants, and a priest shall scoop out of it a handful of its choice flour and oil, as well as all of its frankincense; and this token portion he shall burn on the altar as a fire offering, a pleasing fragrance to God. And the rest of the meal offering shall be for Aaron and his descendants. It is holy of holies among the fire offerings to God."

117. The prohibition against offering up leaven and honey on the altar (Leviticus 2:11): "No meal offering that you offer to the Lord shall be made with leaven, for no leaven or honey may be turned into smoke as an offering to the Lord."

118–119. A negative and positive precept: Not to offer a sacrifice without salt, but to salt all offerings (Leviticus 2:13): "You shall season your every offering of meal with salt, and you shall not omit from your meal offering the salt of your covenant with God; with all your offerings you must offer salt." Abraham Chill notes, "Our present day custom of sprinkling a little salt on our bread before reciting the blessing over it stems from the rabbinic concept that equates our homes with the holy Temple, our table with the altar, and our food with the offerings that were brought in the Temple" (The Mitzvot, page 146).

120. The specification of the sacrifice the Jewish High Court offers when it makes an erroneous ruling that causes the entire people to sin (Leviticus 4:13–14):"If it is the whole community of Israel that has erred and the matter escapes the notice of the congregation, so that they do any of the things which by the Lord's commandments ought not to be done, and they realize their guilt . . . the congregation shall offer a bull of the herd as a sin offering. . . ."

121. The commandment that an offering known as a hattat be brought for unintentional sins (Leviticus 4:27–28): "If any person from among the populace unwittingly incurs guilt by doing any of the things which by the Lord's commandments ought not to be done, and he realizes his guilt, or the sin of which he is guilty is brought to his knowledge, he shall bring a female goat without blemish as his offering for the sin of which he is guilty." While this makes it sound as if every little error entailed the bringing of a sacrifice, the Rabbis understood that a sacrifice was required only for the inadvertent commission of a sin that if committed with premeditation would be punished by karet, a divine punishment of great severity.

122. The duty to offer testimony if one has pertinent knowledge about a crime (Leviticus 5:1): ". . . a person incurs guilt, when he has heard a public-voice conveying a threat [against one who withholds testimony] and he is a witness, who either saw or knows [something relevant], if he does not tell, he bears his iniquity." Verse 5 explains that such a person must confess to withholding testimony and bring a sin offering.

123. The specification of the alternative sin offering to be brought by one who cannot afford to bring a female sheep without blemish (Leviticus 5:7): "But if his means do not suffice for a sheep, he shall bring to the Lord as his penalty for that of which he is guilty, two

turtledoves or two pigeons, one for a sin offering and the other for a burnt offering."

124. The prohibition against completely cutting off the head of a bird brought for a sin offering (Leviticus 5:8): "He shall bring them to the priest, who shall offer first the one for the sin offering, pinching its head at the nape without severing it."

125. The restriction against putting oil into the meal offering brought by an unintentional sinner (this refers to a person who cannot afford to bring an offering of an animal or bird) (Leviticus 5:11): "And if his means do not suffice for two turtledoves or two pigeons, he shall bring as his offering for that of which he is guilty a tenth of an *ephah* [most likely about five eighths of a bushel] of choice flour; he shall not add oil to it . . . for it is a sin offering."

126. The prohibition against putting frankincense into the meal offering brought by an unintentional sinner (Leviticus 5:11): "And if his means do not suffice for two turtledoves or two pigeons, he shall bring as his offering for that of which he is guilty a tenth of an *ephah* of choice flour; he shall not add oil to it, or lay frankincense on it, for it is a sin offering."

127. The requirement to add a twenty percent penalty when making payment for a transgression in which one made personal use of an item that had been consecrated to God (Leviticus 5:15–16): "When a person commits a trespass, being unwittingly remiss about any of the Lord's sacred things, he shall bring as his penalty to the Lord a ram without blemish from the flock, convertible into payment in silver by the sanctuary weight, as a guilt offering. He shall make restitutions for that wherein he was remiss about the sacred things, and he shall add a fifth part to it, and give it to the priest. The priest shall make expiation on his behalf with the ram of the guilt offering, and he shall be forgiven."

128. The specification of an offering known as an *asham taluy*, when a person is uncertain whether he or she has violated a commandment (Leviticus 5:17–18): "And when a person, without knowing it, sins in regard to any of the Lord's commandments about things not to be done, and then realizes his guilt, he shall be subject to punishment. He shall bring to the priest a ram without blemish from the flock, or the equivalent, as a guilt offering." The Rabbis understood this as referring to a situation where the person is unsure whether or not he or she broke a law, the violation of which would entail bringing a sin offering.

129. The specification of the offering brought when one intention-

ally has sinned (*asham vaddai;* Leviticus 5:21–26): "When a person sins and commits a trespass against the Lord by dealing deceitfully with his fellow. . . . Then he shall bring to the priest, as his penalty to the Lord, a ram without blemish from the flock, or the equivalent, as a guilt offering. The priest shall make expiation on his behalf before the Lord, and he shall be forgiven for whatever he may have done to draw blame thereby." The critical offense for which this sacrifice was brought in atonement was for one who lied under oath, and then wished to repent.

130. The commandment to return property that one took dishonestly (Leviticus 5:21–23): "When a person sins . . . by dealing deceitfully with his fellow in the matter of a deposit or a pledge, or through robbery, or by defrauding . . . or by finding something lost and lying about it. . . . When one has thus sinned . . . [one should restore] that which he got through robbery or fraud."

131. The obligation to remove from the altar the ashes of offerings (Leviticus 6:3–4): "The priest . . . shall take up the ashes to which the fire has reduced the burnt offering on the altar and place them beside the altar. He shall then . . . carry the ashes outside the camp to a clean place."

132–133. The requirement to kindle a "perpetual" fire on the altar, and never let it go out (Leviticus 6:5–6): "The fire on the altar shall be kept burning, not to go out: every morning the priest shall feed wood to it, lay out the burnt offering on it. . . . A perpetual fire shall be kept burning on the altar, not to go out."

134–135. The commandment that priests are to eat the remnants of meal offerings, but not cook them so that they become leavened (Leviticus 6:9–10): "What is left of it shall be eaten by Aaron and his sons; it shall be eaten as unleavened cakes. . . . It shall not be baked with leaven."

136. The specification of the daily meal offerings brought by the High Priest—beginning when he is anointed (Leviticus 6:13): "This is the offering that Aaron and his sons shall offer to the Lord on the occasion of his [alternatively "their"] anointment; a tenth of an *ephah* of choice flour as a regular meal offering, half of it in the morning and half of it in the evening." Jewish tradition understood this as meaning that the High Priest was to bring this offering daily, starting with the day on which he was anointed.

137. The requirement that the priest's meal offering should not be eaten (Leviticus 6:16): "So, too, every meal offering of a priest shall be a whole offering; it shall not be eaten."

138. The specification of how priests are to offer the *hattat* or sin

offering (Leviticus 6:18): "The sin offering shall be slaughtered before the Lord, at the spot where the burnt offering is slaughtered." In his *The Taryag Mitzvos*, Rabbi A. Y. Kahan explains: "The sin offering was slaughtered at the north side of the outer Altar. Most of the inner organs were burned upon the Altar, and the rest of the carcass was divided among the *kohanim*. Only the male *kohanim* were permitted to eat of a sin-offering, in the courtyard of the *Beit ha-Mikdash* [Temple in Jerusalem], and only on the same day and following night until midnight. Before the *kohanim* were permitted to partake of the offering, four sprinklings of blood had to be sprinkled on each of the four corners of the outer Altar. The remaining blood was poured at the southern base of the outer Altar" (pages 106–107).

139. The prohibition against eating this offering if any of the animal's blood has been brought into the Tent of Meeting (Leviticus 6:23): "But no *hattat* may be eaten from which any blood is brought into the Tent of Meeting for expiation in the sanctuary; any such shall be consumed in fire."

140. The specification of the *asham*, or guilt offering (Leviticus 7:1–6): "This is the ritual of the guilt offering: it is most holy. The guilt offering shall be slaughtered at the spot where the burnt offering is slaughtered, and the blood shall be dashed on all sides of the altar. All its fat shall be offered. . . . The priest shall turn [the fat] into smoke on the altar as an offering by fire to the Lord; it is a guilt offering. Only the males in the priestly line may eat of it; it shall be eaten in the sacred precinct: it is most holy."

141. The specification of the *shlamim*, or peace offering (Leviticus 7:11–14): "This is the ritual of the sacrifice of peace offering, which one may offer to the Lord. If he offers it for thanksgiving, he shall offer together with the sacrifice of thanksgiving unleavened cakes with oil mixed in, unleavened wafers spread with oil, and cakes of choice flour with oil mixed in, well soaked. This offering, with cakes of leavened bread added, he shall offer along with his thanksgiving sacrifice of well-being. Out of this he shall offer one of each kind of sacrifice as a gift to the Lord; it shall go to the priest who dashes the blood of the sacrifice of peace-offering."

142. The specification against leaving overnight any remains of a *todah*, or thanksgiving offering (Leviticus 7:15): "And the flesh of his thanksgiving sacrifice . . . shall be eaten on the day that it is offered; none of it shall be set aside until morning."

143. The requirement to burn remnants of sacrifices on the third day after they are offered (Leviticus 7:17): "What is then left of the flesh of the sacrifice shall be consumed in fire on the third day." Not all sacrifices were to be burned on the third day; as noted, the *todah* (see preceding commandment) was burned by the next morning.

144. That a sacrifice becomes invalidated because of failure to obey the relevant regulations (Leviticus 7:18): "And if any part whatsoever of the flesh of the sacrifice of his peace offering should be eaten on the third day [see preceding commandment], it shall not be accepted, neither shall it be credited to him who offers it; it shall be an abomination."

145-146. The prohibition against eating the meat of a defiled offering, and the requirement to burn such meat (Leviticus 7:19): "Flesh that touches anything unclean shall not be eaten; it shall be consumed in fire."

147. The prohibition against eating *helev*, or forbidden animal fat (Leviticus 7:23): "You shall eat no fat of ox or sheep or goat. Fat from animals that died or were torn by beasts may be put to any use, but you must not eat of it." Abraham Chill notes that *"helev* refers only to the abdominal fat; i.e., fatty tissue on the stomach, kidney, and flank of oxen, sheep, or goats. A distinguishing feature of this forbidden fat is that it can be peeled like a skin" (*The Mitzvot*, page 167).

148. The prohibition against consuming an animal's blood (Leviticus 7:26): "And you must not consume any blood, either of bird or of animal, in any of your settlements." In its initial formulation, this law was given to Noah and his family, and seems a universal prohibition applicable to all humankind: "You must not, however, eat meat with its life-blood in it" (Genesis 9:4; on the possible reason for the Torah's repeatedly expressed opposition to consuming blood, see entry 149).

149-150. The strictures against priests entering the sanctuary with disheveled hair or torn clothing (Leviticus 10:6): "And Moses said to Aaron and to his sons Eleazar and Ithamar, 'Do not let your hair be disheveled and do not rend your clothes [when you are serving in the sanctuary].'" This instruction is given immediately after God punishes with death Nadav and Avihu, Aaron's two older sons, for behaving inappropriately at the sanctuary (see entry 45). Jewish tradition understood the above verse as obliging priests to trim their hair at least every thirty days (see also Ezekiel 44:20).

151. The requirement that priests, under threat of divinely ordained death, are not to leave the sanctuary during a service (Leviticus 10:7): "And do not go outside the entrance of the Tent of Meeting, lest you die, for the Lord's anointing oil is upon you." Although the verse does not specifically speak of priests leaving the Tent of Meeting while conducting a service there, Jewish tradition understands this verse in light of Leviticus 8:33, which refers to not leaving the Tent during the week-long period of consecration. See also Leviticus 21:12.

152. The stipulation that priests should not enter the sanctuary, or render a legal ruling, after imbibing liquor (Leviticus 10:8–11): "And the Lord spoke to Aaron, saying: 'Drink no wine or other intoxicant, you or your sons, when you enter the Tent of Meeting. . . . This is a law for all time throughout the ages. For you must distinguish between the sacred and the profane, and between the clean and the unclean. And you must teach the Israelites all the laws which the Lord has imparted to them through Moses.' "

153. The specification of the two characteristics that render land animals kosher (Leviticus 11:2–3): "These are the creatures that you may eat from among all the land animals: any animal that has true hoofs, with clefts through the hoofs [i.e., split hoofs], and that chews the cud—such you may eat."

154. The prohibition against eating unkosher animals (Leviticus 11:4–7): "The following, however, of those that either chew the cud or have true hoofs [but not both] you shall not eat: the camel—although it chews the cud, it has no true hoofs: it is unclean for you. The hare—although it chews the cud, it has no true hoofs: it is unclean for you. And the pig—although it has true hoofs, with the hoofs cleft through, it does not chew the cud: it is unclean for you."

155. The specification of the two characteristics that render fish kosher (Leviticus 11:9): "This is what you may eat of all that is in the water: You may eat any creature that lives in the water, whether in seas or rivers, as long as it has fins and scales."

156. The prohibition against eating fish that lack these criteria (Leviticus 11:10–11): "But anything in the seas or in the streams that has no fins and scales . . . they are an abomination for you. And an abomination for you they shall remain: you shall not eat of their flesh. . . ."

157. The stricture against eating unkosher birds (Leviticus 11:13): "The following you shall abominate among the birds—they shall not be eaten, they are an abomination: the eagle, the vulture and the black vulture." Verses 14–19 list an additional eighteen forbidden birds. Without specifying any birds by name, Deuteronomy 14:11 rules: "Of all clean birds you may eat." Jewish tradition ruled that chicken, turkey, goose, and duck, among other fowl, were permitted (see entry 173).

158. The specification of characteristics of permitted locusts (Leviticus 11:21–22): "But these you may eat among all the winged swarming things that walk on fours: all that have, above their feet, jointed legs [i.e., hind legs that can be bent, and that therefore are higher than their other legs] to leap with on the ground. Of these you may eat the following: locusts of every variety, all varieties of bald locust; crickets of every variety, and all varieties of grasshopper." For those readers whose stomachs have suddenly turned squeamish, the "good news" is that Ashkenazic Jewish authorities, having long ago decided that they could no longer distinguish permitted from forbidden crawling creatures, ruled all locusts forbidden.

159. The delineation of the ritual uncleanness of crawling creatures (Leviticus 11:29–31): "The following shall be unclean for you from among the things that swarm on the earth, the mole, the mouse, and great lizards of every variety, the gecko, the land crocodile, the lizard, the sand lizard, and the chameleon. . . . Whoever touches them when they are dead, shall be unclean until evening."

160. A commandment relating to how food or food containers become defiled, and what is to be done with them (Leviticus 11:32–34): "And anything on which one of them [i.e., a mouse, a lizard; see preceding commandment] falls when dead shall be unclean. And if any of those falls into an earthen vessel, everything inside it shall be unclean and [the vessel] itself you shall break. As to any food that may be eaten, it shall become unclean if it came in contact with water; as to any liquid that may be drunk, it shall become unclean if it was inside any vessel." Abraham Chill clarifies how Jewish tradition understood these somewhat confusing verses: "Foods cannot become impure and forbidden for consumption because of contact with something unclean, unless it has first come into contact with water, dew, oil, wine, milk, blood or honey" (*The Mitzvot*, page 179).

161. The law that ritual uncleanness is conveyed by touching an animal's carcass (Leviticus 11:39): "If an animal that you may eat [i.e., a kosher animal: see commandment number 153] has died [of a method other than ritual slaughter], anyone who touches its carcass shall be unclean until evening."

162–163. The prohibition against eating swarming creatures and tiny insects found on grains and fruits (Leviticus 11:41–42): "All the things that swarm upon the earth are an abomination; they shall not be eaten. You shall not eat, among all things that swarm upon the earth, anything that crawls on its belly [i.e., a snake], or anything that walks on fours [i.e., a scorpion], or anything that has many legs;

for they are an abomination." The prohibition against eating tiny insects is derived from the verse's opening, "You shall not eat . . . all things that swarm upon the earth."

164. The prohibition against eating creatures that swarm in water. This is how Jewish tradition understands Leviticus 11:43: "You shall not draw abominations upon yourselves through anything that swarms; you shall not make yourselves unclean therewith and thus become unclean." Since commandment number 156 already forbade eating unkosher fish, this verse is understood as referring to small creatures that live in the water but are not in the category of fish.

165. The stricture against eating swarming creatures (Leviticus 11:44): "You shall not make yourselves unclean through any swarming thing that moves upon the earth." While this seems to be more or less a repetition of commandment number 162, the *Sefer ha-Hinnuch* specifies it as referring to "any swarming thing that crawls upon the earth—even if it does not reproduce" (Volume II, page 199).

166. The specification that a woman becomes ritually unclean after giving birth (Leviticus 12:2, 5): "When a woman at childbirth bears a male, she shall be unclean seven days. . . . If she bears a female, she shall be unclean two weeks." The word *tameh*, translated as "unclean," has nothing to do with hygiene; it refers rather to ritual uncleanness. Abraham Chill explains: "According to biblical law, any discharge from the sex organs renders a person unclean, and defiles any person or object with whom that person comes in contact. . . . A woman who has given birth becomes unclean because of the afterbirth and other postnatal discharges. [When the days of uncleanness have ended] she then immerses herself in a *mikveh* (ritual bath). After this, she is considered ritually clean again" (*The Mitzvot*, page 182).

167. The prohibition of a person who is ritually unclean from eating the meat of a sacrifice offered at the sanctuary. Leviticus 12:4 is cited as the proof text that *any* ritually unclean person shall not eat of a sacrifice, although, in context, the verse is speaking only of a woman rendered unclean through childbirth; indeed, it does not specifically refer to eating: "She shall not touch any consecrated thing, nor enter the sanctuary until her period of purification is complete."

168. The specification of the sacrifice to be brought by a woman who has given birth (Leviticus 12:6–7): "On the completion of her period of purification, for either son or daughter, she shall bring to the priest, at the entrance of the Tent of Meeting, a lamb in its first

year for a burnt offering, and a pigeon or a turtledove for a sin offering . . . she shall then be clean from her flow of blood." A sacrifice was brought for a male child on the forty-first day after the baby's birth, and on the eighty-first day in the case of a female child. Many are puzzled by the regulation that a newborn mother bring a sin offering; for what sin was she atoning? One Rabbi expresses the view that during the painful moments of childbirth the woman might have vowed never to have relations with her husband again (i.e., so that she would never have to undergo the pain of childbirth), and this offering was intended to negate and release her from such a vow.

169. The specification of ritual uncleanness of a *metzora*, a person with a specific sort of skin affliction (Leviticus 13:2–3): "When a person has on the skin of his body a swelling, a rash, or a discoloration, and it develops into a scaly affliction on the skin of his body, it shall be reported to Aaron the priest or to one of his sons, the priests. The priest shall examine the affection on the skin of his body: if hair in the affected patch has turned white, and the affection appears to be deeper than the skin of his body, it is a leprous affection; when the priest sees it, he shall pronounce him unclean."

Metzora was a form of skin affliction which unfortunately is usually translated as leprosy. I say unfortunately because this skin ailment was perceived as a punishment imposed by God, as in the case of Miriam, who was punished with this affliction for speaking against Moses (Numbers 12:10; see also Deuteronomy 24:8–9, which again underscores this disease as punishment). Thus, many people who encountered lepers probably automatically assumed that such individuals were being punished by God, adding to the stigma and isolation caused by the disease.

170. The prohibition against shaving the area of a scaly skin affliction (Leviticus 13:33): "The person with the scall shall shave himself, but without shaving the scall."

171. The commandment that one afflicted with the disease of *tzara'at* should rend his clothes and let his hair grow loose (like a mourner; Leviticus 13:45): "As for the person with a leprous affection, his clothes shall be rent, and the hair of his head shall go loose, and he shall cover over his upper lip; and he shall call out, 'Unclean! Unclean!' "

172. The procedure to be followed when there is an affliction of *tzara'at* on clothing (Leviticus 13:47–54): "When an eruptive affection occurs in a cloth of wool or linen fabric . . . or in a skin or in any-

thing made of skin, if the affection . . . is streaky green or red, it is an eruptive affection. It shall be shown to the priest, and the priests . . . shall isolate the affected article for seven days. On the seventh day, he shall examine the affection: if the affection has spread in the cloth . . . the affection is a malignant eruption; it is unclean . . . it shall be consumed in fire. But if the priest sees that the affection in the cloth . . . has not spread, the priest shall order the affected article washed, and he shall isolate it for another seven days." Verses 55–58 explain precisely what the priest should do at the end of the seven days.

173. The procedure for the ritual rehabilitation of one who has recovered from *tzara'at* (Leviticus 14:2–4): "This shall be the ritual for a leper at the time that he is to be cleaned. . . . If the priest sees that the leper has been healed of his scaly affection, the priest shall order two live clean birds, cedar wood, crimson stuff and hyssop to be brought for him who is to be cleansed." Verses 5–8 describe an unusual sacrificial offering made by the priest on this occasion, which involved slaughtering one bird, then dipping a live bird in the blood of the slaughtered bird. The blood was mixed with water (the birds were slaughtered "over fresh water"), and this was sprinkled seven times on the one "to be cleansed of the eruption."

174–175. The requirement that a *metzora* shall shave all his facial and bodily hair and immerse himself in a ritual bath on the seventh day after the performance of the procedure described in the preceding commandment (Leviticus 14:9): "On the seventh day he shall shave off all his hair—of head, beard, and eyebrows. When he has shaved off all his hair, he shall wash his clothes and bathe his body in water; then he shall be clean."

176. The specification of the offering brought by a *metzora* after he is healed (Leviticus 14:10–11): "On the eighth day he shall take two male lambs without blemish, one ewe lamb in its first year without blemish, three-tenths of a measure of choice flour with oil mixed in for a meal offering, and one log [about two thirds of a pint] of oil. These shall be presented before the Lord, with the man to be cleansed, at the entrance of the Tent of Meeting, by the priest who performs the cleansing."

177. The procedure for how a priest is to treat a house contaminated with *tzara'at* (Leviticus 14:35–42): "The owner of the house shall come and tell the priest, saying, 'Something like a plague has appeared upon my house.' The priest shall order the house cleared before the priest enters to examine the plague. . . . If, when he ex-

amines the plague, the plague in the walls of the house is found to consist of greenish or reddish streaks that appear to go deep into the wall, the priest shall come out of the house . . . and close up the house for seven days. On the seventh day the priest shall return. If he sees that the plague has spread on the walls of the house, the priest shall order the stones with the plagues in them to be pulled out and cast outside the city into an unclean place. The house shall be scraped inside all round, and the coating that is scraped off shall be dumped outside the city in an unclean place. They shall take other stones and replace those stones with them, and take other coating and plaster the house."

178. The ritual uncleanness of a man who has chronic discharges from his penis (Leviticus 15:2): "When any man has a discharge issuing from his member, he is unclean." Jewish tradition understands this verse as referring to one suffering from chronic discharges, as opposed to verse 16, which speaks of a specific incident of seminal emission.

179. The offering to be brought by a man after being healed of chronic discharges (see preceding commandment) (Leviticus 15:13–15): "When one with a discharge becomes clean of his discharge, he shall count off seven days for his cleaning, wash his clothes, and bathe his body in fresh water; then he shall be clean. On the eighth day he shall take two turtledoves or two pigeons and come before the Lord at the entrance to the Tent of Meeting and give them to the priest. . . . Thus, the priest shall make expiation on his behalf. . . ."

180. The specification of ritual uncleanness for one who has a seminal emission (Leviticus 15:16, 18): "When a man has an emission of semen, he shall bathe his whole body in water and remain unclean until evening. . . . And if a man has intercourse with a woman, they shall bathe in water and remain unclean until evening."

181. The specification that a menstruating woman is ritually unclean (Leviticus 15:19): "When a woman has a discharge, her discharge being blood from her body, she shall remain in her impurity seven days; whoever touches her shall be unclean until evening."

182. The stipulation that a woman who has an irregular discharge of blood is ritually unclean (Leviticus 15:25): "When a woman has had a discharge of blood for many days, not at the time of her impurity, or when she has a discharge beyond her period of impurity, she shall be unclean, as though at the time of her impurity, as long as her discharge lasts."

183. The delineation of the offering brought by a woman when her irregular discharge ends (Leviticus 15:28–30): "When she becomes clear of her discharge, she shall count off seven days, and after that she shall be clean. On the eighth day she shall take two turtledoves or two pigeons, and bring them to the priest at the entrance of the Tent of Meeting . . . and the priest shall make expiation on her behalf, for her unclean discharge, before the Lord."

184. The commandment that priests should enter the inner sanctuary only when it is necessary for them to do so. This is how Jewish tradition understands God's instruction to Moses (Leviticus 16:2–3): "The Lord said to Moses: 'Tell your brother Aaron that he is not to come at will into the Shrine behind the curtain . . . lest he die; for I appear in the cloud over the cover. Thus only shall Aaron enter the Shrine: with a bull of the herd for a sin offering and a ram for a burnt offering." In other words, priests should not enter the inner sanctuary at will, but only when they have good reason (i.e., offering a sacrifice) to be there.

185. The specification of the Temple rituals to be performed by the High Priest on Yom Kippur (Leviticus, 16:3ff.). The entire chapter delineates numerous rituals to be performed on this holy day, including a description of the attire the High Priest is to wear and the offering he is to bring, as well as an account of the ceremony of purification.

186. The prohibition against offering a sacrifice outside the sanctuary (Leviticus 17:3–4): "If anyone of the house of Israel slaughters an ox or sheep or goat in the camp, or does so outside the camp, and does not bring it to the entrance of the Tent of Meeting to present it as an offering to the Lord . . . that man shall be cut off from among his people." Verse 7 makes clear that this ordinance was to ensure that the Israelites not offer sacrifices to idols. Deuteronomy 12:20–21, anticipating a time when Israelites would not all be living close to the sanctuary, permits animals to be slaughtered and eaten without being brought there.

187. The commandment to cover the blood of a permissible wild animal or fowl after it has been slaughtered (Leviticus 17:13): "And if any Israelite or any stranger who resides among them hunts down an animal or a bird that may be eaten, he shall pour out its blood and cover it with earth." One does not cover the blood of slaughtered domestic animals.

188. The general prohibition of incest (Leviticus 18:6): "None of you shall come near anyone of his own flesh to uncover nakedness."

189. The prohibition against having sexual relations with one's father (Leviticus 18:7): "Your father's nakedness . . . you shall not uncover."

190. The prohibition against having sexual relations with one's mother (Leviticus 18:7): "She is your mother, you shall not uncover her nakedness."

191. The prohibition against having sexual relations with your father's wife, even if she is not your mother (Leviticus 18:8): "Do not uncover the nakedness of your father's wife." Jewish tradition understands this as applying even if the father divorces the woman, and even after the father's death.

192. The prohibition against having sexual relations with one's full or half sister (Leviticus 18:9): "The nakedness of your sister—your father's daughter or your mother's . . . do not uncover their nakedness."

193–194. The prohibition against having sexual relations with granddaughters, born of either one's son or daughter (Leviticus 18:10): "The nakedness of your son's daughter, or of your daughter's daughter—do not uncover their nakedness."

195. The prohibition against having sexual relations with a daughter. I am following the enumeration of the *Sefer ha-Hinnuch*, which notes that, although no specific Levitical verse says, "the nakedness of your daughter [editor's note: or son, for that matter] you shall not uncover," this prohibition can be deduced by common sense: "Since the Torah forbade a son's daughter and a daughter's daughter, who are more distant relations than she [a daughter] is, there is no need to declare that she is forbidden, as it is a *kal va-homer* [an inference by reasoning from the less to the more; i.e., if it is forbidden to have sex with one's granddaughter, then *kal va-homer* it is forbidden to have sex with one's daughter]."

One can also argue that the prohibition of sex with one's child of either sex is covered by Commandment number 188 (Leviticus 18:6), which outlaws all incest.

196. The prohibition against having sexual relations with a half sister (Leviticus 18:11): "The nakedness of your father's wife's daughter, who was born into your father's household, she is your sister, do not uncover her nakedness." It is hard to understand why this law, a restatement of commandment number 192 (Leviticus 18:9), was repeated. The words "who was born into your father's household" underscore that the woman is a half sister. However, if one's father married a woman who already had a daughter, she is not a half sister, and thus marriage with her is not forbidden.

197–198. The prohibition against having sexual relations with either a paternal or maternal aunt (Leviticus 18:12–13): "Do not uncover the nakedness of your father's sister. . . . Do not uncover the nakedness of your mother's sister." Prior to the giving of the Torah, sex with an aunt apparently was permitted, for Exodus 6:20 records that "Amram [Moses' father] took to wife his father's sister, Jochebed."

199. The prohibition against having sexual relations with an uncle (Leviticus 18:14): "Do not uncover the nakedness of your father's brother." Jewish tradition understood this law as being addressed to males, thereby outlawing a homosexual liaison between a nephew and an uncle. Yet Leviticus 18:22 specifically outlaws homosexuality (commandment number 209). The standard commentaries claim the additional prohibition on homosexual relations with an uncle was to underscore the special severity of homosexual incest. Jewish tradition permits marriage between an uncle and his niece.

200. The prohibition against having sexual relations with an aunt through marriage (Leviticus 18:14): "Do not approach his [i.e., your uncle's] wife; she is your aunt."

201. The prohibition against having sexual relations with a daughter-in-law (Leviticus 18:15): "Do not uncover the nakedness of your daughter-in-law."

202. The prohibition against having sexual relations with a sister-in-law (Leviticus 18:16): "Do not uncover the nakedness of your brother's wife."

203. The prohibition against having sexual relations with a woman and her daughter (Leviticus 18:17): "Do not uncover the nakedness of a woman and her daughter." Jewish tradition understood this commandment as having been violated only if a man married one of the two women and then was intimate with the other.

204–205. The prohibition against having sexual relations with a woman and her paternal and maternal granddaughter (Leviticus 19:17): ". . . nor shall you marry her son's daughter or her daughter's daughter and uncover her nakedness." Of the Torah's still applicable laws, I suspect that these two are the most infrequently violated.

206. The prohibition against having sexual relations with two sisters while both are alive, and if the man is married to one of them (Leviticus 18:18): "Do not marry a woman as a rival to her sister and uncover her nakedness in the other's lifetime." Apparently, prior to the giving of the Torah no such prohibition applied; the Bible's most famous polygamous marriage was that of Jacob to the sisters Rachel and Leah. This marital triangle worked out miserably, which may

help account for the Bible's prohibition of such marriages. However, when a man's wife dies, Jewish law permits him to marry her sister. Throughout history, such marriages were common, it being felt that it was preferable for the orphaned children to be raised by an aunt, rather than an unrelated stepmother.

207. The prohibition against having sexual relations with a woman during her menstrual period (Leviticus 18:19): "Do not come near a woman during her period of uncleanness to uncover her nakedness." The Torah categorically prohibits sexual relations between a couple during the woman's menstrual period, as well as during other times of uterine bleeding. The Rabbis, concerned that women would not be able to distinguish the sources of the bleeding, collapsed all distinctions (see Leviticus 15:25–33) and decreed that sexual relations be prohibited for a full seven days after the woman has experienced the last flow of blood.

208. The prohibition against sacrificing one's child to the idol known as Molech (Leviticus 18:21): "Do not allow any of your children to be offered up to Molech, and do not profane the name of your God." The most common idol to whom children were sacrificed at this time was called Molech, but Jewish law always understood this verse as prohibiting *all* child sacrifice. Indeed, Deuteronomy 18:10 makes the wider prohibition explicit: "Let no one be found among you who consigns his son or daughter to the fire." As the second part of the verse from Leviticus makes clear, one who sacrifices a child to God also is regarded as having profaned God's name.

209. Prohibition of male homosexuality (Leviticus 18:22): "Do not lie with a male as one lies with a woman; it is an abhorrence." There is no explicit biblical prohibition of lesbianism, although later Jewish law condemned it.

210–211. Prohibition of both male and female bestiality (Leviticus 18:23): "Do not have carnal relations with any beast and defile yourself thereby; and let no woman lend herself to a beast to mate with it; it is perversion."

212. To have reverence for one's parents (Leviticus 19:3): "You shall each revere his mother and his father" (see entry 160).

213–214. Prohibition against turning to idol worship or making an idol (Leviticus 19:4): "Do not turn to idols or make molten gods for yourselves."

215. Prohibition against eating meat of a sacrificed animal on the third day after the sacrifice was brought (Leviticus 19:5–8): "When

you sacrifice an offering of well-being to the Lord, sacrifice it so that it may be accepted on your behalf. It shall be eaten on the day you sacrifice it, or on the day following; but what is left by the third day must be consumed in fire. If it should be eaten on the third day, it is an offensive thing. . . . And he who eats of it shall bear his guilt."

216–217. Prohibition against reaping to the very end of one's field; instead, one must leave a portion of one's harvest for the poor and the stranger (Leviticus 19:9–10): "When you reap the harvest of your land, you shall not reap all the way to the edges of your field . . . you shall leave them [the unharvested food] for the poor and the stranger." Although the text doesn't specify what percentage of the field should be left unreaped, Jewish tradition ordains that it should be a minimum of one sixtieth.

218–219. Prohibition against gathering the gleanings (that which falls from the sickle or from the hand); instead, they are to be left for the poor (Leviticus 19:9–10): "[You shall not] gather the gleanings of your harvest . . . you shall leave them for the poor and the stranger."

220–221. Prohibition against reaping all the fruit of one's vineyard; instead, one must leave part of the vineyard unreaped, and available for the poor (Leviticus 19:10): "You shall not pick your vineyard bare . . . you shall leave them for the poor and the stranger."

222–223. Prohibition against gathering the fallen fruit of one's vineyard; instead, the fallen produce should be left for the poor and the stranger (Leviticus 19:10): "[You shall not] gather the fallen fruit of your vineyard; you shall leave them for the poor and the stranger."

224. The prohibition against theft (Leviticus 19:11): "You shall not steal." Jewish tradition understood the prohibition against stealing in the Ten Commandments as referring to kidnapping (the rationale for this understanding is that the violation of the Ten Commandments generally resulted in a capital offense, and kidnapping was the only type of stealing punished by death). This repetition of the commandment against stealing is understood as referring to all other types of thievery.

225. The prohibition against acting deceitfully (Leviticus 19:11): "You shall not deal deceitfully or falsely with one another."

226–227. The prohibition against taking an oath over a false denial (e.g., falsely denying that one received a loan or object to guard), or ever taking any other kind of false oath (Leviticus 19:12): "You shall not swear falsely by My name, profaning the name of the Lord your God."

228. The prohibition against cheating another person (Leviticus 19:13): "You shall not defraud your fellow."

229. The prohibition of robbery (Leviticus 19:13): "You shall not commit robbery." The word for robbery, *gazol*, refers to stealing accompanied by force.

230. The prohibition against delaying payment to a day laborer (Leviticus 19:13): "The wages of a laborer shall not remain with you till morning." In Deuteronomy 24:15, this same stricture is stated in positive terms: "You must pay him [i.e., a day laborer] his wages on the same day" (see commandment number 588). Such workers as cleaning women and handymen must be compensated on the day of their labor, it being assumed that they have immediate need of the money.

231–232. The prohibition against cursing the deaf, or tripping the blind (Leviticus 19:14): "You shall not curse the deaf or place a stumbling block before the blind (see entry 177 for an explanation of how Jewish tradition broadens the scope of these commands).

233–234–235. Directives to judges not to pervert justice, or to favor an eminent person at a trial; instead, they are commanded to render fair judgments (Leviticus 19:15): "You shall not render an unfair decision: do not favor the poor or show deference to the rich; judge your kinsmen fairly."

236. The prohibition against spreading malicious gossip (Leviticus 19:16): "Do not go about as a talebearer among your people" (see entry 178).

237. The obligation to defend victims of violence, or any person whose life otherwise is in danger (Leviticus 19:16): "Do not stand by while your neighbor's blood is shed" (see entry 179).

238. The prohibition against nurturing a silent hatred against another (Leviticus 19:17): "Do not hate your brother in your heart" (see entry 180).

239–240. The obligation to rebuke, but not shame, a person who is behaving wrongly (Leviticus 19:17): "Reprove your kinsmen, and not bear sin because of him" (see entry 181 for an explanation of why the words "and not bear sin because of him" are understood as forbidding shaming the one who is being rebuked).

241–242. The prohibitions against taking revenge or bearing a grudge (Leviticus 19:18): "You shall not take revenge or bear a grudge against your countrymen" (see entry 182).

243. The commandment to love one's fellow human being "as yourself" (Leviticus 19:18): "Love your neighbor as yourself" (see entry 183). The context of the verse, "You shall not take revenge or bear a grudge against your countrymen, but you shall love your neighbor as yourself," suggests that love is being commanded only toward one's countrymen. Leviticus 19:34 and Deuteronomy 10:19 command Israelites to love the stranger, that is, the non-Israelite, as themselves, and this is legislated in commandment number 431.

244–245. Two forbidden mixtures: The prohibitions against mating animals of different species or sowing together different kinds of seed (Leviticus 19:19): "You shall not let your cattle mate with a different kind; you shall not sow your field with two kinds of seed."

246. The prohibition against eating a fruit tree's produce during its first three years (Leviticus 19:23): "When you enter the land [of Israel] and plant any tree for food, you shall regard its fruit as forbidden. Three years it shall be forbidden for you, not to be eaten."

247. The obligation to set aside as sacred the fruit of the fourth year (Leviticus 19:24): "In the fourth year all its fruit shall be set aside for jubilation before the Lord." Jewish law ordained that this fourth-year fruit (*neta revai*) be put aside and eaten in Jerusalem (alternatively, it could be sold, with the money earned thereby taken to Jerusalem and used there to buy fruit, which could then be eaten in the city). From the fifth year onward, all fruit could be eaten (Leviticus 19:25).

248. The prohibition against eating blood (Leviticus 19:26): "You shall not eat anything with its blood." Because other biblical verses already had forbidden consuming blood, Jewish commentaries explained this verse sermonically—forbidding gluttony (i.e., becoming the sort of person who eats like an animal, without even bothering to drain the blood from the meat).

249–250. The prohibitions against practicing divination or soothsaying (Leviticus 19:26): "You shall not practice divination or soothsaying." Deuteronomy 18:10–11 delineates a fuller list of such forbidden activities: "Let no one be found among you . . . who is an augur, a soothsayer, a diviner, a sorcerer, one who casts spells, or one who consults ghosts or familiar spirits, or one who inquires of the dead. In commenting on this verse, Bernard Bamberger notes: "The Bible does not suggest that [these means] are ineffective or fraudulent, but it bans them as idolatrous. In Israel, knowledge of the future could be sought legitimately only through prophets,

through dreams, or through the sacred lot of Urim and Tummim"
(I Samuel 28:6; see entry 42).

251–252. The prohibitions against a man shaving the hair from his
temples and from the corners of his beard (Leviticus 19:27): "You
shall not round off the side-growth on your head, or destroy the
side-growth of your beard." In fulfillment of this commandment,
many of the most traditional Orthodox men grow side-curls (*peyot*).
Jewish law understands this prohibition as applying only to a hand
razor, and permits men to use electric shavers.

Eastern European Jews so identified clergy with beards that they
called a priest a *galach* ("one who is shaven"), since it surprised them
to see a clean-shaven clergyman.

253. The prohibition against tattooing oneself (Leviticus 19:28):
"You shall not incise any marks on yourselves."

254. The obligation to show respect for the sanctuary (Leviticus
19:30): "You shall . . . venerate my sanctuary." In Jewish tradition,
such respect is shown by not going into the area of the Temple with
one's sandals, dirty feet, or change purse, or using it as a shortcut
when going somewhere else.

255–256. The prohibitions against acting as a medium or as a wizard (Leviticus 19:31): "Do not turn to ghosts and do not inquire of
familiar spirits" (a follow-up on commandments 249–250).

257. The obligation to show respect to the elderly (Leviticus
19:32): "You shall rise before the aged and show deference to the
old."

258–259. The prohibitions against using dishonest weights, and the
obligation to use honest ones (Leviticus 19:35): "You shall not falsify
measures of lengths, weight or capacity. You shall have an honest
balance [and] honest weights."

260. The prohibition against cursing one's parents (Leviticus 20:9):
"If any man curses his father and mother, he shall be put to death;
he has cursed his father and mother, his bloodguilt is upon him."
The modern Jewish Publication Society translation renders this verse
as "If anyone insults his father and mother, he shall be put to death."
One suspects that if the law were enforced according to this translation, we would soon hear no more talk about the dangers of world
overpopulation. In actuality, Jewish tradition generally understood
the death sentence as applying only to one who employed God's
holiest name (the four-letter name for God, the Tetragrammaton,
used by the High Priest on Yom Kippur) when cursing his or her
parents.

261. The obligation to execute one convicted of marrying a woman and her mother [as well as the two women] (Leviticus 20:14; see commandment number 203): "If a man marries a woman and her mother it is depravity; both he and they shall be put to the fire, that there be no depravity among you."

262. The prohibition against following the customs practiced by the idolatrous nations living in Canaan in biblical times (Leviticus 20:23): "You shall not follow the practices of the nations that I am driving out before you. For it is because they did all these things that I abhorred them." The previous verses make it clear that the Torah is referring here specifically to sins of sexual decadence, particularly incest. The prohibition against following "the practices of the nations" is understood in Jewish tradition as prohibiting Jews from following inappropriate behavior practiced by gentiles in the societies in which they live.

263–264. The prohibition against a *kohen* (priest) making himself ritually unclean by coming into contact with a corpse, except upon the death of very close relatives, in which case he is commanded to defile himself (Leviticus 21:1–3): "The Lord said to Moses: 'Speak to the priests, the sons of Aaron, and say to them: None shall defile himself for any [dead] person among his kin, except to the relatives that are closest to him: his mother, his father, his son, his daughter, and his brother. Also for a virgin sister, close to him because she has not married, for her he may defile himself.'" He may also "defile" himself for a wife, although the text does not say so. Presumably, a *kohen* was not to defile himself for a non-virgin sister because she had a husband who could mourn for her.

265. The requirement that a priest who becomes defiled during the day and who undergoes ritual immersion not serve at the sanctuary until the evening. This is how the tradition, as interpreted by the *Sefer ha-Hinnuch*, explains Leviticus 21:6: "They [i.e., the priests] shall be holy to their God; for they offer the Lord's offerings by fire, the food of their God, and so must be holy." Thus, the priests cannot serve at the Temple unless they are purified through ritual immersion.

266–267. The prohibition of a priest marrying a harlot or a woman who is the child of a priest who entered into a forbidden marriage (for example, the child of a priest and a divorcee; see following commandment) (Leviticus 21:7): "They shall not marry a woman who is a prostitute or who is profaned."

268. The prohibition against a priest marrying a divorcee (Leviticus

21:7): "Nor shall they marry one divorced from her husband." A priest was even forbidden to remarry his own former wife (see entry 44).

269. The obligation of ordinary Jews to treat *kohanim* as holy (Leviticus 21:8): "And you must treat them as holy, since they offer the food of your God; they shall be holy to you." To this day, Jewish tradition dictates that the first person honored with blessing the Torah must be a person of priestly descent.

270–271. The prohibition against the *Kohen Gadol* (High Priest) entering a place containing a corpse, or defiling himself for any corpse, including those of his closest relatives (Leviticus 21:11): "He shall not go in where there is any dead body; he shall not defile himself even for his father or mother." The sole exception is when a High Priest, while alone, comes across an unburied body; Jewish tradition regards the burial of such a corpse as so significant that it mandates that even a High Priest defile himself in such a case, and bury the corpse.

272. The commandment that the High Priest marry only a virgin (Leviticus 21:13): "He may marry only a woman who is a virgin." One reason for this restriction likely has to do with the dignity of the office: the Israelites did not want some man going around bragging that he had slept with the High Priest's wife.

273–274. The prohibitions against the High Priest marrying or having relations with a widow (Leviticus 21:14): "A widow . . . he may not marry." The verse also specifies that the High Priest is forbidden to marry a prostitute or divorcee, but since such a regulation applied to ordinary priests as well, these restrictions are not listed as separate commandments for the High Priest.

Regarding the prohibition against having sexual relations with a widow outside of marriage, Jewish tradition deduces this from Leviticus 21:15: "That he may not profane his offspring among his kin." The Babylonian Talmud (*Kiddushin* 78a) teaches: "If a High Priest transgressed with a widow, he is to be given two lashings; on account of 'he may not marry,' and on account of 'he may not profane.'"

275–276. The prohibitions against a priest with a permanent physical blemish, or with a temporary one, serving at the sanctuary (Leviticus 21:17–20): "No man of your [i.e., Aaron's] offspring throughout the ages who has a defect shall be qualified to offer the food of his God. No one at all who has a defect shall be qualified: no man who is blind, or lame, or has a limb too short or too long; no man who has a broken leg or a broken arm; or one who is a hunchback, or a dwarf, or who has a growth in his eye, or who has a boil-scar, or scurvy, or crushed testes."

277. The prohibition against a priest with a physical blemish entering those areas of the sanctuary restricted to priests (Leviticus 21:23): "But he shall not enter behind the curtain or come near the altar, for he has a defect." However, such a man could eat the special food designated for priests (Leviticus 21:22).

278. The prohibition against a ritually unclean priest carrying out priestly functions (i.e., offering a sacrifice). That is the understanding Jewish law derives from Leviticus 22:2: "Instruct Aaron and his sons to be scrupulous about the sacred donations that the Israelite people consecrate to Me, lest they profane my Holy name" (i.e., bringing a sacrifice while ritually unclean would profane God's name).

279. The prohibition against a ritually unclean priest eating *trumah* (the produce that is donated to priests; Leviticus 22:4): "No man of Aaron's offspring who has an eruption or a discharge shall eat of the sacred donations until he is clean."

280–281–282. The prohibition against a non-priest eating *trumah* (see preceding commandment)—this includes a priest's Hebrew servant—and against an uncircumcised person eating of this sacred donation (Leviticus 22:10): "No non-priest may eat the sacred offering. Even if a person resides with a priest or is hired by him, that person may not eat the sacred offering." Regarding the prohibition of an uncircumcised person, including an uncircumcised priest,* eating from this offering, while this is not specifically commanded in the text, it is so derived by Jewish tradition.

283. The prohibition against a daughter of a priest who is married to a non-priest eating the *trumah* (Leviticus 22:12): "If a priest's daughter marries a layman, she may not eat of the sacred gifts."

284. The prohibition against Israelites eating *tevel*—produce from which the part to be given to priests has not been deducted—based on Leviticus 22:15: "But [the priests] must not allow the Israelites to profane the sacred donations that they set aside for the Lord . . . by eating such sacred donations."

285–286. The prohibition against a blemished animal being offered as a sacrifice, and the requirement that, to be sacrificed, an animal

---

*For example, if two older brothers of a priest died after being circumcised, a subsequent male child born into the family was freed from the obligation to be circumcised; thus, it could come about that a priest could be uncircumcised.

must be without any disfigurement (Leviticus 22:20–21): "You shall not offer any that has a defect, for it will not be accepted in your favor. And when a man offers . . . a sacrifice to the Lord . . . it must, to be acceptable, be perfect; there must be no defect in it."

287. The prohibition against disfiguring an animal that has been consecrated to be sacrificed, based on Leviticus 22:21, "there must be no defect in it," which a rabbinic text understands as meaning, "no blemish shall come about in it."

288–289–290. The prohibitions against sprinkling the blood of blemished animals on the altar, against ritually slaughtering a defective animal for an offering, and against burning the forbidden parts of blemished animals on the altar. The first of these is derived from Leviticus 22:22's opening words, "Anything blind, or injured, or maimed . . . such you shall not offer to the Lord." Regarding the prohibition against burning the forbidden parts of blemished animals on the altar, this is based on the same verse's final words: ". . . you shall not put *any of them* as offerings by fire to the Lord."

291. The prohibition against castrating an animal, based on Leviticus 22:24: "You shall not offer to the Lord anything [with its testes] bruised or crushed or torn or cut. You shall have no such practices in your own land." "No such practices" was understood as mandating the prohibition of destroying an animal's genitals: Jewish tradition decreed that it was forbidden to castrate or sterilize any creature.

292. The prohibition against offering a defective animal brought by a non-Israelite to the sanctuary (Leviticus 22:25): "Nor shall you accept such [animals; see preceding commandment] from a foreigner for offering as food for your God, for they are mutilated, they have a defect; they shall not be accepted in your favor."

293. The requirement that a sacrificed animal be at least eight days old (Leviticus 22:27): "When an ox or a sheep or a goat is born, it shall stay seven days with its mother, and from the eighth day on it shall be acceptable as an offering by fire to the Lord."

294. The prohibition against slaughtering an animal and its young on the same day (Leviticus 22:28): "However, no animal from the herd or from the flock shall be slaughtered on the same day with its young."

295–296. The prohibition against profaning God's name, and the commandment to sanctify it (Leviticus 22:32): "You shall not profane My holy name, that I may be sanctified in the midst of the Israelite people" (see entry 185).

297–298. The obligation to sanctify the first day of Passover and the prohibition against doing work on it (Leviticus 23:7): "On the first day you shall celebrate a sacred occasion: you shall not work at your occupation."

299. The commandment to bring a *musaf,* or additional offering, on each of Passover's seven days (Leviticus 23:8): "Seven days you shall make offerings by fire to the Lord." To this day, an additional prayer service, also known as *musaf,* is recited on the Sabbath, the New Moon, and on Jewish holidays, the times during which this additional offering was made.

300–301. The obligation to sanctify the seventh day of Passover and refrain from working on it (Leviticus 23:8): "The seventh day shall be a sacred occasion: you shall not work at your occupation."

302. The commandment to bring the priest an *omer,* or offering of barley from one's new harvest on the second day of Passover (Leviticus 23:10–11): "When you enter the land that I am giving to you and you reap its harvest, you shall bring the first sheaf of your harvest to the priest. And he shall wave the sheaf . . . on the day after the Sabbath." Jewish tradition understands the last phrase to mean on the second day of Passover.

303–304–305. The prohibitions against eating cereal grain, roasted grain, and fresh grain until they are brought as an offering (Leviticus 23:14): "Until that very day, until you have brought the offering of your God, you shall eat no bread or roasted grain or fresh grain [of the new crop]; it is a law for all time throughout the ages in all your settlements."

306. The commandment to count the *omer,* here meaning the forty-nine days between the holiday of Passover and Shavuot (Leviticus 23:15): "And from the day on which you bring the sheaf (*omer*) offering . . . you shall count off seven weeks." The count commences on the second night of Passover.

307. The obligation to make a meal offering of two loaves of bread baked from new wheat on the holiday of Shavuot (Leviticus 23:16): "You must count until the day after the seventh week, fifty days, then you shall bring an offering of new grain to the Lord. You shall bring from your settlements two loaves of bread. . . ."

308–309. The commandment to observe Shavuot (the "Festival of Weeks") as a sacred day, and the prohibition against working on it (Leviticus 23:21): "On that same day you shall hold a celebration; it shall be a sacred occasion for you; you shall not work at your occupation."

310–311. The obligation to observe Rosh ha-Shana ("New Year") as a day of solemn rest and the prohibition against working on this day (Leviticus 23:24–25): "In the seventh month, on the first day of the month, you shall observe complete rest, a sacred occasion commemorated with loud blasts. You shall not work at your occupation."

312. The commandment to make a special offering, known as a *musaf* (see commandment number 299), on Rosh ha-Shana (Leviticus 23:25): "And you shall bring an offering by fire to the Lord."

313. The obligation to fast on the tenth day of Tishrei, on the holiday of Yom Kippur. The text (Leviticus 23:27) does not specifically speak of fasting; rather, "It shall be a sacred occasion for you: you shall practice self-denial."

314. The commandment to make a *musaf* offering on Yom Kippur (Leviticus 23:27): "And you shall bring an offering by fire to the Lord."

315–316–317. The prohibition against working on Yom Kippur, the commandment to afflict oneself on this day, and to otherwise make it a solemn day (Leviticus 23:28–29): "You shall do no work throughout that day. . . . Indeed, any person who does not practice self-denial throughout that day shall be cut off from his kin." Jewish law understands self-denial as referring to five Yom Kippur prohibitions: against eating, drinking, bathing, wearing leather shoes, and engaging in sexual relations.

318–319. The commandment to sanctify the first day of Sukkot and the prohibition against working on it (Leviticus 23:34–35): "On the fifteenth day of this seventh month there shall be the Feast of Booths to the Lord [to last] seven days. The first day shall be a sacred occasion: you shall not work at your occupation."

320. The obligation to bring a special *musaf* offering on Sukkot (Leviticus 23:36): "Seven days you shall bring offerings by fire to the Lord."

321–322. The commandments to rest from work on the holiday's eighth day, known as Shmini Atzeret, and to bring a *musaf* offering on this day (Leviticus 23:36): "On the eighth day you shall observe a sacred occasion and bring an offering by fire to the Lord."

323. The prohibition against working on Shmini Atzeret (Leviticus 23:36): "It is a solemn gathering; you shall not work at your occupation."

324. The specifications of the four species which are to be raised and blessed during Sukkot (Leviticus 23:40): "On the first day you shall take the fruit of goodly trees, the branches of date palms, twigs of a plaited tree and brook willows, and you shall rejoice before your God seven days." The first of these is a citruslike fruit known as the *etrog*, while the palm branch is known as the *lulav*.

325. The commandment to dwell in a booth (*sukkah*) seven days

(Leviticus 23:42–43): "You shall live in booths seven days . . . in order that future generations may know that I made the Israelite people live in booths when I brought them out of the land of Egypt."

326–327. The prohibition against working the earth or pruning one's vineyard during the seventh year (Leviticus 25:4): "But in the seventh year, the land shall have a sabbath of complete rest, a sabbath of the Lord: You shall not sow your field or prune your vineyard" (see entry 187).

328–329. The prohibition against harvesting one's land or gathering grapes from one's vines during the seventh year (Leviticus 25:5): "You shall not reap the aftergrowth of your harvest or gather the grapes of your untrimmed vines." Although the text specifies "grapes," Jewish tradition understands this as a general prohibition against systematically gathering the fruit of any of one's trees during the seventh year. One may eat what fields and trees yield naturally during that time (i.e., one may bring home enough food for a day), but it is forbidden to systematically harvest them (see Leviticus 25:6–7).

330. The commandment to count seven sabbatical cycles, after which a Jubilee year is observed (Leviticus 25:8–10): "You shall count off seven weeks of years—seven times seven years. . . . Then you shall sound the horn loud . . . and you shall hallow the fiftieth year. . . . It shall be a jubilee for you . . ." (the specific regulations of the Jubilee year are discussed in entry 187).

331. The obligation to sound a *shofar* (ram's horn) at the beginning of the Jubilee year, which commences in the fiftieth year on Yom Kippur (Leviticus 25:9): "Then you shall sound the horn loud; in the seventh month, on the tenth day of the month, the Day of Atonement, you shall have the horn sounded throughout your land."

332–333–334–335. The commandment to sanctify the Jubilee year, and the prohibitions against farming the land, harvesting wild-growing produce, or systematically gathering fruit from one's trees during this year (Leviticus 25:10–11): "And you shall hallow the fiftieth year . . . you shall not sow, neither shall you reap the aftergrowth or harvest the untrimmed vines . . . you may only eat the growth direct from the vines."

336–337. The obligation to effect justice between buyer and seller, and a prohibition against wronging another in a business deal (Leviticus 25:14): "When you sell property to your neighbor, or buy any from your neighbor, you shall not wrong one another."

338. The prohibition against wronging another with cruel words (Leviticus 25:17): "Do not wrong one another." Since verse 14 had already prohibited wronging another in a business deal (see preceding commandment), the Rabbis understood the word "wronging" here as referring to wronging with words.

339–340. The prohibition against selling land in Israel in perpetuity; instead, one is commanded to return such land to its original owner during the Jubilee year (Leviticus 25:23–24): "But the land must not be sold beyond reclaim, for the land is Mine; you are but strangers and settlers with Me. Throughout the land that you hold, you must provide for the redemption of the land" (see entry 187).

341. The specification of special laws regarding the sale of a house within a walled city (Leviticus 25:29): "If a man sells a dwelling house in a walled city, it may be redeemed until a year has elapsed since its sale. . . . If it is not redeemed before a full year has elapsed, the house in the walled city shall pass to the purchaser beyond reclaim throughout the ages; it shall not be released in the Jubilee."

342. The prohibition against selling land adjoining the cities designated for the Levites so as to assure them their property rights (Leviticus 25:34): "But the unenclosed land about their cities cannot be sold, for that is their holding for all time" (Numbers 35:2 speaks of assigning the Levites "pasture land around their towns").

343. The prohibition against charging interest to a fellow Israelite (Leviticus 25:37): "Do not lend him money at interest" (see entry 206).

344. The prohibition against imposing degrading work on an Israelite slave (Leviticus 25:42): "If your kinsman under you continues in straits and must give himself over to you [as a servant], do not subject him to the treatment of a slave."

345. The prohibition against selling a Hebrew slave at auction (Leviticus 25:42): "They are not to be sold as the sale of slaves." This is the literal meaning of the verse's final clause; the Jewish Publication Society translation, upon which I generally rely, renders it as "they may not give themselves over into servitude."

346. The prohibition against imposing crushing burdens on a Hebrew slave (Leviticus 25:43): "You shall not rule over him ruthlessly; you shall fear your God" (on "fear of God," see entry 153). "Fear of God" is also added as an inducement to fulfill a commandment in instances where the intention is not visible in the action. For example, if a person instructs his servant to dig a well, then, when he has finished, the person says, "Put back the earth. I changed my mind," only the person himself, *and God*, knows if he truly changed his mind, or if he was just imposing arduous work on his servant.

347. The right to hold non-Israelite slaves in perpetuity (Leviticus 25:46): "You may keep them as a possession for your children after you, for them to inherit as property for all time." Although the verse's moral implications are disturbing, it must also be recalled that murdering a slave constituted a capital crime (Exodus 21:20ff.), and that a master who hit a slave and caused him to lose a tooth was compelled to free him (Exodus 21:26).

348. The prohibition against tolerating a non-Israelite's mistreatment of an Israelite slave (Leviticus 25:53): "He shall be under his authority as a laborer hired by the year; he shall not rule ruthlessly over him in your sight."

349. The prohibition against bowing down before a stone image (Leviticus 26:1): "You shall not make idols for yourselves, or set up for yourselves carved images or pillars, or place a decorated stone in your land to prostrate yourselves to it, for I the Lord am your God."

350. The obligation to donate to the sanctuary the value of a human being if one has so vowed (Leviticus 27:1–7): A peculiar law, this refers to a person who promised to give the sanctuary "my value" or "the value of so-and-so." The text goes on to establish the values assigned to people of different ages, possibly based on the price that might be paid for them were they sold as slaves. Thus, the value of a male between twenty and sixty is given as fifty shekels (27:3), of a female of similar age, thirty shekels (27:4), while different values are assigned to younger and older people.

351–352. The prohibition against exchanging an animal that has been consecrated as an offering; if one does so, then both animals must be offered (Leviticus 27:10): "One may not exchange or substitute another for it [i.e., for an animal that has been pledged for an offering], either good for bad, or bad for good; if one does substitute one animal for another, the thing vowed and its substitute shall both be holy."

353–354. The obligation of one who vows the value of an animal to the sanctuary to pay its value as determined by a priest; likewise, the obligation of one who vows the value of a house (Leviticus 27:11–12, 14): "If [the vow concerns] any unclean animal [i.e., an unkosher animal] that may not be brought as an offering to the Lord, the animal shall be presented before the priest, and the priest shall assess it. Whether high or low, whatever assessment is set by the priest shall stand. . . . If anyone consecrates his house to the Lord, the priest shall assess it. Whether high or low, as the priest assesses it, so it shall stand."

355. The commandment that if one vows the value of a field to the sanctuary he must pay this amount in accordance with the expected harvests until the Jubilee year (Leviticus 27:16ff.): "If anyone consecrates to the Lord any land that he holds, its assessment shall be in accordance with its seed requirements [i.e., the number of crops that can be harvested until the next Jubilee year]. . . ." The text then lists various valuations for the consecrated land.

356. The prohibition against exchanging one type of sacrifice for another. For example, it is forbidden to change a peace offering (shlamim) into a guilt offering (asham). Jewish tradition bases this on Leviticus 27:26: "However, a firstborn that is assigned as firstborn to God among animals, no man shall sanctify it." According to the Sefer ha-Hinnuch, this means, "in other words, no one is to make a firstborn animal either an olah (burnt offering) or a peace offering or any other offering . . . no man shall sanctify it; it should rather be left as it is" (volume 3, page 495).

357–358–359. The requirement that if one makes an unspecified vow of one's property, or of one's land, declaring it to be herem [i.e., banning the property's owner from deriving any benefit from it], the sanctified object goes to the priest, and may not be redeemed (Leviticus 27:28): "But of all that anyone owns, be it man or beast or land of his holding, nothing that he has proscribed for the Lord may be sold or redeemed; every proscribed thing is totally consecrated to the Lord." Jewish tradition understands this as meaning that it devolves to the priests; see Leviticus 27:21, which speaks of a field "holy to God," but which then specifies "[and it] shall become the priest's."

360–361. The obligation to tithe one's newborn sheep and cattle and the prohibition against substituting an inferior animal for a superior one (Leviticus 27:32–33): "All tithes of the herd or flock, of all that passes under the shepherd's staff, every tenth one, shall be holy to the Lord. He is not to search between good and bad, he is not to make exchange for it. But if he does substitute one for the other, then it and its substitute shall both be holy, they cannot be redeemed."

NUMBERS

362–363. The commandment to send ritually unclean Israelites outside the Israelite camp, and the prohibition against their entering the sanctuary (Numbers 5:2–3): "Instruct the Israelites to remove from camp anyone with an eruption or a discharge [see Leviticus, chapters 13, 15], and anyone defiled by a corpse. Remove male and female alike; put them outside the camp so that they do not defile the camp of those in whose midst I dwell." While the text does not explicitly prohibit defiled people from entering the sanctuary, Jewish tradition derives this prohibition from the words "so that they do not defile the camp of those in whose midst I dwell," which is understood as meaning "the camp of the Divine presence," i.e., the sanctuary.

364. The obligation to verbally confess one's sins, and to undo the wrong one has done (Numbers 5:6–7): "When a man or woman commits any wrong toward a fellow man, thus breaking faith with the Lord, and that person realizes his guilt, he shall confess the wrong that he has done. He shall make restitution in the principal amount and add one-fifth to it, giving it to him whom he has wronged."

365–366–367. The specification of the procedures to be taken with a *sotah* (suspected adulteress): She is brought before a priest, who puts no oil or frankincense into the *sotah*'s meal offering (Numbers 5:12, 15): "If any man's wife has gone astray and broken faith with him . . . the man shall bring his wife to the priest. And he shall bring as an offering for her one-tenth of an *ephah* of barley flour. No oil shall be poured upon it and no frankincense shall be laid on it, for it is a meal offering of jealousy, a meal offering of remembrance which recalls wrongdoing" (for a description of the other procedures involving a *sotah*, see entry 189).

368–369–370–371–372. The prohibitions against a Nazirite's drinking wine and against drinking other liquor, as well as eating fresh or dried grapes, or grape seeds and skins (Numbers 6:2–4): "If anyone, man or woman, explicitly utters a Nazirite's vow, to set himself apart for the Lord, he shall abstain from wine and any other intoxicant; he shall not drink vinegar of wine or any other intoxicant, neither shall he drink anything in which grapes have been steeped, nor eat grapes fresh or dried. Throughout his term as Nazirite, he may not eat anything that is obtained from the grapevine, even seeds or skins" (see entry 190).

373–374. The prohibition against a Nazirite shaving his hair, and the commandment to let it grow long (Numbers 6:5): "Throughout the term of his vow as Nazirite, no razor shall touch his head; it shall remain consecrated until the completion of his term as Nazirite of the Lord, the hair of his head being left to grow untrimmed."

Samson, who lost all his powers when his hair was cut, was the most famous biblical Nazirite (see entry 66).

375–376. The prohibition against a Nazirite entering a place containing a dead body, even one of a close relative, or allowing himself to become defiled by a corpse (Numbers 6:6–7): "Throughout the term that he has set apart for the Lord, he shall not go in where there is a dead person. Even if his father or mother, or his brother or sister should die, he must not defile himself for them. . . ."

377. The requirement that a Nazirite should shave his head and bring an offering when his period as a *nazir* is complete (Numbers 6:13–20): Verses 14–15 list the offering the Nazirite must make to the Lord when his term is completed, after which "The Nazirite shall then shave his consecrated hair, at the entrance of the Tent of Meeting, and take the locks of his consecrated hair and put them on the fire that is under the sacrifice of well-being" (6:18).

378. The specification of the priestly blessing (Numbers 6:23–27): "Speak to Aaron and his sons: 'Thus shall you bless the people of Israel: Say to them . . .'" (the priestly blessing is cited and discussed in entry 191).

379. The commandment that the priests were to carry the Ark (containing the Ten Commandments) on their shoulders (Numbers 7:9): ". . . for the service of transport of the holy things is theirs, by shoulder they are to carry."

380–381. The obligation of who one was unable to bring a Passover offering at the appropriate time to do so exactly one month later, on the fourteenth of the month of Iyar (Numbers 9:11): "They shall offer it in the second month, on the fourteenth day of the month, at twilight. They shall eat it with unleavened bread and bitter herbs." A person might not have brought the Passover sacrifice at the appropriate time because he or she was away on a long journey or had been defiled through contact with a corpse (Numbers 9:10).

382–383. The prohibitions against leaving over any of the Second Passover sacrifice until the next day and against breaking any of its bones (Numbers 9:12): "And they shall not leave any of it over until morning. They shall not break a bone of it. They shall offer it in strict accord with the law of the Passover sacrifice" (see commandments numbers 8 and 16).

384. The obligation to sound a trumpet when an enemy attack occurs, and during joyous celebrations at the sanctuary (Numbers 10:9–10): "When you are at war in your land against an aggressor who attacks you, you shall sound short blasts on the trumpet, that you may be remembered before the Lord your God and be delivered from your enemies. And on your joyous occasions—your fixed festivals and new moon days—you shall sound the trumpets over your burnt offerings and your sacrifices of well-being. They shall be a reminder of you before your God. . . ." The trumpet used for these ceremonies was not a *shofar* (ram's horn blown on Rosh ha-Shana); it was molded from one piece of silver. The first-century historian Josephus writes that this instrument was a little less than a cubit (18 inches) in length, and somewhat thicker than an ordinary flute (*Antiquities* 3:12:6).

385. The obligation to set aside a portion of *hallah* (dough) for the priest (Numbers 15:18–21): ". . . When you enter the land to which I am taking you, and you eat of the bread of the land, you shall set some aside as a gift to the Lord. As the first yield of your baking, you shall set aside a loaf as a gift. . . . You shall make a gift to the Lord from the first yield of your baking, throughout the ages." In order that the law of *hallah* not be forgotten, Jewish tradition obliges those baking bread to cut or tear off a piece of dough roughly the size of an olive, and burn it; it need no longer be given to a priest since, in the absence of the ashes of a red heifer (see commandment number 397), no priests today are ritually clean.

386. The commandment to wear *tzitzit* (fringes) on a four-cornered garment (Numbers 15:37–38): "The Lord said to Moses: 'Speak to the Israelite people and instruct them to make for themselves fringes on the corners of their garments throughout the ages; let them attach a cord of blue to the fringe at each corner' " (see entry 192).

387. The prohibition going astray after one's heart and eyes (Numbers 15:39): ". . . look at it [the string of the *tzitzit*; see preceding commandment], and recall all the commandments of the Lord and observe them, so that you do not follow your heart and eyes after which you go whoring." Thus *tzitzit* are a kind of ethical-string-around-the-finger to remind Jews of their moral and religious obligations (see entry 192).

388–389–390. The Levites' obligation to guard the sanctuary, and the prohibitions against the priests and Levites doing each other's work, and an outsider serving at the sanctuary (Numbers 18:4): "[The Levites] shall be your [i.e., the priests'] associates and they shall be entrusted with responsibility for the Tent of Meeting and all the Tent's services . . ." From what we know of Temple procedures, of its twenty-four guard positions, twenty-one were occupied by Levites and three by *kohanim*.

The *Sefer ha-Hinnuch* records commandment number 389 as prohibiting priests and Levites from engaging in each other's tasks, basing this on a clause in Numbers 4:19 ("every man to his task and to his burden"). The conclusion of Numbers 18:4, "but a common man shall not draw near to you," prohibited non-Aaronides from engaging in sacred work at the sanctuary.

391. The commandment that the guarding of the sanctuary should be continuous. Jewish tradition understands Numbers 18:5 "and you shall be entrusted with responsibility for the sanctuary and the altar," as mandating perpetual guard duty, both night and day.

392. The obligation of a father to redeem his firstborn son (Numbers 18:15–16): "The first issue of the womb of every being, man or beast, that is offered to the Lord, shall be yours [i.e., the priest's]; but you shall have the firstborn of man redeemed. . . . Take as their redemption price, from the age of one month and up, the money equivalent of five shekels by the sanctuary weight." This still-observed law applies only to the redemption of firstborn sons. On the thirty-first day after the baby's birth (a day or two later if this day falls on the Sabbath or a holiday), a *kohen*, a priest, is presented with five pieces of silver (in the contemporary United States, he is generally given five or six pure silver dollars); in return, he "releases" the son back to the father. The procedure is known as *pidyon ha-ben* (redemption of the [firstborn] son).

393. The prohibition against redeeming the firstborn of a kosher animal (Numbers 18:17): "But the firstlings of cattle, sheep or goats may not be redeemed, they are consecrated . . . ;" in other words, they should be offered as sacrifices rather than redeemed.

394. The Levites' exclusive obligation to perform the sanctuary service (Numbers 18:23): "Only Levites shall perform the services of the Tent of Meetings. . . . It is the law for all time throughout the ages."

395. The commandment to set aside a tithe for the Levites (Numbers 18:24): "For it is the tithes set aside by the Israelites as a gift to the Lord that I give to the Levites as their share. . . ." This tithe was a compensation to the Levites for their spiritual labors on behalf of the community. It might also have been a form of compensation to them for being the only tribe not granted a territorial share in the land of Israel (see Numbers 18:23: ". . . but they shall have no territorial share among the Israelites").

396. The Levites' obligation to donate a tithe from their tithe to the priests (Numbers 18:26): "Speak to the Levites and say to them: 'When you receive from the Israelites their tithes, which I have assigned to you as your share, you shall set aside from them one-tenth of the tithe as a gift to the Lord.'" That this "gift to the Lord" should be presented to the priests is based on the last clause in verse 28,

"and from them you shall bring the gift to the Lord to Aaron the priest."

397. The specification of the law of the Red Heifer (Numbers 19:2): "Instruct the Israelite people to bring you a red cow without blemish, in which there is no defect and on which no yoke has been laid." The intricate laws of using its ashes to purify those ritually unclean from contact with a corpse are discussed in entry 193.

398. The law that everyone and everything that is under the same roof with a corpse becomes ritually unclean (Numbers 19:14–15): "This is the ritual: When a person dies in a tent, whoever enters the tent and whoever is in the tent shall be unclean seven days. And every open vessel, with no lid fastened down, shall be unclean."

399. The requirement that a ritually clean person shall sprinkle the water and ashes of the Red Heifer to purify one who has become ritually unclean (Numbers 19:19): "The clean person shall sprinkle it on the unclean person on the third day and on the seventh day. . . ."

400. The specification of the laws of inheritance when a man dies without a son (Numbers 27:8–11): "If a man dies without leaving a son, you shall transfer his property to his daughter. If he has no daughter, you shall assign his property to his brothers." The subsequent verses take into account further contingencies (i.e., if he has no brothers; for a further discussion of the Torah's laws concerning inheritance, see entry 201).

401. The requirement that a lamb should be offered as a burnt offering every morning and evening (Numbers 28:3): "As a regular burnt offering every day, two yearling lambs without blemish. You shall offer one lamb in the morning, and the other lamb you shall offer at twilight."

402–403–404. The specification of additional offerings for the Sabbath, the New Moon, and on Shavuot (Numbers 28:9–11, 26–31): "On the sabbath day, two yearling lambs without blemish . . . a burnt offering for every sabbath, in addition to the regular burnt offering and its libation. On your new moons, you shall present a burnt offering to the Lord, two bulls of the herd, one ram, and seven yearling lambs, without blemish. . . . On the day of the first fruits, your Feast of Weeks [Shavuot] . . . you shall present a burnt offering of pleasing odor to the Lord: two bulls of the herd, one ram, seven yearling lambs. . . . And there shall be one goat for expiation on your behalf. You shall present them . . . in addition to the regular burnt offering and its meal offering."

405. The commandment to blow the *shofar* on Rosh ha-Shana, the

Jewish New Year (Numbers 29:1): "You shall observe it [i.e., Rosh ha-Shana] as a day when the horn is sounded." According to traditional law, however, the *shofar* is not blown when Rosh ha-Shana falls on a Sabbath.

406–407. The specification of procedures for fulfilling one's vow, and for nullifying it when necessary (Numbers, chapter 30): Numbers 30:3 decrees: "If a man makes a vow to the Lord or takes an oath imposing an obligation on himself, he shall not break his pledge; he must carry out all that has crossed his lips." But if a woman makes a vow or assumes an obligation, if she is still a minor, her father can negate the vow on the day he hears it; if she is married, her husband can do so. However, if "her husband [or her father] learns of [the vow] and offers no objection on the day he finds out, her vow shall stand and her self-imposed obligation shall stand" (30:8). As for a male, who would seem to have no mode of release from a vow, Jewish tradition ordains that a learned scholar, or three ordinary Jews, can release him from a vow, if it is clear that the person making the vow did not anticipate how arduous it would be to abide by its conditions. I recently participated in helping release a woman from an impulsively taken vow whereby she promised that if a young man she knew would remain in remission from cancer, she never again would eat candy or cake.

Because Jewish tradition regards a person's word as his or her bond, many observant Jews, when announcing something that they plan to do, append the Hebrew words *bli neder* ("without a vow"), to protect themselves in case they cannot fulfill their word.

408. The commandment to assign cities to Levites in which to live (Numbers 35:2): "Instruct the Israelite people to assign out of the holdings apportioned to them, towns for the Levites to dwell in." Forty-eight towns were assigned to the Levites, including six cities of refuge for inadvertent manslayers (verse 6; see entry 195).

409. The commandment that murderers not be executed before they stand trial and are convicted (Numbers 35:12): ". . . the killer may not die unless he has stood trial before the assembly."

410. The obligation to confine inadvertent manslayers to a city of refuge until the death of the High Priest (Numbers 35:25): ". . . and the assembly shall [dispatch] him to the city of refuge . . . and there he shall remain until the death of the High Priest. . . ." (see entry 195).

411. The requirement that it takes two witnesses' testimony to convict and execute an alleged murderer (Numbers 35:30): "If anyone kills a person, the manslayer may be executed only on the evidence of witnesses; the testimony of a single witness against a person shall not suffice for a sentence of death."

412. The prohibition against accepting money from a murderer to save him or her from a death sentence (Numbers 35:31): "You may not accept a ransom for the life of a murderer who is guilty of a capital crime; he must be put to death" (on the biblical view of the death sentence for murderers, see entry 150).

413. The prohibition against accepting money from an inadvertent manslayer to free him or her from banishment to a city of refuge (Numbers 35:32): "Nor may you accept ransom in lieu of flight to a city of refuge, enabling one to return to live on his land before the death of the priest" (see entry 195).

DEUTERONOMY

414–415. The judge's obligation to act fairly, and without fear of the litigants (Deuteronomy 1:17): "Do not give anyone special consideration when rendering judgment; hear out low and high alike; you are not to be in fear of any man, for judgment, it is God's. . . ." The *Sefer ha-Hinnuch* explains commandment number 414 as an injunction to the heads of the judicial system to appoint competent judges.

416. The prohibition against desiring what belongs to one's neighbor (Deuteronomy 5:18): ". . . You shall not crave your neighbor's house, or his field . . . or anything that is your neighbor's." This is part of Deuteronomy's statement of the Tenth Commandment; its language differs slightly from the Tenth Commandment's wording in Exodus (20:14), where one is forbidden to covet (*hamod*) that which is his or her neighbor's. Maimonides understands that law as forbidding a person to take—even if one is willing to pay for it— what another owns but does not wish to sell. The injunction here is *Lo titaveh*, "Do not desire," meaning that one should not allow one's wishes to impel one to obsess over acquiring the item (for a further discussion of the rationale behind this commandment, see entry 165).

417. The obligation to acknowledge that God is One (Deuteronomy 6:4): "Hear, O Israel, the Lord is our God, the Lord alone" (see entry 196).

418. The commandment to love God (Deuteronomy 6:5): "And you shall love the Lord your God" (see entry 196).

419–420. The obligation to teach Torah to one's children, and to study it oneself during both the day and at night (Deuteronomy

6:7): "And you shall teach it [i.e., the Torah] diligently to your children, and you shall speak of it when you are at home and when you are away, when you lie down and when you rise up." Jewish tradition understands this final clause as mandating, as a minimum, reciting the words of the *Sh'ma Yisrael* ("Hear, O Israel") in the morning and before one goes to sleep (see entry 196).

421–422. The commandments to put *tefillin* on one's arm and on one's head (Deuteronomy 6:8): "Bind them as a sign on your hand and let them serve as a symbol on your forehead" (see entry 195).

423. The obligation to place a *mezuzah* on one's doorpost (Deuteronomy 6:9): "Inscribe them [i.e., words from the Torah; according to Jewish tradition, Deuteronomy 6:4–9 and 11:13–21 are inscribed on the parchment of the *mezuzah*] on the doorposts of your house and on your gates" (see entry 195).

424. The prohibition against testing God (Deuteronomy 6:16): "Do not test God. . . ." Thus, it would be forbidden for a person to say, "I'll become a fully observant Jew if and when God grants me tremendous wealth." The Rabbis understood this verse as prohibiting the excessive testing of a true prophet by repeatedly asking him to perform miracles.

425–426. The commandment to destroy the seven nations of Canaan, and to show no mercy to these idol worshipers (Deuteronomy 7:12): "When the Lord your God brings you to the land that you are about to enter and possess, and He dislodges many nations before you—the Hittites, Girgashites, Amorites, Canaanites, Perizzites, Hivites, and Jebusites, seven nations much larger than you—and the Lord your God delivers them to you and you defeat them, you must doom them to destruction: grant them no terms and give them no quarter." This is the Torah's most morally problematic commandment; for a discussion of this unusual decree which, in any case, was not carried out, see entry 61.

427. The prohibition against intermarrying with the seven nations then resident in Canaan (Deuteronomy 7:3): "You shall not intermarry with them: do not give your daughters to their sons or take their daughters for your sons. For they will turn your children away from Me to worship other gods. . . ." If the Torah truly had intended the Israelites to wipe out the nations then in Canaan, it made no sense to add this prohibition against intermarrying with them; one cannot intermarry with a corpse! Perhaps the Torah anticipated that the Israelites never would carry out a war of extermination and so wished to underscore that they not intermarry with the Canaanites and become idolaters. Jewish tradition bases on this verse a general prohibition on Jews marrying non-Jews.

428. The prohibition against attempting to profit materially from an idol (Deuteronomy 7:25): "... you shall not covet the silver and gold on them [i.e., idols] and keep it for yourselves, lest you be ensnared thereby. ..."

429. The prohibition against bringing into one's home something disgusting (Deuteronomy 7:26): "You must not bring an abhorrent thing into your house ... you must reject it as abominable and abhorrent." In context, the Torah clearly is referring to an idol or anything used in the practice of idolatry, but the language also could apply to other repellent things (e.g., a person who would collect Nazi souvenirs or shrunken heads as a curiosity).

430. The obligation to bless God after eating (Deuteronomy 8:10): "And you shall eat, and be satisfied, and you shall bless the Lord your God. ..." The commandment to recite the *birkat ha-mazon* (grace after meals) is based on this verse.

431. The commandment to love strangers who live amid the Israelite community (Deuteronomy 10:19): "You must love the stranger, for you were strangers in the land of Egypt." Many traditional Jewish sources restrict applicability of this command to converts to Judaism (in Hebrew, the same word, *ger*, is used for "stranger" and "convert"; as to why I believe such a restriction misinterprets the Torah, see entry 184).

432. The obligation to be in awe, a kind of reverent fear, of God (Deuteronomy 10:20): "You must revere the Lord your God" (see entry 153).

433–434–435. The commandment to pray to God and God alone, to treat nothing else with the reverence with which you treat God, and to swear by God's name (and not the name of any other god) (Deuteronomy 10:20): "... only Him shall you worship, to Him shall you cling, and by His name shall you swear."

436. The obligation to demolish idolatrous temples in the land of Israel (Deuteronomy 12:2): "You must destroy all sites at which the nations you are to dispossess worshiped their gods. ... Tear down their altars, smash their pillars, put their sacred posts to the fire, and cut down the images of their gods, obliterating their name from that site." Clearly, the Torah's central religious message was to establish monotheism and eradicate idolatry.

437. The prohibition against destroying objects deemed Jewishly sacred (Deuteronomy 12:4): "So shall you not do unto the Lord your God" (i.e., destroy sacred temples or scrolls; see preceding commandment).

438. The commandment to fulfill one's vow to bring an offering at the first opportunity one has to do so. This is how Jewish tradition understands Deuteronomy 12:5–6: "But look only to the site that the Lord your God will choose amidst all your tribes as His habitation to establish His name there. There you are to go, and there you are to bring your burnt offerings and other sacrifices. . . ." The connection between this verse and its rabbinic elaboration appears tenuous; instead, Deuteronomy 23:22 seems a clearer proof text for this commandment: "When you make a vow to the Lord your God, do not put off fulfilling it, for the Lord your God will require it of you, and you will have incurred guilt."

439–440. The prohibition against offering a sacrifice outside the sanctuary chosen by God in the Land of Israel; rather, it must be offered there alone (Deuteronomy 12:13): "Take care not to sacrifice your burnt offerings in any place you like, but only in the place the Lord will choose in one of your tribal territories." This commandment applied at various phases in Jewish history, when the Jews had a permanent shrine (e.g., Shilo, but especially Jerusalem).

441. The commandment granting permission to eat meat whenever one wants (as long as it has been properly slaughtered; Deuteronomy 12:15—see also commandment number 451): "But whenever you desire, you may slaughter and eat meat in any of your settlements. . . ."

442–443–444–445–446–447–448–449. A series of prohibitions all derived from Deuteronomy 12:17–18):

- Against eating the second tithe of grain, wine, or oil outside of Jerusalem
- Against a priest eating an unblemished firstborn animal outside Jerusalem (nonpriests were always forbidden to eat an unblemished firstborn animal)
- Against eating the sin-offering (*hattat*) or guilt-offering (*asham*) outside the sanctuary
- Against eating any meat of the burnt-offering (the *olah*)
- Against eating sacrifices of lesser holiness before their blood is sprinkled on the altar
- Against the priests eating the first fruits before they are set down on the sanctuary grounds

As noted, Jewish tradition derives all these prohibitions from Deuteronomy 12:17–18: "You may not eat within your settlements of the tithes of your new grain or wine or oil, or of the firstlings of your herds and flocks, or of any of the vow offerings that you vow, or of your freewill offerings, or the contribution of your hand. These you must consume before the Lord your God in the place that the Lord your God will choose."

450. The prohibition against neglecting the Levites by withholding from them what they are owed (Deuteronomy 12:19): "Be sure not to neglect the Levite as long as you live in your land."

451. The obligation to slaughter ritually an animal whose meat is to be eaten (Deuteronomy 12:21): "If the place where the lord has chosen to establish His name is too far from you, you may slaughter any of the cattle or sheep that the Lord gives you, as I have instructed you. . . ." These last words, suggesting an oral tradition mandating how the slaughter is to be done, serves as the basis for *shechitah*, the Jewish tradition of slaughtering those animals that are kosher and so permitted as food.

452. The prohibition against eating a limb, or any other part, taken from a living animal. This is how Jewish tradition understands the final clause of Deuteronomy 12:23: ". . . you must not consume the life with the flesh."

453. The obligation to bring permitted animals from outside Israel to the sanctuary, which is how the *Sefer ha-Hinnuch* understands Deuteronomy 12:26: "But such sacred and voluntary donations as you may have shall be taken by you to the site that the Lord will choose."

454–455. The prohibitions against adding to or subtracting from the Torah's laws (Deuteronomy 13:1): "Be careful to observe only that which I enjoin upon you: neither add to it nor take away from it" (see entry 197).

456. The commandment to ignore false prophets (Deuteronomy 13:2–4): "If there appears among you a prophet or a diviner of dreams, and he gives you a sign or a portent saying, 'Let us follow and worship another god'—even if the sign or portent that he named to you comes true, do not heed the words of that prophet or that diviner of dreams. For the Lord your God is testing you to see whether you really love the Lord your God with all your heart and soul."

457–458–459–460–461–462. The prohibition against listening to, being seduced by, having affection for, showing pity to, or shielding one who entices people to follow a false idol; rather, one should help bring about such a person's execution (Deuteronomy 13:9): "Do not assent or give heed to him; show him no pity or compassion, and do not shield him, but take his life. . . ." Harsh as these laws sound, it is worth recalling that the twentieth century's two most significant idolatries, Nazism and Communism, led to the murders of tens of millions of people. Had the leaders of these ideologies, Adolf Hitler and Vladimir Lenin (and Lenin's leading disciple after his death, Joseph Stalin), been treated in accordance with biblical justice, these murders almost definitely would not have happened. In Jewish tradition, the words "do not shield" mean, "If you know something pointing to his guilt, you do not have the right to keep quiet" (*Sefer ha-Hinnuch*, volume 4, page 427).

463. The obligation of the judges to examine witnesses carefully to ensure that their testimony is true (Deuteronomy 13:15): "You shall investigate and inquire and interrogate thoroughly. . . ."

464–465. The commandment to destroy and never to rebuild a city that has become filled with idolatry (Deuteronomy 13:16–17): "Put the inhabitants of that town to the sword and put its cattle to the sword. Doom it and all that is in it to destruction. Gather all its spoil into the town square and burn the town and all its spoil . . . and it shall remain an everlasting ruin, never to be rebuilt." The "good news" is that, apparently, this law was never carried out.

466. The prohibition against deriving any benefit from a city destroyed because it had become idolatrous (Deuteronomy 13:18): "Let nothing that has been doomed stick to your hand" (see preceding commandment).

467–468. The prohibition against gashing oneself or tearing one's hair in the manner done by idolatrous mourners (Deuteronomy 14:1): "You are children of the Lord your God. You shall not gash yourselves [i.e., mutilate yourselves] or tear off your hair in the middle of your head, because of the dead."

469. The prohibition against eating animals that Torah law forbids (Deuteronomy 14:3): "Do not eat any abominable thing." Given that the eating of nonkosher animals already is forbidden in earlier commandments, the *Sefer ha-Hinnuch* understands this verse as prohibiting one's consuming consecrated animals that had a defect and so had become disqualified as offerings. In context, however, Deuteronomy 14:3–21 seems to be speaking only about the laws of *kashrut*.

470. The obligation to examine a fowl to determine if it is kosher. This is how Jewish tradition understands Deuteronomy 14:11, "You may eat any clean bird." The Torah goes on to delineate an extensive catalog of forbidden birds, and never specifies which birds are per-

mitted, either by name or characteristics. According to Jewish tradition, birds that have an extra toe, a crop, and a gizzard that can be peeled are permitted. Chicken and duck are kosher. The status of turkey was long disputed, although today it is uniformly regarded as kosher.

471. The prohibition against eating nonkosher winged insects (Deuteronomy 14:19): "Every flying insect that is unclean to you shall not be eaten." The next verse notes that you "may eat every kosher flying creature" (see Leviticus 11:22).

472. The prohibition against eating the meat of a permitted animal that died of itself (Deuteronomy 14:21): "You shall not eat anything that has died a natural death; give it to the stranger in your community to eat, or you may sell it to a foreigner. . . ."

473. The law of the Second Tithe (Deuteronomy 14:22–26): "You shall set aside every year a tenth part of all the yield of your sowing that is brought from the field. You shall consume the tithes of your new grain and wine and oil, and the firstlings of your herds and flocks, in the presence of the Lord your God, in the place where He will choose to establish His name so that you may learn to revere the Lord your God forever. Should the distance be too great for you, should you be unable to transport them, because the place where the Lord your God has chosen to establish His name is far from you and because the Lord your God has blessed you, you may convert them into money. Wrap up the money and take it with you to the place that the Lord your God has chosen, and spend the money on anything you want—cattle, sheep, wine, or other intoxicant, or anything you may desire. And you shall feast there, in the presence of the Lord your God, and rejoice with your household." This tithe was offered in the first, second, fourth, and fifth years of the seven-year Sabbatical cycle.

474. The commandment regarding the Tithe of the Poor, to be offered in lieu of the Second Tithe every third and sixth year (Deuteronomy 14:28–29): "Every third year you shall bring out the full tithe of your yield that year, but leave it within your settlements [during the other two years, the Second Tithe was not left within one's city; see preceding commandment]. Then the Levite, who has no hereditary portion as you have, and the stranger, the orphan and the widow in your settlements shall come and eat their fill. . . ."

475–476–477. The positive commandment to practice remission of debts to fellow Israelites during the seventh year; also, the prohibition against demanding repayment of such a debt from an Israelite and the permission to insist on payment from a non-Israelite (Deuteronomy 15:2): "Every seventh year [in a recurring cycle], you shall practice remission of debts. This shall be the nature of the remission: every creditor shall remit the debt that he claims from his neighbor; he shall not dun his neighbor and brother when God's remission year comes around. You may dun the alien, but if you have any claim against your brother for a debt, you must relinquish it" (see entry 187).

478–479. The prohibition against hardening one's heart against the poor, and the commandment to lend the indigent person what he or she needs (Deuteronomy 15:7–8): "If, however, there is a needy person among you, one of your kinsmen in any of your settlements . . . do not harden your heart and shut your hand against your needy kinsman. Rather, you must open your hand and lend him sufficient for whatever he needs" (see entry 188).

480. The prohibition against withholding a loan to a poor man out of fear that the debt will become uncollectible in the seventh year (see commandments 475 and 476; Deuteronomy 15:9): "Beware lest you harbor the base thought, 'The seventh year, the year of remission, is approaching,' so that you are mean to your needy kinsman and give him nothing. He will cry out to the Lord against you, and you will incur guilt."

481–482. The prohibition against sending off a Hebrew slave empty-handed; rather, one is obligated to give him some goods when his period of service is complete (Deuteronomy 15:12–15): "If a fellow Hebrew, man or woman, is sold to you, he shall serve you six years, and in the seventh year you shall set him free. When you set him free, do not let him go empty-handed. Furnish him out of the flock, threshing floor and vat, with which the Lord your God has blessed you. Remember that you were slaves in the land of Egypt and the Lord your God redeemed you, therefore I enjoin this commandment upon you today" (on slavery in the Bible, see entry 166).

483–484. The prohibition against working the firstling of an animal, and against shearing a firstling sheep, since they are consecrated to God (Deuteronomy 15:19–20): "You shall consecrate to the Lord your God all male firstlings that are born in your herd and flock: you must not work your firstling ox or shear your firstling sheep." Jewish tradition deduces from this verse that it is forbidden to work any animal that has been consecrated to be offered as a sacrifice.

485. The prohibition against eating any leavened food past noon on the day before Passover. Although no such explicit ban exists in the Bible, the Jewish tradition derives this ban from Deuteronomy 16:3,

"You shall not eat anything leavened with it." In context, the verse prohibits eating leavened foods along with the Passover sacrifice.

486. The commandment to eat the Passover sacrifice in its entirety during the night it is offered (Deuteronomy 16:4): ". . . and none of the flesh of what you slaughter on the evening of the first day shall be left until morning." Jewish tradition teaches that along with the Paschal sacrifice, a *korban hagigah* (festival offering) was made. The *Sefer ha-Hinnuch* notes that it is forbidden to leave any flesh of this festival offering to the third day; thus, people have two days, the fourteenth and fifteenth of Nissan, to finish consuming the sacrifice (volume 4, pages 495–499).

487. The prohibition against offering the Passover sacrifice anywhere except the place specified by God (Deuteronomy 16:5–6): "You are not permitted to slaughter the Passover sacrifice in any of the settlements that the Lord your God is giving you, but at the place where the Lord your God will choose to establish His name, there alone shall you slaughter the Passover sacrifice. . . ."

488. The commandment to rejoice on the festival of Sukkot (Booths; Deuteronomy 16:14): "You shall rejoice in your festival, with your son and daughter, your male and female slave, the Levite, the stranger, the orphan and the widow in your communities." Jewish tradition understands the commandment to be joyous as applying to all the pilgrimage holidays (i.e., Passover and Shavuot [Weeks] as well).

489–490. The obligation for males to appear at the sanctuary on the pilgrimage holidays of Passover, Shavuot, and Sukkot, and to bring with them an offering at those times (Deuteronomy 16:16–17): "Three times a year, on the Feast of Unleavened Bread, on the Feast of Weeks, and on the Feast of Booths, all your males shall appear before the Lord in the place that He will choose. They shall not appear before the Lord empty-handed, but each with his own gift, according to the blessing that the Lord your God has bestowed upon you."

491. The commandment to appoint judges and officers in every Israelite community (Deuteronomy 16:18): "You shall appoint judges and officers for your tribes in all settlements that the Lord your God is giving you, and they shall govern the people with due justice." Since the Hebrew Bible's ethos abhors anarchy, it follows that establishing a judicial system is among the first commandments incumbent upon the Israelites as soon as they enter the land (this is also a Noahide law, see entry 149).

492–493. The prohibitions against planting trees and against erecting an idolatrous pillar, in the sanctuary (Deuteronomy 16:21): "You shall not plant for yourself an *Asherah* [sacred idolatrous tree; see Exodus 34:13]—any kind of pole beside the altar of the Lord your God that you may make—or erect a stone pillar; for such the Lord your God detests."

494. The prohibition against offering as a sacrifice an animal with a blemish (Deuteronomy 17:1): "Do not sacrifice to the Lord your God any ox that has a serious blemish, since to do so before the Lord your God is considered revolting." Because this prohibition already has been made, the *Sefer ha-Hinnuch* understands this verse as forbidding even animals with temporary blemishes.

495–496. The obligation to listen to the religious leadership and high court of one's time, and the prohibition against disobeying their rulings (Deuteronomy 17:8–11): "If a case is too baffling for you to decide, be it a controversy over homicide, civil law or assault—matters of dispute in your courts—you shall promptly repair to the place that the Lord your God will have chosen, and appear before the Levitical priests, or the magistrate in charge at the time, and present your problem. When they have announced to you the verdict in the case, you shall carry out the verdict that is announced to you from that place that the Lord chose, observing scrupulously all their instructions to you. You shall act in accordance with the instructions given you and the ruling handed down to you; you must not deviate from the verdict that they announce to you either to the right or to the left."

497. The permission, though not obligation, to anoint a king (Deuteronomy 17:14–15): "If, after you have entered the land that the Lord your God has assigned to you, and taken possession of it and settled in it, you decide, 'I will set a king over me, as do all the nations about me,' you shall be free to set a king over yourself, one chosen by the Lord your God. . . ." (on the Bible's ambivalence regarding kingship, see entry 199).

498–499–500–501–502–503. Six commandments concerning a king (Deuteronomy 17:15–20). He should:

- Be a born Israelite
- Not acquire an unduly large number of horses
- Not settle Israelites in the land of Egypt
- Not take a large number of wives
- Not amass for himself great wealth

• Write for himself a Torah scroll upon his elevation to the kingship

". . . you must not set a foreigner over you, one who is not your kinsman." Jewish tradition applies this even to a righteous convert; something parallel is found in the American Constitution, which restricts the office of president to one born in the United States.

"Moreover, he shall not keep many horses or send people back to Egypt to add to his horses, since the Lord has warned you, 'You must not go back that way again.'" Jewish tradition understood this as forbidding Jews to set up permanent residency in Egypt, a prohibition obviously not observed by the longstanding Jewish community of Egypt, which numbered among its residents Moses Maimonides.

In his compilation of the 613 commandments in his *Sefer ha-Mitzvot* (The Book of Commandments), Maimonides, the great medieval Jewish philosopher, numbers this as negative commandment number 46 and writes: "It is, however, permissible to traverse this area [editor's note: Egypt] for purposes of commerce, or to pass through it on the way to another country. It is said explicitly in the Jerusalem Talmud (*Sanhedrin* 10:8): 'You are not to return to settle, but you may return for purposes of trade, business and conquest of the country.'"

"And he shall not have many wives, lest his heart go astray; nor shall he amass silver and gold to excess." Unfortunately, King Solomon violated all *these* prohibitions, against amassing wives, horses, and wealth, with tragic results (see entry 89).

"When he is seated on his royal throne, he must write a copy of this Teaching [i.e., the Torah] as a scroll edited by the Levitical priests. Let it remain with him and let him read in it all his life, so that he may learn to revere the Lord his God, to observe faithfully every word of this Teaching as well as these laws." The verse's wording about the writing of the Torah is ambiguous; it can be read as translated above, or, as the Jewish Publication Society translation renders the verse, ". . . he shall have a copy of this Teaching written for him on a scroll by the Levitical priests."

This law was intended to remind the king that he was the enforcer of God's law, and not its creator. A contemporary parallel would be if an American president, upon assuming office, had to write out the Constitution by hand, to remind himself that he was bound by its regulations.

504–505. The prohibitions against the tribe of Levi having tribal territory within Israel, and against being given any share of the booty when the land is conquered by the Israelites (Deuteronomy 18:1–2): "The levitical priests, the whole tribe of Levi, shall have no territorial portion with Israel. They shall live only off the Lord's offerings by fire as their portion, and they shall have no portion among their brother tribes: the Lord is their portion, as He promised them." Jewish tradition seems to derive the latter prohibition from the statement that "they shall live only off the Lord's offering by fire as their portion."

506–507–508. The obligations to give to the priests the shoulder, the cheeks, and the stomach of an offering, to give them an offering called *trumah* from one's produce, and also to give them the first shearing of one's sheep (Deuteronomy 18:3–4): "This then shall be the priests' due from the people: Everyone who offers a sacrifice, whether an ox or a sheep, must give the shoulder, the cheeks and the stomach to the priests. You shall also give the first fruits of your new grain and wine and oil, and the first shearing of your sheep."

509. The commandment that the priests and Levites should serve together at the sanctuary in watches. Jewish tradition derives this law from Deuteronomy 18:6–8, although, in context, the verses seem to be addressing other issues concerning Levites: "The Levitical [priest], no matter where he lives among all the Israelites, can come to the place that God shall choose on a festival, or whenever else he wishes to [bring his own sacrifice]. He can then serve before God his Lord just the same as any of his fellow Levitical [priests] whose turn it is to serve before God. [On the festivals], he shall receive the same portion that they do to eat. . . ."

510–511–512–513–514–515. Six prohibitions against forms of magical behavior (Deuteronomy 18:9–11); i.e., against:

- Practicing divination
- Practicing sorcery
- Employing charms (i.e., casting spells)
- Consulting an *ov*, a medium
- Consulting a *yid'oni*, a wizard
- Making inquiries of the dead

"When you enter the land that the Lord your God is giving you, you shall not learn to imitate the abhorrent practices of those nations. Let no one be found among you who . . . is an augur, a soothsayer, a diviner, a sorcerer, one who casts spells, or one who consults mediums or oracles, or one who inquires of the dead."

516. The commandment to heed a truthful prophet of God (Deuteronomy 18:15): "The Lord will raise up for you a prophet from among your own people, like myself [i.e., Moses]; him you shall heed."

517–518. The prohibitions against prophesying falsely in God's name, and against prophesying in the names of idols (Deuteronomy 18:20): "But any prophet who presumes to speak in My name an oracle that I did not command him to utter, or who speaks in the name of other gods—that prophet shall die." The Torah then offers a commonsense guideline for knowing if a prophet is "false": "And should you ask yourselves, 'How can we know that the oracle was not spoken by the Lord?'—if the prophet speaks in the name of the Lord and the oracle does not come true, that oracle was not spoken by the Lord. . . ." (18:21–22).

519. The prohibition against fearing a false prophet (Deuteronomy 18:22): "Do not stand in dread of him" [i.e., a false prophet; see preceding two commandments).

520. The commandment to specify cities of refuge for inadvertent manslayers (Deuteronomy 19:2–3, 9): "You shall set aside three cities in the land that the Lord your God is giving you to possess . . . so that any manslayer may have a place to flee to." This verse also notes that when the land's boundaries were fully established, three additional cities of refuge should be constructed.

521. The prohibition against having pity for pitiless murderers (Deuteronomy 19:11–13): "If, however, a person who is the enemy of another lies in wait for him and sets upon him and strikes him a fatal blow and then flees to one of these towns [i.e., cities of refuge; see preceding commandment], the elders of his town shall have him brought back from there, and shall hand him over to the blood-avenger to be put to death; you must show him no pity. Thus you will purge Israel of the blood of the innocent, and it will go well with you."

522. The prohibition against altering a boundary between one's property and that of one's neighbor's (Deuteronomy 19:14): "You shall not move your countryman's landmarks . . . in the property that will be allotted to you in the land that the Lord your God is giving you to possess."

523. The prohibition against convicting a criminal on the basis of a single witness's testimony; a minimum of two witnesses is required (Deuteronomy 19:15): "One witness [alone] shall not rise up against a man for any [case of] iniquity, for any [case of] sin, in any sin that he sins; at the mouth of two witnesses or at the mouth of three witnesses, a legal matter is to be established."

Since few crimes are carried out in the presence of two witnesses, this law's strict fulfillment would make it virtually impossible to convict any criminals. It is interesting to speculate whether the Torah would have been more sympathetic to conviction on the basis of circumstantial evidence had ancient Israelite society been familiar with the uniqueness of fingerprints and genetic imprints.

524. The commandment to inflict on perjuring witnesses the punishment that the victim of the perjury would have suffered (Deuteronomy 19:18–19): "And the judges shall make a thorough investigation. If the man who testified is a false witness . . . you shall do to him as he schemed to do to his fellow. Thus you will sweep out evil from your midst."

525. The prohibition against the Israelites' quailing in fear before their enemies and fleeing, for they should know that God is in their midst (Deuteronomy 20:1): "When you take the field against your enemies, and see horses and chariots—forces larger than yours— have no fear of them, for the Lord your God who brought you from the land of Egypt, is with you."

526. The commandment to anoint a priest to speak to, and otherwise spiritually guide, the troops during wartime (Deuteronomy 20:2). This verse does not explicitly state that a special priest is appointed for this purpose, but the verse's wording implies the existence of such a clerical office: "Before you join battle, the priest shall come forward and address the troops."

527. The specification of permitted exemptions from army service (Deuteronomy 20:5–9): "Then the officials shall address the troops, as follows:

" 'Is there anyone who has built a new house but has not dedicated it? Let him go back to his home, lest he die in battle and another dedicate it.

" 'Is there anyone who planted a vineyard but has never harvested it? Let him go back to his home, lest he die in battle and another harvest it.

" 'Is there anyone who has paid the bride-price for a wife, but who has not yet married her? Let him go back to his home, lest he die in battle and another marry her.'

"The officials shall go on addressing the troops and say,

" 'Is there anyone afraid and disheartened? Let him go back to his home lest the courage of his comrades flag like his.'

"When the officials have finished addressing the troops, army commanders shall assume command of the troops."

528. The commandment to offer peace to a town before attacking it (Deuteronomy 20:10): "When you approach a town to attack it, you shall offer it terms of peace." While this is a rather humane law, the peace terms to be offered were not particularly generous. If the townspeople surrendered, they were to become subject to forced labor (see verse 11). If they did not do so, in keeping with the then prevailing ethics of warfare, the men were to be slaughtered, and the women, children, and all material possessions taken as booty, these being viewed as a gift from God (verses 13–14).

529. The prohibition of destroying fruit-bearing trees when besieging a city (Deuteronomy 20:19): "When in your war against a city you have to besiege it a long time in order to capture it, you must not destroy its trees, wielding the ax against them. You may eat of them, but you must not cut them down. Are trees of the field human to withdraw before you into the besieged city? Only trees that you know do not yield fruit may be destroyed. . . ." (see entry 200 for the verse's implications in the development of a biblical perspective on ecology).

530. The commandment delineating the responsibility of a city's leaders for a murder committed in its vicinity (Deuteronomy 21:1–8): "If, in the land that the Lord your God is assigning you to possess, someone murdered is found lying in the open, the identity of the killer not being known, your elders and magistrates shall go out and measure the distance from the corpse to the nearby towns. The elders of the town nearest to the corpse shall then take a heifer which has never been worked . . . and the elders of that town shall bring the heifer to an overflowing wadi, which is not tilled or sown. There in the wadi they shall break the heifer's neck. . . . Then all the elders of the town nearest to the corpse shall wash their hands over the heifer whose neck was broken in the wadi. And they shall make this declaration: 'Our hands did not shed this blood, nor did our eyes see it done. Absolve, O Lord, Your people Israel whom You redeemed, and do not let guilt for the blood of the innocent remain among your people Israel.' And they will be absolved of bloodguilt."

531. The prohibition against plowing or sowing in the wadi where the heifer was slaughtered (Deuteronomy 21:4): "And the elders of the town shall bring the heifer down to an overflowing wadi, which

is not tilled or sown. There, in the wadi, they shall break the heifer's neck" (to understand this law within its context, see preceding commandment).

532–533–534. The specification of one positive and two negative laws concerning a beautiful woman taken captive during a war (Deuteronomy 21:10–14):

- Procedures regarding such a woman, including the delineation of her rights during the first month of captivity (the text implies, but does not state explicitly, that one should not be sexually intimate with such a woman unless one intends to take her as a wife)
- The prohibition against selling her as a slave
- The prohibition against turning her into a slave after having been sexually intimate with her

"When you take the field against your enemies, and the Lord your God delivers them into your power and you take some of them captive. And you see among the captives a beautiful woman and you desire her and would take her to wife, you shall bring her into your house, and she shall trim her hair, pare her nails, and discard her captive's garb. She shall spend a month's time in your house lamenting her father and mother; after that you may come to her and possess her, and she shall be your wife. Then, should you no longer want her, you must release her outright. You must not sell her for money; since you had your will of her, you must not enslave her."

535–536. The commandment to execute one guilty of a capital offense and the prohibition against letting the corpse of a hanged criminal remain on the gallows overnight (Deuteronomy 21:22–23): "If a man is guilty of a capital offense and is put to death, and you hang him on a tree, you must not let his corpse remain on the gallows overnight, but you must bury him the same day. For a hanging body is an affront to God. . . ." Concerning the last phrase, the Talmud offers the parable of a king whose identical twin brother was a highwayman. When the latter was caught, tried, and hanged, his body was taken down immediately, lest people pass by and say, "The king is hanging" (Babylonian Talmud, *Sanhedrin* 46b). Because every human being is created in God's image, when even the lowest of criminals is hanged, at some level this constitutes a shame and affront to God.

537. The obligation to promptly bury a criminal after his execution (Deuteronomy 21:23): "You must not let his corpse remain on the gallows overnight, but you must bury him the same day." In ancient times, as well as in more modern eras, many societies let hanging bodies remain exposed to the elements for days and weeks as a way of frightening the general populace. Biblical law forbade this.

Based on this commandment, Jewish law also ruled that dead people are to be buried as quickly as possible. In Jerusalem, the general procedure is to bury a deceased person on the day or night after which he or she has died, so that not even one night passes with the corpse unburied. In most other Jewish communities, burial usually is deferred to the following day.

538–539. The obligation to return a lost object to its owner, and to not pretend that one has not seen it (Deuteronomy 22:1): "If you see your fellow's ox or sheep gone astray, do not ignore it; you must take it back to your fellow."

540–541. The prohibition against ignoring a fallen animal's suffering, and the obligation to help its owner raise it (Deuteronomy 22:4): "If you see your fellow's donkey or ox fallen in the road, do not ignore it; you must help him raise it."

542–543. The prohibition against women wearing male apparel, and against men donning women's clothing (Deuteronomy 22:5): "A woman must not put on man's apparel, nor shall a man wear woman's clothing. . . ."

544–545. The prohibition against taking a mother bird with its young in a nest, and the obligation to send the mother bird away when one wishes to seize her young (Deuteronomy 22:6): "If, along the road, you chance upon a bird's nest, in any tree or on the ground, with fledglings or eggs and the mother sitting over the fledglings or on the eggs, do not take the mother together with her young. Let the mother go, and take only the young. . . ." The rationale for this law is sensitivity to the mother bird's distress, as underscored by Maimonides's observation that "the pain of the animals under such circumstances is very great" (*Guide of the Perplexed* 3:48); thus, it is forbidden in general to cause such pain. The Hebrew term to describe such laws is *tza'ar ba'alei chayyim* (prevention of cruelty to animals; see entry 202).

546–547. The obligation to build a guardrail on one's roof and, by implication, to avoid leaving anything about that can cause serious injury (Deuteronomy 22:8): "When you build a new house, you shall make a guardrail for your roof, so that you do not bring bloodguilt on your house if anyone should fall from it." This law, for example, is violated by people who leave loaded guns in their homes in places where children can find them.

548–549. The prohibition against sowing together mixed seeds, and against eating produce resulting from their planting (Deuteronomy 22:9): "You shall not sow your vineyard with a second kind of seed, else the crop—from the seed you have sown—and the yield of the vineyard may not be used." Rabbinical tradition understands this prohibition as also applying outside of Israel in the case of a mixture of grape seeds, but not in the case of a mixture of two types of grain or vegetables.

550. The prohibition against yoking together two different kinds of animals (Deuteronomy 22:10): "You shall not plow with an ox and a donkey together" (see entry 202).

551. The prohibition against wearing clothing that is *shatnez*, i.e., that contains both wool and linen (Deuteronomy 22:11): "You shall not wear clothing combining wool and linen" (see entry 204).

552. The obligation to marry a woman before living with her (Deuteronomy 22:13): "A man marries a woman and cohabits with her." There is no explicit description of a marriage ceremony in the Torah, and the Rabbis cite this verse as mandating that a man who goes to live with a woman must first marry her.

553–554. The commandment establishing that a woman whose husband falsely accuses her of adultery can insist that he never divorce her; and, that a husband who lodges such a false accusation is never permitted to divorce his wife (Deuteronomy 22:13–19): "A man marries a woman and cohabits with her. Then he takes an aversion to her, and makes up charges against her and defames her, saying, 'I married this woman, but when I approached her, I found that she was not a virgin' [i.e., she had lost her virginity subsequent to the couple's engagement: in Jewish law engagement was a formal ceremony and virtually tantamount to marriage. Hence, its loss subsequent to engagement with anyone other than the future husband was regarded as adultery. If the loss of virginity occurred prior to the engagement, no claim of adultery could be lodged]. . . . [If the charges are found to be false, the man is flogged and heavily fined], for the man has defamed a virgin in Israel. Moreover, she shall remain his wife; he shall never have the right to divorce her."

555. The commandment that those who commit a capital crime are to be executed (Deuteronomy 22:24): "You shall take the two of them out to the gate of that town and stone them to death. . . ."

556. The prohibition against punishing a person who is forced to commit a sin against his or her will (Deuteronomy 22:25–26): "But if the man comes upon the engaged girl in the open country [where she cannot cry out], and the man lies with her by force, only the man who lay with her shall die. But you shall do nothing to the girl. . . ."

557–558. The commandment that a rapist is obligated to marry his victim if she so desires, and the prohibition against his ever divorcing her (Deuteronomy 22:28–29): "If a man comes upon a virgin who is not engaged and he seizes her and lies with her, and they are discovered, the man who lay with her shall pay the girl's father fifty [shekels of] silver, and she shall be his wife. Because he has violated her, he can never have the right to divorce her" (see entry 207; disturbingly, the Torah offers no guidelines as to the rapist's punishment if the woman is unmarried but not a virgin; if she is married, the rapist is executed; see preceding commandment).

559. The commandment excluding from the Jewish community for the purpose of marriage a man who is sexually mutilated (Deuteronomy 23:2): "No one whose testes are crushed or whose member is cut off shall be admitted into the congregation of the Lord [i.e., get married]." Jewish tradition understands this law as applying only to one who intentionally has himself castrated, as was done in some pagan religions. As Abraham Chill comments: "Should the injury to his genitals be inherited or the result of illness—either case being considered an act of God—this prohibition does not apply and the man may marry anyone he chooses. This means that, whereas one who voluntarily allowed himself to be castrated or sterilized is subject to the penalty for having shown that he had no wish or intention of begetting children, one who was impotent or sterile through no fault of his own might hope to be cured of his disability sooner or later and is therefore allowed to marry a Jewess" (*The Mitzvot*, pages 465–466).

560. The commandment classifying a Jewish child resulting from an adulterous or incestuous union as a *mamzer* (bastard) and as forbidden ever to marry any other Jew except another *mamzer* (Deuteronomy 23:3): "A *mamzer* shall not be admitted into the congregation of the Lord; none of his descendants, even in the tenth generation, shall be admitted into the congregation of the Lord" (see entry 205; "tenth generation" is a euphemism for "forever").

561–562–563–564. Three prohibitions and one positive commandment concerning relations between Israelites, and Ammonites, Moabites, Edomites, and Egyptians (Deuteronomy 23:4–10):

- Against Ammonites and Moabites ever becoming Hebrews
- Against concerning oneself with their well-being

- Against hating Edomites and Egyptians
- In addition, there is the positive stipulation that Edomites and Egyptians can be admitted into the Israelite community in the third generation.

"No Ammonite or Moabite shall be admitted into the congregation of the Lord; none of their descendants, even in the tenth generation, shall ever be admitted into the congregation of the Lord, because they did not meet you with food and water on your journey after you left Egypt, and because they hired Balaam, son of Beor . . . to curse you [see entry 50]. . . . You shall never concern yourself with their welfare or benefit as long as you live. You shall not abhor an Edomite, for he is your kinsman [i.e., the descendant of Esau, Jacob's twin brother]. You shall not abhor an Egyptian for you were a stranger in his land. Children born to them may be admitted into the congregation of the Lord in the third generation."

The above is difficult to understand: Ammon's and Moab's sins certainly seem less substantial than those of Egypt, which enslaved the Israelite people and ordered the drowning of every male infant. Yet the Israelites are forbidden to hate Egyptians,* but are encouraged to hate Moabites and Ammonites.

Why? It is not clear, particularly given that Deuteronomy 2:29 states that Moab did sell bread and water to the Israelites. The Torah's attitude notwithstanding, a later biblical book, Ruth, glorifies a Moabite convert to the Israelite religion, and informs us that she is the ancestress of King David, from whom Jewish tradition asserts the Messiah will descend. Thus, among the Messiah's ancestors will be a Moabite convert to Judaism. Rabbinic law dealt with this conundrum by declaring that Moabite and Ammonite *women* were permitted to convert to the Israelite religion and marry Israelite men.

For some two thousand years, Jewish law has ruled that the nations of the ancient Near East have lost their genealogical identities; thus, any gentile who wishes to convert is in principle accepted, without any concern that he may be a descendant of Ammon or Moab.

565. The prohibition against a man who is ritually unclean remaining in the Israelite camp (Deuteronomy 23:11): "If anyone among you has been rendered unclean by a nocturnal emission, he must leave the camp, and he must not reenter the camp" (for one day, until he purifies himself). The *Sefer ha-Hinnuch* notes that the ritually

---

*Dr. Michael Berger has suggested to me that since Egypt was punished, its crime was deemed forgiven.

unclean person was restricted only from the Levite camp (volume 5, page 263).

566–567. The commandments to maintain sanitary conditions within the Israelite army by establishing a privy outside the camp, and by requiring soldiers to carry an implement to dispose of their excrement (Deuteronomy 23:13–14): ". . . there shall be an area for you outside the camp, where you may relieve yourself. With your [military] gear you shall have a spike [something like a shovel], and when you have squatted you shall dig a hole with it and cover up your excrement." The next verse almost seems to serve as the basis for the proverb "Cleanliness is next to Godliness": "Since the Lord your God moves about in your camp to protect you and deliver your enemies to you, let your camp be holy; let Him not find anything unseemly among you and turn away from you."

568–569. The prohibitions against returning a runaway slave to his master, and against oppressing an ex-slave when he comes to live among Israelites (Deuteronomy 23:16–17): "You shall not turn over to his master a slave who seeks refuge with you from his master. He shall live with you in any place he may choose among the settlements in your midst, wherever he pleases; you must not ill-treat him" (see entry 166).

570. The prohibition against an Israelite man or woman becoming a prostitute (Deuteronomy 23:18): "There must not be any prostitutes among Israelite women. Similarly, there must be no male prostitutes among Israelite men."

571. The specification forbidding offering to the sanctuary donations that are unacceptable (Deuteronomy 23:19): "Do not bring a prostitute's fee or the price of a dog to the Temple of the Lord your God. . . ." By implication, this would seem to preclude a charitable organization accepting a contribution derived from illegal, immoral, or otherwise inappropriate activities.

572–573. The prohibition against taking interest on a loan to an Israelite, and the permission to take interest from one to a non-Israelite (Deuteronomy 23:20–21): "You shall not deduct interest from loans to your countrymen . . . but you may deduct interest from loans to foreigners. Do not deduct interest from loans to your countrymen, so that the Lord your God may bless you in all your undertakings in the land that you are about to enter and possess (see entry 206).

574. The obligation to promptly carry out a vow (Deuteronomy 23:22): "When you make a vow to the Lord your God, do not put off fulfilling it. . . ."

575. The commandment to fulfill what one has said one will do (Deuteronomy 23:24): "You must fulfill what has crossed your lips and perform what you have voluntarily vowed to the Lord your God, having made the promise with your own mouth."

576–577–578. The permission to a worker to eat what he can take with his hands while working in a vineyard or field, but the prohibitions against loading food into a vessel and taking it away. Jewish tradition also understands these verses as forbidding one from stopping work in order to eat from one's employer's crops (Deuteronomy 23:25–26): "When you enter another man's vineyard [to work there], you may eat as many grapes as you want, until you are full, but you must not put any in your vessel. When you enter another man's field of standing grain [to work there], you may pluck ears with your hand, but you must not put a sickle to your neighbor's grain." Abraham Chill explains: "The laborer may not interrupt his work in order to partake of the crop. When harvesting the vineyard, he may eat only while he is actually working, while turning at the end of a row or while on his way from the winepress to refill his basket. He may not transfer this right to his wife and children. But, so long as he does not steal any of his employer's time, he may eat as much of the crop as he wishes" (*The Mitzvot*, page 474).

579. The obligation of a man divorcing his wife to issue her a legally binding bill of divorce (Deuteronomy 24:1): ". . . he shall write her a bill of divorce, and place it in her hand, thus releasing her from his household" (see entry 207).

580. The prohibition against remarrying one's former wife, if she has married another since the divorce (Deuteronomy 24:2–4): "When she leaves his household [after the divorce], she may go and marry another man. However, if her second husband rejects her, and writes her a bill of divorce . . . or if her second husband dies, then her first husband who divorced her cannot remarry her, since she has been defiled [i.e., is now forbidden to him]. . . ." Gunther Plaut comments: "She is disqualified [to her first husband] because her second marriage appears now as a promiscuous interlude. According to Nachmanides, the prohibition was intended to prevent wife swapping" (*The Torah: A Modern Commentary*, page 1498).

581–582: The right of a groom not to be drafted into the army for a year after his marriage; and his responsibility during this year to make his bride happy (Deuteronomy 24:5): "When a man has taken a bride, he should not go out with the army or be assigned to it for any purpose; he shall be exempt one year for the sake of his household, to give happiness to the woman he has married." According to Jewish law, the sole instance in which a groom can be taken into the army is to fight in a war of national defense (also, in the original war to capture Israel).

583. The prohibition against taking as collateral for a loan a utensil needed by the borrower to prepare food (Deuteronomy 24:6): "A handmill or an upper millstone shall not be taken in pawn, for that would be taking someone's life in pawn." Handmills were needed to make bread; therefore, seizing such a utensil threatened the borrower's family with starvation, and so was forbidden.

584. The community's obligation to execute a kidnapper who enslaved or sold into slavery a fellow Israelite (Deuteronomy 24:7): "If a man is found to have kidnapped a fellow Israelite, enslaving him or selling him, that kidnapper shall die; thus you will sweep out evil from your midst."

585–586–587. Three commandments, two negative and one positive, concerning taking collateral for a loan (Deuteronomy 24:10–13):

- The prohibition against entering the borrower's house to seize the pledge
- The prohibition against sleeping in a pledged garment
- The obligation to return the pledge, if it is a garment, to the borrower when he needs it

"When you make a loan of any sort to your neighbor, you must not enter his house to seize his pledge. You must remain outside, while the man to whom you made the loan brings the pledge out to you. If he is a needy man, you shall not go to sleep in his pledge: you must return the pledge to him at sundown, that he may sleep in his cloth and bless you; and it will be to your merit before the Lord your God." This exceedingly cumbersome process presumably was intended to discourage lenders from taking such pledges in the first place.

588. The obligation to pay a hired day worker promptly (Deuteronomy 24:14–15): "You shall not abuse a needy and destitute laborer, whether a fellow countryman or a stranger in one of the communities of your land. You must pay him his wages on the same day, before the sun sets, for he is needy and urgently depends on it; else he will cry to the Lord against you and you will incur guilt." The law draws no distinctions between obligations to an Israelite and a non-Israelite; God will hear the cry of either.

589. A prohibition against punishing children for their parents' sins or parents for those of their children (Deuteronomy 24:16): "Parents shall not be put to death for [the sins of] children, nor children be put to death for [the sins of] parents: a person shall be put to death only for his own crime." Jewish tradition derives from this verse the law that close relatives are prohibited from testifying against each other, interpreting the verse as if it read: "Parents shall not be put to death on the basis of the testimony of their children, nor children be put to death on the basis of the testimony of their parents."

590–591. The obligation to treat justly society's weakest members (Deuteronomy 24:17): "You shall not subvert the rights of the stranger and the orphan; you shall not take a widow's garment in pledge."

592–593. The specification of responsibility toward society's weakest members (Deuteronomy 20:19):

- To leave a forgotten sheaf in the field
- To ensure that this food is made available to the stranger, orphan, and widow

"When you reap the harvest in your field and overlook a sheaf in the field, do not turn back to get it; it shall go to the stranger, the orphan and the widow—in order that the Lord your God may bless you in all your undertakings."

594–595. The commandment to lash those convicted of doing evil, but the prohibition against degrading a criminal by administering too many lashes (Deuteronomy 25:2–3): "If the guilty one is to be flogged, the magistrate shall have him lie down and be given lashes in his presence, by count, as his guilt warrants. He may be given up to forty lashes, but not more, lest being flogged further, to excess, your brother be degraded before your eyes." Regarding the "forty lashes," Jewish law understands the maximum permissible number of lashes to be thirty–nine.

596. The prohibition against muzzling an animal working in a field (Deuteronomy 25:4): "You shall not muzzle an animal while it is threshing" (see entry 202).

597–598–599. Three positive commandments concerning a *yevamah*, a widow whose husband dies before the couple has had children (Deuteronomy 25:5–10):

- The commandment to the deceased husband's brother to marry the widow, in what is known as a levirate marriage (in Latin, "levir" means "husband's brother")

- The couple's firstborn son is to be accounted to the dead man (e.g., when the child grows up he inherits his mother's late husband's estate as if the dead man were his father)
- The specification of the procedure to be enacted if the brother-in-law refuses to marry the widow

"When brothers dwell together [Jewish law understands this as applying even when the brothers do not reside near each other] and one of them dies childless, the wife of the deceased shall not be married to a stranger, outside the family. Her husband's brother must cohabit with her, take her as his wife and perform the levir's duty. The first son that she bears will then perpetuate the name of the dead brother, so that his name will not be blotted out in Israel. But if the man does not want to marry his brother's widow, his brother's widow shall appear before the elders in the gate and declare, 'My husband's brother refuses to perpetuate his brother's name in Israel, and he will not perform the duty of a levir.' The elders of his town shall then summon him and talk to him. If he insists, saying, 'I do not want to marry her,' his brother's widow shall go up to him in the presence of the elders, take off his shoe, spit in his face, and make this declaration: 'This is what shall be done to the man who will not build up his brother's house!' And he shall go in Israel by the name of 'the horse where the shoe was removed.' "

The tradition of levirate marriage predates Moses; see the discussion of such a marriage on entry 23. Today, however, this law no longer is practiced, even if the couple wish to marry. Among Orthodox Jews, *halitza*, the ceremony of unbinding the shoe, is still performed so as to release the widow to marry others.

Because this law is biblical and is still regarded as binding, it can periodically result in unpleasant complications. In Israel, on several occasions, young married soldiers have been killed in battle, leaving behind childless widows. Yet the dead soldier's brother may himself be a young child. Since a boy under the age of thirteen (*bar mitzvah*) has no legal standing, the widow must wait until he turns thirteen before the ceremony of *halitza* can be performed, and she be permitted to marry someone else.

600–601. The commandment to punish and to show no mercy to a woman who uses impermissible and obscene means to help her husband (Deuteronomy 25:11): "If two men get into a fight with each other, and the wife of one comes up to save her husband from his antagonist and puts out her hand and seizes him by his genitals, you shall cut off her hand; show no pity."

This law, which commands mutilation, caused the Rabbis no little aggravation; ultimately, they ruled that, despite the Torah's explicit command, no woman's hand was ever to be cut off; instead, a monetary fine was imposed. And if her action was necessary in order to save her husband's life, no punishment at all was imposed.

602. The prohibition against ever possessing, let alone using, dishonest weights and measures (Deuteronomy 25:13–16): "You shall not have in your pouch alternate weights, larger and smaller. You shall not have in your house alternate measures, a larger and a smaller. You must have completely honest weights and completely honest measures, if you are to endure long on the soil that the Lord your God is giving you. For everyone who does those things, everyone who deals dishonestly, is abhorrent to the Lord your God." The reward promised, "to endure long on the soil that the Lord your God is giving you," brings to mind another commandment which is followed by this promised reward, "Honor your father and mother."

603–604–605. Two positive and one negative commandment concerning Amalek (Deuteronomy 25:17–19; see also entry 38):

- To remember the evil Amalek did to Israel in the desert
- To wipe out Amalek
- Not to forget the evil Amalek did to Israel

"Remember what Amalek did to you on your journey, after you left Egypt, how, undeterred by fear of God, they surprised you on the march, when you were famished and weary, and cut down all the stragglers in your rear [see Exodus 17:8–13; the detail about Amalek striking Israel's weakest members is not mentioned there]. Therefore, when the Lord your God gives you peace from all your enemies around you, in the land that the Lord your God is giving you as a hereditary portion, you must blot out the memory of Amalek from under heaven. Do not forget!"

606. The obligation to recite a specific prayer upon bringing one's first fruits to the sanctuary (Deuteronomy 26:1–10): "When you enter the land that the Lord your God is giving you as a heritage, and you occupy it and settle in it, you shall take some of every first fruit of the soil . . . put it in a basket and go to the place where the Lord your God will choose to establish His name. . . . The priest shall take the basket from your hand and set it down in front of the altar of the Lord your God. You shall then recite as follows before the Lord your God: "My father was a fugitive Aramean. He went down to Egypt with small numbers and sojourned there; but there he became

a great and very populous nation. The Egyptians dealt harshly with us and oppressed us; they imposed heavy labor upon us. We cried to the Lord, the God of our fathers, and the Lord heard our plea and saw our plight, our misery, and our oppression. The Lord freed us from Egypt by a mighty hand, by an outstretched arm and awesome power, and by signs and portents. He brought us to this place and gave us this land, a land flowing with milk and honey. Wherefore, I now bring the first fruits of the soil which You, O Lord, have given me. . . ."

607–608–609–610. One positive and three negative commandments concerning the various tithes (Deuteronomy 26:12–15):

- The obligation to make a certain declaration when the portions and tithes are paid
- The prohibition against eating the Second Tithe while in mourning (Jewish tradition restricts the mourner's right to eat from the tithe to a very short period: from the time an immediate relative has died until the person is buried)
- The prohibition against eating this tithe while ritually unclean
- The prohibition against spending any money exchanged for the Second Tithe on anything other than food and drink

"When you have set aside in full the tenth part of your yield—in the third year, the year of the tithe—and have given it to the Levite, the stranger, the orphan, and the widow, that they may eat their fill in your settlements, you shall declare before the Lord your God, 'I have cleared out the consecrated portion from the house; and I have given it to the Levite, the stranger, the orphan, and the widow just as You commanded me; I have neither transgressed nor neglected any of Your commandments: I have not eaten of it while in mourning; I have not cleared out any of it while I was unclean, and I have not deposited any of it with the dead [this verse is the basis for the last prohibition listed above]. I have obeyed the Lord my God; I have done just as You commanded me. Look down from Your holy abode, from heaven, and bless your people Israel and the soil You have given us, a land flowing with milk and honey, as You swore to our fathers.' "

611. The commandment to emulate God's behavior by walking in His ways (Deuteronomy 28:9): "The Lord will establish you as His holy people, as He swore to you, if you keep the commandments of the Lord your God and walk in His ways" (see entry 208).

612. The obligation of the entire Israelite community to assemble every seven years to hear the Torah publicly read (Deuteronomy 31:10–13; according to Jewish tradition, the text read was certain designated sections of the Book of Deuteronomy): "And Moses instructed them as follows: Every seventh year, the year set for remission [of debts; see Deuteronomy 15:1], at the Feast of Booths, when all Israel comes to appear before the Lord your God in the place which He will choose, you shall read this Teaching [i.e., the Torah] aloud in the presence of all Israel. Gather the people—men, women and children, and the strangers in your communities—that they may hear and so learn to revere the Lord your God and to observe faithfully every word of this Teaching. Their children, too, who have not had the experience, shall hear and learn to revere the Lord your God as long as they live in the land which you are about to cross the Jordan to occupy." According to Jewish tradition, the reading occurred on the second day of Sukkot (the Feast of Booths) in the year following the *shmittah* (the year during which the land lies fallow; see entry 187).

613. The commandment that each Jew should write a Torah scroll during his lifetime. This is how Jewish tradition understood Deuteronomy 31:19, a divine directive to Moses to write down what he has heard from God: "Therefore, write down this poem and teach it to the people of Israel; put it in their mouths. . . ."

Jewish tradition considers a person to have fulfilled this commandment by contributing money to have a Torah scroll written, or even by purchasing religious books, which one will use to acquire knowledge of Torah.

APPENDICES

APPENDIX I:
THE BOOKS OF THE
HEBREW BIBLE
IN ORDER OF APPEARANCE

In Hebrew, the name for the Bible is Tanakh, an acronym for the three categories of books that make up the Bible: *Torah, Nevi'im (Prophets)*, and *Ketuvim (Writings)*. As noted, observant Jews do not generally refer to the Bible as the Old Testament. That is a Christian usage.

The Hebrew Bible contains thirty-nine books; however, the order in which the books appear in Jewish editions of the Bible is somewhat different from Christian editions. What follows is a listing of the thirty-nine books as they appear in traditional Hebrew Bibles. Following the English name of each book, I have transliterated the Hebrew name. The "ch" sound in Hebrew is pronounced as the "ch" in Bach (see, for example, #10).

TORAH

1. Genesis *(Brei-sheet)*
2. Exodus *(S'hmot)*
3. Leviticus *(Va-Yikra)*
4. Numbers *(Ba-Midbar)*
5. Deuteronomy *(D'varim)*

PROPHETS *(NEVI'IM)*

6. Joshua *(Ye-ho-shua)*
7. Judges *(Shof-tim)*
8. First Samuel *(Shmu-el Aleph)*

595

9. Second Samuel (*Shmu-el Bet*)
10. First Kings (*Me-lachim Aleph*)
11. Second Kings (*Me-lachim Bet*)
12. Isaiah (*Ye-sha-ya-hu*)
13. Jeremiah (*Yir-mi-ya-hu*)
14. Ezekiel (*Ye-chez-kel*)
15. Hosea (*Ho-shea*)
16. Joel (*Yo-el*)
17. Amos (*Ah-mos*)
18. Obadiah (*O-vad-ya*)
19. Jonah (*Yo-na*)
20. Micah (*Mee-cha*)
21. Nahum (*Na-chum*)
22. Habakkuk (*Cha-ba-kuk*)
23. Zephaniah (*Tze-fan-ya*)
24. Haggai (*Cha-gai*)
25. Zechariah (*Ze-char-ya*)
26. Malachi (*Mal-a-chi*)

WRITINGS (*KETUVIM*)

27. Psalms (*Te-hee-lim*)
28. Proverbs (*Mish-lei*)
29. Job (*Ee-yov*)
30. The Songs of Songs (*Shir ha-Shirim*)
31. Ruth (*Root*)
32. Lamentations (*Ei-cha*)
33. Ecclesiastes (*Ko-hel-let*)
34. Esther (*Es-ter*)
35. Daniel (*Da-nee-ayl*)
36. Ezra (*Ez-ra*)
37. Nehemiah (*Ne-chem-ya*)
38. First Chronicles (*Divrei ha-Yamim Aleph*)
39. Second Chronicles (*Divrei ha-Yamim Bet*)

APPENDIX II:
DATES OF MAJOR BIBLICAL
EVENTS AND CHARACTERS

Attempts to date the opening episodes of Genesis, stories such as Noah and the Flood and the Tower of Babel, are purely speculative. It is also impossible to be precise in dating the rest of Genesis, which tells the stories of the Patriarchs. One can simply note that the narratives about Abraham, Isaac, and Jacob occur at some point after 2000 and before 1500 B.C.E. We also have no way of knowing the precise dates of the events described in the last four books of the Torah and in the earlier books of the prophets. However, by the time we come to the events described in II Kings and the later prophets, we often can determine the dates quite accurately.

In compiling this listing I have relied in the main, but not exclusively, on Judah Gribetz's exhaustive *The Timetables of Jewish History: A Chronology of the Most Important People and Events in Jewish History* (New York: Simon & Schuster, 1993).

1230 The Exodus from Egypt and the revelation at Mount Sinai. The events described in the last three and a half books of the Torah, starting with Exodus, chapter 13, occur in the years following the Exodus.

1190 The Israelites, under the leadership of Joshua, Moses' successor, enter Canaan and start to capture the land.

1125 The Israelites are living under Canaanite domination when Deborah, a prophetess and judge, accompanied by Israelite general Barak, rallies Israelite troops to defeat Canaanite forces at Mount Tabor.

1050 The Philistines inflict a stunning defeat on the Israelites and capture the Ark of the Lord (the holiest object in ancient Jewish life, the Ark contained the Ten Commandments).

1020 Saul is anointed as Israel's first king.

1005 Saul is killed in battle against the Philistines.

1004 David becomes king over the tribe of Judah and in 998 over all Israel. During his forty-year reign, David captures Jerusalem and establishes it as Israel's capital, and consolidates the whole land of Israel under Israelite rule.

967 Solomon succeeds his father David as king.

950 Solomon completes construction of the *Beit ha-Mikdash*, the Great Temple in Jerusalem.

931 After Solomon's death, the ten northern tribes revolt against his son Jeroboam and form the kingdom of Israel. They anoint Rehoboam as king.

860 The prophet Elijah repeatedly confronts Ahab and Jezebel, among Israel's most wicked kings and queens.

750 The prophets Hosea and Amos denounce the disparities between the rich and poor that increasingly pervade Israelite society. Amos warns the people of Israel that their kingdom will be destroyed because of its moral corruption.

722 Assyria defeats the ten tribes of Israel and deports many of its residents. Most of the members of the Ten Lost Tribes assimilate into the societies into which they are exiled and become lost to the Jewish people.

720 The prophets Micah and Isaiah criticize the remaining Jewish kingdom of Judah for its religious hypocrisy and cruelty toward the poor. They warn that Judah will be destroyed if its people do not repent.

715 King Hezekiah of Judah heeds the prophetic warnings and promotes religious reform.

698 Manasseh, among the most evil kings of Judah, assumes the throne, reigns for fifty-five years, and undoes all the good done by his father, Hezekiah. He promotes idolatry and sheds much innocent blood.

640 Josiah, Manasseh's grandson, becomes king and institutes extensive religious and moral reforms. Unfortunately, the reform is short-lived.

625 The prophets Jeremiah and Zephaniah warn the people of impending catastrophe if they do not abandon pagan practices and immoral conduct.

587 Babylon puts down a second revolt by Judea (the first was in 598) and destroys the Jerusalem Temple and the city of Jerusalem.

586 Gedaliah, the Babylon-appointed Jewish governor of Judea, is assassinated by extremist Judean nationalists.

539 King Cyrus of Persia defeats Babylon and permits the Judean exiles to return to, and rebuild, Israel.

515 The Second Temple is completed.

450 Nehemiah, a Jewish official in Persia, is dispatched to Jerusalem to supervise the community.

428 Ezra comes to Judea and is authorized by Persia to establish a theocracy in which the Jews are required to live according to Torah law.

BIBLIOGRAPHY

JEWISH TRANSLATIONS AND COMMENTARIES ON THE TORAH

Fox, Dr. Everett. *The Five Books of Moses*. New York: Schocken Books, 1995.

Hertz, Rabbi J. H. *The Pentateuch and Haftorahs*. London: Soncino Press, 1980.

Kaplan, Rabbi Aryeh. *The Living Torah: The Five Books of Moses and the Haftarot*. New York: Moznaim Publishing, 1981.

Levine, Baruch A. *The JPS Torah Commentary: Leviticus*. Philadelphia: Jewish Publication Society, 1989.

Milgrom, Jacob. *The JPS Torah Commentary: Numbers*. Philadelphia: Jewish Publication Society, 1990.

————. *Leviticus 1–16: A New Translation with Introduction and Commentary*. Garden City, N.Y.: Doubleday/Anchor Bible, 1991.

Plaut, Rabbi W. Gunther, ed. *The Torah: A Modern Commentary*. New York: Union of American Hebrew Congregations, 1981.

Sarna, Nahum. *The JPS Torah Commentary: Exodus*. Philadelphia: Jewish Publication Society, 1991.

————. *The JPS Torah Commentary: Genesis*. Philadelphia: Jewish Publication Society, 1989.

Scherman, Rabbi Nosson. *The Chumash: The Stone Edition*. Brooklyn, N.Y.: Mesorah Publications, 1993.

Tanakh: A New Translation of the Holy Scriptures. Philadelphia: Jewish Publication Society, 1985.

Tigay, Jeffrey H. *The JPS Torah Commentary: Deuteronomy*. Philadelphia: Jewish Publication Society, 1996.

Weinfeld, Moshe. *Deuteronomy 1–11: A New Translation with Introduction and Commentary*. Garden City, N.Y.: Doubleday/Anchor Bible, 1991.

BOOKS CITED AND CONSULTED

Alter, Robert. *The Art of Biblical Narrative*. New York: Basic Books, 1981.

———. *The World of Biblical Literature*. New York: Basic Books, 1992.

Berger, David. "On the Morality of the Patriarchs in Jewish Polemic and Exegesis," in Clemens Thoma and Michael Wyschogrod, eds., *Understanding Scripture: Exploration of Jewish and Christian Traditions of Interpretation*. Mahwah, N.J.: Paulist Press, 1987, pp. 49–62.

Bergren, Richard Victor. *The Prophets and the Law*. Cincinnati: Hebrew Union College, 1974.

Bialik, Hayim Nahman, and Yehoshua Hana Ravnitzky. *The Book of Legends: Legends from the Talmud and Midrash*, translated from the Hebrew *Sefer Ha-Aggadah* by William Braude. New York: Schocken Books, 1992.

Bright, John. *A History of Israel*. 2nd ed. Philadelphia: Westminster Press, 1975.

———. *Jeremiah* (a commentary). Garden City, N.Y.: Doubleday/Anchor Bible, 1965.

Chill, Abraham. *The Mitzvot: The Commandments and Their Rationale*. New York: Bloch Publishing Company, 1974.

Comay, Joan. *Who's Who in the Bible*. New York: Bonanza Books, 1980.

Crenshaw, James. "Samson," in David Noel Freedman, ed., *Anchor Bible Dictionary*, Vol. 5. Garden City, N.Y.: Doubleday, 1992, pp. 950–954.

Day, A. Colin. *Roget's Thesaurus of the Bible*. San Francisco: Harper San Francisco, a division of HarperCollins Publishers, 1992.

Eliach, Yaffa. *Hasidic Tales of the Holocaust*. New York: Oxford University Press, 1982.

Elman, Yaakov. *The Living Nach: Early Prophets: A New Translation [with commentary] Based on Traditional Jewish Sources*. New York: Moznaim Publishing, 1994.

Exum, J. Cheryl. *Fragmented Women: Feminist (Sub)Versions of Biblical Narratives*. Valley Forge, Pa.: Trinity Press International, 1993.

Feldman, David. *Birth Control in Jewish Law: Marital Relations, Contraception, and Abortion as Set Forth in the Classic Texts of Jewish Law*. New York: New York University Press, 1968.

Fewell, Danna Nolan. "Joshua" and "Judges," in Carol Newman and

Sharon Ringe, eds., *The Women's Bible Commentary*. Louisville, Ky.: Westminster/John Knox Press, 1992, pages 63–66 and 67–77.

Friedrich, Otto. *The End of the World: A History*. New York: Coward, McCann, 1982.

Gold, Michael. *Does God Belong in the Bedroom?* Philadelphia: Jewish Publication Society, 1992.

Goldstein, Rebecca. "Looking Back at Lot's Wife," in *Out of the Garden: Women Writers on the Bible*. New York: Fawcett Columbine (paperback), 1995, pp. 3–12.

Goodman, Hannah Grad. *The Story of Prophecy*. New York: Behrman House, 1965.

Graetz, Heinrich. *A History of the Jews*. Philadelphia: Jewish Publication Society, 1891–1898.

Greenberg, Irving. "Cloud of Smoke, Pillar of Fire: Judaism, Christianity and Modernity After the Holocaust," in Eva Fleischner, ed., *Auschwitz: Beginning of a New Era? Reflections on the Holocaust*. Published jointly by Ktav Publishing, The Cathedral Church of St. John the Divine, and the Anti-Defamation League: New York, 1977, pp. 7–55.

Greenberg, Moshe. "Reflections on Job's Theology," in *The Book of Job: A New Translation According to the Traditional Hebrew Text*. Philadelphia: Jewish Publication Society, 1980, pp. xvii–xxiii.

———. "Some Postulates of Biblical Criminal Law," in Moshe Greenberg, *Studies in the Bible and Jewish Thought*. Philadelphia: Jewish Publication Society, 1995, pp. 25–41.

Gunn, David M., and Danna Nolan Fewell. *Narrative in the Hebrew Bible*. Oxford and New York: Oxford University Press, 1993.

haLevi, Aaron. *Sefer ha-Hinnuch*, ascribed to Rabbi Aaron haLevi of Barcelona and translated by Charles Wengrov. 5 vols. Jerusalem and New York: Feldheim Publishers, 1984.

Herzog, Chaim. *Heroes of Israel*. Boston: Little, Brown, 1989.

Heschel, Abraham Joshua. *The Prophets: An Introduction*. 2 vols. New York: Harper Torchbooks, 1969.

Jacobs, Louis. *The Jewish Religion: A Companion*. Oxford and New York: Oxford University Press, 1995.

———. *A Jewish Theology*. New York: Behrman House, 1973.

Kahan, Rabbi A. Y. *The Taryag Mitzvos*. Brooklyn, N.Y.: Keser Torah Publications, 1987.

Kam, Rose Sallberg. *Their Stories, Our Stories: Women of the Bible*. New York: Continuum, 1995.

Kasher, Menachem. *Encyclopedia of Biblical Interpretation: Exodus*, Vol. 9. New York: American Biblical Encyclopedia Society, 1953.

Kaufmann, Walter. *The Faith of a Heretic*. Garden City, N.Y.: Doubleday, 1961.

————. *Religions in Four Dimensions: Existential, Aesthetic, Historical, Comparative.* New York: Reader's Digest Press, 1976.

Kaufmann, Yehezkel. *The Religion of Israel,* trans. and abridged by Moshe Greenberg. Chicago: University of Chicago Press, 1960.

Lamm, Norman. "Ecology in Jewish Law and Theology," in his *Faith and Doubt: Studies in Traditional Jewish Thought.* New York: Ktav, 1986, pp. 162–185.

Landis, Joseph. *The Great Jewish Plays.* New York: Horizon Press, 1972.

Leibowitz, Nehama. *Studies in Shemot: The Book of Exodus.* 2 vols. Jerusalem: World Zionist Organization, Department for Torah Education and Culture, 1976.

————. *Studies in the Book of Genesis: In the Context of Ancient and Modern Jewish Bible Commentary.* Jerusalem: World Zionist Organization, Department for Torah Education and Culture, 1972.

Lockyer, Herbert, ed. *Nelson's Illustrated Bible Dictionary.* Nashville: Thomas Nelson Publishers, 1986.

Maimonides, Moses. *Code of Maimonides.* New Haven: Yale University Press, published in a multivolume translation starting in 1949.

Midrash Rabbah. London: Soncino Press, published in a multivolume translation, 1983.

Milgrom, Jacob. "The Biblical Diet Laws as an Ethical System." *Interpretation,* July 1963.

Pardes, Ilana. *Countertraditions in the Bible: A Feminist Approach.* Cambridge, Mass.: Harvard University Press, 1992.

Pellegrino, Charles. *Return to Sodom and Gomorrah: From the Location of the Garden of Eden to the Parting of the Red Sea—Solving the Bible's Ancient Mysteries Through Archaeological Discovery.* New York: Avon Books, 1995.

Prager, Dennis. *Think a Second Time.* New York: Regan Books/HarperCollins, 1995.

Rabinowitz, Abraham Hirsch. *Taryag: A Study of the Tradition That the Written Torah Contains 613 Mitzvot.* Northvale, N.J.: Jason Aaronson Inc., 1996.

Riedel, Eunice, Thomas Tracy, and Barbara Moskowitz. *The Book of the Bible.* New York: William Morrow and Company, 1979.

Rosenblatt, Naomi, and Joshua Horwitz. *Wrestling with Angels: What the First Family of Genesis Teaches Us About Our Spiritual Identity, Sexuality, and Personal Relationships.* New York: Delacorte Press, 1995.

Sarna, Nahum M. *Exploring Exodus: The Heritage of Biblical Israel.* New York: Schocken Books, 1986.

————. *On the Book of Psalms.* New York: Schocken Books, 1993.

————. *Understanding Genesis: The Heritage of Biblical Israel.* New York: Schocken Books (paperback), 1970.

Segev, Tom. *The Seventh Million: The Israelis and the Holocaust.* New York: Hill and Wang, 1993.

Shapiro, David. *Studies in Jewish Thought.* New York: Yeshiva University Press, 1975.

Spiegel, Shalom. "Amos vs. Amaziah," in Judah Goldin, ed., *The Jewish Expression.* New York: Bantam Books, 1970, pp. 38–65.

Steinmetz, Devora. *From Father to Son: Kinship, Conflict and Continuity in Genesis.* Louisville, Ky.: Westminster/John Knox Press, 1989.

Steinsaltz, Adin. *Biblical Images,* trans. Yehuda Hanegbi and Yehudit Keshet. Northvale, N.J.: Jason Aaronson Inc., 1994 (originally published in 1984).

Sternberg, Meir. *The Poetics of Biblical Narrative.* Bloomington, Ind.: Indiana University Press, 1987.

Telushkin, Joseph. *Jewish Literacy: The Most Important Things to Know About the Jewish Religion, Its People, and Its History.* New York: William Morrow and Company, 1991.

————. *Jewish Wisdom: Ethical, Spiritual, and Historical Lessons from the Great Works and Thinkers.* New York: William Morrow and Company, 1994.

————. *Words That Hurt, Words That Heal.* New York: William Morrow and Company, 1996.

Weiner, Herbert. *9½ Mystics.* New York: Holt, Rinehart and Winston, 1969.

Wiesel, Elie. *Five Biblical Portraits.* Notre Dame, Ind.: University of Notre Dame Press, 1981.

Wigoder, Geoffrey, ed. *Illustrated Dictionary and Concordance of the Bible.* Jerusalem: The Jerusalem Publishing House Inc., 1986.

Willmington, Harold L. *Willmington's Complete Guide to Bible Knowledge.* Wheaton, Ill.: Tyndale House Publishers, 1990.

Wilson, James Q., and Richard J. Herrnstein. *Crime and Human Nature.* New York: Simon & Schuster, 1985.

INDEX

Aaron, 110–111
  blessing instituted by, 126, 478
  childhood of, 96
  death of, 138, 145, 153
  descendants of, 125, 142, 387
  in desert, 112, 115, 132–133, 137
  firstborn status of, 498
  Golden Calf constructed by, 122, 123
  Moses' preeminence resented by, 129–130, 131
  Pharaoh confronted by, 103, 104–105, 107, 129
  as priest, 119, 120, 125, 126, 134, 194, 478
  punishment of, 131, 137–138
  rebellions against, 132–133, 134–136, 137, 424
  sons of, 127–128
Abednego (Azariah), 379, 380
Abel, murder of, xxi, 11–12, 13, 31, 54, 70, 87, 402, 407
Abigail, 215–217, 227
Abijah, 394
Abimelech (Gideon's son), 173, 174–176, 412
Abimelech, king of Gerah, 25–26, 45, 130n
Abiram, 134, 135
Abishag, 239
Abner, 213, 214, 220–222, 242, 244
abolitionists, 442
Abraham:
  burial of, 31, 42–43, 87
  circumcision of, 408, 409, 509
  death of, 60
  fatherhood of, 29–31, 37–41, 44, 59, 497, 499
  genealogy of extended family of, 41
  God challenged by, xxi–xxii, xxv, 14n, 25, 32–34, 38, 307n, 493
  God's choice of, 22–24
  God's promises to, 25, 28–29, 30, 40
  idolatry rejected by, 22, 171
  Isaac offered as sacrifice by, 37–41, 43, 451
  Ishmael fathered by, 29–31, 497
  lies promulgated by, 24–27
  marriage of, 21, 24–27, 29–31, 39, 40, 41, 167, 455
  name change of, 21, 60
  as patriarch of Israel, 18, 20, 21, 25, 52, 77
  polygamy practiced by, 29, 410, 411
  Sarah buried by, 41, 42
  as Sarah's half brother, 26, 455
Abravanel, Isaac, 93, 163, 421–422, 423
Absalom, 230
  Amnon murdered by, 233–234, 412, 462, 505
  death of, 237, 239, 243–244
  uprising led by, 217, 235–237, 238, 239, 243, 245, 246, 331, 412
Achan, 120, 160, 161
Achimelech, 207–208
Adam:
  creation of, 399
  descendants of, 10, 13, 18
  in Garden of Eden, 7–9, 10, 20, 496
  labor as punishment for, 10
  mortality and, 240

607

Adam (*cont.*)
  original sin based on, 10–11, 402
  procreative obligation on, 400, 403
  single mate created for, 413
  vegetarian diet of, 6, 7, 403, 500
Adams, John, xxv
Adonijah, 217, 237–240, 244, 245, 412
Adoni-zedek, 163
Adriel, 205
adultery:
  Abraham's exposure of Sarah to, 24–27
  children of, 503–505
  Noahide prohibition of, 404
  ordeal as test for, 475–476
  polygamy vs., 413, 435
  punishment for, 435, 504n–505n
  resistance to, 75–77
  Seventh Commandment on, 207, 213,
    418, 420, 434–435, 456, 503n, 505,
    518
  spousal forgiveness for, 310–312, 435
  woman's marital status as biblical
    determinant of, 434–435, 476, 503
African Americans:
  spirituals of, 104, 160, 333
  U.S. slavery and, 94, 106, 440, 442,
    444
Agag, 114, 199, 208, 369, 370
agriculture:
  animal labor in, 500–501
  charity in harvest of, 360n, 473, 545
  prophetic references to, 285–286, 306
  punishment for thievery in, 436, 447
  Sabbatical years of fallowness in, 472,
    525
  warfare renounced for, 285–286
Agur, 344
Ahab, 159n, 254–260, 264, 265, 266, 267,
    313, 438, 494n
Ahad Ha'am, 430
Ahasuerus, 226n–227n, 368–378, 383n
Ahaz, 269, 283, 288, 289
Ahaziah, 264, 265–266, 494n
Ahikam, 278
Ahitophel, 235–236, 237
akedah, 37–41, 43
Akiva, 53–54, 357–358, 400, 466, 488
Al Aksa, 251
alcoholism, 460
  biblical drunkenness and, 16, 17, 36–37
Alexandri, 524–525
Allen, Woody, 121
Alter, Robert, 47n, 55, 72, 74
Amalek, 113–115, 116, 199, 208, 369,
    370

Amasa, 243, 244
Amaziah (high priest), 314, 316
Amaziah, king of Judah, 283, 514
Amidah, 191
Ammonites:
  ancestry of, 37
  god of, 248
  immorality of, 315
  Israelites' battles with, 176, 198, 219,
    226, 228, 483
  Jewish conversion of, 391
Amnon, 217, 237
  as firstborn son, 233, 240, 498
  incestuous rape by, 232–233, 239, 243,
    245, 462, 498
  murder of, 233–234, 239, 243, 412, 462,
    505
Amon, 272
Amos, 128, 304, 312–318, 319–320, 337,
    493
Amoz, 289
Amram, 240, 456
anarchism, 402, 403
Anchor Bible Dictionary (Freedman), 183
Anchor Bible Series, 274, 404
animals:
  dietary laws on, 403, 404, 453–454, 500,
    535–537
  Egyptian plagues visited upon, 106
  extinction of, 480–481
  God's creation of, 5, 6n
  humane treatment for, 140–141, 496,
    499–501, 524–525, 581
  humankind considered as higher than,
    399, 496
  lack of moral awareness in, 399
  Sabbath observance for, 428, 500, 525
  sacrifices of, 15, 28, 40, 301, 409, 451–
    453, 481–482, 530–531
  survival of flood by, 14
  talking, 8, 9, 109, 140–142
  theft of, 436, 447
Anski, S., 250–251
antisemitism:
  biblical justification used for, 50, 317
  family history of, 425
  nationalistic arguments for, 370–371
Arabs:
  as descendants of Ishmael, 30, 31, 43
  terrorist attack on, 320
Aramaic, 387
arelim, 410
Aristotle, 101, 422
Ark of the Covenant, 193–194, 214, 223,
    250

army service, religious objection to, 433, 434
Arnaud-Amalric, 320
arrogance, 18, 19, 327
Artaxerxes I, 387, 390
Artaxerxes II, 387n
Art of Biblical Narrative, The (Alter), 74
Asa, 394
Asahel, 242
asceticism, Nazirite, 179, 182, 190, 476–478, 559–560
Ashkenazi, Eliezer, 53, 55
Ashtar-Chemosh, 150
Ashtoreth, 248
Assyria:
   fall of, 307
   Israelites conquered by, 253, 267, 270, 283, 307, 323, 394
Astar, 376
atheistic philosophy, subjective ethics of, 466
Auschwitz, 462
Auschwitz (Fleischner), 352
Avihu, 127–128
Azariah (Abednego), 379, 380

Baal, 136n, 147, 170–171, 173, 254, 255–256, 258, 266, 302, 311, 438
Baalis, 279
Ba'al Shem Tov, Israel, 466
Babel, Tower of, 18–19, 20
Babylon:
   Assyria conquered by, 307
   fall of, 381–382, 385
   Gilgamesh epic of, 16
   Jewish exile in, xxiii, xxiv, 121, 277, 290, 297, 299–300, 303, 341–342, 376–378, 386
   Judah conquered by, 253, 296–298, 299, 308, 362
Baha'i religion, 416n
Balaam, 139–142
   talking donkey of, 8, 9, 109, 140–141, 142
Balak, 139, 140, 141
Balfour Declaration, 267
Bamberger, Bernard, 547–548
baptism, 10, 402
Barak, 167–169
Bardin, Shlomo, 10
Bar Mitzvah, 401
Baruch, 296, 299
Barzillai, 246
bastardy (*mamzerut*), 230, 503–505

Bathsheba, 224–227, 228–230, 231, 236, 238, 239, 243, 435, 438
Begin, Menachem, 341n
Beit ha-Mikdash, 118n
   see also Temple
Bellow, Saul, 335
Belshazzar, 381–382
Ben-ammi, 37
Ben Azzai, Simeon, 400
benediction, priestly, 104, 126, 478–479
Benjamin (Jacob's son), 60, 73, 82, 83, 84–86, 240
Benjamin (kingdom), 89, 223, 253
Benjamites, 184–187, 195, 197, 204
Berger, Michael, 234n, 584n
Bergren, Richard Victor, 274
Berman, Saul, 118, 119, 427–428
bestiality, 404, 456
Bethuel, 41
Bialik, Hayim Nahman, 24, 174, 525
Bible, Hebrew:
   authorship of, 136, 153–154, 247, 331, 340
   components of, xxii–xxiv
   first parable of, 174–175
   first recorded prayers in, 26, 44
   genealogical records in, 41, 393
   given names taken from, xxvi, 21, 347
   Jacob's vision as first dream recounted in, 55–56
   life after death in, 217–218, 366
   narratives vs. laws in, xxii–xxiii, 96, 497–498
   warfare ethics in, 165
   wide influence of, xxv–xxvi
   younger sons favored in, 201, 497–498
Biblical Images (Steinsaltz), 183
Bichri, 240, 241
Bigtan, 376
bikur holim, 510
Bildad, 350
Bilhah, 59, 88–89
birds, dietary laws on, 454
birth control, 401
Birth Control in Jewish Law (Feldman), 401
birth order, 414, 497–498
blasphemy, 404
blessings, priestly, 104, 126, 478–479
blind people, ethical treatment mandated for, 416, 459–460, 546
blood:
   Nile water transformed to, 102, 105, 106
   prohibition against consumption of, 403, 453, 534, 547
B'nai B'rith, 29

b'nai Noach, 403–404

B'nai Yisra'el, 88

Boaz, 356, 360–361

Book of Legends, The (Bialik and Ravnitsky), 24, 174

Book of the Bible, The (Reidel, Tracy, and Moskowitz), 166

Book of the Commandments (Maimonides), 421

Brandeis-Bardin Institute, 10

Braude, William, 525

bribery, judicial system corrupted by, 335, 336, 525

Bright, John, 274

brit (covenant), 29

brit milah, 409

brothers:
    alienation of, xxi, 11–12, 31, 50, 51, 53, 54, 61–64, 67–70, 74, 78–79, 87–88, 129–130, 233–234, 402, 411–412, 413
    reconciliations between, 61–64, 82–88

Buchmann, Christina, 37

business ethics, 314–315

Cain:
    Abel murdered by, xxi, 11–14, 31, 54, 70, 87, 402
    mark of, 13
    protest to God made by, 12–13, 32
    punishment of, 12, 407n
    responsibility for others dismissed by, 12, 88

Caleb, 132, 133, 157

Canaan (Ham's son), 17, 18, 393

Canaan (place name):
    Abraham sent to, 23, 24
    God's bestowal of, 28–29, 42, 146, 150
    fruitfulness of, 132
    Israelites' arrival in, xxiii, 125, 132–134, 146–147, 150, 157–166
    tribal territories within, 89, 125, 144, 147
    warfare in, 160–173

cannibalism, 362

capitalism, biblical limitations on, 471–472

capital punishment:
    for adultery, 504n–505n
    for behavior toward parents, 431, 520
    for kidnapping and slavery sale, 73, 435–436, 440, 444, 545
    for murder, xxvii, 12, 73, 403, 405–408, 419n, 520

Catholic Church, Ten Commandments in, 419

Cave of Machpela, 42–43, 60

celibacy, 293

cemeteries, *kohanim* barred from, 126

Chaim, Chaffetz, 514–515

chametz, Passover ban of, 516, 517

charity, 35, 119, 326, 360, 402, 449, 473–474, 483, 488–489

Chen, Abraham, 41

childbirth, 9, 194, 401, 537–538

children:
    blessings for, 90, 478
    disciplinary action for, 344
    firstborn, 107, 414, 497–498, 516–517
    genocide effected through murder of, 94–96
    illegitimate, 176, 178, 230, 503–505
    inheritance rights of, 143–145, 361
    messianic reconciliation with, 309
    mourning for, 69–70, 73, 128
    naming of, xxvi, 21, 347, 409
    as orphans, 448–449
    parental favoritism and, 11, 46–47, 52, 54, 55, 63, 67–70
    parental guilt devolved upon, 266, 342, 383n, 424–425
    of polygamous fathers, 411–412, 413
    as property in Babylonian law, 445
    sacrifice of, 35, 37–41, 177–178, 406, 417n, 451, 484
    as slaves, 441
    Torah study for, 489, 517

Chileab, 217, 240

Chill, Abraham, 514, 519, 523, 530, 534, 536, 537, 583, 586

chosenness, xxv, 23, 128, 305, 315, 316, 319–320, 468

Christianity:
    on acceptance of injury, 445–446
    blood sacrifice as theme in, 37, 452–453
    celibacy in, 293
    chosenness appropriated by, xxv
    ethical issues superseded by faithfulness to, 319–320, 325–326
    family supported in, 430
    fundamentalist, 288–289, 402
    on Isaiah's prophecies, 288–289
    Jewish persecution by, 317, 445n
    Judaism split from, 410
    offering of Isaac as precedent for, 37
    original sin in, 10–11, 402
    Protestant, 288–289, 325–326, 402
    shepherd imagery of, 337
    on Sixth Commandment, xxviin
    unconditional love linked with, 311
    on virgin birth, 288–289

Chronicles, 393–395

Chushai, 235, 236

circumcision, 30, 65–66, 206, 254, 258, 261, 408–410, 441, 509, 515
cities of refuge, 405n, 406, 407, 484–486
civil disobedience, 92–94
cleanliness, ritual, 482, 537–541, 549, 558–559, 563
clothing, fabric mixtures in, 502
Cohen, David, 477
Cohen, Hermann, 467
Comay, Joan, 256
Communism, 105, 415–416, 570
concentration camps, 363–364, 399, 425, 462
Constitution, U.S., 419n, 495, 575
contraception, 401
conversion, Jewish, 356, 359, 362, 389–390, 410, 467–468
corpses, 126, 477, 482, 549, 563
Countertraditions in the Bible (Pardes), 145
cousins, marriage permitted between, 51, 456
covenant (*brit*), 29
covetousness, Tenth Commandment against, 224, 259, 418, 419, 420, 438–439, 519
Cozbi, 143
creation:
    of capacity for moral choice, 399–400
    in God's image, 6, 399–400, 405n
    humankind as partner in, 7
    of man and woman, 6, 8, 13, 399–400, 413
    as monogamous model, 413
    of nature, 496
    order of, 5–6
    of Sabbath, 150–151, 428
Crenshaw, James, 183
Crescas, Hasdai ibn, 421–422, 423
Crime and Human Nature (Wilson and Herrnstein), 404
criticism:
    effective delivery of, 228–230, 463–464
    prophets revered despite, 317
Cromwell, Oliver, 175
Crusades, 320, 426
cult religions, 430
Cyrus (the Great; Darius the Mede), king of Persia, 277, 290, 382–384, 385–386

damnation, Christian belief as determinant of, 319–320, 402
Daniel, Book of, 379–384
Darius the Mede, *see* Cyrus, king of Persia
Datan, 134, 135

daughters:
    incestuous relations with, 36–37
    inheritance claims of, 143–145
    Sabbath blessing for, 90
    see also children
David:
    abdication by, 238–239, 245
    adulterous relationship of, 224–229, 236, 243, 393–394, 435, 438, 499
    ancestry of, 72, 127, 201, 241, 361, 391–392
    anointing of, 196, 220n
    in battle, 114, 201–203, 220–221, 236
    character flaws of, 224
    death of, 222
    fatherhood of, 127, 192, 217, 230–231, 232–240, 245–246, 412, 413, 498, 505
    Gibeonite treaty reinstated by, 163
    God's choice of, 174, 218
    Goliath slain by, 201–203, 205, 209, 220
    Israelite empire consolidated by, xxiv, 220–222, 249, 272, 394
    Jerusalem established as capital by, 222–223
    Joab's service under, 242–244
    Jonathan's friendship with, 200, 206, 207, 209–211, 213, 358
    Messiah as descendant of, xxiv, 224, 236, 271, 284, 362
    on priestly service, 125
    psalms of, 331, 340
    punishment of, 229–231, 236
    Saul's enmity toward, 200, 203, 205–213, 219, 220, 221, 228
    as shepherd, 202, 337
    Solomon as successor to, 231, 238–239, 244–246, 412, 498
    Temple construction prohibited for, 223, 250, 394
    Uriah's death arranged by, 226, 228, 229–230, 243, 438
    wives and concubines of, 44, 200, 202, 205–207, 211, 212–217, 221–222, 227, 231, 236, 239, 410, 412, 435
    as younger son, 201
Day of Judgment, 306
deafness, 459–460, 546
death:
    from hunger vs. sword, 363–364
    life after, 218, 366
    resurrection from, 303–304
death sentences, xxvii, 12, 73, 403, 405–408, 419n, 431, 435–436, 440, 444, 504n–505n
Deborah, 167–169, 183

debts:
  Sabbatical year cancellation of, 471–472
  slavery for restitution of, 314, 391, 449
Declaration of Independence, 419n, 498n
Delilah, 181–182, 183, 477
Deuteronomy, Book of, xxiiin, 149
dietary laws:
  on animal species, 379, 453–454, 535–537
  against consumption of blood, 403, 453, 534, 547
  in Garden of Eden, 7, 453n
  holiness as reason for, 454
  for meat, 6, 7, 403, 453, 454, 526, 529
  for Nazirite ascetics, 477
  Noahide laws on, 403, 404
  for Passover, 515–516, 517
  sacrificial offerings and, 529
  salt in, 530
  on sciatic nerve, 62, 515
Dinah, 64–67, 83, 505
disarmament, 285–287
divination, 119–121, 146, 161, 173
divorce, 126, 310, 504, 505, 508–509
dogs, obedience of, 399
Dome of the Rock, 251
dreams, 55–56, 68, 78–81, 130, 381n–382n
Dred Scott decision, 440
drunkenness, 16, 17, 36–37, 190, 191, 460
Dybbuk, The (Anski), 250–251

Eban, Abba, 462
Ecclesiastes, 247, 355, 365–367
ecological awareness, 495–497
Eden, *see* Garden of Eden
Egypt:
  Abraham and Sarah's visit to, 24–25, 27
  Hebrew enslavement in, xxii, 91–92, 151, 417, 423
  Israelites' departure from, xxi, 107–110, 515, 517
  ten plagues inflicted upon, xxii, 102, 106–107, 108, 111, 194, 417, 439
Ehrlich, Arnold, 136
Eichmann, Adolf, 370
Eighth Commandment, 259, 418, 420, 435–436, 439
Elah, 265n
Elazar, 120, 146
Elchanan, 203
elderly, care for, 416, 492, 548
Eli, 190, 191, 192–194
Eliab, 202, 203, 220n
Eliach, Yaffa, 364

Eliezer, xxv, 28, 44–45, 57, 499
Elihu, 351
Elijah, 136n, 265, 293, 309, 312, 326n, 432
  Ahab denounced by, 254, 255, 259–260, 494n
  ascent to heaven made by, 261
  as folk hero, 254, 257–258, 261
  idolatry opposed by, 254–258
Elimelech, 359, 360, 361
Eliphaz, 350, 351
Elisha, 257, 261–263, 264, 449
Elkanah, 59, 189, 191, 412
Elman, Yaakov, 185, 187
Encyclopedia Judaica, 358
Encyclopedia of Biblical Interpretation (Kasher), 420
End of the World, The (Friedrich), 320
Endor, necromancer of, 217–218
ends vs. means, xxii
England, Gandhi's pacifist advice for, 286
Enlightenment, 401–402, 403
Enoch, 13
environmental awareness, 495–497
envy, 402
Ephraim, 89–90
Ephraimites, 172, 177–178
Ephron, 42, 43
Epstein, B. H., 143
Er, 70–71, 74
Esau, 483
  as favorite son, 46
  firstborn status lost by, 21, 47, 48–55, 60, 70, 90n, 497
  at Isaac's burial, 43
  Jacob's reconciliation with, 61–64, 87–88, 215
  non-Jewish status of, 20
  wives of, 432
Esther, 226n–227n, 355, 367, 371–378
Esther, Book of, xxiv, 114, 355, 358, 367–378, 383n
Ethbaal, 265
ethical behavior:
  toward animals, 428, 496, 499–501, 524–525, 581
  in business dealings, 314–315
  fear of God as support for, 93, 415–416
  general directive on, 151
  of gentiles, 92–96, 116
  as God's primary demand on humankind, 20, 23, 284, 301–302, 315, 317–318, 326–327, 422–423, 468
  holiness mandate and, 456–457
  last six commandments on, 302, 420
  for prevention of others' injuries, 461–462

ritual observance vs., 274, 284, 301–302, 308, 313–316
theological roots for, 465–466, 468–470
Torah as basis for lessons on, 317–318, 489
toward vulnerable people, 284, 301–302, 313, 314, 335–336, 391, 415, 416, 448–449, 459–460, 461–462
ethical monotheism, 302, 423, 467
ethical will (*tzava'a*), 149–151
Ethiopians, 320
Eve, 6, 7–11, 13, 18, 20, 240, 400, 402, 403, 500
evil:
    existence of, xxiv, 340, 350–352
    fear of God as deterrent to, 415–416
    first knowledge of, 8
    generational transfer of, 424–425
    human capacity for resistance to, 12, 399–400
    internal propensity for, 13, 15, 401–403
    local influence of, 34, 332–333, 335
    murder as infinite commission of, 407
    of Sodom, 34–36
    transformation from, 33–34, 286, 304, 321, 323, 333
Exodus, Book of, xxii–xxiii
Exploring Exodus (Sarna), 99
Ezekiel, 303–304, 305
Ezekiel, Book of, 35
Ezra, 386–390, 391, 394
Ezra, Book of, 385–390, 391

fabrics, prohibited mixtures of, 502
faith, ethical behavior vs., 319–320, 325–326
Faith of a Heretic, The (W. Kaufmann), 166
false prophets, 299
fasting, 325n
Fathers According to Rabbi Nathan, The, 204
Fear No Evil (Sharansky), 338
Feinstein, Moshe, 443
Feldman, David, 401
Feldman, Leonid, 135
fences, legal, 491
Fewell, Danna Nolan, 74, 161, 169, 178
Fifth Commandment, 418, 420, 430–433
firstborn sons, 107, 414, 497–498, 516–517
First Commandment, 418–419, 425, 517–518
First Jewish Commonwealth, 296
fish, dietary restrictions on consumption of, 453–454
Five Scrolls, xxiv, 355–378

Fleischner, Eva, 352
Flood, 14–17
food:
    manna given for, 111–113
    see also dietary laws
forgiveness, 445–446
Fourth Commandment, 7, 418, 420, 427–430, 441, 470, 500
Fox, Everett, 522
Frank, Anne, 366n
Freedman, David Noel, 183
freedom:
    conduct and, 105
    political, xxi
Free-Loan Societies, 473, 507
free will, 290, 417
Friedman, Theodore, 318
Friedrich, Otto, 320
friendship, biblical examples of, 209–211, 358–359
fringes, ritual (*tzitzit*), 479–480, 481, 561
From Father to Son (Steinmetz), 74
fundamentalism:
    Christian, 6, 288–289, 402
    Islamic, 416n
    Jewish, 351–352
funerals, 126, 338

Gamliel, 336
Gandhi, Mohandas, 286
Garden of Eden, 7–10, 15, 496
    Christian original sin based on, 402
garments:
    fabric mixtures forbidden in, 502
    for priests, 118–119, 173, 527
    ritual, 479–481
Gedaliah, 276, 278–279
Gehazi, 263
Genesis, Book of:
    Hebrew name for, xxiiin
    narrative style of, xxii
Gershom, 98
Gibeonites, 161, 162–164
Gideon (Jerubaal), 170–173, 174, 176, 177, 412, 493–494
Gilgamesh epic, 16
God:
    biblical characters' arguments with, xxi–xxii, xxiv–xxv, 14n, 25, 32–34, 38, 100–104, 123, 133, 307–308, 323–324, 352–353, 493
    blasphemy of, 348, 404
    commandment of belief in, 421–422, 468
    as creator, 5–7, 150–151, 294
    denial of, 404

God (*cont.*)
    depth of love from, 305, 308, 310, 311,
        323–324, 425
    evil permitted by, xxiv, 307–308, 340,
        351–352
    fear of, 93, 343, 415–416
    in first three of Ten Commandments,
        418, 419, 420, 421–427, 517–518
    humankind created in image of, 6, 399–
        400, 405*n*
    human righteousness desired by, 20, 23,
        284, 301–302, 315, 317–318, 422–
        423, 468–469
    Jewish mission to spread message of,
        xxv, 287–288, 324, 468–470
    love for, 149, 467, 488–489
    misuse of name of, 163, 426–427, 470,
        518
    non-Hebrew prophet's messages from,
        139–142
    protection sought from, 337–340, 362–
        363
    right to confrontation of, xxi–xxii, xxiv–
        xxv, 62
    universality of, 422
    world destruction forsworn by, 123, 403,
        405
Gold, Michael, 504
Golden Calf, 32, 89, 122–124, 125, 132
Golden Rule, xxi, 465
Goldin, Judah, 318
Goldstein, Baruch, 320
Goldstein, Rebecca, 36, 37
Goliath (of Gath), 201–203, 205, 209, 220
Goliath the Gittite, 203
Gomer, 310–311
goodness:
    Enlightenment presumption of, 401–402
    as moral choice vs. obedience, 399–400
    see also ethical behavior; righteousness
Goshen, 106
gossip, 335, 460–461, 524
Graetz, Heinrich, 298
gratitude, 220
Great Britain, Nazi attack on, 286
Great Events of Bible Times (Harpur), 251
Greenberg, Irving, 352
Greenberg, Moshe, 349
grudges, revenge vs., 464–465, 546
Gunn, David, 74, 178

Habakkuk, 306, 307–308
Hagar, 21, 26, 29–31, 59, 411, 413
Haggai, 306, 308–309, 386
haLevi, Aaron, 513–514

Halevi, Judah, 117
Ham, 17–18
Haman, 114, 355, 367, 369–375, 377–378,
    383*n*
Hamas, 320
Hammurabi's Code, 230, 445, 448
Hamor, 64–66
Hanamel, 299
Hananiah (false prophet), 299
Hananiah (Shadrach), 379, 380
Hannah, 59, 189–191, 412
Hannuka, 5*n*, 471, 491
Harbonah, 373
Harpur, James, 251
harvest, holidays linked with, 470, 471
Hasidic Tales of the Holocaust (Eliach), 364
Hasidism, 466, 481
hatred, unwise repression of, 462–463
Hauptmann, Bruno, 444
Heber, 168
Hebron, 222, 320
herbivorousness, 6, 7, 403, 500
herem, 159, 160–161
heresy, 320, 416*n*–417*n*
Herodotus, 269
Heroes of Israel (Herzog), 183
Herrnstein, Richard, 404
Hertz, Joseph, 290, 291, 524
Herzl, Theodor, 341
Herzog, Chaim, 183
Heschel, Abraham Joshua, 314–315, 318
Hezekiah, 268–270, 289, 308, 344*n*, 394
Hiel of Beth-el, 159*n*–160*n*
Hilkiah, 272
Hillel, 327, 401, 466, 472
Hiram, king of Tyre, 250
Hitler, Adolf, 91, 95*n*, 103, 115, 286, 366*n*,
    416, 434, 570
Hofni, 193–194
holiness, general mandate for, 456–458
Holocaust, 12
    God's allowance of, 170, 338–340
    Israeli state established after, 304
    remembrance of, 341*n*
    victims blamed for, 351–352
holy days, 251, 470–471, 525–526
    see also Sabbath; specific holidays
Holy of Holies, 118, 250–251
home safety, 501–502
homosexuality, 35, 211, 404, 456, 544
Horwitz, Joshua, 14
Hosea, 266, 305, 310–312, 317–318, 435
Hoshea, 267
hospitality, 35
hospitals, visits to, 510

Huldah, 272n–273n
humankind:
  animals vs., 399, 496
  brotherhood of, 309
  creation in God's image for, 6, 399–400, 405n
  God's desire for righteous behavior of, 20, 23, 284, 315, 317, 318, 323–324, 326–327, 422–423, 468–469
  God's eradication of, 13, 14, 403, 405
  propensity for evil behavior of, 13, 15, 401–403
  as responsible for welfare of others, 12, 88, 434, 461–462
  suffering experienced by, 348–353
human nature, God's negative assessment of, 401–403
humility, 327

ibn Ezra, Abraham, 128, 290, 439
Ichabod, 194
idolatry:
  Abraham's rejection of, 22, 23, 171
  absolute ban on, 302, 413, 416n, 518, 547
  by Canaanites, 146, 147, 170–171
  child sacrifice and, 406
  commandment against, 424–425
  as denial of God, 404
  Elijah's efforts against, 254–258
  of Golden Calf, 32, 89, 122–124, 125
  human sacrifice and, 147, 406
  immorality linked to, 416n–417n
  Israelite reversions to, 122–124, 147, 170–171, 173, 195, 248, 253–258, 266, 267, 269, 273, 274
  nationalism as form of, 425
  Noahide prohibition of, 404
  Torah law opposed to, 149–150, 317, 519, 544, 557
  of wealth, 124, 488–489
illness, visits to those with, 509–510
Illustrated Dictionary and Concordance of the Bible (Wigoder), 395
incest, 541–543
  children born from, 503–505
  cousin relationships not viewed as, 456
  of Lot's daughters, 17–18, 36–37
  Noahide law on, 404
  specific prohibitions against, 455, 456
  as universal crime, 404
infertility, 22, 25, 29, 59, 189–191, 214
injury, responsibility for prevention of, 461–462
Innocent III, pope, 320

intellectualism, 301
interest, prohibition of, 335–336, 416, 473, 506–507, 523
intermarriage, 566–567
  Ezra's dissolution of, 387, 388–389
  Moses' opposition to, 150
  for political reasons, 413n–414n
  of Ruth, 359, 361–362, 391–392
  of Samson with Philistine woman, 179–180, 183
Isaac:
  Abraham's offering of, 37–41, 43, 451
  birth of, 21, 31, 179, 411
  burial of, 42–43, 63
  death of, 60–61
  fatherhood of, 401, 432, 497
  Ishmael's relationship with, 31, 43, 87
  Jacob blessed by, xxii, 21, 46–55, 90n, 479
  marriage of, xxv, 41, 43–45, 46, 54–55, 57, 167, 499
  passive aspect of, 43–46, 47
  as patriarch, 20, 21
  as younger son, 497
Isaiah:
  ancestry of, 283, 289
  ethical teachings of, 284
  messianic age predicted by, 284–287
  prophetic task of, 283–284
  universal peace described by, 285–287
Isaiah, Book of, 267, 268–269, 283–291, 305, 318, 386, 429, 449, 500
  multiple authorship of, 289–291
Isaiah Wall, 286
Ish-Boshet, 210–211, 213–214, 220–221, 222, 242
Ishmael (Abraham's son), 21, 26, 29–31, 40, 43, 87, 404, 411, 497
Ishmael (Gedaliah's murderer), 279
Islam:
  biblical lineage of, 404
  fanatical behavior and, 320, 470
  fundamentalist, 416n
  in Jerusalem, 251
  Jewish chosenness appropriated by, xxv
  murder for heresy against, 320, 416n
  theft punishment and, 448
Israel, Kingdom of:
  dispersion of, 266–268, 316
  establishment of, 89, 242, 394
  freedom of speech in, 316n–317n
  Judah separated from, 252–253, 394

Israel, State of:
  creation of, 285, 304
  modern boundaries vs. biblical promise
    of, 29*n*
Israelites:
  in Babylonian exile, xxiii, xxiv, 121, 277,
    290, 297, 299–300, 303, 341–342, 376–
    378, 386
  in battle, 113–115, 120, 133, 147, 150,
    158–160, 163, 164–165, 167–173,
    176, 177–178, 185–186, 193–194,
    195, 198–203, 217–219, 226
  Canaanite arrival of, 132, 146–147, 150,
    157–166
  class divisions among, 313
  Egyptian persecution of, 81, 91–99, 101–
    102, 105, 107, 108–110
  forty-year desert sojourn of, 111–154,
    410, 429
  God's revelation made to, 116–117
  idolatrous practices of, 122–124, 147,
    170–171, 173, 195, 248, 253–258,
    266, 267, 273, 274, 308
  kingship of, 172–173, 174–175, 196–
    197, 493–495
  Lot's descendants as enemies of, 37
  in messianic age, 284–285
  moral deterioration of, 184–187, 284,
    308, 312–318
  name of, 62, 88
  paternal determination of identity for,
    494*n*
  under Persian rule, 121, 290, 300, 382–
    387, 390
  return to homeland prophesied for, 290,
    299–300, 303, 307, 386
  Ten Lost Tribes of, 253, 266–268, 300,
    307
  tribal disputes among, 184–187, 195,
    220–222
  twelve initial tribes of, 88–90
Isserles, Moses, 504*n*

Jabin, 167–168
Jacob:
  death of, 43, 88
  Esau reconciled with, 61–64, 87–88, 215
  as father, 59–60, 64–70, 82, 84–85, 88–
    90, 234*n*, 411–412, 497–498, 505
  God in dream of, 55–56, 130
  Isaac's blessing procured by, xxii, 46–55,
    90*n*, 479
  as Israel, 60–62
  Joseph mourned by, 69–70, 73
  journey to Egypt made by, 27, 87

  marriages of, 44, 51, 53, 57–60, 61,
    67, 88–89, 167, 410, 411–412, 454–
    455
  as patriarch, 20, 21, 23, 52, 88–90, 497
  shrewdness of, 43, 47, 50, 61
  tithing vowed by, 483
Jacob, Benno, 423
Jacobs, Louis, 10–11, 23*n*, 395, 458, 482
Jael, 168, 169
Janowska, 363–364
Jehoiachin, 275, 297
Jehoiakim, 272, 275, 278, 296, 298
Jehoram (Joram), 260, 264–265, 497
Jehoshaphat, 394, 497
Jehovah's Witnesses, 433
Jehu, 260, 264–266
Jephtah, 172*n*, 176–178, 483–484
Jeremiah, 293–302, 305, 323, 449
  on acceptance of Babylonian rule, 275–
    276, 277, 278, 279, 296–298, 299
  background of, 158, 296, 299
  celibacy of, 293–294
  desolation experienced by, 293–295
  on God's emphasis of ethical behavior,
    274, 299, 301–302, 326–327, 423
  hopeful transformation of, 295, 299–300
  Lamentations attributed to, 355, 362
  prophetic vocation resisted by, 103, 294–
    295
  on return to Israel, 277, 299–300, 386
Jericho:
  battle of, 157–160, 164
  illegal looting of, 120, 160–161
  restoration of, 159*n*–160*n*
Jeroboam I, king of Israel, 253, 316*n*
Jeroboam II, king of Israel, 316
Jerubaal (Gideon), 170–173, 174, 176, 177,
    412, 493–494
Jerusalem:
  Babylonian conquest of, 275–276, 295,
    297, 299, 303, 355, 362
  as capital of Israel, 214, 222–223
  defenses rebuilt for, 390–391
  Jewish exile from, xxiii, 275
  psalm on remembrance of, 340–342
  Temple built in, 223, 249–251, 275, 276;
    see also Temple
Jesse, 201, 207, 210, 240, 242, 253, 284
Jesus:
  celibacy of, 293
  Christian insistence on belief in, 319–
    320, 325–326
  Christianity's beliefs of human sins
    atoned by death of, 10–11
  circumcision of, 410

Jethro (Reuel), 97–98, 102, 103, 115–116, 337

Jewish Biblical Exegesis (Jacobs), 458

Jewish Expression, The (Goldin), 318

Jewish Literacy (Telushkin), 166

Jewish Publication Society Bible, 169*n*, 365

Jewish Religion, The (Jacobs), 10, 395, 482

Jewish Theology, A (Jacobs), 23*n*

Jewish Wisdom (Telushkin), 465

Jews:
  Ashkenazic vs. Sephardic, 126
  chosenness of, xxv, 23, 128, 305, 315, 316, 319–320, 468
  God's message to be spread by, xxv, 287–288, 324, 468–470
  matrilineal identification of, 409*n*, 494*n*
  Nazi persecution of, 91, 338–340, 363–364, 462
  Orthodox, 126, 251, 290, 344, 472, 473, 475, 480, 482, 498, 510
  Reform, 409
  world population levels of, 267–268

Jezebel, 254, 255, 257, 258, 259, 260, 264–265, 313, 438, 494*n*

Jezreel, 310

jihad, 251

Joab, 220, 224, 225, 226, 234, 235, 237, 238–244, 245, 406

Joan of Arc, 169

Joash, 171

Job:
  daughters as heirs to, 145
  as fictional character, 348–349
  friends of, 130*n*, 350–352
  protests to God made by, xxiv–xxv, 32, 307*n*, 352–353
  righteousness of, 347, 348, 449
  sufferings of, 128, 348–349

Job, Book of, xxiv, 347–353, 365

Joel, Book of, 287, 306

Jonadab, 232

Jonah, Book of, 195, 262, 295, 305, 306, 321–325, 501

Jonathan:
  David's friendship with, 200, 206, 207, 209–211, 213, 358
  death of, 211, 358
  inadvertent transgression of, 120, 177, 197, 199, 211*n*
  military involvement of, 120, 210–211

Joram (Jehoram), 260, 264–265, 497

Joseph:
  betrayals experienced by, 79
  birth of, 60
  brothers reconciled with, 82–88, 89
  dreams interpreted by, 78–81, 381*n*–382*n*
  fraternal enmity toward, 53, 67–70, 73, 74, 78–79, 82, 87, 234*n*, 411–412, 413
  Mordechai vs., 378
  as Pharaoh's official, 80–83, 91, 378
  prophetic dreams of, 68, 77, 79*n*, 81, 82
  righteousness of, 75, 77
  as slave, 3, 53, 69, 70, 73, 74–77, 78–79, 82, 86–87, 412
  sons of, 89–90, 497

Josephus, Flavius, 93, 120, 298, 561

Joshua:
  Canaanite conquest and, 113–114, 132, 133, 157, 158–160, 162–166
  circumcisions reestablished by, 410
  as successor to Moses, 120, 123, 145–146, 149, 153–154, 164

Joshua ben Korchah, 104

Josiah, 271–274, 278, 294, 308, 394

Jotham, 174–175, 412

JPS Torah Commentary, The (Milgrom), 131, 139, 143

JPS Torah Commentary, The (Sarna), 17, 94, 104

Jubilee years, 472, 555, 556, 558

Judah (Jacob's son):
  birth of, 59
  descendants of, 89, 127, 201
  Joseph wronged by, 69
  moral transformation of, 72–74, 84–85, 86, 87, 88
  Tamar's son fathered by, 70–73, 82

Judah (kingdom), 89, 220–222, 241–242, 253, 267, 278–279, 283, 306–307
  Babylonian rule of, 275–279, 296–298, 299, 308
  kings of, 268–276, 283, 294, 297, 394
  Lamentations on, 362–363

Judah ben Tabbai, 204

Judaism:
  Christian split from, 410
  conversion to, 356, 359, 362, 389–390, 391, 410, 467–468
  historical truth of, 117
  Orthodox, 126, 251, 290, 344, 472, 473, 475, 480, 482, 498, 510
  patriarchs and matriarchs of, 20–21
  Reform, 409
  three essences of, 325, 326–327

judiciary:
  in biblical legal system, 492–493
  bribery of, 335, 336, 525
  deterioration of, 183

judiciary (*cont.*)
  Jewish laws for, 436–437, 490, 492–493, 521, 546
  kohanim in, 183
  mandate for establishment of, 404
  need for, 116, 402
  vigilantism and, 142–143
  women in, 167, 183
Judith, 432
justice:
  for enemies, 493
  fugitives from, 405–406
  Moses' commitment to, 14n, 23, 96–99
  revenge vs., 444–446, 464
  strong emphasis on, 326–327, 492–493

kabbalah, 11
Kahan, A. Y., 514, 533
Kam, Rose Sallberg, 227
Kaplan, Aryeh, 524, 526
Kasher, Moshe M., 420
Kaufmann, Walter, 152–153, 165, 166, 317–318, 327, 457, 458
Kaufmann, Yehezkel, 165, 166, 315, 318
Kelman, Wolfe, 74
Kennedy, John F., 111
Kennedy, Joseph P., Jr., 111
Kennedy, Robert F., 110–111
Khomeini, Ruholla, 320, 416n, 470
kidnapping, 435–436, 440, 443–444, 448, 518, 545
Kierkegaard, Søren, 41
Kimhi, David (Radak), 27, 220
King, Martin Luther, Jr., 426
kings:
  biblical views on, 174–175, 196–197, 493–495
  examples of covetousness in, 438
  limitation on wives for, 249, 413
knowledge, tree of, 7, 8–9
kohanim, 125–127, 267
Kook, Abraham Isaac, 477
Korah, 134–136, 137, 424
kosher foods, *see* dietary laws
Kovner, Abba, 339
Kula, Irwin, 151

Laban, 44, 45, 46, 48n, 51, 55, 60, 455
  Jacob deceived by, 53, 57–58, 61, 411
labor:
  of domestic animals, 500–501, 546
  prompt payment for, 458–459
  as punishment, 10
  Sabbath ban of, 112, 427–429, 518
  Yom Kippur prohibition of, 471

Lamech, 13, 413
Lamentations, Book of, 355, 362–364, 365
Lamm, Norman, 496, 497
land, Jubilee year restoration of, 472
Landis, Joseph, 251
languages, multiplicity of, 18–19
Lapidot, 167
laws:
  equality under, 407, 436–437, 524, 525
  on ethical treatment of vulnerable people, 416, 439–442
  evolutionary nature of, 413–414, 439
  on female legal rights, 144–145
  natural human requirements for, 402–403
  Noahide, 403–404
  reconciliation of conflict between, 325–326
  on rights vs. obligations, 461
  vigilantism vs., 143
Leah:
  burial of, 42–43
  marriage of, 53, 57–59, 60, 61, 89, 167, 411, 413
  as matriarch, 20–21
  motherhood of, 59, 64, 411
Lee, Harper, 77
Leibowitz, Nehama, 53, 55, 67, 99, 420, 423
Lemuel, 245n, 344
Lenin, V. I., 570
leprosy, 126, 262–263
Levi, 66–67, 89, 90
levirate marriage, 71
Levites, 89, 123–124, 125, 126, 134, 135, 251, 267, 388
Leviticus, Book of, xxiiin
life:
  after death, 218, 366
  infinite value of, 407
Lincoln, Abraham, 91, 439
Lindbergh, Charles A., 444
linen, wool mixed with, 502
literary prophets, 326, 422
Living Nach, The (Elman), 187
Lo-ammi, 310
loans:
  prohibition of interest on, 335–336, 416, 473, 506–507, 523
  Sabbatical year debt forgiveness and, 471–472
Lockyer, Herbert, 121, 477, 604
Lo-ruhamah, 310
Lot, 17, 32, 35–37, 489
love:
  forgiveness and, 310–312, 345

in friendship, 209–211, 358–359
for God, 149, 467, 488–489
God's capacity for, 305, 308, 310, 311, 323–324, 425
of neighbor as self, xxi, 211, 344, 400, 460–461, 464, 465–467, 546–547
for strangers, 467–468
Luther, Martin, 319–320, 325–326, 327
lying, 24–27, 93, 207, 436–437

Machpela, Cave of, 42–43, 60
magic, prohibitions on, 522, 548, 576–577
Maimonides, Moses, 34, 88, 421, 423, 482, 519, 565, 581
    on additions to Torah law, 491
    on animal sacrifice, 451
    charitable deeds categorized by, 473
    effective criticism described by, 464
    on free will, 290
    gratuitous destruction condemned by, 496
    on rationality of Torah laws, 151
    on repentance, 87
    on restitution for murder, 406n
    Torah laws enumerated by, 513–514
    on treatment of widows and orphans, 449
Malachi, 306, 308, 309, 432
mamzerut (bastardy), 230, 503–505
Manasseh (Hezekiah's son), 269, 270–271, 272, 394
Manasseh (Joseph's son), 89–90
manna, 111–113, 429
Marmer, Stephen, 111n, 489
marriage:
    adultery and, 24–27, 75–77, 207, 213, 310–312, 404, 413, 418, 420, 434–435, 456, 475–476, 503n
    annulment of, 504
    criteria for partner in, xxv
    divorce and, 126, 310, 504, 505, 508–509
    between first cousins, 51, 456
    forgiveness within, 310–312, 435
    husband's obligations in, 442–443, 519–520
    inheritance rights and, 144, 360–361
    between Jews and non-Jews, 150, 179–180, 183, 359, 361–362, 388–390, 391–392, 413n–414n, 566–567
    kinship prohibitions and, 26, 58, 411, 455–456
    levirate, 71
    male domination within, 9, 368
    for monarchs, 221–222, 249, 495

polygamy in, 13, 191, 410–414, 435, 443, 498, 503
of priests, 126, 549–550
procreative obligation and, 400, 401
rabbinic law on, 414
with redeeming kinsman, 360–361
sexuality within, 55, 443, 454–455
unconditional love within, 310–312, 435
wedding ceremonies for, 300n, 341, 342, 442
martyrs, 488
masturbation, 74
matriarchs, 20–21, 42–43
means vs. ends, xxii
Me'arat ha-Machpela, 42–43, 60
meat consumption:
    milk foods separated from, 454, 526, 529
    prohibition lifted for, 6, 403, 453, 500
Meir, Rabbi, 333
Melanchthon, Philip, 326, 327
Memucan, 368
men:
    circumcision of, 30, 65–66, 206, 254, 258, 261, 408–410, 441, 509, 515
    dominance of, 9, 368, 484
    God's creation of, 6, 13, 399–400, 413
    marital obligations of, 442–443, 519–520
    ritual garments for, 480–481
Merab, 205
Merchant of Venice, The (Shakespeare), 446n, 506
mercy, 323–324
Meshach (Mishael), 379, 380
Mesha Stone, 150
Meshech Hokhma (Simcha), 400–401
Messiah, xxiv, 224, 236, 271, 284–285, 309, 356, 361, 362
mezuzah, 490, 566
Micah, 305, 318, 325–327, 344, 422
Michal, 200, 205–207, 212–214, 215, 221–222, 227
Midrash, 8
Milcom, 248
Milgrom, Jacob, 130n, 131, 138, 139n, 143, 403, 404n, 453, 454n, 475n, 478–479, 481, 485
military service, religious objection to, 433, 434
milk, meat separated from, 454, 526, 529
Milton, John, 6n, 175
mincha, 452
minor prophets, 305–327
    Amos, 128, 304, 312–318, 319–320, 337, 493
    Habakkuk, 306, 307–308

minor prophets (*cont.*)
  Haggai, 306, 308–309, 386
  Hosea, 266, 305, 310–312, 317–318, 435
  Joel, 287, 306
  Jonah, 195, 262, 295, 305, 306, 321–325, 501
  Malachi, 306, 308, 309, 432
  Micah, 305, 318, 325–327, 344, 422
  Nahum, 306, 307
  Obadiah, 305, 306–307
  Zechariah, 306, 308–309, 386
  Zephaniah, 306, 308
miracles, 102, 109, 111–114, 121–122, 137–138, 163, 171, 256–257, 261, 268–269
Miriam, 93, 95–96, 110–111, 129–131, 137, 167, 498
Mishael (Meshach), 379, 380
Mishnah, 485n–486n
Mishneh Torah (Maimonides), 34, 290, 406n
Moab, 37
Moabites, 37, 139–141, 150, 355–356, 362, 391–392
moderation, 366–367
mohel, 409
Molech, 406
monarchy, biblical ambivalence on, 174–175, 196–197, 493–495
moneylending, 335–336, 416, 473, 506–507, 523
monogamy, biblical preference for, 413–414
monotheism:
  Canaan consecrated to, 146, 165
  essential tenets of, 487–488
  ethical, 302, 423, 467
  expansion of, 165
  fallibility of prophets tied to, 138
  First Commandment on, 421–423
  intermarriage as threat to, 388n
  Israelites' return to, 195–196
  Jewish initiation of, 23
  moral implications of, xxv, 26n, 39
  Prophets as history of, xxiii–xxiv
  Solomon's loss of commitment to, 413
  universal morality linked to, xxv
morality:
  belief in God linked to, 26n
  evolutionary views of, 317
  fear of God seen as support for, 93, 415–416
  general holiness mandate vs. specific laws on, 456–458
  human capacity for, 399–400
  idolatry as deterrent to, 416n–417n

  monotheism as basis for, xxv, 26n, 39
  of ritual observance vs. moral behavior, 274, 284, 301–302, 308, 313–316
Mordechai, 367, 369–370, 371–378
mortality, introduction of, 10, 240
Moses:
  ancestry of, 96–97, 456
  in arguments with God, 32, 100–104, 123, 133
  birth of, 95–96, 111
  death of, xxiiin, 138, 145, 152–154
  farewell speeches by, xxiiin, 149–151
  fatherhood of, 98, 115, 401, 409
  God's revelations to, 100–104, 112, 116–120, 122, 127–128, 130, 133, 144–146, 153, 478, 480
  Israelite slaves championed by, 80, 100–105
  Joshua chosen as successor to, 120, 145–146, 149, 153–154, 164
  leadership of, 100–104, 106, 108–116, 122–124, 129–139, 143–154, 323, 337
  marriage of, 44, 98, 115, 129
  Pharaoh confronted by, 80, 99, 100–101, 103–105
  punishment of, 137–139, 151, 152, 409
  rebellions against, 122–124, 134–136, 424
  reluctance shown by, 100–104, 294
  righteousness of, 14n, 23, 96–99
  Samuel vs., 194–195
  siblings of, 95–96, 129–130, 498
  singular preeminence of, 130, 152–153, 154, 388
  slavemaster killed by, 97, 99
  as teacher, 77, 115, 138, 149–151, 312
  Ten Commandments given to, xxii, 419
  Torah revealed to, xxiii, 153
  warfare overseen by, 113–114, 150
Moskowitz, Barbara, 166
mosques, Jerusalem erection of, 251
Mount Abarim, 145
Mount Ararat, 15
Mount Carmel, 255–257, 258
Mount Nebo, 152, 153
Mount Sinai, xxii, 116–117, 118, 122, 257
Mount Tabor, 167, 168
mourning, 69, 70, 73, 153, 237, 348, 432
murder, 402–408
  of Abel, xxi, 11–13, 31, 54, 70, 87, 402, 407
  death sentences for, xxvii, 12, 403, 405–408, 419n, 520
  false testimony on, 407
  of household intruder, 433–434

idolatrous sacrifice as, 406, 484
money as restitution for, 406–407
premeditation of, 405, 520
religious fanaticism involved in, 319–
  320, 416n–417n, 470
responsibility for prevention of, 241,
  434, 461, 462
Sixth Commandment on, xxvi–xxvii,
  259, 418, 433–434, 518
of slaves, 407n, 440, 442, 520
two witnesses needed for capital
  punishment of, 408, 564–565
as universal crime, 404
unpremeditated, cities of refuge for, 405,
  406, 484–486
vigilantism and, 143
Muslims, *see* Islam
mussar haskel, 27
Mussolini, Benito, 286n

Na'aman, 262–263
Nabal, 215–216, 227
Nabopolassar, 307
Nachmanides, Moses (Ramban), 27, 457,
  458
Nadav, 127–128
Nahash, 198
Nahor, 41, 57
Nahum, 306, 307
nakedness, 9, 17–18
Naomi, 356, 358–360, 361n
Narrative in the Hebrew Bible (Gunn and
  Fewell), 74, 178
Nathan, 223, 227, 228–231, 238, 245, 312,
  499
nationalism, unethical acts based on, 425
Native Americans, harvest celebrated by,
  267
nature, divine creation vs. pagan worship
  of, 5, 496
Navot, 258–260, 264, 265, 313, 438
Nazirite vows, 179, 182, 190, 476–478,
  559–560
Nazis, 91, 114–115, 208, 286, 363, 339,
  363, 399, 415–416, 425, 462, 570
Nebuchadnezzar, 253, 275–276, 277, 278,
  297, 379–381, 386
Nebuzaradan, 276
Necho, 273
necromancy, 217–218
Nehemiah, 390–392, 394–395
Nehemiah, Book of, 387, 390–392, 429
Nelson's Illustrated Bible Dictionary
  (Lockyer), 121, 269, 477
9½ Mystics (Weiner), 41

Nineveh, fall of, 195, 307, 321–324, 501
Ninth Commandment, 259, 418, 420, 436–
  437, 439
Noa, 144
Noah, 13, 14–18, 20, 32, 402, 451
  God's covenant with, 15, 403, 405
  laws revealed to, 403–404, 405
  meat consumption permitted to, 6, 403,
    453, 500
Nob, Saul's massacre of residents of, 208
Non-Violence in Peace and War (Gandhi),
  286n
Numbers, Book of, xxiiin

oaths, 163, 276–277, 278, 335, 366, 483–
  484, 564
Obadiah (Ahab's aide), 255, 257
Obadiah (prophet), 305, 306–307
Obed, 361
Old Testament, xxii, xxiiin
  see also Bible, Hebrew
Omer, 470
Omri, 265n
Onan, 71, 74
On the Book of Psalms (Sarna), 334–336
original sin, 10–11, 402
Orpah, 359, 361n
orphans, care for, 284, 336, 448–449, 523
Orthodox Jews, 126, 251, 290, 344, 472,
  473, 475, 480, 482, 498, 510
Out of the Garden (Buchmann and Spiegel),
  37

pacifism, 286
Palgi, Yoel, 339
Palti (Paltiel), 213, 214, 222, 227
Pardes, Ilana, 145
parents:
  children punished for misdeeds of, 266,
    342, 383n, 424–425
  discipline administered by, 344
  favoritism felt by, 11, 46–47, 52, 54, 55,
    63, 67–70, 233
  honor toward, 418, 420, 430–433, 518,
    548
  inheritance from, 143–145
  joys experienced by, 232
  messianic reconciliation with, 309
  mourning period for, 230–231, 432
parole, 407
Paschal lamb, 107, 451, 515, 516, 526
Passover (*Pesach*), 525–526, 552–553
  dietary laws for, 515–516, 517
  as festival of matzot, 470
  sacrifice for, 273, 526, 560

Passover (*cont.*)
  seder rituals for, 107, 111, 254, 258, 261, 355, 451, 515, 516, 517
patriarchs, 20–21, 42–43
Paul, 410
peace, prophecies of, 285–287, 309
Pellegrino, Charles, 286–287
Peninah, 189, 190, 412
Pentateuch and Haftorahs, The (Hertz), 291
Peretz, 72
perjury, 259, 407, 418, 436–437, 524
Pesach, see Passover
Peshur, 296, 298
Pethuel, 306
Pharaoh:
  Israelites persecuted by, 91–96, 97, 101–102, 105, 415
  in Joseph's time, 79–81, 381*n*–382*n*
  Moses' confrontation of, 80, 99, 100–101, 103, 105
  punishment of, 102, 106–109, 417
Philistines:
  circumcision not practiced by, 206, 410
  immoral behavior of, 315
  intermarriage with, 179–180
  Israelites' battles with, 120, 193–194, 195, 198–203, 208, 210–211, 217–220
  Samson's conflict with, 180–183
Phineas, 193–194
phylacteries, 489*n*
Pinchas, 142–143, 186
Plaut, Gunther, 101, 116, 123, 127, 131
Plutarch, 428
Poetics of Biblical Narrative, The (Sternberg), 227
political asylum, 440
political dissent, 338, 415–416
polygamy, 13, 191, 410–414, 435, 443, 498, 503
Potiphar, 75–77, 78
poverty, poor:
  burial costs and, 510
  ethical behavior toward, 313, 314, 335–336, 391, 416, 436–437, 473, 523
  judicial equality and, 492, 524, 525
  Sabbatical year debt forgiveness and, 471–472
  tithe in aid of, 119, 449
Prager, Dennis, 64, 426, 432, 434, 488, 490
prayer:
  intervention of wronged party through, 130
  protocols for, 190, 191
  for restoration of Temple, 251

pregnancy, 401
priests:
  ancestry of, 125–127
  benediction from, 104, 126, 478–479
  divination devices used by, 119–121
  garments for, 118–119, 173, 527–528
  higher moral standards for, 127–128
  laws for, 532–535, 549–551
  ordination of, 146
  riches of, 313
primogeniture, 107, 414, 497–498
procreative obligation, 7, 400, 401, 403, 405
property rights, female claims of, 143–145
prophets:
  false, 299
  literary, 326, 422
  minor, 305–327
  Moses as unique among, 130, 152–153, 154
  warnings vs. oracles from, 268
  see also specific prophets
Prophets, xxii
  books of, xxiii–xxiv
  historical period covered in, xxiii
Prophets, The (Heschel), 314–315, 318
Prophets and the Law, The (Bergren), 274
prosbul, 472
prostitution, 71–72, 157–158, 273, 480
Protestantism:
  fundamentalist, 288–289, 402
  on preeminence of faith vs. deeds, 325–326
  see also Christianity
Proverbs, Book of, 247, 343–345
Psalms, Book of, xxiv, 331–342
  authorship of, 136, 331, 340
  protests to God in, 32, 307*n*
Puah, 93–94, 415
puberty rites, 408
punishment:
  of Adam and Eve, 9–10
  for adultery, 435, 504*n*–505*n*
  of Cain, 12–13
  of children for sins of parents, 266, 342, 424–425
  of descendants, 266
  of Egyptians, 417
  for false witness on murder, 407
  for involuntary homicide, 484–486
  for kidnapping, 435–436, 440, 444, 448
  labor as, 10
  limitations on, 444–446
  for mistreatment of widows and/or orphans, 448–449

of Moses, 137–139
for murder, xxvii, 12–13, 403, 405–408, 419*n*
necessity for, 446, 448
for perjury, 407, 437
for rapists, 505–506
revocation of, 323–325
for theft, 161, 419*n*, 436, 441, 447–448
vicarious infliction of, 230, 504–505
for violation of Ten Commandments, 419*n*, 420, 424–425
Purim, xxiv, 114, 355, 373, 378, 471, 491

rabbinical ordination, 146
Rabin, Yitzhak, 470
Rachel, 337
death of, 43, 48*n*, 60, 69
marriage of, 44, 53, 57, 58–60, 61, 67, 89, 167, 411, 455
as matriarch, 20–21
motherhood of, 60, 67, 82, 411
racism, 320, 389, 426–427, 468
Radak (David Kimhi), 27, 220
rage, 402
Rahab, 157–158, 159, 161
rainbows, 15, 403
Ralbag, 163
Ramban (Moses Nachmanides), 27, 457, 458
Ramses II, king of Egypt, 95
rape, 3, 64–67, 184–185, 505–506, 583
false accusation of, 75–77
Rashi, 93, 111, 163, 441*n*, 492
Ravnitzsky, Yehoshua Hana, 17, 174, 525
Rebecca:
ancestry of, 41
burial of, 42–43
decisive behavior by, 44–45, 52, 61
Hebrew name for, 21
Isaac's blessing of Jacob engineered by, 21, 48–49, 51, 52, 54
marriage of, 43–45, 46, 54–55, 57, 167, 499
matriarchal role for, 20–21, 41, 46–47, 497, 499
as mother-in-law, 432
Red Heifer, rite of, 481–482, 563
Red (Reed) Sea, parting of, 109, 157
Reform Judaism, 409
refuge, cities of, 405*n*, 406, 407, 484–486
Rehoboam, 249, 252–253
Religion of Israel, The (Y. Kaufmann), 166, 318
Religion on the Line, 434

Religions in Four Dimensions (W. Kaufmann), 318, 327, 458
repentance, 87, 88
as internal transformation vs. outward ritual, 306, 323
limitation on, 427
for New Year, 470
Nineveh model for, 323–325
provocation for, 321
test of, 83
restitution, 406–407, 441, 447, 449
retribution, limitation of, 444–446
Return to Sodom and Gomorrah (Pellegrino), 287
Reuben, 59, 68–69, 83–85, 88–89, 90, 497
Reuel (Jethro), 97–98, 102, 103, 115–116, 337
revenge, 444–446, 464–465, 546
Riedel, Eunice, 166
Riemer, Jack, 116
righteousness:
eleven psalmic attributes of, 334–335
of Noah, 14*n*, 16
transformation to, 33–34
see also ethical behavior; goodness
Roman Catholic Church, Ten Commandments in, 419
Rome, Jewish revolt against, 298
Rosenblatt, Naomi, 14
Rosh Chodesh, 331, 515
Rosh ha-Shana, 279, 387, 470, 553–554, 561, 563–564
Rousseau, Jean-Jacques, 401–402
Russell, Bertrand, 466
Ruth, 355–356, 358–362, 389–390, 391–392

Sabbath (Shabbat), 104
for animals, 428, 500
blessings for children on, 90, 478
business suspended for, 314–315, 388, 391
of Comfort, 291
Fourth Commandment on, 7, 150–151, 418, 420, 427–430, 441, 470, 500, 518
holiness of, 251, 518
initial establishment of, 6–7
as innovative concept, 428
Jewish unity maintained through, 429–430
manna supplied for, 112, 113
prohibitions vs. positive laws for, 513
for slaves, 428, 429, 440, 500
Torah specifics on, 287, 513, 517, 529

Sabbath (*cont.*)
two rationales for, 150–151, 428–429
Sabbatical years, 388, 471, 472
sacrifices, 529–534
agricultural products for, 11, 452, 523,
526
of animals, 15, 28, 40, 301, 409, 451–
453, 481–482, 516, 530–531
ethical behavior vs. rituals of, 301–302,
313–316
human, 35, 37–41, 147, 177–178, 301,
406, 417n, 451, 453, 484
Isaac offered as, 37–41, 43, 451
loving acts as replacement for, 452
for Passover, 273
in Temple, 250, 253, 451, 452
Safra, 334
salt, 530
Samson, 178–182, 219, 477
Samuel, 187, 230n, 437
on Amalekite foe, 114, 199, 369
ancestry of, 136, 424
birth of, 190–191
God's revelations to, 193, 196, 197, 204
Israelite kings anointed by, 196, 197,
204, 220n
on kingship vs. divine authority, 175,
196–197, 494
monotheism restored by, 195–196
Moses vs., 194–195
as Nazirite, 190, 477
Saul's death prophesied by, 211, 217–
218, 219
sons of, 192, 196
Samuel, Rabbi, 469
Sanhedrin, 336
Sarah:
as Abraham's half sister, 26, 455
adultery risked by, 24–27
beauty of, 24
death of, 41, 42, 45
God's renaming of, 21
infertility of, 22, 25, 29, 59
Ishmael's expulsion demanded by, 21, 26,
31, 40, 411
marriage of, 21, 24–27, 29–31, 40, 41,
167, 411, 455
as matriarch, 18, 20–21, 25
motherhood of, 30–31, 39, 41, 411
Sarna, Nahum, 17, 66, 67, 94, 99, 104, 334–
336
Satan, 348–349, 393
Saul, 195
in battle, 114, 120, 198–199, 201, 202,
208, 210–211
character flaws of, 197, 200, 230n
David as enemy of, 200, 203, 205–213,
219, 220, 221, 224, 228
Endor necromancer consulted by, 121,
217–218
fatherhood of, 120, 177, 197, 199, 200,
205, 207, 210, 211n, 215, 222
as first Israelite king, 173n, 174, 196, 197–
198, 204, 494
Gibeonite treaty violated by, 163–164
Nob population murdered by, 208
Samuel's lie to, 437
successor for, 213
suicide of, 208, 211, 219–220, 237n
Urim consulted by, 120, 121
Scherman, Nosson, 104
Schumann, Robert, 345
Second Commandment, 418, 419, 420, 424–
425
seder:
Elijah's cup at, 254, 258, 261
liberation story told at, 517
Paschal lamb for, 107, 451, 515, 516
Ten Plagues recited in, 111
Sefer ha-Hinnuch (haLevi), 456, 458, 513–514
Segev, Tom, 341n
self-defense, killing in, xxvii, 241, 433–434
semikha, 146
Seneca, 428
servants:
ethical treatment of, 416, 500
see also slavery; slaves
Seth, 13, 54
Seventh Commandment, 207, 213, 418,
420, 434–435, 456, 503n, 505
Seventh Million, The (Segev), 341n
sexual behavior:
adulterous, 24–27, 75–77, 310–312, 404,
413, 418, 420, 434–435, 456, 475–
476, 503n
biblical love poem and, 357–358
celibacy and, 293
of harassment, 360n
homosexual, 35, 211, 404, 456
with kings' consorts, 236, 239
kinship restrictions on, 26, 58, 315, 411,
455–456, 541–544
within marriage, 55, 443, 454–455
menstrual period as bar to, 456, 491,
544
Noahide laws on, 404
perversity in, 17–18, 544
prohibitions against, 454–456, 541–544
of rape, 3, 64–67, 75–77, 184–185, 505–
506, 583

ritual fringes for resistance of, 480
Yom Kippur abstention from, 471
sexuality, first human knowledge of, 9*n*
Shabbat, *see* Sabbath
Shabbat Nachmanu, 291
Shadrach (Hananiah), 379, 380
Shakespeare, William, 506, 507
shalshelet, 75
shamash, 5*n*
Shammai, 508
Shaphan, 278
Shapiro, David, 325
Sharansky, Natan, 338
shatnez, 502, 582
Shavuot, 355, 470, 525–526, 553, 563, 573
Shecaniah, 389
Shechem, 64–66, 84, 505
Shemaiah, 253
Shemini Atzeret, 471, 554
shepherds, 202, 337
Sheshbazzar, 386
Sheva, 240–241
shibboleth, 178
Shifra, 93–94, 415
Shimei, 203, 246
Shirat ha-Yam ("Song at the Sea"), 110
Sh'ma Yisra'el, 487–490, 566
Shmoneh Esray prayer, 20
shoes, ritual removal of, 100, 104, 478
shofar, 117, 159, 470, 555, 563–564
Shulkhan Arukh, 461, 504
siblings:
    alienation between, xxi, 11–12, 31, 50,
        51, 53, 54, 61–64, 67–70, 74, 78–79,
        87–88, 129–130, 233–234, 402, 411–
        413
    marriage restrictions on, 455–456
Simcha of Dvinsk, Meir, 400–401
Simeon, 66–67, 83–84, 85, 89
Simeon ben Gamliel, 54
Simeon ben Lakish, 16, 208, 218, 241,
    348
Simeonites, 89, 143
Simlai, 513
Simon, Uriel, 37–38, 106, 191, 325
Singer, Isaac Bashevis, 12
Sisera, 167–168, 169
Sixth Commandment, 259, 418, 433–434,
    439
    precise translation of, xxvi–xxvii, 433
Sixth Zionist Congress, 341
slander, 335
slavery, 439–442, 498*n*
    active remembrance of, 81
    capital punishment for sales into, 73

Israelites' experience of, xxi, 81, 91–99,
    101–102, 105, 108, 133–134
kidnapping for sale into, 435–436, 440,
    444, 448
as restitution for theft or debt, 314, 391,
    441, 447, 449
in U.S., 94, 106, 440, 442, 444
slaves:
    biblical laws on treatment of, 439–440,
        441–442, 447, 556–557
    capital punishment for murder of, 407*n*,
        440, 442
    conditions for emancipation from, 440,
        442, 519
    gentiles vs. Hebrews as, 440–442
    Jubilee year freedom for, 472
    as property, 440–441
    runaway, 440, 442
    Sabbath observance for, 428, 429, 440,
        500
Sodom, xxi, 14*n*, 23, 25, 32–37, 38
Solomon:
    character deterioration of, 248–249, 367,
        394, 413
    as David's successor, 231, 238–239, 245–
        246, 412, 498
    death of, 266, 394
    executions ordered by, 244, 245–246,
        406, 412
    God manifested in dream of, 130, 246
    Messiah's descent from, 236
    son of, 241–242, 249, 252, 253
    taxes imposed by, 248–249, 252, 392
    Temple built by, 118*n*, 223, 236, 249–
        250, 252, 309, 394, 452
    wealth of, 248–249, 494, 495
    wisdom attributed to, 246–248, 249,
        253, 367, 392, 481
    wives of, 183, 248, 399, 410, 412–413*n*,
        495
    writings of, 247, 343–344, 357, 365, 367
"Some Postulates of Biblical Criminal Law"
    (Greenberg), 448
"Song at the Sea" (*Shirat ha-Yam*), 110
Song of Songs, 212*n*, 247, 355, 356, 357–
    358, 455
sons:
    firstborn, 107, 414, 497–498, 516–517
    naming of, 409
    Sabbath blessing for, 90
    see also children
sotah, 475–476, 560
soul, prenatal existence of, 294
Soviet Union, 105, 317, 338
Spiegel, Celina, 37

Spiegel, Shalom, 313n, 316n–317n, 318
Spinoza, Baruch, 409
Spira, Israel, 363–364
Stalin, Joseph, 416, 570
Steinmetz, Devora, 74
Steinsaltz, Adin, 179, 183
Sternberg, Meir, 227
strangers, love of, 467–468, 522–523, 567
Studies in Jewish Thought (Shapiro), 325
Studies in Shemot (Leibowitz), 99, 420, 423
Studies in the Book of Genesis (Leibowitz), 55
suffering, God's allowance of, 348–353, 362–363
suicide, 208, 211, 219–220, 231, 237
Sukkot, 267, 355, 387–388, 471, 525–526, 554–555, 573
sun gods, 5
Supreme Court, U.S., slavery decision of, 440
surnames, of *kohanim* vs. Levites, 126
Szonyi, David, 134n

Tabernacle, 118–119, 336
Tacitus, 428
tallit, 480–481
Talmud, 414
Tamar (Amnon's half sister), 232–233, 234, 243, 462, 505
Tamar (Judah's daughter-in-law), 70–74, 82
TaNaKh, xxiin
Taney, Roger Brooke, 440
Tanhuma, 400
Taub, Daniel, 446n
Teacher's Resource Guide for the Rabbi's Bible, The (Friedman), 318
tefillin, 489, 566
Telushkin, Dvorah, 189
Telushkin, Helen, 431–432
Temple (*Beit ha-Mikdash*):
    Babylonian destruction of, 250, 275–276, 278, 291, 295, 297, 355, 381, 386
    future restoration of, 251, 341
    Holy of Holies in, 250–251
    Islamic mosques built on site of, 251
    resanctification of, 272–273, 274, 392
    sacrifices offered in, 250, 253, 301–302, 451, 452
    Second, 250, 303, 308–309, 386, 452, 472
    size of, 250
    Solomon's construction of, 118, 223, 236, 249–250, 252, 309, 394, 452
    Tabernacle as forerunner of, 118, 336
    wood used in construction of, 250, 496

Temple, The (Berman), 119
Ten Commandments, xxvi–xxviii, 418–439
    in Ark of the Lord, 193–194, 214, 223, 250
    community membership conditions formulated by, 419n
    ethical behavior prescribed by, 302, 420
    holy place for, 118
    issuance of, xxii, 116–117, 419, 470
    in Jethro passage of Torah, 116
    Moses' reiteration of, 150–151
    penalties for violation of, 419n, 420, 424–425
    progression of, 419–420
    reverence for, 251
    Roman Catholic list of, 419
    speech prohibitions from, 418, 420
    synagogue recitation of, 110
    see also specific commandments
Ten Plagues, xxii, 106–107, 108, 111, 194, 417
Tenth Commandment, 224, 259, 418, 419, 420, 438–439, 565
Ten Tribes, disappearance of, 253, 266–268, 300, 307
Terah, 22, 23, 26, 171, 173–174
Teresh, 376
Tetrachordon (Milton), 6n
theft, 546
    Eighth Commandment on, 418, 420, 435–436, 439, 518
    Noahide law against, 404
    penalties for, 161, 419n, 436, 441, 447–448, 521
    as universal crime, 404
Their Stories, Our Stories (Kam), 227
theodicy, 351
Think a Second Time (Prager), 490
Third Commandment, 418, 419, 426–427
Tiglath-Pileser, 267
Tirzah, 144
Tisha Be'Av, 291, 355
tithing, 449, 483, 558, 562–563
To Kill a Mockingbird (Lee), 77n
tolerance, 327
Torah:
    authorship of last passages in, 153–154
    chanting of, 75
    democratization of, 388
    five books of, xxii–xxiii
    Josiah's reinstitution of, 272–273
    names for books of, xxiiin
    prophets' ethical views derived from, 317–318
    Shavuot linked with receiving of, 470

study of, 488, 489, 565–566
two major principles of, 423
Torah, laws of:
  for kings, 494–495
  on love of God, 149
  necessity for, 402–403, 489
  no additions to or diminishment of, 490–491
  rational roots of, 151
  vows in violation of, 176–177, 178
Torah, The (Plaut), 101, 131
totalitarian societies, 93, 415–416, 440
Tower of Babel, 18–19, 20
Tracy, Thomas, 166
tree of knowledge, 7, 8–9
trees, preservation of, 495–496
Tummim, 119–121, 146, 161
Twelve Tribes, 59, 88–90
tzava'a (ethical will), 149–151
Tzipporah, 98, 115, 129, 409
tzitzit (ritual fringes), 479–480, 481, 561

unconditional love, 311–312
United Nations, 286
universalism, 327
Unterman, Jeremiah, xxvii, 173*n*, 226*n*,
  230*n*, 300, 340*n*, 369, 379, 479
Uriah (prophet), 278
Uriah the Hittite, 224–227, 228–230, 231,
  243, 438
Urim, 119–121, 146, 161
Uzziah, 283

Valéry, Paul, 131
Vashti, 367–369, 371, 374
vegetarianism, 6, 7, 403, 500
vengeance, 444–446, 464–465
vigilantism, 143
virgin birth, 288–289
virginity, 505, 522
vows, fulfillment of, 163, 176–177, 178,
  335, 366, 483–484, 564
vulnerable people, ethical treatment for,
  284, 301–302, 335–336, 415, 416, 448–449, 459–460, 461–462

wages, prompt payment of, 458–459
warfare:
  biblical ethics of, 165–166
  ecological limitations for, 495
  against Israelites, 113–115, 120, 133,
    147, 150, 158–160, 163, 164–165, 167–173, 176, 177–178, 185–186, 193–194, 195, 198–203, 217–219, 226
  killing in, 433, 434

messianic renunciation of, 285–287, 309
  necessity for, 286–287, 306
  opposition to, 296–298
wealth:
  ethical behavior and, 301, 312–315, 391
  idolatry of, 124, 488–489
  of kings, 248–249, 494, 495
  of priests, 313
wedding ceremony, 300*n*, 341, 342, 442
Weiner, Herbert, 41
Weinfeld, Moshe, 419*n*, 420
Wengrov, Charles, 458
Who's Who in the Bible (Comay), 256
widows, care for, 284, 336, 448–449, 523
Wiesel, Elie, 324
Wigoder, Geoffrey, 395
Wilde, Oscar, 59, 333
will, ethical (*tzava'a*), 149–151
Wilson, James, 404
Winds of War (Wouk), 286
wisdom, 343
women:
  adultery based on marital status of, 434–435, 476, 503
  adultery test administered to, 475–476
  as biblical heroines, 96, 167–169, 355–356, 376
  birth control for, 401
  divorced, 484, 504
  God's creation of, 6, 8
  husband's sexual responsibility to, 443
  inheritance rights for, 143–145
  male domination of, 9, 484
  menstrual periods of, 456, 491
  no procreative obligation for, 400–401
  proverbial ideal for, 334, 344–345
  rape of, 35, 64–67, 75–77, 185, 505–506, 583
  ritual garments and, 480, 481
  as widows, 448–449, 484
Women's Bible Commentary, The (Fewell), 161,
  169
Words That Hurt, Words That Heal
  (Telushkin), 228, 461
World of Biblical Literature, The (Alter), 55
Wouk, Herman, 110, 286, 287
Writings, xxii, xxiv

Xerxes I, king of Persia, 378

Yavesh-Gilead, Saul's protection of, 198,
  219–220
Yevtushenko, Yevgeny, 264
Yochanan bar Nappacha, 16, 241
Yochanan ben Kareah, 279

Yochanan ben Zakkai, 452, 482
Yocheved, 93, 96, 97, 456
Yom Kippur, 118, 195, 250–251, 257, 324–
    325, 470–471, 541, 554, 555

Zadok, 245
Zangwill, Israel, 317
Zebulun, 64, 89
Zechariah, 306, 308–309, 386

Zedekiah, 275–276, 297, 298, 494
Zelophehad, 143–145
Zephaniah, 306, 308
Zeresh, 372–373
Zeruiah, 242
Zilpah, 59, 89
Zimri, 142–143, 237n, 265
Zionism, 341
Zophar, 350, 351